Encyclopedia of
Gun Control
and Gun Rights

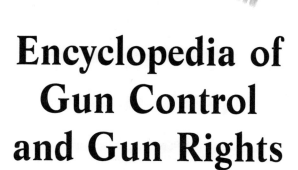

Encyclopedia of Gun Control and Gun Rights

Glenn H. Utter

Oryx Press

2000

The rare Arabian Oryx is believed to have inspired the myth of the unicorn. This desert antelope became virtually extinct in the early 1960s. At that time, several groups of international conservationists arranged to have nine animals sent to the Phoenix Zoo to be the nucleus of a captive breeding herd. Today, the Oryx population is over 1,000, and over 500 have been returned to the Middle East.

© 2000 by Glenn H. Utter
Published by The Oryx Press
4041 North Central at Indian School Road
Phoenix, Arizona 85012-3397
http://www.oryxpress.com

Published simultaneously in Canada
Printed and bound in the United States of America

∞ The paper used in this publication meets the minimum requirements of American National Standard for Information Science—Permanence of Paper for Printed Library Materials, ANSI Z39.48, 1984.

Library of Congress Cataloging-in-Publication Data

Utter, Glenn H.
   Encyclopedia of gun control and gun rights / Glenn H. Utter.
      p.   cm.
   Includes bibliographical references and index.
   ISBN 1-57356-172-X (alk. paper)
    1. Firearms—Law and legislation—United States Encyclopedia.
    2. Gun control—United States Encyclopedia. I.Title.
KF3941.A68U88   2000
363.3'3'097303—dc21

99-43449
CIP

CONTENTS

PREFACE

Gun control is a fascinating public policy area that creates extremely emotional reactions among both those who advocate greater regulation and those who oppose further restrictions on firearms ownership. The issues raised in the debate deal with fundamental questions of constitutional law and the rights of individuals, opportunities for self-protection, and the control of violence. A long-time gun collector informed me of an additional factor making this area especially intriguing. Whenever he displays his gun collection, he can be assured of an attentive audience. Firearms are inherently interesting to many people. Thousands of admiring firearms fans flood gun shows, admiring the many displays of guns, both new and old.

Both sides of the gun control debate have their heroes and villains. Gun rights advocates often portray the Bureau of Alcohol, Tobacco and Firearms (BATF) as a power-hungry group of government officials intent on limiting the liberties of law-abiding citizens and consider the National Rifle Association (NRA) a champion of individual liberty. Gun control supporters often see gun manufacturers as profit-hungry exploiters of Americans' fascination with firearms who take advantage of a too ready willingness to settle disputes violently. They perceive the NRA as a politically ruthless organization, but view the BATF as a well-intentioned if ineffectual government agency. This book is an attempt to present varying views on gun rights and gun control, treating all sides of the gun control question as fairly and accurately as possible.

Gun-related Web sites have proliferated in recent years, contributing greatly to the resources available on firearms and gun control. Initially gun rights groups had the advantage in putting their message before the Internet audience, but more recently gun control organizations have begun to narrow the information gap. These Web sites have been an extremely valuable source of information in preparing this book. In addition, a large number of books, periodicals, and organization newsletters, pamphlets, and monographs were consulted.

Included among the entries are various organizations that have taken stands on gun control. Although many organizations are on the same side of the gun control question, they do not necessarily hold the same views on the issue. Many individuals who have promoted or opposed gun control, both inside and outside of government, have been included, as well as those who have conducted research in the area. Various laws dealing in some way with gun policy are discussed and many judicial decisions, both at the national and state levels, are described. These decisions are especially important, given the emphasis on constitutional questions by several pro-gun forces. Various events, such as the 1999 Littleton, Colorado, school shooting and the 1997 Empire State Building shooting, are discussed. Such events take on special importance because gun control proponents have often mounted campaigns for further firearms legislation closely following their occurrence. At the same time, gun rights advocates have vigorously defended gun rights, arguing that other factors, such as the mass media, lack of parental discipline, and general moral decline, are responsible for the violence.

Although the book concentrates on gun control in the United States, several entries examine the experience of other countries, such as Israel, Switzerland, Japan, and the United Kingdom, with firearms policy. In addition to current issues, historical events and persons are included. Many on both sides of the gun control debate find such historical occurrences as the American Revolution and the passage of Black Codes in southern states following the Civil War significant to their interpretation of the motives of those either supporting or opposing more stringent legislation dealing with firearms. Although peripheral to the contemporary debate over gun control, some of the more renowned persons in the development of the gun industry, such as Oliver Winchester, Samuel Colt, and Eliphalet Remington, are included as important contributors to the special place firearms take in American culture.

The book's over 300 entries are heavily cross-referenced to guide users to related topics. Each entry concludes with a list of further readings, and most entries on organizations and associations provide the group's Web site. The book also includes a brief chronology of some of the most important events in the history of guns and gun control in the United States, a select bibliography of information resources, an introductory essay with facts and statistics on gun control in the U.S., appendices of state constitutional provisions, state firearms laws, and organization addresses, and an index.

Several colleagues at Lamar University have contributed to the writing of this book. Dr. James Love, professor of criminal justice, provided invaluable help. We had many productive discussions in which he offered his personal insights from the perspective of a former police officer. Dr. James True, Jack Brooks Chair of Government and Public Service, assisted with data analysis, and Dr. Terri Davis, assistant professor of political science, conducted legal research. Dr. Larry Osborne, chair of the Computer Science Department, provided practical assistance regarding computer resources. Colleen Barry, an undergraduate research assistant during summer 1998, conducted bibliographical searches. People on both sides of the gun control question contributed helpful information. They include Richard Aborn, Massad Ayoob, David Kopel, Alan Korwin, Bill McGeveran, Josh Sugarmann, David Hemenway, and Franklin Zimring. Although recognizing the assistance of many people, I accept full responsibility for any errors of judgment or fact.

INTRODUCTION

Perhaps with the one exception of abortion, gun control is the most controversial issue in American politics, and it appeals strongly to the emotions of those who support as well as those who oppose further regulation of firearms. Although people take many different positions on the issue, supporting some proposals for control and rejecting others, the more uncompromising on both sides tend to collapse pro- and anti-gun control categories into two. The pro-gun forces see themselves as the supporters of a vital constitutional right to keep and bear arms pitted against the "gun grabbers." Strong advocates of gun control see themselves struggling for a more civilized society against the "gun nuts" and profit-hungry firearms manufacturers and dealers. Like many other subjects, the issue of gun control is preeminently a political question in that the competitors attempting to influence public policy have an intense interest in the ultimate outcome. Therefore, positions tend to harden and proponents of one position tend to deny any merit in the stand taken by others, each side attributing dishonest motives to those with whom they disagree. Scholars who otherwise are meticulous in presenting research results can become as impassioned in their argumentation as the most openly partisan supporter of a fervently held political position.

Supporters and opponents of gun control disagree over the significance of firearms as an independent variable in explaining the high level of violence in the United States. The term "gun culture" is used by both sides in explaining their respective views of the special role firearms have played in American history and continue to play in contemporary society. Gun rights advocates point with pride to the role that average Americans played in the Revolutionary War, especially because of the skill they demonstrated with firearms against an intimidated British force. Firearms are seen as an important ingredient in the unique ability of Americans to maintain their independence from a potentially oppressive government. Those less impressed with the gun tradition see that the American love affair with firearms has contributed to a violent past and a continuing belief that many problems can be resolved through violence. While not denying this predilection for violence, gun supporters note that other cultures not having as extensive a supply of firearms also experience high levels of violence, that some societies with high concentrations of firearms have much lower levels of violence, and that the level of violent crime in the United States did not increase proportionately with a marked increase in the number of firearms available. Gun rights advocates state their position with the popular saying, "Guns don't kill people, people kill people." However, Franklin Zimring and Gordon Hawkins have argued that firearms have had an independent influence on violence in the United States in that the number of violent crimes that lead to serious injury are significantly higher in the United States than in other countries. Table 1 indicates that the homicide rate is much higher in the United States, where firearms are easily obtainable, than in England and Wales, where firearms are far less available to the general public.

TABLE 1

GUN AND HANDGUN HOMICIDES, ENGLAND AND WALES AND THE UNITED STATES, 1980–1984[a]

Type of Murder	Homicides		Average annual rate per one million population		England and Wales to United States ratio
	England and Wales	United States	England and Wales	United States	
All gun[b]	213	63,218	.86	54.52	1 to 63.4
Handgun[b]	57	46,553	.23	40.15	1 to 174.6
Nongun[b]	2,416	41,354	9.75	35.67	1 to 3.7
Total[c]	2,629	104,572	10.61	90.19	1 to 8.5

[a]Annual average population for 1980-1984; United States, 231.9 million; England and Wales, 49.55 million.
[b]Figures for the U.S. involved some extrapolation from homicides for which weapon was known.
[c]Figures for England and Wales relate to offenses currently recorded as homicide.

Source: Ronald V. Clarke and Pat Mayhew, "The British Gas Suicide Story and Its Criminological Implications," *Crime and Justice: A Review of Research,* ed. Michael Tonry and Norval Morris, vol. 10 (Chicago: University of Chicago Press, 1988), p. 107. Reprinted with permission from the University of Chicago Press.

Supporters of an individual right to keep and bear arms rely on two basic arguments to make their case. First, they claim that the right can be defended as a basic natural, or human, right independent of any positive law, or has evolved through a long tradition of common law stretching back in English history and subsequently recognized and protected in the Second Amendment to the U.S. Constitution. They view the Second Amendment guarantee of the right to keep and bear arms as the premier right that must be preserved to protect the remaining rights listed in the Bill of Rights. In recent years, scholars advocating the position that the Constitution protects an individual right to possess and carry firearms, not just a corporate right of state governments to maintain a militia independent of the federal government, have published a large body of literature, primarily in law journals.

The second major defense of a right to keep and bear arms makes a utilitarian argument, relying on empirical claims that law-abiding citizens can use firearms effectively to protect themselves against law-breakers. Contrary to the gun control position that certain firearms such as handguns have no legitimate use outside their application to certain limited sports, gun supporters claim that such weapons have a definite defensive use. Such researchers as John R. Lott conclude that concealed carry laws give the law-abiding citizen a definite advantage over the potential criminal.

Although firearms supporters consider the Second Amendment the heart of their defense of gun rights and the most important protection in the Bill of Rights, other guarantees are often cited as important to their cause. The Fourth Amendment protection against unreasonable searches and seizures is considered important to protect gun owners against searches conducted by government officials enforcing gun control laws. Gun rights advocates believe that such searches are conducted according to unconstitutional laws and therefore represent inappropriate harassment. The Ninth Amendment, which guarantees rights to the people not specifically stated in the Constitution, has been used by firearms supporters to argue for an additional protection for the right to keep and bear arms, which they consider a fundamental right established in natural law, common law, and the American political tradition. Gun rights supporters consider the Fourteenth Amendment important because of the tendency of the U.S. Supreme Court in recent decades to apply specific protections found in the Bill of Rights to the states. They argue that the Second Amendment should also be applied to the states, thus limiting state government power to restrict firearm ownership.

Contrary to the gun rights position, gun control supporters argue that the Second Amendment, like any other freedom, is not absolute. Some gun rights advocates agree that government can institute reasonable firearms restrictions to maintain an ordered society. However, those more suspicious of the motives of gun control advocates hold that any gun control measure represents yet another step down a slippery slope toward banning firearms and in the direction of a national confiscation effort. If any consensus exists on the gun control issue, it is that guns should be kept from particular individuals, such as felons and those who are mentally unstable. However, conflict arises over where to draw the boundary. For instance, should those convicted of misdemeanor domestic violence charges lose their right to possess firearms? May those convicted of more serious crimes ever reclaim their right to possess firearms? The greatest controversy arises over proposals that regulate the firearms ownership of the vast majority of people who have not violated the law in any way to deny ownership to those most likely to misuse firearms.

Beyond the arguments presented by both sides in the gun control debate, groups have made various efforts to influence the decisions of the national and state governments and the contest among the various participants has been played out in legislative chambers as well as the courts. Modern efforts at gun control began in 1934 with passage of the National Firearms Act, which placed limitations on certain types of weapons, such as machine guns. The National Rifle Association (NRA), which was established in 1871, had a significant influence on the contents of the legislation. In 1938, the Federal Firearms Act was passed, the last major piece of gun control legislation to receive serious consideration for the next 30 years. The 1968 Gun Control Act was passed following the assassinations of President John Kennedy in 1963 and Martin Luther King, Jr., and Robert Kennedy in 1968. However, the legislation came under criticism from pro-gun groups, which fought for revisions in the legislation. The 1986 Gun Owners Protection Act repealed those sections that gun interests considered more objectionable. The passage of this act over the objections of opponents and police organizations resulted in the mobilization of the gun control movement. Handgun Control, Inc., the most influential of the gun control organizations, captured two major allies in James and Sarah Brady. James Brady, President Ronald Reagan's press secretary, had been badly wounded in the assassination attempt on the president in 1981. The Reagan administration's strong opposition to gun control notwithstanding, the Bradys came to the forefront of the pro-regulation movement.

Passage of the Brady Handgun Violence Prevention Act in 1994 represented a significant shift in the fortunes of the gun control movement. The act established a five-day waiting period so that local law enforcement agencies could conduct background checks on prospective handgun purchasers to determine if they fell into a class of those prohibited from owning a firearm. In 1997, the U.S. Supreme Court dealt a minor setback to the Brady Act when it ruled that the provision mandating law enforcement agencies to run background checks was an unjustified federal intrusion into state affairs. However, the waiting period ended in November 1998, when a national instant check system (NICS) went into effect. Therefore, the Printz decision had minimal effect on the application of the Brady Act.

The effectiveness of the Brady Act has been a matter of debate. Supporters, including President Bill Clinton, have claimed that thousands of purchases have been prevented because of the background check requirement. However, others note that the act is a limited measure that requires enhancement through passage of additional provisions. Gun supporters doubt the effectiveness of the legislation, questioning the accuracy of claims about the prevention of purchases and noting that few prosecutions have occurred under the law. However, gun advocates have perhaps neglected the potential deterrent effect of the law. Most of those who are disqualified from purchasing firearms may not try to make a legal purchase. Gun rights advocates respond that such people receive weapons from alternative sources, thus nullifying any beneficial effect the legislation might achieve, while still inconveniencing law-abiding citizens.

Some gun control organizations, such as the Violence Policy Center (VPC), are nearly as critical of the Brady Act as gun rights groups, claiming that the legislation is ineffective. They contend that the best way to limit gun violence is to institute a general ban on handguns. Such a proposal confirms the fears of pro-gun organizations, which claim that more moderate gun control measures must be resisted because the logic of gun control leads inevitably to more extreme proposals. Any compromise on gun control will lead inexorably to greater pressure to compromise further. Given that gun ownership is considered a basic constitutional right, compromise appears very ominous to gun advocates. Gun rights advocates express concern about the increase in federal firearms legislation, beginning especially in the 1940s, as indicated in Table 2.

Gun control advocates have attempted to confront efforts to circumvent the law, concentrating their efforts on controlling the illegal gun trade. To restrict so-called "straw purchases," in which someone buys several handguns from a legitimate dealer and then resells them to those not legally qualified to make a purchase, some gun control supporters have advocated limiting the purchase of handguns to one per month, arguing that no legitimate purchaser needs to buy more than twelve weapons in one year.

Gun control advocates have also focused on the issue of gun safety, particularly to prevent accidents involving unauthorized access to firearms by children. This issue of gun-related injuries and deaths among young people has inspired calls for mandatory use of locks on handguns and the development of technology that would prevent the use of a handgun by anyone other than the owner. Although pro-gun groups have been somewhat suspicious of such calls for the mandatory sale of a gun lock with each new handgun, the industry has responded to this proposal by developing several types of locking devices. The more skeptical among gun rights supporters question whether the value of a handgun for self-defense can be maintained if they are kept locked, but some companies have advertised their safety products as compatible with keeping the weapon readily accessible in an emergency.

Date	Words Added	New USC Sections	% Increase at the Time	% Increase as of 1996
1791	0	0	—	0
1894	547	1	—	0.7
1910s	1,481	7	271	1.8
1920s	1,543	8	43.2	1.8
1930s	1,736	9	32.7	2.1
1940s	7,498	37	58.6	8.9
1950s	7,102	42	35.7	8.5
1960s	27,908	51	58.4	33.4
1970s	11,407	26	19.3	13.6
1980s	6,777	28	10.3	8.1
1990-95	7,687	22	10.4	9.2
1996	9,898	not codified	13.4	11.8
Totals	83,584	231 (through 1995)		

TABLE 2

GROWTH IN FEDERAL GUN LAWS

Source: Alan Korwin with Michael P. Anthony, *Gun Laws of America—Every Federal Gun Law on the Books, with Plain English Summaries* (Phoenix: Bloomfield Press, 1997), p. 23. Reprinted with permission from Alan Korwin and Bloomfield Press.

Gun rights groups have cautioned that an emphasis on gun locks and other technology to maintain the safety of firearms neglects the importance of educating the owners of firearms about safe handling and storage, and teaching young people to stay away from firearms when unsupervised. The NRA developed the Eddie Eagle program to teach gun safety to children. However, gun control organizations doubt the ultimate effectiveness of such a program, arguing that keeping firearms out of the home represents the surest way to avoid a tragic accident. Because children, even when instructed, tend to act irresponsibly, the best strategy involves keeping firearms completely inaccessible. Some gun control groups even suspect that the Eddie Eagle program encourages a positive attitude toward firearms among children that promotes future ownership, a charge that the NRA and its supporters readily deny.

With a Republican Congress and the legislatures of several states passing preemption laws preventing local governments from passing gun control ordinances more stringent than state statutes, some gun control organizations and municipal governments have shifted their focus to the courts, suing firearms manufacturers and retailers for compensation for the damage done by their products. Such lawsuits instituted by municipal governments in Chicago, Atlanta, New Orleans, and elsewhere resemble the state government lawsuits against the tobacco industry to recover the costs of medical care attributed to the ill effects of smoking. Gun supporters fear that such lawsuits could bankrupt the firearms industry and claim that gun control groups have that outcome as their ultimate goal.

In February 1999, a federal jury in New York raised the concern of the firearms industry by awarding $500,000 to a survivor of a shooting incident. The jury found that 15 of 25 manufacturers named in the lawsuit were responsible for injuries because they had negligently marketed a legal product. Among the companies found liable were Beretta USA, Colt, and Jennings Firearms. The plaintiffs argued that the companies oversupplied states with more lenient gun control laws, mainly in the South, aware that the excess guns would ultimately make their way through the black market into the hands of criminals in states with more stringent regulations, such as New York. The firearms companies had argued that their responsibility ended with delivery to distributors. Tables 3 and 4 report domestic firearms production (1899–1995) and imports (1987–1994), respectively.

TABLE 3

DOMESTIC PRODUCTION OF CIVILIAN FIREARMS, 1899-1995 (IN THOUSANDS)

Year	Handguns	Rifles	Shotguns	Total Production
1899 to 1945	11,722	20,651	13,338	45,711
1946	176	729	621	1,526
1947	257	953	860	2,070
1948	427	1,170	1,013	2,610
1949	256	862	1,050	2,168
1950	261	847	1,324	2,432
1951	307	668	1,001	1,976
1952	398	521	899	1,818
1953	355	541	948	1,844
1954	327	437	707	1,471
1955	362	556	739	1,657
1956	451	554	830	1,835
1957	460	514	688	1,662
1958	440	406	531	1,377
1959	519	517	610	1,646
1960	475	469	564	1,508
1961	447	482	575	1,504
1962	431	529	591	1,551
1963	453	579	639	1,671
1964	491	713	746	1,950
1965	666	790	899	2,355
1966	700	850	976	2,526
1967	926	909	1,044	2,879
1968	1,259	1,100	1,155	3,514
1969	1,255	1,297	1,119	3,671
1970	1,394	1,195	1,144	3,733
1971	1,448	1,269	1,141	3,858
1972	1,805	1,677	1,135	4,617
1973	1,934	1,637	1,271	4,842
1974	1,715	2,105	1,803	5,623
1975	2,024	2,126	1,595	5,745
1976	1,833	2,112	1,337	5,282
1977	1,880	1,933	1,225	5,038
1978	1,077	1,788	1,196	4,061
1979	2,124	1,876	1,320	5,320
1980	2,370	1,936	1,339	5,645
1981	2,537	1,681	1,156	5,374
1982	2,629	1,623	879	5,131
1983	1,967	1,110	960	4,037
1984	1,680	1,107	1,086	3,873
1985	1,550	1,141	770	3,461
1986	1,428	971	641	3,040
1987	1,659	1,006	858	3,523
1988	1,746	1,145	928	3,819
1989	2,031	1,407	936	4,374
1990	1,839	1,156	849	3,844
1991	1,757	681	352	2,790
1992	1,525	677	806	3,008

TABLE 3				
DOMESTIC PRODUCTION OF CIVILIAN FIREARMS, 1899-1995 (IN THOUSANDS) *(CONT.)*				
1993	2,825	1,160	1,145	5,130
1994	2,582	1,324	1,255	5,161
1995	1,723	1,332	1,174	4,229
Totals	73,503	75,019	61,768	210,290

Source: Violence Policy Center, *Firearms Production in America* (Washington, DC: 1997), Appendix Four. Reprinted with permission.

TABLE 4	
TOTAL GUN IMPORTS, 1987–1994	
1987	1,138,806
1988	1,240,581
1989	1,100,789
1990	1,025,476
1991	1,084,891
1992	1,541,706
1993	2,081,266
1994	2,239,460

Source: U.S. Census Bureau, Foreign Trade Division; reprinted in Tom Diaz, *Making a Killing: The Business of Guns in America* (New York: New Press, 1999), p. 74. Reprinted with permission from the Violence Policy Center and Tom Diaz.

Related to the lawsuit strategy, gun control advocates have called for regulating firearms as consumer products. The firearms industry is essentially self-regulating, setting its own standards of safety. So-called Saturday night specials or junk guns, inexpensive handguns that are claimed to be less safe than higher quality firearms, are the focus for much of the concern for consumer protection. The 1968 Gun Control Act prohibited the importation of such weapons, but domestic production expanded greatly to fill the demand. By requiring high production standards, the manufacture of Saturday night specials could possibly cease.

Gun rights groups have attempted to counter the initiatives of gun control organizations, challenging gun laws in the courts and sponsoring legislative initiatives at the national and state levels. When Massachusetts passed a stringent gun control bill in 1998, the NRA quickly began a legal challenge to the law. Pro-gun organizations have supported the liberalization of concealed carry laws, backing "shall issue" provisions that require law enforcement agencies to issue a concealed carry license to anyone not specifically prohibited from owning a firearm. The NRA has also challenged NICS, questioning the keeping of purchase records by the BATF even for a brief time. On the national level, gun groups, with the support of some law enforcement organizations, have lobbied for a reciprocity measure whereby each state would be required to recognize the concealed carry licenses of other states, just as each state recognizes the drivers' licenses of other states.

The participation of health care professionals in firearms research has created a good deal of controversy. Those more sympathetic to gun ownership claim that this research fails to meet the standards of good social science methodology. At the most extreme, gun rights supporters claim that such research is biased, prejudging firearms as dangerous items that should not be kept in the home. Arthur Kellermann's claim that a firearm kept in the home is far more likely to be used to harm a family member or friend than to fend off an attack by an intruder has been challenged by those more sympathetic to gun ownership, who argue that the use of firearms to harm others is more likely to occur among those with criminal histories. For their part, health care researchers have criticized research indicating that carrying concealed weapons (CCW) laws at the state level have a measurable deterrent effect on crime, questioning the methodology employed and the assumptions made. The controversy over appropriate research methodologies and objectives reached the political realm in 1997 when Congress was strongly lobbied to cut the budget for the Centers for Disease Control's (CDC) National Center for Injury Prevention and Control (NCIPC) to limit NCIPC-sponsored research on firearms, which was claimed to be politically motivated, biased, and, hence, "unscientific." Doctors for Integrity in Policy Research (DIPR), a pro-gun organization, led the criticism leveled at the Centers. Health care researchers employ the epidemiological model in their research on firearms, the same procedure used in studying the progression of a disease. The use of this methodology raises suspicions among some pro-gun supporters that these researchers have already judged firearms, like a disease, as something bad that deserves to be eliminated.

In response to calls for additional gun control, gun rights advocates argue that existing legislation covers virtually any illegal action committed with a firearm. They recommend the more judicious application of existing statutes, but also raise doubts about the possibility of keeping firearms out of the hands of criminals. Some researchers have focused on the illegal gun trade, attempting to trace the typical routes of firearms from manufacturers to those who use them in illegal activities. Gun control advocates suggest that registration of firearms would assist in tracing firearms used in criminal activity back to their original purchasers. Such a plan would place greater legal responsibility on gun owners for the safe and secure storage of firearms. Some states already have instituted measures holding gun owners responsible if young people harm themselves or others with weapons to which they have gained access.

In 1994, Congress passed an assault weapons ban. Gun control advocates contend that such semi-automatic weapons with large capacity ammunition clips have been used disproportionately in criminal activity. Some gun researchers and gun rights advocates contend that the banning of specific weapons represents a distinctly ineffective way to limit firearms violence because other types of firearms can easily be substituted for the prohibited models. Firearms not classified as assault weapons can have as much, or more, destructive effect as the banned guns.

In the debate over gun control, gun control groups are at a definite disadvantage, given the large membership in gun rights organizations and the many publications dealing with firearms. Table 5 provides circulation figures for the major publications. Such magazines as *Guns and Ammo, Guns, Gun Journal, Gun Week, Women and Guns, Gun News Digest,* and the NRA's *American Rifleman* provide colorful descriptions of new firearms along with articles highly critical of gun control measures and supportive of gun rights. Gun control advocates have attempted to counteract this advantage by enlisting the support of public relations firms to produce public service advertisements that caution the public about the dangers of firearms in the home. Such campaigns have included television announcements, billboards, and special marches to raise concern about firearms-related violence, especially among youth.

TABLE 5	
MAJOR COMMERCIAL GUN PUBLICATIONS: CIRCULATION	
Publication	**Circulation**
American Rifleman (National Rifle Association)	1,480,074
American Hunter (National Rifle Association)	1,059,000
North American Hunter (North American Hunting Club)	715,725
Guns and Ammo	575,000
Shooting Times	189,634
Guns	168,000
Handguns	150,000
American Guardian (National Rifle Association)	140,000
American Handgunner	133,648
Combat Handguns	126,498
Gun World	126,402

Source: Tom Diaz, *Making a Killing: The Business of Guns in America* (New York: New Press, 1999), p. 52. Reprinted with permission from the Violence Policy Center and Tom Diaz.

The focus on guns and young people includes a concern for students who take firearms to school. Estimates are that several thousand young people take guns to school each year. Reasons for carrying a weapon include the desire to impress others and the belief that a weapon will guarantee personal security. In 1994, Congress passed the Gun-Free Schools Act, a measure geared to deter such activity. The highly publicized school shootings in 1997, 1998, and 1999 continued to raise concerns about firearms in schools. However, some more avid gun rights supporters argued that firearms in schools–in the hands of authorized persons– would likely deter such shooting incidents.

The focus of gun control campaigns on youth is especially troubling for gun interests. They believe that such a focus threatens a tradition that has been passed from father to son for generations. The sporting industry is concerned that the demand for their products, which in the past depended on generational transfer, may be headed for a decline because the next generation may not become as firmly tied to the sporting tradition. When Charlton Heston began a public relations campaign for the NRA in 1997, he focused his attention on transferring positive attitudes about gun ownership to a new generation. Trade associations encourage such transfer, recommending that fathers take not only their sons but also their daughters on hunting trips. Gun control organizations disapprove of such attempts, viewing firearms as a clear threat of injury and death to youth.

Gun control advocates are especially critical of what they consider the efforts of the firearms industry to increase sales by manipulating the emotions of women. They claim that gun manufacturers, finding that the male market had been saturated, decided to develop a new market among women to maintain sales. They also charge that gun interests focused on women's fears of being attacked by a stranger to encourage them to become firearms owners. Gun rights supporters respond that women have the same rights as men to protect themselves and charge that the women's rights movement is inconsistent in demanding equal rights for women, while at the same time denying women the right to self-protection. Gun control advocates note that the most probable threat of violence that women face is not from a stranger, but from people that women know, such as husbands and boyfriends. In any event, gun ownership among women lags considerably behind that for men.

The question of militia groups lies at the edge of the gun control debate. Militia supporters argue that their organizations are protected by the Second Amendment. They believe that the amendment provides the opportunity to defend individual freedom against a tyrannical government. This position involves what many consider a curious argument that the Constitution guarantees a right to revolt against the governmental structure that it established: The governing document plants the seeds of its own destruction. Supporters of the militia idea contend that the protection of liberties against a powerful government must include the possibility of violent resistance. Therefore, gun control legislation is viewed with special suspicion because it is seen as denying the ability to take the ultimate step to defend freedom against tyranny. Those less skeptical of government respond that freedom ultimately depends on a legal order and a strong government that is able to defend citizens against the encroachment on the rights of some by others in society.

One of the more extreme arguments against gun control, made by such organizations as Jews for the Preservation of Firearms Ownership, involves the charge that it has often accompanied genocide. The nineteenth-century attempt to disarm Native Americans, the effort to keep African Americans disarmed in the South following Reconstruction, and the Nazi gun control policies that preceded the Holocaust are often mentioned as examples of the dangers of gun control. Such disarmament is thought to put the people at the mercy of an oppressive government. Those more sympathetic to gun control conclude that such arguments are historically inaccurate and less than persuasive, especially given that black youth are particularly prone to suffer injury and death from firearms that appear to be readily available, a limited form of genocide in itself. Therefore, it is not surprising that groups representing minorities often support measures intended to limit minority youth access to firearms. For instance, the National Organization of Black Law Enforcement Executives (NOBLE) has taken positions in favor of various gun control legislation, as have such African-American legislators as John Conyers, Democrat from Michigan.

The future of gun control depends on several factors. The outcome of lawsuits being lodged against firearms manufacturers can have a significant impact on the availability of firearms to the general public, especially if juries award damages to claimants at the expense of companies. Such outcomes depend upon the willingness of juries and courts of appeals to hold gun manufacturers responsible for the marketing of their products. At the national level, partisan control of Congress may have an important effect on the fortunes of such measures as mandating gun locks and the one-gun-per-month limitation. If Democrats regain control of Congress, the chances of further gun control legislation may improve significantly. Finally, public opinion may play a role in future action. If the American public remains supportive of specific gun control proposals, gun control advocates will be able to argue more persuasively that they are carrying out a popular mandate. The future will likely mirror the past, with gun interests strongly opposing additional regulations, but with compromises being reached as the interests supporting legislation make their case for additional legislation.

GUIDE TO SELECTED TOPICS

Firearms and Ammunition

AK-47
Black Talon Bullet
Long Gun
Saturday Night Special
Sawed-Off Shotgun
Smart Guns
Tommy Gun

Firearms Industry Organizations

American Firearms Council
American Shooting Sports Council
National Association of Federally
Licensed Firearms Dealers
National Shooting Sports
Foundation
Sporting Arms and Ammunition
Manufacturers' Institute

Firearms Researchers

Cook, Philip J.
Hemenway, David
Kates, Don B., Jr.
Kellermann, Arthur
Kleck, Gary
Kopel, David B.
Lott, John R.
Ludwig, Jens Otto
Wintemute, Garen J.
Zimring, Franklin

Government Agencies and Policies

Background Checks
Bureau of Alcohol, Tobacco, and
Firearms
Canadian Firearms Centre
Civil Forfeiture
Concealed Weapons Detectors
Gun Buyback Programs
Gunshot Detection Technology
National Center for Injury Prevention
and Control
National Instant Check System
National School Safety Center
National Tracing Center

Project Exile
Sporting Purposes Test
United Nations
Washington, D.C.
Youth Crime Gun Interdiction
Initiative

Groups Supporting Gun Control

American Academy of Pediatrics
American Bar Association
American Civil Liberties Union
American Jewish Congress
Americans for Democratic Action
Cease Fire, Inc.
Center for the Study and Prevention
of Violence
Center to Prevent Handgun Violence
Central Conference of American
Rabbis
Children's Defense Fund
Coalition to Stop Gun Violence
Drive-By-Agony
Educational Fund to End Handgun
Violence
Firearms Litigation Clearinghouse
Fraternal Order of Police
Gun Control Resource Center
Handgun Control, Inc.
Harborview Injury Prevention and
Research Center
HELP Network
International Organization of Chiefs
of Police
Johns Hopkins Center for Gun Policy
and Research
Klanwatch Project
Legal Action Project
Legal Community Against Violence
Mennonite Central Committee
Militia Watchdog
Mothers Against Violence in America
National Association of Police
Organizations
National Association of School
Psychologists
National Crime Prevention Council
National Education Association

National Organization of Black Law
  Enforcement Executives
National SAFE KIDS Campaign
Pacific Center for Violence
  Prevention
PAX
Physicians for Social Responsibility
Police Executive Research Forum
Potomac Institute
Presbyterian Church (U.S.A.)
Project Lifeline
Safe Range Association
Stop Handgun Violence, Inc.
Student Pledge Against Gun
  Violence
United States Conference of Mayors
Violence Policy Center
Violence Prevention Research
  Program

Groups Supporting Gun Rights

Academics for the Second
  Amendment
American Firearms Council
American Shooting Sports Council
Arming Women Against Rape and
  Endangerment
Citizens Committee for the Right to
  Keep and Bear Arms
Congress of Racial Equality
Democrats for the Second
  Amendment
Doctors for Integrity in Policy
  Research
Doctors for Responsible Gun
  Ownership
Firearms Coalition
Firearms Owners Against Crime
Firearms Research and Identification
  Association
Gun Owners' Action League
Gun Owners of America
Gun Rights Policy Conference
Heartland Institute
Independence Institute
Institute for Legislative Action
International Defensive Pistol
  Association
Izaak Walton League of America

Jews for the Preservation of Firearms
  Ownership
John Birch Society
Law Enforcement Alliance of
  America
Lawyer's Second Amendment
  Society
Libertarian Party
Michigan Militia
Militia of Montana
National Association of Federally
  Licensed Firearms Dealers
National Center for Policy Analysis
National Concealed Carry
  Incorporated
National Firearms Association
National Firearms Association of
  Canada
National Muzzle Loading Rifle
  Association
National Rifle Association
Paul Revere Network
Safety for Women and Responsible
  Motherhood
Second Amendment Committee
Second Amendment Foundation
United States Practical Shooting
  Association
Women Against Gun Control
Women's Firearm Network

Gun Control Issues

Accidents Involving Guns
African Americans and Guns
Black Talon Bullet
Collectors
Consumer Product Safety
Drive-By Shootings
Eddie Eagle
Fatalities
Gun Culture
Gun Owners
Gun Shows
Health Care Professionals
Instrumentality Effect
Media Violence
Native Americans
Product Liability Lawsuits
Schools and Guns

Self-Defense
Suicide
Survivalism
Taggants
Trigger Locks
Violent Crime Rate
Women and Guns
Youth and Guns

Historical Events

American Revolution
Beecher's Bibles
Black Codes
Dueling
Empire State Building Shooting
Federalist Papers
Jonesboro, Arkansas, School
    Shooting
Kennesaw, Georgia
Littleton, Colorado, School Shooting
Minutemen, Revolutionary
Morton Grove, Illinois
Oklahoma City Bombing
Ruby Ridge
Stockton, California, Shooting
Texas Tower Shooting
Waco, Texas, Raid

Historical Individuals and Groups

Black Panther Party
Browning, John Moses
Colt, Samuel
Dodd, Thomas J.
Jefferson, Thomas
Ku Klux Klan
Minutemen, Modern
Remington, Eliphalet, II
Ruger, William Batterman (Bill)
Smith and Wesson
Whitney, Eli
Winchester, Oliver Fisher

Individuals Supporting Gun Control

Aborn, Richard
Boxer, Barbara
Brady, James

Brady, Sarah
Clinton, William Jefferson (Bill)
Conyers, John
Dodd, Thomas J.
Feinstein, Dianne
Kellermann, Arthur
Lautenberg, Frank R.
Reno, Janet
Schumer, Charles E.
Wintemute, Garen J.
Zimring, Franklin E.

Individuals Supporting Gun Rights

Ayoob, Massad
Barr, Bob
Chenoweth, Helen
Craig, Larry E.
Gottlieb, Alan Merril
Gritz, James (Bo)
Halbrook, Stephen P.
Harder, Chuck
Heston, Charlton
Kates, Don B.
Knox, Neal
Kopel, David B.
LaPierre, Wayne
Lott, John R.
McClure, James Albertas
McCollum, William (Bill)
Metaksa, Tanya K.
Paul, Ron
Pratt, Larry
Reagan, Ronald
Thompson, Linda
Volkmer, Harold Lee

Legislation and U.S. Constitutional Amendments

Antiterrorism and Effective Death
    Penalty Act
Assault Weapons Ban
Brady Handgun Violence
    Prevention Act
Concealed Carry Laws
Dick Act
Federal Firearms Act
Firearm Sentence Enhancement
    Laws

Firearms Owners Protection Act
Fourteenth Amendment
Fourth Amendment
Gun Control Act of 1968
Gun-Free Schools Act
Lautenberg Amendment
Law Enforcement Officers
    Protection Act
Mailing of Firearms Act
Maryland One-Gun-Per-Month Law
Massachusetts Gun Violence
    Prevention Law
Militia Act of 1792
National Firearms Act
Ninth Amendment
Roberti-Roos Assault Weapons Act
Second Amendment
State Firearms Preemption Laws
Sullivan Law
Undetectable Firearms Act

Legislators and Government Officials

Barr, Bob
Boxer, Barbara
Bush, George
Chenoweth, Helen

Clinton, William Jefferson (Bill)
Conyers, John
Craig, Larry E.
Dodd, Thomas J.
Feinstein, Dianne
Lautenberg, Frank R.
McClure, James Albertas
McCollum, William (Bill)
Paul, Ron
Reagan, Ronald
Reno, Janet
Schumer, Charles E.
Volkmer, Harold Lee

Publications

American Rifleman
Gun Journal
Gun News Digest
Gun Week
Gun World
Guns and Ammo
Guns Magazine
Handguns Magazine
Paladin Press
Shotgun News
Small Arms Review
Soldier of Fortune
The Turner Diaries
Women and Guns Magazine

Aborn, Richard (1952–)

As president of Handgun Control, Inc. (HCI) and the affiliated Center to Prevent Handgun Violence (CPHV) until 1996, Richard Aborn has been an active supporter of more stringent gun control legislation. Since 1979, Aborn has been active in the campaign to reduce gun violence. From 1979 to 1984, he worked in the Manhattan District Attorney's Office, investigating and prosecuting homicide and illegal gun distribution cases. After leaving government, Aborn worked as a volunteer for HCI and was elected to the board of trustees in 1988 and to the presidency in 1992.

Aborn worked to implement CPHV's STAR program (Straight Talk About Risks) in New York City public schools. The program, which is aimed at children from prekindergarten through the twelfth grade, is intended to educate youth about the dangers of firearms to reduce injuries resulting from their misuse. Aborn contributed to former New York Governor Mario Cuomo's publication project, *New York State Strategy to Reduce Gun Violence*. He has been a consultant to the Ford Foundation on violence and youth and has worked with a New York task force of public health officials to consider solutions to the problem of violent crime.

Aborn supports a comprehensive federal gun control bill that would include licensing and registration of handgun purchases and transfers, the limitation of gun purchases to one per month, and a ban on Saturday night specials. He advocates a tax at a "reasonable level" on ammunition, dealers' licenses, and firearms to be used to pay for the medical costs of gun-related injuries. He insists that HCI does not want to ban all guns or interfere in the lawful acquisition of firearms, but instead strives to stop the illegal gun market. Aborn sees no contradiction between gun ownership and gun control.

Aborn notes that illicit gun traffickers acquire firearms in jurisdictions with weak gun control laws and then sell them illegally in jurisdictions with more stringent laws. He claims that Virginia was the primary source of illegal firearms until that state passed a one-gun-a-month law. Aborn holds that Saturday night specials (which he defines as a handgun that has a barrel less than two inches long, is made of non-homogeneous metal, is unsafe, and cannot pass a drop test from more than five feet) are disproportionately used as crime weapons and have little self-defense use.

Aborn claims that gun control laws already passed have been effective. He cites a U.S. Justice Department estimate that the Brady Handgun Violence Prevention Act prevented over 70,000 felons from purchasing guns from retail outlets during its first year in effect. In addition, he asserts that the assault weapons ban has effectively restricted the supply of such firearms.

In an effort to reassure gun owners that the HCI does not intend to ban guns, Aborn states that anyone who wishes to have a firearm for self-defense should be allowed to do so. However, he is careful to indicate that a firearm in the home poses serious risks to the residents. In arguing for more stringent gun control laws, Aborn refers to public opinion polls that have consistently indicated that a majority of U.S. citizens support such legislation. In 1996, Robert Walker succeeded Aborn as president of HCI and CPHV. Aborn continued his activities in the gun control movement, working with PAX and other gun control organizations. *See also* BRADY HANDGUN VIOLENCE PREVENTION ACT; CENTER TO PREVENT HANDGUN VIOLENCE; HANDGUN CONTROL, INC.; PAX; SATURDAY NIGHT SPECIAL.

Further Reading: Kevin Pursglove, "Interview with Richard Aborn," at the Handgun Control, Inc. Web site <http://www.irsociety.com/recent/tranabor.html>.

Academics for the Second Amendment (ASA)

Academics for the Second Amendment (ASA) is an organization composed of law professors, political scientists, philosophers, and historians who support the individual right to keep and bear arms. Although ASA notes that the view of the Second Amendment as guaranteeing only the right of states to maintain militias has gained many adherents, the organization contends that this position results from a general hostility among academicians toward guns and gun owners. The organization sponsors legal, philosophical, and historical scholarship that seeks to establish that the right to bear arms applies to individual citizens. To disseminate the results of such scholarship, ASA has conducted professional meetings attended by scholars, lawyers, news reporters, and students.

ASA argues that in the eighteenth century the term "militia" referred not to a formal military organization but to a system of universal military service in which each male citizen of military age was required to possess a firearm for defense against foreign invasion, tyranny, and criminal activity. The organization claims that after the Civil War debates in Congress regarding the nature of citizenship affirmed the need to protect the individual right of African Americans in the South to keep and bear arms for self-defense.

ASA contends that the individual right to keep and bear arms guaranteed in the Second Amendment is not absolute, just like the First Amendment rights of freedom of speech and assembly. Unlike some other gun rights organizations, ASA believes reasonable people may have genuine differences of opinion regarding the application of the right of gun ownership, thus leaving the door open for "sensible gun laws" that are constitutional.

ASA is headquartered in St. Paul, Minnesota, and Joseph E. Olson, the organization's president, teaches business courses at Hamline University. Olson serves on the board of directors of the National Rifle Association (NRA). He has served as administrative law judge for the state of Minnesota and has been a consultant for state legislators and the Minneapolis City Council. ASA has received financial support from the NRA. Of a total of $90,000 reported raised by the organization, $6,000 was donated by the NRA. When ASA held a conference in 1992, the NRA's Legal Defense Fund contributed $5,000 toward expenses. While those involved in the organization consider their efforts necessary to counteract a fundamental prejudice against firearms among academics, gun control advocates see the organization as biased in favor of the NRA and other gun rights organizations. *See also* NATIONAL RIFLE ASSOCIATION; SECOND AMENDMENT.

Further Reading: Scott Heller, "The Right to Bear Arms," *Chronicle of Higher Education* 21 (July 1995), A12; Robert J. Spitzer, *The Politics of Gun Control*, 2nd ed. (New York: Chatham House, 1998).

Accidents Involving Guns

Gun control advocates have cited accidents involving guns as a major reason for introducing greater regulation of firearms, including such measures as mandated training for gun purchasers, firearm safety locks, and outright banning of handguns. Opponents of such measures argue that decreases in the number of gun accidents in recent years make any additional legislation unnecessary. Employing 1987 data from the Metropolitan Life Insurance Company, Gary Kleck, a leading firearms researcher, estimates that fatal gun accidents (FGAs) amount to less than 5 percent of all gun deaths and just over 1 percent of all accidental deaths. He puts the total number of FGAs each year at less than 1,400. Table 6 presents Kleck's estimates of FGAs from 1933 to 1995, based on data from the U.S. National Center for Health Statistics and the National Safety Council. Employing data gathered by the Consumer Product Safety Commission in 1980–81, Kleck observes that guns ranked as the thirty-sixth most common cause of nonfatal accidents. He speculates that the infrequency with which gun owners use their weapons accounts for the low rate of injuries due to firearms.

Kleck notes that the rate of FGAs declined by 33 percent from 1967 to 1987. He attributes the decline in part to improved medical treatment of gunshot wounds and possibly to the increasing number of so-called Saturday night specials, small-caliber handguns with lower power. However, another possibility is that the gun control movement's warnings about the dangers of firearms, particularly handguns, may have reached many gun owners. In more recent years, gun rights organizations such as the National Rifle Association (NRA) have placed greater emphasis on firearm safety through such initiatives as the Eddie Eagle program.

Recent gun control initiatives have been defended as ways of preventing gun accidents involving children. However, Kleck estimates that the probability of a gun accident in gun-owning households involving a child from 0 to 14 years old to be approximately 1 in 58,000, and for handgun-owning households, 1 in 60,000. Kleck claims that handguns are particularly difficult for a young child to fire, a position gun control advocates dispute. While keeping guns locked away is the most effective method of preventing gun accidents involving children, people primarily have handguns in the home for self-protection and some people believe that an unloaded

gun or a gun kept in a locked place defeats the purpose of having the weapon.

Kleck associates the probability of gun accidents with age, sex, and racial groups. Blacks and males aged 15 to 24 have higher accident rates than the general population. In addition, Kleck notes that gun accidents are related to social class: lower income people are more likely to have gun accidents, just as they are more likely to have accidents in general. These are just the people that gun safety programs are less likely to reach. Some evidence also indicates that gun accidents are related to the characteristics of individual gun owners. Accident-prone owners are more likely to be impulsive, alcoholic, or willing to take risks, and more likely to have a flare for the sensational. Kleck notes that a large proportion of gun accidents are related to reckless behavior.

To decrease further the number of accidents involving guns, various groups have advocated mandatory training and proficiency tests to receive a permit to purchase a firearm, although gun rights organizations are less likely than gun control groups to support such measures. Training, which may help reduce accidents due to lack of knowledge, would have little effect on incidents involving intentional, or semi-intentional, reckless activity. Greater attention to possible safety flaws in particular guns may reduce some types of gun accidents. For instance, particular models may be prone to firing when dropped. Trigger locks or other devices to protect against accidental firing could be mandated.

While gun control supporters suggest various measures that may help reduce firearm accidents and other causes of gun deaths and injuries, gun rights advocates quickly become suspicious of any restrictions on the right to own a firearm. In addition, some gun rights supporters question the effectiveness of existing gun control legislation in reducing gun accidents. Even with recent reductions in the numbers of gun accidents, which could to some extent be attributed to gun control legislation, calls for further measures will continue as long as highly emotional incidents

TABLE 6

Fatal Gun Accidents, U.S., 1933–1995

Year	Total	FGAs per 100,000 Resident Population	Handguns (%)	Estimated Handgun	Handgun FGAs per 100,000 Resident Population
1933	3014	2.40			
1935	2799	2.20			
1940	2390	1.80			
1945	2454	1.84			
1950	2174	1.43			
1955	2120	1.28			
1960	2334	1.30			
1965	2344	1.21			
1970	2406	1.18			
1975	2380	1.10			
1980	1955	0.86	41.1	803	0.35
1985	1649	0.69	36.7	605	0.25
1990	1416	0.57	50.8	720	0.29
1991	1441	0.57	49.8	718	0.28
1992	1409	0.55	49.1	691	0.27
1993	1521	0.59	55.2	840	0.33
1994	1356	0.52			
1995	1225	0.47			

Source: Reprinted with permission from Gary Kleck, *Targeting Guns: Firearms and Their Control* (New York: Aldine de Gruyter, 1997), pp. 323-24. Copyright © 1997 by Walter de Gruyter, Inc., New York.

(especially involving children) occur. *See also* AMERICAN ACADEMY OF PEDIATRICS; EDDIE EAGLE; FATALITIES; KLECK, GARY; NATIONAL CENTER FOR INJURY PREVENTION AND CONTROL; NATIONAL RIFLE ASSOCIATION; SATURDAY NIGHT SPECIAL; TRIGGER LOCKS.

Further Reading: Susan Glick and Kristen Rand, eds., *Kids Shooting Kids: Stories from Across the Nation of Unintentional Shootings among Children and Youth* (Washington, DC: Violence Policy Center, 1997); Gary Kleck, *Point Blank: Guns and Violence in America* (New York: Aldine de Gruyter, 1991).

African Americans and Guns

Researchers indicate that African Americans face a far greater risk of being victims of gun violence than the American population as a whole. African-American males in their teens and early 20s are especially prone to suffer from gun violence. In 1990, it was estimated that while the homicide rate associated with firearms for all individuals in their early 20s was 17.1 per 100,000, the rate for African-American males was 140.7, over eight times as great. For all teenagers between the ages of 15 and 19, the homicide rate was 14.0 per 100,000, while for African-American teenagers the rate was 105.3, indicating that gun violence among African Americans represents a major problem for this minority community. "Black-on-black" violence remains a significant problem.

While youth suicide by firearms or other means has raised major concerns among social scientists, this phenomenon is even more critical among young African Americans. The suicide rate among African-American males under 25 increased 20 percent from 1980 to 1992, and during the same period the rate rose from 0.5 per 100,000 to 2.0 among black youths aged 10 to 14. Among all youths under 25 who commit suicide, 50 percent use a firearm; among black youths, over 70 percent employ a firearm. Gun control advocates point to the increasing availability of guns as one important factor in explaining the differences in homicide and suicide rates between blacks and the population as a whole. The African-American population appears to have arrived at the same conclusion, for surveys indicate that African Americans support gun control at higher rates than whites.

Although data indicate that African Americans are at higher risk of being victims of gun violence than the American population as a whole, gun rights supporters emphasize that African Americans have an equal right to possess firearms for sporting purposes and self-defense, and encourage gun ownership among minorities. The young man shown here is engaged in benchrest shooting. *Courtesy of Browning.*

Despite such figures, gun rights advocates argue from a broader historical perspective that African Americans from the time of slavery to the present have suffered from discrimination that prevented them from possessing firearms they could have used to defend themselves. They argue that despite Fourteenth Amendment (ratified in 1868) guarantees of equal protection under the law for all Americans, blacks were denied basic rights, particularly in the South, and thus reduced to a status inferior to whites. Although in *United States v. Cruikshank* (1876) the Supreme Court refused to allow the national government to intervene to protect the rights of blacks to keep and bear arms, numerous tales are told of blacks who used firearms to protect themselves during the dark days of segregation and intimidation.

Lynchings of blacks by whites encouraged some blacks to acquire firearms for self-defense. Although at times blacks took collec-

tive action to arm themselves, southern states established legal policies intended to disarm them. Firearms laws did not ban the possession of guns, but made it more difficult for African Americans to own guns. Gun rights advocates note that even during the height of nonviolent opposition to discrimination during the 1960s, some southern blacks decided to protect themselves by owning firearms. For instance, in 1964, a group of armed blacks in Jonesboro, Louisiana, formed the Deacons of Defense and Justice, vowing to resist any racist attacks. The organization established chapters in Louisiana, Mississippi, and Alabama as a deterrent to the violent attacks conducted against civil rights workers.

Gun rights advocates argue that today the crucial violence problem for African Americans is not a need for more stringent gun control efforts in the minority community. Rather, because government has demonstrated an inability to provide adequate protection, blacks must assert their right to keep and bear arms. When applied to African Americans, gun rights supporters label gun control a racist policy, based on the long history of attempts to prevent blacks from exercising what is considered a basic civil right of self-defense. Gun control advocates respond to the claimed racist history of gun control measures by arguing that African Americans have suffered historically and are still experiencing the harmful effects of a society inundated with firearms. *See also* BLACK CODES; BLACK PANTHER PARTY; FATALITIES; FOURTEENTH AMENDMENT; STATE GUN STATUTES; SUICIDE; *UNITED STATES V. CRUIKSHANK* (1876).

Further reading: Gregg Lee Carter, *The Gun Control Movement* (New York: Twayne, 1997); Robert J. Cottrol and Raymond T. Diamond, "The Second Amendment: Toward an Afro-Americanist Reconsideration," in David B. Kopel, ed., *Guns: Who Should Have Them?* (Amherst, NY: Prometheus, 1995).

AK-47

In 1997, the news media noted the fiftieth anniversary of the most successful assault rifle ever made, the AK-47, also called the Kalashnikov after its Russian developer, Mikhail Kalashnikov, a sergeant in the Soviet army. The AK-47 was celebrated for its exceptional reliability, highly accurate semiautomatic fire, and controllable automatic burst fire. Because the AK-47 proved relatively inexpensive and required little sophistication to produce, underdeveloped countries, especially those associated with the former Soviet Union, became major sources of the weapon. The AK-47 was used throughout the world in various guerrilla wars supported by the Soviet Union. Other countries, including China, Finland, Israel, North Korea, South Africa, and Eastern European nations then under Soviet control, produced versions of the weapon.

Kalashnikov developed the weapon in the highly secretive atmosphere of the Stalinist regime, basing the design on a German assault rifle, or *Sturmgewehr,* used during World War II. The assault rifle met the criteria set by the Soviet military establishment of the

time: simplicity of manufacture and operation, reliability, and firepower. For his accomplishment, the Russian sergeant received a monetary reward and gained recognition as a Hero of Socialist Labor.

In 1959, the AK-47 was even further simplified, thus reducing its costs of production. The revised weapon was called the AKM. Countries within the Soviet bloc, which produced their own weapons, standardized parts for the assault rifle. The United States failed to develop a similarly efficient system of small arms production. Many argue that the more technically sophisticated weapons produced by American and European manufacturers were no more effective than the AK-47 and were considerably more expensive.

American forces first faced the legendary Soviet assault rifle in Vietnam, where the AKM was generally judged more reliable than the American M-16. Unlike the M-16, the AKM withstood the harshest conditions, further increasing the weapon's reputation for dependability. The AKM could also be used to great effect by relatively untrained soldiers, an important feature in a guerrilla war.

Nations outside the Soviet bloc, including Israel, South Africa, and Finland, also produced variations of the AK-47, which retained the basic features of the Soviet weapon with certain additions, such as a bipod stand, carrying handle, folding stock, or grenade launcher. Semi-automatic versions of the AK-47 have been available to private citizens in the United States. The call for a ban on assault rifles gained momentum in part due to the reputation of the Kalashnikov and similar automatic and semi-automatic weapons. Their widespread availability throughout the world and the mystique that developed around them made these weapons an attractive possession and a prime good in illegal foreign trade. *See also* ASSAULT WEAPONS BAN; ISRAEL; STOCKTON, CALIFORNIA, SHOOTING.

Further reading: Virginia Ezell, "The 50th Anniversary of the AK-47: A Visit to the Izhevsk Machine Plant," *Small Arms Review* 1 (April 1998), 42-48; Michael R. Gordon, "Russians Honor Inventor of AK-47 Assault Rifle," *New York Times* (March 13, 1997); Jack Lewis, ed., *The Gun Digest Book of Assault Weapons*, 4th ed. (Northbrook, IL: DBI Books, 1996).

Aliens

In February 1997, following the shooting at the Empire State Building in New York City, in which an alien who had been in the United States for just five weeks killed one person and wounded several others with a firearm he purchased in Florida, Senators Richard J. Durbin, Democrat from Illinois, and Edward M. Kennedy, Democrat from Massachusetts, introduced the Empire State Building Counter-Terrorism Act. The bill was intended to amend the Brady Handgun Violence Prevention Act by prohibiting the purchase or possession of a firearm or ammunition by an alien admitted to the United States under a non-immigrant visa.

The bill contained exceptions for aliens admitted to the United States for legitimate hunting or sporting purposes and for official government representatives, "distinguished foreign visitors," and foreign law enforcement officers of governments friendly to the United States. According to the provisions of the proposed legislation, a person admitted into the country under a non-immigrant visa could receive a waiver by submitting a petition to the U.S. attorney general indicating that waiving the prohibition "would be in the interests of justice" and "would not jeopardize the public safety." Gun rights organizations reacted negatively to the proposed legislation, arguing that such proposals demonstrated an anti-foreign bias and could deny individuals the needed means for self-defense.

The Durbin-Kennedy bill was approved as part of the Omnibus Appropriations Act for fiscal 1999. In November 1998, an official of the Bureau of Alcohol, Tobacco, and Firearms (BATF) announced at the National Association of Sporting Goods Wholesalers show in Tampa, Florida, that the new federal restrictions on the sale of firearms to aliens included in the Durbin-Kennedy bill were being instituted. Individuals included in the ban are those traveling temporarily in the country, those attending school in the country but maintaining a residence abroad, and certain foreign employees. In addition to aliens admitted to the U.S. for lawful hunting or sporting purposes, the prohibition does not apply to official representatives of a foreign government accredited to the U.S. government or to an international organization with headquarters in the U.S.

BATF Form 4473, which was revised in October 1998 to accommodate the National Instant Check System, was altered in early 1999 to provide for a declaration regarding alien status. However, questions arose regarding the effectiveness of a system that depends on a statement by the purchaser and an instant check system that may not have the required information to flag an alien with a non-immigrant visa. *See also* BRADY HANDGUN VIOLENCE PREVENTION ACT; BUREAU OF ALCOHOL, TOBACCO, AND FIREARMS; EMPIRE STATE BUILDING SHOOTING; GUN SHOWS; NATIONAL INSTANT CHECK SYSTEM.

Further reading: Durbin-Kennedy Empire State Building Counter-Terrorism Act of 1997 <www.thomas.loc.gov/cgi-bin/query/z?c105:S.380>; Robert M. Hausman, "ATF Announces New Gun Restrictions for Aliens," *Gun Week* 33 (December 20, 1998), 3.

American Academy of Pediatrics (AAP)

The American Academy of Pediatrics (AAP), concerned with what it considers an unacceptable level of firearms deaths and injuries among children and adolescents, has taken a strong stand against the possession of firearms in the home. Two groups within the organization, the committee on injury and poison prevention and the committee on adolescence, have made extensive policy recommendations to reduce the number of deaths and injuries among children and adolescents due to firearms. AAP supports model state legislation that would prohibit the manufacture, sale, distribution, or ownership of handguns.

The organization expresses concern that no safety regulations exist for handguns, which are considered potentially deadly consumer products. AAP notes that the American culture, including the mass media, encourages dangerous gun use. Firearm safety programs are considered of questionable worth, given that children and adolescents often lack good judgment and tend to act impulsively. The organization cautions that some gun education programs may actually encourage or promote firearm use among children and recommends that schools and local groups choose such a program with care. The Academy supports a collective interpretation of the Second Amendment, claiming that it was intended to prohibit the national government from interfering with state militias. The organization concludes that the Second Amendment is no barrier to legislation geared to reduce the availability of handguns to children.

AAP asserts that the most dependable way of reducing firearms-related deaths and injuries among children is to remove handguns from their environment. To accomplish this end, restrictions should be placed on the private purchase of handguns and on their possession in the home, which could involve a complete ban on such weapons. As another way of reducing the danger handguns pose to children, AAP suggests reducing the destructive capability of ammunition. The Academy recommends that pediatricians and other health care providers inform parents about the dangers of handguns in the home and calls for reducing the romantic portrayal of guns in the media.

The Academy estimates that 20 percent of fatalities among older youth are due to firearms, three-quarters of teenage homicides involve the use of firearms, and 80 percent of child accidental firearm deaths occur among youth aged 10 to 19. The organization recommends that health care providers ask patients if a gun is present in the home and counsel gun owners to remove weapons, or at least to store them safely. Health care providers are asked to identify adolescents who may be at greater risk of firearm violence, and provide appropriate counseling.

AAP has called for the formation of coalitions of health care professionals, parents, schools, police, the media, and others to work to reduce firearm injury and death. Educational programs would involve curricula that cover such topics as coping skills, conflict management, and risk awareness. The organization advocates research to better understand those variables related to firearm injuries and to arrive at additional policies to reduce gun violence.

The Academy distributes a pamphlet that recommends always keeping guns unloaded and locked away. It advises keeping bullets locked in a separate location, making sure that children do not have access to keys. For families that do not have a firearm, the pamphlet recommends that parents tell their children to stay away from guns when at their friends' homes. Although parents who possess guns are urged to unload them and lock them away from children, the brochure emphasizes that the safest way to prevent gun accidents is not to keep a gun in the home. Parents are asked to tell their children that movie and television violence is not real and that guns could seriously hurt them. Parents should also counsel their children in nonviolent ways of settling arguments. The brochure also cautions against allowing children to participate in shooting activities. *See also* ACADEMICS FOR THE SECOND AMENDMENT; ACCIDENTS INVOLVING GUNS; HEALTH CARE PROFESSIONALS; MEDIA VIOLENCE; SECOND AMENDMENT; TRIGGER LOCKS.

Further reading: American Academy of Pediatrics, "Firearms and Adolescents," *Pediatrics* 89 (April 1992), 784-87; American Academy of Pediatrics, "Firearm Injuries Affecting the Pediatric Population," *Pediatrics* 89 (April 1992), 788-90; American Academy of Pediatrics, *Keep Your Family Safe from Firearm Injury*, brochure (n.d.); AAP web site <www.aap.org/advocacy/firearms>.

American Bar Association (ABA)

The American Bar Association (ABA) recognizes that gun safety is a major public concern, citing data that identify firearms as the most often used instrument in homicides. Referring to the more than 35,000 deaths attributed to firearms in 1995, the ABA notes that the overall homicide rate in the United States far exceeds that of other industrialized nations. The organization considers gun violence among youth a serious public policy problem. Citing a United Nations report, the ABA notes that 9 out of 10 killings of youth in industrialized nations occur in the United States.

The ABA was formed in 1878 and subsequently became the primary representative of the legal profession in the United States. In 1936, the House of Delegates was created as the organization's major policy-making body. In 1997, the House of Delegates had 525 members, including, among others, delegates from the states, state and local bar associations, and affiliated organizations. Members of the Board of Governors are also members of the House of Delegates. The Board acts and speaks for the ABA, following the direction of the House.

Among its stated goals, the ABA promotes improvements in the justice system and the law, serves as the legal profession's national representative, and represents the interests of the membership. Approximately half of American lawyers are members. The organization informs members, policy makers, and the general public about its recommendations on various issues, including gun control.

In the past, the ABA focused on possible legal strategies to keep firearms away from youth and adult criminals. More recently, the organization has entertained proposals originating with public health professionals and community leaders. While recognizing the legitimacy of gun ownership, especially in a nation with a long tradition of firearms possession, the ABA supports efforts to control illegal or unauthorized access to firearms to reduce the death rate from suicides, accidents, and homicides related to firearms.

The ABA supports policies geared to regulate firearms sales and transfers to ensure that minors are prevented from gaining access to guns. The organization supports legislation establishing consumer safety standards for firearms. Such a measure would effectively ban the domestic manufacture of Saturday night specials, handguns generally considered of inferior quality. Such standards would include a mandate that each new firearm sale to a private individual include a safety lock and a device to indicate if weapons contain ammunition. The organization recommends such safety features to ensure that teenagers

and children cannot inadvertently fire a gun. *See also* ACCIDENTS INVOLVING GUNS; LAWYER'S SECOND AMENDMENT SOCIETY; LEGAL COMMUNITY AGAINST VIOLENCE; SATURDAY NIGHT SPECIAL; UNITED NATIONS.

Further Reading: American Bar Association Web site <http://www.abanet.org>.

American Civil Liberties Union (ACLU)

On many civil liberties issues, the American Civil Liberties Union's (ACLU) positions coincide closely with those of gun rights groups such as the National Rifle Association (NRA). The ACLU, like the NRA, calls for greater accountability of federal law enforcement procedures, especially in light of such events as the Ruby Ridge standoff in 1992 and the raid on the Branch Davidian compound in Waco, Texas, in 1993. Each organization believes that additional authority should not be granted to law enforcement agencies until procedures have been established to secure every person's constitutional rights. For instance, both the ACLU and the NRA have expressed concern that the rights of citizens not be violated in the federal government's war on drugs. On subjects such as the Fourth Amendment protection against unreasonable searches and seizures, the Fifth Amendment guarantee against self-incrimination, and other safeguards in the Bill of Rights, the two organizations tend to agree. However, on the Second Amendment, which is of greatest importance to the NRA and other gun rights groups, the ACLU holds a significantly different interpretation. Due to that difference, the relationship between the ACLU and the NRA is sometimes amicable, but often uneasy.

The 275,000-member ACLU is headquartered in Washington, D.C., but has offices in all 50 states, as well as staffed affiliate offices in major cities and over 300 chapters in smaller towns. The organization maintains regional offices in Denver and Atlanta. Ira Glasser, who has written extensively on civil liberties, has served as executive director since 1978, and Nadine Strossen, law professor at the New York Law School, has been presi-

The logo of the American Civil Liberties Union, which holds positions similar to those of the National Rifle Association on many gun rights issues, but denies that the Second Amendment guarantees an unlimited right of individuals to own firearms. *Courtesy of the American Civil Liberties Union.*

require possession of weapons far more deadly than handguns or rifles. While many gun rights advocates argue that circumstance should have no bearing on an absolute right protected by the Constitution, the ACLU concludes that the Second Amendment does not guarantee an unlimited right of individuals to own firearms and other weapons, and that such measures as licensing and registration constitute reasonable restrictions.

The organization believes any reasonable person will conclude that the right to bear arms does not apply to such modern weapons as bazookas, torpedoes, missiles, and submachine guns. If government has the right under the Constitution to restrict arms, then there must be a determination of what constitutes a reasonable restriction, which may include regulations that do not violate any of the other rights guaranteed by the Bill of Rights. *See also* NATIONAL RIFLE ASSOCIATION; RUBY RIDGE; SECOND AMENDMENT; WACO, TEXAS, RAID.

Further Reading: ACLU, "Guardian of Liberty: American Civil Liberties Union," briefing paper, 1997; ACLU, "Gun Control," ACLU library resource, 1996; ACLU Web site <www.aclu.org>.

dent since 1991. An 84-member board of directors representing state affiliates governs the organization. The ACLU has had significant influence in many civil liberties areas, including the rights of prisoners, children, voters, workers, and women.

The ACLU adheres to a collectivist interpretation of the constitutional right to keep and bear arms. The national board, after much discussion, agreed that the original intention of the Second Amendment was to guarantee the right of states to establish militias to protect their security and freedom against the national government. According to the ACLU, this intention is "somewhat anachronistic" in the contemporary world because its implementation would logically

American Firearms Council (AFC)

The American Firearms Council (AFC) describes itself as "an industry educational foundation whose purpose is to study the issues, conduct and collect research, and disseminate information to educate the public and the media on public safety, and about firearms for sport [and] self-protection." The organization led the firearms industry's opposition to the various gun control initiatives that followed passage of the 1994 Brady Handgun Violence Prevention Act, including proposals to ban assault weapons, institute mandatory gun registration, and restrict juvenile acquisition and possession of guns. The AFC objects to the attempt to convert gun violence from a criminal justice to a public health issue. It has publicized research findings indicating that crime rates have fallen in states that adopted provisions allowing the carrying of concealed weapons.

The Council recognizes various legitimate reasons for owning guns, "from the thrill of watching the sun rise on an early morning hunt–the challenge and discipline of competition–the appreciation of collecting fine craftsmanship–to the sense of security for one's self and family." Responding to those who advocate further gun control to reduce accidental gun injuries and deaths, the organization notes that, compared to other causes, fatalities from firearm accidents represent a small and decreasing problem. The AFC reports a 15-percent decline in fatal firearm accidents from 1985 to 1995 and attributes this decline to gun safety programs, not gun control.

In 1996, the AFC initiated a national firearm safety effort intended to reach those who did not own firearms. In organization-supported ads that appeared in major newspapers, law enforcement officers presented specific gun safety rules. AFC President Richard Feldman emphasized that the campaign would focus on the importance of individual responsibility for gun safety. The organization holds an annual Firearm Education Day and invites politically influential individuals to participate. Participants are given the opportunity to shoot a variety of firearms.

The Council publicizes three basic safety rules:

1. "Treat every gun as if it's loaded!"
2. "Never point a gun at anything you don't mean to shoot!"
3. "Keep your finger off the trigger until ready to fire!"

The AFC does not believe any safety mechanism is a substitute for proper gun handling, and the organization urges all firearms owners to become familiar with guidebooks accompanying guns and to undergo training in the use of weapons. While using a firearm, the owner should protect it from unauthorized use. If not in use, a firearm should be locked away unloaded, with ammunition kept in a separate place. Although gun control advocates agree with such advice, many contend that a home would be much safer without any guns at all.

The AFC has expressed concern about efforts to hold gun manufacturers, retailers, and the industry in general responsible for illegal acts committed with firearms. According to the organization, even though manufacturers have successfully defended themselves in several cases, the costs of legal defense can be high. Because the suits often are not based on the claim that the product is defective, insurance companies may not cover the costs of litigation. The Council contends that lawsuits supported by gun control organizations are being used as a way to put firearms manufacturers out of business. The Council reacted strongly against a suit brought in New York federal circuit court in 1996 that accused firearms companies and trade associations of illegally conspiring to prevent passage of legislation to regulate firearms commerce. *See also* ACCIDENTS INVOLVING GUNS; ASSAULT WEAPONS BAN; BRADY HANDGUN VIOLENCE PREVENTION ACT.

Further Reading: American Firearms Council, Inc. Web site <http://www.assc.org/afchome.html>.

American Jewish Congress (AJC)

The American Jewish Congress takes a strong pro-gun control position on several firearms-related issues, holding that more stringent legislation is required. In May 1998, following a series of school shootings, the Congress announced that it was initiating a campaign in the Jewish community to mobilize support for more effective gun control laws. In the announcement, AJC President Jack Rosen and Executive Director Phil Baum stated that firearms "have exacted a terrible toll on American life," and asserted that the those opposing gun control do not represent the majority position. They labeled absurd the claim that "rapid-firing assault weapons are designed for personal use," rejected assertions about gun rights based on "specious constitutional arguments," and called foolish the pro-gun slogan "guns don't kill people, people kill people." Rosen and Baum pointed to "the unspeakable killings of children by children," claiming that gun violence in the United States kills 16 youths each day. The announcement noted that the president of

AJC's Northern Pacific Region was among eight people who were shot and killed in 1993 by a gunman in San Francisco.

In June 1997, the Congress reacted against the U.S. Supreme Court ruling in *Printz v. United States* that a provision of the Brady Handgun Violence Prevention Act requiring background checks of prospective gun purchasers by local law enforcement officers violated the constitutional separation of powers between the federal and state governments. AJC President David V. Kahn and Executive Director Baum issued a statement criticizing the Court's narrow interpretation of federal power. Kahn and Baum asserted that the Court was adhering to an outdated eighteenth-century conception of federalism and urged Congress to find alternative ways of dealing with the problem of handguns and their relation to criminal activity.

In September 1997, Baum issued a statement on behalf of the Congress regarding assault weapons. Baum supported Senator Dianne Feinstein's request that Israel cease exporting assault weapons to the United States and expressed the hope that Israel would comply. However, Baum claimed that the ultimate fault did not lie with Israel, stating that "it is problematic to call upon another country to exercise restraints on behalf of the people of the United States which the people of the United States have been unwilling to impose upon themselves." Baum pledged that the AJC would cooperate with Senator Feinstein to enhance legislation prohibiting the importation of assault weapons "so that the door to them will be closed firmly, once and for all." *See also* ASSAULT WEAPONS BAN; BRADY HANDGUN VIOLENCE PREVENTION ACT; FEINSTEIN, DIANNE; ISRAEL; *PRINTZ V. UNITED STATES* (1997).

Further Reading: American Jewish Congress Web site <www.ajcongress.org>.

American Revolution

For gun rights advocates, the causes and conduct of the American Revolution are a vital support for their interpretation of the Second Amendment as guaranteeing an individual right to keep and bear arms. According to this view, the British maintenance of a standing army in their American colonies threatened the basic rights of colonists, who, in any event, had learned through necessity the value of arming themselves against the elements, the Indians, and, ultimately, a tyrannical foreign power. Key moments in the revolution stand out in this interpretation. In March 1770, the "Boston Massacre," a confrontation between British soldiers and an unruly mob of Bostonians, ended in bloodshed as the troops shot into the unarmed crowd. Five men were killed and the soldiers responsible were placed on trial. Gun supporters also focus on the April 19, 1775, battles of Lexington and Concord, which marked the true beginning of the war. British forces attempting to regain control of munitions taken by the colonists suffered moderately heavy losses at the hands of militia bands.

According to gun rights advocates, Americans can derive a fundamental lesson from the revolutionary experience: The ultimate defense of individual and nation against tyranny depends upon a citizenry willing and able to take up arms, not upon an organized standing army that can easily become the instrument of oppression. Therefore, any attempt to limit an individual right to keep and bear arms must be vigorously resisted because it may foreshadow attempts to tyrannize the population.

Despite this pro-gun interpretation, the revolutionary experience with arms contains mixed lessons. In May 1775, the Second Continental Congress, seeking to devise an effective military strategy, struggled against the strong aversion that many colonists had to a standing army. Despite this antipathy, the British army had defended the colonies during the French and Indian War. Congress therefore created an American military force to improve the chances of victory against the professional British army. Members of Congress realized that dependence on militias alone could not achieve their objective. As the war proceeded, the standing Continental army became the most important military instrument for the Americans. In winter

1778, Baron Friedrich Wilhelm von Steuben, a Prussian army officer serving with General George Washington at Valley Forge in Pennsylvania, molded American troops into an effective fighting force.

The American Revolution was not a clear conflict pitting the united colonists against the tyrannous British, but was to some extent a civil war. The American population divided into three groups: the pro-independence faction, those who remained loyal to Great Britain (Tories), and those who were neutral, prudently supporting one side or the other depending upon the fortunes of war. The revolutionaries struggled not only with the British, but with the loyalists, a significant segment of the population composed of a varied group of small farmers, large landowners, and professional people.

Marksmanship contributed significantly to the ultimate American victory. Living on the edge of the wilderness, Americans had a long experience with firearms, which many colonists learned to handle at an early age. Revolutionary forces attempted to impress and intimidate the British with their proficiency in firearms. British General William Howe, commenting on his enemy's prowess, once referred to the "terrible guns of the rebels." To reinforce this image, General George Washington ordered his troops to wear hunting shirts, symbolizing the adeptness of the riflemen. However, a lack of arms presented a serious problem for the American army. Historians estimate that in summer 1776 one-fourth of Washington's troops had no guns. British confiscation was not the only source of difficulty. Although local gun makers worked feverishly to produce weapons, and contracts were signed with foreign producers, gun-making was slow and tedious in this pre-industrial age. The French helped the Americans acquire desperately needed arms to continue the struggle, contributing an estimated 100,000 firearms by 1781.

Many factors contributed to the final American victory formalized in the 1783 Treaty of Paris, including the transition from militia units to regular troops, French assistance, and British difficulties in supporting and supplying troops. However, following the war, Americans focused on the role of a militia composed of citizen soldiers, and continued to venerate the abilities of the individual marksman. Although Washington wished to continue at least a limited standing military force following the end of hostilities, the Continental Army was allowed to dwindle to less than 100 soldiers. Fear of centralized government, combined with suspicion of a standing army, resulted in a postwar emphasis on militias. The Second Amendment, whether interpreted as a right to keep and bear arms guaranteed to Americans individually, or as a right granted to states in the formation and maintenance of their respective organized militia units, arises out of this historical context. *See also* MINUTEMEN, REVOLUTIONARY; NATIVE AMERICANS; SECOND AMENDMENT; UNITED KINGDOM.

Further Reading: Lee Kennett and James LaVerne Anderson, *The Gun in America: The Origins of a National Dilemma* (Westport, CT: Greenwood, 1975); Wayne R. LaPierre, *Guns, Crime, and Freedom* (Washington, DC: Regnery, 1994).

American Rifleman

The official journal of the National Rifle Association (NRA), the *American Rifleman* contains articles on such topics as new handguns and rifles, hunting and shooting techniques, the history of firearms in the United States, and the activities and meetings of the Association. Of all the gun magazines, the *American Rifleman*, in its 114th year of publication in 1999, stands as the primary voice for pro-gun interests. Each issue contains material on the politics of gun ownership, focusing on the protection of what the NRA contends is the Second Amendment's guarantee of the individual's right to keep and bear arms. Members of the organization receive the magazine, which is published 11 times per year.

Several regular features advocate the rights of gun owners. "The Armed Citizen" offers several accounts of gun owners who were able to defend themselves against crime because they had access to a firearm. Wayne LaPierre, NRA executive vice president, writes a regular column about the status of gun rights in the United States and abroad. LaPierre has dedicated the organization to electing a pro-gun president, keeping a pro-gun Congress, and educating a pro-gun generation. LaPierre reports on legislative proposals to regulate gun sales and ownership. He reports critically on gun control efforts, including President Bill Clinton's support for gun registration and allegations that the president seeks to appoint anti-Second Amendment federal judges, as well as a United Nations-backed gun control campaign involving a ban on the import of handguns.

Another feature of the magazine, "ILA Report," offers detailed news of legislative action from the NRA's Institute for Legislative Action (ILA). The ILA provides members with information about the progress of NRA-backed legislative proposals and reports on state legislative action, such as the passage of versions of the NRA-ILA's model Crime Victims' Protection Act. "ILA Report" also publishes the names of those who have made monetary contributions to the Institute.

"NRA Woman's Voice," a column written by women active in the NRA, offers information about the special place of women in the organization and the problems they sometimes face in acquiring training in the use of firearms. The "NRA Regional Report" includes news about NRA activities from around the nation, including legislative activity at the state level, training workshops, shooting events, law enforcement activities, and a schedule of gun shows. Each issue contains at least one feature article relevant to the NRA's position on the Second Amendment. *See also* CLINTON, WILLIAM JEFFERSON (BILL); GUN SHOWS; INSTITUTE FOR LEGISLATIVE ACTION; NATIONAL RIFLE ASSOCIATION; LAPIERRE, WAYNE; SECOND AMENDMENT; UNITED NATIONS; WOMEN AND GUNS.

Further Reading: *American Rifleman* (National Rifle Association, Fairfax, VA).

American Shooting Sports Council (ASSC)

Founded in 1989, the American Shooting Sports Council (ASSC) is the trade associa-

tion of the firearms industry, conducting lobbying activities on legislative and legal issues. The organization represents all parts of the industry, including firearms, ammunition, and various accessory producers. Approximately 2,000 firearms, ammunition, and accessory manufacturers and importers belong to the organization, plus several hundred wholesale distributors, over 25,000 retailers, and several thousand industry representatives, such as salespeople, suppliers, and trade and consumer publications. The ASSC campaigns against what the organization considers unreasonable limitations on the right to keep and bear arms. The group constitutes a large lobbying force in Washington, D.C., and the state capitals.

Each year since 1992, ASSC members have rallied in Washington, D.C., meeting with their congresspeople and senators and their staffs and with government officials in federal agencies involved in regulating the firearm industry. At the Annual Wild Game Banquet, the Council presents a favored legislator with the Congressional Leader of the Year Award. In 1997, Republican Representative Bob Barr of Georgia received the award, and in 1998 the recipients were Republican Senator Jeff Sessions of Alabama and Democratic Representative John Tanner of Tennessee.

Along with gun rights organizations, the ASSC strongly disagrees with those who claim a close relationship between guns and crime, contending instead that firearms do not play a major independent role in illegal activities. The Association claims that American citizens owning firearms contribute significantly to the individual and collective security of the people. Contrary to charges that the industry's products are an inherently unsafe product, ASSC Executive Director Richard Feldman asserts that "our industry markets safety," and argues that firearms, when used "properly and responsibly," are inherently safe and protect law-abiding citizens from criminals.

The ASSC strives to protect the industry from national or state government actions that would limit the possession of firearms. In January 1998, Feldman announced that the Council had taken legal action against Massachusetts Attorney General Scott Harshbarger, who had intended to institute new restrictions on gun ownership in the state. Feldman charged that the Massachusetts attorney general had acted unilaterally, ignoring input from ASSC; Feldman stated that his organization was willing to work with the state on "feasible, rational solutions." Fearing that new regulations in the guise of consumer safety would include a ban on handgun sales in Massachusetts, the ASSC charged Attorney General Harshbarger with attempting to achieve gun prohibition by issuing regulatory orders without the appropriate interest group and constituent input. Although enforcement of the Massachusetts attorney general's regulations was halted temporarily due to a firearms industry lawsuit and an appeal by Harshbarger, a strict new Massachusetts gun control law went into effect in October 1998.

On the national level, the ASSC has disputed Handgun Control, Inc.'s claim that a significant number of prosecutions have resulted from passage of the Brady Handgun Violence Prevention Act. According to Feldman, crime rates have declined in recent years because more Americans have purchased firearms and many states have enacted provisions allowing citizens to carry concealed weapons, not because of the Brady Law's provisions. Like other gun rights groups, the Council is concerned by calls from various international organizations for a cross-national gun control policy. Representing the ASSC at the Americas Regional Workshop on Firearm Regulation in Sao Paulo, Brazil, in December 1997, Feldman cautioned the representatives that they must respect the right to possess a firearm in nations, such as the United States, that recognize such a right. Feldman also declared that the ASSC supported efforts to obstruct illegal arms trading and the criminal misuse of firearms, but strongly objected to any efforts to prevent law-abiding citizens from owning guns. *See also* BARR, BOB; BRADY HANDGUN VIOLENCE PREVENTION ACT; CONCEALED CARRY LAWS; HANDGUN CONTROL, INC; MASSACHUSETTS GUN VIOLENCE PREVENTION LAW.

Further Reading: Richard Feldman, "From the Capital: Pro Safety or Anti-Gun?," *Guns and Ammo* (September 1997) 34–35; Richard Feldman, "America's Regional Workshop on Firearm Regulation," American Shooting Sports Council statement (December 1997).

Americans for Democratic Action (ADA)

Americans for Democratic Action (ADA), a liberal organization founded in 1947 by such noted individuals as Eleanor Roosevelt, Walter Reuther, Arthur Schlesinger, Jr., Reinhold Niebuhr, and Hubert Humphrey, has taken a consistently pro-gun control stand. ADA members include professionals, businesspeople, labor leaders, educators, political leaders, and other persons who subscribe to a liberal political ideology. Its members associate with 22 local chapters that work to elect liberal candidates and to lobby progressive measures at the state and local levels. The national organization maintains a political action committee, ADA/PAC, which makes campaign donations to liberal candidates seeking seats in the U.S. Congress.

ADA takes a strong position against the use of weaponry of any sort, particularly when the use of force is perceived as threatening the democratic political process. The organization advocates decreasing the national military budget by at least 50 percent and using the funds for development programs in the United States and other countries. Believing that demilitarization and democracy are closely linked, the organization advocates an American foreign policy that encourages other nations, particularly developing countries, to reduce the political role of their armed forces, thereby stimulating progress toward freedom of speech, fair elections, and the elimination of human rights abuses.

The ADA supported passage of the Brady Handgun Violence Prevention Act and advocates its maintenance in the face of court challenges, noting that the legislation has been effective in preventing illegal firearms purchases. The Lautenberg Amendment, which prohibits firearms sales to those previously convicted of a misdemeanor involving domestic violence, also received ADA support. The group has opposed attempts in the U.S. Congress to limit the ability of gun violence victims to sue gun manufacturers for damages, and supports passage of state consumer protection laws to protect the consumer against low-quality firearms. The organization has opposed proposals to allow the importation of surplus military weapons. To protect children from the misuse of handguns, the ADA advocates measures mandating the use of trigger locks and safety courses for gun owners.

The ADA supports control of firearms trafficking, especially among youth, noting that the Bureau of Alcohol, Tobacco, and Firearms (BATF) has insufficient authority to trace weapons. The ADA also advocates a policy that would hold gun owners responsible for failing to store firearms properly if children who gain access to the weapons use them to injure or kill others. The organization supports bans on Saturday night specials and recognizes the need for greater safety in schools against the possibility of gun violence. Gun rights advocates claim the ADA has taken inconsistent positions by refusing to recognize the individual right to keep and bear arms, which gun rights supporters believe is protected by the Second Amendment. *See also* BRADY HANDGUN VIO-LENCE PREVENTION ACT; BUREAU OF ALCOHOL, TOBACCO, AND FIREARMS; LAUTENBERG AMEND-MENT; SATURDAY NIGHT SPECIAL; SECOND AMENDMENT; TRIGGER LOCKS.

Further Reading: Americans for Democratic Action Web site <http://www.adaction.org>; Steven M. Gillon, *Politics and Vision: The ADA and American Liberalism* (New York: Oxford University Press, 1987).

Antiterrorism and Effective Death Penalty Act

The Antiterrorism and Effective Death Penalty Act of 1996 introduced several changes in federal firearms laws. According to the act. anyone who knowingly provides "material support or resources," including firearms, to a foreign terrorist organization, or conspires to do so, is subject to a fine or to imprisonment for a term of up to 10 years. The act also made it a crime to provide, or hide, firearms, knowing or intending that they be used to commit a crime.

The act directed the U.S. attorney general and secretary of defense to conduct a joint study of the "number and extent of thefts from military arsenals (including National Guard armories) of firearms, explosives, and other materials that are potentially useful to terrorists." Referring to acts of terrorism beyond the nation's borders, the law declared that an act of terrorism includes the use of a firearm to assault any person in the United States if the assault involves "conduct transcending national boundaries," and if the offense involves one or more of the following: the use of the mail or interstate or foreign commerce or has an effect on interstate or foreign commerce; the victim is employed in the federal government or the military; any federally owned building or property is damaged, or the offense occurred in a U.S. territorial jurisdiction. Non-lethal assault with a firearm carries a maximum sentence of 30 years. The law also provides penalties for threatening or conspiring to commit an assault with a firearm.

The act significantly increased the penalty for carrying a firearm onto an airplane. Punishments are provided for anyone who kills or attempts to kill an officer or employee of the federal government, including any member of the armed forces while engaged in official duties. This provision also applies to former government personnel. The definition of a deadly weapon includes a weapon "intended to cause death or danger" but that fails to operate due to a defective component.

The act directed the secretary of the treasury to conduct a study of tagging explosive materials "for purposes of detection and identification," to explore the possibility of making inert those chemicals commonly used to manufacture explosives and the feasibility of controlling "certain precursor chemicals used to manufacture explosive materials," and to investigate state licensing requirements for the purchase and use of commercial high explosives. At the request of firearms organizations, the act excluded black or smokeless powder from the mandated study.

Also mandated was a Treasury Department study of law enforcement officer deaths and serious injuries over the preceding decade, including felonies and accidents, shootings, the type of firearm involved, whether officers were shot with their own firearms or with other officers' firearms, and instances in which bullet-resistant vests or helmets were penetrated by armor-piercing ammunition. In the examination of ammunition, the study was to determine the effect a ban on particular calibers would have on uses for civilian self-defense and sports. The act authorized up to $10 million for the National Institute of Justice Office of Science and Technology to develop technologies to be employed to combat terrorism, including detection devices for weapons, explosives, and chemicals, and to evaluate technologies to assist state and local law enforcement agencies in efforts to resist terrorism. *See Also* TAGGANTS.

Further Reading: Alan Korwin, with Michael P. Anthony, *Gun Laws of America* (Phoenix: Bloomfield, 1997).

Armijo v. Ex Cam, Inc. (1987)

Armijo v. Ex Cam, Inc. (656 F. Supp. 771, 1987) raised the question whether a manufacturer of a gun that is used in a murder or assault can be held liable for damages to a victim of the crime. The U.S. District Court for New Mexico granted the defendant's motion to dismiss, stating that the New Mexico courts would not recognize any cause for action except under existing theories of liability accepted in the state.

On April 3, 1983, Dolores Armijo's brother, Steven, shot and killed James Saulsberry, Dolores' husband. Steven turned the gun on Dolores and her daughter, but it misfired. Ex Cam, Inc., had imported and distributed the gun used in the shooting. Dolores sued the company, employing various bases for liability, including the special product liability argument for Saturday night specials articulated in the Maryland case, *Kelley v. R G. Industries, Inc.*, which had established a special area of liability for gun manufacturers.

The court enunciated the doctrine of liability under New Mexico law, indicating that the plaintiff must demonstrate five conditions: the product was defective; the product was defective when it left the defendant and reached the consumer in the same condition; the defect made the product dangerous to the user; the consumer was injured; and the defect in the product was the immediate cause of the injury. The court concluded that the handgun performed as it was intended, and therefore could not be considered defective under the laws of New Mexico.

As to the potential criminal misuse of the firearm, the court indicated that New Mexico case law does not support any such theory. Any gun purchaser could reasonably recognize that it might be used as a murder weapon, just as a knife, an axe, or a bow and arrows. The court also disallowed the plaintiff's contention that marketing handguns should be labeled "ultrahazardous." The plaintiff attempted to establish a negligence standard for liability, claiming that the manufacturers failed to exercise reasonable care in selling a product that involved a significant risk of its use in criminal activity. The court rejected the prospect that New Mexico courts would recognize such an obligation on a manufacturer under existing liability statutes.

All firearms may be used in criminal activity, but in *Kelley v. R.G. Industries, Inc.*, the Maryland Court of Appeals ruled that manufacturers of a particular type of handgun could be held liable for its misuse. Therefore, the New Mexico court argued that an interesting situation resulted in Maryland: Only victims shot by Saturday night specials are able to recover damages; those shot by any other weapon lack any basis for a liability suit, even though the more expensive guns are agreed to be more deadly and accurate. The court concluded that the New Mexico courts could not adopt such a doctrine. *See also* KELLEY V. R.G. INDUSTRIES, INC. (1983); SATURDAY NIGHT SPECIAL.

Further Reading: *Armijo v. Ex Cam, Inc.,* 656 F. Supp. 771 (1987).

Arming Women Against Rape and Endangerment (AWARE)

Arming Women Against Rape and Endangerment (AWARE) is an organization that strives to make women aware of the possibility of being a victim of crime, assists women in avoiding violence through education and training, and provides women with information about dealing with unavoidable violent situations. AWARE claims that "defending yourself is okay," that fighting back is the best strategy because women who resist attacks suffer fewer injuries and stop attacks more successfully. According to AWARE, its name implies that a woman should be armed "with courage, spirit, knowledge, and determination, whether or not one is armed with an extrinsic weapon." Firearms are recognized as one possible means of self-defense that women may wish to consider.

AWARE provides information and advice about such criminal threats as rape, carjacking, purse snatching, stalking, domestic abuse, and attempted or threatened murder. In addition, the organization provides advice about protecting children from violence. With regard to firearms, AWARE refers to the National Rifle Association's (NRA) Eddie Eagle warning: "don't touch it, leave the area immediately, tell an adult." Unlike organizations such as the Violence Policy Center, which is critical of the NRA's Eddie Eagle training program, AWARE recommends the program highly and offers information about obtaining available materials from the NRA.

AWARE provides advice regarding various methods of fending off an attack. Although the martial arts are good for exercise and building confidence, they are considered of questionable value to women for self-defense. Personal alarms and rape whistles are not recommended as a primary defense because they depend on the assumption that someone else will come to a woman's defense.

AWARE does not recommend the use of stun guns, which they consider overrated by manufacturers. Experience indicates that stun guns hurt but do not always incapacitate, and they require actual contact with the attacker. The organization evaluates chemical defensive sprays, such as pepper spray (oleoresin capsicum), which cause vision impairment, a burning sensation to the skin, and difficulty in breathing if inhaled. AWARE cautions that these products may not be effective against some violent people and results depend on appropriate use.

Although AWARE takes no explicit stand on gun control and recognizes that many women dislike firearms, the organization supports the option of firearms as a means of self-defense. AWARE states that "whatever you might think of the NRA, they have created excellent introductory courses." The two recommended NRA courses, Home Firearm Safety and Basic Pistol, are called "good in theory," but value may depend on the quality of particular instructors. AWARE suggests that the interested person ask the NRA for a list of certified instructors, several of whom are women. The organization recommends the magazine *Women and Guns* as a source of information on the selection of firearms and self-defense. AWARE board members contribute articles to the magazine. *See also* EDDIE EAGLE; NATIONAL RIFLE ASSOCIATION; WOMEN AND GUNS; *WOMEN AND GUNS* MAGAZINE.

Further Reading: Arming Women Against Rape and Endangerment Web site <www.aware.org>.

Assault Weapons Ban

In the late 1980s and early 1990s, an intense political struggle occurred between the pro- and anti-gun control forces over passage of an assault weapons ban, a measure to prohibit the sale of certain military-style semiautomatic firearms. After more than five years in which such a proposal came to a floor vote six times in the Senate and six times in the House of Representatives, a ban was placed in the Violent Crime Control and Law Enforcement Act (P.L. 103-322, 108 Stat. 1796) that finally became law in September 1994.

The 1993 assault weapons ban prohibited the sale and possession of various types of firearms, such as this Uzi pistol. *Courtesy of Handgun Control, Inc.*

Much controversy still rages over the definition of an assault weapon and the significance of such a definition in categorizing a particular type of firearm. Assault weapons include semi-automatic firearms that fire a single round of ammunition with each pull of the trigger. Among other characteristics, they have large ammunition clips that can hold up to 30 rounds; are compact; have barrels less than 20 inches long; weigh from 6 to 10 pounds; are made for military use; and have pistol grips.

Opponents of a ban challenged the method of defining assault weapons. They insisted that the original definition included the ability to fire several rounds with one pull of the trigger, thus making assault weapons synonymous with machine guns. Because machine guns had been under strict federal government regulation since passage of the National Firearms Act in 1934, opponents saw no need for additional legislation. Referring to the 1939 Supreme Court decision in *United States v. Miller,* opponents argued that the military character of these weapons placed them under Second Amendment protection as just those types of firearms crucial to the maintenance of a militia. Relying on their interpretation of the militia's purpose, opponents maintained that assault weapons could prove especially useful should citizens find themselves resisting a tyrannical government.

Opponents further noted that the number of assault weapons used in crimes was small, claiming that just 4 percent of the nation's homicides involved any type of rifle at all. Employing Bureau of Alcohol, Tobacco, and Firearms (BATF) data, opponents observed that just 1 percent of military-style semi-automatic weapons are "misused." Supporters of a ban responded that drug traffickers and urban gangs were using such weapons in increasing numbers, and that Congress should take steps to limit their distribution before they became more widespread. The weapons' offensive and destructive capabilities and their lack of legitimate hunting and sporting uses added to the need for a ban. On the other hand, opponents of a ban insisted that gun control advocates had decided to target assault weapons because of a few cases of their misuse and because of their ominous appearance.

Two events spurred the introduction of an assault weapon ban in Congress: the January 1989 schoolyard shooting in Stockton, California, that left five children dead and 29 others wounded; and the Killeen, Texas, cafeteria shooting in which 22 people were killed and 23 others wounded before the shooter took his own life. Republican President George Bush, who had previously rejected calls for regulating assault weapons, reversed his position in March 1989 with an executive order instituting a temporary ban on the importation of some assault weapons. He soon extended the import ban to include several more weapons, and ultimately made the ban permanent. Democratic President Bill Clinton expanded the ban in 1993 to include assault-type handguns.

Proposals to institute a ban were introduced in Congress in 1989, 1990, and 1991, but failed to gain approval in both houses. In November 1993, the Senate passed a ban on the manufacture of 19 assault weapons, and in spring 1994 the House began to consider the measure, with President Clinton actively lobbying for the bill. In April, the House Judiciary Committee approved the measure, although the committee chair, Jack Brooks of Texas, vehemently opposed it. After approval in the full House, the assault weapons ban, as part of a larger bill, went to conference committee to resolve differences between the House and Senate. In August, after long discussions leading to compromises, the bill was returned to both chambers for final approval. However, opposition to the bill remained strong in the House, where it was defeated on a close floor vote, due largely to Republican concern for proposed expenditures of $33 billion, and both Democratic and Republican opposition to the assault weapons measure. Despite the defeat, President Clinton, with the backing of police organizations and congressional leaders, insisted on continuing the struggle to pass the bill. After intense negotiation, the House approved the measure, with support from 46 Republicans. When the revised bill went to the Senate, supporters succeeded in mustering sufficient support to win procedural votes, thus paving the way for final approval.

The assault weapons ban outlawed the sale and possession of 19 types of weapons, along with several replica models sharing certain characteristics, for a period of 10 years. Gun clips holding more than 10 bullets were also prohibited. The measure exempted over 650 sporting rifles as well as existing assault rifles. Researchers will have a difficult task discovering the effects of the assault weapons ban. Although advocates of the ban argued that the danger from such weapons was largely a potential for increased violence, they have no way of determining the number of people who would have been killed or wounded had the measure not passed. *See also* BUREAU OF ALCOHOL, TOBACCO, AND FIREARMS; BUSH, GEORGE; CLINTON, WILLIAM JEFFERSON (BILL); NATIONAL FIREARMS ACT OF 1934; STOCKTON, CALIFORNIA, SHOOTING; *UNITED STATES V. MILLER* (1939).

Further Reading: Alan M. Gottlieb, *Gun Rights Fact Book* (Bellevue, WA: Merril, 1989); Jeffrey A. Roth and Christopher S. Koper, "Impacts of the 1994 Assault Weapons Ban: 1994–96," *National Institute of Justice Research in Brief* (March 1999), 1–12; Robert J. Spitzer, *The Politics of Gun Control*, 2nd ed. (Chatham, NJ: Chatham House, 1998).

Australia

Like the United States, gun control measures in Australia were avidly pushed following well-publicized multiple killings involving firearms. In December 1987, eight people were killed; in August 1991, seven people lost their lives; and in 1996, the most serious of all shooting incidents occurred in Port Arthur, where a shooter used two semi-automatic weapons to kill 35 people. As a result of these incidents, Australia established a national gun registration program and enacted national uniform firearm regulations that required gun purchasers to submit to a 28-day "cooling-off period" before taking possession of a firearm to allow for a background check for criminal offenses. Also, the ownership of dangerous weapons was restricted. In 1997, a national gun buy-back program was instituted.

The parents of two children who were killed by guns in 1968 and 1970 dedicated themselves to strengthening the gun laws in Australia. They established the Council to Control Gun Misuse in 1981. Following the 1987 killings, the movement gained new momentum and in 1988 Gun Control Australia was formed. The organization began to distribute books on social, ethical, and legal issues regarding firearm use. The organization has used the occurrence of multiple gun deaths, which it calls "gun massacres," in its lobbying efforts for more stringent gun control. In the 10-year period beginning in 1987, three such events occurred each year, leaving an average of five people dead. Gun Control Australia contends that only in the United States does the "massacre rate" exceed Australia's.

The Australian Labor Party (ALP) has supported uniform gun control legislation. The party concedes that sporting shooters, hunters, collectors, and people in hazardous occupations have legitimate reasons for owning firearms, but considers high-caliber firearms and automatic weapons too dangerous to be possessed by the civilian population.

Gun Control Australia claims that current gun control legislation has serious weaknesses. The Australian Clay Target Association (ACTA) was granted an exemption from the prohibition on the use of semi-automatic and pump action shotguns. The requirement that hunters must receive written permission from landowners to shoot has been weakened by offering a lifetime approval. The organization contends that guns used in hunting are the most dangerous, when stored in the home, because they are "available for domestic impropriety." Most disturbing for Gun Control Australia is that the granting of gun ownership and use to members of gun clubs has led to increased membership in these organizations. Gun Control Australia believes that new firearms legislation has not altered the number of guns in homes, 25 percent of which are estimated to contain at least one weapon. The organization also believes that storage requirements for guns kept in the home must be improved to reduce the probability of accidents.

Pro-gun organizations, such as the Sporting Shooters Association, have vehemently resisted the push toward stricter gun control. In 1993, the Association formed a lobbying arm called the Institute of Legislative Action. Proposals have been made to allow semi-automatic weapons to be used at shooting ranges, to allow target shooting on private property, to permit some people to carry guns in urban areas, to allow unlicensed minors to shoot pistols at approved shooting ranges, and to exempt existing gun owners from the cooling-off period before purchasing another weapon.

Further Reading: Australian Labor Party Web site <www.ssaa.org.au/alpolicy.html>; Gun Control Australia Web site <http://home.vicnet.net.au/~guncontrol>; David B. Kopel, *The Samurai, the Mountie, and the Cowboy* (Buffalo, NY: Prometheus, 1992).

Aymette v. The State (1840)

In *Aymette v. The State* (21 Tenn. 154–162, 1840), a Tennessee court of appeals ruled on the constitutionality of an 1837 Tennessee statute that prohibited any person from wearing "any bowie knife, or Arkansas toothpick, or other knife or weapon in form, shape or size resembling a bowie knife or Arkansas tooth-pick under his clothes, or concealed about his person." The court determined that this provision did not conflict with the first article of the state constitution which stated that "the free white men of this State have a right to keep and bear arms for their common defense." The court emphasized the qualifying phrase "for the common defense" in allowing restrictions on arms bearing, ruling that the state constitution did not guarantee the right to keep and bear weapons that have no recognized military use. Nearly 100 years later, in 1939, the U.S. Supreme Court in *United States v. Miller* followed a similar line of reasoning regarding the Second Amendment right to keep and bear arms.

In 1839, William Aymette was indicted for violating the statute prohibiting the carrying of a concealed Bowie knife. He went in search of a person with whom he had argued earlier in the day, issuing verbal threats and brandishing the knife. The jury found Aymette guilty and the court sentenced him to three months imprisonment and fined him $200. Amyette appealed the verdict, claiming that the law violated the state constitution.

In rendering its decision, the appeals court investigated the purpose for which citizens are granted the right to bear arms. Referring to Great Britain under the rule of James II in the late seventeenth century, the court indicated that Protestants had been denied the right to bear arms in defense of their rights against the government: "The grievances to which they were thus forced to submit, were for the most part of a public character, and could have been redressed only by the people rising up for their *common defence* to vindicate their rights." The court noted that the provision of the Tennessee constitution was adopted "in reference to these historical facts."

The court emphasized that the words "bear arms" refer to the military use of weapons and do not apply to wearing arms on the person "as part of the dress." For the purpose of defense, citizens do not need weapons that are used primarily in "private broils" and that have little value in warfare: "They could not be employed advantageously in the common defence of the citizens."

The court declared that although the right to keep and bear arms for the common defense must be zealously preserved, the state constitution does not prohibit the legislature from enacting legislation to regulate the manner in which weapons may be used. For the court to deny the legislature the authority to pass legislation regarding the use of arms would be "to pervert a great political right to the worst of purposes." An individual may legitimately be prevented from carrying weapons "merely to terrify the people, or for purposes of private assassination." While the court was willing to suggest that the right to *keep* arms was unqualified, the right to *bear* arms could be limited according to the purpose for which arms were carried, which must ultimately involve maintaining the common defense.

The Tennessee court respectfully dissented from a Kentucky court's decision in *Bliss v. Commonwealth* in 1822. That court had ruled that a similar statute in Kentucky was contrary to the state constitution and hence void. The Tennessee court argued that a legitimate distinction could be made between a law prohibiting the right to bear arms and a law that regulated the manner in which a weapon may be carried. Given the relation of bearing arms to the common defense, the Tennessee court refused to regard such activities as carrying a dagger or a pistol under clothing as examples of bearing arms. Applying the practical criterion of usefulness during war or for the defense of citizens, the court declared that such weapons simply did not meet this qualification for protection and therefore could be restricted. *See also* BLISS V. COMMONWEALTH (1822); STATE GUN STATUTES; *UNITED STATES v. MILLER* (1939).

Further Reading: *Aymette v. The State* (21 Tenn. 154–162, 1840); "*Aymette v. The State* (1840)," in Robert J. Cottrol, ed., *Gun Control and the Constitution: Sources and Explorations on the Second Amendment* (New York: Garland, 1994), pp. 2-10.

Ayoob, Massad (1948–)

Massad Ayoob, director of the Legal Force Institute, a self-defense training program for police officers and civilians, has been a vocal advocate of the right to carry firearms for self-defense. He is considered an expert in self-defense techniques and firearms training. Ayoob serves as handgun editor for *Guns* magazine, and his monthly column, "Defense," often contains commentary on issues related to gun control. In addition, he serves as law enforcement editor of *American Handgunner* and as associate editor of *Combat Handguns, Gun Week,* and *Guns and Weapons for Law Enforcement.*

Early in his career as a self-defense expert, Ayoob concentrated on hand combat, writing for such martial arts journals as *Black Belt Official Karate* and *Karate Illustrated.* In 1979, concerned about the legal problems faced by individuals who use force in self-defense, Ayoob published *In The Gravest Extreme: The Role of the Firearm in Civilian Self Defense.* In 1981, he established the Lethal Force Institute to offer instruction in self-defense. An expert pistol shooter, Ayoob created an intensive training course that includes actual combat shooting as well as lectures, video presentations, and discussion. One course, titled "Judicious Use of Deadly Force," deals with such topics as the legally permissible circumstances for using a firearm in self-defense, the selection of firearms and ammunition, shooting stances, street gun-fighting tactics, psychological preparation for violent encounters, and choosing an attorney for defense in court.

In 1987, Ayoob was named national director of firearms and deadly force training for the American Society of Law Enforcement Trainers. Although not himself a lawyer, he has served as co-vice chair of the

Forensic Evidence Committee of the National Association of Criminal Defense Lawyers. He has served as a senior research associate for the Center for Advancement of Applied Ethics at Carnegie-Mellon University and as a part-time police officer for over 23 years. He is also a certified prosecutor. Ayoob has been called on a number of occasions as an expert witness, testifying for police officers who have used deadly force.

In the book *The Truth About Self Protection*, Ayoob offers advice on avoiding violent crime, covering such topics as mental alertness, alarms, martial arts, firearms, and auto security. He adheres to the basic premise that it is morally superior to resist evil action than to acquiesce in it. In *The Ayoob Files: The Book*, Ayoob describes several shooting incidents and suggests what the reader might do in similar circumstances. Ayoob has produced several video tapes, including *Shoot to Live*, in which he provides strategies for surviving a gunfight and advice about where to shoot an assailant for maximum effect. *Cute Lawyer Tricks* is a video intended to prepare police officers and civilians for the techniques lawyers use in the courtroom.

Ayoob staunchly defends the individualist interpretation of the Second Amendment. He portrays the gun control issue as one of civil rights, claiming that such policy proposals as needs-based licensing of firearms and increased taxes on guns and ammunition discriminate against the poor and minorities. He contends that any ban on particular weapons would require that the government pay fair market value to gun owners under the provisions of eminent domain. Such compensation would require billions of dollars that Ayoob maintains would be better spent for medical research or housing for the homeless. He argues that women should have the same rights of self protection as men. Holding that affordable handguns give disadvantaged women the opportunity to protect themselves, Ayoob singles out women's groups for special criticism because they discourage women from acquiring firearms for self-defense. *See also* GUN WEEK; GUNS MAGAZINE; SECOND AMENDMENT; SELF-DEFENSE; WOMEN AND GUNS.

Further Reading: Massad Ayoob, *The Truth About Self Protection* (Concord, NH: Police Bookshelf, 1999); Massad Ayoob, *Ayoob Files: The Book* (Concord, NH: Police Bookshelf, 1995); Massad Ayoob, *In the Gravest Extreme: The Role of the Firearm in Civilian Self Defense* (Concord, NH: Police Bookshelf, 1980).

B

Background Checks

The Brady Handgun Violence Prevention Act went into effect on February 28, 1994. It mandated background checks of those intending to purchase a handgun. From March 1, 1994, when the act required background checks to begin in most states, through December 1996, the Bureau of Justice Statistics estimates that approximately 7,782,000 presale checks were performed on people applying to purchase a handgun from federally licensed firearms dealers. Of that total, 173,000, or 2.2 percent of the total number of applicants, were not allowed to purchase a handgun. Nearly 68 percent of the rejections were associated with a felony conviction or current felony indictment. While gun control supporters lauded the results of checks, gun rights advocates focused on what they considered a small percentage of rejections.

The Gun Control Act of 1968 specified that the following individuals be denied the opportunity to purchase a handgun:

1. juveniles (under 18 years old)
2. fugitives from justice
3. persons under indictment for, or already convicted of, a crime punishable by imprisonment for more than one year
4. persons unlawfully using controlled substances
5. persons legally determined to be mentally defective or committed to a mental institution
6. aliens illegally in the United States
7. persons dishonorably discharged from the armed forces
8. persons who have renounced U.S. citizenship
9. persons subject to a court order restraining them from harassing, stalking, or threatening an intimate partner or a child
10. persons convicted of a felony or misdemeanor related to domestic violence

Thirty-two states were originally covered by the Brady law while the 18 remaining states (called Brady-alternative states) had their own legislation mandating background checks. By the end of 1996, nine additional states had enacted their own legislation, creating 23 Brady states and 27 Brady-alternative states. The Bureau of Justice Statistics reported that during 1996, the 32 original Brady states had a rejection rate of 3.6 percent while the original Brady-alternative states rejected 1.9 percent of applications, a statistically significant difference. The 23 current Brady states had a rejection rate of 3.1 percent while the current Brady-alternative states had a 2.5-percent rate, which was not statistically significant.

After felony indictment or conviction, the reasons for rejecting an application included being a fugitive from justice (6.0 percent), violating a state law prohibition (5.5 percent), being under a restraining order (3.9 percent), having been judged mentally ill or suffering from a mental disability (1.5 percent), addicted to drugs (1.2 percent), and violating a local law prohibition (.7 percent). The remainder were rejected for a variety of reasons, including applications by illegal aliens, juveniles, those dishonorably discharged from the military, and those convicted of domestic violence.

Through 1996, background checks were conducted under the interim provisions of the Brady Act, which required a five-day waiting period to allow time for chief law enforcement officers (CLEOs) at the state and local levels to conduct the investigation of each applicant. In 1997, the Supreme Court, in *Printz v. United States*, disallowed the federal provision in the Brady Law requiring CLEOs to conduct background checks. Therefore, supporters of background checks anxiously awaited the completion of a national computerized instant check system. In November 1998, the Federal Bureau of Investigation (FBI) initiated the National Instant Check System (NICS), a computerized system allowing federal firearms officials to run an immediate background check on potential firearms purchasers.

Because background checks apply only to federally licensed firearms dealers selling new handguns, a potentially vast market in used handguns continues without any limitation on purchasers who would otherwise fall into one or more of the prohibited categories. Gun control advocates call for more restrictive background check laws, while gun rights supporters divide on the issue. Some support the replacement of the five-day waiting period with the instant check. Others advocate the elimination of background checks, arguing that the present checks have had little effect on limiting handgun sales except to inconvenience the law-abiding purchaser. *See also* Brady Handgun Violence Prevention Act; Gun Control Act of 1968; National Instant Check System; *Printz v. United States* (1997); State Gun Statutes.

Further Reading: Donald A. Manson and Darrell K. Gilliard, "Presale Handgun Checks, 1996," *Bureau of Justice Statistics Bulletin* (September 1997); Regional Justice Information Service, St. Louis, Missouri, *Survey of State Procedures Related to Firearm Sales, 1996* (Washington, DC: Bureau of Justice Statistics, 1997).

Bailey v. United States (1996)

In *Bailey v. United States* (516 U.S. 137, 1996), the U.S. Supreme Court ruled on what the term "use" meant in the context of a federal statute [18 U.S.C. section 924 (c) (1)] that established a minimum five-year sentence for anyone found guilty of using or carrying a firearm "during and in relation to any crime of violence or drug trafficking crime." The Court established a narrow interpretation of "use," thus spurring a move by gun control advocates in Congress to expand the term's definition to include instances the Court did not recognize as being covered under existing legislation.

In May 1989, police stopped Roland Bailey's automobile when they noticed the vehicle lacked a front license plate and an inspection sticker. After officers ordered Bailey to leave the vehicle, they discovered he had no driver's license and their search of the car revealed plastic bags containing 30 grams of cocaine. When officers discovered a 9-mm. pistol in the trunk, violation of 18 U.S.C. 924 (c) (1) was added to several other charges. A jury, informed by the prosecution that drug dealers often carry firearms for self-protection and to safeguard their drugs and money, found Bailey guilty on all charges. On the weapons charge, the defendant received a five-year prison term.

Bailey appealed his conviction to the Court of Appeals for the District of Columbia Circuit, which upheld the lower court decision. The court interpreted the notion of "use" broadly, stating that the statute applied in this case because the jury could reasonably conclude that the firearm found in the trunk of Bailey's car had aided drug transactions, having been used to protect the illegal drugs and the money received from sales.

Meanwhile, in another drug case, Candisha Robinson was arrested for selling crack cocaine to an undercover officer. When police officers found an unloaded .22 caliber Derringer stored in a trunk she kept in her apartment, Robinson was charged with a firearm violation under section 924 (c) (1) and subsequently found guilty. However, the Court of Appeals in this case reversed the conviction, ruling that the evidence showing a gun close to the drugs was insufficient to establish a violation of the "use" provision of the firearms statute. Given the inconsistent outcomes of the Bailey and Robinson cases, the District of Columbia Circuit Court of Appeals combined the two cases for a consistent ruling. A majority of the court, by deciding that evidence in each case was adequate to uphold conviction under the firearms statute, established a proximity and accessibility test for determining when a firearm has been "used," thus reversing the original Appeals Court decision in the Robinson case and affirming Bailey's conviction.

The defendants in each case argued that "use" should be interpreted in the narrow sense of "active employment of a firearm." On appeal, the Supreme Court agreed with the appellants that the proximity and accessibility test provided a too-broad interpretation of use, concluding that this test offered virtually no limitation on the type of possession to be considered criminal. The Court declared that the government must demonstrate "active employment of the firearm," that the statute requires actual, not merely intended, use. The Court also indicated that the active meaning of "use," includes "brandishing, displaying, bartering, striking with, and most obviously, firing or attempting to fire, a firearm." The "inert presence" of a firearm, such as its storage, does not justify prosecution under the statute.

Recognizing that its interpretation of congressional intent restricted the statute's range of application, the Supreme Court noted that the government may charge offenders under the "carry" provision of the statute. Because the District of Columbia Court of Appeals did not consider the defendants' liability un-

der the "carry" provision, the Supreme Court returned the Bailey and Robinson cases to the trial courts for reconsideration of the convictions on that basis. *See also* FIREARM SENTENCE ENHANCEMENT LAWS.

Further Reading: *Bailey v. United States*, 516 U.S. 137 (1996).

Barr, Bob (1948–)

When Republican Congressman Bob Barr entered the U.S. House of Representatives in January 1995, he quickly established himself as a major opponent to new gun control proposals and existing gun legislation and as a strong supporter of the individualist interpretation of the Second Amendment. Having serious reservations about the power of federal law enforcement agencies, Barr worked for elimination of the Bureau of Alcohol, Tobacco, and Firearms (BATF), for downsizing other federal law enforcement agencies, and for repeal of the Brady Handgun Violence Prevention Act and the assault weapons ban.

Representative Bob Barr (R-GA), a congressional opponent of gun control, has worked for elimination of the BATF and for repeal of the Brady Act. *Courtesy of the Second Amendment Foundation.*

A native of Iowa, Barr received a B.A. from the University of Southern California in 1970, an M.A. from George Washington University in 1972, and a law degree from Georgetown University in 1977. While a student in Washington, D.C., Barr worked for the Central Intelligence Agency (CIA) as an intelligence analyst. After completing his law degree, Barr moved to Georgia to practice law. From 1986 to 1990, he served as a U.S. attorney. In 1992, he sought the Republican nomination for a seat in the U.S. Senate, but lost in a runoff. Two years later he won the Republican nomination for a seat in the U.S. House of Representatives and defeated the five-term incumbent in a nationwide conservative tide. Gun control supporters point out that the new congressman received $5,000 from the Georgia Gun Owners' Political Action Committee during the primary, and an additional $4,950 from the National Rifle Association (NRA) during the general election campaign.

When House Speaker Newt Gingrich established a Republican task force on firearms, he chose Barr to head the group. In that capacity and as a member of the Judiciary Committee, Barr attempted to revise a domestic and international terrorism bill. Voting against the bill as it was reported from the committee in June 1995, Barr worked with committee chairman Henry J. Hyde, Republican of Illinois, to develop an alternative that would be more appealing to House conservatives. In March 1996, Barr proposed an amendment to the bill that eliminated a section allowing the introduction of evidence obtained through illegal wiretaps and a provision facilitating prosecution of those who sell guns subsequently used in a crime.

Barr successfully opposed the reintroduction of the excluded measures in the House-Senate conference committee. He insisted that federal law enforcement officers did not need the increased authority that the deleted provisions would provide. The bill became law in April 1996. Despite subsequent terrorist acts, including the bombing at the Centennial Olympic Park in Atlanta, Georgia, Barr's home state, the congressman remained un-

willing to support a more stringent anti-terrorism measure, objecting to any quick reaction to a specific criminal act.

Barr proposed repealing the 1994 ban on particular types of assault weapons. He argued that longer prison sentences were a better deterrent to crime than attempting to ban weapons. Tanya Metaksa, executive director of the NRA's Institute for Legislative Action, commended Barr for his efforts to schedule a House vote on the repeal, which occurred in March 1996. Neal Knox, then first vice president of the NRA, also credited Barr for his efforts to repeal the assault weapons ban. The measure included a provision to increase sentences for committing violent or drug-related crimes. Although the bill passed in the House by a vote of 239-173, it failed in the Senate. In March 1999, Barr introduced legislation to limit the liability of firearms manufacturers for the criminal use of their products. He has also supported legislation to limit federal asset forfeiture authority. *See also* ASSAULT WEAPONS BAN; BRADY HANDGUN VIOLENCE PREVENTION ACT; BUREAU OF ALCOHOL, TOBACCO, AND FIREARMS; CIVIL FORFEITURE; KNOX, NEAL; LEGAL ACTION PROJECT; METAKSA, TANYA K.; NATIONAL RIFLE ASSOCIATION.

Further Reading: Bob Barr Web Site <www.house.gov/bar>; Robert Dreyfuss, "Uzi Does It," *Mother Jones* 21 (September/October 1996), 46-47; Philip D. Duncan and Christine C. Lawrence, *Politics in America: The 105th Congress* (Washington, DC: CQ Press, 1997).

Barrett v. United States (1976)

In *Barrett v. United States* (423 U.S. 212, 1976), the U.S. Supreme Court ruled on a provision of the Gun Control Act of 1968 [18 U.S.C. 992 (h)] which prohibited a convicted felon, among other categories of individuals, from receiving "any firearm or ammunition which has been shipped or transported in interstate or foreign commerce." The major issue to be decided was whether the provision applies more broadly to a person who makes an intrastate purchase of a firearm that has been transported in interstate commerce from the manufacturer to a distributor and ultimately to a dealer, or whether the law can be interpreted more narrowly as having application only to direct interstate sales or acquisitions.

In 1967, a Kentucky state court convicted Pearl Barrett of housebreaking, imposing a two-year sentence. In April 1972, Barrett purchased a .32-caliber revolver from a federally licensed firearms dealer. The firearm, which had been manufactured in Massachusetts, was shipped to a distributor in North Carolina and then to the Kentucky dealer. Within an hour of the purchase, a county sheriff stopped Barrett for driving while intoxicated and discovered the fully loaded firearm lying on the floorboard. At his trial on the charge of having violated section 922 (h), Barrett moved for a directed verdict of acquittal, arguing that the statute did not apply to his receipt of a firearm because the purchase was in no way associated with the interstate transfer of the weapon. The judge denied the motion and Barrett was found guilty. The Court of Appeals, in a divided opinion, affirmed the verdict.

Because of the significance of the issue and a contradictory decision by another Court of Appeals, the Supreme Court decided to accept the appeal. Barrett admitted that Congress has the authority under the Commerce Clause of the Constitution to regulate interstate firearms trafficking, but argued that Congress intended the legislation to apply to interstate trafficking alone, not to isolated intrastate transfers within a state that have no connection to interstate commerce. In response, the Court noted that while the prohibited action ("to receive any firearm") is in the present tense, the statute's reference to interstate commerce is stated in the present perfect tense ("has been shipped or transported"), which indicates that the interstate transfer has been completed before acquisition by the purchaser. If Congress had intended to restrict the statute to direct interstate receipt, it would have explicitly stated the limitation. The Court disagreed with the charge that the statute was ambiguous and therefore rejected the call to decide the case with leniency.

According to the Court, the structure of the Gun Control Act indicated that Congress "did not intend merely to restrict interstate sales but sought to keep firearms away from the persons Congress classified as potentially irresponsible and dangerous." For instance, section 922 (d) prohibits a federally licensed dealer from "knowingly selling or otherwise disposing of any firearm . . . to the same categories of potentially irresponsible persons." The Court noted that other sections of the Act, such as licensing provisions, apply both to exclusively intrastate as well as interstate actions. Therefore 922 (h) can be consistently interpreted, with the intent of the entire act, to apply to intrastate retail firearms sales. To decide otherwise would eliminate the statute's application to the typical circumstance—a felon purchasing or receiving a firearm from a local dealer.

The Supreme Court declared that the narrow interpretation in *United States v. Tot* (1942) of a similar provision limiting interstate transactions that was included in the Federal Firearms Act of 1938 had no relevance to the task of determining Congress's intentions in the present case. The justices concluded that nothing in the legislative history of the Gun Control Act argued persuasively that Congress intended to apply the limited interpretation presented in the Tot decision. *See also* FEDERAL FIREARMS ACT; GUN CONTROL ACT OF 1968; *UNITED STATES V. TOT* (1942).

Further Reading: *Barrett v. United States*, 423 U.S. 212 (1976).

Barron v. Baltimore (1833)

The U.S. Supreme Court case *Barron v. Baltimore* (32 U.S. 7 Pet. 243, 1833) established the principle that the Bill of Rights of the U.S. Constitution only limited the actions of the national government and did not apply to the states. Although subsequent constitutional history resulted in much of the Bill of Rights being applied to state and local governments, the Second Amendment has remained under the precedent set by the Barron case. Gun rights advocates have called for a court ruling applying the Second Amendment to the states.

In the 1830s, when the City of Baltimore, Maryland, under the authority of the Maryland legislature, diverted the flow of some streams, Barron's wharf became useless for shipping due to deposits of silt. Barron argued that the state legislature and the actions of the city had divested him of his property without just compensation, a violation of the Fifth Amendment of the U.S. Constitution. Chief Justice John Marshall, speaking for the Supreme Court, denied that the Court had jurisdiction to declare state legislation unconstitutional. Marshall stated that the provision of the Fifth Amendment regarding just compensation for property taken for public use limited the power only of the national government and was not applicable to state laws and actions. He claimed that the limitations generally established in the Constitution applied only to the government created by that document, noting that during ratification proceedings for the Constitution calls were made for a bill of rights to protect the people specifically against possible encroachments by the national government.

Gun rights supporters contend that the Supreme Court ruling in *Barron v. Baltimore* no longer applies, given the long series of Supreme Court rulings establishing that most of the provisions within the Bill of Rights limit the states via the Fourteenth Amendment. They claim that the logic of Supreme Court rulings indicates that the Second Amendment protection of the right to keep and bear arms applies to the states as well as to the national government. However, gun control supporters, arguing that the Second Amendment established a state right to maintain militias independent of the national government, would deny that the Barron case and subsequent decisions applying portions of the Bill of Rights to the states ever had any potential applicability to the Second Amendment. *See also* FOURTEENTH AMENDMENT; SECOND AMENDMENT.

Further Reading: *Barron v. Baltimore*, 32 U.S. 7 Pet. 243 (1833).

Beecham v. United States (1994)

In *Beecham v. United States* (511 U.S. 368, 1994), the U.S. Supreme Court dealt with the issue of a convicted felon's eligibility under federal law to own firearms. Federal legislation was intended to keep firearms away from those considered most likely to misuse them, but there remained the difficult question of how a convicted felon's right to possess firearms might be restored. Specifically, does the removal of felony status by a state also apply to felony status resulting from a federal conviction? The Court ruled that for persons convicted of a felony to receive relief from the Gun Control Act of 1968, the federal statute that prohibits a convicted felon from possessing a firearm [18 U.S.C. 922 (g)], "they must have had their civil rights restored under federal law."

The Court ruled simultaneously on cases involving two defendants, Beecham and Jones, who had both been found guilty of violating the federal statute prohibiting firearm ownership to convicted felons. In 1979, Beecham had been convicted in Tennessee of a federal firearms violation, and Jones had two West Virginia state convictions and one 1971 federal conviction in Ohio for interstate transportation of a stolen automobile. West Virginia had subsequently restored Jones's civil rights, and Beecham claimed that Tennessee had restored his civil rights. The district courts in the two cases were asked to decide whether these state restorations of civil rights eliminated the application of the gun ownership restriction for the two defendants. The courts had to decide which jurisdiction— state or federal—determines whether the restoration of civil rights applies to a prior federal conviction.

While the district courts determined that state restoration removed the imposed disabilities under federal law, the Fourth Circuit Court of Appeals reversed the lower court rulings, concluding that state restoration of civil rights did not free a convicted felon from restrictions resulting from a federal conviction. The Supreme Court agreed with the Fourth Circuit. Although states had restored the defendants' civil rights, these restorations applied only to the jurisdiction in which the conviction occurred.

Justice Sandra Day O'Connor, arguing for the Court, faced an issue raised by the Ninth Circuit Court's original ruling. That court stated that because no federal process existed for restoring civil rights to a federal felon, Congress must have intended that other jurisdictions, not the federal government, should perform the function. The Supreme Court rejected this interpretation, noting that nothing in the statute sustains the view that felons in all jurisdictions were intended to have access to all the procedures, including pardon, expungement, set-aside, and civil rights restoration. As O'Connor observed, since "some jurisdictions have no procedure for restoring civil rights," a person convicted of a felony in a federal court has no greater disadvantage than someone convicted in the court of a state that has no provision for restoring civil rights. The Beecham decision maintained the federal government's discretion in applying firearm ownership restrictions for convicted felons. *See also* GUN CONTROL ACT OF 1968.

Further Reading: *Beecham v. United States*, 511 U.S. 368 (1994).

Beecher's Bibles

The term Beecher's Bibles refers to the Sharps rifles that Northern opponents of slavery sent to Kansas after 1854 to assist those who desired to keep the territory free of slavery. Supporters of gun rights today argue that the events in Kansas during the 1850s are a prime example of the need for the right of individuals to possess firearms to defend themselves against tyranny and oppression. The conflict in Kansas, a prelude to the Civil War, began with Congress's passage of the Kansas-Nebraska Act in May 1854. The act intended to allow the residents of Kansas to decide whether slavery would be legal in the territory, but rather than allowing a peaceful resolution to the conflict by local citizens, the act led to violence that ignited the emotions of both North and South.

Although the bona fide settlers from the North outnumbered the supporters of slavery, slaveowners in Missouri, fearful that a free Kansas would threaten their financial holdings and ultimately their way of life, sent thousands of men into Kansas to coerce the population to favor legalization of slavery. The invasion of Missourians carrying revolvers, shotguns, and other weapons overwhelmed Free State forces. In November 1854, an election was held to select a territorial representative to Congress. Approximately 2,000 Missourians crossed the border to coerce voters and election officials and to cast their own ballots in the election. A pro-slavery candidate was elected. In March 1855, a second invasion of an estimated 5,000 Missourians led to the election of a pro-slavery territorial legislature in Kansas.

News of the events in Kansas spread through an indignant North, leading many to call for assistance of the anti-slavery forces in "Bleeding Kansas." Many people were encouraged to emigrate to Kansas to serve the anti-slavery cause. As part of this campaign, many individuals and groups donated funds to purchase Sharps rifles for the anti-slavery forces in Kansas. Reverend Henry Ward Beecher, pastor of Plymouth Church in Brooklyn, New York, raised funds among his parishioners. Beecher declared that the rifles served a greater redeeming role for Kansas than the Bible, noting that at times self-defense was a man's religious duty. Due to Beecher's strong appeals for funds, the Sharps rifles became known as Beecher's Bibles.

Charles Robinson, representative for the Emigrant Aid Company in Lawrence, Kansas, formed two military companies and requested rifles and other weapons to arm the groups. The Sharps rifles, highly effective weapons for that time, were early models of the breech loader that could fire up to 10 rounds per minute with a greater range than comparable weapons. For two years, appeals were made in churches throughout the North for funds to purchase these weapons. Due to Beecher's noted success, Plymouth Church became known as the Church of the Holy

Rifles. Although prominent individuals made donations, they were fearful of the potential political consequences. The rifles could help the Free Staters defend themselves against southern slave holding interests, but the donors recognized that they were defying a national government that at least nominally supported the slave position.

Although gun rights supporters see in this historical event a key example of the value of the right to keep and bear arms, historians comment that as soon as the Free State forces, including John Brown, used violence in response to the disruption caused by Missourians, they lost their claim to moral superiority. Both sides shed blood in a mini-civil war that no government sanctioned. Not armed force, but the continued push toward fair elections, proved the more effective strategy. Historian Oswald Garrison Villard (1943) contends that the movement toward freedom for all in Kansas occurred in part because of the "abandonment of the policy of carrying on an unauthorized war, and of meeting assassination with assassination" (p. 307). Historical examples such as Beecher's Bibles do not necessarily present a clear lesson about the value of firearms; at best, they indicate the delicate balance between resisting tyranny with armed force and maintaining a commitment to legal procedure.

Further Reading: Richard O. Boyer, *The Legend of John Brown: A Biography and a History* (New York: Alfred A. Knopf, 1973); Oswald Garrison Villard, *John Brown* (New York: Alfred A. Knopf, 1943).

Bernethy v. Walt Failor's Inc. (1978)

Bernethy v. Walt Failor's Inc. (97 Wash. 2d 929, 1978) is an example of a tort case, which is a lawsuit involving a wrongful act, damage, or injury willfully caused. In cases like Bernethy, victims of firearm violence have attempted to establish the legal and financial responsibility of a gun manufacturer or retail outlet for injuries resulting from firearm use. Because gun control advocates believe that dealers should show greater caution about the people to whom they are willing to sell firearms, they regard such judicial actions an important means to keep firearms away from those who are likely to commit acts of violence. Walt Failor, owner of a gun store in Washington state, became the defendant in a wrongful death suit after Robert Fleming, using a 30-30 rifle he had taken from Failor's store, shot and killed his wife, Phoebe, in a tavern where they had been drinking.

On April 11, 1978, Fleming, who had been drinking with his wife and friends at a local tavern, went to Failor's store to purchase a weapon. Although Failor claimed that Fleming demonstrated no significant symptoms of drunkenness, others reported that he was most definitely intoxicated when he entered the store. Fleming told Failor he wished to purchase a rifle for his son. Failor laid the weapon and ammunition on the counter and began completing the necessary forms and processing the credit card sale. At this point, Fleming walked out of the store with the gun and ammunition. When Failor followed him into the street, asking for payment, Fleming threatened the store owner with the gun.

When arrested for killing his wife, Fleming had a blood alcohol level over twice that accepted in many states for drunk driving. A wrongful death suit was brought against Failor on behalf of Phoebe Fleming's three children, claiming that he had shown negligence in providing the rifle to Fleming. When the court dismissed the case, determining that the store owner was not negligent in providing a firearm to Fleming, even though the purchaser was intoxicated, the case was appealed. In turn, the Court of Appeals requested that the Supreme Court of Washington determine the appropriateness of the original court's summary judgment in favor of the defendant.

Citing a provision within tort law, the Washington Supreme Court indicated that a seller may be found liable for providing a piece of property if the purchaser is evidently incompetent or the seller can reasonably anticipate that the transfer will result in physical harm. Although Failor argued that the principle did not apply in this case because Fleming's actions were ultimately criminal, the court ruled that if "intervening criminal acts" are found to be foreseeable, then a claim of negligence may be made.

Although Failor argued that he did not sell the gun to Fleming, but that the man had in fact stolen the weapon, the court noted that Failor had nearly completed the sale, and that Fleming was able to leave the store with the weapon because Failor had left it within reach. The court ruled that actual liability in Phoebe Fleming's death must be determined in a jury trial. Ultimately important for the gun control question is that the court established the principle of liability of a gun retailer for the actions of the purchaser at least under circumstances where the seller can reasonably anticipate the use to which the purchaser may put the weapon. *See also* FATALITIES.

Further Reading: *Bernethy v. Walt Failor's Inc.*, 97 Wash. 2d 929 (1978); Mark A. Siegel, Nancy R. Jacobs, and Carol D. Foster, eds., *Gun Control: Restricting Right or Protecting People?* (Wylie, TX: Information Plus, 1991).

Black Codes

Supporters of the view that the Fourteenth Amendment made the Second Amendment applicable to the states employ the history of the Black Codes in the post-Civil War South to bolster their position. These Codes, which restricted the rights of formerly enslaved African Americans, were one of the factors that motivated Congress to propose the Fourteenth Amendment to assure that all Americans, regardless of race or color, could enjoy equal rights under the Constitution.

In 1865-1866, the former states of the Confederacy passed a series of laws that established, state by state, the basis of citizenship for newly freed African Americans. The Codes granted certain basic civil rights to blacks, including the right to marry, to own personal property, and to sue in the state judicial system. However, their basic rights were severely limited through such measures as establishing segregated public facilities, limiting the ability to gain work and the right to own real estate, and denying the right to testify in court. To protect the rights of former slaves and prevent what amounted to re-enslavement, Congress established the Freedmen's Bureau, an agency that opposed enforcement of the Codes. Radical Republi-

can governments under Reconstruction later repealed this legislation.

Of great concern to those interested in applying Second Amendment protections to the states, the southern states of Alabama, Louisiana, and Mississippi enacted measures that prohibited blacks from owning firearms without first gaining a license, a legal procedure not required of whites. For instance, an 1865 Louisiana statute declared that any black not in military service could not carry a firearm unless granted special permission by an employer and a law enforcement officer. Punishment for violating the statute included forfeiting the weapon and being fined $5. To the dismay of northern Republicans, southern legislation protected the right of former members of the Confederate forces to bear arms while at the same time denying that right to blacks, a group that had demonstrated its loyalty to the Union.

Contemporary Second Amendment supporters contend that when Congress began to debate the substance of the Fourteenth Amendment, southern efforts to disarm blacks played a clear role in their thinking. Specific congressmen are quoted as saying that they believed the new Amendment would apply the Bill of Rights to the states, including the Second Amendment with its guarantee of the right to keep and bear arms.

However, application to the states of the Second Amendment or any of the other provisions of the Bill of Rights did not occur for the remainder of the nineteenth century. The first of the few cases regarding the Fourteenth Amendment and the right to bear arms came before the Supreme Court in 1876. In *United States v. Cruikshank*, William Cruikshank was charged with denying the rights of two black men to peaceably assemble and bear arms. The Supreme Court held that the national government could not protect the rights of citizens against the actions of other private citizens. Because the First and Second Amendments were not applicable in this case, the plaintiffs were required to seek a remedy from state legislatures and state judicial systems.

Despite the Black Codes connection, the Supreme Court has so far been unwilling to accept the position that one of the objectives of the Fourteenth Amendment was to protect the rights of all Americans to keep and bear arms as enunciated in the Second Amendment. *See also* AFRICAN AMERICANS AND GUNS; FOURTEENTH AMENDMENT; SECOND AMENDMENT; *UNITED STATES V. CRUIKSHANK* (1876).

Further Reading: Robert J. Cottrol and Raymond T. Diamond, "The Second Amendment: Toward an Afro-Americanist Reconsideration," in David B. Kopel, ed., *Guns: Who Should Have Them?* (Amherst, NY: Prometheus, 1995); Walter L. Fleming, ed., *Documentary History of Reconstruction: Political, Military, Social, Religious, Educational and Industrial, 1865 to the Present Time* (Gloucester, MA: P. Smith, 1960).

Black Panther Party

An organization of the late 1960s that gained fame and notoriety far beyond its numbers, the Black Panther Party gave new significance to the notion of a right to bear arms. Two young African Americans, Bobby Seale and Huey Newton, officially created this self-defense group in Oakland, California, on October 15, 1966. Seale assumed the office of party chairman and Newton took the position of minister of defense. They had read Robert Williams's *Negroes with Guns*, and had resolved to abide by Mao Tse-tung's revolutionary principle that "Power also grows out of the barrel of a gun." Following the lead of another local organization, the Panthers planned to patrol the streets of Oakland, observing arrests and informing those arrested of their legal rights. However, they decided on the novel tactic of carrying firearms. In November 1966, the Panthers began to patrol the streets, harassing the police at opportune moments. Newton discovered a California statute that allowed the carrying of a loaded shotgun or rifle provided that it was not concealed. Newton and Seale acquired an M-1 rifle and a 9-mm pistol.

Members of the Black Panther Party, an African-American self-defense group founded in California in the 1960s by Bobby Seale and Huey Newton, openly carried firearms as they patrolled the streets seeking to end police harassment of African Americans. *Roz Payne/Archive Photos.*

In January 1967, Newton, Seale, and fellow Panther Bobby Hutton, all of whom worked for antipoverty programs, used their paychecks to open the first Black Panther Party office in North Oakland. They soon acquired new recruits and new weapons. With money received from selling copies of *Quotations from Chairman Mao Tse-tung*, they purchased additional firearms. The ability to handle handguns and rifles became a major prerequisite for membership. The party leadership ultimately established a six-week training period for recruits.

The Black Panthers received widespread publicity for their new practice of carrying firearms. Their clothing, consisting of a blue shirt and black pants, black leather jacket and black beret, gave the Panthers the look of a militia unit and contributed to the attention they received in the media. However, they also gained the keen attention of law enforcement officers. In April 1967, when state legislator Donald Mulford proposed legislation restricting the carrying of loaded firearms in public places, the Panthers played the role of gun rights advocates. On May 2, a group of Panthers traveled to Sacramento, armed with handguns and rifles and accompanied by reporters and cameramen. They were arrested for conspiracy to disrupt a legislative session. Those Panthers charged pleaded guilty to committing a misdemeanor and were sentenced to six months in prison. In July, the state legislature enacted the provision prohibiting the carrying of a loaded firearm.

By early 1968, the influence of the Panthers appeared to be increasing, even though Newton had been convicted of voluntary manslaughter, the result of a gun fight with a police officer the previous October. The officer died in the shootout and Newton was wounded. Another Panther, Eldridge Cleaver, advocated preparation for impending revolutionary violence. In September 1968, he spoke before a group of lawyers in San Francisco, where he stated that the lawyers could help the movement by donating machine guns. Demonstrating the audacity so characteristic of the Black Panthers, Cleaver declared that the Panthers needed to buy guns to kill judges, police, and corporation lawyers.

The Black Panthers hit their peak in 1969, obtaining a nationwide membership of 1,500 to 2,000. However, trouble with the police continued. Nearly 350 members were arrested on a variety of charges from murder to bank robbery. In 1970, the membership declined significantly. Increasing disagreements, particularly between Newton and Cleaver, contributed to the party's steady decline.

Following the demise of the Black Panthers in the early 1970s, the party leadership led less than successful lives. In 1989, Newton, who experienced drug problems, was shot and killed outside a crack house. That same year Seale, a recovering alcoholic, pleaded guilty to charges of passing bad checks. Cleaver, who fled the country to live in Cuba and Algeria, returned to the United States. In the late 1980s and early 1990s he also experienced drug problems. In summer 1990, he entered a drug rehabilitation center due to crack cocaine addiction, but was arrested again for cocaine possession in June 1992. He died in 1998.

The history of the Black Panthers demonstrates the complexity of the gun control issue. Ronald Reagan, while president of the United States in the 1980s, strongly opposed any gun control legislation (although after leaving the presidency, he announced his support for the Brady bill). However, while governor of California from 1967 to 1975, he signed the 1967 bill to limit the carrying of firearms, legislation prompted by the activities of a small group of African-American revolutionaries in the Black Panther Party. *See also* AFRICAN AMERICANS AND GUNS; BRADY HANDGUN VIOLENCE PREVENTION ACT; REAGAN, RONALD; STATE GUN STATUTES.

Further Reading: G. Louis Heath, *Off the Pigs! The History and Literature of the Black Panther Party* (Metuchen, NJ: Scarecrow Press, 1976); Hugh Pearson, *The Shadow of the Panther: Huey Newton and the Price of Black Power in America* (Reading, MA: Addison-Wesley, 1994); Robert Franklin Williams, *Negroes with Guns* (Detroit, MI: Wayne State University Press, 1998 [1962]).

Black Talon Bullet

In the early 1990s, the Black Talon bullet came under severe attack for its destructive capacity. Bills were introduced in Congress to ban the bullet, including a measure supported by Senator Daniel Patrick Moynihan, Democrat of New York, that would have levied a 10,000 percent tax on the ammunition. Originally, the Black Talon was touted as the ideal ammunition to resolve a dangerous situation for law enforcement officers. At times, police cannot stop violent criminals even after shooting them several times. The Black Talon increased the likelihood that incapacitating damage had been done to anyone endangering the life of a police officer. However, Winchester-Olin, the manufacturer of the Black Talon, distributed the ammunition to the general public and by 1993 the bullet gained notoriety when it was used in several violent crimes, including the murder of a Washington, D.C., police officer.

In 1987, Marty Fackler, a U.S. army researcher and veteran combat trauma surgeon, had recommended to the Federal Bureau of Investigation that the light and fast ammunition they were using did not penetrate deeply enough or produce sufficient tissue damage. He recommended a heavier bullet with greater destructive capability. Tom Burczynski, who had been working with hollow-point bullets, developed a bullet with a cone-shaped post in the point, which he called the Hydra-Shok. Federal Cartridge purchased the license to manufacture the new ammunition and in 1989 won a contract with the Federal Bureau of Investigation (FBI) to supply agents with the new bullets. Fackler, not convinced that the Hydra-Shok was the best solution to the problem, became involved in improving Winchester's soft copper-jacketed OSM. Alan Corzine and David Schluckebier finally designed a new bullet, which Winchester christened the Black Talon. The bullet derives its name from the six sharp petals, or talons, that are produced on impact, and from the black oxide coating, included both for cosmetic reasons and to reduce bore friction. The Black Talon retains the OSM's soft copper jacket which, after entering the body, peels back to expose the six sharp points. After traveling four inches into the body, the Black Talon expands to nearly three times its original diameter. The devastation produced by the bullet increases as it rotates within the body. Fackler considered it to be the greatest advance in handgun ammunition since the original development of the hollow-point bullet, which is composed of a lead slug with an indentation at the tip to allow for expansion upon impact.

Winchester aggressively marketed the new bullet, introducing it at a gun show in the New Orleans Superdome in January 1992. Demonstrations were given for law enforcement agencies, and police forces in Baltimore, Dallas, and New York City switched to the new ammunition. The bullets were packaged in black boxes on which the words "deep penetrator" were printed in red. The company provided gun store displays, showing spent bullets with the six distinguishing tines. Hunting magazines praised the new bullet, calling it a "top-flight big-game bullet." David B. Petzal, reviewing ammunition in *Field and Stream*, commented that the Black Talon and bullets like it "penetrate deeply, destroy major organs, break major bones, and exit the far side, leaving a blood trail."

In July 1993, a man used Black Talons to kill eight people in a San Francisco law office before shooting himself. Health care professionals, who witnessed the effects the ammunition had on victims, spoke out against its sale. Some physicians expressed fear of being cut by the sharp barbs as they operated on gun shot wounds. In November 1993, after two bills had been introduced in Congress to ban the Black Talon, Winchester announced it would limit sales to law enforcement agencies. On December 7, six people were killed on a Long Island Railroad car by an individual wielding a semi-automatic weapon loaded with Black Talon bullets. Despite the voluntary ban on sales to the general public, the Black Talon and similar ammunition remained widely available. *See also* Fatalities; Gun Shows.

Further Reading: Jonathan Alter, "Curb Violence by Targeting Bullets," *Washington Monthly* 26 (January/February 1994), 45-46; Julie Petersen, "This Bullet Kills You Better," *Mother Jones* 18 (September/October 1993), 15; David E. Petzel, "Bullet-In," *Field and Stream* 97 (February 1993), 65-67; Peter Richmond, "The Black Talon," *Gentlemen's Quarterly* 64 (July 1994), 100-05); Martin D. Topper, "The Truth About Hollow Points," *Handguns* 12 (February 1998), 36-38, 40-41, 74-75.

Bliss v. Commonwealth (1822)

In 1822, a Kentucky state court decision, *Bliss v. Commonwealth* (12 Ky. [2 Litt.] 90, 1822), affirmed the individual citizen's right to keep and bear arms as protected in the Kentucky state constitution. The court regarded such a right in the strongest terms, declaring it absolute and immune from any attempt by the legislature or any other government office either to ban or to regulate the right to bear arms.

Found in possession of a sword in a cane, Bliss was charged under state law with carrying a concealed weapon. The jury in the court of original jurisdiction found him guilty and assessed a fine of $100. Bliss appealed the decision, claiming that the statute under which he was convicted violated article 10, section 23 of the state constitution. The section stated "that the right of the citizens to bear arms in defence of themselves and the state, shall not be questioned." In contrast, the statute under which Bliss was convicted stated that any person in the commonwealth of Kentucky who wears a pocket pistol, dirk, large knife, or sword in a cane, "unless when traveling on a journey," shall be subject to a fine of $100 or more.

The court argued that it had the right to declare acts of the legislature contrary to the state constitution. Reminiscent of the U.S. Supreme Court in the 1803 case *Marbury v. Madison*, the state court declared that "it is emphatically the duty of the court to decide what the law is." The court has the responsibility to compare the law with the constitution, and when the two conflict, decide in favor of the constitution. Although recognizing that deciding such conflicts was a delicate matter, the court affirmed the judicial branch's responsibility to decide in favor of the constitution over any ordinary act of the legislature.

The court referred to a section in article 10 of the Kentucky state constitution, which declared that everything in the article shall forever remain inviolate from government power, and that laws contrary to its provisions shall be void. Foreshadowing justifications used in subsequent cases for limiting the right to bear arms, the state attorney in his argument before the court distinguished between prohibiting the exercise of a right, and simply regulating the way in which the right may be exercised. However, the court responded that any restraints on the full exercise of the right, whether a complete prohibition, or any measure short of complete restriction, violated the provisions of the constitution.

Using an absolutist interpretation of the right to bear arms, the court ruled that the act under which Bliss was convicted failed to agree with the state constitution and thus was void. The absolute right existed at the time the constitution was adopted, limited only by the individual decisions of citizens to bear or not to bear arms. Therefore, restricting that liberty inevitably meant violating the right guaranteed in the constitution. The legislature did not have the right to prohibit the wearing of weapons that were lawful to wear when the constitution was adopted. The Court also ruled that no valid distinction could be made between concealed weapons and weapons carried openly—if one practice was protected under the constitution, so was the other. *See also* STATE GUN STATUTES.

Further Reading: *Bliss v. Commonwealth*, 12 Ky. [2 Litt.] 90 (1822); Earl R. Kruschke, *The Right to Keep and Bear Arms* (Springfield, IL: Charles C. Thomas, 1985).

Boxer, Barbara (1940–)

Barbara Boxer, a Democratic senator from California, outspokenly advocates gun control. She has initiated legislation to ban domestic manufacture and sales of junk guns, or Saturday night specials, and supports efforts to require locks for handguns. Her campaign for gun regulation focuses on the danger that firearms present to children and adolescents. In 1998, the final year of her first term in the Senate, Boxer stepped up efforts in support of firearms regulation.

Senator Barbara Boxer (D-CA) is an outspoken advocate of gun control. *Courtesy of Senator Boxer's Office.*

Born in Brooklyn, New York, Boxer earned a B.A. in economics from Brooklyn College in 1962. She became a stockbroker and journalist before entering politics. After serving on the Marin County, California, Board of Supervisors from 1977 to 1983, where she became the first woman board president, Boxer was elected to the U.S. House of Representatives. In 1992, she was elected to the U.S. Senate, winning a second term in 1998. Boxer's committee assignments include Appropriations, Banking, Housing and Urban Affairs, Environment and Public Works, and Budget. In addition to gun control, she has supported legislation dealing with such issues as the pensions of working people, lower trade barriers, improvements in public education, abortion rights, environmental protection, and health care. Although Boxer has backed legislation to protect the property rights of California computer and entertainment companies, she has challenged the legitimacy of California companies that produce inexpensive handguns.

In January 1997, along with three other senators, Boxer reintroduced a bill, called the American Handgun Standards Act, that would apply production norms to American-manufactured handguns that the Gun Control Act of 1968 already imposed on imported weapons. The legislation would subject handguns to product safety standards from which they are presently exempt. Boxer argued that the less expensive handguns are at least three times more likely than other handguns to be used in the commission of a crime. Although some gun rights advocates profess that junk guns, or Saturday night specials, can be reliable defense weapons, especially for the less well-to-do, Boxer noted that they are subject to unpredictable firing and inaccuracy, making them poor prospects either for hunting or for self-protection.

When the California legislature began considering a prohibition on junk guns, Boxer urged passage of the measure. Because nearly 40 California municipalities had already approved bans on the sale of junk guns, the chances of passage were considered good. In June 1997, the senator commended the legislature for passing the measure, and publicly encouraged Republican Governor Pete Wilson to sign the bill. When Wilson vetoed the legislation, claiming that junk guns presented no extraordinary danger, Boxer offered to meet with him to present information about their unreliability. Despite Boxer's characteristically aggressive strategy, the governor's veto remained unchanged.

In October 1997, after President Bill Clinton reached an agreement with eight handgun manufacturers to include safety locks with newly manufactured handguns, Boxer sent letters to California manufacturers of inexpensive handguns, urging them to join in the agreement. She recommended that manufacturers select high-quality locks that cannot be opened by a young child, and encouraged companies to make improvements in the guns themselves to meet quality and safety standards imposed on imported handguns. Although recommending voluntary compliance, Boxer also introduced legislation mandating that gun locks be included with the sale of all new handguns. In 1998, Boxer urged newly elected National Rifle Association (NRA) president Charlton Heston to support safety locks. *See also* CLINTON, WILLIAM JEFFERSON (BILL); FEINSTEIN, DIANNE; GUN CONTROL ACT OF 1968; HESTON, CHARLTON; NATIONAL RIFLE ASSOCIATION; SATURDAY NIGHT SPECIAL.

Further Reading: Philip D. Duncan and Christine C. Lawrence, *Politics in America, 1998: The 105th Congress* (Washington, DC: CQ Press, 1997); Senator Barbara Boxer Web site <www.senate.gov/~boxer>.

Brady Handgun Violence Prevention Act

The Brady Handgun Violence Prevention Act (Pub. Law 103–159), which became law in November 1993 and went into effect in February 1994, imposed a five-day waiting period so that background checks could be run on those wishing to purchase a handgun. It was the first significant piece of federal gun control legislation to be enacted since 1968. The legislation was named after James S. Brady, press secretary to President Ronald Reagan, who was severely wounded during an assassination attempt on the president in 1981. After the attempt, Brady and his wife Sarah became avid gun control advocates and spearheaded much of the effort for passage of the Brady bill.

The introduction of the bill into Congress in 1987 began a battle between pro- and anti-gun control forces that lasted nearly seven years. Although the National Rifle Association (NRA) had supported a waiting period in the 1970s, the organization became increasingly militant and worked hard to prevent adoption of the measure. The NRA questioned the effectiveness of such waiting periods, arguing that most criminals acquire guns from illicit sources, not from reputable dealers. Therefore, the law supposedly would have little effect on criminals but would unduly inconvenience law-abiding citizens.

The long battle and strong opposition notwithstanding, advocates of the measure were spurred on by an awareness of the huge number of handguns already available in the United States and the support most Americans were expressing for stricter control of handguns. Proponents noted that similar requirements in some states had prevented sales to criminals and had led to some arrests. They argued that the law could also provide for a cooling-off period that would deter crimes of passion committed by such people as angry employees and jealous spouses looking for immediate revenge. The long struggle to have the bill enacted symbolized the strong feelings on both sides of the issue and became a test of antagonistic political forces. Passage finally came when the Republican leadership (the Republicans then being in a minority in Congress), recognizing strong public support, ended attempts to obstruct a vote on the measure.

The provisions of the Brady law are generally considered moderate. The legislation does not ban any firearms, such as inexpensive handguns, called Saturday night specials, or assault weapons, but imposes a waiting period of five business days before an individual may take possession of a purchased handgun. The waiting period was intended as a temporary measure, remaining in effect for five years to allow the federal government time to institute a national computerized system for instantly checking the backgrounds of handgun purchasers. States that had waiting periods of at least five days to conduct background checks were not subject to the new law. The legislation required gun dealers in states subject to the law to provide local chief law enforcement officers with the names of people purchasing handguns and directed officials to conduct background checks. In this way, felons and the mentally unstable could be prevented from legally purchasing handguns.

Justice Department estimates in 1997 indicated that since the Brady bill became law, at least 250,000 sales of handguns had been prevented. More than 70 percent of these cases involved people convicted or indicted on felony charges. The Justice Department figures also revealed that over 70 federal prosecutions and 52 convictions had occurred since the law's passage. However, pro-gun groups were unimpressed with the figures, noting that the number of aborted sales and convictions were small compared to the total number of checks.

A legal challenge led to a 1997 Supreme Court decision invalidating a key portion of the Brady law requiring local chief law enforcement officers to run background checks on handgun buyers. However, other provisions of the law were left intact and a national instant check system became operational in November 1998, obviating the need for assistance from local law enforcement. In addition, by 1998, 27 states had enacted their own laws requiring a background check. *See also* BRADY, JAMES; BRADY, SARAH; BACKGROUND CHECKS; NATIONAL INSTANT CHECK SYSTEM; NATIONAL RIFLE ASSOCIATION; *PRINTZ V. UNITED STATES*; REAGAN, RONALD; SATURDAY NIGHT SPECIAL.

Further Reading: Gregg Lee Carter, *The Gun Control Movement* (New York: Twayne, 1997); Robert J. Spitzer, *The Politics of Gun Control*, 2nd ed. (New York: Chatham, 1998).

Brady, James (1940–)

Since the mid-1980s, James Brady, along with his wife Sarah, has played an important role in furthering gun control policies. Brady, who was shot and seriously wounded during the March 30, 1981, attempt to assassinate President Ronald Reagan, became a strong advocate for more stringent federal and state gun laws. However, he did not join the gun control effort as early as his wife. Officially still on the White House staff until the end of the Reagan administration in 1989, he did not wish to publicly oppose the administration's policy positions. Although confined to a wheelchair and experiencing speech difficulties, Brady traveled with his wife to present what they jovially called a "dog and pony show," advocating greater control of firearms.

Brady entered politics as a campaign manager and in 1980 worked for John Connally in the former Texas governor's bid for the presidency. When that effort failed, Brady joined Ronald Reagan's campaign. Following the Reagan victory, Brady was named presidential press secretary. He was at Reagan's side when an assassin's bullet exploded in his head, leaving him with only 80 percent of his brain. Although doctors initially did not expect Brady to live, he walked out of the hospital, with great difficulty, eight months later. He will remain largely paralyzed and in pain for the rest of his life. The recovery was slow and difficult. At first Brady had difficulty controlling his emotions, laughing or crying unexpectedly, a condition common to those suffering head injuries. Although he recovered some use of his left side, his left arm remained paralyzed. He could walk, at least a few steps, with the aid of a cane. Just getting in and out of automobiles presented a major challenge. Brady, who continued to have speech and memory problems, was a living example of the damage a handgun can inflict.

After January 1989, Brady decided to join his wife in support of Handgun Control, Inc. (HCI). In November 1989, Brady testified before the Senate Judiciary Committee in favor of proposed legislation that would ultimately be called the Brady bill. Presenting himself as an example of what true inconvenience meant, he asked the committee members if they would continue to satisfy the wishes of special interests who might be inconvenienced by new legislation. Brady said that although he had watched from his wheelchair as the gun lobby opposed "one sane handgun control bill after another," he was no longer going to watch passively. He called on Congress to pass the bill that would mandate a waiting period before purchasing a handgun. Brady noted that congresspeople had "closed their eyes to tragedies like mine" and cited polls indicating that over 90 percent of Americans supported the bill. Although the legislation did not pass that year, Brady continued his active support until final passage in 1994.

Brady described the National Rifle Association as "the evil empire." He had become, in his own words, the gun lobby's "worst nightmare," a living example of the dangers of firearms. Since passage of the bill, Brady has continued to advocate further measures to limit handgun violence, such as instituting education programs, limiting traffic in private transfers of handguns, and defending already existing gun laws. *See also* BRADY, SARAH; BRADY HANDGUN VIOLENCE PREVENTION ACT; HANDGUN CONTROL, INC.; NATIONAL RIFLE ASSOCIATION; REAGAN, RONALD.

Further Reading: Wayne King, "Target: The Gun Lobby," *New York Times Biographical Service* (December 1990), 1156-61; Philip Shenon, "Wife of Aide Cut Down with Reagan Scoring Hits Against the Gun Lobby," *New York Times Biographical Service* (May 1990), 500-01.

Brady, Sarah (1942–)

In the 1980s and 1990s, Sarah Brady, chairperson of Handgun Control, Inc. (HCI), perhaps contributed more than anyone else to the push toward more stringent gun control legislation. Wife of James Brady, press secretary to President Ronald Reagan who was shot during an attempt on the president's life in 1981, became an ideal spokesperson for the gun control movement. HCI membership doubled after she became the organization's chairperson, a position for which her previous political experience had provided excellent training. Her greatest triumph came with passage of the Brady Handgun Violence Prevention Act in 1994, which required a five-day waiting period and background check before a potential buyer could take possession of a firearm. She is also credited with assisting in the passage of several state gun control measures.

The daughter of an agent for the Federal Bureau of Investigation (FBI), Sarah Kemp Brady graduated from the College of William and Mary in 1964. She became assistant to the campaign director for the National Republican Congressional Committee in 1968. From 1970 to 1974, Brady served as administrative aide to Republican Representatives Mike McKevitt of Colorado and Joseph J. Maraziti of New Jersey. She met her future husband, James Brady, at a Republican campaign cocktail party. After the birth of her son Scott, Sarah Brady devoted her time to married life.

When her husband was shot and seriously wounded during the Reagan assassination attempt on March 30, 1981, Sarah Brady began a long and arduous period assisting her husband's partial recovery. She devoted herself to volunteer work with such organizations as the March of Dimes and the Foundation for Critical Care Medicine. An incident that occurred in 1984 while she and her son were visiting James Brady's relatives in Illinois motivated her to become involved in the gun control movement. While driving in a friend's truck, Scott, then five years old, discovered what he thought was a toy pistol under the seat and pointed it at his mother. She became angered by what she perceived to be the laxness of gun laws. Passage of the Firearms Owners Protection Act of 1986, backed by the National Rifle Association (NRA) and other gun rights organizations, convinced Brady of the need to work for maintaining existing laws and initiating stronger controls on gun ownership. When she contacted HCI, the organization's president, Charles J. Orasin put her to work writing letters to senators about repealing the Protection Act. She also spoke to senators personally and wrote to national newspapers about the issue.

Sarah Brady meets reporters outside the Supreme Court on June 27, 1997, to comment on the Court's recent invalidation of a portion of the Brady Handgun Violence Prevention Act. *REUTERS/Luc Novovitch/Archive Photos.*

As an advocate for the gun control cause, Brady had instant credibility. She spoke from personal experience. Gun rights advocates soon realized they had a formidable opponent. She was constantly on the move, speaking in favor of stricter gun laws, especially the Brady bill. She challenged members of Congress to be courageous and defy the NRA by supporting gun control legislation. She expressed her lack of respect for members of Congress, calling them "weak-kneed" and "gutless" for voting with the NRA. Brady has called the NRA a "horrible organization," the leaders of which "lie a lot."

During the 1988 presidential campaign, Brady warned aides to Republican candidate George Bush that she would denounce Bush if he opposed the Brady bill and the waiting period it mandated. Although the bill failed to pass that year, Bush maintained his silence. Gun rights advocates found it difficult to respond publicly to Brady, apparently realizing the sympathy the public had for her and her husband. Magazines with a large proportion of women readers ran articles about the ordeal Brady and her husband endured and reported on her efforts in support of gun control. Brady remains the chairperson of HCI. That organization's ability to challenge the NRA at the state and national levels is due in large part to the efforts of Sarah Brady, whose name has become closely associated with gun control efforts. *See also* BRADY, JAMES; BRADY HANDGUN VIOLENCE PREVENTION ACT; BUSH, GEORGE; FIREARMS OWNERS PROTECTION ACT; HANDGUN CONTROL, INC.; NATIONAL RIFLE ASSOCIATION; REAGAN, RONALD; WOMEN AND GUNS.

Further Reading: Mary Huzinec, "Brady's Battle," *Ladies Home Journal* 108 (March 1991), 61-62; Wayne King, "Target: The Gun Lobby," *New York Times Biographical Service* (December 1990), 1156-61; Rita Rooney, "Sarah Brady's Fighting Spirit," *McCalls* 114 (November 1986), 150, 153; Philip Shenon, "Wife of Aide Cut Down with Reagan Scoring Hits Against the Gun Lobby," *New York Times Biographical Service* (May 1990), 500-01.

Britain. See United Kingdom

British American Security Information Council (BASIC)

In 1987, Daniel Plesch founded the British American Security Information Council (BASIC), a nongovernmental organization based in Washington, D.C., and London that conducts research on international security issues, including regulation of the legal and illegal distribution of small arms to conflict areas around the world. Plesch continues to serve as the organization's director. BASIC claims that legally manufactured and distributed weapons contribute as much to conflict and crime as do weapons that are transferred illegally. BASIC has received funding from various private sources, including the Ford Foundation and Rockefeller Family Associates. The organization claims that light weapons have caused approximately 90 percent of war casualties since 1945. Through its efforts, the Council hopes to increase international security and decrease the probability of armed conflict.

BASIC's Project on Light Weapons works to create more effective procedures to control international weapons transfers. The organization provides information to governmental and nongovernmental organizations about weapons sales and disseminates proposals for more effective control. BASIC has explored the relationship between ammunition and armed conflict and researchers associated with the organization have investigated such topics as ammunition production, trade routes for small arms, and the adverse effects of ammunition availability on national and regional stability and security. The organization has explored strategies for controlling the illicit as well as the legal ammunition market that focus on both governmental and private trade. Policies that BASIC recommends include destroying collected weapons, establishing codes of conduct for weapons manufacturers, initiating more stringent domestic gun control, marking and registering firearms, and improving international cooperation among law enforcement agencies.

The Council has published several reports dealing with small arms, including a directory of individuals and organizations involved in limiting such weapons and an overview of the illicit light weapons trade and investigations of light weapons manufacturing in particular countries. The Council warns against focusing too intently on the illicit firearms market while ignoring the spread of small arms through legal transfers and the so-called "gray" market involving sales of guns to legally qualified purchasers, which are ultimately transferred to people involved in criminal activities. Another BASIC report offers information on the various legislative initiatives countries have taken to deal with the light weapons trade.

The Council informs individual and organizational members and others about the outcome of meetings to discuss the control of small arms. The Council has distributed Natalie J. Goldring's report on the meeting of a United Nations panel of governmental experts on small arms, which includes recommendations for the destruction of surplus weapons and weapons remaining after cessation of armed conflict, improvement of border controls and better training for customs officials, and expanded firearm buyback programs. Goldring notes that the panel endorsed a feasibility study of marking newly manufactured weapons to improve traceability and restricting production and sales of small arms to manufacturers and dealers that have received government authorization.

Gun rights advocates have expressed serious reservations regarding BASIC's attempts to institute international small arms control, fearing that any intergovernmental agreements will result in further firearms limitations in the United States, which, they believe, would constitute further violations of the Second Amendment right to keep and bear arms. Although BASIC emphasizes primarily the illegal distribution of small arms worldwide, gun rights advocates are particularly concerned by the organization's support for additional controls on the legal trade in firearms. *See also* UNITED NATIONS; UNITED KINGDOM.

Further Reading: British American Security Information Council Web site <www.basicint.org>.

Browning, John Moses (1855–1926)

The modern weapons that provide an important part of the context for the heated debate over gun control differ markedly from the firearms available in the early nineteenth century. John Moses Browning vies for the position of the greatest of all firearms inventors. His innovations in the late nineteenth and early twentieth centuries contributed greatly to the fortunes of Winchester and other gun manufacturers.

Browning acquired an interest in firearm design from his father, Jonathan, who also manufactured guns. Born in Tennessee in 1805, the elder Browning first encountered a firearm in his early teens when he was given an old flintlock rifle in payment for some farmwork. He repaired the gun and sold it back to the previous owner. Working in a blacksmith shop, Jonathan acquired metalworking skills. After converting to the Mormon faith, Jonathan moved to Utah, where Brigham Young selected him as the community's gunsmith.

As a youth, John Moses found himself surrounded by the firearms business. When he made a primitive firearm at the age of 10, the elder Browning, unimpressed, commented that a boy nearly 11 years old could do a better job. In 1878, after examining a rifle, Browning commented to his father that he could improve on the design. Jonathan encouraged his son to try. The son made his first serious attempts at firearm construction, receiving a patent for one of them, a single-shot cartridge rifle. Browning and his brothers produced some 600 of the rifles before he sold the patent to Oliver F. Winchester and the Winchester Repeating Arms Company for an outright payment of $8,000 in lieu of royalties.

As Browning continued to develop new firearms, he would build a model by hand, from which he made drawings. In 1884, Browning displayed a well-designed lever-action hunting rifle. A cautious person, he made sure to receive a patent before reveal-

John Browning was one of the most innovative American inventors of firearms in the nineteenth century. *Courtesy of Browning.*

In 1902, Browning offered Thomas Bennett, president of Winchester, a newly produced automatic shotgun. However, this time Browning opted for royalties rather than a single payment. When Bennett refused, the 20-year Browning-Winchester collaboration came to an end. Browning explored new business collaborations with other gun manufacturers. Using Browning patents, Colt produced the first American automatic pistol, the Model 1900. Remington manufactured a semi-automatic rifle, the Model 8, from a Browning patented design. Browning, still active, died in 1926 from a heart attack in his son's office in Liege, France. By the time of his death, Browning had altered the landscape of firearms production. His work had laid the groundwork for many future developments in the arms industry. *See also* COLT, SAMUEL; REMINGTON, ELIPHALET, II; WINCHESTER, OLIVER FISHER.

Further Reading: Sam Fadala, *Great Shooters of the World* (South Hackensack, NJ: Stoeger, 1990); Wayne Van Zwoll, *America's Great Gunmakers* (South Hackensack, NJ: Stoeger, 1992).

ing the innovative design to Winchester. The new rifle became the Winchester Model 1886. Through 1935, Winchester manufactured 160,000 of these rifles. In the late 1880s, Browning designed some of the best firearms of the time, including a single-shot cartridge rifle, a repeating lever-action rifle, and a repeating shotgun. During this same period, he also developed the idea for a gas-operated firearm that would fire nearly 1,000 rounds per minute.

When Winchester wanted to produce a miniaturized version of the Model 1886, it offered Browning $10,000 for a model delivered in three months, or $15,000 if forthcoming in two months. Browning responded that he could design the firearm in 30 days if Winchester were willing to pay $20,000 for it. Browning received the $20,000 for developing what became the Model 1892. Had Browning opted for royalties, his return would have been far greater. The company sold over one million of the rifles before discontinuing production in 1941.

Bryan v. United States (1998)

In *Bryan v. United States* (Docket No. 96-8422, U.S. Supreme Court, 1998), the U.S. Supreme Court ruled on the meaning of a section of the Firearms Owners' Protection Act (FOPA). The section [U.S.C. 924 (a) (1) (D)] prohibits any person without a federal firearms license from engaging in a business involving firearms dealing. Although widely considered a general weakening of the Gun Control Act of 1968, FOPA clarified provisions of that act, such as providing a definition for the term "engaged in the business." Gun rights advocates were concerned that federal firearms legislation could be used to prosecute individuals who might sell their gun collections, not knowing they were doing anything that could be considered illegal. The Bryan case dealt with the kind of knowledge an individual must possess to be found culpable under the law. Did conviction of violating section 924 require the defendant to have knowledge of the law, or less restrictively, knowledge that he or she was acting unlawfully?

The original prosecution of Sillasse Bryan determined that the defendant, who did not have a federal license to deal in firearms, used other individuals to purchase pistols in Ohio under false pretenses, assuring these purchasers that he would file the serial numbers off the guns. He then resold the handguns in areas of Brooklyn, New York, known for illegal drug activity. The evidence demonstrated that Bryan knew that his actions were unlawful. However, the prosecution presented no grounds for concluding that he was aware of the federal law prohibiting firearms dealing without a license. The judge denied a defense request to instruct the jury that they could arrive at a guilty verdict only if Bryan knew about the federal licensing requirement. The jury subsequently found Bryan guilty of violating federal firearms regulations.

When the Appeals Court affirmed the conviction, the Supreme Court decided to hear the case because an Appeals Court for another circuit had ruled that the government must demonstrate that a defendant was aware of the licensing requirement. The Court rejected the defendant's argument that knowledge of the law is required for conviction because the statute's use of the term "knowingly" regarding the commission of the relevant act "does not necessarily have any reference to a culpable state of mind or to knowledge of the law;" in other words, the term knowingly "merely requires proof of knowledge of the facts that constitute the offense."

Bryan had argued that the Supreme Court, in cases dealing with violations of the tax code, determined that conduct is criminal only when done "willfully;" in other words, the defendant must be aware of the specific provision he is charged with violating. Because certain statutes containing technical provisions may trap people who genuinely believe they are engaged in innocent conduct, the Court employed a more specific sense of "willful," referring to knowledge of the specific statute. However, in the Bryan case the jury found that the defendant knew he was involved in unlawful conduct even though the prosecution did not determine that he was aware of the specific statute prohibiting firearms dealing without a federal license. Therefore, the Court ruled that the Bryan case does not qualify as an exception to the general rule that ignorance of the law is no excuse. *See also* GUN CONTROL ACT OF 1968.

Further Reading: *Bryan v. United States*, Docket No. 96-8422 (U.S. Supreme Court, 1998).

Bureau of Alcohol, Tobacco, and Firearms (BATF)

The Bureau of Alcohol, Tobacco, and Firearms (BATF) is responsible for overseeing compliance with federal policies regarding the production, taxation, and distribution of alcohol, tobacco, and firearms. In 1972, the agency was given bureau status in the Treasury Department. The Bureau is composed of two sections, one for regulatory enforcement and the other for criminal enforcement. Matters such as gun licensing and tracing, illegal firearms transport and possession, and explosives are the domain of the criminal enforcement section. The political battle over gun control has focused on the BATF, with gun control supporters frustrated by an agency they consider ineffective, and gun control opponents expressing concern over what they call a power-grabbing and rights-violating behemoth.

The BATF has a long heritage. Its roots extend back to 1791 when Secretary of the Treasury Alexander Hamilton established a mechanism for collecting a liquor tax. In 1919, with the beginning of Prohibition, a Bureau of Prohibition was created within the Treasury Department. In 1933, when Prohibition ended with ratification of the Twenty-First Amendment, the Bureau of Prohibition was renamed the Alcohol Tax Unit. Having become part of the Internal Revenue Service (IRS), the unit was renamed the Alcohol and Tobacco Tax Division in 1951. It was granted authority to collect a newly created federal tobacco tax. Although the agency first assumed responsibility for gun regulation in 1942 as a result of the National Firearms Act

In April 1993, BATF agents gather at the FBI command center before leaving Waco, Texas, at the end of their 51-day siege of the Branch Davidian compound. *REUTERS/G. Reed Schulman/Archive Photos.*

of 1934 and the Federal Firearms Act of 1938, it achieved its current status and title with the Gun Control Act of 1968. The BATF has always lacked the status of an independent regulatory agency.

The Bureau's capacity to enforce gun control legislation has never been extensive. It issues licenses for gun manufacturers and dealers, but lacks any regulatory authority. It has little access to information about the number of guns sold each year. In 1965, just five full-time employees were engaged in enforcing the 1934 and 1938 laws and the Bureau achieved few convictions under these laws. It conducted few firearm investigations and revoked the licenses of just a handful of firearms dealers. Today, monitoring over 280,000 firearms dealers is an overwhelm-

ing task for the Bureau's 250 agents. In the 1980s, to assist in its legal responsibility of tracking firearms, the BATF proposed a plan to computerize records. This proposal prompted the National Rifle Association (NRA) to encourage its membership to write representatives and senators and object to the agency's attempts to make its operations more efficient. In response, the Treasury Appropriations Subcommittee cut funds from the BATF's budget that would be designated for computerization. The BATF was denied the authority to expend any funds for the purpose of centralizing records dealing with the acquisition and status of firearms that are maintained by federal firearms licensees. This prohibition became part of the 1986 Firearms Owners' Protection Act.

Because the BATF lacks independent agency status and does not have the prestige of some federal agencies, it must depend on the president and Congress for its continuation. In 1981, the agency escaped President Ronald Reagan's attempt to disband it, but still suffered significant budget cuts. A proposal to shift BATF duties to the Internal Revenue Service was also aborted. The Bureau recouped some of its limited prestige and financial support in the late 1980s due to successful operations involving investigations of extremist groups. However, the BATF's mishandling of the 1993 raid on the Branch Davidian compound near Waco, Texas, along with evidence that officials attempted to conceal their mistakes, proved a serious blow to the agency. A committee headed by Vice President Al Gore recommended merging the BATF into the Federal Bureau of Investigation (FBI), but the plan was not implemented.

The NRA, already a fierce BATF critic, attacked the agency for its performance in Waco as well as for the 1992 assault, in cooperation with the FBI and federal marshals, on the Randy Weaver home at Ruby Ridge, Idaho. Weaver, a white supremacist, lost family members in skirmishes with BATF agents. Since these events, a new director has attempted to improve morale and management within the agency. However, pro-gun groups have continued their attacks on the agency. *See also* GUN CONTROL ACT OF 1968; NATIONAL RIFLE ASSOCIATION; REAGAN, RONALD; RUBY RIDGE; WACO, TEXAS, RAID.

Further Reading: Bureau of Alcohol, Tobacco, and Firearms Web site <www.atf.treas.gov>; James Moore, *Very Special Agents: The Inside Story of America's Most Controversial Law Enforcement Agency–The Bureau of Alcohol, Tobacco, and Firearms* (New York: Pocket Books, 1997); Robert J. Spitzer, *The Politics of Gun Control*, 2nd ed. (New York: Chatham House, 1998); Josh Sugarmann, *National Rifle Association: Money, Firepower and Fear* (Washington, DC: National Press, 1992).

Bush, George (1924–)

George Bush, Republican president of the United States from 1989 to 1993, was a life member of the National Rifle Association (NRA) until his resignation in 1995 in pro-

test against remarks made by the organization's executive vice president, Wayne LaPierre, in a verbal attack on federal law enforcement agents. The resignation was especially notable because Bush had been a strong supporter of the gun rights movement throughout his political career, and had often received the backing of gun rights groups.

In 1988, because of his consistent support of gun rights, Bush received the NRA's endorsement for the presidency. The NRA spent $1.5 million during the campaign to support Bush and to oppose the Democratic candidate, Michael Dukakis, who was considered a major enemy of the organization for his advocacy of gun control. In December 1988, the NRA named Bush its "Person of the Year," declaring him to be the only candidate who would defend the rights of gun owners. However, Bush's honored position in the NRA did not last much longer. Although Bush had opposed any ban on assault weapons, in March 1989 he reversed his position following extensive media reporting on the Stockton, California, shooting in which school children were injured and killed by an assailant wielding an assault rifle.

William Bennett, Bush's director of the Office of Drug Policy, announced an import ban on five types of assault weapons. Soon afterward, Bush announced an extension of the temporary ban to 24 types of assault weapons. Speaking in favor of the ban, Bush noted that assault weapons were the "guns of choice" for criminals and stated that the ban was meant to keep sophisticated firearms out of the hands of criminals. Bush also announced proposals to double minimum sentencing for criminal use of a semi-automatic firearm, to enact a permanent ban on the import of assault weapons, and to prohibit future production and sale of high-capacity ammunition magazines (greater than 15 rounds). Bush opposed the Brady Handgun Violence Prevention bill through the rest of his term, but gave hints that he might approve the legislation as part of an acceptable crime bill. The Brady bill was passed after Bush left office.

Initially, the NRA refrained from blaming Bush for the assault weapons ban, opting instead to focus criticisms on Bennett and the administration in general and to ask the president to reverse the shift in administration policies. However, although Bush's Democratic opponent in 1992 was Bill Clinton, a major advocate of restrictions on firearms, the NRA refused to endorse Bush for reelection or to contribute to his campaign, concluding that Bush had failed the organization by supporting restrictions on the import of assault weapons.

In 1995, Bush reacted strongly against an NRA fund-raising letter distributed just before the bombing of the Oklahoma City federal office building. The letter, signed by Wayne LaPierre, compared federal government agents to Nazis who wore "Nazi bucket helmets and black storm trooper uniforms" and harassed, intimidated, and even murdered law-abiding citizens. In his letter of resignation addressed to NRA President Thomas Washington, Bush stated that LaPierre's comments left him outraged. He considered the verbal attack "a vicious slander on good people." Although Bush admitted that he had long agreed with most of the organization's objectives, the attack on federal agents offended his own "sense of decency and honor" and his "concept of service to country." Bush regarded LaPierre's statements to be a slander on officials "who are out there, day and night, laying their lives on the line for all of us." Bush decided to resign his life membership in the NRA because Washington had failed to repudiate LaPierre's attack. Washington responded to Bush's letter, defending LaPierre's remarks, but LaPierre ultimately apologized, stating that he regretted having offended federal law enforcement officials. *See also* Brady Handgun Violence Prevention Act; Clinton, William Jefferson (Bill); LaPierre, Wayne; National Rifle Association; Oklahoma City Bombing; Stockton, California, Shooting.

Further Reading: Jack Anderson, *Inside the NRA: Armed and Dangerous* (Beverly Hills, CA: Dove, 1996); Robert J. Spitzer, *The Politics of Gun Control*, 2nd ed. (New York: Chatham House, 1998); Josh Sugarmann, *National Rifle Association: Money, Firepower and Fear* (Washington, DC: National Press, 1992).

C

Canada

Gun rights advocates, such as the National Firearms Association (NFA) of Canada, as well as organizations in the United States, have criticized more stringent gun control in Canada, arguing that such laws violate the individual right to bear arms. Given the close geographical proximity of the two countries, gun rights groups in the United States fear that stricter laws in Canada foreshadow similar statutes in the United States. Inspection authority granted to Canadian government officials by the Firearms Act, which went into effect in 1998, is intended to ensure compliance with statutes regarding safe storage of firearms.

As in the United States, violence involving firearms has increased Canadian support for gun control. In 1989, following the murder of 14 women at the University of Montreal, additional types of weapons were restricted or banned and tighter standards for acquiring a gun permit were instituted. Canadians wishing to purchase a gun had to undergo evaluation and were required to take a safety course. Automatic firearms and semiautomatics capable of being adapted to automatic fire were banned. Still, millions of firearms remained in private hands, a troubling condition for many Canadian gun control advocates.

In 1994, after a series of highly publicized violent incidents involving firearms, the Coalition for Gun Control, supported by several groups representing such interests as the police, lawyers, teachers, health workers, and women, campaigned for stricter gun control legislation. The Liberal Party, which won the 1993 federal elections, promised to support stronger legislation. The NFA argued that further gun control would restrict the average Canadian's ability to defend him or herself against criminal activity. Opponents of stricter legislation noted that guns were consistently involved in only 32 percent of homicides, and just 27 percent of all robberies. Gun control supporters responded that the use of handguns in crimes had risen sharply. The general public strongly supported stricter gun control legislation. In 1993, 86 percent of respondents in a national poll supported registration of all firearms, 84 percent favored a prohibition on assault weapons, and 71 percent wanted to ban all handguns.

The new Firearms Act provides for inspection of businesses, gun collectors, owners of prohibited firearms, and owners with more than 10 firearms. Inspectors must give owners reasonable notice regarding the place to be inspected and must gain the consent of the resident. Police cannot use force to enter a home to conduct a search. Gun owners can be required to show their weapons to the police, but can bring them to the front door of the residence or to a police station.

Like the legal codes of most states in the United States, the Canadian criminal code treats as a separate offense the use of a firearm during the commission of a crime. The Firearms Act specifies minimum sentences for certain crimes, such as manslaughter, kidnapping, hostage-taking, robbery, or extortion, if committed with a firearm. An individual could also be prosecuted for possessing a firearm without being licensed to do so, or for failing to register the firearm. The act increased the Canadian government's authority to prevent firearms smuggling. Canadian residents wishing to import or export firearms must acquire licenses and registration certificates.

Information contained in the computerized registration system is governed by the Privacy Act to prevent unauthorized individuals from acquiring information. Firearms dealers can submit information to the system, but they will be unable to access information contained in the system. Data regarding the types and number of firearms owned will not be directly matched with the owner's name and address, but rather with a firearms identification number.

Supporters of the new registration system expect that it will assist the police in several ways. If a firearm is stolen, the police will have a better chance of returning the weapon to the legal owner. If all legal owners have registered their firearms, then those failing to register can be charged under the criminal code, thus providing the police with an additional weapon in the fight against crime. If domestic violence in a home appears likely, registration will allow the police to know more accurately how many firearms need to be removed from the premises. If weapons are registered and entered in a computerized database, then police can more easily trace the legal owner of a firearm. Traceability is expected to increase gun owner responsibility for maintaining the security of weapons. Owners may be more likely to report the loss or theft of a firearm and more hesitant to lend firearms to those with whom they are not familiar. *See also* CANADIAN FIREARMS CENTRE; NATIONAL FIREARMS ASSOCIATION OF CANADA.

Further Reading: Marshall J. Brown, "New Canadian Gun Law Faces Budget, Legal Problems," *Gun News Digest* (Summer 1998), 38-39; Canadian Government Web site <canada.just.gc.ca/>; "Gun Control," *Economist* 333 (October 29, 1994), 50.

Canadian Firearms Centre (CFC)

The Canadian Firearms Centre (CFC) is an agency of the Canadian government responsible for coordinating the enforcement of Canada's firearms statutes, especially the more stringent provisions of the Firearms Act of 1998. Both sides of the American gun control debate can look to the operation of the CFC when considering how more stringent gun control legislation might be implemented in the United States. The CFC's duties include registering firearms, providing education for firearms owners, and restricting the illegal trafficking in firearms.

The Centre is composed of four separate organizations: the Department of Justice Firearms Policy and Programs Branch, the Firearms Implementation Project, the Public Affairs Unit, and the International Unit. The Centre operates in cooperation with other federal agencies, including the Royal Canadian Mounted Police (RCMP), Revenue Canada Customs, the Department of Foreign Affairs and International Trade, Human Resources Development Canada, and Public Works and Government Services Canada. Each has responsibility for administering provisions within Canada's firearms legislation.

The CFC is responsible for verifying the registration of firearms. Beginning in December 1998, firearms owners were required to meet with a firearms verifier to confirm the accuracy of the description of a firearm on the registration application. The CFC then provides the owner with a registration certificate recording the verification. Because the verification process is a recently implemented policy, the CFC registrar has invited firearms experts, such as collectors and employees of firearms businesses, to become firearms verifiers.

The CFC is responsible for training all persons who carry firearms as part of their official duties. The Centre has cooperated with regional law enforcement agencies in producing a series of videos for viewing by police officers, who also receive a handbook explaining the provisions of the firearms laws. The CFC trains firearms officers and those who process information gathered from the implementation of the Firearms Act. Judges, prosecutors, and justices of the peace are furnished with information to assist them in interpreting firearms laws. To reach the average citizen, the CFC sends representatives to hunting and gun shows to distribute pamphlets and fact sheets that clarify the new firearms provisions. In addition, the CFC maintains a toll-free number that people may call to receive advice, and publishes information in hunting and firearms magazines. The Centre distributes a newsletter, *Insight*, which contains information on various topics dealing with recent changes in firearms legislation.

A program manager for safety education and awareness who is attached to the CFC has led an effort to create two new safety education courses for those who wish to obtain a firearm. These courses became available in late 1998. The first course treats the safe use and storage of rifles and shotguns and the second deals with handgun safety. Individuals may bypass the course and become eligible for possession and acquisition of a license if they succeed in passing a firearms test or if they have already taken a previous safety course.

The Firearms Act includes greater restrictions on importing and exporting firearms and the Canadian criminal code includes new penalties for smuggling and illegal trafficking in guns. CFC officials believe that the new requirement to register rifles and shotguns and the automated registration system will help law enforcement trace the illegal market in firearms. Law enforcement agencies in Canada and the United States share information regarding the illegal use of firearms. Such information includes the make, model, and serial number of guns found at crime scenes. *See also* CANADA; NATIONAL FIREARMS ASSOCIATION OF CANADA.

Further Reading: Canadian Firearms Centre Web site <www.cfc-ccaf.gc.ca>; *In Sight: The Newsletter of the Canadian Firearms Centre.*

Caron v. United States (1998)

In *Caron v. United States* (Docket No. 97-6270, U.S. Supreme Court, 1998), the U.S. Supreme Court ruled that a felon could have the right to own firearms restored under federal law only if a state conferred the right to own all types of firearms, not just some. If federal authorities discover a convicted felon in possession of specific firearms that the state has granted him or her a right to possess, he or she still may have violated federal prohibitions on the ownership of firearms. The federal government uses state determinations of whether an individual is too dangerous to possess a firearm, but need not follow a state's policies regarding the ownership of specific categories of firearms in applying prohibitions on gun ownership or for enhanced sentencing for a convicted felon who uses a firearm in another crime. The federal statute [921 (a) (20)] states that a previous conviction is not to be considered for enhanced sentencing if the offender's civil rights have been restored, "unless such . . . restoration . . . expressly provides that the person may not . . . possess . . . firearms."

On three separate occasions (in 1958, 1959, and 1963), Gerald Caron had been convicted in Massachusetts state court of attempted breaking and entering. In 1970, a California state court convicted him of assault with intent to commit murder and attempted murder. Subsequently residing in Massachusetts, Caron was allowed under state law to possess rifles or shotguns because his conviction was more than five years old and he had obtained a firearm permit. In 1993, federal agents arrested him for threatening a man and his family with a semi-automatic rifle. Agents seized six rifles and over 6,000 rounds of ammunition from Caron's home. After conviction, the Federal District Court in Massachusetts enhanced his sentence for having been convicted at least three times as a violent felon.

Taking an appeal from the Court of Appeals for the First Circuit, the U.S. Supreme Court, in a 6-to-3 decision, affirmed the lower court's ruling that the defendant's previous convictions counted toward enhanced sentencing. The Court stated that the phrase "may not . . . possess . . . firearms" can be understood in two "all-or-nothing" ways. The first interpretation, which the government attorneys supported, holds that the phrase applies to all firearms at the federal level when a state *forbids* possession of one or more types of firearms. According to the second interpretation, the phrase does not apply if a state *permits* possession of one or more types of firearms. The Court sided with the government contention that a state limitation on firearms possession, regardless of how extensive, "activates the uniform federal ban on possessing any firearms at all."

The Court declared that the federal government has "an interest in a single, national, protective policy, broader than required by state law," for determining when a convicted felon should continue to be denied the right to possess firearms. States cannot provide the "positive assurance" that an individual no longer presents a risk of danger. Federal law offers that assurance by considering "primary conduct not covered by state law." Because federal law refers to firearms possession generally and not to specific types of weapons, the Court has interpreted the relevant statute to establish a more stringent standard for reestablishing the right to possess firearms than states have at times adopted.

Further Reading: *Caron v. United States*, Docket No. 97-6270 (U.S. Supreme Court, 1998).

Cases v. United States (1942)

On an appeal from the District Court of the United States for Puerto Rico, the U.S. Court of Appeals for the First Circuit in *Cases v. United States* (131 F.2d 916, 1942) reviewed the sentencing of the appellant, who was found guilty of violating two sections of the Federal Firearms Act (FFA) of 1938, which made it unlawful for anyone under indictment or convicted of a crime of violence to ship or transport any firearm or ammunition in interstate or foreign commerce, or to receive a firearm or ammunition that had been transported in interstate or foreign trade. Firearm or ammunition possession is presumptive evidence that the firearm was transported or received by the individual in violation of the law.

In August 1941, the defendant received 10 rounds of ammunition from a friend who had purchased it for him in a hardware store. Three days later he went to a beach club in the municipality of Carolina, carrying a .38 caliber Colt revolver. He became angry with another patron, shooting him with the revolver. The defendant had been convicted in a Puerto Rican court in 1922 of aggravated assault and battery, thus bringing him under the prohibition of the FFA and making illegal his possession of the weapon and ammunition.

The defendant employed several arguments in claiming that the FFA was unconstitutional. First, he argued that it was an ex post facto law, establishing additional punishment for an act already committed. The court disagreed, ruling that in no sense was the FFA an ex post facto law because no one transporting or receiving a firearm or ammunition prior to passage of the act could be prosecuted under its provisions. With regard to the law instituting additional punishment, the court stated that the statute represented a valid exercise of legislative authority to regulate, even though certain conduct was made dependent on past behavior, including acts committed prior to passage of the legislation. The court focused on the nature of the past behavior in establishing the ineligibility of a person to engage in a future activity. Citing a related Supreme Court ruling, the court indicated that a felony conviction can be used to disqualify a person in the practice of medicine. In the present case, the intention of Congress was to protect the citizenry from those who, by their past conduct, had demonstrated their unfitness to own dangerous weapons.

In response to the appellant's argument that his Second Amendment right to possess a firearm had been violated, the court stated that the right to keep and bear arms is not an individual right and that the sole purpose of the Second Amendment is to prevent the federal government from encroaching on a right that could be established in local legislation. The circuit court cited *United States v. Miller* (1939), in which the U.S. Supreme Court in a limited ruling declared that weapons having no relation to the preservation of a well regulated militia are not protected by the Second Amendment. The circuit court noted that under a strict interpretation of the Miller decision, the only firearms that could be regulated would be "weapons such as a flintlock musket or a matchlock harquebus." To hold that only antiquated weapons with no relation to a well regulated militia could be subject to regulation would in effect make the untenable assertion that the Second Amendment right to bear arms is absolute.

The appellant further argued that the FFA denied him equal protection under the law because it did not apply equally to all who were included in the disqualifying category. Crimes used to define the category were differently defined in different states and territories, a potential difficulty that arose because a federal law depended on criminal definitions provided by varying state statutes. The court agreed that this was true, but concluded that the definitions of crimes were not sufficiently varied in different states to make the classification unconstitutional. Congress had achieved "practical uniformity" among the states and territories in the application of the act.

The appellant also charged that the ammunition he was accused of having acquired three days before the incident at the beach club was not covered under the act. However, the court determined that the evidence sufficiently indicated that the appellant had no other weapon than the .38 caliber revolver. This fact justified the conclusion that the ammunition acquired was for the .38 caliber weapon and hence satisfied the definition of ammunition within the FFA. Therefore, all objections of the appellant were rejected and the appeals court upheld the district court

judgment. *See also* FEDERAL FIREARMS ACT; SECOND AMENDMENT; *UNITED STATES V. MILLER* (1939).

Further Reading: *Cases v. United States*, 131 F.2d 916 (1942).

Cease Fire, Inc.

Founded by Jann Wenner, editor-in-chief of *Rolling Stone* magazine, Cease Fire, Inc., is a nonprofit organization concerned with reducing the number of handgun-related deaths and injuries, especially among children and teenagers. It engages in nationwide education campaigns to inform people about the dangers of handguns kept in the home. In 1997, Cease Fire developed public service announcements for radio and television and a series of advertisements for newspapers and magazines.

Associated with Cease Fire is a 38-member advisory panel composed of individuals from the media and entertainment industries, the legal and medical professions, law enforcement organizations, and the political realm. The advisory panel includes Senators John H. Chafee, Republican from Rhode Island, and Dianne Feinstein, Democrat from California; former Democratic President Jimmy Carter; actors Michael Douglas and Paul Newman; former CBS News anchor Walter Cronkite; Gilbert Gallegos, national president, Fraternal Order of Police; Larry Bedard, president of the American College of Emergency Physicians; and Jerome J. Shestack, president of the American Bar Association. Elizabeth Schmidt serves as the organization's executive director.

Cease Fire emphasizes two basic themes: firearm violence as a public health problem, and guns as unsafe and dangerous products that do not have a legitimate place in homes, especially where there are children. In September 1997, during an event held at the National Medical Center in Washington, D.C., to initiate a new advertising campaign, Wenner claimed that 10 children are killed each day by handguns. In addition, an estimated 1.2 million elementary school children go home each day to a home with a gun and without adult supervision. Just as Americans have been made aware of the health risks of smoking cigarettes and driving without seat belts, Wenner stated that the ad campaign was intended to raise public awareness of the dangers of having a handgun in the home.

The campaign's print advertisements and public service announcements were produced by BBDO, a New York-based advertising agency. The announcements presented actual accounts of children finding handguns, even when hidden or locked away. The accounts end tragically. Michael Douglas narrated four of the announcements that were broadcast nationwide on major cable networks, network affiliates, and cable systems. The print advertisements ran in such national magazines as *People, Time, Rolling Stone,* and *Vanity Fair.* The day after the Washington meeting, a gathering was held in Boston for the unveiling of a large billboard intended for use in cities nationwide. Six cities—Albuquerque, Austin, Cleveland, Miami, Portland, and Salt Lake City—were targeted for prolonged public awareness campaigns, including placement of posters at bus and train stations, distribution of brochures to parents, broadcast of public service announcements, and printing of ads in local and regional publications.

In a prior media campaign, more than $5 million was devoted to seven public service announcements describing tragic incidents involving children and guns. The ads, which were placed with national cable networks, cable systems, network affiliates, independent stations, and movie theater chains, featured Paul Newman and his wife Joanne Woodward, Walter Cronkite, and Oprah Winfrey. In addition, funds were used to run print ads in 26 national magazines. Gun rights groups, which emphasize the defensive value of firearms, reject the emotional appeal used in Cease Fire ads, noting that the probability of children being involved in gun accidents has fallen in recent years. *See also* FEINSTEIN, DIANNE.

Further Reading: Cease Fire, Inc., Web site <www.ceasefire.org>.

Center for the Study and Prevention of Violence (CSPV)

The Center for the Study and Prevention of Violence (CSPV), located at the University of Colorado at Boulder, was established in 1992 with a grant from the Carnegie Corporation of New York as an organization dedicated to understanding and preventing violence, including violence involving the use of firearms. Although the Center provides information about the prevalence and prevention of firearms-related violence, it is cautious about identifying firearms as an independent cause of violence and does not focus on gun control policy in sponsored research.

The Center has three basic missions. First, CSPV's Information House, which is the core of the organization, gathers research reports on the causes and prevention of violence, maintains databases, conducts literature searches, and provides information to the public upon request. Second, the Center provides assistance to those wishing to develop a violence prevention program. Third, CSPV conducts research on the causes of violence and the effectiveness of programs intended to prevent violent behavior.

CSPV reports that from 1984 to 1993 handgun homicides among youth aged 15 to 19 increased more than 450 percent. In 1992, 5,262 youths aged 5 to 19 died of gunshot wounds. Among the causes, 62 percent were homicides, 27percent were suicides, and 9 percent were unintentional injuries. Among children aged 5 to 9, firearm injuries were the fifth leading cause of death, and among those aged 10 to 14, such injuries were the second leading cause of death. The Center also focuses on the availability of guns among youth, citing survey data indicating that 13 percent of respondents in the sixth through twelfth grades had been threatened with a firearm. The Center reports that increasing numbers of children are being exposed to gun violence, which can traumatize young people and disrupt the educational system. The Center cites data indicating that in 1992 the average cost of a violent injury, fatal or nonfatal, was $44,000. That year the total medical cost of violence was estimated to be $13.5 billion.

Although the Center reports that the increase in lethal firearm injuries is associated with greater youth access to firearms and less hesitancy to use them, it concludes that the problem of firearms violence must be addressed in a larger social context.

Through funding from the Colorado Trust, CSPV has begun a study of youth handgun violence in cooperation with the Center for Public-Private Sector Cooperation at the University of Colorado at Denver. The research project involves investigating the extent of the problem, analyzing information gathered from focus groups within Colorado, and identifying prevention or intervention initiatives that demonstrate promise of success. The Center states that the research project will not involve the issue of handgun control, nor will it take a position on legislation to control handguns.

CSPV concludes that the public health approach to the study and prevention of youth violence is a valuable research tool. According to the Center, the public health approach focuses on primary prevention, which involves searching for ways of preventing disease or injury. According to the primary prevention strategy, researchers should conduct an epidemiological analysis to discover the behavioral and environmental "risk factors" (such as the availability of firearms to youth) that are related to injury. According to the Center, "the public health approach allows one to think about violence not as an inevitable fact of life, but as a problem that can be prevented."

Further Reading: Center for the Prevention of Violence Web site <www.colorado.edu/cspv>.

Center to Prevent Handgun Violence (CPHV)

In 1983, Handgun Control, Inc. (HCI), the leading gun control organization, established the Center to Prevent Handgun Violence (CPHV) to assume the educational role of informing citizens about the dangers of handgun ownership and use. Noting that 16 children in the United States die each day from suicide, homicide, or accidents involving firearms, CPHV focuses on the dangers of handguns to minors. The Center coordinates HCI's media relations and acts as a repository for donations because contributions to it are tax deductible. CPHV is chaired by Sarah Brady.

Through its "Straight Talk About Risks" (STAR) program, the organization provides training, curricula, and videos to train educators, parents, and others who wish to inform young people, from pre-school through high school, of the dangers of firearms. Converse, the tennis shoe manufacturer, has helped to organize "The Converse STAR Team," a program in which athletes present public service announcements about alternatives to gun violence. STAR materials, available in Spanish and English, include posters, classroom handouts, and videos. In 1993-1994, STAR materials were introduced in a sample of schools in 30 cities around the nation. More than 2,000 teachers received training in the curriculum and over 150,000 students were exposed to the materials. Both the National Education Association and the American Federation of Teachers endorse the STAR curriculum.

In cooperation with the American Academy of Pediatrics, CPHV sponsors "Steps to Prevent Firearm Injury" (STOP). Health care professionals counsel parents and children about avoiding the dangers of gun availability in the home and in the community. Educational materials for parents and children were given to over 6,500 pediatricians during the early 1990s. Nearly all major medical associations have endorsed STOP. An associated activity, Project Lifeline, is a public education campaign in cooperation with the health community that trains health care professionals to educate the public about gun violence.

CPHV's Legal Action Project (LAP), formed in 1989, provides free legal representation for victims of gun violence who are suing gun owners, dealers, or manufacturers for recklessness in the production, use, or sale of handguns. The Project counters the arguments of pro-gun groups that are based on the Second Amendment. The Entertainment Resources Department, a branch of CPHV located in Los Angeles, California, cooperates with the entertainment industry to promote the prevention of gun violence through appropriate portrayals in film, television, and other media.

CPHV's Research Department collects evidence that gun control laws are successful and analyzes data to measure the impact of guns in society. The Department suggests ways to improve violence prevention programs. The Law Enforcement Relations Department and its Gun Interdiction Project cooperates with police departments and other criminal justice professionals in the attempt to eliminate illegal guns. Acting as a clearinghouse for law enforcement, the Project encourages the sharing of information among police agencies. *See also* BRADY, SARAH; HANDGUN CONTROL, INC.; HEALTH CARE PROFESSIONALS; LEGAL ACTION PROJECT; MEDIA VIOLENCE.

Further Reading: Center to Prevent Handgun Violence, "We Can End the Violence," (pamphlet, n.d.); Center to Prevent Handgun Violence Web site <www.handguncontrol.org>; Gregg Lee Carter, *The Gun Control Movement* (New York: Twayne, 1997).

Central Conference of American Rabbis (CCAR)

For many years, the Central Conference of American Rabbis (CCAR) has taken a strong stand in favor of stricter gun control measures. In 1975, at its 86th annual convention, delegates adopted a resolution advocating gun control. The preamble to the resolution stated that increasing numbers of handguns in the United States have led to ever greater loss of life. The handgun was identified as the weapon most often involved in "cases of rage and passion" that result in injury or death. The resolution declared that easy access to firearms has increased the number of deaths among young people aged 1 to 19 and that greater numbers of high school students fall victim to handguns each year.

Founded in 1889, the Conference is composed of Reform rabbis ordained at the Hebrew Union College-Jewish Institute of Religion as well as rabbis ordained at liberal European seminaries. The group is an authoritative force for many American Jews on public policy issues, including gun control.

CCAR has resolved that the United States Congress and state legislatures should enact legislation to ban the sale of handguns. The ban should not apply to military personnel, police officers, security personnel while on the job, and target shooters who have received licenses from local authorities. The Conference concludes that legislation should provide for the collection of all handguns presently possessed by "citizens, aliens, residents and visitors of the United States." Just compensation would be given to those whose firearms were confiscated. In addition, the Conference resolved that its members would assist those working for passage of legislation.

At its 98th annual convention in 1987, the Conference approved another resolution regarding the effort to enact more stringent gun control legislation. Noting the organization's continuing support for gun control, the resolution stated that stricter laws are intended to "eliminate the senseless slaughter of humans in our land by those who easily obtain unlicensed hand guns." CCAR declared its opposition to the National Rifle Association (NRA) for its "dedicated pursuit of unlicensed gun ownership." Observing that the NRA contributes to congressional election campaigns, and claiming that legislators' voting records are influenced by these contributions, CCAR urged members of Congress to refuse financial support from the NRA and to support strict gun control legislation.

At its 100th Annual Convention in June 1989, CCAR approved a resolution which noted that firearms and "automatic weapons" continued to proliferate and that deaths and injuries resulting from such weapons were increasing "astronomically." The Conference resolved that local, state, and national officials restrict handgun sales and ban automatic weapons sales to the general public. Because federal law already severely limits the sale of automatic weapons, the Conference likely meant semi-automatic versions of automatic weapons, or assault rifles, which may be converted to automatic use. *See also* AMERICAN JEWISH CONGRESS; ASSAULT WEAPONS BAN; JEWS FOR THE PRESERVATION OF FIREARMS OWNERSHIP; NATIONAL RIFLE ASSOCIATION.

Further Reading: Central Conference of American Rabbis Web site <www.ccarnet.org>.

Chenoweth, Helen (1938–)

Helen Chenoweth, congresswoman from Idaho since 1995, has established a strong reputation for defending gun rights against what she considers federal government encroachment. She bases her gun rights position, as well as stands on other issues, on the belief that the people have certain rights independent of government and that government is created to protect those rights. She has gained the support of several pro-gun organizations in her attempts to pass legislation to ensure gun rights, particularly a proposal to repeal the Lautenberg Amendment, a measure included in the 1996 Omnibus Appropriations Bill that prohibits anyone convicted of a misdemeanor involving domestic violence from purchasing or owning a firearm. The repeal effort proved unsuccessful in the 105th Congress.

Although a relatively recent arrival to Capitol Hill, Chenoweth has considerable political experience. In 1978, after serving as chief of staff to Congressman Steve Symm, Chenoweth established Consulting Firms, Inc., a business that focused on environmental and energy policy issues and the protection of private property rights. Earlier in her career Chenoweth became a medical and legal management consultant, speaking frequently on political issues in these areas. Once elected to Congress, her strong background in conservative politics prepared the way for an active role in the new Republican congressional majority. A representative from the state in which the Ruby Ridge standoff occurred, Chenoweth has championed the call for less federal government involvement in the states.

Chenoweth has supported many conservative objectives, including a proposal for a constitutional amendment that would abol-ish the federal income tax by repealing the Sixteenth Amendment. The income tax would only be valid during a congressionally declared war. Given her strong support for individual rights and opposition to federal government power, pro-gun groups find Chenoweth an ideal legislator to whom to appeal for assistance.

In 1997, Chenoweth directed her attention toward the Lautenberg Amendment, passed the year before. She had voted against the omnibus appropriations bill that contained Democratic Senator Frank Lautenberg's provision denying gun ownership to those convicted of a domestic violence misdemeanor. In March 1997, Chenoweth introduced legislation to repeal the Lautenberg Amendment, deploring what she considered the inappropriate and unethical procedures by which the amendment became law. In addition to the procedural criticisms, she cited several substantive objections to the amendment. First, Chenoweth claimed the gun legislation amounted to an ex post facto law that applied to individuals long after they were initially charged with the misdemeanor. In

Representative Helen Chenowith (R-ID) is a strong defender of gun rights. *Courtesy of Rep. Chenowith's office.*

addition, she claimed that the provision established punishment for a minor offense completely out of proportion to the seriousness of the infraction. Chenoweth also charged that the amendment denied judicial discretion to states in determining suitable penalties in specific cases.

The congresswoman claimed that the Lautenberg provision allowed the federal government to assume powers not specifically delegated to it in Article I, Section 8 of the Constitution. The constitutional framers, she argued, intended that the enactment and enforcement of criminal law be a state and local function. Also, the Lautenberg Amendment constituted an unfunded federal mandate that shifted costs for enforcement onto state and local police agencies. Most fundamentally, Chenoweth contended that the provision violated the Second Amendment right to keep and bear arms. She regarded this constitutional issue to be especially important for women involved in domestic disputes who may have been charged and convicted along with their husbands for misdemeanor domestic violence. She argued that the Lautenberg Amendment left abused women defenseless against attack. *See also* LAUTENBERG, FRANK R.; LAUTENBERG AMENDMENT; RUBY RIDGE; SECOND AMENDMENT; WOMEN AND GUNS.

Further Reading: Helen Chenoweth, "Testimony on Proposed Legislation Relating to the Lautenberg Gun Ban," Judiciary Subcomittee on Crime, March 5, 1997; Helen Chenoweth Web site <www.house.gov/chenoweth/>; Gun Owners of America, "Rep. Chenoweth Introduces Lautenberg Repeal," *The Gun Owners* 16 (April 25, 1997), 1-3.

Children's Defense Fund (CDF)

The Children's Defense Fund (CDF), an organization that promotes the interests of poor, minority, and disabled children, has advocated policies to limit youth access to firearms and to hold adults responsible for the illegal use of guns by youth. More broadly, the organization promotes programs to improve the health and education of children and to prevent broken families and youth crime and violence. Although some social scientists and gun rights advocates have claimed that guns represent a minimal danger to children under 10 years old, organizations like the CDF present powerful emotional arguments in favor of gun control measures.

Marian Wright Edelman, president of the CDF, founded the organization in 1973. In the late 1960s, she worked for the Poor People's March and subsequently founded the Washington Research Project, a public interest law firm and precursor of the CDF. The Fund receives financial support from foundations, corporations, and individuals. The organization opposes any policy that involves taking primarily punitive actions against juveniles involved in illegal activities. Rather than devoting resources to incarceration after crimes have been committed, the CDF advocates preventive measures to keep youth in school and away from illegal activities. This conviction could have led to a position on firearms closer to that of gun rights organizations, which claim that guns are not dangerous, youth in trouble are. Instead, the organization recommends locking up guns, not children.

The CDF claims that since the 1980s nearly all the increase in violent crime involving youth can be associated with access to firearms. From 1983 to 1995, gun homicides committed by juveniles tripled, although homicides committed with other weapons declined. Data are cited indicating that child gun deaths have risen from 8 per day in 1983 to 14 per day in 1995. Although the CDF admitted in 1998 that violent crime arrests had declined 12 percent since 1994 and homicide rates among children aged 10 to 17 had decreased 31 percent since 1993, the organization still considers youth violence a major problem, especially because weapons violations doubled between 1985 and 1994.

The CDF believes that any legislation dealing with youth crime must address the problem of firearms. The CDF supported legislation being considered in the 105th Congress that would impose penalties for transferring firearms to youths and for assisting young people to make illegal purchases. The organization has advocated a measure that would hold adults accountable if children gain access to guns. In July 1998, President Bill Clinton announced his support for this proposal. The organization supports collaboration among federal, state, and local law enforcement agencies to trace the sources of firearms that youths use in crimes. Like many other groups, the CDF advocates the introduction of safety locks that are integral to the design of handguns. Although several manufacturers have agreed to include locks, the organization believes that legislative mandates would ensure the maintenance of basic standards.

The CDF supported the 1998 Children's Gun Violence Prevention Act, which was introduced by Representative Carolyn McCarthy, Democrat of New York, a recently elected congresswoman whose husband was killed during the Long Island Railroad gun incident. Among its provisions, the bill would mandate studies to determine the most effective means of making guns child-resistant, and would impose a fine and prison sentence for adults who allow their firearms to be used by children to commit acts of violence. The CDF expects further reductions in firearms violence among youth with the adoption of legislation to establish adult responsibility for gun safety, and to institute after-school programs that would occupy youth during times when violent acts are most likely occur. *See also* ACCIDENTS INVOLVING GUNS; CLINTON, WILLIAM JEFFERSON (BILL); TRIGGER LOCKS.

Further Reading: Children's Defense Fund Web site <www.childrensdefense.org/safestart>.

Citizens Committee for the Right to Keep and Bear Arms (CCRKBA)

The Citizens Committee for the Right to Keep and Bear Arms (CCRKBA) was established in 1971 to promote the interpretation of the Second Amendment to the U.S. Constitution that all citizens have the right to own and carry firearms. The organization operates on the principle that "an armed populace is more likely to be a free populace."

The CCRKBA has a staff of 40 to 50 people, a budget of over $3.6 million, and offices in Washington, D.C., and Bellevue, Washington. The organization claims a membership of over 600,000, with groups in all 50 states and 140 local organizations. More than 150 members of Congress serve on CCRKBA's national advisory committee. Membership comes with a $15.00 annual donation to the organization. Five-year memberships ($50) and lifetime memberships ($150) are also available. Members receive "action alerts"—bulletins that provide information about proposed gun control legislation and advice on what actions to take to prevent passage.

In Washington, D.C., the CCRKBA public affairs staff interacts with public officials and other pro-gun groups to initiate and assist in the passage of pro-gun legislation and to defeat gun control measures. In 1986, CCRKBA cooperated with the National Rifle Association (NRA) and Gun Owners of America (GOA) in an intensive lobbying campaign to gain passage of the Firearms Owners Protection Act. CCRKBA maintains a political action committee (Right to Bear Arms Political Victory Fund) that raises funds to donate to political candidates who support the organization's pro-gun positions.

The Bellevue, Washington, headquarters is responsible for grass-roots lobbying in state legislatures. State offices monitor the state and local activities of gun control groups. With the assistance of local organizations, the Committee works to defeat anti-gun legislation in many states and localities. To achieve its objectives nationwide, the organization strives to inform members about gun issues and encourages them to participate in efforts to protect gun rights.

As part of its educational campaign, CCRKBA maintains a speakers bureau that promotes speaking engagements by pro-gun activists. Committee representatives appear at conferences, schools, gun shows, and on television and radio. It conducts research to indicate the positive impact of guns on society. For instance, a 1996 news release from the organization reported the results of a study demonstrating that states that have enacted laws that are less restrictive in granting the right to carry a concealed weapon have considerably lower violent crime rates than states with more restrictive laws.

Various literature is available through the organization, including such monographs as *The Good Side of Guns: The Role of Firearms in Self Defense, Armed and Alive,* and *The Great Assault Weapon Hoax.* Books by the Committee's chairman, Alan Gottlieb, including *The Rights of Gun Owners* and *Gun Rights Fact Book,* are also available. CCRKBA publishes a monthly newsletter, *Point Blank,* and holds an annual conference. *See also* GOTTLIEB, ALAN MERRIL; GUN OWNERS OF AMERICA; FIREARMS OWNERS PROTECTION ACT; NATIONAL RIFLE ASSOCIATION; SECOND AMENDMENT.

Further Reading: Citizens Committee for the Right to Keep and Bear Arms, "States Allowing Citizens to Carry Concealed Firearms Have Less Violent Crime" (news release, March 27, 1996); CCRKBA Web site <www.ccrkba.org>; Alan M. Gottlieb, *Things You Can Do to Defend Your Gun Rights* (Bellevue, WA: Merril Press, 1993).

City of Las Vegas v. Moberg (1971)

The Court of Appeals of New Mexico, in *City of Las Vegas v. Moberg* (82 N.M. 626, 1971), ruled that any ordinance denying people the right to bear arms violates Article II, Section 6 of the state constitution of New Mexico, which states that "The people have the right to bear arms for their security and defense, but nothing herein shall be held to permit the carrying of concealed weapons." The court decided that while this constitutional provision allows local governments to prohibit the carrying of concealed weapons, ordinances cannot limit the right of persons to carry weapons openly.

When Leland Moberg discovered that his automobile had been burglarized, he went to the booking room of the police department of the city of Las Vegas, New Mexico, to report the crime. When police officers noted that he was carrying a pistol openly in a holster, Moberg was arrested for "carrying a concealed and deadly weapon" and was convicted in municipal court of violating a city ordinance making it unlawful for anyone to carry a weapon, concealed or not, within the city limits of East Las Vegas. The ordinance defined deadly weapons to include guns, pistols, knives with blades longer than two and a half inches, slingshots, sandbags, metallic knuckles, concealed rocks, and "all other weapons, by whatever name known, with which dangerous wounds can be inflicted."

Moberg appealed the conviction to the district court, which granted him a new trial. At this trial, no evidence was presented that the defendant was carrying a concealed weapon. Both the defense and the prosecution dealt with the charge as involving the carrying of a deadly weapon as such. The district court found him guilty of violating the city ordinance prohibiting the carrying of a deadly weapon, but one which was in plain view and not concealed. Moberg then appealed the conviction to the Court of Appeals of New Mexico, contending that the ordinance under which he was convicted violated his right to bear arms as guaranteed under the state constitution.

The court first established the obvious: an ordinance that denies rights protected in the state constitution is void. Ordinances that specifically prohibit the carrying of *concealed* weapons are considered a proper exercise of the police power because they do not deprive citizens of the right to bear arms but simply regulate that right. The constitution specifically provides for this exception. However, the court noted that the Las Vegas ordinance prohibited the carrying of all weapons, whether concealed or not, thereby denying to citizens the constitutionally guaranteed right to bear arms. Therefore, that portion of the Las Vegas ordinance that prohibited the carrying of weapons openly was determined to violate the state constitution. *See also* CONCEALED CARRY LAWS.

Further Reading: *City of Las Vegas v. Moberg,* 82 N.M. 626 (1971).

City of Salina v. Blaksley (1905)

In 1905, the Supreme Court of Kansas, in *City of Salina v. Blaksley* (83 P. 619, 72 Kan. 230, 1905), ruled that there was no absolute right to possess or carry a handgun for self-defense. The court declared that the state constitution did protect an individual right to bear arms, but the right belongs only to the people collectively when associated with membership in authorized military groups. The court ruled that the state could restrict possession of weapons to those employed in "civilized warfare."

James Blaksley was arrested for carrying a revolver within the Salina city limits while under the influence of alcohol. After he was found guilty in the city police court, the defendant appealed the conviction to the district court, which upheld the original verdict. Blaksley then appealed to the Kansas Supreme Court, claiming that section 1003 of the General Statutes of 1901 violated the state constitution. The statute stated that "The [city] council may prohibit and punish the carrying of firearms or other deadly weapons, concealed or otherwise." Section four of the bill of rights within the state constitution declared that "The people have the right to bear arms for their defense and security; but standing armies, in time of peace, are dangerous to liberty, and shall not be tolerated."

In response to Blaksley's contention that the constitution limited the legislature's power to prevent an individual from possessing or carrying arms, the court concluded that the provision in the bill of rights regarding the bearing of arms refers to the people collectively rather than to the rights of individual persons. The court believed that the expression of concern for standing armies and their threat to liberty established the relationship between the right to bear arms and the nature of the military establishment. Therefore, the framers did not intend to establish a right of individuals independent of a concern for military organization. Article eight of the state constitution clarified the way in which the people could exercise the right to bear arms. In preserving the general security, all able-bodied citizens between the ages of 21 and 45 were to serve in the militia. In time of peace, the militia would serve as the sole means for maintaining security. However, no one had the right to assume that responsibility without the sanction of the legislature through the authority of the constitution.

The court also focused on the Second Amendment to the U.S. Constitution in support of its position that the right to bear arms applied only to membership in the state militia or other legitimate military organization. Similar to the state constitution, the objective of the national document was to maintain security by guaranteeing to people, as members of a well-regulated militia or other legally sanctioned military organization, the right to bear arms. According to the court's interpretation of the exercise of this right, the defendant could not satisfy the condition of membership in an organized militia or any other legal military organization that would sanction the bearing of arms. His carrying a weapon was not covered under the state bill of rights and therefore no constitutionally protected right was involved. *See also* BLISS v. COMMONWEALTH (1822); SECOND AMENDMENT.

Further Reading: *City of Salina v. Blaksley*, 83 P. 619, 72 Kan. 230 (1905); Earl R. Kruschke, *The Right to Keep and Bear Arms* (Springfield, IL: Charles C. Thomas, 1985).

Civil Forfeiture

Civil forfeiture refers to government confiscation of property, including such things as automobiles, trucks, airplanes, sea vessels, cash, and real property that in some way has been involved in a crime. Although federal, state, and local governments have generally used forfeiture to discourage the drug trade, the procedure applies to many other unlawful acts, such as transporting illegal aliens, violating conservation laws, counterfeiting, sale of obscene materials and contraband cigarettes, and illegal gambling. Gun rights advocates fear that the procedure may be used more extensively against gun owners who have in some way inadvertently violated a firearms statute. Although civil forfeiture has been upheld by the U.S. Supreme Court, many have expressed concern that the federal program grants extensive powers to government officials.

The Controlled Substances Act, in Title 21, Section 881, provides for a forfeiture program aimed primarily at drug smugglers and dealers. The acquittal of a defendant on criminal charges may not end civil action. Although no criminal guilt may be established, property can still be confiscated because the courts require a less demanding level of proof in civil forfeiture than in criminal proceedings. While criminal cases employ "beyond reasonable doubt" as the standard of proof, civil forfeiture cases employ "probable cause." Although a forfeiture can be challenged in court, those concerned with the process, including gun rights advocates, note that the claimant may not have the right to counsel, a jury trial, or the opportunity to confront witnesses or informants.

The Department of Justice pursues three major goals: 1) punishing and deterring criminal activity by denying persons the property used in or obtained through illegal activities; 2) improving collaboration among federal, state, and local law enforcement agencies by sharing recovered resources, and 3) accumulating revenues to be used in further law enforcement operations involving forfeiture. The last goal includes providing legal training for law enforcement officers engaged in the civil forfeiture process. Those troubled by the civil forfeiture process claim that law enforcement agencies may demonstrate great zeal in confiscating property even when a criminal conviction seems unlikely, given the lower burden of proof and the incentive of monetary gain. Although forfeiture statutes contain exemptions for property owners who are ignorant of any illegal use, the courts have upheld forfeitures even when the owner most likely was innocent of any involvement or collaboration in criminal activity.

Gun rights advocates are most concerned about the possible forfeiture authority of the Bureau of Alcohol, Tobacco, and Firearms (BATF). Congress provided the BATF with seizure authority, specifically with regard to customs violations, in the Gun Control Act of 1968. However, the Firearms Owners' Protection Act of 1986, for which the Na-

tional Rifle Association (NRA) and other gun rights organizations lobbied extensively, limited that authority. BATF agents may seize only those firearms actually used in a specific illegal activity. Any other property owned by the accused cannot be seized. To confiscate a weapon, the owner must have been charged with a "willful or knowing" violation of firearms laws. Confiscation also requires a higher burden of proof: clear and convincing evidence. If acquitted, the gun owner must have his or her weapon returned.

The more limited firearms forfeiture rules notwithstanding, gun rights advocates express concern that Congress and the president may be willing to establish more extensive forfeiture authority, especially in relation to bans on certain firearms such as assault rifles. The nightmare scenario for gun advocates is a BATF granted the authority to confiscate, on the word of a confidential informant, guns and possibly other property for "minor" violations of firearms laws. Such fears may lead gun rights groups to lobby for weakening existing forfeiture statutes. *See also* Bureau of Alcohol, Tobacco, and Firearms; Firearms Owners Protection Act; Gun Control Act of 1968; National Rifle Association; *United States v. One Assortment of 89 Firearms* (1984).

Further Reading: May Ferguson Bradford, *Asset Forfeiture* (Beaumont, TX: United States Attorney's Office, Eastern District of Texas, n.d.); Diane Cecilia Weber, "Civil Forfeiture: The 'War on Drugs' Could Become the 'War on Gun Owners,'" *Guns and Ammo* 42 (June 1998), 16, 18-19; 42 (July 1998), 12, 14, 96.

Clinton, William Jefferson (Bill) (1946–)

Since taking office in 1993, Democratic President Bill Clinton has been a major supporter of more stringent gun control, and has become a major target of gun rights groups such as the National Rifle Association (NRA). During Clinton's administration, the Brady Handgun Violence Prevention Act and a ban on assault weapons were enacted. At the signing ceremony for the Brady Act, Clinton reminisced about his boyhood experiences with guns, stating that "I live in a place where we still close schools and plants on the first day of deer season." However, he claimed that this aspect of American life had been transformed into "an instrument of maintaining madness. It is crazy."

The 1992 Democratic platform on which Clinton first campaigned for the presidency contained an explicit endorsement for additional gun control legislation. The platform supported a waiting period for handgun purchases and a ban on assault weapons, advocated increased penalties for crimes committed with firearms, called for a halt to the illegal gun market, and backed severe punishment for those selling firearms to youths. However, Clinton's platform stated that no restrictions should be placed on firearms used for "legitimate hunting and sporting purposes."

The Brady bill languished in Congress during the Republican administrations of Ronald Reagan and George Bush, but when Clinton became president in January 1993 the measure gained a major advocate. On November 30, 1994, Clinton signed the bill into law. A more difficult fight for Clinton was passage of the assault weapons ban. In 1993, he expanded the import ban instituted by President George Bush, issuing an executive order that included assault-style handguns. In 1994, Clinton supported an assault weapons ban being considered by the U.S. House of Representatives as part of the crime bill. Although the bill was initially defeated in a House vote, Clinton stated that the fight was not over. He obtained the support of police organizations in a public relations campaign. Although many who supported the crime bill asked Clinton to remove the assault weapons ban, the president refused. A compromise bill, which included decreased spending, passed the House in August, gained Senate approval, and was signed by the president in September. Unpopular among gun rights advocates, the ban came under attack in 1996 in the new Republican-controlled Congress. In March, a repeal was approved by the House, but not by a sufficient margin to survive a Clinton veto, and the Senate never

took up the measure. In 1998, Clinton further expanded the ban on assault weapons, announcing a permanent prohibition on the importation of 58 additional firearms.

In an August 1994 press conference, Democratic President Bill Clinton denounces the National Rifle Association and Republican members of Congress for opposing his crime bill. *REUTERS/Gary Cameron/ Archive Photos.*

Although a national instant background check system was inaugurated on November 30, 1998, to replace the five-day waiting period imposed by the Brady law, Clinton stated that he would ask Congress to institute a new waiting period. In a speech given shortly after the new system went into effect, Clinton praised the instant check, stating that in the first four days of operation, 100,000 prospective firearms sales were examined and 400 purchases were stopped. Nonetheless, Clinton argued that a waiting period would provide a "cooling-off period" to prevent purchases made in anger or desperation and would allow for a more thorough check of records that are not yet computerized. Clinton criticized the NRA for initiating a lawsuit against the instant check system.

In addition to reestablishing the waiting period, Clinton announced that he would ask

Congress to impose a lifetime prohibition on gun ownership for juveniles convicted of violent crimes. Under current law, the criminal records of youths are disregarded after they turn 21. In addition, Clinton asked Attorney General Janet Reno and Treasury Secretary Robert Rubin to propose strategies to require people who purchase firearms at gun shows to undergo background checks. *See also* ASSAULT WEAPONS BAN; BRADY HANDGUN VIOLENCE PREVENTION ACT; BUSH, GEORGE; GUN SHOWS; LITTLETON, COLORADO, SCHOOL SHOOTING; NATIONAL RIFLE ASSOCIATION; REAGAN, RONALD; RENO, JANET.

Further Reading: Alice Ann Love, "Clinton Eyes Handgun Waiting Period," Associated Press (December 5, 1998), *Yahoo!* News Website <http://dailynews.yahoo.com/headlines/ap/a.../?s=v/ap/19981205/ts/clinton_radio_4.html>; Jack Nelson, "Clinton to Introduce Gun Control Measures, Challenge NRA Lobby," Los Angeles Times (November 19, 1993); Robert J. Spitzer, *The Politics of Gun Control*, 2nd ed. (New York: Chatham House, 1998).

Coalition to Stop Gun Violence (CSGV)

The Coalition to Stop Gun Violence (CSGV) works toward banning the importation, manufacture, sale, and transfer of handguns and assault weapons to the general public. The only exceptions to such a ban would include law enforcement, military, and security personnel, gun clubs where weapons would be securely stored, and gun dealers buying and selling inoperable antique firearms. The organization does not call for a similar ban on shotguns and rifles used for hunting because they are not considered a serious threat to public safety.

The CSGV was established in 1974 as the National Coalition to Ban Handguns. Initially operating in collaboration with Handgun Control, Inc. (HCI), CSGV soon separated from its partner organization because of disagreements about the basic strategy to pursue. The National Coalition called for stronger policies on gun control than did HCI. In 1990, the organization assumed its present name. The CSGV, a coalition of over 40 associations, including religious, labor,

medical, and educational groups, claims a membership of over 100,000 individuals. In 1993 and 1994, the CSGV joined with broadcast networks like MTV and Nickelodeon and with several movie studios to produce a media campaign against violence.

Although the CSGV champions a complete ban on handguns and assault rifles, the organization also advocates what it considers 'intermediate steps" to limit the level of violence. Observing that in 1994 over half of the guns used in crimes that the Bureau of Alcohol, Tobacco, and Firearms (BATF) could trace originated with federally licensed firearms dealers, the CSGV calls for measures to limit the availability of federal licenses for firearms dealers. The organization observes with approval that from 1994 to 1996 the number of licensed dealers declined from over 245,000 to 142,000. The 1994 Brady Handgun Violence Prevention Act had increased the three-year license fee from $30 to $200.

The CSGV advocates restrictive licensing and registering of gun owners and opposes attempts on the state level to liberalize laws allowing for the carrying of concealed weapons. The organization has expressed concern over the costs of treating victims of firearm violence, most of which are passed on to the taxpayer. The organization estimates that while 35,000 to 40,000 firearms-related deaths occur each year, the number of injuries are three times as great, with medical costs approximately $300,000 per injury. Therefore, the CSGV supports measures to increase taxes on handguns and ammunition, with the revenues to be earmarked for health care costs. The organization also supports legislation to establish strict liability for firearms manufacturers and dealers. A related measure would allow for regulating firearms as consumer products that must meet certain safety standards.

Banning Saturday night specials, or "junk guns," has been one of the organization's longstanding objectives. Citing BATF data, the CSGV identifies junk guns as a major culprit in crime. Although the Gun Control Act of 1968 banned import of such weapons, domestic production has continued. The organization hopes to stop manufacturers from producing the weapons, or at least to convince manufacturers to set higher production standards. Hoping to limit the illegal transfer and use of handguns, the CSGV supports a national one-handgun-a-month limit on purchases.

The organization believes that greater controls on legal gun owners and dealers, called the "gatekeepers" of firearms used in crimes, will result in lowered gun violence. The CSGV rejects the argument that the Second Amendment guarantees an individual right to keep and bear arms, asserting that ever since *United States v. Miller* (the 1939 decision that held that firearm possession is not a right protected by the Constitution unless related to the maintenance of a well-regulated militia), the Supreme Court has refused to hear a case based on the Second Amendment.

The greatest challenge to the organization's position that private handgun ownership should be prohibited is the claim that firearms offer an effective means of self-defense. Responding to that claim, the CSGV cites data indicating that suicides are five times more likely to occur in homes with firearms, and homicides are three times more likely. The CSGV emphasizes the extremely restricted instances in which a firearm may be used legally against another person. *See also* BRADY HANDGUN VIOLENCE PREVENTION ACT; BUREAU OF ALCOHOL, TOBACCO, AND FIREARMS; GUN CONTROL ACT OF 1968; HANDGUN CONTROL, INC.; SATURDAY NIGHT SPECIAL; SECOND AMENDMENT; *UNITED STATES V. MILLER* (1939).

Further Reading: Coalition to Stop Gun Violence Web site <www.gunfree.org>; Robert J. Spitzer, *The Politics of Gun Control* (Chatham, NJ: Chatham House, 1995).

Collectors

Gun collectors have been a sticking point in discussions of firearms regulation proposals, given their concern that such measures could threaten hobbies and economic enterprises. According to Roland Docal, "[The gun collector's] focus is on the beauty, craftsmanship, rarity, and profit potential that accom-

pany the possession of firearms. While the collector usually sides with pro-gun forces, he does so to ensure the continued legality of his activity and to protect the value of his investment." Gun control supporters often express sympathy for the concerns of gun collectors, realizing that to be successful, they cannot afford to alienate a potentially influential group that does not necessarily have the same overriding concern with the Second Amendment that gun rights organizations have.

The number of collectors burgeoned during the twentieth century. In 1939, there were an estimated 50,000 collectors in the United States. Twenty years later, that estimate had increased to 650,000 and has continued to increase. Fascination with the art and technology of firearms and the expectation of rising values have contributed to the enterprise. Since 1979, the National Rifle Association (NRA) has published *Man at Arms*, one of the major magazines devoted to historical guns, swords, and related collectable items.

The assault weapons ban of 1994, known as the Public Safety and Recreational Firearms Use Protection Act, while making it unlawful "to manufacture, transfer, or possess a semiautomatic assault weapon," made exceptions, including "any firearm that (i) is manually operated by bolt, pump, lever or slide action; (ii) has been rendered permanently inoperable; or (iii) is an antique firearm." This attempt to accommodate gun collectors notwithstanding, some collectors have remained pessimistic regarding the future prospects for firearms restrictions, especially given the general public sentiment in favor of further controls.

Collectors contend that any measure banning the manufacture, sale, and possession of particular firearms would be a violation of the Fifth Amendment protection against being deprived of property without just compensation. Docal estimates that the "fair market value" of the approximately 222 million privately owned firearms in the United States is $66.6 billion. However, he notes that this figure represents less than 5 percent of the annual federal budget, and therefore is seen as a realistic amount for gun control advocates to recommend paying to confiscate firearms.

Docal expresses apprehension about so-called "practical confiscation," legal requirements that stop short of actual confiscation but effectively eliminate firearms from a jurisdiction. For instance, a statute could offer several alternatives to gun owners, such as selling their firearms, keeping them outside a given jurisdiction, or surrendering them to authorities. Any of these options is less than palatable to gun collectors whose major concern is not with the use to which a firearm may be put, but primarily its possession as an object of value. *See also* ASSAULT WEAPONS BAN; GUN SHOWS; NATIONAL RIFLE ASSOCIATION; SECOND AMENDMENT.

Further Reading: Ronald Docal, "The Second, Fifth, and Ninth Amendment–The Precarious Protectors of the American Gun Collector," *Florida State Law Review* 23 (Spring 1996), FSU Web site <http://www.law.fsu.edu/journals.lawreview/frames/234/docatxt.html>; Lee Kennett and James La Verne Anderson, *The Gun in America: The Origins of a National Dilemma* (Westport, CT: Greenwood, 1975).

Colt, Samuel (1814–1862)

Samuel Colt, an inventive gunsmith and astute businessman, made the repeating handgun a common possession in the United States. He called his sixshooter "the peacemaker," a description with which contemporary gun supporters would agree, for it coincides with the view that a gun can play a crucial role in maintaining security and tranquility among people by keeping at bay those who would threaten the safety of the community.

Although his guns are most often associated with the winning of the West, Colt was born in Hartford, Connecticut. Colt lived in the East, where he established his firearms manufacturing plants. His interest in guns began at the age of 7, when he was given a horse pistol. Colt's mother died when he was 11 years old; his father sent him to live on a farm, where he was expected to contribute to the daily chores, and then to Amherst Academy. However, Samuel's fascination with explosives resulted in his ouster when an explosion rocked the school. At age 16, Colt found himself aboard a sailing vessel where he served a one-year stint as a sailor. Colt then returned to Hartford and put himself to work making two model pistols, neither of which proved successful. His father advised Colt to abandon the project.

Despite his father's counsel, Colt continued to develop his repeating pistol. Muzzleloaders placed settlers at a disadvantage in confrontations with Indians. Reloading was laborious and potentially dangerous, involving several complex steps. An Indian with a bow and arrows could shoot far more quickly than a pioneer with a muzzleloader, and with deadly effect. For four years, Colt, who was still in his teens, abandoned his firearm project, traveling around the country as "Dr. Coult" and entertaining audiences, at times passing himself off as a healer of sorts. By the mid-1830s, Colt returned to his revolver and improved it sufficiently to obtain

Samuel Colt was a nineteenth-century gunmaker whose sixshooter, the "peacemaker," made the repeating handgun a common possession in the United States. *Archive Photos.*

patents on it in England and France. In February 1836, at the age of 21, he received a U.S. patent for the revolving breech pistol, which granted him a 20-year monopoly on the production of revolvers. That same year he opened the Patent Arms Manufacturing Company in Paterson, New Jersey, and maintained a showroom in New York City.

Colt's repeating handgun, while not an innovation, encompassed the best of prevailing ideas. However, the first model had several disadvantages. At times it malfunctioned due to fouling or broken parts, and it was relatively expensive. Although the gun sold slowly, Colt, with a knack for advertising, made the public aware of his product by taking part in an advertising tour. His sales efforts notwithstanding, Colt was unsuccessful in interesting the federal government in his weapon. His financial situation grew worse because he tended to spend profits before they were made. In 1842, Colt was forced to close the Paterson plant.

War ultimately saved Colt's business. When the United States declared war on Mexico in 1846, the national government placed an order for 1,000 revolvers. Colt reached an agreement with Eli Whitney, Jr., to produce a new revolver Colt had developed in collaboration with Samuel Walker, a .44-caliber weapon that came to be called the Colt Walker. Colt resolved to improve the design of his successful revolver and opened his own manufacturing plant in Hartford. By 1850, his plant was operating successfully. That same year, the Connecticut State Militia commissioned him as a lieutenant-colonel, a title he used in promotional efforts targeted at government and military officials.

Colt traveled to Europe several more times to establish a market for his product. He opened a firearms manufacturing plant in London. A generous man who also knew how to promote his revolver, Colt presented several noted individuals with commemorative models, including Prince Albert, husband to Queen Victoria of Great Britain; Presidents Zachary Taylor and Franklin Pierce; the Prince of Wales, heir to the British throne; and Czar Nicholas I of Russia. These gifts helped spread the Colt name to many nations.

Colt continued to improve his handgun, replacing the Walker with newer models. When the Crimean War broke out in Europe in the 1850s, demand rose once again for Colt firearms.

As the American Civil War approached in 1861, Colt anticipated the increased demand for weapons. During the war, Colt's factory operated around the clock. Pushing himself too hard, Colt died in January 1862 at the age of 48. At the time of his death, his company was worth over $11 million. It has been said that "God made men, [but] Sam Colt made them equal." Colt's innovation made possible the production of repeating firearms through mass production methods, thus making these weapons available to people of all stations around the world. *See also* BROWNING, JOHN MOSES; REMINGTON, ELIPHALET, II; RUGER, WILLIAM BATTERMAN (BILL); WHITNEY, ELI; WINCHESTER, OLIVER FISHER.

Further Reading: Sam Fadala, *Great Shooters of the World* (South Hackensack, NJ: Stoeger, 1990); William N. Hasley, *Colt: The Making of an American Legend.* (Amherst: University of Massachusetts Press, 1996); Wayne Van Zwoll, *America's Great Gunmakers* (South Hackensack, NJ: Stoeger, 1992).

Commonwealth v. Davis (1976)

The Supreme Judicial Court of Massachusetts, in *Commonwealth v. Davis* (369 Mass. 886, 1976), ruled that a state statute providing penalties for the illegal possession of a shotgun with a barrel less than 18 inches long, does not violate either the Massachusetts Declaration of Rights or the Second Amendment to the United States Constitution. The court was guided in its ruling by the precedent of past federal appeals court decisions, such as *United States v. Tot* (1942), *United States v. Miller* (1939), and *Cases v. United States* (1942).

In January 1974, while conducting a search with a warrant of an apartment for narcotics, police discovered firearms and ammunition in the possession of Hubert Davis. Indicted for possession of a shotgun with a barrel less than 18 inches long, Davis was tried and found guilty. Moving for a new trial, Davis argued that the statute under which he was convicted violated his right to bear arms under both the Massachusetts and U.S. constitutions.

Article 17 of the Massachusetts Declaration of Rights states that, "The people have a right to keep and to bear arms for the common defence. And as, in time of peace, armies are dangerous to liberty, they ought not to be maintained without the consent of the legislature; and the military power shall always be held in an exact subordination to the civil authority, and be governed by it." The court ruled that the intention of this provision was not to guarantee individual ownership or possession of weapons. Article 17 arose from a distrust of standing armies and the decision to rely instead on a militia. Thus, the right guaranteed in the article refers to provision for the common defense and citizen participation in an organized militia.

Although the court ruled that the statute in question, which limits the possession of arms by individuals, might at one time have interfered with the operation of the militia because weapons were provided by individual citizens, today the militia, or National Guard, is equipped by public moneys. The court further ruled that even in the distant past regulation of the possession or carrying of firearms, so long as it did not involve a blanket prohibition, would not have been considered an unconstitutional limitation on individual liberty or a restriction on the militia.

Deciding that the Massachusetts constitution did not support Davis's claim regarding the right to keep and bear arms, the court also rejected the claim that the statute was beyond the police power, arguing that a sawed-off shot gun, because it is a dangerous weapon and can be concealed, is reasonably subject to regulation. Therefore, the state legislature can justifiably treat such a weapon as related to violent crime and make it subject to rigorous licensing and even a ban.

The court considered the claim that the statute violated the Second Amendment to the U.S. Constitution. Making reference to the precedent established by previous Supreme Court decisions, especially in *United States v. Miller*, the court argued that the amendment resulted from the apprehension during the time the Constitution was being debated that the power of the national government over the state militias established in Article I, section 8, clauses 15 and 16, could have a deleterious effect on state militia organizations. The court interpreted the amendment as a declaration that the militias may be protected from national government action. Therefore, the amendment limits only the national government, not the states.

The court saw little likelihood that the Second Amendment might some day be interpreted as limiting the states as well as the national government, because, unlike other provisions in the Bill of Rights, the Second Amendment does not focus on guaranteeing the rights of individuals, but protects state militias against national government interference. Even if the Supreme Court should one day decide that the amendment applies to the states, the states would still have the ability to exercise their regulatory authority in the realm of firearms. *See also* CASES V. UNITED STATES (1942); SECOND AMENDMENT; UNITED STATES V. MILLER (1939); UNITED STATES V. TOT (1942).

Further Reading: *Commonwealth v. Davis*, 369 Mass. 886 (1976).

Concealed Carry Laws

Concealed carry laws provide for the issuance of carrying concealed weapons (CCW) licenses, which allow individuals to bear loaded, hidden weapons on their persons. Some state legislatures have enacted measures that completely prohibit carrying concealed weapons. Other states have "may-issue" provisions that allow local law enforcement agencies the discretion of approving or denying applications for a CCW license after investigating an applicant's record and confirming the need to carry a weapon. Still other states have instituted "shall-issue" laws that direct law enforcement officials to issue CCW licenses to anyone who applies, unless the person is disqualified for some designated reason, such as having been convicted of a felony. One state, Vermont, does not require a license of any kind to carry a concealed weapon.

Many advocates of the right to carry a concealed weapon claim that the right to bear arms is nearly absolute and therefore no demonstration of need should be established as a criterion for carrying a concealed weapon. They contend that a major benefit of a CCW law is to reduce crime generally. Proponents argue that if those contemplating crime realize that a targeted victim may be armed, they are less willing to risk the physical danger to themselves of carrying out the assault.

In 1996, the Citizens Committee for the Right to Keep and Bear Arms (CCRKBA) issued the results of a study of data from the FBI's *Uniform Crime Reports* for 1994 to demonstrate that crime rates in states that have instituted CCW provisions are significantly lower than rates in states lacking such provisions. The organization claimed that states with restrictive concealed carry laws had murder rates nearly 99 percent higher than non-restrictive states. The CCRKBA data summary indicated that the robbery rate in restrictive states was 109 percent higher than the rate for non-restrictive states, and the aggravated assault rate for restrictive states was 65 percent higher than for non-restrictive states. The Committee concluded that concealed carry laws should receive major credit for the differences in crime rates among the various states.

CCW advocates have been successful in gaining acceptance of concealed carry provisions in several states. In 1995, for instance, Arkansas, North Carolina, Oklahoma, and Texas enacted "shall-issue" ordinances. Nevada, Utah, and Virginia replaced "may-issue" with "shall-issue" provisions, and Florida, Idaho, and Pennsylvania modified "shall-issue" provisions, making them more acceptable to gun advocates. By 1998, 31 states had shall-issue CCW laws.

Although CCW advocates argue that when citizens carry weapons, society becomes safer and more "polite," opponents claim that this position demonstrates a cynical view of human relationships and is basically untrue. They argue that because the United States already has over 200 million firearms owned by private citizens, we should already have the safest and most polite society in the world.

However, in the United States the death rate attributed to firearms remains high. The anti-CCW advocates also argue that the primary beneficiaries of such provisions are gun manufacturers, who, they claim, look upon concealed carry laws as an opportunity to bolster sales.

Opponents of CCW provisions also argue that law enforcement officers face greater danger with liberalized concealed carry laws. Police confront a greater chance that the persons they stop on the highway or meet in other potentially volatile situations may be carrying a concealed firearm. Opponents, noting that the FBI's *Uniform Crime Reports* indicate that almost one-third of all murders result from arguments, contend that such encounters, which otherwise would end in shouting matches or fistfights, are more likely to result in serious injury when guns are present. They also claim that suicides, criminal homicides, and gunshot accident deaths are far more likely to occur than homicide resulting from legitimate self-protection efforts. *See also* CITIZENS COMMITTEE FOR THE RIGHT TO KEEP AND BEAR ARMS; CONCEALED WEAPONS DETECTORS; HANDGUN CONTROL, INC.

Further Reading: Citizens Committee for the Right to Keep and Bear Arms, "States Allowing Citizens to Carry Concealed Firearms Have Less Violent Crime," (Bellevue, WA, 1996); Susan Glick, *Concealed Carry: The Criminal's Companion* (Washington, DC: Violence Policy Center, 1995); Susan Glick, *Concealing the Risk: Real-World Effects of Lax Concealed Weapons Laws* (Washington, DC: Violence Policy Center, 1996); Handgun Control, Inc., "Carrying Concealed Weapons (CCW) Fact Sheet" (Washington, DC, n.d.).

Concealed Weapons Detectors

In 1995, the United States Justice Department provided $2.15 million for a project to develop test models of concealed weapons detectors. The Department's National Institute of Justice (NIJ) was granted supervision over the project, which has involved work at three laboratories. The object of the project is to produce an instrument capable of identifying and describing a concealed weapon from a distance of 12 feet that an individual is carrying in his or her clothing. The hope is that the distance at which a weapon may be identified can be increased.

A concealed weapons detector would represent a technological advance on current airport metal detectors and could be made mobile, allowing it to be used in a variety of circumstances. With an estimated cost of $10,000 or less per unit, such instruments could become standard equipment for police vehicles. By pointing the instrument from the window, police would be able to determine if someone on the street were carrying a firearm. Those who support the development of such devices indicate that liberalized concealed carry laws may make the ability to detect firearms a crucial factor in effective policing.

Although the Fourth Amendment guarantee against unwarranted searches and seizures, a right that gun advocates take seriously, limits standard frisking without reasonable suspicion that a person may be armed, a detector might avoid such legal restrictions. If a detecting device could identify the presence of a concealed weapon without a search, then a subsequent frisk and confiscation may be legally justifiable.

The projects that were granted funding investigated different methods of detection. One method involves the measurement of irregularities in the human body's natural electromagnetic waves caused by the presence of a firearm. Another method, similar to radar, measures the reflection of an emitting pulse. A third procedure attempts to detect irregularities in the earth's magnetic field caused by a firearm. Each method includes a monitor and a computer system that, with sufficient sophistication, could even identify the type of firearm being detected.

With regard to the politics of gun control, improved technology has the advantage of avoiding many of the traditional issues that divide the opponents and proponents of firearms restrictions. David Van Biema reported that the prospect of improved technology that allows concealed weapons detectors has gained the support of liberal politicians, such as former congresswoman Patricia Schroeder, and conservative politicians, such

as Representative Fred Heineman. Although civil liberties issues may arise regarding the use of the new technology, at least one spokesperson for the American Civil Liberties Union (ACLU) has expressed cautious acceptance, perhaps due in part to the ACLU's willingness to entertain the constitutionality of gun control legislation. However, guns rights advocates may not support the ability of potentially oppressive government agents to ferret out the firearms of law-abiding citizens. *See also* AMERICAN CIVIL LIBERTIES UNION; CONCEALED CARRY LAWS; FOURTH AMENDMENT.

Further Reading: David Van Biema, "Peekaboo: The New Detector," *Time* 145 (March 27, 1995), 29; A. Trent De Persia, Suzan Yeager, and Steve Ortiz, eds., *Surveillance and Assessment Technologies for Law Enforcement* (Bellingham, WA: International Society for Optical Engineering, 1997); Department of Energy, "Bannock County Courthouse to Be 'Secure' Using INEEL Technology," *Department of Energy News* (April 22, 1997).

Congress of Racial Equality (CORE)

The Congress of Racial Equality (CORE), a civil rights organization that has taken a position on gun control sympathetic to the National Rifle Association (NRA), was established in 1942 by James Farmer. CORE maintains a national headquarters in New York City and has local affiliates and chapters throughout the United States and in parts of Africa, Central America, and the Caribbean. The organization prides itself on striving for equal rights for all and works to achieve self-determination and self-government. CORE believes all people can have the right "to decide for themselves what social and political organizations can operate in their best interest."

Initially, CORE worked to desegregate restaurants and other public accommodations in Chicago. The organization sponsored non-violent sit-ins at segregated public places in the South and sponsored the interracially supported Freedom Rides through the southern states, a strategy intended to end segregation on interstate bus routes. CORE helped sponsor the 1963 civil rights march on Washington, D.C. Subsequently, the organization engaged in black voter registration efforts in southern states and improvement in slum housing and police conduct.

In the 1980s, the NRA began to collaborate with CORE and its leader, Roy Innis, on crime prevention strategies. In 1984, Innis and the NRA initiated a campaign to liberalize the handgun laws in the state of New York. Innis, who had two sons who were victims of gun violence, declared that some way needed to be found to "bring some kind of fear into a criminal" and to "make the streets unsafe for criminals." In 1986, the NRA joined with CORE in developing the National Crime Fighters' Crusade. Josh Sugarmann, director of the Violence Policy Center, has reported that the NRA donated $5,000 to CORE to conduct the initiative. NRA representative Richard Feldman declared that the intentions of CORE and the NRA were to "let decent citizens know how to lawfully obtain firearms." Sugarmann claims that at the opening of the crusade, New York State Rifle and Pistol Clubs "demonstrated gun safety techniques and handed out handgun permit applications." In 1986, the NRA continued its support for CORE, contributing over $4,000 to Innis's unsuccessful bid for a seat in the U.S. House of Representatives.

CORE is considered a more moderate civil rights organization that emphasizes the need for self-help. The gun rights perspective found a comfortable home with the organization's overall philosophy. For instance, a current program, Project Independence, a welfare reform and job training program, focuses on alleviating the costs of welfare, unemployment, and the criminal justice system by providing workforce training and "welfare-to-work" assistance. The organization strives to instill in individuals technical skills, work values, and self-esteem. Recognizing the importance of personal security, CORE has been willing to join forces with the NRA to achieve that end. *See also* NATIONAL RIFLE ASSOCIATION; VIOLENCE POLICY CENTER.

Further Reading: Congress of Racial Equality Web site <www.core-online>; Josh Sugarmann, *National Rifle Association: Money, Firepower and Fear* (Washington, DC: National Press, 1992).

Consumer Product Safety

Gun control advocates note that no federal agency has been granted the authority to regulate the consumer product safety of firearms. Although Congress authorized the Bureau of Alcohol, Tobacco, and Firearms (BATF) to regulate commerce in guns and ammunition, that agency has little authority to oversee the safety of firearms as a consumer product. Supporters of consumer gun safety claim that firearms meet the basic conditions for legitimate regulation because they are obviously dangerous, exacting a high yearly death toll.

Consumer product safety advocates suggest that the BATF be granted the same authority that three other federal regulatory agencies already have to determine product safety. The Consumer Product Safety Commission (CPSC), established in 1972, regulates over 15,000 varied consumer products. When Congress originally passed legislation creating the CPSC, firearms and ammunition were exempted from its control. The CPSC relies on a series of about 90 hospital emergency rooms, called the National Electronic Injury Surveillance System (NEISS) to record injuries associated with consumer products. This reporting system allows the agency to respond to potentially hazardous products. The two other regulatory agencies are the National Highway Traffic Safety Administration (NHTSA), which was established under the National Traffic and Motor Vehicle Safety Act of 1966 to regulate automobile safety, and the Environmental Protection Agency (EPA), which was given the authority under the Federal Insecticide, Fungicide and Rodenticide Act (FIFRA) of 1947 to regulate the manufacture, sale, and use of pesticides, and manages the enforcement of the Toxic Substances Control Act (TSCA), which limits the use of harmful chemicals.

Gun control advocates argue that if various other potentially dangerous products are regulated by federal agencies, firearms are a reasonable candidate for such consumer safety regulation. Although this regulation might be considered best handled by an independent regulatory agency, the BATF has long experience with regulating firearms. The agency would need the authority to set firearms safety standards, to be able to oversee compliance, and have the capability to order recalls of defective weapons. However, the BATF, long a target of severe criticism by gun rights groups, would have to receive significantly increased powers from Congress to act as a consumer agency.

According to gun control supporters, the BATF should be given the authority to limit the availability of especially hazardous firearms and be able to order an end to selling firearms that present an immediate danger to the public. They also contend that air and pellet guns, presently under the jurisdiction of the CPSC, should be transferred to the BATF. If given powers similar to other product safety agencies, the BATF would have the ability to gather data regarding injuries and deaths associated with firearms. Prior to marketing, if a firearm presents a serious risk to consumer safety, the BATF could prevent the weapon from being offered to consumers.

The call for banning handgun sales, more than any other proposal, leads gun rights advocates to conclude that the ultimate purpose of applying consumer product safety policy to firearms is to take guns away from law-abiding American citizens. Gun control advocates argue that firearms legitimately used for hunting and other sports would not be subject to any ban. However, critics of such bans indicate that, in terms of product hazards, long guns, which include shotguns and rifles, arguably present a far greater danger than do handguns and therefore would become the next target for prohibition. They conclude that firearms, like automobiles, are inherently dangerous products and that safety can best be ensured not through prohibition but by effective consumer training in their use. *See also* BUREAU OF ALCOHOL, TOBACCO, AND FIREARMS; PRODUCT LIABILITY LAWSUITS.

Further Reading: Wayne R. LaPierre, *Guns, Crime, and Freedom* (Washington, DC: Regnery, 1994); Josh Sugarmann and Kristen Rand, *Cease Fire: A Comprehensive Strategy to Reduce Firearms Violence* (Washington, DC: Violence Policy Center, 1997).

Conyers, John (1929–)

U.S. Congressman John Conyers, liberal Democrat from Detroit, Michigan, has consistently advocated more stringent gun control. In 1985, he supported the ban on armor-piercing ammunition; in 1986, he opposed passage of the Firearms Owners' Protection Act, which allowed for the interstate sale of rifles and shotguns and the easing of record-keeping for firearms transactions; in 1988, he supported the ban on the production and importation of firearms that could not be detected by X-ray machines and metal detectors; and in 1993, he voted in favor of the Brady Handgun Violence Prevention Act. His positions on gun-related issues are consistent with his generally liberal stand.

The son of a Detroit auto worker, Conyers attended Wayne State University, where he received a B.A. in 1957 and a law degree in 1958. He first won election to the U.S. House of Representatives in 1964 from a newly created black majority district. He is presently the ranking Democrat on the Judiciary Committee, where he has offered tenacious opposition to the Republican majority. Conyers is described as a "cranky idealist fighting the GOP to save programs for the poor." He has often been at odds with Judiciary Committee chairman Henry Hyde, particularly over the Republican anti-crime bill during the 104th Congress. Conyers believed that the Republicans were attempting to federalize too many crimes, in contradiction to their program of returning authority to the states. However, Conyers and Hyde found common ground in a bill making it a federal crime to destroy religious property. During the impeachment hearings for President Bill Clinton in 1998, Conyers remained one of the staunchest opponents of Republican-drafted impeachment articles.

During the Democratic-controlled 103rd Congress (1993–1994), Conyers played an important role in crafting President Clinton's crime bill. He lobbied with the Democratic leadership to maintain an assault weapons ban, as well as crime prevention funding, in the bill. Conyers also supported a provision to direct the attorney general to gather data on incidents of police brutality. However, some members to the Black Caucus, which Conyers helped found, were not satisfied with the bill. To resolve the discrepancy between his commitment to the Black Caucus and his responsibility as a senior Democrat to support the party's legislative agenda, Conyers voted twice to have the crime bill considered on the House floor, but then opposed final passage. In the 105th Congress, Conyers continued his support for gun control, proposing an amendment to federal firearms statutes that would "prohibit the transfer of a firearm to, and the possession of a firearm by, a person who is intoxicated." *See also* ASSAULT WEAPONS BAN; BRADY HANDGUN VIOLENCE PREVENTION ACT; CLINTON, WILLIAM JEFFERSON (BILL); FIREARMS OWNERS PROTECTION ACT.

Further Reading: Congressman John Conyers Web site <www.house.gov/conyers>; Philip D. Duncan and Christine C. Lawrence, POLITICS IN AMERICA, 1998: THE 105TH CONGRESS (Washington, DC: Congressional Quarterly, 1997).

Cook, Philip J. (1946–)

Philip J. Cook has conducted research on firearms and violence for over 20 years. Cook is Terry Sanford Professor of Public Policy Studies at the Terry Sanford Institute of Public Policy at Duke University where he is also professor of economics and sociology. He has published articles dealing with the causal links between gun control ordinances and levels of crime, the effect of gun availability on robbery and murder committed during robbery, state programs for screening handgun buyers, the effect of gun availability on violent crime patterns, and gun markets. He argues that the availability of firearms has an independent effect on the seriousness of crime. With regard to suicide rates, he has concluded that the availability of deadly instruments can affect the resolve to complete the act. Therefore, depriving suicidal persons of the means, including firearms, to complete the act of self-destruction can save lives.

Cook received a B.A. from the University of Michigan in 1968 and a Ph.D. in economics from the University of California at Berkeley in 1973. In the latter year, he went to

Duke University as an assistant professor and in 1984 became professor of public policy and economics. In 1992, he attained his present position as a professor of public policy, economics, and sociology. He has received several research grants, including support from the Center for the Study and Prevention of Handgun Violence in 1979–80 to investigate major gun regulation proposals and from the Harry Frank Guggenhein Foundation in 1993–94 to examine markets for stolen guns. In a project funded by the National Institute of Justice, Cook, along with Jens Ludwig, investigated the private ownership of firearms, exploring such topics as the methods of firearms acquisition, storage and carrying of firearms, and the defensive use of firearms against criminal attacks.

In 1996, Cook served as editor for a symposium on youth, firearms, and public policy. Among the motivations for organizing the symposium was the observation that violent crime among youth has increased significantly in recent years. The purpose of the

Philip J. Cook has conducted extensive research on the link between violence and firearms. *©Duke University Photography/Photo by Jim Wallace.*

symposium was to investigate more promising policies to discourage potentially violent youths from acquiring, carrying, and employing firearms. The symposium concluded that firearms have made youth violence more lethal and gun use has been transmitted among youth groups in a fashion similar to the spread of disease. Although keeping guns away from youth will not solve the more basic causes of violence, the symposium participants reasoned that a focus on restricting access to firearms could save lives and reduce fear.

Cook, along with co-authors Jens Ludwig and David Hemenway, has criticized the widely disseminated claim that citizens use firearms 2.5 million times each year for self-defense. Re-analyzing the data from which that claim was derived, Cook concluded that some survey respondents must have misreported self-defense incidents and suggested that many "false positive" reports occur when attempting to measure a rare event in a large population. He claimed that medical researchers in epidemiology employ screening methods to avoid the problem of false positives, but social surveys still ignore this threat to validity.

Cook, along with James A. Leitzel, has responded to the major arguments against gun control. Noting the limits of punishing crime after the fact, Cook supports measures to preempt the violent use of firearms. Responding to the argument that gun control laws are ineffective in keeping firearms from criminals, Cook claims that regulations, such as a tax on guns, may ultimately affect the illegitimate market. Cook argues that, contrary to belief, guns are scarce goods and can be made scarcer through law enforcement policy. He concludes that any right to keep and bear arms is not absolute and therefore is subject to reasonable limitations to guarantee public safety. *See also* ACCIDENTS INVOLVING GUNS; CENTER FOR THE STUDY AND PREVENTION OF VIOLENCE; HEMENWAY, DAVID; LUDWIG, JENS OTTO; SUICIDE.

Further Reading: Thomas B. Cole and Philip J. Cook, "Strategic Thinking about Gun Markets and Violence," *Journal of the American Medical Association* 275 (June 12, 1996), 22; Philip J. Cook, "The Technology of Personal Violence," in Michael Tonry, ed.,

Crime and Justice: An Annual Review of Research (Chicago: University of Chicago Press, 1991); Philip J. Cook and James A. Leitzel, "Perversity, Futility, Jeopardy: An Economic Analysis of the Attack on Gun Control," *Law and Contemporary Problems* (Winter 1996).

Craig, Larry E. (1945–)

U.S. Senator Larry E. Craig, conservative Republican from Idaho, serves on the National Rifle Association's (NRA) board of directors, the Congressional Advisory Board of the Second Amendment Foundation, and the National Advisory Council of the Citizens Committee for the Right to Keep and Bear Arms (CCRKBA). He is an officer of the Congressional Sportsman's Caucus. The NRA has a strong congressional ally in Senator Craig. A firm advocate of limited government, Craig believes that gun control proposals represent an illegitimate intrusion into citizens' lives. He has consistently opposed legislative proposals to restrict firearms, voting against passage of the Brady Handgun Violence Prevention Act in 1993. In another key vote in 1993, Craig voted in favor of a motion to kill an amendment to prohibit the manufacture, sale, and future possession of 19 semi-automatic assault weapons. In 1994, Craig opposed the Omnibus Crime Bill, which contained a freeze on the manufacture and sale of assault weapons. When Democratic President Bill Clinton addressed the nation on his weekly radio broadcast to pressure Congress into passing the crime bill, Craig presented the Republican response, criticizing the inclusion in the bill of the assault weapons ban.

Craig grew up on the Idaho ranch his grandfather homesteaded in 1899. He received a B.A. from the University of Idaho in 1969. A farmer and rancher, Craig won election to the U.S. House of Representatives in 1981, where he served for 10 years. In 1990, he ran for the seat of retiring Republican Senator James A. McClure, who had sponsored the Firearms Owners Protection (McClure-Volkmer) Act of 1986. This act had eased the restrictions on firearms imposed by the Gun Control Act of 1968. An original

Senator Larry Craig (R-ID) serves on the National Rifle Association's board of directors and is a leading congressional opponent of gun control. *Courtesy of Senator Craig's office.*

supporter of the Firearms Owners Protection Act, Craig proved to be an effective successor to McClure's anti-gun control advocacy.

After Majority Leader Bob Dole of Kansas resigned his Senate seat in June 1996 to campaign for the presidency, Craig was chosen chairman of the Senate Republican Policy Committee, an influential leadership position. Craig had previously chaired the Republican Steering Committee, a caucus of mostly conservative senators. In his new position, Craig became a major opponent of the Clinton administration's legislative proposals, including those concerned with gun control. However, in 1996, Craig worked with the Clinton administration, leading a bipartisan task force to develop an anti-terrorism bill following the bombing at the Olympic Games in Atlanta. Craig's concern for federal intervention in state and local affairs led him to propose that federal officers administering national forests and parks cease carrying firearms. Democrats responded that Craig and other Republicans were attempting to engender a fear of the federal government in the public. *See also* Assault Weapons Ban; Brady Handgun Violence Prevention Act; Citizens Committee for the Right to Keep and Bear Arms; Clinton, William Jefferson (Bill); Firearms Owners Protection Act; Gun Control Act of 1968; McClure, James Albertas; National Rifle Association; Second Amendment Foundation.

Further Reading: Larry Craig Web site <www.senate.gov/~craig/>; Philip D. Duncan and Christine C. Lawrence, *Politics in America: The 105th Congress* (Washington, DC: CQ Press, 1997).

D

Democrats for the Second Amendment (D2A)

Although many congressional Democrats, especially those from the South, have been strong opponents of gun control, Democrats for the Second Amendment (which calls itself "D2A") claims to include those exceptional Democrats who do not support gun control. While otherwise supporting the liberal political agenda of the Democratic Party, D2A refuses to back what it considers the national party's pro-gun control position. The organization claims that prior to the 1994 congressional elections, the Democratic Party had lost touch with the American public on the issue of gun control. Following the Republican capture of both houses of Congress in 1994, D2A commented, "You wouldn't listen to us until November, maybe now we have your attention."

D2A states that the organization began in 1994 with several pro-gun Democrats communicating on the Internet. They voiced mutual concerns about the direction their party was taking on the gun control issue. They established a more formal organization and began producing a bimonthly newsletter, *D2A*, which is distributed to the membership and to members of Congress and is made available at several gun shops and firing ranges around the nation. The newsletter contains brief articles about the organization, the defensive value of hand-

guns, the meaning and value of a well regulated militia, and the current politics of gun control. Members communicate primarily via the Internet.

The members of D2A consider their organization a "think tank" that communicates with Democratic members of Congress regarding the attitudes of constituents on the issue of gun rights. They support the Democratic Party as "the party of heart and the party of help." Arguing that contemporary Democrats have strayed from the Democratic tradition of advocating the interests of common people that can be traced from Thomas Jefferson, the founder of the party, to modern presidents like Franklin Delano Roosevelt, Harry Truman, John F. Kennedy, Lyndon Johnson, and Jimmy Carter, D2A fails to note that Roosevelt and Johnson were strong supporters of gun control measures.

The organization claims that many constituents of Democratic senators and representatives believe in the right of citizens to own firearms for defense against violent crime and object to the Democratic Party's support for gun control legislation. D2A members say they differ with congressional Democrats only on the gun control issue. Therefore, members will work with non-Democrats only on the gun rights issue, lobbying against further gun control legislation and for repeal of existing legislation that the organization considers unconstitutional.

D2A supports policies to institute instant unrecorded background checks that gun purchasers can appeal, liberalization of state concealed weapon carry laws, voluntary firearms training, and firearms safety education in schools. The organization opposes the imposition of waiting periods before purchasing a firearm, licensing gun owners (except for hunting licenses), any sort of gun registration system, limitations on the ownership of semi-automatic weapons (which D2A believes are misnamed as assault weapons), and restrictions on magazine capacity.

The organization recommends that Democrats who support gun rights inform others of their position. They should contact public officials at the national, state, and local levels about their opposition to gun control, and become familiar with pro-gun control arguments to more effectively argue against them. D2A has two membership categories: participatory members are registered Democrats, while supporting members are not. The difference between the two categories is that only participatory members may be officers of the organization. The organization states that it endorses only Democratic candidates who oppose gun control. The membership is willing to vote for pro-gun rights Republicans when Democratic candidates advocate gun control. *See also* ASSAULT WEAPONS BAN; JEFFERSON, THOMAS; SECOND AMENDMENT.

Further Reading: Democrats for the Second Amendment Web site <www.d2a.org>; *D2A Newsletter.*

Dick Act

The Dick Act, or Militia Act, of 1903 repealed the Militia Act of 1792. The act revived state militias, or, as they had come to be called, National Guard units, based on voluntary recruitment and greater national government control over their organization and operation. The national army gained some control over the militia and was granted the authority to create a reserve force under its own control. Gun control advocates argue that the modern militia, beginning with the Dick Act, eliminated any notion of universal citizen membership in the militia and with it the claim that citizens in general have a right to bear arms as members of at least the "unorganized militia." Gun rights advocates contend that the National Guard as established under the Dick Act does not satisfy the constitutional reference to an organized militia.

The Militia Act of 1792 never operated well in maintaining a militia force in each of the states. The inadequacies of American military preparedness during the Spanish American War of 1898 motived Republican President William McKinley's secretary of war, Elihu Root, to begin an inquiry into possible strategies for modernizing and rationalizing the military organization. Noting that the militia system was still operating under the 111-year-old Militia Act and recognizing the value of an effective reserve system, Root asked Colonel William Sanger, inspector general of the New York National Guard, to investigate the citizen reserve systems in other nations. In 1900, following a tour of European nations, Sanger submitted a report on the English and Swiss systems.

Sanger developed the legislation in collaboration with Ohio Congressman Charles Dick, who was a major general in command of the Ohio National Guard, president of the National Guard Association, and chairman of the House Committee on the Militia. In 1902, Dick presented a plan to the annual meeting of the National Guard Association. Supporters of militia reform, including local militias, desired not only greater funds for state organizations, but also greater recognition for the militia's role in the national military system. Republican President Theodore Roosevelt strongly supported reform, as did the regular army.

Meanwhile, the War Department proposed its own reform bill, which included a measure that, although rejected, had a significant impact on the final version of the act. Section 24 of the failed reform bill would have mandated the creation of a national reserve force of up to 100,000 men with prior military service. This force would have had no relationship to any state. Although the House passed the bill, the Senate refused to concur.

However, the Senate quickly passed the bill when Root agreed to withdraw Section 24. States' rights advocates, who had strongly opposed the national force, supported the revised bill even though it established significant national government supervision over the state militias. Not until after World War II did state militias protest expansion of national supervision, but by then such objections were too late to force a policy change.

According to Elihu Root, the Dick Act would not simply replace state with national funds, but create an effective training ground for volunteer soldiers. The act required states to meet national standards to receive grant-in-aid funds. Funds were contingent upon a state having at least 100 militiamen for each senator and representative the state had in Congress. A state's militia units had to drill at least 24 times each year with at least two-thirds of its strength, and attend a five-day summer camp. Summer maneuvers had to be held jointly with regular troops, and could not occur unless federal inspectors certified that the militia was prepared. Federal inspections of all units were to be held annually and any deficiencies corrected. State governors were required to request additional arms before the War Department would provide them. Congressional appropriations for state militias increased from $3.5 million in 1903 to $5 million in 1908, while states collectively contributed from $5.8 to $9 million each year. The act succeeded in achieving one of its major objectives: to bring states with inadequate militia organizations up to national minimum standards.

Whatever anyone might argue about the purpose of state militias in opposing a possibly tyrannous national government, the Dick Act essentially placed militias (by 1903 commonly referred to as the National Guard) under federal control. Rather than representing a force potentially opposed to the national government, the National Guard and the regular army served as complementary organizations with a common objective. However, gun rights advocates insist that if the National Guard, which they are not willing to equate with the militia as designated in the Constitution, is the first line of reserve, then another constitutionally protected force is the unorganized militia, potentially composed of all adult citizens armed with weapons they provide for themselves through the Second Amendment right to keep and bear arms. The practicality of such an interpretation does not matter so much to them as the asserted constitutional relationship between militia service and an individual right to possess firearms. *See also* MILITIA ACT OF 1792; SECOND AMENDMENT.

Further Reading: John K. Mahon, *History of the Militia and the National Guard* (New York: Macmillan, 1983); William H. Riker, *Soldiers of the State: The Role of the National Guard in American Democracy* (Washington, DC: Public Affairs Press, 1957).

Dickerson v. New Banner Institute, Inc. (1983)

The U.S. Supreme Court decision in *Dickerson v. New Banner Institute, Inc.* (460 U.S. 103, 1983) dealt with Title IV of the Gun Control Act of 1968 [18 U.S.C. 922 (g) (1) and (h) (1)], which prohibits any person convicted of a crime punishable by more than a year in prison from shipping, transporting, or receiving any firearm or ammunition in interstate commerce. The case involved the expungement of a guilty verdict in state court and whether this state action exempted the defendant from the relevant provisions of the Gun Control Act. Although the Court ruled that it did not in 1983, in 1986, Congress passed the Firearms Owners Protection Act, a provision of which overruled the decision by indicating that a state law governed a state conviction.

David Kennison, chairman of the board and shareholder of the New Banner Institute, Inc., had pleaded guilty in an Iowa state court to a charge of carrying a concealed handgun. Although the conviction could have brought a fine and imprisonment for up to five years, Kennison was placed on probation. After completion of the probationary period, his record of deferred judgment was expunged. In May 1976, he applied to the Bureau of Alcohol, Tobacco, and Firearms (BATF) for licenses to manufacture, deal in, and collect firearms and ammunition, but failed to reveal his guilty plea in the Iowa case. Although Kennison received the license, it was later withdrawn when the BATF discovered the Iowa conviction. The case ultimately reached the U.S. Court of Appeals for the Fourth Circuit, which ruled that Kennison could not be denied a federal firearms license because the conviction had been expunged under Iowa's deferred judgment procedure. The Supreme Court agreed to hear the case to resolve conflicting decisions rendered by other Courts of Appeals.

The Supreme Court first noted Kennison's guilty plea to a state charge punishable by more than one year in prison, which it considered equivalent to a conviction. Whether Kennison actually received a prison term was considered irrelevant; the statute simply referred to violations punishable by imprisonment for more than a year. Therefore, the Court considered that Kennison had been convicted according to the language of the relevant provision within the Gun Control Act.

The Court referred to other provisions within federal gun control legislation to support its conclusion that Congress did not intend expunction of a state conviction to remove any legal prohibition regarding firearms. Noting that the secretary of the Treasury was granted the authority to issue exemptions to such prohibitions, the Court declared that Congress likely did not intend to allow this grant of authority to the secretary "to be overcome by the vagaries of state law." The Court noted that a search of the legislative history of Title IV and related federal firearms statutes resulted in no support for state expunction as a method of removing the disabilities of 922 (g) (1) and (h) (1).

The Court emphasized Congress's intention to establish a uniform national policy to deter illegal firearm use and observed that Congress used state convictions to activate federal prohibitions. But by employing state court convictions, Congress did not intend "to tie those disabilities to the intricacies of state law." Rather, state convictions were conducive to identifying those considered at

risk for committing violent crime. The Court concluded that "the circumstances surrounding the expunction of his conviction provide little, if any, assurance that Kennison is a person who can be trusted with a dangerous weapon." *See also* BUREAU OF ALCOHOL, TOBACCO, AND FIREARMS; CONCEALED CARRY LAWS; FIREARMS OWNERS PROTECTION ACT; GUN CONTROL ACT OF 1968.

Further Reading: *Dickerson v. New Banner Institute, Inc.*, 460 U.S. 103 (1983).

Doctors for Integrity in Policy Research (DIPR)

Edgar A. Suter, a San Ramon, California, physician, established Doctors for Integrity in Policy Research (DIPR) in response to firearms studies conducted by medical researchers who view guns as a major cause of violence and accidents. The 500-member organization attempts to expose what it considers bias, incompetence, and dishonesty in research reports, particularly those published in the *New England Journal of Medicine* and the *Journal of the American Medical Association*, and criticizes medical researchers for treating firearms as "evil talismans." The DIPR has singled out for especially harsh criticism the Centers for Disease Control's National Center for Injury Prevention and Control (NCIPC). NCIPC-supported studies resulted in conclusions critical of firearms. The DIPR, along with the National Rifle Association (NRA) and other pro-gun organizations, attempted to have congressional funding for the National Center cut, arguing that the agency supported politically motivated research.

The DIPR claims that medical researchers ignore a large body of social science research that suggests that firearms can have positive consequences and that only a small proportion of firearms are ever misused. Contrary to research indicating that firearms kept in the home threaten the lives of residents, the organization cites studies indicating that there are 2.5 times as many beneficial uses of guns each year as there are harmful uses. The DIPR notes that a majority of the gun deaths each year are suicides. No gun ban would reduce the total suicide rate because people determined to kill themselves would substitute other means. The organization notes that, contrary to the pro-gun control portrait of gun violence where victims are family members or friends of the shooter, over three-quarters of murderers have histories of violence. Countering claims about the economic costs of firearms violence, the organization asserts that the economic benefits of firearms used to save lives and protect property amounts to a half trillion dollars each year.

The DIPR recommends "oversight of the competence and integrity of further tax-funded research" by introducing more careful congressional monitoring of publicly funded research and an improved peer review process for professional journals. Rather than calling for additional legislation, the organization advocates the enforcement of existing statutes against violent crime. However, the DIPR does not advocate any further sentence enhancement provisions. Any enforcement efforts should be focused on the illegal trafficking in firearms and those guns held legally should be left alone.

In response to the pro-gun control argument that gun ownership should be regulated in a manner similar to the registration of automobiles and the issuing of drivers licenses, the DIPR holds that guns should be treated "completely, consistently, and constitutionally" like cars. The organization opposes any "need" provision that would require prospective firearm owners to provide a reason, such as self-defense, for ownership, and contends that just as with automobiles, no licensing or registration should be required for firearms used on private property. Like automobiles, firearms should be kept from "the mentally incompetent, the criminal, and the irresponsible." Voluntary safety training programs should be made available.

The DIPR strongly opposes any focus on firearms as an independent cause of violent crime. Instead, the organization calls for welfare policy reform, contending that government programs have destroyed families and social stability. Opportunities for the poor should be created, particularly in the private sector. To make the illegal drug trade less attractive, the organization suggests examining the feasibility of decriminalizing personal drug use by adults. Although the organization deplores media violence, it advocates parental discretion as the major way of handling the problem. The DIPR recommends teaching children nonviolent means of conflict resolution. The organization holds that the "scapegoating of guns and gun owners" should end, given that gun ownership is "a neutral or positive social phenomenon of half of American households." *See also* DOCTORS FOR RESPONSIBLE GUN OWNERSHIP; HEALTH CARE PROFESSIONALS; MEDIA VIOLENCE; NATIONAL CENTER FOR INJURY PREVENTION AND CONTROL; SUICIDE.

Further Reading: *Doctors for Integrity in Policy Research-related* Web site <www.dipr.org>.

Doctors for Responsible Gun Ownership (DRGO)

Doctors for Responsible Gun Ownership (DRGO), a program of the Claremont Institute located in Claremont, California, was established in 1994 to respond to health care professionals and organizations that were supporting further gun control policies by taking an epidemiological approach to firearms and gun violence. Founded in 1979, the Claremont Institute encourages a return to what it considers the nation's founding principles: a limited government held accountable to the people, respect for private property, stable family life, and a strong defense. Adhering to the principles of the parent organization, the DRGO promotes individual freedom and responsibility against government intervention. Sister programs supported by the Institute include the Center for the American Constitution, the Center for the Study of Natural Law, and the International Affairs Center. The DRGO has worked with other organizations in an attempt to discredit the research findings of medical professionals who claim that gun ownership represents a serious threat to public health.

The DRGO claims a membership of 800 physicians and other health professionals who are not only trained in medical research, but are familiar with firearms. Timothy Wheeler, a head and neck surgeon practicing in Fontana, California, heads the organization. Employing a medical analogy similar to those it criticizes pro-gun control health professionals for using, the DRGO claims to be the "antidote" to what it considers dishonest research and mistaken ideological positions of pro-gun control groups. The organization contends that an alternative body of research conducted by criminologists and other social scientists demonstrates that firearms owned by law-abiding citizens deter crime and prevent far more deaths and injuries than they cause.

Representatives of the DRGO testified before the U.S. House of Representatives Appropriations Committee regarding what the organization considered the Centers for Disease Control's (CDC) anti-gun bias. The DRGO takes some of the credit for congressional cuts in CDC funding earmarked for firearms research. Wheeler has publicly criticized the CDC and its director, David Satcher, for supporting what he labels biased research.

The DRGO participated with two other organizations, Doctors for Integrity in Policy Research (DIPR) and the Lawyer's Second Amendment Society (LSAS), in an *amicus curiae* brief submitted to the U.S. Supreme Court, supporting a challenge, based on the Tenth Amendment, to the Brady Handgun Violence Prevention Act. Filed in 1995, the brief claims that extensive benefits are derived from firearms ownership and that gun control legislation, especially the Brady law, has been ineffective in controlling crime. The DRGO and the other organizations participating in the brief challenged the claim that the Brady law has prevented over 60,00 illegal handgun purchases. The brief contended that the Brady law costs more lives than it saves because citizens are denied the right to defend themselves and their families.

Although raising objections to any limitations on what is considered an individual right to keep and bear arms and a right of self-defense, the brief stated that if the Supreme Court allows "an infringement of the right to keep and bear arms," the limitation should be as unintrusive as possible. Therefore, an "instant check" system was supported as a replacement for the five-day waiting period. However, the brief urged that this system be voluntarily adopted by the states, not mandated by the Brady law, which would constitute a violation of the Tenth Amendment guarantee of state powers. *See also* BRADY HANDGUN VIOLENCE PREVENTION ACT; DOCTORS FOR INTEGRITY IN POLICY RESEARCH; HEALTH CARE PROFESSIONALS; LAWYER'S SECOND AMENDMENT SOCIETY; NATIONAL CENTER FOR INJURY PREVENTION AND CONTROL; NATIONAL INSTANT CHECK SYSTEM.

Further Reading: Claremont Institute Web site <www.claremont.org>; Steven A. Silver, "Amicus Brief on Behalf of Doctors for Integrity in Policy Research, Doctors for Responsible Gun Ownership, and The Lawyer's Second Amendment Society in Support of Petitioner Sheriff Richard Mack" (Encino, CA: Lawyer's Second Amendment Society, 1996); Timothy Wheeler, "The Bully Pulpit and the Right of the People," *Pasadena Star News* (June 26, 1997).

Dodd, Thomas J. (1907–1971)

Although Democratic Senator Thomas J. Dodd played a major role in the negotiations that ultimately brought about passage of the 1968 Gun Control Act, he was an unlikely leader on the gun control issue. He hailed from Connecticut, a major gun manufacturing state; he had a penchant for alcohol that became widely known among his colleagues; and he came under investigation by the Senate for misappropriation of campaign funds that led finally to a censure vote by his senatorial colleagues.

Dodd began his political career with a sterling reputation. Before World War II, he spent a year working in the Federal Bureau of Investigation (FBI). As a special assistant to a United States attorney, he prosecuted southern public officials for civil rights violations at a time when the issue had little national saliency. During the war, he brought to justice leaders of the German-American Bund, a pro-Nazi group supporting the German war effort, and prosecuted officials of the Anaconda Wire and Cable Company for supplying defective telephone wire to the military. At the Nuremberg war crimes trials following the war, Dodd served as executive trial counsel. In 1952, he withstood the Republican presidential and congressional victories to become the only Connecticut Democrat to be elected to Congress. In 1958, Connecticut voters elected him to the U.S. Senate. During the Cold War era, he was a moderate Democrat with strong anti-Communist credentials.

Former Senator Thomas J. Dodd (D-CT) was instrumental in achieving passage of the Gun Control Act of 1968. *Thomas J. Dodd Papers, Archives and Special Collections, Thomas J. Dodd Research Center, University of Connecticut Libraries.*

Like fellow senators from Massachusetts and Connecticut, who wished to protect the domestic firearms industry, Dodd attempted but failed to add riders to bills that would ban importation of military firearms. In 1963, Dodd developed a new strategy, focusing the fight on the claim that cheap imported guns contributed to violent crime, especially among youth. At least initially, Dodd did not alienate the major American firearms manufac-

turers because he concentrated his investigations on inexpensive mail-order guns and the surplus military weapons imported from abroad. In January 1963, Dodd, as chairman of the Senate Subcommittee on Juvenile Delinquency, opened the Hearings on Interstate Traffic in Mail-Order Firearms. Gun dealers testified about current practices, police officials related the tragic results of firearms reaching the hands of juveniles, and private citizens told stories about the misuse of firearms, especially by youth.

In August 1963, with the support of the National Rifle Association (NRA), Dodd introduced a bill that was referred to the Committee on Commerce, where it languished until President John F. Kennedy's assassination by a gunman using an Italian-made Mannlicher-Carcano rifle purchased through a mail-order firm. The assassination gained nationwide publicity for Dodd's legislative agenda. Originally, Dodd proposed to ban mail-order handgun purchases, but he agreed to expand the bill to include rifles and shotguns. Strong opposition from gun interests blocked the new legislation, despite support from New England firearms manufacturers. In 1965, Dodd again failed to get a bill out of committee. The following year his censure by the Senate severely limited the senator's ability to push the gun control bill. However, Dodd insisted on maintaining his leadership on the firearms issue, negotiating with the NRA for support of his proposed legislation. Frank Orth, executive vice president of the NRA, was willing to back Dodd's call to include rifles in the bill, but he did not necessarily represent a majority of the organization's board of directors.

Gun control legislation continued to be debated extensively for the next four years. Dodd became frustrated by the NRA, which pledged its support personally, but voiced strong opposition in the pages of the organization's publications. In 1968, the assassinations of Robert Kennedy and Martin Luther King, Jr., opened the way to passage of the Gun Control Act. Two years later, Dodd failed to gain re-election. Although the NRA claimed responsibility for defeating

Dodd and other public officials who supported gun control, in Dodd's case, the Senate censure reduced his chances for re-election. If someone other than the beleaguered Dodd had led the fight for gun control, the 1968 act might have contained more extensive provisions. *See also* GUN CONTROL ACT OF 1968; NATIONAL RIFLE ASSOCIATION.

Further Reading: Bill R. Davidson, *To Keep and Bear Arms* (New Rochelle, NY: Arlington House, 1969); Robert Sherrill, *The Saturday Night Special* (New York: Charterhouse, 1973).

Drive-By-Agony

Lorna Hawkins founded Drive-By-Agony in 1992 to increase awareness of gun violence and its effects on families and communities. The organization, headquartered in Lynwood, California, is governed by a five-member board of directors, an executive director, and a project director. In 1988, after her eldest son was killed in a drive-by shooting, Hawkins began her efforts with a program on a local cable television station. Subsequently, a second son was killed in an attempted car jacking. The television program gives victims of violent crime, particularly in the low-income, minority communities in the Los Angeles area, an opportunity to help themselves and others "by talking out their pain." The show, with the same name as the organization, refers survivors and families to professional counselors. Young people are offered the opportunity to speak about their own experiences. Drive-By-Agony offers assistance with contacting law enforcement agencies, conducts self-help support group sessions, and initiates action-awareness campaigns. The organization provides information about summer activities for at-risk youth and supports efforts to limit the access youth have to firearms.

In 1991, Hawkins began an annual March for Peace in support of victims of violence. The event, which focuses on school-age youth, includes discussions about anger management and career development assistance. In 1993, she began making presentations on crime prevention counseling to various community organizations, including hospitals,

churches, schools, Parent-Teacher Associations, drug abuse prevention organizations, and victims groups. She currently works with the California Youth Authority, assisting in programs for youth offenders. In 1993 and 1996, Hawkins helped organize the national Silent Shoe March in Washington, D.C., in which shoes that belonged to victims of gun violence were presented as a graphic demonstration of the lives lost to firearms.

In 1995, Hawkins developed a curriculum for youth, called Straight Talk About Violence, which deals with methods of conflict resolution. Straight Talk About Violence provides the opportunity for students to discuss the problems of violence and allows them to understand its origins and prevent its spread. Those who have lost family members or friends to violence have the opportunity to express their feelings. In 1994, the organization began Saving American Families Everywhere (SAFE), a youth leadership program that provides young people with employment skills and teaches conflict management and child care. In these programs, the organization emphasizes the danger of owning and carrying a firearm. *See also* DRIVE-BY SHOOTINGS.

Further Reading: Drive-By-Agony Web site <http://www.drive-by-agony.org>.

Drive-By Shootings

In the 1970s, drive-by shootings began to replace the traditional rumble, or gang fight, as the characteristic violent interchange among street gangs. The combination of two technologies–the firearm and the automobile–made the drive-by shooting a preferred strategy of gangs. Gang researcher William B. Sanders reports that the percentage of San Diego, California, gang assaults that were drive-by shootings increased from 23.7 in 1981 to 40.8 in 1988. In many American cities in the late 1980s, the crack cocaine trade and related drive-by shootings had become extensive. Such shootings contributed to the large number of adolescent firearms victims, especially innocent bystanders, and consequently to increased calls for additional gun control legislation.

According to Sanders, a drive-by shooting occurs "when members of one gang drive a vehicle into a rival gang's area and shoot at someone." The drive-by shooting, or foray, is contrasted with the melee or rumble, where rival gang members meet at a specific time and place to fight. The introduction of firearms altered this strategy because mass shootouts were an impractical alternative to the rumble. Instead, youths ventured into a rival gang's territory for a brief encounter, and returned quickly to home territory. Initially, in more densely populated areas on the East Coast, with neighborhoods close together, forays would occur on foot or on bicycle. On the West Coast, with neighborhoods geographically dispersed, the automobile became the primary mode of transportation. After a shooting, gang members could quickly return to their home neighborhood located miles from the incident.

According to Sanders, gangs develop mythologies about rivals, labeling them dangerous people deserving of violent attack. Revenge for the past misdeeds of rivals plays an important role. Because forays are considered dangerous for the perpetrators, involving the risk of arrest and of becoming a target themselves, participation demonstrates the appropriate virtues of gang membership, including heart, courage, and honor. The drive-by is equivalent to a tactic in warfare. Just as in combat, innocents are not intentionally targeted, but they may become victims nonetheless. In part because they consider themselves engaged in warfare against a dangerous enemy, gang members generally demonstrate little remorse over the injury or death of innocents, including young children.

Innocents can become victims if a drive-by targets a party held by a rival gang. Although women are usually not targets, they may become so simply by being present at a gathering. In addition, if a house is the focus of an attack, the gang member's family can become victims. No group norms appear to prohibit the wounding or killing of family members. The injury or killing of innocents in drive-by shootings have led to calls for further gun control measures. The assumption of gun control supporters is that the frequency of injury and death resulting from gang activities would decrease if firearms could be kept from gang members. *See also* DRIVE-BY-AGONY.

Further Reading: William B. Sanders, *Gang-bangs and Drive-Bys: Grounded Culture and Juvenile Gang Violence* (New York: Aldine de Gruyter, 1994).

Dueling

The decline of dueling as a method of resolving disputes represents an area in which gun control and the control of other deadly weapons was successful, at least in limiting a particular use. Dueling reached its peak in the United States between 1770 and 1860, but could not be declared extinct until the early decades of the twentieth century. However, gun control advocates wonder if many contemporary altercations involving the use of firearms are a throwback to the time when gentlemen defended their honor, one-on-one, on the field of combat.

Dueling originated in Europe during medieval times as a means of resolving judicial disputes. Judicial combat, where the two sides to a disagreement resorted to arms to arrive at a settlement, was based on the belief that the victory would go to the person who had God on his side. During the Middle Ages, thousands of men lost their lives in this form of conflict resolution. Although the Roman Catholic Church and, subsequently, various Protestant denominations condemned dueling, and several European monarchs banned the practice and imposed severe punishments for disobedience, dueling continued largely unabated. The inability of legal sanction to end the practice of dueling is echoed in contemporary pronouncements by gun defenders that gun control legislation simply does not keep firearms away from those who truly want them.

European colonists brought the tradition of dueling to the New World. Practices similar to dueling occurred among Native Americans, although some historians argue that these were copied from the Europeans. The first recorded duel in America occurred in

Between about 1770 and 1860, dueling with pistols was a common method for gentlemen to defend their honor and to settle disputes. The death of Alexander Hamilton in a duel in 1804 (depicted here) helped destroy public acceptance of dueling. *Archive Photos.*

1621 between two servants in Plymouth, Massachusetts. Fighting with daggers, the two men succeeded in wounding each other, but no one suffered any lethal damage. The community reacted with disapproval, not so much because of the duel itself, but because the participants were servants. Only gentlemen were thought to have the privilege to engage in the practice. Most Americans never approved of dueling, including Benjamin Franklin, who once remarked that dueling allowed each person to assume the position of judge for his own complaint, and to act as the jury and ultimate executioner. Popular opinion notwithstanding, laws prohibiting the practice were either ineffective or nonexistent. Prior to 1850, several states had no statute making dueling illegal. Even the District of Columbia had no law banning dueling until 1838.

Historians have suggested various explanations for the ultimate disappearance of dueling. The passage and enforcement of stringent laws certainly had its effect. In addition, people became more aware that dueling over relatively minor affronts resulted in the squandering of human life. School children today learn about the famous duel in 1804 in which Aaron Burr shot and killed Alexander Hamilton, a signer of the Constitution, a member of President George Washington's cabinet, and one of the most brilliant statesmen in American history. Burr, who was vice president under President Thomas Jefferson, never regained his stature in national politics. The appalling loss of such talent to the shot of a pistol did not bode well for a practice increasingly labeled as barbaric.

A change in the conception of a man's honor occurred in the last half of the nineteenth century. No longer were gentlemen willing to risk their lives over a slight offense. The spread of the democratic ideology throughout American society undoubtedly contributed to this change. Rather than resorting to mortal combat, men increasingly viewed a fist fight as the appropriate response to a crude comment. Contemporary gun control advocates oppose concealed carry laws in part because, when guns are readily available, the offhand remark can quickly escalate into the use of deadly firepower, thus harking back to a time when the duel, in a more formal way, led to the same consequences.

By the mid-nineteenth century, the practice of dueling came under increasing derision, which contributed to its extinction. Even at its height, the press and the general public often reacted to an announced duel with taunting, mockery, and even contempt. A practice intended to defend a gentleman's honor could not survive for long under public ridicule. The gun control movement has attempted to accomplish a similar result today by portraying in an unflattering way those who possess firearms, especially handguns.

See also Jefferson, Thomas; Native Americans.

Further Reading: Robert Baldick, *The Duel: A History of Duelling* (New York: Clarkson N. Potter, 1965); Hamilton Cochran, *Noted American Duels and Hostile Encounters* (Philadelphia, PA: Chilton, 1963).

E

Eddie Eagle

In 1988, the National Rifle Association (NRA) selected Eddie Eagle, a cartoon character in the form of an eagle, as the mascot for the organization's firearms safety for children program. The program involves a school-based curriculum for children in preschool through the sixth grade. Despite the asserted civic virtue of the program, Eddie Eagle created the same sort of controversy in the gun control debate that Joe Camel prompted in the dispute over cigarette smoking. While the NRA stated that the cartoon character added to the appeal of the safety program, gun control advocates claimed that it attracted young children to essentially unsafe products and diverted attention away from more effective ways of ensuring the safety of children from firearms.

NRA President Marion Hammer began the Eddie Eagle program in Florida in response to state legislative efforts to enact child access prevention (CAP) legislation that would establish criminal penalties for adults who failed to keep firearms away from children. Hammer argued that the best way to protect children from firearms was to educate them about the potential dangers of guns. Although the bill ultimately passed the Florida legislature, Hammer was able to include an amendment that required the Florida Department of Education to generate a framework for a gun awareness program to by introduced

in the Florida public schools. The Dade County school system passed over the Eddie Eagle program and funded a Center to Prevent Handgun Violence (CPHV) gun violence prevention program. However, Hammer succeeded in having the Eddie Eagle materials included along with the CPHV program.

The NRA has campaigned for the introduction of its firearm safety program as a substitute for child access prevention legislation that would initiate penalties for unsafe storage of weapons. For instance, in February 1997 the Indiana General Assembly replaced a CAP bill with an amendment mandating an Eddie Eagle program. Proponents of CAP legislation argue that the NRA substitute inappropriately relieves the gun owner of responsibility for firearm storage and in effect places that responsibility on children.

The NRA noted that the Eddie Eagle program had received the National Safety Council's (NSC) Silver Award of Merit in 1995 for initiating the training program for children. Opponents of the program quickly noted that the president of the National Safety Council informed Hammer that the NRA had improperly cited the award issued to the organization by the Council's Youth Activities Division when lobbying against a bill requiring trigger lock safety devices, a bill that the National Safety Council endorsed. The organization requested that the NRA stop referring to the NSC or the safety award in their lobbying campaign. *See also* CENTER TO PREVENT HANDGUN VIOLENCE; NATIONAL RIFLE ASSOCIATION.

Further Reading: *Joe Camel with Feathers: How the NRA with Gun and Tobacco Industry Dollars Uses its Eddie Eagle Program to Market Guns to Kids* (Washington, DC: Violence Policy Center, 1997).

Educational Fund to End Handgun Violence

The Educational Fund to End Handgun Violence was established in 1978 as an educational charity devoted to ending firearms violence. Joshua Horwitz is the organization's executive director. The Educational Fund places special emphasis on preventing firearms-related injuries among children. The organization, located in Washington, D.C., is composed of parents, teachers, and journalists who are concerned about firearms-related violence. The Educational Fund's activities include Hands without Guns, an anti-violence program for teenagers; Citizens' Conference to Stop Gun Violence, a grassroots initiative to limit gun violence; and Ceasefire Action Network (CAN), a source of information for local groups interested in preventing firearms violence. CAN is a coalition of state gun control organizations, public health professionals, local anti-violence activists, religious groups, and individuals that facilitates communication among its various individual and group members. A bimonthly publication, the *Ceasefire Action Network Newsletter*, provides information about anti-gun violence activities.

The Educational Fund participated in the formation of the Citizens' Conference to Stop Gun Violence, an annual meeting to disseminate knowledge and techniques to make communities safe from gun-related violence. During the November 1998 conference, which was held in Washington, D.C., the Educational Fund, in cooperation with the Center to Prevent Handgun Violence, conducted a symposium in which the presenters treated gun violence as a public health issue. Presenters examined research conducted from a public health perspective, reported on the activities of public officials to reduce gun violence, and provided advice to community activists regarding the use of the public health issue to organize anti-gun violence initiatives. Such firearms researchers as Arthur Kellermann and Garen Wintemute spoke at the conference.

The Educational Fund's Hands without Guns initiative provides information to youth, anti-violence groups, and schools in local communities. The program was created by the Educational Fund in cooperation with 2PM Media, a communications firm specializing in assisting small organizations to publicize their message to the general public. The program adheres to an epidemiological explanation of gun violence among youth, arguing that in the early 1990s, as youths involved in the drug trade began to carry firearms, other young people responded by also acquiring weapons. Hands without Guns hopes to break what it considers a cycle of contagion by engaging youth in more productive activities and establishing more positive role models. Hands without Guns has tested a workshop approach in four cities: Boston; Washington, D.C.; Chicago; and Holland, Michigan. Michael MacDonald, a youth organizer in Boston, initiated the first workshops. The workshops encourage discussions among youth on such topics as personal safety, peer pressure, ways that violence can be avoided, drugs, racism, and unemployment. David Hemenway of the Harvard School of Public Health developed a survey to evaluate the success of the program. Advice and literature are provided to assist local groups and individuals in coordinating efforts to reduce youth violence. *See also* CENTER TO PREVENT HANDGUN VIOLENCE; HEMENWAY, DAVID; KELLERMANN, ARTHUR; WINTEMUTE, GAREN J.

Further Reading: Educational Fund to End Handgun Violence Web site <www.gunfree.org/edfund/ceasefir.htm>.

Empire State Building Shooting

Like other acts of violence involving firearms, the February 23, 1997, Empire State Building shooting evoked renewed calls for more stringent gun control legislation at the national, state, and local levels. Other voices, more sympathetic to gun rights, emphasized the self-protection value of firearms. The incident began when Ali Abu Kamal, a 69-year-old Palestinian from Ramallah in the West Bank, who had arrived in the United States just five weeks before, opened fire on a group of approximately 100 tourists on the observation deck of the Empire State Building. New Yorkers were shocked by the shooting, in which one tourist from Denmark was killed, several people were wounded, and others were injured in the resulting panic. Abu Kamal died of a self-inflicted gunshot wound to the temple.

Many public officials and citizens were troubled to discover that a loophole in existing gun control legislation allowed Abu Kamal to purchase a .380-caliber semi-automatic Beretta handgun from a gunshop in Melbourne, Florida. Kamal had lost his life's fortune and blamed Zionists and Zionist sympathizers for his financial troubles. Apparently realizing that the New York City gun laws, which required fingerprinting and a background check, a process that could take from six months to a year, would make it extremely difficult for him to purchase a firearm locally, Abu Kamal traveled to Florida to acquire a weapon. Although Florida had a five-day waiting period in compliance with the Brady Handgun Violence Prevention Act, nothing on the form required a statement of length of residence in the United States. A 1994 federal law prohibited gun purchases by anyone who had been in the country for less than 90 days. Abu Kamal acquired a picture identification card from the Florida Department of Highway Safety and Motor Vehicles, which proved sufficient identification to purchase a handgun.

Almost immediately after Abu Kamal's brief shooting spree, public officials began to call for gun control reform. Three days after the shooting, the Clinton administration announced that gun purchase forms would be reworded to notify gun dealers that a 90-day residency in the United States was required to purchase a gun. The administration also

indicated that ways were being explored to combine FBI records with those of the Immigration and Naturalization Service. On February 28, Democratic Senators Edward M. Kennedy of Massachusetts and Richard J. Durbin of Illinois announced they were introducing legislation that would prohibit foreign visitors from buying and carrying firearms. Noting that the United States was a potential terrorist target, Durbin stated that the nation should not permit guns to be placed in the hands of "would-be terrorists." Kennedy commented that there was no justifiable reason to allow temporary visitors to the nation to purchase and carry a firearm. The legislative proposal would hold gun dealers liable for knowingly selling a firearm to a foreigner not qualified to own a weapon. Gun purchasers would have to certify that they were not foreigners prohibited from buying firearms.

On March 5, President Bill Clinton, at a ceremony attended by James S. Brady, the presidential press secretary who was shot and seriously wounded during an assassination attempt on President Ronald Reagan in 1981, announced that he had ordered the Bureau of Alcohol, Tobacco, and Firearms (BATF) to more rigorously apply the law requiring legal immigrants to prove that they had been a resident in the United States for at least 90 days. The president also declared his support for the Durbin-Kennedy bill, which ultimately was passed as part of the Omnibus Appropriation Act for fiscal 1999. In addition, he took the opportunity to announce a legislative proposal to ban armor-piercing bullets, and stated that federal agencies had been directed to require trigger locks on every handgun issued to law enforcement agents.

While gun control supporters were advocating various legislative measures, including federally imposed national uniformity in gun control policy to prevent out-of-state purchases of handguns, the National Rifle Association (NRA) cautiously announced its opposition to any new legislation. Chip Walker, a spokesman for the organization, stated that Clinton's proposals were inappropriate because one incident of gun violence involving an alien should not lead to a denial of gun ownership to peaceful and productive foreign visitors who, just like American citizens, have the right of self-protection. Given the equal protection guarantees of the Fourteenth Amendment, Walker doubted that the courts would support gun ownership restrictions based solely on citizenship. *See also* ALIENS; BRADY, JAMES; BRADY, SARAH; BRADY HANDGUN VIOLENCE PREVENTION ACT; BUREAU OF ALCOHOL, TOBACCO, AND FIREARMS; CLINTON, WILLIAM JEFFERSON (BILL); FOURTEENTH AMENDMENT; NATIONAL RIFLE ASSOCIATION; REAGAN, RONALD; TRIGGER LOCKS.

Further Reading: *New York Times*, February 24, 1997 (pp. A1, B4); February 25 (pp. A26, B5); February 26 (p. B3); February 27 (p. A22); February 28 (p. B3); March 6 (p. B3).

F

Farmer v. Higgins (1990)

The case of *Farmer v. Higgins* (907 F.2 1041, 1990) concerned a challenge to restrictions on the right to make or own a machine gun, an area of gun control that for years has troubled the more uncompromising defenders of the right to own firearms, especially those who engage in gun collecting. Although the Firearms Owners' Protection Act of 1986 generally weakened federal gun control legislation, one provision of the act prohibited private individuals from owning machine guns unless they had possession of the weapons prior to May 19, 1986. Except for more avid gun rights supporters, the prevailing view is that because machine guns lack sporting value and are extremely deadly weapons, private citizens should not be allowed to possess them.

In October 1986, J.D. Farmer, Jr., a gun collector, applied to the Bureau of Alcohol, Tobacco, and Firearms (BATF) for authorization to make and register a machine gun. The BATF refused Farmer's request, referring to the new firearms law as the basis for its ruling. Farmer challenged the decision in court, claiming that the BATF had misinterpreted the intent of the law. Farmer's argument depended on the meaning of the phrase "under the authority" because the law stated that the prohibition on the transfer or possession of a machine gun does not apply to "a transfer to or by, or possession by or *under the authority* of, the United States or any department or agency thereof or a State, or a department, agency, or political subdivision thereof." Farmer argued that by applying under the National Firearms Act of 1934 to manufacture a machine gun, he satisfied this provision of the 1986 law. He claimed the BATF was legally obligated to grant him permission to manufacture a machine gun.

A Federal District Court upheld Farmer's claim. However, a United States Court of Appeals overruled the lower court decision, concluding that the intent of Congress was clear. The court referred to section 922 (o)(2)(B) of the statute. The law stated that the prohibition on transferring or owning a machine gun did not apply to "any lawful transfer or lawful possession of a machine gun that was lawfully possessed before the date this subsection takes effect." The court ruled that if Congress had not intended to alter the 1934 legislation, then this clause exempting from the prohibition any owners prior to May 19, 1986, would lack any meaning.

The court further determined that the phrase "under the authority" of a government agency had a delimited application that did not cover Farmer's interpretation. The phrase referred to machine guns manufactured for the military, for police forces, or under government jurisdiction for export to a foreign nation. On January 15, 1991, the U.S. Supreme Court refused to hear the appeal, thus letting stand the Appeals Court ruling. *See also* BUREAU OF ALCOHOL, TOBACCO, AND FIRE-ARMS; FIREARMS OWNERS PROTECTION ACT; NATIONAL FIREARMS ACT OF 1934.

Further Reading: *Farmer v. Higgins*, 907 F.2 1041 (1990); Mark A. Siegel, Nancy R. Jacobs, and Carol D. Foster, *Gun Control: Restricting Rights or Protecting People?* (Wylie, TX: Information Plus, 1991).

Fatalities

The rate of fatalities from firearms varies according to age, race, and sex, and specific circumstance (homicide, suicide, or accident). The observation of overall trends in firearm fatalities has contributed to the call for further efforts to restrict access to guns, particularly among youth. In *Gun Control: An American Issue* (1997), Nancy Jacobs, Mark Siegel, and Mei Ling Rein provide a summary of data regarding firearm-related fatalities compared to other causes of death. In 1995, firearm injuries were the second leading cause of accidental fatalities in the United States (24 percent), behind motor vehicle traffic injuries (29 percent).

In 1995, 13 percent of all deaths among children aged 10 to 14 were attributed to firearms, the second leading cause of death for this age group. The death rate from firearms increased significantly from 1980 to 1994. In 1980, the number of deaths per 100,000 population for those aged 15 to 19 attributable to motor vehicle accidents was 42.5, while the rate for firearms was 14.8. In 1994, the rate for motor vehicle accidents had declined to 29.1 but the firearm rate had increased to 28.4. The Centers for Disease Control and Prevention (CDC) predicted that firearms would become the leading cause of injury by the year 2000, although falling crime rates, including homicide, may invalidate that projection.

The increase in firearms-related fatalities has been most pronounced among African-American males. In 1980, the death rate among black males aged 15 to 19 was 46.7 per 100,000, which was over three times the rate for the total population in that age group. By 1994, the rate for all youth aged 15 to 19 had nearly doubled while for black males the

rate more than tripled. The rate for black males stood at 152.7, over five times the rate for all youth aged 15 to 19. Among white males, the rate increased from 21 per 100,000 in 1980 to 30.6 in 1994. For white females, the rate increased only slightly from 4.2 in 1980 to 4.8 in 1994.

In 1994, the firearm death rate among males aged 15 to 24 exceeded that for motor vehicle accidents (54 and 41 per 100,000, respectively). The death rate from firearms among males aged 15 to 24 was eight times higher than that for females in that age group. The firearm-related murder rate was twice as high as the suicide rate from firearms. For those aged 25 to 64, males were five times more likely than females to die from firearm injuries. Among all males in the United States, the firearm death rate was considerably higher than for other developed countries (averaging 11-12 per 100,000 in Canada, Israel, and Norway, and 1 per 100,000 in The Netherlands, England, and Wales).

Older Americans are more likely to die from disease than either automobile accidents or firearms. Of those aged 45 to 64 who died from firearm injuries, suicide was the cause of death two to four times more often than homicide. For persons 65 years old and over, firearms caused 14 percent of injury deaths, compared to 23 percent for falls and 22 percent for motor vehicles. Nearly 90 percent of firearm deaths in this age group were suicides. Males aged 65 to 74 were 11 times more likely to die from firearm suicides than were females. For the oldest Americans, firearm suicide was primarily a male phenomenon. The suicide rate for males over 85 years old was 45.7 per 100,000, compared to 1.2 for females.

Jacobs, Siegel, and Rein report CDC estimates of potential years of life lost to firearm-related fatalities. From 1980 to 1991, firearms ranked fourth among the causes of potential life lost before age 65, behind unintentional injuries from causes other than firearms, cancer, and heart disease. In that same time period, the potential years lost increased 13.6 percent for firearm-related deaths, but decreased by 25.2 percent for non-firearm related unintentional injury deaths, declined 18.1 percent for heart disease, and remained the same for cancer. Table 7 provides a listing of fatalities due to firearms in 1996 by age categories.

TABLE 7	
FIREARM DEATHS, 1996	

Age	Deaths
0-4	88
5-9	95
10-14	510
15-19	3,950
20-24	4,816
25-29	3,989
30-34	3,414
35-39	3,318
40-44	2,746
45-49	2,289
50-54	1,693
55-59	1,317
60-64	1,077
65-69	1,191
70-74	1,161
75-79	1,027
80-84	785
85+	546
Unknown	28
Total	34,040

Source: National Center for Health Statistics.

See also ACCIDENTS INVOLVING GUNS; CANADA; ISRAEL; SUICIDE; UNITED KINGDOM; VIOLENT CRIME RATE.

Further Reading: Nancy R. Jacobs, Mark A. Siegel, and Mei Ling Rein, eds., *Gun Control: An American Issue* (Wylie, TX: Information Plus, 1997).

Federal Firearms Act

The Federal Firearms Act of 1938 was the last piece of major gun control legislation passed in the pre-World War II era. The objective of the act was primarily to regulate the interstate sale of firearms and other weapons. The act mandated that firearms manufacturers, dealers, and importers be licensed. The fee charged for registration, which was set at just one dollar, was collected by the Internal Revenue Service (IRS). At the time of passage, the National Rifle Association (NRA) contended that the fee should have been even lower. The law prohibited those

convicted of a felony, fugitives from justice, persons under indictment, or those failing to meet local licensing requirements from acquiring firearms. In addition, the act made it a crime to transport stolen firearms if the manufacturer's identification mark had been altered.

The act fell short of Attorney General Homer Cummings's hope to institute a national system of registration for all firearms. Cummings insisted that firearms registration should be no more objectionable to Americans than registering automobiles. In 1937, he declared, "Show me the man who does not want his gun registered and I will show you a man who should not have a gun." The NRA, leading a coalition of pro-gun groups, including the American Legion, the American Wild Life Institute, the American Game Association, and the Izaak Walton League, won concessions from Congress and the Justice Department. Losing these battles with pro-gun interests, President Franklin Roosevelt withdrew from the process leading to passage of the act. Although the law granted the Treasury Department control over the national licensing system for gun manufacturers and dealers, the authority to keep firearms from prohibited classes of people was significantly weakened by requiring that any prosecution had to show that a dealer who sold firearms to criminals did so knowingly. Those selling firearms were not required to determine the eligibility of buyers.

The Federal Firearms Act, which was replaced by the Gun Control Act of 1968, was generally considered ineffective in controlling the gun trade. In their book, *The Citizen's Guide to Gun Control* (1987), Franklin Zimring and Gordon Hawkins have commented that the measure amounted to "a symbolic denunciation of firearms in the hands of criminals, coupled with an inexpensive and ineffective regulatory scheme that did not inconvenience the American firearms industry or its customers." *See also* GUN CONTROL ACT OF 1968; IZAAK WALTON LEAGUE OF AMERICA; NATIONAL RIFLE ASSOCIATION.

Further Reading: Federal Firearms Act (P.L. 75-785); Earl R. Kruschke, *Gun Control* (Santa Barbara, CA: ABC-CLIO, 1995); Eric Larson, *Lethal Passage: The Story of a Gun* (New York: Vintage, 1995); Franklin E. Zimring and Gordon Hawkins, *The Citizen's Guide to Gun Control* (New York: Macmillan, 1987).

Federalist Papers

From 1787 to 1788, Alexander Hamilton, James Madison, and John Jay, under the collective pseudonym "Publius," wrote and published the *Federalist Papers*, a series of newspaper articles defending the adoption of the new United States Constitution. Although their arguments possess no official status, they have often been used to interpret the intent of the constitutional framers. Publius did not discuss the notion of a right to bear arms, for the Second Amendment was not proposed until the Constitution had been ratified and the first Congress had convened. However, Hamilton and Madison did investigate the merits of militias in the several states, which are relevant to the right to bear arms because the Second Amendment refers to "a well regulated Militia being necessary to the security of a free State," as opposed to a standing army.

However, contrary to the belief that standing armies should not be allowed under the new constitution, Hamilton in Federalist No. 24 noted that only two state constitutions contained prohibitions on the formation of standing armies in peacetime and that the Articles of Confederation imposed no limitation on the ability of the United States government to form a standing army. In addition to arguing that there was no precedent for denying the new national government the authority to establish a standing army, Hamilton claimed that the nation required the services of such a military force even in peacetime. Small garrisons on the Western frontier would provide defense against the "ravages and depredations of Indians," and a professional military would ward off any possible aggressive actions by the British or Spanish. Militias, he argued, could not meet these defense needs, for citizens would constantly be dragged from their private occupations for military service. The loss to society

of their labor and the burden such service would represent for these men indicated that a permanent army paid by the government could better fulfill the nation's defensive needs.

In Federalist No. 25, Hamilton argued for the natural superiority of a standing army over a militia force. He questioned the argument that a militia was primarily responsible for the American victory in the war for independence, stating that "the liberty of [the militiamen's] country could not have been established by their efforts alone, however great and valuable they were." Although Hamilton admitted in Federalist No. 28 that a minor disturbance in part of a state could be handled adequately by the militia, sometimes a more extensive military force would be necessary to preserve peace and maintain the authority of the laws against insurrection and rebellion. A national standing army would at the same time guarantee that the state government did not exceed its authority.

In Federalist No. 29, Hamilton defended the new Constitution's provision for national control over militias, especially in periods of insurrection and invasion when a common authority would become vital to the maintenance of defense: "This desirable uniformity can only be accomplished by confiding the regulation of the militia to the direction of the national authority." Thus, if an insurrection or invasion occurred in one state, the proper action would be for the militia in a neighboring state to come to its aid against a common enemy, under the control of the national authority.

Despite Hamilton's conclusion that a regular army can out-perform a militia, Madison in Federalist No. 46 assured Americans that a regular army under the control of the national government would pose no serious threat because the people and their state governments could stave off the threat. State militias composed of nearly a half-million men could not be defeated by a much smaller regular army. As evidence to support this contention, Madison referred to the recent war for independence and the fact that Americans, unlike citizens of most other nations, were well armed. These citizens, joined by their state governments, would form a "barrier against the enterprises of ambition, more insurmountable than any which a simple government of any form can admit of."

Madison was surely in favor of a significantly stronger national government and believed that the new Constitution would accomplish this objective. However, for the states to ratify the document, many had to be convinced that the new national government would not pose a threat to the integrity of the states and to individual liberties. Therefore, Madison's argument might be seen as an attempt to allay fears rather than any sort of endorsement of the notion that states, with the aid of militia composed of citizen soldiers, could back an insurrection against a repressive national government. *See also* AMERICAN REVOLUTION; MILITIA ACT OF 1792; SECOND AMENDMENT.

Further Reading: Alexander Hamilton, James Madison, and John Jay, *The Federalist Papers* (New York: Mentor, 1961); Robert J. Spitzer, *The Politics of Gun Control* (Chatham, NY: Chatham, 1995).

Feinstein, Dianne (1933–)

Dianne Feinstein, Democratic Senator from California, has gained the ire of gun rights organizations for her avid support of gun control measures. In 1994, the Senate passed two bills she supported, the assault weapons ban and the Gun-Free Schools Act. Although generally considered a liberal who supports abortion rights (in 1996 the liberal organization Americans for Democratic Action gave her a 95 percent approval rating while the American Conservative Union rated her at 20 percent), Feinstein has supported the death penalty and advocated a constitutional amendment prohibiting desecration of the U.S. flag. Throughout her public career, Feinstein has maintained an interest in criminal justice issues, and considers gun control a major priority in the campaign to limit violence.

Feinstein received a B.A. in history from Stanford University in 1955. She was a member of the California Women's Parole Board from 1960 to 1966 and in 1968 served as a member of the San Francisco Committee on Crime. In 1969, she was elected to the San Francisco Board of Supervisors, serving as president in 1970-71, 1974-75, and 1978. When San Francisco Mayor George Moscone and fellow Board member Harvey Milk were assassinated (an event that influenced her subsequent position on gun control), Feinstein succeeded to the office of mayor.

Senator Dianne Feinstein (D-CA), an advocate of gun control, supported both the assault weapons ban and the Gun-Free Schools Act. ©*Thomas John Gibbons.*

In 1979, Feinstein was elected mayor in her own right, a position she held until 1989. During her tenure as mayor, Feinstein focused on public safety and improving the efficiency of the police force. In 1990, Feinstein lost the California gubernatorial election to Pete Wilson, but two years later won the U.S. Senate seat formerly held by Wilson, defeating Wilson's personally chosen replacement in a special election to fill the remaining two years in Wilson's senate term. In 1994, she won election to a full term. Feinstein serves on the Judiciary Committee; the Subcommittee on Technology, Terrorism, and Government Information; and the Subcommittee on Youth Violence.

Feinstein's assault weapons ban was included in the 1994 Crime Bill, which prohibits the manufacture, transfer, and possession of 19 specific types of semi-automatic assault weapons, such as the Uzi and the M-11 Sub-Machine pistol. Arguing in favor of passage, Feinstein advocated common sense laws to stop the distribution of military-style assault weapons. She was careful to emphasize the legitimate use of firearms for home defense, hunting, and recreation. When a fellow senator who opposed the ban suggested that Feinstein had insufficient knowledge of weapons, she related a very personal experience with firearms, telling of her attempt to find Harvey Milk's pulse after he had been shot.

Feinstein, along with Democratic Senator Byron Dorgan of North Dakota, sponsored the Gun-Free Schools Act, which mandated that schools enforce a gun-free policy or face the loss of federal funding. Claiming that 100,000 guns are brought to school each day, she declared that schools should be "safe havens" for children, a place where they can be protected from the violence too often present in the world. Because state and local policies regarding students who take guns to school vary widely, Feinstein argued that uniform national guidelines were necessary.

In 1998, Feinstein sponsored an amendment to an appropriations bill to ban the importation and sale of high-capacity ammunition magazines. She intended the legislation to fill a gap left by the 1994 Crime Bill. Although the 1994 legislation prohibited the future manufacture and sale of ammunition clips with a capacity over 10 rounds, it allowed the importation and sale of clips manufactured prior to enactment of the ban. The senator claimed that such ammunition magazines had no legitimate sporting purpose and represented a serious threat to public safety. She pointed to the Jonesboro, Arkansas, school shooting to illustrate the dangers of such large ammunition clips. The intent of the proposed legislation was to prohibit the further importation of clips and to prevent the sale of present stocks. Those already legally possessing high capacity clips could keep them, but could not transfer them to another person. In July 1998, the Senate voted to table Feinstein's amendment.

Feinstein's concern for public safety proceeded in areas complementary to her interest in gun control policy. In April 1998, the senator announced her support for a proposed constitutional amendment that would protect the victims of violent crime. The Victims' Rights Amendment would guarantee various rights to crime victims, including the right to attend any judicial proceedings, to be heard in the process, to receive restitution from the convicted offender, and to be provided safety from any future action by the offender. *See also* ASSAULT WEAPONS BAN; BOXER, BARBARA; GUN-FREE SCHOOLS ACT; JONESBORO, ARKANSAS, SCHOOL SHOOTING.

Further Reading: Philip D. Duncan and Christine C. Lawrence, *Politics in America: The 105th Congress* (Washington, DC: CQ Press, 1997); "Senators Launch Effort to Ban High Capacity Ammunition Clips," *News from Senator Dianne Feinstein* (March 31, 1998); Dianne Feinstein Web site <www.senate.gov/~feinstein>.

Firearm Sentence Enhancement (FSE) Laws

Firearm Sentence Enhancement (FSE) laws at the state and national levels establish minimum sentences or mandate additional prison time for felonies committed with firearms. Both pro- and anti-gun control advocates tend to support such laws, as does the general public. Those supporting sentence enhancement laws argue that the threat of greater punishment deters crime and that longer sentences keep violent offenders in prison where they cannot victimize even more people. However, researchers have raised serious questions about the effectiveness of longer sentences for crimes committed with a firearm.

Wayne R. LaPierre, executive vice president of the National Rifle Association (NRA), supports mandatory prison sentences for those who are convicted of using a deadly weapon in the commission of a felony. LaPierre advocates "real-offense sentencing," which mandates that a judge consider the fact that a defendant used a firearm or other weapon, or caused bodily harm in the commission of a crime, even though the official charge does not reflect that fact. Further, LaPierre advocates a mandatory life sentence with no chance of release for anyone convicted a third time for a violent felony.

In January 1997, Congresswoman Sue Myrick, Republican from North Carolina, introduced a measure, titled the Mandatory Minimum Sentences for Criminals Possessing Firearms Act, which would amend the existing federal criminal code regarding mandatory additional sentences for crimes committed with firearms. The bill was meant to clarify the intentions of Congress in previous legislation establishing sentence enhancement for criminal firearm use. In 1995, the Supreme Court had ruled that a person committing a crime had to fire or brandish a weapon before enhanced or minimum penalties became applicable. The bill provided for imprisonment for an additional 10 years beyond the sentence imposed for the violent crime if the criminal possesses a firearm in carrying out the criminal act. Anyone who brandishes a firearm would be sentenced to 15 years imprisonment in addition to the original sentence for the crime of violence. The bill defined "brandishing" to mean "to display all or part of the firearm so as to intimidate or threaten, regardless of whether the firearm is visible." Finally, anyone who fires a gun during a crime of violence shall receive an additional 20-year sentence. In February 1998, the House passed the bill and referred it to the senate, which took no action.

Although firearm sentence enhancement laws have proven to be popular, serious questions have been raised regarding their effectiveness. For instance, in a 1995 article in *Criminology*, Thomas Marvell and Carlisle Moody analyzed the effects of such laws in the states that had passed sentence enhancement or minimal sentencing measures. They noted that measuring consequences is complicated by alternative social theories that offer conflicting predictions: sentence enhancement statutes can arguably both in-

crease and reduce prison populations, crime rates, and the use of firearms in the commission of crimes. Marvell and Moody concluded that FSE laws generally do not reduce crime rates or gun use nationwide.

Available data indicate that only a small proportion of state FSE laws are significantly associated with decreased crime or gun use, and that a corresponding proportion of laws are associated with increased levels of violent crime. Various other factors, including judges who find ways to bypass mandatory sentencing, the minimal deterrent value of additional sentencing, the limited capacity of existing prison facilities, and criminals' increased ability to evade arrest for gun crimes may militate against the effectiveness of FSE laws. *See also* BAILEY V. UNITED STATES (1996); LAPIERRE, WAYNE; NATIONAL RIFLE ASSOCIATION.

Further Reading: Dan Carney, "Crimes Committed with Guns May Carry Higher Penalties," *Congressional Quarterly Weekly Report* 55 (September 13, 1997), 2149; Wayne R. LaPierre, *Guns, Crime, and Freedom* (Washington, DC: Regnery, 1994); Thomas B. Marvell and Carlisle E. Moody, "The Impact of Enhanced Prison Terms for Felonies Committed with Guns," *Criminology* 33 (1995), 247-78; Sue Myrick Web site <www.house.gov/myrick>.

Firearms Coalition

Neal Knox established the Firearms Coalition in 1982 following his removal from the National Rifle Association's (NRA) Institute for Legislative Action. Initially called the Neal Knox Hard Corps, the Coalition functions as a rallying point for those members of the NRA who take a more uncompromising position on the issue of gun control. The Coalition operates through Knox's consulting firm, Neal Knox Associates. Since 1984, Knox has been a registered lobbyist for the Coalition. On the organization's membership application, the contribution is called a "retainer" for Knox's services as a Washington lobbyist. Josh Sugarmann, head of the Violence Policy Center, has estimated that the Coalition receives approximately $100,000 per year in contributions.

The organization provides Knox with a base from which to further his anti-gun control agenda within the NRA. Coalition supporters, many of whom are NRA members, oppose more moderate elements in the NRA who are considered too willing to compromise on gun control measures. When Charlton Heston was elected NRA president in 1998, the Coalition reported his support for the Gun Control Act in 1968, claiming that the new president's views on gun control had not changed noticeably since then. The Coalition has participated in fights over rules within the NRA, particularly those dealing with the nomination of candidates to the board of directors.

Wishing to activate gun owners politically, the Coalition keeps members and others interested in gun rights regularly informed about the activities of Congress regarding proposals related to firearms policy. The Coalition maintains the Online Bulletin as a means of communication among pro-gun advocates. In December 1998, with the National Instant Check System scheduled to begin, the Coalition paid close attention to legislative proposals to prevent federal government agencies from keeping a file of those who applied for a firearm purchase. The Coalition emphasized that the Brady Handgun Violence Prevention Act prohibits the retention of information on the subjects of background checks who were found to be qualified to purchase a firearm.

Although the Coalition recognizes that there are more pro-gun Republicans in Congress than pro-gun Democrats, it recommends that gun owners not become overly committed to a political party. The Coalition criticized Heston for supporting the Republican opponent of a pro-gun incumbent Democratic congressman who had received the endorsement of the NRA's Institute for Legislative Action (ILA) and a contribution from the ILA's Political Victory Fund. Although the Coalition recognizes that a Republican-controlled Congress is much more likely to support the interests of gun owners, it holds that the actions of Republicans as well as Democrats must be monitored closely so that no politician takes support from gun rights groups for granted.

In 1998, the Coalition opposed a measure to mandate the sale of trigger locks with new handguns. It objected to a proposal to require the safe storage of firearms, calling it "one of the most far-reaching 'gun control' laws pushed in recent years." Neither measure cleared Congress. The Coalition supported a measure to allow law enforcement officers and civilians with concealed weapons permits in their home states to carry concealed firearms in other states. The organization has strongly criticized President Bill Clinton and his administration for supporting additional gun control legislation. *See also* CLINTON, WILLIAM JEFFERSON (BILL); CONCEALED CARRY LAWS; GUN CONTROL ACT OF 1968; HESTON, CHARLTON; INSTITUTE FOR LEGISLATIVE ACTION; KNOX, NEAL; NATIONAL INSTANT CHECK SYSTEM; NATIONAL RIFLE ASSOCIATION; *SHOTGUN NEWS*; TRIGGER LOCKS; VIOLENCE POLICY CENTER.

Further Reading: Firearms Coalition Web site <www.nealknox.com>.

Firearms Litigation Clearinghouse (FLC)

The Firearms Litigation Clearinghouse, run by the Washington, D.C.-based Educational Fund to End Handgun Violence, was founded in 1981 to provide assistance to victims of firearms violence and their attorneys. The organization states that its ultimate goal is to serve as a means of reducing firearms injuries and deaths through the use of civil lawsuits. Among its objectives, the organization strives to eradicate firearms that have manufacturing or design defects, to broaden the legal definition of design defect to include those firearms that most typically are used to injure people, to require manufacturers to equip firearms with child-proof safety devices, and to provide attorneys with information and support so that they can initiate lawsuits in gun-related injury cases.

The Clearinghouse provides plaintiffs' attorneys with various types of assistance, including access to a list of expert witnesses, case consultations, information about previous cases, and data about firearms manufacturing. The organization distributes a quarterly newsletter, the *Firearms Litigation Reporter*, which provides updated information regarding product liability law, negligent entrustment as a means of holding gun manufacturers and retailers legally responsible for the criminal use of firearms, and various constitutional issues. The newsletter reports on recently filed cases and settled lawsuits and offers current information about the firearms industry.

While the Clearinghouse estimates that less than 10 percent of unintentional shooting injuries are ever reviewed for possible litigation, it claims that most of these injuries are potentially subject to legal action. Those concerned about gun violence are encouraged to consider the potential of litigation as an effective tactic in reducing firearms violence. According to the Clearinghouse, anti-gun-violence activists should advise victims of gun violence and their families to engage an attorney to examine the shooting in preparation for possible legal action. The Clearinghouse notes that on many occasions the courts have held firearms and ammunition manufacturers, firearms dealers, and distributors responsible for injuries caused by their products.

The Clearinghouse is critical of the fact that firearms are specifically exempted from the regulatory jurisdiction of the Consumer Product Safety Commission (CPSC). The Clearinghouse also notes that the Bureau of Alcohol, Tobacco, and Firearms (BATF) has no authority to regulate the safety of domestically produced firearms and only weak authority to regulate imported weapons. The BATF has no power to require recalls of any defective firearms and may not establish safety standards. The Clearinghouse contends that the failure to regulate firearms safety contributes to the disproportionately high number of persons injured or killed by firearms each year in the United States.

The Clearinghouse believes that the courts can provide an effective alternative means of controlling firearms violence. The organization also holds that although the criminal justice system may prosecute those directly responsible for firearms injuries and deaths, civil procedure can also be used to gain monetary compensation for the injured party from those who supply firearms. The Clearinghouse operates under the tenet that "every shooting should be reviewed by a competent attorney." Worthy of special attention are situations in which negligence or product liability may be demonstrated, including circumstances where a child is the shooter, a firearm discharged after being dropped or bumped, a gun discharged while being cleaned, the shooter claims he or she did not pull the trigger, or a gun fired even though the magazine had been removed. Other situations subject to civil action involve negligent entrustment, in which a firearms dealer or other person provides a firearm to a person determined to be incompetent to use it, such as a minor, a felon, or a person addicted to drugs. *See also* BUREAU OF ALCOHOL, TOBACCO, AND FIREARMS; EDUCATIONAL FUND TO END HANDGUN VIOLENCE; LAWYER'S SECOND AMENDMENT SOCIETY; LEGAL ACTION PROJECT; LEGAL COMMUNITY AGAINST VIOLENCE; PRODUCT LIABILITY LAWSUITS; TRIGGER LOCKS.

Further Reading: Firearms Litigation Clearinghouse Web site <www.firearmslitigation.org>.

Firearms Owners Against Crime (FOAC)

Firearms Owners Against Crime (FOAC) is one of many state organizations dedicated to the preservation of what is considered a constitutional right to keep and bear arms. The organization was established by several people who had worked unsuccessfully to defeat a 1993 ordinance in Pittsburgh, Pennsylvania, that banned certain firearms and ammunition. The FOAC became a political action committee in 1994, focusing on electoral politics in an attempt to influence government policy toward firearms.

The FOAC urges like-minded voters to support candidates friendly to gun rights and to help persuade others to do the same. Recommendations are made for national as well as state and local offices. The organization plans to expand its activities beyond electoral politics to focus on legislative proposals of concern to the group. Although gun control legislation has been enacted, the organization holds that "laws can be repealed, bureaucracies abolished, judges impeached, and jurisdiction limited."

The FOAC monitors the state legislative agenda and the voting records of elected officials and publishes a voting guide that it distributes to the constituents of state legislators. The organization produced 80,000 guides for the 1994 elections and 250,000 for the 1996 elections. The FOAC holds that a vote choice should never be one between two evils. If no candidate for a particular office has demonstrated sufficient support for the interests of firearms owners, the organization will not make a recommendation to voters.

The FOAC holds to a fundamental principle: "In a free society, no citizen should ever have to justify the assertion of a fundamental right." Gun control advocates might well agree with that assertion, but deny that the right to keep and bear arms falls into the category of fundamental rights. The organization also holds to the position that government is best when it governs least. The FOAC believes that, contrary to this basic principle, government bureaucracy is intruding into the lives of private citizens more than at any other time in the nation's history. If violent crime is a problem with which government must deal, the FOAC believes that it must enforce laws already in existence to punish and deter criminal acts before considering additional legislation that would infringe on the rights of law-abiding citizens to keep and bear arms. The organization complains about what it considers the high-handed activities of federal officers, such as agents of the Federal Bureau of Investigation (FBI).

Pennsylvania Governor Thomas J. Ridge, a Republican, came under attack for his support of gun control. He was accused of initiating "the most striking anti-individual rights campaign in history" by attacking "almost every amendment in the Bill of Rights in the U.S. Constitution as well as the Declaration of Rights in the Pennsylvania Constitution."

The governor was criticized for supporting a state law establishing an instant check system for those wishing to purchase a handgun and making the seller of a firearm responsible for the criminal use of the weapon. The FOAC has also expressed opposition to a measure allowing the confiscation of firearms from individuals under psychiatric treatment who have been declared threats to themselves and to others. *See also* SECOND AMENDMENT; NATIONAL INSTANT CHECK SYSTEM.

Further Reading: Firearms Owners Against Crime Web site <www.hhi.com/foac/>.

Firearms Owners Protection Act

The first piece of significant national firearms legislation since 1968, the Gun Owners Protection Act , which became law in 1986, was in fact a measure that weakened many of the provisions of the Gun Control Act of 1968. The leadership of the National Rifle Association (NRA) lobbied intensely for the act's adoption, while police organizations were either ambivalent toward, or actively opposed to the legislation.

In the early 1980s, the Gun Control Act of 1968 came under intense criticism. Opponents claimed that the act unnecessarily limited the freedoms of law-abiding citizens while failing to keep firearms out of the hands of criminals. The Bureau of Alcohol, Tobacco, and Firearms (BATF), the government agency given responsibility for enforcing the law, was singled out as a major violator of individual rights. Senator James A. McClure, Republican of Idaho, and Representative Harold L. Volkmer, Democrat of Missouri, were the bill's chief sponsors. McClure argued that the provisions of the 1968 act were vague and imprecise, allowing abuses that must be remedied. Volkmer expressed concern that the law branded as criminal the perfectly legitimate actions of individual citizens.

Senator McClure proposed amendments to the 1968 act that were intended to eliminate the perceived abuses. His amendments dealt with such subjects as the law's restrictions on the interstate sales of firearms, the alleged harassment of citizens by the BATF and other government agencies, and the forfeiture of property for violations of the act's provisions. He called for limiting such seizures only to those weapons actually used in the commission of a crime.

Referring to various guarantees of individual rights within the Constitution (the Second Amendment guarantee of the right to bear arms, the Fourth Amendment prohibition against illegal searches and seizures, the Fifth Amendment due process declaration, and the Tenth Amendment reservation of powers to the states and to the people), the new Firearms Owners Protection Act declared that it was not the intention of Congress to restrict unnecessarily the rights of American citizens who acquired, possessed, or used firearms for such lawful purposes as hunting, target shooting, or personal protection.

The act permitted the sale once again of ammunition through the mail. Weapons dealers were allowed to resume the interstate sale of rifles and shotguns, although a provision to permit the sale of mail-order handguns was deleted from the bill. Ammunition dealers were no longer held to stringent record keeping regulations. Violations of record keeping requirements for weapons dealers were reduced from a felony to a misdemeanor and more stringent criteria were established to prove guilt. Officials must be able to demonstrate the intentions of dealers, determining whether they knowingly or willingly violated the law. The act also established time limitations for officials administering provisions of the legislation. The BATF was prohibited from centralizing the records of firearms dealers or from establishing a firearms registration system. The act also restricted the authority of BATF officials to inspect dealer records, and allowed an individual wishing to reclaim a firearm seized by law enforcement agents to shift defense attorney fees to the prosecuting agency.

The McClure-Volkmer bill emphasized that gun ownership by itself constituted no legitimate reason for limiting the rights of citizens. The law focused instead on the mis-use of firearms, requiring minimum and mandatory penalties for such misuse. Those engaging in drug trafficking who carry a firearm were subject to additional penalties. The bill also banned the future production of machine guns for sale to individuals, and prohibited the importation of barrels for Saturday night specials. *See also* BUREAU OF ALCOHOL, TOBACCO, AND FIREARMS; FOURTH AMENDMENT; GUN CONTROL ACT OF 1968; MCCLURE, JAMES ALBERTAS; NATIONAL RIFLE ASSOCIATION; SATURDAY NIGHT SPECIAL; SECOND AMENDMENT; VOLKMER, HAROLD LEE.

Further Reading: Gregg Lee Carter, *The Gun Control Movement* (New York: Twayne Publishers, 1997); Earl R. Kruschke, *Gun Control* (Santa Barbara, CA: ABC-CLIO, 1995); Josh Sugarmann, *National Rifle Association: Money, Firepower and Fear* (Washington, DC: National Press, 1992).

Firearms Research and Identification Association (FRIA)

Limited to a few professionals in the fields of engineering, safety, insurance, finance, and business, the Firearms Research and Identification Association (FRIA) is dedicated to the study of firearms. John A. Caudron founded FRIA in 1978 as an appendage to his company, Fire and Accident Reconstruction, located in Walnut, California. Organization members investigate the authenticity and history of firearms, analyze their involvement in accidents, and provide reports on defective weapons. The organization certifies the authenticity of firearms and makes appropriate identification of weapons. FRIA has been involved in the development of a test to certify firearm professionals.

Caudron, a forensic engineer, personally conducts approximately 200 investigations each year into the causes of injuries, product failures, property damage, and fire. He recreates the circumstances that might have contributed to accidents, including those involving firearms. When investigating losses attributed to firearms, Caudron conducts a detailed study of the weapon in question, determining its intended use and specific design.

Caudron emphasizes that the Firearms Research and Identification Association is a nonpolitical organization and does not take an official position on the gun control issue. However, the organization revolves around an interest in the use of firearms and Caudron's company exists in part due to a cultural situation in which guns are readily available and subject to use in a variety of circumstances. Above all, Caudron emphasizes that guns, like any tool, must be understood before they can be used properly.

The FRIA and Caudron's Fire and Accident Reconstruction company investigate cases involving lost or stolen guns, the misuse of weapons, and possible design defects. In one case, the organization investigated the trajectory of shots fired at lights on the nets of fishermen. After examining the angles and types of holes in the lamps, conducting simulated tests and making actual rifle firings, the investigators determined that the shots came from a nearby oil platform. In another case involving a shotgun breech that exploded, Caudron determined that the metal chemistry and heat treatment of the component parts failed to meet specifications.

Caudron is an instructor in the use of the rifle, pistol, and shotgun and is certified by the National Rifle Association (NRA). He is an expert in the use of a variety of firearms and maintains a practice range. Caudron has conducted accident analyses in firearms cases for attorneys and insurance companies and has qualified as an expert witness in firearms cases involving personal injury, product defect, product failure, design defect, and property damage. *See also* NATIONAL RIFLE ASSOCIATION; PRODUCT LIABILITY LAWSUITS.

Further Reading: *San Bernardino County Bar Association, Bulletin* 21 (July 1993), 10; Fire and Accident Reconstruction, "Firearms Background" (unpublished statement, n.d.).

Fourteenth Amendment

Gun rights advocates look to the Fourteenth Amendment as the vehicle by which the Second Amendment, which they claim protects an individual's right to keep and bear arms, limiting the power of state governments as well as the national government to control firearms. When first adopted in 1789, the Bill of Rights was understood to limit only the powers of the national government against encroachment on the rights of citizens. States had their own bills of rights to protect citizens against the power of these subordinate governments within the federal system. However, ratification of the Fourteenth Amendment in 1868 began a slow and halting process (termed selective incorporation) by which the Supreme Court in various cases interpreted various rights guaranteed in the Bill of Rights as applying to states as well as to the national government.

Section 1 of the Amendment states that, "All persons born or naturalized in the United States, and subject to the jurisdiction thereof, are citizens of the United States and of the State wherein they reside. No State shall make or enforce any law which shall abridge the privileges or immunities of citizens of the United States; nor shall any State deprive any person of life, liberty, or property, without due process of law; nor deny to any person within its jurisdiction the equal protection of the laws." The significance of this provision did not become established until many decades later, when the Supreme Court decided, in many separate cases, that selected rights guaranteed in the U.S. Constitution limit states as well as the federal government. For instance, in *Gitlow v. New York* (1925), the Supreme Court ruled that the First Amendment freedoms of speech and press are protected, via the Fourteenth Amendment, against state limitation. However, early Supreme Court decisions—including rulings on the right to keep and bear arms (*United States v. Cruikshank* [1876] and *Presser v. Illinois* [1886]) as well as the First Amendment freedoms of speech, press, and religion, the Fourth Amendment guarantee against unreasonable search and seizure, and the Fifth Amendment protection from self-incrimination—determined that the Bill of Rights still applied only to the federal government.

The consistent refusal of the Court to apply the Bill of Rights to the states began to crumble in 1925 when the Supreme Court, in *Gitlow v. New York*, ruled that the First Amendment right of freedom of speech applied to the states. Since then a long list of decisions have selectively incorporated portions of the Bill of Rights into the Fourteenth Amendment. Those portions that the Supreme Court has so far not applied to the states include the Third and Seventh Amendments, the indictment by grand jury requirement of the Fifth Amendment, and the Second Amendment guarantee of the right to keep and bear arms. Gun rights advocates, arguing in favor of Second Amendment incorporation, indicate that one of the primary purposes of the Fourteenth Amendment was to protect the right of African Americans to own and carry firearms, one of many rights threatened by the so-called Black Codes. Gun rights advocates claim that senators considering the proposed amendment were especially concerned by the denial of the right to own firearms. Whether or not this right played a major role in the proposing of the Fourteenth Amendment, the Supreme Court for 130 years has declined to incorporate the Second Amendment within the Fourteenth. However, gun rights advocates contend there is no clearer guarantee within the Bill of Rights to be protected against state encroachment. Supposing the validity of state application of the Second Amendment, interpreted as guaranteeing an individual right, many of the several thousand state and local gun laws could be judged violations of the Constitution.

Gun control advocates respond that the Supreme Court has rightly refused to incorporate the Second Amendment into the Fourteenth. They argue that unlike other rights in the Constitution, the right to keep and bear arms refers to a collective right of individual states to form and maintain a militia through the maintenance of armed militia units. Gun control advocates further contend that even should the Amendment be applied to the states, its protections are not absolute, just as the protection of free speech in the First Amendment does not preclude any and all limitations on free speech, as in cases of libel, slander, and pornography.

Gun rights supporters, noting that the Supreme Court has altered precedents in the past, remain hopeful that future challenges to gun control legislation will lead to the desired decision that the Second Amendment does apply to the states in the way they most desire: That the Second Amendment protects the right of individual citizens to keep and bear arms, and that neither local, state, nor the national government may violate that claimed right. *See also* AFRICAN AMERICANS AND GUNS; BLACK CODES; FOURTH AMENDMENT; GOTTLIEB, ALAN MERRIL; *PRESSER V. ILLINOIS* (1886); SECOND AMENDMENT; STATE GUN STATUTES; *UNITED STATES V. CRUICKSHANK* (1876).

Further Reading: Alan M. Gottlieb, *The Rights of Gun Owners* (Bellevue, WA: Merrill, 1991); William E. Nelson, *The Fourteenth Amendment: From Political Principle to Judicial Doctrine* (Cambridge, MA: Harvard University Press, 1995).

Fourth Amendment

Gun rights supporters consider the Fourth Amendment protection against unreasonable searches and seizures to be a significant supplement to their arguments, based on the Second Amendment, against gun control legislation at the state and national levels and in opposition to the efforts of police officials to enforce such legislation. Gun rights supporters contend that many of the searches and seizures conducted against gun owners violate the rights of law-abiding citizens.

The Fourth Amendment states that, "The right of the people to be secure in their persons, houses, papers, and effects, against unreasonable searches and seizures, shall not be violated, and no Warrants shall issue, but upon probable cause, supported by Oath or affirmation, and particularly describing the place to be searched, and the persons or things to be seized." Under standard circumstances, police officials must demonstrate "probable cause" before a judge or other magistrate will issue a search warrant. This order specifies the place to be searched and objects that may be seized. If officials can demonstrate that the situation did not allow time, securing a warrant may not be essential to the legality of a search to acquire incriminating evidence. However, if the court rules that the evidence was not obtained legally, the "exclusionary rule" may apply, that is, evidence obtained by illegal or unreasonable means cannot be admitted in either a federal or state criminal trial. The courts in effect must decide between the presence of probable cause and an individual's right to privacy in determining the appropriateness of a search warrant in a given circumstance.

The meaning of "unreasonable" has been subject to interpretation. More recently, the Supreme Court has tended to allow greater leeway for the police in conducting searches and seizures. More general searches, such as administrative inspections for health or safety reasons, and blanket searches such as those conducted at airports, potentially pose troubling questions regarding citizen rights because the wording of the Fourth Amendment usually is taken to refer to suspicion directed at an individual person.

With regard to the Fourth Amendment, gun rights advocates may be arguing one of two points. First, they can claim that police officials, in their zeal to ferret out illegal firearms, in fact violate citizen rights under the constitutional protection against unreasonable searches and seizures. When police officers search a home, an automobile, or an individual, they may conduct the search in such a way as to violate the reasonableness proviso. On the other hand, gun rights advocates may contend that because gun control laws are, from their perspective, clearly unconstitutional, any searches and seizures of weapons involve harassment of law-abiding citizens who have been made criminals by unconstitutional laws. The very conduct of a search violates a gun owner's protection against unreasonable searches and seizures because such searches have been conducted to enforce an unconstitutional law.

Gun control supporters would not necessarily have any difficulty with the first position, in that all searches and seizures, whether involving illegal firearms or the illegal use of them, or any other violation of the law, must be conducted within the boundary of the Fourth Amendment protection, although each

side may draw the line at different places. However, to the extent that the second argument is invoked, gun control advocates reject the claim that gun laws are unconstitutional and hence that the Fourth Amendment should be employed to limit enforcement. *See also* FOURTEENTH AMENDMENT; GOTTLIEB, ALAN MERRIL; SECOND AMENDMENT.

Further Reading: George Anastapol, *The Amendments to the Constitution: A Commentary* (Baltimore: Johns Hopkins University Press, 1995); Alan M. Gottlieb, *The Rights of Gun Owners* (Bellevue, WA: Merril, 1991); Robert J. Spitzer, *The Politics of Gun Control* (Chatham, NJ: Chatham House, 1995).

Fraternal Order of Police (FOP)

In 1994, the Fraternal Order of Police (FOP), along with several other law enforcement organizations, supported passage of the Brady Handgun Violence Prevention Act. Gun control advocates saw this support as weakening the relationship between police organizations and the National Rifle Association (NRA), which opposed the Brady Act. The national FOP organization, called the Grand Lodge, continues to support the Brady Act as a means of preventing criminals from acquiring firearms. In addition, the Grand Lodge has declared its opposition to any legislation that would repeal or weaken the ban on assault weapons. The organization supports a ban on "cop killer" bullets, ammunition capable of penetrating the body armor used by police officers.

The FOP has voiced opposition to the Lautenberg Amendment, also known as the Domestic Violence Offender Gun Ban. The law, which prevents those convicted of domestic violence misdemeanor charges from purchasing or owning a firearm, has been applied to police officers around the country. According to the FOP, the law has forced police departments to dismiss veteran officers with good records for a misdemeanor offense that occurred many years ago.

The Fraternal Order initiated a judicial challenge to the Lautenberg Amendment, claiming that the provision is unconstitutional because it applies retroactively to convictions

In February 1993, Dewey Stokes (standing), then president of the Fraternal Order of Police, holds an NRA ad attacking the Brady bill at a news conference called to support the reintroduction of the bill. Seated is James Brady, the former White House press secretary after whom the bill is named. *Corbis/Reuters.*

that occurred prior to passage. The statute adversely affects a large group of people who have been "ensnared" by the new prohibition. The organization supports an amendment to the original measure that would make the restriction apply only to future cases of domestic violence. Then the law would apply equally to private citizens as well as to police officers and those in the military who subsequently are convicted of misdemeanor domestic violence charges.

With regard to other firearms-related measures, the FOP supports the imposition of greater penalties for those who use body armor while committing a crime. Another measure the organization favors would increase criminal penalties for those who use laser sights on firearms when committing a crime. The organization has expressed its opposition to the proposed one-gun-a-month

legislation that would limit individuals to purchasing no more than one firearm in a 30-day period.

The FOP supports a mandate to federal law enforcement agencies to issue locks to gun-carrying employees and legislation requiring the sale of a gun safety lock with each purchase of a new firearm. Following the Empire State Building shooting in February 1997, which was committed by a recent immigrant to the United States, the organization expressed its support for the more effective enforcement of a statute that would not allow resident aliens to purchase a firearm until they have lived in a state for at least 90 days. The organization also advocates a requirement that federally licensed firearms dealers post notices in gun stores informing customers that it is a federal offense for a juvenile to possess a handgun, advising customers that handguns are a major cause of death among youth, and recommending safe storage and locking devices as means for preventing firearms accidents.

As an organization representing law enforcement officers, the FOP supports legislation that would exempt presently employed officers in good standing and retired officers from state and local prohibitions on carrying concealed firearms. Such legislation would permit officers to carry concealed firearms when traveling in jurisdictions other than their own. According to the FOP, such a provision would accomplish two major objectives. First, officers with the appropriate knowledge and training would have the means of enforcing the law and keeping the peace if called on to do so when not on active duty. Second, law enforcement officers may become the targets of criminals they helped to convict and therefore have special requirements for self-protection that should supersede state and local regulations. *See also* ASSAULT WEAPONS BAN; BRADY HANDGUN VIOLENCE PREVENTION ACT; EMPIRE STATE BUILDING SHOOTING; LAUTENBERG AMENDMENT; NATIONAL RIFLE ASSOCIATION; TRIGGER LOCKS.

Further Reading: Fraternal Order of Police Web site <www.grandlodgefop.org>.

G

Gottlieb, Alan Merril (1947–)

For over 20 years, Alan Gottlieb has played a central role in the campaign for recognition of a constitutional right of individuals to keep and bear arms and has worked vigorously to defeat measures that would impose more stringent gun control. Before entering a career as a gun rights advocate, Gottlieb served in the Army National Guard, entering as a private in 1968 and leaving as a Specialist Fourth Class in 1974. In 1971, he received a B.S. from the University of Tennessee. A political conservative, Gottlieb served as the national director of Young Americans for Freedom in 1971-72 and has been the national treasurer of the American Conservative Union. In 1974, Gottlieb established the Citizens Committee for the Right to Keep and Bear Arms (CCRKBA) to proclaim his interpretation of the Second Amendment and to serve as a source of information for individuals with the same goal. At the same time, Gottlieb founded the Second Amendment Foundation (SAF), the research and education affiliate of CCRKBA.

Gottlieb has authored or co-authored several books dealing with the rights of gun owners, including *The Gun Owner's Political Action Manual* (1976); *The Rights of Gun Owners* (1981); *The Gun Grabbers* (1986); *Gun Rights Fact Book* (1988); *Things You Can Do to Defend Your Gun Rights* (1993) and *More Things You Can Do to Defend Your Gun Rights* (1995), both co-authored with

David Kopel; and *Guns for Women* (1988), co-authored with George Flynn. Much of Gottlieb's publications offer practical advice to those who want to further the gun rights cause. For instance, *Things You Can Do to Defend Your Gun Rights* contains information about ways to influence government, including registering to vote, writing letters to elected officials, circulating petitions, visiting public officials personally, working for political candidates who take pro-gun rights stands, and testifying at public hearings. He gives advice on ways to gain publicity for the gun rights movement.

Alan M. Gottlieb founded the Citizens Committee for the Right to Keep and Bear Arms and the Second Amendment Foundation. *Courtesy of Alan M. Gottlieb.*

Gottlieb and Flynn's *Gun Rights for Women*, which is dedicated to Annie Oakley, the famous trick-shot artist, offers practical advice to women who wish to purchase a handgun (a disclaimer at the beginning of the book states that the authors are not recommending the purchase of a handgun, but are simply offering guidance for those who have already made the decision to buy a weapon). A chapter titled "Armed Citizens" provides 100 accounts of women who used a firearm to save their own or others' lives. Other chapters describe handgun features and specific makes and models, offer tips about firearm safety, and present the names and addresses of organizations that the reader might wish to join.

Gottlieb has received several recognition awards for his active support of gun rights, including the Good Citizenship award from the Citizens Home Protective Association (1978); the Good Citizen award from the Hawaii Home Protective Association (1978); the Cicero award from the National Association of Federally Licensed Firearms Dealers (1982); the Top Ten Outstanding American Handgunners award from the American Handgunner Award Foundation (1984); and the Kentucky Freedom Fighter award, presented by the Kentucky House of Representatives (1985).

Gottlieb's tenure as chairman of the CCRKBA has not been entirely smooth. In May 1984, he pleaded guilty to a federal charge of income tax evasion for failing to report income in 1977 and 1978 from his company, Merril Associates, a consulting firm for direct mailing clients. He was sentenced to one year in jail and a $5,000 fine. Gottlieb served eight and a half months of the sentence before being released. He claimed that the indictment was part of the Treasury Department's strategy of targeting gun rights groups.

In another incident, members of the CCRKBA who complained about his handling of the organization's affairs were excluded from the group. These individuals launched a court challenge, but Gottlieb maintained his leadership position.

Gottlieb has continued to campaign for gun rights, publishing various periodicals for the CCRKBA and SAF, including the *Gun Week* newspaper and *Gun News Digest*, a quarterly publication. Gottlieb has also made appearances on various news programs, including *Good Morning America*, *McNeil-Lehrer*, and *PBS Late Night*. Gottlieb's combative dedication to the Second Amendment has kept him at the forefront of the anti-gun control forces. *See also* CITIZENS COMMITTEE FOR THE RIGHT TO KEEP AND BEAR ARMS; *GUN NEWS DIGEST; GUN WEEK*; KOPEL, DAVID B.; SECOND AMENDMENT; SECOND AMENDMENT FOUNDATION; WOMEN AND GUNS.

Further Reading: Alan M. Gottlieb, *Gun Rights Fact Book* (Bellevue, WA: Merril, 1989); Josh Sugarmann, *National Rifle Association: Money, Firepower and Fear* (Washington, DC: National Press, 1992).

Gritz, James (Bo) (1939–)

In the 1980s and 1990s, James "Bo" Gritz, a Vietnam-era Green Beret colonel and a leader in the Patriot Movement, played a prominent role in far-right fringe and paramilitary survivalist groups, combining an appeal to patriotism with conservative Christian beliefs. Gritz has maintained associations with such Christian Identity figures as Pete Peters. He has identified an enemy composed of "seditious bankers" and "satanic globalists" led by the United Nations. Gritz is an avid opponent of gun control legislation, counseling supporters to resist any federal government attempt to confiscate their firearms. In the 1980s, Gritz made unsuccessful attempts to find American prisoners of war allegedly still held in Southeast Asia. In 1988, he joined Populist Party presidential candidate David Duke, a former Ku Klux Klan Imperial Wizard, to run for vice president, but resigned from the ticket to make an unsuccessful bid for the Republican nomination for a U.S. House seat from Nevada. In 1992, Gritz became the Populist Party presidential candidate. Comparing his campaign to a second American revolution, Gritz promised to restore states rights, reject global government, and safeguard personal liberty.

With FBI agents and Montana highway patrolmen standing behind him, James "Bo" Gritz meets reporters in April 1996 after being refused entry to the Freemen compound near Jordan, Montana. *REUTERS/Gary Caskey/Archive Photos.*

In 1992, Gritz gained national publicity during the standoff at Ruby Ridge between Randy Weaver and federal authorities in which Weaver's wife and son and a U.S. marshal were killed. Gritz served as an intermediary, helping Weaver, a fellow Green Beret veteran, surrender to authorities. In 1996, he persuaded Federal Bureau of Investigation (FBI) agents to permit him to mediate a standoff with the Freemen of Montana, but he was unable to convince them to surrender. The standoff ultimately ended peacefully. In 1998, he led a group into the rural North Carolina woods to try to persuade accused abortion clinic bomber Eric Rudolph to surrender. Gritz ultimately condemned federal agents for the handling of the Randy Weaver situation, as well as the Waco, Texas, Branch Davidian raid in 1993.

Gritz offers a military training regime called SPIKE Delta Force Training (Specially Prepared Individuals for Key Events). The training is said to provide "classified, secret information so that you will never be a victim again." Among the topics covered are gun control, counter-terrorist driving, medical emergencies, and lock-picking. Gritz offers the training on over 70 hours of video tapes.

In 1994, Gritz established a Christian Covenant Community in Kamiah, Idaho, on land purchased from a Native American reservation. The community was intended to serve as a haven where patriotic Americans could survive the anticipated devastation. He called the land Almost Heaven, and began selling lots to families wishing to move to the remote Idaho site. By 1996, the community had not developed as quickly as expected and some residents became critical of Gritz for failing to commit more completely to the community.

Gritz continued to maintain an organization in Sandy Valley, Nevada, called the Center for Action, broadcasting a short-wave radio show, "Freedom Calls." In September 1998, after his wife had filed for a divorce, Gritz was found lying by a remote road in rural Idaho, suffering from a self-inflicted gunshot wound. He survived the incident. *See also* RUBY RIDGE; UNITED NATIONS; WACO, TEXAS, RAID.

Further Reading: Aaron Delwiche, "Propaganda Examples: James Bo Gritz," <www.carmen. artsci.washington.edu/propaganda/gritz.htm>; Bo Gritz Web site <www.bogritz.com>; *The Militia Watchdog*, "Patriot Purgatory: Bo Gritz and Almost Heaven," <www.militia-watchdog.org/gritz.htm>.

Gun Buyback Programs

Gun buyback programs have been established in some cities to decrease the number of firearms, reduce gun-related criminal activity, and prevent gun accidents, particularly involving children. Such programs have gained support in the international community as a way of decreasing tensions in nations facing civil unrest. Gun rights supporters have responded to gun buyback programs with skepticism about their effectiveness and with concern that a political message is being conveyed that guns, independent of the human beings who use them, are evil. Although gun buyback programs appear to have had little impact on the level of crime and violence, and gun rights supporters object to the program's assumption that firearms are themselves dangerous and possibly worthy of confiscation, supporters hope to have some impact, however minimal, on what they consider to be a serious social problem, and to raise general public awareness of the problem of gun violence.

Gun buyback programs have been attempted in such cities as Houston, Dallas and Fort Worth, Los Angeles, Buffalo, and Boston. In 1994, a program in Baltimore, Maryland, offered $100 for each working handgun surrendered. One thousand guns were gathered during the first day of the offer, depleting funds devoted to the buyback program. The city continued the buyback program after a private citizen donated additional funds, but decreased the offer to $50 per gun.

In November 1995, Texans Against Gun Violence conducted a gun buyback program in Houston, called "Operation Safe and Secure." Participants could exchange a firearm for a gift certificate worth a minimum of $50 in merchandise at two local retail outlets. Residents at participating apartment complexes could receive a voucher for $100 toward their rent. Those turning in firearms also received tickets to a Houston Aeros hockey game. This in-kind payment avoided the criticism leveled at cash payment programs because the funds could not be used to purchase drugs or additional firearms. For instance, a program in Baton Rouge, Louisiana, offered cash for guns, which, according to some reports, encouraged some participants to purchase inexpensive firearms and redeem them for more than their value. Supporters believe that even though some cheating may occur, the programs have led participants to turn in guns kept in the home that could result in accidental shootings.

The Houston buyback program, which was funded by donations from local businesses, collected 133 weapons, including small-caliber handguns, rifles, and shotguns, some of which were reported to have sawed-off barrels. Civilian volunteers conducted the operation, in part to assure participants that they would not be arrested for illegal possession of a firearm. Organizers of the program indicated that weapons would be melted down to prevent them from re-entering society.

Further Reading: Julie Mason, "No Questions About Guns: Participants in Buyback Won't Face Police Scrutiny," *Houston Chronicle* (November 18, 1995), 40A; Mike Tolson, "Program Collects 133 Weapons: Houston's First Gun Buyback Also Draws Group of Protestors," *Houston Chronicle* (November 19, 1995), 42A.

Gun Control Act of 1968

The Gun Control Act of 1968 was the first major piece of gun control legislation to be enacted since the Federal Firearms Act of 1938. The act was contained in two statutes: Titles IV and VII of the Omnibus Crime Control and Safe Streets Act (82 Stat. 225, 236), and the Gun Control Act (82 Stat. 1213). The act placed controls on those people engaged in the sale of firearms and essentially replaced the Federal Firearms Act of 1938.

The effort to pass a new gun control law began in 1963 when the Senate Judiciary Committee considered a bill prohibiting mail-order sales of handguns to minors. The long trail of events leading to final passage in 1968 included several assassinations. After President John Kennedy was shot and killed in November 1963, supporters expanded the bill to include a ban on mail-order sales of shotguns and rifles. However, the lobbying efforts of anti-gun control forces, headed by the National Rifle Association (NRA), were successful in keeping the bill locked in committee.

Growing concern over violence led several states and municipalities to enact legislation of their own, which proved to be another impetus toward national action. The assassinations of Martin Luther King, Jr., and Robert Kennedy in 1968 provided the crucial momentum toward congressional action. The legislation, the result of considerable compromise, pleased few. Those opposing gun control finally accepted the bill, fearing the possibility of even more rigorous provisions, and supporters were disappointed that stronger restrictions were not included.

Among its provisions, the legislation strengthened the firearms licensing process to limit foreign and interstate transport of firearms to legitimate manufacturers, dealers, and importers. The act prohibited the interstate shipment of pistols and revolvers to private individuals. Gun buyers could only purchase a handgun in the state in which they resided. The licensing fee for federal firearms dealers was increased from $1 to $10 and minors were forbidden from receiving a license. Dealers could not sell rifles, shotguns, or ammunition to anyone under 18, or pistols and ammunition to anyone under 21. Dealers and collectors were required to keep more complete records. The legislation prohibited importation of foreign military surplus firearms, except those used in hunting, and extended the National Firearms Act of 1934 by requiring registration and a transfer tax on such "destructive devices" as anti-tank guns, bazookas, and mortars.

Focusing on criminal activity, the act forbade convicted felons, the mentally incompetent, and drug addicts from shipping or receiving weapons via interstate commerce, and licensed dealers could not knowingly sell weapons to these categories of people. Anyone who used a firearm to commit a crime that involved breaking a federal law was subject to additional punishment, which included a minimum of one year in prison. Although the legislation represented a significant step forward for those advocating gun control, the measure failed to meet Democratic President Lyndon Johnson's primary objective: to require national registration and licensing of firearms. *See also* DODD, THOMAS J.; FEDERAL FIREARMS ACT; FIREARMS OWNERS PROTECTION ACT; NATIONAL FIREARMS ACT; NATIONAL RIFLE ASSOCIATION.

Further Reading: Lee Kennett and James La Verne Anderson, *The Gun in America: The Origins of a National Dilemma* (Westport, CT: Greenwood, 1975); Earl R. Kruschke, *Gun Control* (Santa Barbara, CA: ABC-CLIO, 1995); Robert J. Spitzer, *The Politics of Gun Control* (Chatham, NY: Chatham, 1995).

Gun Control Resource Center (GCRC)

The Gun Control Resource Center (GCRC), a Web site located at Temple University in Philadelphia, Pennsylvania, advertises itself as "a starting point for those seeking information about handgun violence in America." The site describes American culture as "steeped in violence." In that context, a person requires "a lot of courage" not to possess a firearm and anyone who refuses to own a gun deserves commendation. The GCRC's major goal is "to reduce the bloodshed" produced by firearms.

The GCRC looks favorably on the policies other nations have instituted to reduce gun violence, including Great Britain's 1997 ban on the possession of handguns, and Australia's prohibition of pump-action shotguns and certain types of assault weapons and establishment of a gun registration system. The site claims that Japan, Colombia, India, and Russia have blamed the United

States for the firearms smuggled across their borders.

The GCRC supports passage of gun control legislation that would require licensing of handgun owners and registration of handgun sales and transfers, limit handgun purchases to one per month, mandate gun safety training for gun owners, ban the sale of Saturday night specials, and require such safety features as ammunition load indicators. The bill would grant authority to the Bureau of Alcohol, Tobacco, and Firearms (BATF) to regulate firearm and ammunition safety, to ban the sale of firearms that were deemed unsafe, and to create a clearinghouse to gather and analyze information about firearms-related deaths and injuries.

The GCRC publicizes the "gun owner's bill of responsibilities," which includes the following provisions: use maximum care when handling a firearm, take a safety course once a year, store firearms securely to prevent accidents or theft, and support legislative proposals to keep guns away from criminals. The GCRC has shown sympathy for the call for a ban on the sale or possession of all handguns as a way of reducing violence. *See also* BRADY HANDGUN VIOLENCE PREVENTION ACT; BUREAU OF ALCOHOL, TOBACCO, AND FIREARMS; JAPAN; RUSSIA; SATURDAY NIGHT SPECIAL; UNITED KINGDOM.

Further Reading: Gun Control Resource Center Web site <http://astro.ocis.temple.edu/~hunka/handgun.html>.

Gun Culture

The term "gun culture" has been used to refer to the strong American attraction to firearms. Proponents of gun control have used the term pejoratively to explain what they consider the extremely serious problem of firearms violence in the United States and to offer a reason for the strong resistance to effective firearms legislation, while gun rights supporters use the term to indicate what they consider the long and honorable American tradition of firearms ownership. In 1970, historian Richard Hofstadter identified the origin of the American gun culture in the history of the nation. Early settlers who expanded the frontier westward needed firearms to shoot wild game and farmers used guns to shoot vermin and predatory animals. Hofstadter noted that in 1675–76 Indians "damaged half the towns of New England, destroyed a dozen, and killed an estimated one out of every sixteen males of military age among the settlers." In such a dangerous environment, the firearm became a necessity of life.

By the time of the American Revolution, Americans had become adept at the use of firearms and that experience contributed significantly to the colonists' success in revolutionary battles. According to Hofstadter, British troops became so fearful of the hunter's marksmanship that General George Washington asked his troops to dress in hunting shirts to terrorize the enemy. Although Washington had little faith in the militia and preferred to rely instead on the regular army, Americans became convinced that the minutemen had demonstrated their military superiority over the professional soldiers upon which the decadent nations of Europe relied.

Despite the popular view that developed about the use of firearms during the Revolution, historian Michael A. Bellesiles (1996) has noted that Americans in the early 19th century were largely uninterested in gun ownership and use. In the early years of the nation, the federal government largely failed in its efforts to increase citizen participation in militias and to encourage gun ownership. Following the Civil War, Union soldiers were allowed to keep their firearms and, with declining gun prices that followed decreased government demand, weapon ownership in the civilian population became far more common. The Civil War also established the general belief that firearms were necessary for the preservation of an orderly society, an important element of the gun culture.

In addition to the influence of the Civil War on the development of an American gun culture, Hosftadter claimed that before the development of the entertainment industry and organized competitive sports, hunting and fishing became major pastimes. For many American youth, receiving their first real rifle

Although gun control advocates use the term "gun culture" to describe the problem of violent crime in the U.S., supporters of the right to bear arms, such as this man protesting anti-NRA demonstrations in Denver in May 1999, use the term to describe what they consider the long and honorable American tradition of firearms ownership. *Corbis/AFP.*

symbolized passage to manhood. However, while some have argued that the gun is so important to Americans because it is a symbol of masculinity, Hosfstadter responded that this claim does not explain why men in other societies did not come to associate firearms with masculinity.

Although the percentage of the nation's population engaged in farming declined markedly, the gun remained a prevalent feature in American life. Hostadter attributed this phenomenon partially to basic political beliefs: the fear of a standing army as a threat to liberty and a continuing "faith in the civic virtue and military prowess of the yeoman." The firearm, which played such a crucial role in settling the West and defending settlers against the Indian, entered popular culture through novels, movies, and, ultimately, television. Hofstadter observed a unique tendency in the United States to prefer "the isolated, wholly individualistic detective, sheriff, or villain," and to resolve conflicts through "ready and ingenious violence." The Second Amendment came to be regarded as guaranteeing a basic individual right to keep and bear arms, despite the tendency of the courts to interpret the amendment in terms of the need for a well regulated militia.

Hofstadter identified as an ingredient in the notion of a gun culture the belief that ac-

cess to firearms served as an important deterrent to tyranny. In 1970, Hofstadter disputed an argument gun rights advocates have used more recently–that gun control laws in Nazi Germany contributed to the establishment of tyranny–contending that the Weimar Republic failed to respond decisively to Nazi terror tactics. According to Hofstadter, "It is not strong and firm governments but weak ones, incapable of exerting their regulatory and punitive powers, that are overthrown by tyrannies." Contrary to the prevailing gun culture, which holds that firearms in private hands provide a basic defense of freedom, Hofstadter considered the presence of groups of individuals in possession of arms a threat to public order.

The recognition of underlying cultural beliefs about firearms help to explain the deep-seated disagreements that exist in the American debate over gun control. While proponents of stronger gun control, such as Hofstadter, identify a disturbing pattern of attitudes toward the use of firearms in the United States, gun rights advocates find a similarly emotional belief system among gun opponents. Gun rights supporters claim that gun control advocates want to brand all firearms as evil in and of themselves, regardless of the person using them. *See also* AMERICAN REVOLUTION; MINUTEMEN, REVOLUTIONARY; NATIVE AMERICANS; SECOND AMENDMENT.

Further Reading: Michael A. Bellesiles, "The Origins of Gun Culture in the United States, 1760–1865," *Journal of American History* 83 (September 1998), 425–455. Richard Hofstadter, "America as a Gun Culture," *American Heritage* (October 1970), 4-11, 82-85; David Kopel, *The Samurai, the Mountie, and the Cowboy* (Buffalo, NY: Prometheus, 1992).

Gun-Free Schools Act

Co-sponsored by Senators Dianne Feinstein, Democrat of California, and Byron Dorgan, Democrat of North Dakota, the Gun-Free Schools Act was signed by President Bill Clinton in October 1994 as part of the Elementary and Secondary Education Act. The Education Act provided $12 billion in federal funding for public schools for the next

TABLE 8

NUMBER OF STUDENTS EXPELLED FOR GUN-FREE SCHOOLS ACT VIOLATIONS PER 1,000 STUDENTS OF THE SCHOOL-AGE POPULATION, 1996–1997

State	Number of Students Expelled in 1996-97	School-Age Population 1996	Expelled Students Per 1,000 of Pop.
Alabama	91	780,000	0.117
Alaska	19	135,000	0.141
Arizona	152	807,000	0.188
Arkansas	62	484,000	0.128
California	723	6,132,000	0.118
Colorado	475	728,000	0.652
Connecticut	19	575,000	0.033
Delaware	7	126,000	0.056
Florida	202	2,467,000	0.082
Georgia	244	1,401,000	0.174
Hawaii	0	215,000	0.000
Idaho	33	258,000	0.128
Illinois	250	2,241,000	0.112
Indiana	109	1,089,000	0.100
Iowa	40	537,000	0.074
Kansas	43	507,000	0.085
Kentucky	70	710,000	0.099
Louisiana	88	906,000	0.097
Maine	13	228,000	0.057
Maryland	73	927,000	0.079
Massachusetts	54	1,031,000	0.052
Michigan	92	1,865,000	0.049
Minnesota	18	931,000	0.019
Mississippi	11	552,000	0.020
Missouri	318	1,027,000	0.310
Montana	12	177,000	0.068
Nebraska	20	329,000	0.061
Nevada	54	293,000	0.184
New Hampshire	15	220,000	0.068
New Jersey	57	1,415,000	0.040
New Mexico	71	365,000	0.195
New York	128	3,220,000	0.040
North Carolina	163	1,321,000	0.123
North Dakota	1	127,000	0.008
Ohio	937	2,089,000	0.449
Oklahoma	0	653,000	0.000
Oregon	85	597,000	0.142
Pennsylvania	200	2,133,000	0.094
Rhode Island	7	172,000	0.041
South Carolina	94	684,000	0.137
South Dakota	7	153,000	0.046
Tennessee	98	958,000	0.102
Texas	532	3,870,000	0.137
Utah	80	490,000	0.163
Vermont	5	111,000	0.045
Virginia	92	1,777,000	0.052
Washington	146	1,051,000	0.139
West Virginia	27	315,000	0.086
Wisconsin	54	1,006,000	0.054
Wyoming	0	102,000	0.000

Source: Report on State Implementation of the Gun-Free School Acts—School Year 1996–97 (Washington, DC: U.S. Department of Education, 1998), Table 1.

five years, the receipt of which was made dependent on a school's adherence to the provisions of the Gun-Free Schools Act. The act was a response to the perception that violence had increased significantly in American schools and that too many students were taking guns to school. It is an attempt to establish national standards for dealing with instances of gun-carrying by students on school property.

The provisions of the law require schools to expel for a least one year any student found carrying a firearm. In addition, each school is required to report to their state education agencies any incidents involving a student carrying a gun. Schools are to include in their reports the number of occurrences and the types of guns involved. Although state and local governments may have their own policies regarding gun-carrying in schools, the federal law provides a minimum standard for such policies. Although the law requires public schools receiving federal funding to abide by its provisions, individual schools may alter the expulsion policy in response to local circumstances. Table 8 provides data on the enforcement of the Gun-Free Schools Act for the 1996–1997 school year.

Americans have traditionally preferred a decentralized system of public education. Not only have states assumed the primary role in school policy, but in some states, local school districts enjoy considerable autonomy. In 1994, when the Gun-Free Schools Act was approved, all states had some form of expulsion guidelines for their school districts. These policies ranged from suspension for being caught with a gun at school to a one-year expulsion. Some states had no express policy regarding the discovery of weapons at school, or had not specified a period of expulsion. The Los Angeles Unified School District had formulated an expulsion policy, but with no stated minimum length of time. Maryland allowed county boards to establish suspension, expulsion, and other disciplinary policies on a county-by-county basis. New York authorized the board of education of each school district to enact provisions for suspension and expulsion. Texas law provided

for a student's expulsion for, among other things, possessing a firearm, an illegal knife, or other prohibited weapons while present at school or attending a school-sponsored event.

While supporters of the legislation believe its merits are obvious, some proponents of the defensive use of firearms contend that gun-free schools become easy targets for those wanting to harm students and teachers. In a 1998 *Wall Street Journal* article, John Lott stated that "attempts to outlaw guns from schools, no matter how well meaning, have backfired. Instead of making schools safe for children, we have made them safe for those intent on harming our children." However, it is not clear what the consequences might be of a policy that allowed people other than trained security officers to carry guns at school. *See also* CLINTON, WILLIAM JEFFERSON (BILL); FEINSTEIN, DIANNE; LOTT, JOHN R., JR.

Further Reading: Dianne Feinstein, "Gun-Free Schools Act," *Fact Sheet*, Washington, DC, 1998 A14; Dianne Feinstein Web <site www.senate.gov/~feinstein>; John Lott, "The Real Lessons of the School Shootings," *Wall Street Journal* (March 27, 1998); Beth Sinclair, Jennifer Hamilton, Babette Gutman, Julie Daft, and Dee Bolick, *Report on State Implementation of the Gun-Free Schools Act–School Year 1996-1997*, Final Report (Washington, DC: U.S. Department of Education, 1998).

Gun Journal

Since 1991, the Collector Arms Dealers Association (CADA) has sponsored the *Gun Journal*, which is published monthly by Blue Book Publications, Inc. The magazine appeals to serious gun collectors. The editor encourages readers to join firearms organizations, attend gun shows, read about gun collections, keep their own gun collections in good condition, stay abreast of the classified ads, and check the Web sites for information about antique firearms. The magazine contains a list of firearms sites on the Internet. The bulk of the publication includes classified advertisements for various categories of antique firearms, providing a wealth of information for the collector. The editors often publish articles on the history of guns in the United States and worldwide.

In addition to the extensive classified column, the magazine contains advertisements for Blue Book Publications, including books dealing with combat shotguns, Colt firearms, single shot rifles, and Spencer repeating firearms. Another section titled "Auction Update" reports on recent auction sales of antique arms. The sale prices, which range from a few thousand dollars up to as much as $20,000, provide incentives for collectors to be on the watch for that especially valuable serendipitous find. Also included are several pages of advertisements for gun shows around the nation at which antique arms and other gun products can be purchased or traded.

In the March 1998 issue, Chris Wolf, in an article titled "How Bad Can It Get?," warned of the imminent confiscation of all firearms in the United States. He compared government policy toward guns to laws regulating smoking and predicted that just like cigarettes, guns will be branded a health hazard. Wolf argued that just as government has determined to control the loss of lives and wealth related to smoking, the same will be done with firearms. The author associated the anti-gun crusade with liberalism, but quickly tied that more moderate ideology with communism. In explaining and criticizing the desire to control guns, he used such terms as democratic socialism, liberalists, liberal moralist dictatorship, and moralist puritanism. Wolf stated that he fears a puritanical regime that will ban all firearms in the United States, following the pattern he saw occurring in Canada, Great Britain, and Australia. A Canadian himself, Wolf expressed his displeasure with the Royal Canadian Mounted Police, who are enforcing the new gun control provisions in Canada. He predicted that firearms periodicals will disappear as they are subjected to pressures to be "politically correct" and fail to gain advertising. He predicted that the whole economy would be adversely affected by government restrictions on the manufacture and sale of firearms.

Articles on gun control take fervent stands against laws that limit the right to possess firearms. *Gun Journal* portrays collectors' interests in guns to be far removed from any criminal activity and strongly opposes government regulation or restrictions on collectors' activities. The magazine presents the image of antique gun collectors as enthusiastic participants in a hobby and business who wish that the government would leave them alone in their honest and peaceful activities. The publication considers government interference by such agencies as the Bureau of Alcohol, Tobacco, and Firearms (BATF) to be not only inconvenient but illegitimate. *See also* AUSTRALIA; BUREAU OF ALCOHOL, TOBACCO, AND FIREARMS; CANADA; COLT, SAMUEL; UNITED KINGDOM.

Further Reading: *Gun Journal* (Blue Book Publications, Inc., Minneapolis, MN).

Gun News Digest (GND)

Gun News Digest (GND) is a publication of the Second Amendment Foundation. Alan M. Gottlieb, Massad Ayoob, and Joseph P. Tartaro, members of the Foundation's board of trustees and strong pro-gun advocates, were instrumental in establishing the magazine in 1994. The pages of *GND* are devoted almost exclusively to promoting the right to keep and bear arms. Published quarterly, the magazine contains minimal advertising, but entries often refer to specific firearms manufacturers and products.

Each issue of *GND* contains an editorial that introduces the major subjects discussed in that issue, thus establishing the overall pro-gun position of the publication. A "Reader Feedback" column publishes letters from readers on various topics related to the debate over gun control. A "News Briefs" section summarizes gun-related news stories from the previous three months. The news stories cover state legislative and gubernatorial activities and initiatives. Other topics include the use of guns to deter criminals and updates on presidential and congressional gun control proposals.

The magazine has focused on the attacks gun control groups have made on so-called Saturday night special handguns. In "What's So Special About Saturday Night?," which appeared in the Winter 1997–1998 issue, Robert Hausman claimed that the basic objective of banning such handguns is the disarming of the poor. Contrary to the general impression that Saturday night specials are weapons of choice for criminals, Hausman stated that, "Among the principal buyers of these firearms are tens of thousands of members of law-enforcement." They are the "first choice" of the general public and police officers who use them as back-up weapons and off-duty arms.

The internal politics of the pro-gun movement receives detailed attention. Each year *GND* provides extensive coverage of the Gun Rights Policy Conference, an annual meeting of pro-gun researchers sponsored by the Citizens Committee for the Right to Keep and Bear Arms (CCRKBA) and the Second Amendment Foundation. *GND* has reported on such Conference topics as criticism of the effort to portray firearms ownership as a public health question, the usefulness of so-called junk guns, and the value of education in saving children from gun violence.

GND reprinted resolutions adopted by the Twelfth Annual Gun Rights Policy Conference, including one affirming an absolutist position called the "NATO Doctrine," which declared that, "Any attack on one class of firearms or firearm owners shall be considered an attack on all classes of firearms or firearm owners, and shall be fought with all efforts and resources by the entire pro-gun community." *See also* AYOOB, MASSAD; CITIZENS COMMITTEE FOR THE RIGHT TO KEEP AND BEAR ARMS; GOTTLIEB, ALAN MERRIL; SATURDAY NIGHT SPECIAL; SECOND AMENDMENT FOUNDATION.

Further Reading: *Gun News Digest* (Second Amendment Foundation, Bellevue, WA).

Gun Owners

To determine their most likely sources of support, both gun rights and gun control groups need to identify those groups with the highest and lowest levels of gun ownership. According to the results of a 1998 survey reported in Figure 9, more men (43 percent) than women (30 percent) own firearms. A considerably larger percentage of whites own firearms (40 percent) than do blacks (20 percent). The most gun-owning age group includes those over 50 years old. High school graduates have a higher rate of gun ownership than either college graduates or those with less than a high school education.

People in various income categories have roughly equal levels of firearm ownership, except for those with incomes under $20,000, who have a significantly lower level of ownership. Those with incomes greater than $50,000 have the highest level of ownership. Farmers have the highest level of gun ownership among the occupations (72 percent) and those in service positions have the lowest (29 percent). Gun ownership tends to be highest in the South (42 percent) and lowest in the Northeast (22 percent). Among religious groups, Protestants have the highest level of gun ownership (42 percent) and Jews have the lowest (12 percent). Republicans have a higher level of gun ownership (46 percent) than Democrats (30 percent) or Independents (32 percent). See Table 9 for more data on gun ownership in the United States.

Further Reading: Gary Kleck, *Targeting Guns: Firearms and Their Control* (Hawthorne, NY: Aldine De Gruyter, 1997); John R. Lott, Jr., *More Guns, Less Crime: Understanding Gun-Control Laws* (Chicago: University Press, 1998).

Gun Owners' Action League (GOAL)

The Gun Owners' Action League (GOAL) is the state firearms association of Massachusetts, the state with possibly the most stringent firearms legislation. The organization describes itself as "an association of law-abiding citizens who believe in the basic right of firearms ownership for competition, recreation, and self-protection." GOAL, a strong critic of state gun control provisions, initiated a legal challenge to the Massachusetts Gun Violence Prevention Law in October 1998, the day the provision went into effect. Michael Yacino, executive director of GOAL, declared that the Massachusetts statute is "too vague to understand, too obscure to enforce, and too unintelligible to obey." The organization expressed its concern regarding what

TABLE 9

FIREARM OWNERSHIP

By demographic characteristics, United States, 1998.
Question: "Do you happen to have in your home (or garage) any guns or revolvers?" If yes, "Is it a pistol, shotgun, rifle, or what?"

| | Firearm in the home | | Type of firearm | | |
	No	Yes	Pistol	Shotgun	Rifle
National					
	65%	35%	20%	21%	21%
Gender					
Male	57	43	25	28	26
Female	70	30	16	15	17
Race					
White	60	40	22	25	24
Black	80	20	12	7	8
Other	89	11	7	6	7
Ages					
18-29 years	77	23	13	15	12
30-39 years	67	33	17	18	19
40-49 years	57	42	24	25	26
50-59 years	57	43	27	25	28
60-69 years	59	41	22	28	26
70 years and over	68	32	17	19	17
Education					
Less than high school	65	34	17	22	19
High school graduate	57	43	24	24	25
Some college	65	35	22	22	21
College graduate	74	26	13	14	17
Post college	72	28	18	17	19
Family Income					
Under $20,000	78	22	12	11	12
$20,000 to $29,999	68	32	18	17	17
$30,000 to $49,999	58	42	23	24	24
$50,000 and over	56	43	27	29	29
Occupation					
Manager/professional	68	32	19	18	20
Technical/sales/					
admin support	67	33	19	19	20
Service	71	29	17	17	14
Farming/fishing/					
forestry/logging	28	72	24	48	48
Production/craft	47	53	31	35	35
Operator/laborer	60	39	18	25	21
Region					
Northeast	77	22	9	13	16
Midwest	62	37	17	24	20
South	58	42	27	26	24
West	68	32	19	16	21
Religious Preference					
Protestant	58	42	23	26	26
Catholic	72	27	15	16	17
Jewish	88	12	12	3	3
None	73	26	17	14	13
Other	81	19	10	14	14
Political Party					
Democrat	70	30	17	14	16
Independent	68	32	18	19	17
Republican	54	46	26	32	33
Other party	63	37	19	26	23

Note: Percentage of respondents who reported having a pistol, shotgun, or rifle add to more than the overall percentage answering yes because some respondents reported having more than one type of firearm.

Source: National Opinion Research Center—General Social Survey 1998 Data File (The Roper Center for Public Opinion Research at the University of Connecticut).

it considered "fuzzy descriptions" of assault weapons, large capacity firearms, and feeding devices. Due to vagueness in the law, GOAL claimed that Massachusetts firearms owners could not be sure if they are complying with its provisions.

GOAL's headquarters, located in Northboro, Massachusetts, has a full-time staff. The executive director oversees the organization's various activities, including fund raising, publishing, and legislative work, and manages the office. A board of directors, elected by the membership, establishes organization policy. GOAL emphasizes various educational programs and advocates teaching children safety and responsibility in handling firearms. Members have encouraged use of the National Rifle Association's (NRA) Eddie Eagle Gun Safety Program in Massachusetts elementary schools. GOAL provides firearms training courses for older youths. Organization representatives speak at schools about firearms ownership and the association makes available information packets to students. GOAL provides information to adults about national, state, and local firearms laws and distributes a booklet about Massachusetts gun regulations.

Association members receive a directory of state legislators and information on candidates for public office and their positions on firearms policy. Candidates are invited to speak to organization members in their districts to express their views on firearms issues. Each year the organization conducts a Firearms Safety and Education Day for state legislators, assistant district attorneys, media people, and administration officials who are offered personal instruction in safe firearms handling. GOAL has a professional lobbyist at the state capital to monitor the progress of firearms-related legislation and court cases.

GOAL presents its views on firearms issues to the general public through the dissemination of literature and video tapes. The organization maintains a speakers bureau for presentations before various civic groups. GOAL publishes a monthly newsletter, *The Message*, which contains information about politics and legislative activities as well as sporting news and advertisements for products. The newsletter contains a calendar of shooting competitions, sporting events, gun shows, and firearms courses. GOAL supports a weekly radio program, The GOAL Line, which deals with firearms issues, hunting topics, and various sports subjects. *See also* EDDIE EAGLE; GUN SHOWS; MASSACHUSETTS GUN VIOLENCE PREVENTION LAW; NATIONAL RIFLE ASSOCIATION; STATE GUN STATUTES.

Further Reading: Gun Owners Action League Web site <www.goal.org>; "Suit Challenges Massachusetts Gun Law," *Gun Week* 33 (November 10, 1998).

Gun Owners of America (GOA)

Established in 1975 by California state senator H. L. "Bill" Richardson, Gun Owners of America (GOA) strives to preserve what it considers an individual right to keep and bear arms. The organization identifies its membership as "patriotic Americans working together to preserve the right to keep and bear arms, protecting and safeguarding our Constitutional freedoms for future generations," and prides itself on being the most uncompromising anti-gun control organization in the U.S. The organization claims to have invested more money than any other group in the successful fight to pass the Firearms Owners' Protection Act of 1986, and takes credit for being the only organization to have fought to repeal the Brady Handgun Violence Prevention Act's background check requirement. GOA also advocates the right of law-abiding citizens to carry a firearm without a permit.

Three other organizations are associated with the GOA. Gun Owners of America Victory Fund is the GOA's political action committee. This organization raises funds to be donated to candidates for public office at all levels of government who support the right of gun ownership. Also associated with the GOA is Gun Owners of California, an entity that is active only in the state of California. It was founded by Bill Richardson to deal with any issues concerning firearms that arise in that state. Gun Owners Foundation is the non-profit educational arm of the GOA to

GUN
OWNERS
OF AMERICA

The logo of the Gun Owners of America, one of the country's leading pro-gun rights groups. *UPI/Corbis-Bettmann.*

which supporters can make tax deductible contributions. The Foundation organizes seminars that are intended to inform the media, government officials, and the general public about Second Amendment issues, and is a source of books and other publications dealing with gun issues.

The Gun Owners, the GOA's newsletter, includes articles about current legislation being considered at the national, state, and local levels. Sample headlines from the newsletter indicate the concerns of the organization: "Senate Crime Bill Threatens to Put Second Amendment Out of Business" (April 25, 1997), "New Gun Ban Stripping Self-Defense Right from Millions–GOA Continues Offensive Against Onerous Law" (February 28, 1997), and "Congress 'Ganging Up' on the Bill of Rights" (June 20, 1997). The organization's general theme is that the right to privacy of law-abiding citizens is threatened by gun laws, and that these citizens face unwarranted arrest and imprisonment simply for trying to defend themselves. *The Gun Owners* reports the votes of senators and representatives on measures of concern to the organization.

The GOA interprets any measure to control firearms as an attempt to take away the guns of law-abiding citizens. For instance, in the 1980s, when the Bureau of Alcohol, Tobacco, and Firearms (BATF) was giving school children who visited the Department of the Treasury cards designating them honorary agents of the Bureau, GOA executive director Larry Pratt warned that the Bureau was encouraging children to spy on their parents and neighbors.

The GOA engages in a number of activities to further its objective of preventing the passage of gun control legislation. The organization conducts surveys of the membership, the results of which are sent to congresspeople and the president to inform them about the attitudes of gun owners. A 1997 GOA fact sheet argues for the self-defense value of firearms ("Guns save more lives than they take; prevent more injuries than they inflict"), claims that the Brady law has been unsuccessful, and insists that licensing or registration of firearms leads inevitably to confiscation.

Members who have access to fax machines can use GOA's Fax Alert Network (FAN), which distributes up-to-date information on gun legislation proposals. The GOA provides its membership with Candidate Rating Guides each general election year, in which candidates are rated on their support of gun owners. At the local level, the organization maintains a field staff that attends town meetings and state legislative sessions where gun control measures may arise. In this way, the Washington, D.C., headquarters of the GOA can be kept informed of any proposals that local gun control groups are attempting to have passed. The GOA also maintains a Legal Defense Program that provides assistance to gun owners who find themselves involved in a legal action with the government. Although a smaller organization, the GOA has played an active role in opposing gun control legislation. *See also* BRADY HANDGUN VIOLENCE PREVENTION ACT; BUREAU OF ALCOHOL, TOBACCO, AND FIREARMS; FIREARMS OWNERS PROTECTION ACT; PRATT, LARRY; SECOND AMENDMENT.

Further Reading: Josh Sugarmann, *National Rifle Association: Money, Firepower and Fear* (Washington, DC: National Press, 1992); Gun Owners of America "Firearms Fact-Sheet" (membership brochure, 1997); Gun Owners of America, *The Gun Owners* (monthly newsletter); Gun Owners of America Web site <www.gun-owners.org>.

Gun Rights Policy Conference (GRPC)

The Gun Rights Policy Conference (GRPC) is an annual meeting of firearms rights activists representing national and state gun organizations and scholars who support the right to keep and bear arms. Begun in 1986, the Conference is sponsored by the Second Amendment Foundation (SAF) and the Citizens Committee for the Right to Keep and Bear Arms (CCRKBA) and includes such major pro-gun advocates as Alan Gottlieb, Joseph Tartaro, Don Kates, and David Kopel. Conference presentations deal with the major political issues confronting the gun rights movement, including mandatory trigger locks and other gun safety proposals, challenges to shooting ranges, the National Instant Check System to determine eligibility to purchase a firearm, the treatment of gun advocates in the media, and reciprocity for state concealed carry laws.

The thirteenth annual meeting of the GRPC was held in Seattle, Washington, in September 1998, an appropriate meeting place given the pro-gun movement's defeat of a 1997 ballot initiative in that state. Various gun-related organizations and companies, such as the American Firearms Council, the American Shooting Sports Council, Heckler and Koch, North American Arms, Smith and Wesson, and Beretta USA provided financial assistance for holding the conference.

U.S. Senator Larry Craig, an Idaho Republican, delivered the keynote address; he emphasized constitutional rights and the individual right to keep and bear arms. Referring to the Clinton administration, Craig stated that "if they succeed in their mission of disarming Americans' will to defend themselves, then they will have gotten our guns." The senator claimed that gun control advocates believe firearms owners are criminals and "less than American." Craig referred to the right to bear arms "the first right above all rights, the right of self-preservation and self-defense." Sally Brodbeck, a National Rifle Association (NRA) board member, speaking at a panel on gun control measures, commented that, "Mandatory background checks and fingerprints for firearms purchases, mandatory trigger locks, 'smart' guns, or one-gun-a-month limitations–even instant check–are all prior restraint on a Constitutional right."

At a panel on United Nations efforts to introduce international control over small arms, NRA board member Irv Benzion stated that the greatest external danger confronting the gun rights movement is gun control proposals emanating from the United Nations. The 1998 conference approved a resolution advocating that the United States government "provide no funds or support of any kind to the United Nations or to any of its entities or subdivisions" until that international organization ceases to support policies contrary to "the traditional, individual right of law-abiding American citizens to keep and bear arms." *See also* AMERICAN FIREARMS COUNCIL; CITIZENS COMMITTEE FOR THE RIGHT TO KEEP AND BEAR ARMS; CLINTON, WILLIAM JEFFERSON (BILL); CONCEALED CARRY LAWS; CRAIG, LARRY E.; GOTTLIEB, ALAN MERRIL; KATES, DON B.; KOPEL, DAVID B.; NATIONAL INSTANT CHECK SYSTEM; NATIONAL RIFLE ASSOCIATION; SECOND AMENDMENT FOUNDATION; TRIGGER LOCKS; UNITED NATIONS.

Further Reading: Nancy Norell, "1998 GRPC Celebrates Victory, Looks to Future Challenges," *Gun News Digest* 3 (Winter 1998-99), 10-25; Jim Schneider, "12th Annual Gun Rights Policy Conference," *Gun New Digest* 3 (Winter 1997-98), 26-39.

Gun Shows

In recent years, the United States has experienced a proliferation of gun shows, also called sportsmen shows, expos, arms shows, or weapons fairs. In 1998, over 1,200 shows were scheduled throughout the United States. This number is an underestimate because it does not include events in smaller towns and cities. Usually occurring on the weekend, these shows attract large numbers of people who, for a relatively small admission fee, can view a wide variety of products. The National Rifle Association (NRA) often has a booth established just outside the arena, offering free admission to those who join the organization.

Gun shows display a wide variety of handguns, rifles, and shotguns, both new and used. The participant can find in one place a vast display of firearms that far exceeds the inventory of any one gun shop. By purchasing a used handgun, a buyer can avoid the Brady Act's background check because only new weapons are covered under the statute. However, President Bill Clinton has proposed closing this loophole in federal regulations. Collectors of antique firearms also congregate at these shows, trading, purchasing, or selling weapons. A show may also include an auction of collectable firearms.

Other items on display include knives and military memorabilia, especially German equipment from World War II. Booths offer a wide variety of literature to attendees, including used books and magazines. In addition to standard treatments of firearms, books and pamphlets deal with such topics as converting a semi-automatic weapon to fully automatic, with the disclaimer that the activity is forbidden by federal law. Gun safe manufacturers have prominent displays. Booths offering merchandise less directly related to firearms, such as jewelry, clothing, and popular art, can also be found at gun shows. Other defense items besides firearms are available, including pepper spray and other non-lethal weapons.

Until recently, agents of the Bureau of Alcohol, Tobacco, and Firearms (BATF) frequently observed the happenings at gun shows to determine if any illegal gun activity was occurring. However, with pressure being placed on the agency, such surveillance has lessened. Gun shows are large economic enterprises, and the National Association of Arms Shows (NAAS), the official organization representing businesses and individuals promoting weapons fairs, has a strong interest in the survival of gun shows and their continued operation unhampered by official limitations.

Members of NAAS meet annually and deal with issues of concern to gun show promoters. NAAS officials make presentations on such topics as obtaining favorable press coverage for gun shows and taking part in legislative lobbying and relevant court cases. Participants share information about the difficulties encountered from national, state, and local governments when attempting to organize and conduct shows. *See also* BRADY HANDGUN VIOLENCE PREVENTION ACT; BUREAU OF ALCOHOL, TOBACCO, AND FIREARMS; CLINTON, WILLIAM JEFFERSON (BILL); COLLECTORS; NATIONAL RIFLE ASSOCIATION.

Further Reading: *Gun Show Calendar* 11 (January, February, March 1998) (Iola, WI: Krause Publications, 1997); Kristen Rand, *Gun Shows in America: Tupperware Parties for Criminals* (Washington, DC: Violence Policy Center, 1996).

Gun Week (GW)

Established in 1966, *Gun Week (GW)* magazine is a vocal advocate of gun rights and an avid opponent of attempts to institute gun control measures. The Second Amendment Foundation (SAF) publishes *GW* 36 times per year. Each issue is approximately 16 pages, printed on newsprint. Typical of other gun magazines, *GW* carries articles on new weapons, especially handguns, but contains less advertising. The magazine contains advertisements for gun shows and provides a list of events that will occur during the next month. Those conducting shows are invited to list the event free of charge in the pages of *GW*. Advertisements for various literature as well as other gun magazines appear in *GW*.

A column, "Industry News," by Robert M. Hausman, reports on occurrences in gun manufacturing, including corporation mergers and the introduction of new products, such as laser sighting systems, new handgun hunting ammunition, and innovative firearms. *GW* prints brief news stories for hunting enthusiasts, reporting on hunting activities in the various states. A classified advertising section begins with a disclaimer, part of which states that, "The legal ownership of machine guns, submachine guns, silencers and silencer-equipped firearms and most conversion parts or kits requires compliance with federal laws, plus compliance with any applicable state and local laws." Books dealing with various firearm subjects are regularly reviewed.

A large portion of each issue is devoted to the politics of gun control. Gun supporters are encouraged to make their views known to their congresspeople. *GW* suggests that supporters meet with their representatives in district offices when Congress is in recess. Attempts to thwart gun control measures at the state level are detailed. Reports of the internal politics of the National Rifle Association (NRA), including battles over the leadership of the organization, appear in the pages of *GW*. Legislators supporting the right to bear arms are given the opportunity to present their views.

GW reports on attempts to institute gun control measures, usually emphasizing what the magazine considers the folly of such proposals. For instance, in 1997, Nelson Kester of Fresno, California, owner of three Auto Mart dealerships, began a month-long buy-up of guns. *GW* reported that anyone purchasing a car would receive a $500 rebate by surrendering a gun, and persons who could not qualify for financing would receive $100 for a gun. The response, claimed *GW*, was so overwhelming that Kester had to suspend the program. The magazine reported that people who had just purchased a gun for much less turned it in for the $100. One person was quoted as saying that he would purchase five $20 guns with the money he received for turning in one firearm. By reporting such stories, *GW* emphasizes what it considers the foolishness of gun control mea-

sures. Other articles deal with such topics as the selection of federal judges, the Bureau of Alcohol, Tobacco, and Firearms (BATF), state and federal court rulings, and congressional policy on the gun trade. *See also* BUREAU OF ALCOHOL, TOBACCO, AND FIREARMS; GUN BUYBACK PROGRAMS; GUN SHOWS; NATIONAL RIFLE ASSOCIATION; SECOND AMENDMENT FOUNDATION.

Further Reading: *Gun Week* (Second Amendment Foundation, Buffalo, NY).

Gun World

Published monthly by Y-Visions Publishing, *Gun World* contains articles and columns that support the right of gun owners against attempts to enact gun control legislation. *Gun World* covers subjects that typically appear in gun magazines, including various hunting topics, reports on new gun products, and stories on various aspects of the gun industry, such as holster making and locking mechanisms. "Gun Spots," a report on a wide variety of products, appears throughout the magazine.

Editor Steve Comus writes a regular column titled "Editorial License," in which he defends the right to bear arms against the "evil interference" of government. According to Comus, citizens are always in danger of losing their freedoms, especially the Second Amendment guarantee of the right to keep and bear arms. Comus has touched on the policy of banning firearms from public housing, viewing this policy as racially motivated. He has also referred to the claimed racial origin of the term "Saturday night special." The editor warned of the government compilation of data and the efforts of "media elitists" who support gun control.

"Kopel's Komment," a regular column by gun rights advocate David Kopel, reports on current political events having to do with efforts to oppose gun control. Reporting on the defeat of a handgun licensing initiative in the state of Washington, Kopel mentioned that if the measure had passed, it would have required individuals to obtain a new license and submit to a new police investigation every five years. Kopel claimed that the measure was intended to "disarm as many people as possible," and therefore violated the Washington state constitution.

Charlton Heston, movie actor and president of the National Rifle Association (NRA), contributes articles to *Gun World*, as he does to other pro-gun magazines, reporting on legislative activities in Washington, D.C. Noting that 31 states presently have provisions allowing for the carrying of concealed weapons, and that permit holders are "among the most law-abiding people around," Heston has emphasized the importance of passing a law to establish a national right to carry concealed weapons. Heston warned against the increasing role of the federal government in law enforcement and the dissipation of state sovereignty and individual rights, urging readers to observe their legislators' voting behavior, and make choices accordingly at the next election. *See also* CONCEALED CARRY LAWS; HESTON, CHARLTON; KOPEL, DAVID; NATIONAL RIFLE ASSOCIATION; SATURDAY NIGHT SPECIAL; SECOND AMENDMENT; WASHINGTON, D.C.

Further Reading: *Gun World* (Y-Visions Publishing, Anaheim, CA).

Guns and Ammo (G&A)

Like *American Rifleman*, each issue of *Guns and Ammo (G&A)* contains articles that support the right to bear arms and oppose initiatives to regulate gun purchases, ownership, and use. Beginning its forty-second year in 1999, *G&A* is published monthly by the Petersen Publishing Companies, Inc. While not as obviously political as *American Rifleman*, the magazine contains regular features concerning gun policy. Most articles deal with topics related directly to firearms, including reports on new weapons, technical advances, tips for better shooting, and antique weapons, especially those used in the "Old West." The magazine is divided into sections by type of firearm: handgun, rifle, and shotgun. Interspersed among the articles are advertisements for handguns, rifles and rifle scopes, ammunition, collectible guns, knives, gun safes, and other paraphernalia related to firearms.

"Armed Response," a column similar to a feature in the *American Rifleman*, contains accounts submitted by readers relating their "use of a firearm to prevent a crime or save a life." Typically, the column describes an innocent citizen who succeeds in defusing a dangerous situation by relying on a handgun. Many of the stories involve the value of concealed carry laws.

Each month a column titled "Second Amendment" deals with topics related to the protection of what is considered to be the constitutionally guaranteed right of individuals to keep and bear arms. The December 1997 column was titled "Instant Check: A Trojan Horse." The author, Larry Pratt, labeled the Brady Act's instant registration and check system a "Trojan horse that gun banners will use later on to grab people's firearms." Unlike many gun advocates who welcomed an instant check as a substitute for the five-day waiting period, Pratt strongly opposed it, claiming that although the Brady law has not effectively kept guns out of the hands of criminals, the check procedure amounts to a national gun-owner registration system.

Another regular column, "From the Capitol," to which actor, pro-gun advocate, and National Rife Association (NRA) President Charlton Heston began to contribute in late 1997, chronicles the struggle over gun control measures in the national and state capitals. The column focuses its critiques on the major gun control advocates, such as Handgun Control, Inc. (HCI), President Bill Clinton, and Democratic Senators Barbara Boxer of California and Herb Kohl of Wisconsin. Heston has suggested that "young killers and thugs" should be locked up, not guns. Heston has focused on the importance of state legislatures, urging gun owners to communicate with their state legislators and to make their position felt in national and state elections: "Put your governor and statehouse on notice that you're paying attention to what they're doing and that you'll vote accordingly in the next election."

While not dealing overtly with gun control issues, the column "Personal Security" assumes that law-abiding citizens live in a dangerous world and therefore need to take appropriate steps to ensure self-defense. In the July 1997 issue, Jim Grover discussed the construction of a "safe room," a "personal haven to protect your family from intruders until reinforcements arrive." Requirements include a solid door that can be securely locked with dead bolts, a cellular phone, a fire extinguisher, and an appropriate firearm. The December 1997 column, titled "Be a Tough Nut to Crack," provided 20 steps to improve home security, such as installing 3M Scotchshield on ground-floor windows and buying a storage container that keeps handguns secure but accessible.

"Street Cop," written by Jim Fotis, executive director of the Law Enforcement Alliance of America, treats questions of firearms and gun rights from the perspective of law enforcement officers. Unlike many police organizations that have in recent years backed such gun control measures as the Brady Act, Fotis regards guns as an inappropriate target in the attempt to determine the causes of crime. In the January 1998 issue, Fotis claimed that Handgun Control, Inc., and other anti-gun organizations have tried to drive a wedge between pro-gun forces by characterizing law enforcement officials as supporters of gun control. *See also* AMERICAN RIFLEMAN; BOXER, BARBARA; BRADY HANDGUN VIOLENCE PREVENTION ACT; CLINTON, WILLIAM JEFFERSON (BILL); HANDGUN CONTROL, INC.; HESTON, CHARLTON; NATIONAL INSTANT CHECK SYSTEM; NATIONAL RIFLE ASSOCIATION; PRATT, LARRY; SECOND AMENDMENT.

Further Reading: *Guns and Ammo* (Petersen Publishing, Los Angeles, CA).

Guns Magazine (GM)

Guns Magazine (GM) contains articles opposing gun control measures and advocating the self-defense value of firearms. The magazine, which appears monthly, is published by Firearms Marketing Group. While opposing gun control legislation, *GM* prints a disclaimer informing readers that "Products mentioned or advertised may not be legal in all states or jurisdictions." The warning also states that "Firearms are dangerous and if used improperly may cause serious injury or death."

Each issue contains a letters column, titled "Crossfire," which includes communications from those who protest various gun control proposals in the United States and other nations. Although pro-gun interests generally oppose any suggestion of making gun locks mandatory, one writer expressed his enthusiasm for new gun locks on the market. *GM* and other gun magazines have carried advertisements for such gun locks.

Advertisements in *GM* include a wide variety of products and services, including knives, ammunition, concealed carry holsters, souvenir pistols (for instance, "The Audie Murphy Tribute .45,"), books and book clubs (for instance, the Military Book Club), gun security safes, rifle scopes, bullet proof vests, night vision viewers, gunsmith schools, and firearms training schools. Each issue contains classified advertisements, including sections for accessories, ammunition, books, collectibles, fireworks, guns and gun parts, knives and swords, military surplus, and police equipment. A "New Products" section presents brief descriptions of recently marketed items, such as pistol grips, ammunition, gun cases, holsters, and knives. Another column, "Guns Insider," by Scott Farrell, offers information about the gun industry and its products.

GM contains articles critical of proposed gun control measures that present research findings supporting the position of anti-gun control groups and questioning the findings of pro-gun control researchers such as David Hemenway, professor of health policy at the Harvard School of Public Health. For instance, a January 1998 article by Joanne Eisen and Paul Gallant, titled "A Product of the Incessant Fear Mongering," referred to Hemenway as a "prolific contributor to the junk-science medical literature on firearms and violence." Hemenway is suspected of wishing to ban firearms while advocating a variety of measures to make guns useless for self-defense, including such legal provisions as holding adults criminally liable for children's accidental deaths, taking the purchaser's thumb prints prior to acquiring a gun, and requiring trigger locks on new firearms. *See also* CONCEALED CARRY LAWS; HEMENWAY, DAVID; TRIGGER LOCKS.

Further Reading: *Guns Magazine* (San Diego, CA).

Gunshot Detection Technology (GDT)

Gunshot detection technology (GDT) may contribute to limiting illegal gun use without initiating additional gun control legislation. GDT involves the placement of sensors in urban areas to detect the sound of gunshots. Transmitters send information to a police dispatch center where a computer receives and reports the messages, indicating the location of the gunshot. On the basis of this information, a decision can then be made whether to send a police unit to the spot of the report. The sensors may be contained in boxes mounted on telephone or light poles or camouflaged as birdhouses or roof vents.

In 1997, a GDT study was conducted by the Center for Criminal Justice Research at the University of Cincinnati. In *Using Gunshot Detection Technology in High-Crime Areas* (1998), Lorraine Green Mazerolle, director of the Center, reported on the research findings. The Center conducted field trials involving two systems, Trilon Technology's ShotSpotter, which was tested in Redwood City, California, and Alliant Techsystems's System for Effective Control for Urban Environment Security (SECURES), tested in Dallas, Texas. The ShotSpotter, which employs a triangulation method, was deployed in a one square mile area divided into 319 sectors. The system was accurate 80 percent of the time in detecting gun shots, and in 72 percent of instances was able to determine the location of the gunshot within 25 feet. Accuracy varied according to the weapon fired.

During the two months of the test, the SECURES system reported 182 firearm shots, 151 of which were not reported by citizens. The additional electronic reports represented a major increase in workload for police officers, which may explain why there was little measured change in response time. The increase in reported incidents was attributed to two possible sources. First, given the recent development of the technology, false alarms may have been a factor. However, the large number of electronic alerts not reported by citizens may indicate a high rate of unreported gunshots. If the latter is true, the increased workload may be worth the effort, for electronic gunshot detection could significantly alter police strategies for controlling random gunfire.

Researchers concluded that gunshot detection systems potentially can serve three purposes. First, if a police department has a rapid response policy, the new technology could enhance response time. However, a department may wish to devote resources to preventive measures rather than to a detection system, in which case rapid response to such incidents would not have high priority. Gunshot detection could also serve as a problem-solving tool, allowing for the identification of areas with many incidents of gunshots, determination of the demographic characteristics of such areas, and evaluation of responses to the problem. Finally, gunshot detection systems may act as a deterrent to crime.

Crime reduction would depend on publicizing the introduction of electronic detection, and on whether the presence of detection systems in fact leads to the apprehension of those who fire guns. Sensing devices could be moved randomly to various locations, thereby reducing the cost of the system. However, random moves would depend upon the portability of the system. Researchers concluded that as accuracy increases, gunshot detection systems could become a valued instrument for local law enforcement in controlling one aspect of illegal firearms use.

Further Reading: Lorraine Green Mazerolle, *Using Gunshot Detection Technology in High-Crime Areas* (Washington, DC: National Institute of Justice Research Preview, June 1998); Lorraine Green Mazerolle, *Gunshot Detection Technology in High-Crime Areas* (videotape) (Washington, DC: National Institute of Justice, 1998).

H

Halbrook, Stephen P. (1947–)

Stephen P. Halbrook has focused his Fairfax, Virginia-based law practice on cases dealing with firearms legislation and Second Amendment issues. He has specialized in litigation involving the Bureau of Alcohol, Tobacco, and Firearms (BATF), federal mandates to the states (such as the Brady Handgun Violence Prevention Act requirement that local law enforcement officers run background checks on prospective handgun purchasers), and civil

This drawing shows gun rights attorney Stephen Halbrook (standing, right) arguing a case before the U.S. Supreme Court. *Courtesy of Stephen P. Halbrook.*

and criminal litigation at the state and local levels regarding firearms prohibitions, license and permit practices, and product liability lawsuits. He has authored three books on gun rights, including a guide for attorneys involved in firearms cases. One of Halbrook's most noted cases is *Printz v. United States* (1997), in which he represented Sheriff Jay Printz before the U.S. Supreme Court regarding the Brady background check. He argued successfully that the background check violated the Tenth Amendment and the principle of separation of powers between state and national governments.

Halbrook received a B.S. in business in 1969 and a Ph.D. in philosophy in 1972 from Florida State University. He received a law degree from Georgetown University Law Center in 1978. From 1972 to 1981, he taught philosophy at Tuskegee Institute, Howard University, and George Mason University. In addition to cases involving firearms regulations, Halbrook represented Virginia in a challenge to the federal mandate to states contained in the National Voter Registration (Motor-Voter) Act. On several occasions, Halbrook has testified before congressional committees concerned with firearms issues.

In *That Every Man Be Armed: The Evolution of a Constitutional Right*, originally published in 1984, Halbrook examines the philosophical, historical, and legal roots of the right to bear arms. Beginning with Plato and Aristotle in ancient Greece, he provided a comprehensive historical treatment of statements about arms: Cicero in ancient Rome, Machiavelli in Renaissance Italy, English common law, the American revolutionaries and the framers of the Constitution, pre-Civil War writers, the Fourteenth Amendment, Supreme Court decisions, and state court rulings.

In *A Right to Bear Arms: State and Federal Bills of Rights and Constitutional Guarantees*, Halbrook detailed the provisions in the first state constitutions that dealt with the right to bear arms. Halbrook's *Firearms Law Deskbook: Federal and State Criminal Practice*, first published in 1995, provides infor-

mation about previous firearms decisions for lawyers and litigants involved in legal cases. Halbrook treats federal prosecutions initiated by the BATF and provides detailed information about pretrial proceedings, jury trials, sentencing procedures, and appeals. He analyzes the congressional intent of the Gun Control Act of 1968 and the National Firearms Act of 1934; presents the various regulations pertaining to the sale, manufacture, transfer, transportation, licensing, importation, and possession of firearms; summarizes state gun control laws; and explains the extent of BATF authority. Halbrook also suggests litigation strategies, including advice about challenging recently enacted laws, particularly on the grounds of excess vagueness. Halbrook provides regular updates to the book. *See also* AMERICAN REVOLUTION; BRADY HANDGUN VIOLENCE PREVENTION ACT; BUREAU OF ALCOHOL, TOBACCO, AND FIREARMS; FOURTEENTH AMENDMENT; GUN CONTROL ACT OF 1968; NATIONAL FIREARMS ACT OF 1934; *PRINTZ V. UNITED STATES* (1997); SECOND AMENDMENT; STATE GUN STATUTES.

Further Reading: Stephen P. Halbrook, *Firearms Law Deskbook: Federal and State Criminal Practice* (Deerfield, IL: Clark Boardman Callaghan, 1995); Stephen P. Halbrook, *A Right to Bear Arms: State and Federal Bills of Rights and Constitutional Guarantees* (Westport, CT: Greenwood, 1989); Stephen P. Halbrook, *That Every Man Be Armed: The Evolution of a Constitutional Right* (Albuquerque: University of New Mexico Press, 1984); "Stephen P. Halbrook Resume," <http://www.mcs.net/~lpyleprn/sphresum.html>.

Handgun Control, Inc. (HCI)

Mark Borinsky, founder of Handgun Control, Inc. (HCI), is a prime example of an interest group entrepreneur—a person who, through individual efforts, creates an organization to further a cause. Borinsky's ordeal of being robbed at gunpoint when he was a student in Chicago inspired him to do something about the gun problem. Some individuals respond to such a situation by buying their own gun for self-protection, but Borinsky took another path. He decided to form an organization dedicated to controlling handgun ownership. After moving to Washington,

D.C., in 1974, he ran a newspaper ad inviting like-minded individuals to join him in the fight against handguns. Edward Welles, a retired Central Intelligence Agency (CIA) employee, responded to the call. They opened an office for the newly formed organization, the National Council to Control Handguns (NCCH), the precursor of HCI. Pete Shields, a marketing manager whose 23-year-old son had been murdered with a handgun, joined the organization in 1975. His organizational skills and political abilities opened doors in Washington for the fledgling organization. Subsequently, he became chairman of HCI.

At about the same time Borinsky was establishing HCI, the Board of Church and Society of the Methodist Church founded the National Coalition to Ban Handguns (NCBH), an organization that HCI joined. Originally HCI supported the NCBH's mission to ban the sale of all handgun ammunition. However, public opinion survey results convinced the HCI leadership that while Americans willingly accepted the prospect of the licensing and registering handguns and the imposition of waiting periods for their purchase, they tended to reject a total ban. The organization left the alliance with the NCBH and changed its goal to creating controls on the sale of handguns, while accepting them as appropriate possessions if acquired for legitimate purposes. No longer

in association with HCI, the NCBH continued to pursue the more ambitious goal of banning handguns.

In its effort to become an effective lobbying instrument for the gun control movement, HCI received assistance from the *pro bono publico* work of two Washington law firms that supported the organization's mission. The firms helped HCI become legally established and develop into an effective legislative lobbying organization. HCI succeeded in enlisting the assistance of sports and entertainment personalities such as Steve Allen, Leonard Bernstein, Ann Landers, and Neil Simon.

In 1976, after establishing a friendly relationship with members of the House Judiciary Committee, HCI appeared on the way to attaining a ban on the manufacture of Saturday night specials. However, when the National Rifle Association (NRA), spurred on by the initial success of the new gun control organization, activated its membership to contact their congresspeople, four members of the Judiciary Committee withdrew their support for such a ban. This loss, largely a result of inexperience, was reversed by events in the early 1980s. Following the 1981 assassination attempt on President Ronald Reagan that left his press secretary, James Brady, seriously wounded, HCI found a potent ally in Brady's wife, Sarah, who joined

The logo of Handgun Control, Inc., one of the country's leading gun control groups. *UPI/Corbis-Bettmann.*

the organization in 1985 and ultimately became its chairperson. After an assailant wielding a cheap handgun killed famed singer John Lennon on the streets of New York in 1980, HCI's membership increased 16-fold.

Gruesome events continued to improve the prospect for HCI's gun control objectives. The January 1989 murder of school children in Stockton, California, by a gunman using an AK-47 rifle spurred a call to ban assault weapons. HCI achieved a major victory when the 1994 Violent Crime Control and Law Enforcement Act included a ban on 19 types of assault weapons. The Brady Handgun Violence Prevention Act went into effect the same year, establishing a five-day waiting period so that a background check could be conducted by local law enforcement officers on those wishing to purchase a handgun. HCI, working with legislative allies, pushed for further measures to curb handgun violence that involved added regulations on gun owners and manufacturers and the taxation of guns and ammunition. However, in the November 1994 election many gun control supporters in Congress were defeated and the mood on Capitol Hill became far less sympathetic to HCI goals.

HCI continues to lobby for limitations on gun trafficking and child access to handguns, federal firearms licensing reform, a ban on assault weapons, and maintenance of existing gun laws against attacks from pro-gun groups. At the state level, HCI acts to preserve existing laws and to enact further legislation intended to prevent gun violence. It files *amicus curiae* briefs when gun laws are challenged in the courts. The HCI national headquarters encourages the establishment of grassroots organizations at the state and local levels and supports existing groups. However, HCI derives its greatest support from larger urban areas, with regional offices in Chicago, Los Angeles, San Diego, and San Francisco. HCI admits that the NRA agenda tends to dominate in smaller communities.

As part of its recruitment efforts, HCI reaches out to those who have experienced gun violence. In 1995, the organization sponsored a Mother's Day Memorial for families whose members have experienced gun vio-lence. Tragedies involving the use of firearms are used to promote the cause of the organization. When such an event occurs, HCI experiences an increase in membership and requests for information about gun control.

HCI continues its lobbying efforts in Congress and supports candidates who approve of their gun control agenda. The National Handgun Control Political Action Committee, the political arm of the organization, raises funds to be contributed to the campaigns of candidates who have demonstrated support for gun control. Three newsletters, *Legal Action Report*, *The Outreach*, and *Rx for Gun Violence*, inform the membership and other interested persons about the group's activities and the status of gun control legislation at the national and state levels.

In January 1997, a bill strongly backed by HCI, the "American Handgun Standards Act" (S. 70/H.R. 492), was introduced in Congress. The bill was intended to eliminate Saturday night specials, cheap handguns banned from import but still produced in the United States. The bill would require all domestically produced firearms to meet the same quality and safety standards required of imported guns. HCI also supports mandatory child safety locks on handguns and the "One-Handgun-Per-Month" proposal, which would prohibit anyone from purchasing more than one handgun in a 30-day period. *See also* AK-47; ASSAULT WEAPONS BAN; BRADY, JAMES; BRADY, SARAH; BRADY HANDGUN VIOLENCE PREVENTION ACT; NATIONAL RIFLE ASSOCIATION; REAGAN, RONALD; SATURDAY NIGHT SPECIAL; STOCKTON, CALIFORNIA, SHOOTING; TRIGGER LOCKS; WASHINGTON, D.C.

Further Reading: Gregg Lee Carter, *The Gun Control Movement* (New York: Twayne, 1997); Handgun Control, Inc., "Key Legislative Issues for the 105th Congress," (brochure, n.d.); Handgun Control, Inc. "Gun Laws Work," (brochure, n.d.); Handgun Control Inc., Web site <www.handguncontrol.org>.

Handguns Magazine

Although not as explicitly political as other publications, *Handguns* magazine, which has been published since 1986 by Petersen Publishing Company in Los Angeles, California, emphasizes the defensive use of firearms by law-abiding citizens, one of the major themes of pro-gun groups that defend the right to keep and bear arms.

"Gun Rights," a column written by gun advocate Don B. Kates, Jr., offers explicit arguments for the right to keep and bear arms. In 1997 and 1998, Kates wrote a series of columns about gun policy and violence in other countries. For instance, commenting on the Republic of Ireland, he observed that in 1972 the government decreed that citizens surrender all handguns and rifles. One purpose of the new policy was to prevent the transfer of arms to Northern Ireland. Kates claimed that if the prohibition policy was also intended to decrease the national murder rate, it failed. While the Irish averaged 11 murders per year in the four years prior to the gun ban (1968-71), the average rose to 21 homicides in the four years following the ban (1972-75). From 1981 to 1990, the rate increased to 30.3 per year. Kates concludes that any explanation of homicide rates cannot rely solely on the availability of particular types of firearms, but must take into account social, economic, and institutional variables.

Jerry Usher writes a regular column on the defensive use of firearms, titled "Defensive Combat." In one issue, Usher examined the defensive value of miniguns. Although noting the limitations of such guns (for instance, their range is often not much more than three yards), he concluded that "there are times when a minigun is preferable to no gun at all." He claimed that a minigun has real defensive value when an encounter is very close and the gun is a weapon of last resort, and advised that a person should carry the largest and most powerful weapon possible, which at times may be a minigun.

Chuck Taylor writes a column titled "Handguns in Combat," in which he relates accounts of successful uses of firearms for self-defense. In each issue, Taylor builds suspense as terrorists begin their attack. However, the cool-headed target successfully uses a handgun to fell the aggressor. Taylor describes the proper procedure in using a hand-

gun. For instance, in the January 1998 depiction, the defender, after firing at an intruder, carefully uses safety procedures: "Jenkins released the trigger, placed his trigger finger outside the triggerguard and lowered his weapon back to Ready." The intended lesson is clear: If handled correctly, a handgun is not dangerous to the defensive user, but certainly presents a serious threat to the attacker. *See also* KATES, DON B.

Further Reading: HANDGUNS (PETERSEN PUBLISHING COMPANY, LOS ANGELES, CA).

Harborview Injury Prevention and Research Center (HIPRC)

Founded in 1985, the Harborview Injury Prevention and Research Center (HIPRC) seeks to develop injury prevention strategies by conducting studies of the causes and nature of the injuries people suffer. Located in Seattle, Washington, the Center is associated with the University of Washington. Similar to other organizations that investigate injuries from an epidemiological perspective, the Center includes firearms injury prevention as one of its many research topics. Frederick P. Rivara and David Grossman, the Center's co-directors, have both conducted research involving injury prevention, including injuries caused by firearms.

Rivara, who serves as George Adkins Professor of Pediatrics and adjunct professor of epidemiology at the University of Washington, has focused his research on several areas related to the epidemiology and prevention of injuries, including those associated with bicycle, pedestrian, motor vehicle, alcohol-related, and firearms-related accidents. He is interested in developing ways to prevent violence among young children. Among his publications, Rivara co-authored a study of a Seattle, Washington, gun buyback program, a comparative study of firearms injuries, and an investigation of the role of the pediatrician in preventing violence.

Grossman, associate professor of pediatrics at the University of Washington, has investigated motor vehicle-related injuries, intentional injury and suicide prevention, and rural injury control. Among his publications, he has co-authored studies dealing with pediatrician and family physician counseling to prevent firearm injury, police recommendations regarding the safe storage of handguns, and an evaluation of an elementary school violence prevention curriculum.

The Center is involved with several injury prevention projects, including the development of a motor vehicle trauma surveillance system in cooperation with General Motors. Pedestrian safety, especially for older adults, has also received the Center's attention. The Center has begun a study involving the protection of abused women and the efficacy of court orders in preventing future violence and injury. The study results will include recommendations for altering the nature of police, court, and health care intervention in cases of domestic violence.

The Center cooperates with the Seattle Police Department to evaluate aspects of the city's Domestic Violence Unit, including comparison of the Unit with other cities, examination of recidivism rates, possible impediments to police intervention, and data collection and management practices. These studies are indirectly related to firearms violence because guns are sometimes used in domestic violence, and women threatened with violence are often encouraged to purchase a firearm for self-protection.

The Center has conducted two initiatives directly related to firearms. The HIPRC entered an agreement with the Washington State Department of Health to appraise a firearms injury surveillance system (FISS), which gathers information about deaths and injuries caused by firearms. The system could provide a more reliable source of information from which to draw conclusions about firearm safety. The second initiative involves the development and evaluation of a community-based project to provide information about the safe storage of handguns. To disseminate information, the project planned to enlist the assistance of health care providers and public health workers, law enforcement agencies, the broadcast and print media, and public schools. *See also* ACCIDENTS INVOLV-ING GUNS; FATALITIES; HEALTH CARE PROFESSIONALS; PACIFIC CENTER FOR VIOLENCE PREVENTION; SUICIDE; WOMEN AND GUNS; YOUTH AND GUNS.

Further Reading: Harborview Injury Prevention and Research Center Web site <www.weber.u. washington.edu/~hiprc>.

Harder, Chuck (1944–)

A heavy-set man with a melodious voice, Chuck Harder has established himself as a prominent figure in the talk-radio business. He adds to the gun control debate by claiming that, like many other activities, gun control policy initiatives are geared to deny the American people a basic right, in this case, the right to keep and bear arms. Harder broadcasts on the Peoples Radio Network, which is located in the renovated Telford Hotel in White Springs, Florida. He expanded his radio station outlets from just a few in 1987 to nearly 300 in 1995, placing second only to Rush Limbaugh, who broadcasts on over 600 stations. Harder's stations are located primarily in the South and Southwest. His radio program contains a definite anti-government message. In one program, he was quoted as saying, "We have a government, ladies and gentlemen, that is lying to the people, raping the people, defrauding the people. . . . These [federal officials] are very power hungry and, in my opinion, evil people. They want all the marbles."

Harder portrays a federal government in partnership with large corporations, both of which threaten the freedom and well-being of the average American. He claims that "New York power brokers," "New York bankers," and "the global elite" have nearly succeeded in gaining control of the American government. During congressional debates over the North American Free Trade Agreement (NAFTA), Harder campaigned vigorously against its passage, asserting that he was defending the average American worker's interests. Such positions have attracted the surprising support of some liberals. For instance, consumer advocate Ralph Nader has been a frequent guest on Harder's radio program.

Harder emphasizes the possibility of government conspiracies to divest the American people of their freedoms, a message welcomed by certain groups in society, such as the militia movement. He once interviewed Ken Adams, an officer of the Michigan Militia, an organization Harder described as a group of citizens prepared to serve in "the time of need." He emphasized the intention of the militia to remain independent of any government control so that Attorney General Janet Reno could not call them to "go invade Waco." Comparing the United States with Russia, Harder referred to the Waco incident as "America's Chechnya." Harder's views on the purpose of a militia and his insistence on the right to bear arms assume the right of citizens to use weapons against their own, supposedly tyrannical, government.

Harder depends on radio audience contributions to support his organization, For the People. An estimated 40,000 individuals have joined the organization at a fee of $15 per year. For the People publishes a biweekly newsletter, *News Report*, which has an estimated 30,000 subscribers. Harder advertises merchandise on his program to obtain financial support for the organization. In 1995, this practice drew the attention of the Internal Revenue Service (IRS). To maintain his tax-exempt status, Harder agreed to sell the radio operations to a nonprofit group called the National Center for Manufacturing Sciences, which is led by Pat Choate, Ross Perot's 1996 presidential running mate.

The National Center ultimately objected to the more extreme statements Harder made on the air, such as comparing President Bill Clinton to Adolf Hitler and calling the president a "cheat and liar." Supporting conspiracy theories about the Clinton administration, Harder stated that the difference between Watergate and Whitewater was "a very, very big pile of bodies." He has warned that a declining economic system may lead to political violence. *See also* CLINTON, WILLIAM JEFFERSON (BILL); MICHIGAN MILITIA; RENO, JANET; RUSSIA; WACO, TEXAS, RAID.

Further Reading: Marc Cooper, "The Paranoid Style," *Nation* 260 (April 10, 1995), 486; Gail DeGeorge, "For Pat Choate, Talk Radio Turns to Static," *Business Week* (November 4, 1996), 50; Morris Dees, *Gathering Storm: America's Militia Threat* (New York: HarperCollins, 1996).

Health Care Professionals

A large number of health care workers and health care institutions have taken stands in favor of more stringent gun control legislation. Motivated by the large number of gun-related injuries and deaths they regularly face, physicians have produced a body of literature criticizing the widespread availability of firearms in American society. Health care professionals have adopted the epidemiological model to describe the distribution of firearms in American society, describing guns as something akin to a virus causing an epidemic of injuries and death. Many in the medical profession look upon guns not as inanimate objects that may be used for good or ill, but as a distinct social evil. To rid the nation of deaths and injuries, the virus—that is, the guns—must be eliminated. Gun control becomes the method to immunize the nation from the devastation caused by guns.

The disease metaphor contains a psychiatric component. The very presence of guns, called the "weapons effect," is claimed to encourage violent behavior. Findings from several social psychological experiments suggest that the presence of guns can lead to the commission of violent acts that otherwise would not occur. To the extent that violent actions are impulsive rather than planned, these experiments indicate that the presence of firearms may increase the likelihood of assaults. The possibility of a weapons effect has been used to argue in favor of more stringent gun control measures that would limit the availability of firearms.

Closely related to the claimed weapons effect is the assertion that many people who participate in violent incidents involving guns are not criminals. Law-abiding citizens have no trouble with the law until they engage in an argument that escalates into violence. If firearms are available, they either magnify the violent confrontation, or increase the probability of serious injuries.

Critics of pro-gun control medical professionals argue that such assertions conceal additional information regarding the characteristics of violent persons. They note that approximately 75 percent of murderers have adult criminal records. In addition, they assert that in 90 percent of homicides committed in the home, police were called to the same address one or more times in the previous two years, indicating a pattern of violent behavior. Such data suggest that the relationship between guns and violence is not as direct as health professionals claim.

In 1979, the Public Health Service announced a goal of reducing the number of privately owned handguns by 25 percent by 2000. The medical profession's view of guns appears similar to its view of cigarettes. Health professionals wish to disseminate information stigmatizing guns as a socially unacceptable health hazard, just as smoking cigarettes became a widely recognized health hazard. In their campaign against guns, health professionals target not only homicides and other crimes committed with guns, but also suicide, especially among youth.

Critics, who are often social science researchers, look elsewhere for the causes of violence. Rather than focusing on the availability of firearms, they identify what they consider more plausible causal factors such as persisting poverty, especially among certain ethnic minority groups; a feeling of hopelessness; a lack of education and promising employment opportunities; the prevalence of the drug trade; and inadequate prison facilities that lead to early release of repeat offenders. Critics reject the weapons effect touted by medical professionals, arguing that law-abiding citizens do not undergo the risk of becoming criminals simply through the possession firearms. This alternative research has failed to discover any significant relationship between the availability of firearms and the incidence of homicide, suicide, assault and rape, robbery, or burglary. Critics assert that more radical gun control involving widespread denial of gun ownership would prevent the ordinary citizen from exercising his or her personal choice to own firearms for protecting self, home, and family. They fault health care professionals for failing to provide the average citizen with any reasonable recommendations for protection against crime.

Social science researchers critical of the medical professionals' position on gun control note that a series of existing laws already makes it illegal for felons, those convicted of acts of violence, and those convicted of drug crimes, from possessing guns. However, because these laws have proved ineffective, the researchers doubt the value of additional gun control statutes. Once more, law-abiding citizens are the ones most likely to obey firearms laws, thereby limiting their capacity for self defense.

Critics claim that publications of the health care profession are far more likely to include articles that support the anti-gun position. The *New England Journal of Medicine* has faced severe criticism for a long-standing anti-gun policy, consistently choosing to publish articles on the various negative aspects of gun ownership while at the same time ignoring research that fails to discover statistically significant relationships between the level of gun possession and rates of violence. Health care professionals respond that critics display the same bias they claim to have discovered in pro-gun control advocates. Health care professionals also claim that their research techniques are superior to those used by social scientists. *See also* DOCTORS FOR INTEGRITY IN POLICY RESEARCH; DOCTORS FOR RESPONSIBLE GUN OWNERSHIP; FATALITIES; PHYSICIANS FOR SOCIAL RESPONSIBILITY; SUICIDE; VIOLENT CRIME RATE; YOUTH AND GUNS.

Further Reading: Harborview Injury Prevention and Research Center Web site <www.weber.u.washington.edu/~hiprc>; Don B. Kates, Henry E. Schaffer, John K Lattimer, George B. Murray, and Edwin H. Cassem, "Bad Medicine: Doctors and Guns," in David B. Kopel, ed., *Guns: Who Should Own Them?* (Amherst, NY: Prometheus, 1995); Physicians for Social Responsibility Web site <www.psr.org>.

Heartland Institute

The Heartland Institute, a libertarian "think tank" located in Chicago, Illinois, takes a resolute stand against gun control and other legislation intended to impose regulations on the behavior of citizens. Among other publications, the organization distributes *Intellectual Ammunition*, a bimonthly public policy magazine in which anti-gun control articles appear. The board of directors includes individuals from major corporations, such as Philip Morris, Amoco, and Procter and Gamble. The members of the board of policy advisers hail largely from the academic community. The organization has a staff of eight and a budget of over $1 million.

The Institute claims status as "the first think tank in the nation to focus on free-market solutions to state and local public policy problems." In its various analyses, the Institute maintains the overarching theme that government is the problem, not the solution. With regard to gun control, the Institute contends that the provision of the Brady Handgun Violence Prevention Act mandating background checks on all those wishing to purchase a handgun forced local law enforcement officials to devote scarce resources to investigating citizens, the vast majority of whom are law-abiding.

The Institute published a policy study prepared by Daniel D. Polsby and Dennis Brennen presenting what the authors term 10 myths about gun control. The authors emphasize not only the inability of gun control legislation to prevent crime, but the limitations such legislation places on citizens to protect themselves. Employing the findings of such researchers as Gary Kleck, Polsby and Brennen conclude that no credible relationship exists between the number of guns available in society and increases in crime. In response to the claim that gun control laws prevent friends from killing friends, the authors assert that most murderers and homicide victims have criminal records. They argue that waiting periods imposed for the purchase of a handgun could actually increase killings because many criminals will substitute more deadly weapons, such as rifles and shotguns, that are not covered by such laws. Gun accidents provide a weak justification for gun control laws, the authors claim, because the number of accidents has been declining in recent years. Finally, referring to the work of David Kopel, the authors assert that legal scholarship has conclusively determined that the Second Amendment was intended to protect an individual right to possess arms.

The Heartland Institute notes that several judicial rulings have determined that the police cannot protect everyone, nor do they have the legal responsibility to do so. Attempting to give law enforcement officials a duty to protect all individuals would result in a huge police force likely to endanger liberty. The Institute contends that the carrying of concealed firearms offers an effective means of self-protection, and that a national concealed carry law would act as a significant deterrent to violent crime. Citing data that citizens often use firearms to kill and wound criminals, the Institute concludes that guns are an excellent means of self-defense.

The Institute claims that political considerations often determine a politician's position on gun control. For instance, Al Salvi, who ran unsuccessfully for a U.S. Senate seat from Illinois, switched from an anti- to a pro-gun control position. The Institute, lamenting this switch by a winner of the Heartland Liberty Prize, claims that the public's failure to understand the basic issues underlying firearms policy forced Salvi to abandon the basic principle that less government means more freedom, a position "he knows to be right," to increase his chances for election. More generally, the organization holds that the call for gun control lacks any rational justification, being based instead on the political ambitions of those exploiting public misinformation. *See also* ACCIDENTS INVOLVING GUNS; BRADY HANDGUN VIOLENCE PREVENTION ACT; CONCEALED CARRY LAWS; HEALTH CARE PROFESSIONALS; KLECK, GARY; KOPEL, DAVID B.; SECOND AMENDMENT.

Further Reading: Heartland Institute Web site <www.heartland.org>.

HELP Network

The HELP Network, or Handgun Epidemic Lowering Plan, was established in 1993 to assist in reducing firearm-related violence. The organization is located at the Violent

Injury Prevention Center (VIPC) of the Children's Memorial Medical Center in Chicago. Like other health-care organizations, the Network takes an epidemiological approach to gun violence, regarding it as a disease to be investigated in the same way medical researchers treat standard illnesses. The Network supports legislation mandating child safety locks for handguns and liability laws that allow victims of gun violence to sue firearms manufacturers.

HELP has four major policy objectives: 1) to develop procedures for tracking handguns and firearm injuries; 2) to support the research activities of the National Center for Injury Prevention and Control (NCIPC); 3) to reduce the availability of especially dangerous handguns to civilians; and 4) to restrict minors' access to firearms. The organization particularly emphasizes the need to establish an effective nation-wide system for monitoring non-fatal firearms-related injuries, noting that less than half of health departments in the nation collect information on such injuries. The Network believes that data on injuries is crucial to the public health approach to preventing firearm injuries.

Katherine Kaufer Christoffel serves as chair and medical director of the HELP Network. Christoffel is a professor of pediatrics and preventive medicine at Northwestern University School of Medicine and an attending pediatrician at Children's Hospital in Chicago. In addition to firearms-related injuries, she has conducted research on motor vehicle injuries, consumer product-related injuries, and child abuse. She notes that just as the federal deficit cannot be controlled without reducing health care costs, health care costs cannot be controlled without lowering the costs of treating firearm injuries, which number as many as 100,000 each year. Christoffel claims that a firearm injury can cost more than $1,000,000 over the life of the victim. She argues that the only way to lower the monetary and personal costs of firearm-related deaths and injuries is through preventive strategies.

Network membership includes over 100 organizations, including the American Academy of Pediatrics, the American Medical As-

sociation, the American College of Physicians, and such gun control organizations as the Center to Prevent Handgun Violence (CPHV) and Cease Fire, Inc. Individual members include health care professionals, especially trauma doctors. The Network distributes a quarterly newsletter, *HELP Network News*, and a monthly mailing containing information about legislative activity and reports on recent statistics. Member organizations are provided with various audio-visual materials, databases, and other technical support. A speakers bureau locates speakers to make presentations at medical conventions and other meetings.

The Network believes that firearms make domestic violence especially dangerous and argues that guns are not the solution for women seeking greater security, stating that "once a gun is brought into [a woman's] home, it puts her and her family at increased risk of gun homicide, suicide, or unintentional shooting." To assist in the removal of firearms from the home, the Network distributes *The HELP Handgun Disposal Handbook: A Prescription for Safety* to health organizations, violence prevention groups, and the general public. The handbook presents information about ways to dispose of a handgun and provides advice for those interested in initiating a community program to prevent handgun injury. The organization has produced a brochure for patients presenting the dangers of handguns in the home.

Associated with the Network is HELP for Survivors, a Chicago support group for people who have lost someone to firearm violence. The organization helps members cope with their personal loss. The program offers assistance to those wishing to control the spread of handguns and assault weapons. Individuals are prepared for various advocacy activities aimed at reducing handgun violence, including contacting policy makers and working with community groups. *See also* ACCIDENTS INVOLVING FIREARMS; CEASE FIRE, INC.; CENTER TO PREVENT HANDGUN VIOLENCE; HEALTH CARE PROFESSIONALS; NATIONAL CENTER FOR INJURY PREVENTION AND CONTROL; TRIGGER LOCKS; VIOLENT CRIME RATE; WOMEN AND GUNS; YOUTH AND GUNS.

Further Reading: HELP Network Web site <www.childmmc.edu/help/helphome.htm>.

Hemenway, David (1945–)

David Hemenway, director of the Harvard Injury Control Research Center and professor at the Harvard School of Public Health, conducts research on firearms from a public health perspective and has published several articles on the subject. His work has been criticized by those who conclude that firearms are an important means of defense against crime, a position Hemenway rejects. Hemenway's research interests include the costs and benefits of gun ownership, gun use among adolescents, the use of guns in self defense, guns on college campuses, the relationship between firearm availability and completed suicide, and National Rifle Association (NRA) membership characteristics.

Hemenway founded the New England Injury Prevention Center in 1986, where he assumed responsibility for injury prevention training programs. He chairs the Injury Prevention Council of the National Association for Public Health Policy. He has conducted research and written journal articles on a number of subjects, including motor vehicle crashes, falls, fires, suicide, and child abuse. At the Harvard Injury Control Research Center, Hemenway supervises the scientific and administrative staff and is responsible for budget and fund-raising activities and the completion of research projects.

In a co-authored article titled "Firearms and Community Feelings of Safety," which appeared in a 1995 issue of the *Journal of Criminal Law and Criminology*, Hemenway reported the results of a study indicating that gun ownership imposes psychic costs on others in society. Eighty-five percent of non-gun owners surveyed stated they would feel less safe if gun ownership increased in their community. Only 8 percent reported that they would feel safer. Paul Gallant and David Kopel, writing for the Independence Institute, a pro-gun organization, have criticized the study, claiming that psychic costs are "imaginary" and that non-gun owners actually receive advantages from increased gun

David Hemenway, director of the Harvard Injury Control Research Center, conducts research on firearms from a public health perspective. *Courtesy of Harvard Injury Control Research Center.*

ownership. Citing studies by such researchers as John R. Lott, they claim that burglars tend to avoid dwellings that appear occupied for fear the owner may be armed.

In a co-authored 1995 *Journal of the American Medical Association* article, Hemenway focused on the risks of keeping a firearm in the home. The article was based on a survey of 800 randomly selected gun owners. He concluded that guns kept for protection and handguns generally are more likely to be stored loaded or both unlocked and loaded. Twenty-nine percent of those surveyed reported keeping a loaded gun in the home and 21 percent responded that they kept a firearm loaded and unlocked. Contrary to the claims of gun rights advocates that training is the key to firearm safety, Hemenway discovered that owners who had received training were almost twice as likely to keep a loaded and unlocked firearm in the home. The study results suggest that residents would be far safer not having guns in the home.

Hemenway has questioned the claim, originating with firearm policy researcher Gary Kleck, that there are 2.5 million cases of defensive firearm use in the United States each year, a figure that has been used to argue against restrictions on firearm ownership. Hemenway claims that the type of survey on which the figure is based tends to overestimate the occurrence in the population of a reported activity, such as defensive gun use. Hemenway does not accept the conclusion that if the legitimate uses of firearms outnumber criminal uses, then extensive firearm ownership contributes to overall public safety.

In 1997, Hemenway received a health policy research grant to conduct a three-year public health study of firearms policies in the United States and to determine approaches to decrease the level of lethal violence. Among the topics Hemenway planned to investigate are gun carrying practices, gun storage, the use of firearms for self-defense, and gun brandishing. The research includes an examination of the public health literature and a survey of college students and adults. In addition to several articles, Hemenway intends to write a book on firearms from the public health perspective. *See also* COOK, PHILIP J.; HEALTH CARE PROFESSIONALS; INDEPENDENCE INSTITUTE; KLECK, GARY; KOPEL, DAVID B.; LOTT, JOHN R.; LUDWIG, JENS OTTO; NATIONAL RIFLE ASSOCIATION; SUICIDE; TRIGGER LOCKS.

Further Reading: Philip J. Cook, Jens Ludwig, and David Hemenway, "The Gun Debate's New Mythical Number: How Many Defensive Uses Per Year?" *Journal of Policy Analysis and Management* 16 (Summer 1997), 463-69; Paul Gallant and David Kopel, "The 'Psychic Cost' of Holiday Gift-Giving" (Golden, CO: Independence Institute opinion editorial, n.d.); David Hemenway, S.J. Solnick, and D.R. Azreal, "Firearm Training and Storage," *Journal of the American Medical Association* 273 (1995), 46-50; David Hemenway, S.J. Solnick, and D.R. Azreal, "Firearms and Community Feelings of Safety," *Journal of Criminal Law and Criminology* 86 (Fall 1995), 121-32.

Heston, Charlton (1924–)

In the 1990s, actor Charlton Heston's public comments in favor of gun rights made his name virtually synonymous with the National Rifle Association (NRA). While he is widely recognized by the American public, he has not been treated as seriously as he might because of his association with a number of film epics. In 1997, in an effort to rescue the NRA from reported financial difficulties, Heston invited members to join him in raising $100 million in the following three years for a media campaign to present the pro-gun position on the Second Amendment. In June 1998, after serving a term as NRA first vice president, he was elected to a three-year term on the board of directors and was chosen as the organization's president.

Heston, born Charles Carter, had a long and successful career in the movies. Early in his career, he became typecast as a historical hero. He starred in a series of epics, including *The Ten Commandments*, (1956), *Ben-Hur* (1959), *El Cid* (1961), and *The Agony and the Ecstacy* (1965). In addition, the public remembers him in such movies as *Planet of the Apes* (1968), *The Omega Man* (1971), and *Soylent Green* (1973). In the 1980s, Heston began to support various conservative causes, including gun rights.

Heston refers to the Second Amendment as "America's First Freedom" because, he claims, it protects all other freedoms contained in the Bill of Rights: It is "the first among equals." Heston has stated that just as the First Amendment protects tabloid newspapers despite most people's dislike of them, so the Second Amendment protects assault weapons. In his effort to assist the pro-gun movement, Heston writes a column for *Guns and Ammo* titled "From the Capitol," in which he reports on the politics of gun control in the United States and other countries. Heston's defense of gun rights contains an element of nostalgia. He harks back to an America where people could "pray without feeling naive, love without being kinky, sing without profanity, be white without feeling guilty, own a gun without shame." He has been criticized for broadening the struggle for gun rights into a cultural warfare in which white, middle class, Protestant values are preferred.

On May 1, 1999, less than two weeks after the school shooting in nearby Littleton, Colorado, Charlton Heston, president of the National Rifle Association, addresses the NRA's annual meeting in Denver. *REUTERS/Rick Wilking/Archive Photos.*

Heston's election as president of the NRA was opposed by a faction in the organization led by Neal Knox. Opponents within the gun rights movement as well as gun control advocates publicized Heston's early support for the Gun Control Act of 1968. Documents uncovered at the Lyndon Baines Johnson Library at the University of Texas revealed that Heston, along with other actors, supported an expansion of the bill to ban the interstate sale or transfer of rifles and shotguns. Following the assassination of Robert Kennedy, Heston appeared with four other actors on a television talk show to make a nationwide appeal for passage of the Gun Control Act. A 1968 *American Rifleman* column identified Heston as one of several film stars who were staunch supporters of gun control.

In response to the revelations about his past support for gun control, Heston stated that this was one of the mistakes he made. However, Knox claimed that Heston had not changed his views on gun control substantially since supporting the 1968 act, pointing to a May 1997 statement in which Heston commented that some guns were inappropriate for private ownership. Such revelations notwithstanding, Heston and his allies succeeded in gaining leadership positions at the 1998 NRA meeting, even though Knox's opposition indicates that Heston does not represent the most uncompromising stance within the gun rights movement. However, Heston is an extremely articulate individual and a vocal representative of the nation's largest gun rights group. *See also* AMERICAN RIFLEMAN; ASSAULT WEAPONS BAN; GUN CONTROL ACT OF 1968; *GUNS AND AMMO*; KNOX, NEAL; NATIONAL RIFLE ASSOCIATION; SECOND AMENDMENT.

Further Reading: Charlton Heston, "Speech by National Rifle Association First Vice President Charlton Heston Delivered at the Free Congress Foundation's 20th Anniversary Gala" (December 7, 1997); Charlton Heston, "My Crusade to Save the Second Amendment," *American Rifleman* 145 (September 1997), 30-34; Neal Knox, "The Heston File" *Neal Knox Report* (March 2, 1998), <www.nealknox.com>; "Stars Fall from Anti-Gun Bandwagon," *American Rifleman* 116 (October 1968), 10.

Huddleston v. United States (1974)

In *Huddleston v. United States* (415 U.S. 814, 1974), the U.S. Supreme Court dealt with a provision of the Gun Control Act of 1968 [18 U.S.C. (a) (6)] that makes unlawful the making of a false statement "in connection with the acquisition . . . of any firearm . . . from a . . . licensed dealer." The Court was asked to determine whether this provision applied to the redemption of a firearm from a pawnshop.

In 1965, William C. Huddleston, Jr., was convicted in a California state court of the felony charge of writing checks without sufficient funds. Under the Gun Control Act, the conviction precluded him from acquiring a firearm. In 1971, Huddleston pawned three rifles belonging to his wife. The pawnshop owner was a federally licensed firearms dealer. When Huddleston redeemed the rifles, he was asked to complete Treasury Form 4473, "Firearms Transaction Record," which contained the following question: "Have you been convicted in any court of a crime punishable by imprisonment for a term exceeding one year?" The question was derived from 18 U.S.C. 922 (d) (1) which prohibits selling or otherwise disposing of a firearm to someone who "has been convicted in any court of . . . a crime punishable by imprisonment for a term exceeding one year." Huddleston responded "no" to the question and signed each of three forms, certifying that he had answered the questions truthfully and accurately and that he was aware of the penalty for making a false statement.

When Huddleston was charged for violating 922 (a) (6), he moved to dismiss the indictment, arguing in part that the statute was not intended to apply to the redemption of a pawned firearm. The district court denied the motion and found the defendant guilty. The U.S. Court of Appeals for the Ninth Circuit affirmed the conviction. In an appeal to the U.S. Supreme Court, Huddleston argued that the legislative history and language of the statute demonstrated that Congress did not intend that "acquisition" apply to redemption from a pawnshop. He further argued that even if Congress did have that intention, the ambiguity of the statute required a decision favoring the defendant. The Court concluded that while a redemption is not a sale, it can be included under some "other disposition" of a firearm, a situation it determined is covered under the statute. The Court noted that Congress did not make an explicit exception for a pawnshop redemption and that it was reasonable for Congress to view a pawn transaction as different from a situation in which a firearm is returned to the owner after being repaired. The Court noted that the terms "acquisition" and "sale or other disposition" are closely associated. A pawnbroker could "dispose" of a firearm through a "redemptive transaction."

The Court declared that the statute's legislative history supported this interpretation, observing that Congress intended the legislation to deter crime by keeping "firearms out of the hands of those not legally entitled to possess them because of age, criminal background, or incompetency." To enforce the legislation, a person making a false statement regarding eligibility to acquire a firearm from a licensed dealer was subject to criminal penalty. The statute channeled weapons sales through firearms dealers to limit sales to those who did not present a threat to the public interest. To achieve this broader objective, it is reasonable to conclude that Congress intended pawnshop redemptions to be covered by the statute.

The Court perceived no underlying constitutional questions at issue. No claim was made on Second Amendment grounds, and the Court rejected the claim that Huddleston's property had been taken without just compensation as well as the argument that the defendant's Treasury form responses had been coerced. *See also* GUN CONTROL ACT OF 1968; SECOND AMENDMENT.

Further Reading: *Huddleston v. United States,* 415 U.S. 814 (1974).

I

Independence Institute

The Independence Institute is a public policy research organization that takes a fervent pro-gun rights position, providing a voice for an essentially libertarian perspective on firearms and the criminal justice system. Located in Golden, Colorado, the Institute was founded in 1985 by David S. D'Evelyn and John Andrews. The Institute conducts studies of various public policy issues in such areas as education, health care, transportation, the environment, government reform, and criminal justice and violent crime. Largely through the efforts of its research director, David Kopel, the Institute has focused much of its attention on firearms issues. The organization has a definite free-market, pro-individual freedom perspective and emphasizes private-sector, community-based solutions to policy problems.

The Institute publishes research reports, offering recommendations from a pro-freedom perspective, and distributes to the media a weekly commentary on current events that emphasizes civil liberties and economic freedom. The Institute broadcasts a weekly television program, *Independent Thinking*, from a Denver television station, along with a public affairs discussion program. The organization sponsors public debates and weekend conferences at the Institute headquarters.

The Institute regards itself as a primary source of research on the right to keep and bear arms. It has published many reports on gun control and solutions to crime that respect civil liberties. People associated with the Institute have treated a number of issues on the gun control agenda, such as the ideological origins of both pro- and anti-gun attitudes in the United States. This study investigates the phenomenon of guns substituting as scapegoats for the actual causes of violence. The entrance of medical professionals into the gun control movement is regarded as an attempt to use professional status to influence the debate. The effort to ban particular types of firearms has come under investigation. Banning of weapons by type, such as assault rifles, is rejected as unconstitutional because banned guns cannot be rationally distinguished from other weapons. The Institute has investigated and rejected the anti-gun claim that firearms should not be kept in the home for self-protection because they are too dangerous.

Institute reports defend state laws permitting carrying concealed handguns, claiming that permit holders are in fact more law-abiding than the general population. Papers defending the Second Amendment have been issued, including an analysis of the Supreme Court's ruling in *United States v. Miller* (1939), the major twentieth-century decision on the right to keep and bear arms. The view that the Second Amendment involves a collective right granted only to state governments is examined and rejected. Other projects include investigations of gun control laws in other countries, including the former Warsaw Pact countries and Japan. Other topics of investigation include evaluations of the success of existing gun control laws, guns as defensive tools for women, biblical and other religious authorizations for the use of arms in the defense of the innocent, and the reliability of media polls that often report significant public support for gun control. Other criminal justice topics closely related to the question of firearms policy, such as media violence, the federalization of criminal law, and sentencing policy, have received the Institute's attention. *See also* ASSAULT WEAPONS BAN; HEALTH CARE PROFESSIONALS; KOPEL, DAVID B.; JAPAN; MEDIA VIOLENCE; SECOND AMENDMENT; *UNITED STATES V. MILLER* (1939); WOMEN AND GUNS.

Further Reading: Independence Institute Web site <www.i2i.org>.

Institute for Legislative Action (ILA)

An organization established in 1975 within the National Rifle Association (NRA), the Institute for Legislative Action (ILA) concentrates on lobbying members of the U.S. Congress and state legislatures. Since its foundation, the ILA has become an influential voice within the parent organization, having become skillful at influencing members of the national and state legislatures. The ILA has been successful in mobilizing membership support for its policy stands. The organization's activities absorb 25 percent of the NRA's yearly budget, which in 1992 amounted to nearly $29 million.

The ILA conducts mailings to NRA members that include legislative alerts informing the rank and file regarding the organization's efforts to protect gun rights in the national and state legislatures. In addition to warning members about upcoming gun control efforts, the ILA has conducted mass mailings to raise funds to support the organization's activities. Such fund-raising mailings alert the membership to gun control measures proposed in the national and state legislatures. The ILA supervises the Political Victory Fund (PVF),

which is the NRA's political action committee. the PVF raises money to be donated to political candidates who have taken a supportive stand on the gun control issue.

The ILA has focused its attention on a number of issues nationwide. Pro-gun control Senator Barbara Boxer, a California Democrat, has come under strong criticism for her 1997 gun control bill, the American Handgun Standards Act, which would ban inexpensive handguns that are easily concealed. U.S. Senator Charles Schumer, a New York Democrat, earned the disapproval of the ILA for his advocacy of the "Twelve Is Enough Anti-Gunrunning Act," which would limit to one per month the number of guns a federally licensed dealer could sell to a non-licensed person, and would limit non-licensed individuals to purchasing no more than one gun in a 30-day period.

The ILA actively supports pro-gun legislation, such as a measure that would institute reciprocity among states having laws allowing the carrying of concealed weapons. Members were encouraged to sign petitions and phone and write their representatives to support the bill. The ILA has lobbied in state legislatures to pass versions of the NRA-ILA model Crime Victims Protection Act intended to prevent those convicted of crimes from suing victims who inflicted injuries on them, thus protecting those gun owners who use their weapons in self-defense. In 1997, Mississippi and North Dakota passed variants of the model bill and the ILA has encouraged lobbying in other states for passage.

The Institute keeps track of other activities that may threaten pro-gun interests and publicizes the opinions of public officials who support its position on the right to keep and bear arms. The Bureau of Alcohol, Tobacco, and Firearms (BATF) is a consistent focus of attention. In 1997, the BATF, in cooperation with the Clinton administration, was accused of working to reduce the number of federally licensed firearms dealers. As evidence of this charge, the ILA reported that the number of federal firearms licensees declined from 287,000 in 1993 to 124,000 in 1997. The ILA has reported on BATF activities that the

ILA claims amount to harassment of gun dealers and private citizens. The National Center for Injury Prevention and Control of the Centers for Disease Control (CDC) has come under attack for labeling gun ownership a "health hazard." The ILA has been critical of the United Nations' firearms regulation proposals, expressing concern that U.S. policy might be dictated by the international organization.

The ILA has provided publicity for the NRA-ILA program titled "Crime Strike" and publicizes the success of the "Keep Killers in Prison" campaign. At the invitation of murder victims' families, Crime Strike assists these families in their efforts to prevent paroles for convicted murderers. The ILA welcomes support from those legislators opposing gun control. *See also* BOXER, BARBARA; BUREAU OF ALCOHOL, TOBACCO, AND FIREARMS; CLINTON, WILLIAM JEFFERSON (BILL); CONCEALED CARRY LAWS; HEALTH CARE PROFESSIONALS; NATIONAL RIFLE ASSOCIATION; SCHUMER, CHARLES; STATE GUN STATUTES; UNITED NATIONS.

Further Reading: "ILA Report," *American Rifleman* (monthly); Institute for Legislative Action Web site <www.nraila.org>; Josh Sugarmann, *National Rifle Association: Money, Firepower and Fear* (Washington, DC: National Press, 1992).

Instrumentality Effect

Advocates of gun control claim that the weapons instrumentality effect is a significant factor in determining the seriousness of intentionally inflicted injuries. The instrumentality effect states that the presence of a lethal weapon increases the probability of a fatal injury. As Philip J. Cook has asserted, "case fatality rates for assaults, robberies, and other violent encounters are much higher when the assailant uses a gun than a knife, club, or bare hands." Although Marvin Wolfgang, in a study conducted in the 1950s, concluded that the unavailability of firearms would have little effect on the number of firearms-related homicides because other weapons are readily at hand, Frank Zimring in the 1960s determined from his study of gun and knife as-

saults in Chicago that gun assaults led to fatalities five times as often as knife fights.

Attempting to explain his results, Zimring offered an ambiguity hypothesis, suggesting that in many cases, the assailant does not clearly intend to kill the victim. Because firearms are more deadly than other weapons, the chance that an attack will lead to death increases markedly when a gun is used. If the attacker does not have a clear intent to kill the victim, the attack may not be sustained beyond the first blow. Therefore, the lethality of the weapon may be a crucial factor in whether the attack will result in a fatality. Zimring also discovered that the fatality rate increased with the caliber of firearm used, a finding that appeared to support the instrumentality effect. A possible alternative explanation for lower fatality rates with other weapons and lower caliber firearms is that, counter to Zimring's ambiguity of intent hypothesis, those using firearms and higher caliber firearms have a greater intention to inflict harm and choose weapons accordingly. However, a large proportion of the knife attacks could be categorized as serious, leading to the conclusion that had attackers used firearms instead, a higher percentage of injuries would have resulted in death.

In the 1980s, Cook conducted a study to test the weapon instrumentality effect in robbery. He hypothesized that if the type of weapon is an independent causal factor in the probability of death, then there should be a positive relationship between a city's gun robbery rate and the robbery murder rate. Examining changes in robbery and robbery murder in 43 cities from 1976 to 1983, Cook discovered that for each additional 1,000 gun robberies, there occurred 4.8 murders, but every 1,000 non-gun robberies resulted in only 1.4 murders. Cook concluded that the murder and robbery rates are related and that the outcome depends at least in part on the type of weapon used in the robbery.

Research suggests an instrumentality effect with regard to the successful completion of a robbery: success for cases involving guns is higher than for other weapons. Although the chance that violence will occur is less with firearms, if such violence does occur, the presence of a gun increases the chance that injuries will be more serious. Some people have argued that stricter control of handguns would lead to criminals substituting more lethal long guns. However, others observe that handguns are disproportionately used in crime and are preferred because they are more easily concealed. Therefore, those advocating stricter controls on handguns reject the substitution argument, contending that handgun control will result in fewer firearms being involved in crime.

Cook has concluded that "if violent people did not have access to guns, there would still be as much violence in the United States as there is now, or more, but it would be much less deadly." Gun control advocates extend this conclusion, proposing that the presence of firearms in various conflict situations increases the probability that serious injury or death will occur. Contrary to this conclusion, those more supportive of the gun rights position argue that the presence of firearms among citizens acts as a deterrent to crime because criminals fear that their intended victims are armed. *See also* COOK, PHILIP J.; FATALITIES; VIOLENT CRIME RATE; ZIMRING, FRANKLIN E.

Further Reading: Philip J. Cook, "The Technology of Personal Violence," in Michael Tonry, ed., *Crime and Justice: A Review of Research*, vol. 14 (Chicago: University of Chicago Press, 1991); Marvin E. Wolfgang, *Patterns in Criminal Homicide* (Philadelphia: University of Pennsylvania Press, 1958); Franklin E. Zimring, "Is Gun Control Likely to Reduce Violent Killings?" *University of Chicago Law Review* 35 (1968), 721-37.

International Association of Chiefs of Police (IACP)

The International Association of Chiefs of Police (IACP), which labels itself "the world's senior law enforcement executive association," has actively opposed efforts on the state and federal levels to enact liberalized carrying concealed weapons (CCW) laws and has objected to proposals to institute a federal law that would establish a more uniform national right to carry concealed weapons by preempting, or superseding, state concealed carry laws. By taking these positions on CCW laws, the IACP has come into conflict with many gun rights organizations. Established in 1893, the IACP has over 14,000 members from 80 countries. The organization has its headquarters in Alexandria, Virginia, and maintains a professional staff of 50 people. An advisory board of 52 individuals representing international, federal, state, and local law enforcement agencies oversees the professional staff and establishes policy for the organization.

In July 1997, Darrell L. Sanders, president of the IACP, presented testimony regarding proposed CCW legislation before the Subcommittee on Crime of the U.S. House of Representatives Committee on the Judiciary. Sanders declared that his organization opposed preemption of local law enforcement discretion in issuing CCW permits. He observed that no adequate studies had been conducted that would support a decision to federalize concealed weapons policy. Such laws differ widely from state to state, reflecting the varied wishes of citizens in different states. Sanders was concerned with a provision in proposed legislation allowing current or retired police officers to carry concealed weapons in any jurisdiction. Federal legislation would impose a uniform national standard and thus deprive state and local jurisdictions of the right to maintain their own qualifications for police officers and policies for off-duty carrying.

Sanders referred to the "slippery slope" approach of the proposed legislation that involved a dual strategy of liberalizing CCW laws for private citizens and police. He reported that the IACP opposed any federal legislation that would liberalize CCW laws with regard to interstate carrying of concealed weapons by police officers when not on duty. If some legislation were to be enacted, Sanders recommended measures that only allowed states to enter into reciprocal agreements to regulate the carrying of concealed weapons. He advocated a version that would exempt only qualified law enforcement officers on active duty and that would allow state and local agencies to establish policies regarding carrying weapons off-duty or out of jurisdiction.

The IACP has asked members to form coalitions among groups that share a similar concern over liberalized CCW laws. The coalitions should investigate proposed bills carefully and contact sponsors to recommend ways of amending them to make the legislation more restrictive. Provisions that could be added to CCW bills include such requirements as fingerprinting applicants; checking for criminal history, drug or alcohol addiction, and mental health status; requiring a minimum number of hours per year of firearms training instruction; charging fees for processing applications; increasing penalties for those who carry concealed weapons without a permit; and issuing CCW permit stickers to be affixed to state drivers licenses.

IACP members are encouraged to lobby for strict CCW license revocation policies for such criminal activity as stalking and domestic abuse, to call for CCW laws to be approved by referendum election, and to work for the inclusion of a provision requiring reauthorization after a limited number of years. CCW laws could also contain a requirement that permit applicants show proof of gun liability insurance. The IACP is especially concerned with maintaining some local police discretion in processing applications for CCW licenses. *See also* Concealed Carry Laws; State Gun Statutes.

Further Reading: International Association of Chiefs of Police Web site <www.theiacp.org>.

International Brotherhood of Police Officers (IBPO)

The International Brotherhood of Police Officers (IBPO), one of the largest police unions in the nation, representing over 50,000 law enforcement personnel, has supported several gun control initiatives. Priding itself on a militant advocacy of the rights of police officers, the organization maintains a professional lobbying staff in Washington, D.C., and works aggressively for the passage of legislation to benefit it members. The Brotherhood has lobbied for legislation that would prohibit mail-order sales of body armor so that police officers would be less likely to face violent criminals who are well armed and well protected.

Established in 1964, the IBPO grew out of a controversy over the firing of seven police officers in Cranston, Rhode Island. As a result of the controversy, the Rhode Island legislature passed the Police Officers Arbitration Act, which granted to police officers the right to organize and negotiate. The organization has defended its members in many court cases and labor relations hearings and before Civil Service commissions.

The IBPO has endorsed the proposal of California Democratic Senator Barbara Boxer to require trigger locks on all new handgun sales. Kenneth T. Lyons, the organization's national president, noted that a difficult job for police officers is to enter a home where a child has been injured or killed by an unsecured gun. Citing Centers for Disease Control (CDC) data indicating that over one million children have unsupervised access to loaded and unlocked firearms, Lyons declared that the proposed legislation "simply put will save lives."

The IBPO has supported legislation to establish a permanent waiting period for purchasing a handgun. The Brady Handgun Violence Prevention Act provided for a temporary five-day waiting period that was replaced by a National Instant Check System (NICS) in November 1998. The proposed legislation would establish a minimum three-day waiting period for purchasing a handgun. Lyons holds that such a waiting period would help prevent impulsive purchases of handguns in crisis situations. In addition, a waiting period would allow for a more thorough background check than an instant check system.

The IBPO supports several other gun control initiatives. Firearms dealers should be made more accountable by a policy of revoking the license of any dealer who knowingly sells a gun to a minor. Two forms of identification should be required to purchase a firearm. Steps should be taken to improve the ability to trace firearms used in crimes committed by juveniles. Firearms manufacturers should be required to improve safety features on their products. The Brotherhood supports the proposed Children's Gun Violence Prevention Act, which is intended to keep guns away from young people. The bill includes a proposal for gun violence awareness programs and an initiative to identify and prosecute anyone providing guns to minors.

The IBPO objects to the 1996 Lautenberg Amendment which bans firearms possession for anyone convicted of a misdemeanor related to domestic violence. The organization holds that the legislation is "extreme in its scope" and "short-sighted" because it does not include an exception for weapons possession by government personnel in the performance of their duties. The Brotherhood supports legislation that would exempt law enforcement officers, at least while they are on the job. Arguing that police officers often face threats while performing their official duties, the organization supports legislation that would permit active and qualified retired officers to carry a firearm in any jurisdiction. *See also* BOXER, BARBARA; BRADY HANDGUN VIOLENCE PREVENTION ACT; INTERNATIONAL ASSOCIATION OF CHIEFS OF POLICE; LAUTENBERG AMENDMENT; NATIONAL INSTANT CHECK SYSTEM; YOUTH AND GUNS.

Further Reading: International Brotherhood of Police Officers Web site <www.ibpo.org>.

International Defensive Pistol Association (IDPA)

The International Defensive Pistol Association's (IDPA) emphasis on defensive shooting reflects the growing perception that handguns serve as highly useful defensive weapons for the average citizen. The organization was established by a group of individuals dissatisfied with the United States Practical Shooting Association, which they claim "has lost touch with the original principles of practical shooting and has become just another shooting game." Bill Wilson serves as the organization's president. Viewing pistol shooting competition as a simulation of defensive tactics, the IDPA wishes to "create a level playing field for all competi-

tors to test the skill and ability of the individual, not his equipment or gamesmanship."

Competition supported by the IDPA involves defensive pistol shooting in realistic self-defense situations. Competitors must use practical handguns, full charge service ammunition, and holsters that are considered appropriate for self-defense use. The IDPA encourages close range shooting at moving targets. Shooting distances are usually under 15 yards. Shooting stages often begin with the pistol in the holster and concealed. Among its goals, the Association promotes safe and competent use of firearms and equipment intended for self-defense, provides shooters with courses that simulate "potentially life-threatening encounters," and tests skills required for surviving such situations. Competitors in IDPA matches must use service type pistols or revolvers, 9mm/.38 Special or larger caliber. Holsters must be of the concealed carry type. Matches are open to anyone who can legally own a handgun. Competition is divided into four divisions: stock service pistol, enhanced service pistol, custom defensive pistol, and service revolver. Clubs affiliated with the IDPA are located in 42 states and seven foreign countries.

The IDPA emphasizes safe firearms use, suggesting that the more often persons handle a gun, the more likely they will have a "negligent discharge." The first IDPA pistol competition rule states that any competitor who handles a firearm unsafely will be disqualified from the match. Bill Nottingham, who is associated with the organization, has presented his version of "The Four Laws of Gun Safety" that are meant to decrease the probability of a tragedy occurring if a gun owner experiences "brain-fade," a momentary lapse in safe handling. While many gun control supporters advocate limitations on the use of firearms to prevent tragedy, Nottingham suggests basic rules to minimize the results of a negligent discharge. According to the first rule, assume that a gun is always loaded. This tenet calls for constantly inspecting a firearm to determine if it contains ammunition. The second rule states, "Never point a gun at something you're not prepared to destroy."

Always aim a firearm in a safe direction. The third rule mandates making sure of the target and what is behind it. Firearms users should be aware of the penetrating power of their weapons and aim only at a bullet-proof backstop. According to the fourth rule, shooters should keep their finger off the trigger until the sight is on the target: "The finger should not touch the trigger until the instant you are prepared to fire." Nottingham concludes that firearms should be kept from children, those not trained in their use, and "especially thieves." *See also* CONCEALED CARRY LAWS; UNITED STATES PRACTICAL SHOOTING ASSOCIATION.

Further Reading: International Defensive Pistol Association Web site <www.idpa.com>.

Israel

Gun rights advocates point to Israel as a nation with a high gun density in the population but with a low murder rate (40 to 60 murders each year in a population of less than 5 million), thus dismissing any claim of a relationship between the availability of firearms and the level of violence. Robert W. Lee, a gun rights advocate, notes that in April 1984 three terrorists began shooting in a Jerusalem café with automatic weapons. They killed just one individual before being shot by Israelis armed with handguns. Lee concludes that certain mass murders in the United States could be prevented if gun carrying were as widespread as in Israel.

However, gun control advocates note that the distribution of firearms in Israel is strictly regulated. Anyone wishing to carry a firearm must demonstrate a valid reason for doing so, although any person without a criminal record may fairly easily acquire a permit. The Interior Ministry must issue a special permit, which requires the approval of the police. The permit contains basic information about the gun owner and the type of gun possessed. The owner of a weapon is legally responsible for it. If it is lost or stolen, the owner must inform the police within 24 hours, but still may be prosecuted on the misdemeanor charge of negligence.

In the article "Israel Has a Successful Gun Control Policy" (1992), Abraham Tennenbaum, a former Israeli police lieutenant, noted that the United States and Israel differ according to the reasons citizens own firearms. In Israel, although guns are owned for hunting and target shooting, their main function is military defense and protection against terrorism. Tennenbaum found that most firearms in Israel are owned not by private citizens who carry them, but by the army, the police, or other authorities. Due to a system of universal military service, most citizens are issued firearms to take home with them. If school children take a trip, they are accompanied by armed guards, who are often parents and teachers. The local police station assigns them firearms that are returned after the trip. The Civil Guards, a volunteer group operated by the Israeli police, conduct armed night patrols of neighborhoods. Firearms are issued at the start and returned at the completion of each patrol.

Tennenbaum attributed the high concentration of firearms in Israel to the special security needs of the country. The basic policy is to distribute firearms generally to those not specifically prohibited from possessing arms. Although criminals can acquire firearms, it is a more difficult task than in the United States and the punishment can be severe. Illegal weapons are either stolen from private citizens or taken from the army. Tennenbaum noted that because the army is a source of illegal weapons, explosives and automatic weapons are used more often in murders. The case of Israel demonstrates that there is no simple relationship between the prevalence of firearms and acts of violence. Cultural factors may play a role in the low incidence of gun-related violent crime, as do serious attempts to keep weapons out of the hands of known criminals. Israeli gun control policy toward Arab residents would likely not be accepted by gun rights advocates in the United States. In 1996, Israeli firearms laws were modified to permit all civilians who have served in army combat units to carry guns. This policy generally excluded Arab residents from firearm possession.

Further Reading: Robert W. Lee, "Gun Control Would Not Reduce Crime," in Charles P. Cozic, ed., *Gun Control* (San Diego: Greenhaven Press, 1992), pp. 50-58; Abraham N. Tennenbaum, "Israel Has a Successful Gun Control Policy," in Charles P. Cozic, ed., *Gun Control* (San Diego: Greenhaven Press, 1992), pp. 248-51.

Izaak Walton League of America (IWLA)

Although the Izaak Walton League of America (IWLA), one of the nation's oldest conservation groups, usually does not take part in the gun control debate, the organization has on occasion supported gun rights groups. The organization's hunting membership influences its position on this issue. Given the organization's prestige in the area of conservation, it can prove to be a valued ally, along with other groups concerned with wildlife preservation and resource conservation.

In 1922, 54 sportsmen, concerned about the deterioration of the nation's fishing streams, formed the organization to fight water pollution. Named after a seventeenth-century English fisherman and conservationist, the League today has 50,000 members and attempts to protect not only the nation's waterways, but also its soil, forests, and wildlife. Among its many projects, the League campaigned for the creation of the Land and Water Conservation Fund, a revenue source for acquiring land for parks and recreational facilities.

Since its founding, the IWLA has been active in outdoor recreation activities, including hunting and fishing. In 1937, the organization backed the Pittman Robertson Act, which imposed an excise tax on the sale of sporting firearms and ammunition. Money raised by this tax was to be used for wildlife projects. In the 1950s, as millions of Americans took up the sport of hunting, the League began a program to improve hunter behavior. This program continued through the 1970s, and in 1980 the League sponsored the first National Conference on Outdoor Ethics.

In the 1960s, gun rights groups were able to elicit expressions of support from the Izaak Walton League, along with other wildlife and conservation organizations. When Senator Thomas Dodd, a Connecticut Democrat, expanded his gun control proposals to include regulation of the sale of rifles and shotguns, sporting and conservation groups such as the IWLA sensed a potential threat to the interests of their membership, many of whom were hunters. Pro-gun interests argued that the formulation of any reasonable and effective firearms legislation should include input from groups like the League. Pro-gun groups recognized that the prestige of the IWLA, a longtime conservation group that has gained the respect of hunters, could lend significant support to the gun rights position.

In recent years, the League has continued to support outdoor ethics conferences, in which hunters and other outdoor enthusiasts participate. Those engaged in outdoor recreation are urged to take responsibility for preserving and protecting resources. The League's wide interests, including promotion of energy efficiency and lowering greenhouse gas emissions, soil conservation and preservation of agricultural wetlands, and educational projects dealing with natural resource maintenance, assure the organization a respected place in the area of environmental protection. Gun rights groups have benefited from the potential support of such organizations. *See also* DODD, THOMAS J.; GUN CONTROL ACT OF 1968.

Further Reading: Bill R. Davidson, *To Keep and Bear Arms* (New Rochelle, NY: Arlington House, 1969); Izaak Walton League of America Web site <http://www.iwla.org>.

J

Japan

Japan has strict gun control laws and a low crime rate. The nation experiences approximately 200 gun-related violent crimes each year, which, compared to the United States, is extremely low. The robbery rate in Japan is 1.4 per 100,000 population, compared to 220.9 in the United States. Analysts disagree about the nature of the relationship between Japanese gun control policy and that nation's crime rate. While some advocate the introduction of similarly stringent legislation in the United States to curb crime, others observe that the success of Japan's gun control policies cannot be separated easily from Japanese traditions that emphasize social control.

Japanese law prohibits ownership of handguns and rifles. Sportsmen are allowed to own shotguns for hunting and other gun-related sporting activities, but acquiring such a weapon requires undergoing a prolonged licensing process. Applicants must attend classes, take a written examination, and pass a shooting test. They must undergo mental testing and submit an affidavit to police certifying their mental competence to own a firearm. Police run background checks on applicants and their relatives to make sure they have committed no crimes. Police officials are granted extensive discretion to deny a license to anyone they suspect of being a danger to others.

Firearms owners are required to store weapons in a locker and to inform police of its precise location in the home. Ammunition must be kept locked in a separate place. In 1971, the Japanese government prohibited any transfers of rifles, but allowed current licensed owners to keep their weapons. When an owner dies, relatives must surrender the rifle to police. Violation of the handgun prohibition can result in severe punishment. The maximum penalty for possessing a handgun is 10 years in prison and a fine roughly equivalent to $8,000. Even though shotguns and air rifles remained legal, the number of licensed weapons declined by nearly a quarter during the 1980s.

While most analysts admit that Japanese gun control policies have been successful, they have attributed that success to several causes. The police, who generally are held in high regard, have been granted extensive search and seizure powers. Twice each year police make visits to all Japanese homes to gather various types of information. They check on gun licensees to determine if a gun has been stolen, how securely the gun is stored, and the emotional stability of the owner. The Japanese justice system does not ensure protection against police searches, and the right of habeas corpus is not nearly as stringently enforced as in the United States. Police are efficient in clearing criminal cases. Due to this efficiency, no compelling need exists for Japanese citizens to own firearms for self-defense. For instance, Tokyo has been labeled the safest city in the world.

Historically, gun ownership in Japan was limited to a relatively small elite. Unlike the United States, where over 200 million firearms are privately owned, few guns are in private hands. Firearms were introduced into Japan during the sixteenth century and quickly came into use as weapons of warfare. However, largely through the influence of the samurai warrior nobility, which preferred to rely on the sword, firearms distribution was severely limited. Firearms manufacturing never became a significant economic enterprise for private distribution.

Because the Japanese people, traditionally very law-abiding, comply voluntarily with gun control laws, police officials are not required to expend a much time or effort enforcing the laws. However, officials have become concerned about even the small rate of violent crime. In 1995, just 34 gun-related homicides occurred in Japan, but officials still worried that a population exposed to Western popular culture and increasingly concerned about confronting criminals wielding firearms might find gun ownership an attractive option.

Further Reading: Catherine Foster, "Nations Around World Try to Get a Grip on Guns," *Christian Science Monitor* (May 15, 1996), 1, 10-11; David B. Kopel, *The Samurai, the Mountie, and the Cowboy* (Buffalo, NY: Prometheus, 1992).

Jefferson, Thomas (1743–1826)

Gun rights advocates cite the views of such noted early American statesmen as Thomas Jefferson to support their claim that the Constitution guarantees an individual right to keep and bear arms. Jefferson, in the Declaration of Independence, offered a defense of the right of revolution that for over 200 years has inspired those who oppose tyranny. Those supporting gun rights deduce from that defense that the right to bear arms against an oppressive government stands as a major bulwark against the abuse of power.

Gun advocates use several of Jefferson's statements to support the view that he understood the Second Amendment as guaranteeing a fundamental right to bear arms. For instance, National Rifle Association (NRA) executive vice president Wayne LaPierre notes a quote from Italian criminologist Cesare Beccaria that Jefferson "copied . . . in longhand into his own personal compilation of great quotations." The quote declares that laws forbidding the carrying of arms to avoid a "trifling inconvenience" disarms "those only who are neither inclined nor determined to commit crimes." Second Amendment Foundation president Alan Gottlieb quotes Jefferson from a letter written in 1811 commenting that state militias, which could oppose national dictatorship, would be composed of every citizen capable of bearing arms. Gottlieb quotes Jefferson as recommending the use of a gun as exercise to develop a strong body and strong mind. The gun, according to Jefferson, should be "the constant companion of your walks."

After taking part in the drafting and signing of the Declaration of Independence, Jefferson returned to Virginia to take part in writing the new state constitution. He proposed the inclusion of a provision to guarantee "a freeman's right to use arms while forbidding standing armies." During the state convention debates over ratification of the national constitution, Jefferson expressed his own preferences for a bill of rights. He urged that such a document should guarantee freedom of religion, freedom of the press, protection against a standing army, freedom of commerce against the restrictions of monopolies, the right of habeas corpus, and trial by jury. He expressed intense concern, as he had with the Virginia state constitution, with a standing army, which he declared a dangerous instrument against the rights of the nation that places the people at the mercy of the government.

In *The Constitutional Thought of Thomas Jefferson* (1994), David Mayer suggested that Jefferson's influence can be seen in the Second Amendment's guarantee of the right to keep and bear arms. However, others argue that the Second Amendment and concerns over a standing army are closely related constitutionally, and were so related in Jefferson's mind. To soften the national government's power to maintain an army, the Second Amendment placed the control of militias solidly in the hands of the states. Therefore, although Jefferson may have supported the right of citizens to bear arms, his preference may not be directly reflected in the Second Amendment. *See also* AMERICAN REVOLUTION; GOTTLIEB, ALAN MERRIL; LAPIERRE, WAYNE; NATIONAL RIFLE ASSOCIATION; SECOND AMENDMENT.

Further Reading: Alan M. Gottlieb, *Gun Rights Fact Book* (Bellevue, WA: Merril, 1994); David N. Mayer, *The Constitutional Thought of Thomas Jefferson* (Charlottesville: University Press of Virginia, 1994).

Jews for the Preservation of Firearms Ownership (JPFO)

In 1989, Aaron Zelman founded Jews for the Preservation of Firearms Ownership (JPFO) to counter the pro-gun control position of the Anti-Defamation League. Zelman continues to serve as executive director. The JPFO holds to an absolutist interpretation of the Second Amendment and always puts the term gun control within quotation marks to emphasize their complete rejection of its legitimacy. The organization applies lessons from the Holocaust to current debates over gun control, coming to the conclusion that horrible things can happen to people who surrender their right to own firearms. The JPFO recommends that all law-abiding citizens own firearms. The organization supports carrying concealed weapons laws as a method of deterring criminal activity and advocates firearms safety courses in public schools. Those who misuse firearms should undergo severe penalties.

The JPFO maintains that because Jewish law requires self-defense, gun control subverts God's command. Although the organization focuses primarily on activating Jewish gun owners to vocalize their opposition to gun control, non-Jewish members are welcomed. Zelman estimates that 25 percent of JPFO members are not Jewish. While the organization cooperates with other gun rights groups and offers them the results of JPFO investigations, it claims to be the only group that truly understands the importance of the issue. It contends that gun control has historically been an intimate part of genocide campaigns that have led to the deaths of millions of people.

The JPFO promotes a cartoon character similar to the National Rifle Association's (NRA) Eddie Eagle. Gran'pa Jack, who appears in the comic book, *"Gun Control" Kills Kids*, criticizes gun control efforts and tells children that firearms save lives. The character encourages children to make sure their parents own firearms and know how to use them. The comic books are intended for use in school systems.

The organization holds that the Gun Control Act of 1968 is based on a Nazi gun law passed in Germany in 1938. Both laws determine the legality of firearms on the basis of function, contain provisions limiting importation only to those guns judged suitable for sporting purposes, and grant to an unelected bureaucracy the authority to determine the meaning of sporting purpose. The JPFO claims that during the twentieth century, 59 million people were killed worldwide as a result of gun control laws that left them defenseless. However, in contrast to Nazi Germany, the United States has a Constitution that, according to the JPFO, guarantees individuals an absolute right to own firearms.

Consistent with its absolutist stand on gun control, the JPFO opposes the instant check system, which in November 1998 replaced the federal five-day waiting period for purchasing a handgun. The organization claims that the instant check database is equivalent to national gun registration. According to the JPFO, the Nazi model of gun registration will lead to further citizen acceptance of federal government interference in their lives, the classification of gun owners as a dangerous class of people to be watched with suspicion (just as Jews were stigmatized in Nazi Germany), and ultimately confiscation of firearms.

Although gun control supporters have used various mass shootings, including those at schools, in campaigns advocating more stringent regulations on firearms ownership, the JPFO asserts that gun control allows such incidents to occur in the first place. Teachers and school officials are unable to defend students because gun control laws leave them unarmed. A prospective terrorist or anyone wishing to gain publicity knows that schools are an undefended target. The organization recommends enactment of the policies followed in Israel, where PLO terrorist attacks on schools are deterred because teachers and parents carry firearms. *See also* AMERICAN JEWISH CONGRESS; CENTRAL CONFERENCE OF AMERICAN RABBIS; CONCEALED CARRY LAWS; EDDIE EAGLE; GUN CONTROL ACT OF 1968; ISRAEL; NATIONAL INSTANT CHECK SYSTEM; NATIONAL RIFLE ASSOCIATION; SECOND AMENDMENT; YOUTH AND GUNS.

Further Reading: "Interview with Aaron Zelman," *Guns and Ammo* (April 1996), 10-13; Jews for the Preservation of Firearms Ownership Web site <www.jpfo.com>.

John Birch Society (JBS)

The John Birch Society (JBS), a conservative organization that gained much publicity during the 1960s for its strong anti-communist stand, is a firm supporter of an individual right to keep and bear arms. Society members believe that the American system of government, which they call a constitutional republic, is "the finest yet developed by man." The Second Amendment, as part of the revered governing document, is understood to guarantee the right of free individuals to possess firearms. Members believe that this right to keep and bear arms must be defended against those who would limit the freedoms of Americans. The Society holds the Constitution in such high regard that it has opposed calls for a constitutional convention to amend the document, even when the organization supports the intent of the proposed changes.

Robert Welch founded the Society in 1958 following a meeting of business friends at which he presented his plan to fight collectivism and what he considered treasonous activities in American government. Welch named the organization after an American missionary to China who aided the Chinese in their struggle against the Japanese. Birch was killed by the new communist regime that came to power in China in 1949. For over 35 years, the Society has operated as an educational organization, warning Americans

against what it considers ever expanding government power and socialist tendencies in American government. In addition to gun control, the organization opposes proposals for national health care, a national school curriculum and teacher certification, government-mandated food and vitamin labeling, and any other measure that would result in greater government control over the lives of citizens.

The Society has expressed its opposition to the Brady Handgun Violence Prevention Act, claiming that the law has inconvenienced many law-abiding citizens without demonstrating any positive benefit for fighting crime. Robert W. Lee writes a regular column for the organization's bimonthly publication, *The New American*, in which he reports on the gun rights issue. In response to school shootings in the 1990s in Arkansas, Kentucky, and Mississippi, Lee rejected the conclusion that firearms in the hands of youth are always dangerous. He recounted cases in which young people employed guns successfully to defend themselves against criminal attacks.

In 1998, when Charlton Heston was being considered for the presidency of the National Rifle Association (NRA), Lee raised doubts about Heston's commitment to gun rights, discussing Heston's support for passage of the Gun Control Act of 1968. Heston was described as a "gun control diehard" for maintaining his commitment to a gun control organization led by actor Tom Laughlin after many other actors had dropped away from the group. Lee expressed concern regarding Heston's expressed intention to move the NRA to a more moderate position.

The Society has supported several items on the gun rights agenda, including state concealed carry statutes, which require local law enforcement officers to grant a license to carry a concealed weapon to anyone, such as a convicted felon, who is not expressly forbidden to do so. The Society emphasizes that concealed carry laws have not resulted in increased homicides among normally law-abiding citizens. The organization notes with approval that women are increasingly assuming the right to bear arms for self-defense. *See also* Brady Handgun Violence Prevention Act; Concealed Carry Laws; Gun Control Act of 1968; Heston, Charlton; National Rifle Association; Second Amendment; State Gun Statutes; Women and Guns; Youth and Guns.

Further Reading: John Birch Society Web site <www.jbs.org>; Robert W. Lee, "Heston, For the Record," *The New American* (April 13, 1998), 15-16; Robert W. Lee, "Guns in the Right Hands," *The New American* (August 17, 1998), 33-34.

Johns Hopkins Center for Gun Policy and Research

The Johns Hopkins Center for Gun Policy and Research was established in 1995 through funding from the Joyce Foundation. The Center labels gun violence a health issue and strives to reduce gun violence by providing research results to policy makers, organizations, the mass media, and the general public on subjects such as firearms-related injuries and the consequences of various gun policies. The Center takes a pro-gun control stance and questions the value of research conducted by social scientists who conclude that firearms possession can be an effective means of personal defense. Stephen P. Teret serves as director of the Center and John S. Vernick is the associate director. The Center employs three additional faculty members and collaborates with gun policy researchers at other universities and foundations.

The Center has developed a model handgun safety standard act that state and local governments may use as a guide to revising firearms policy. Formulated in 1996, the model law calls for establishing a commission that will determine an appropriate handgun safety performance standard. Each handgun should be equipped with technologically sophisticated devices that prevent it from being fired by anyone but the owner. The technology must be integral to the gun's design and not an addition to it, and the personalized component should not be subject to easy alteration. The law would mandate that a manufacturer submit a model of a personalized handgun to an independent laboratory where its compliance with the performance standard will be determined.

The model legislation provides for specific exemptions, including handguns that are categorized as antiques, manufactured before the effective date of the law, acquired by law enforcement officers and members of the armed forces, or attached to a federal agency. Although exempted weapons may not be sold, traded, shipped, or distributed by dealers after the law has gone into effect, sales and transfers among private individuals would be allowed.

Law enforcement officers would be authorized to confiscate any handgun not covered by an exemption that fails to meet the performance standard, as long as they comply with constitutional restrictions on searches and seizures. Attorneys general of the various states would have the authority to take legal action against those failing to comply with the regulations. A violation of the law would constitute a felony punishable by fine and imprisonment. If an owner of a handgun or an unauthorized person fires the weapon, causing personal injury to another person, the owner could be held liable for damages.

The Center has criticized research conducted by social scientists such as John R. Lott and David B. Mustard of the University of Chicago, who conclude that allowing those without criminal records or histories of mental illness to carry concealed handguns can provide a higher level of personal safety. The Center claims that the University of Chicago researchers used a discredited methodology, disregarded established theories within criminology, ignored the possible effects of gun laws other than "shall issue" statutes, failed to observe precise dates when laws went into effect, and used an ambiguous definition for "shall issue" laws, which require law enforcement officers to issue a license to carry a concealed firearm to any applicant not specifically prohibited from doing so. *See also* Concealed Carry Laws; Lott, John R.

Further Reading: Johns Hopkins Center for Gun Policy and Research Web site <http://infosys.jhsp.edu/centers/gunpolicy>; John R. Lott, Jr., *More Guns, Less Crime: Understanding Crime* *and Gun-Control Laws* (Chicago: University of Chicago Press, 1998).

Jonesboro, Arkansas, School Shooting

The 1998 Jonesboro, Arkansas, school shooting involved two adolescents, one 11 and the other 13, who were arrested for killing four fellow students and one teacher, and wounding 11 others at the Westside Middle School. The shooting followed a series of other gun incidents at schools around the country. When the Jonesboro shooting occurred, the news media and the nation were already sensitized to the troubling repetition of firearms violence committed by adolescents a little older than children. President Bill Clinton, on a tour of African nations, took time to comment publicly that he and his wife were "deeply shocked and heartbroken." The incongruous image of two young boys employing firearms with such deadly effect shocked many around the nation, especially when the

news media reported that under Arkansas law the two boys had only limited responsibility for their actions. They had missed school that day to prepare for the shooting. One of the boys pulled the fire alarm and then took position with the other, taking aim from a wooded area as the unsuspecting students and teachers exited the school building. Wearing camouflage outfits and carrying a Ruger .44-caliber rifle and a 30.06 hunting rifle, they began firing at their classmates and teachers.

The press reported that the stepfather of one of the boys charged in the incident had trained his son in the use of rifles and shotguns and had begun training the boy in handgun shooting competition involving moving targets. He was also an official in a local gun club. A club member commented that the boy had been taught firearm safety and was a good student of gun handling.

The Jonesboro shooting set the stage for another round of debates over gun control. Many news programs and talk shows dis-

Students of Westside School bow their heads in prayer at the burial service of teacher Shannon Wright, who was killed on March 24, 1998, when two youths opened fire on fellow students at the school. *REUTERS/John Kuntz/Archive Photos.*

cussed the possible causes of the incident and the potential consequences. The Violence Policy Center (VPC) quickly issued a press release about the "massacre of children by children" that should focus national attention on "America's youth gun culture." The organization strongly implied that such gun groups as the National Rifle Association (NRA) and the National Shooting Sports Foundation (NSSF) were partly responsible for the gun culture, given that they "court America's children and actually encourage the use and possession of guns by kids." The VPC claimed that gun organizations intend to create future customers for the firearms industry and to recruit supporters for the pro-gun movement. The organization cited the NRA youth magazine *In Sights* and the 1997 Browning firearms catalog which displays a photograph of a child wearing a Browning cap and playing with spent shotgun shells.

Gun control critics responded that firearms did not cause the Jonesboro incident. The troubled youth, who were intent on doing harm to their fellow students, could just as well have used the vehicle in which they had intended to escape, driving it into the school and achieving a similarly deadly effect. Gun supporters balance what they perceive as the benefits of exposing young people to guns against the occasional tragedy caused for reasons other than the simple availability of firearms. In the meantime, pro-gun control groups continued to cite such incidents in their call for more stringent controls on the sale and possession of firearms in the United States. *See also* CLINTON, WILLIAM JEFFERSON (BILL); GUN CULTURE; LITTLETON, COLORADO, SCHOOL SHOOTING; NATIONAL RIFLE ASSOCIATION; NATIONAL SHOOTING SPORTS FOUNDATION; RUGER, WILLIAM BATTERMAN (BILL); STOCKTON, CALIFORNIA, SHOOTING; VIOLENCE POLICY CENTER; YOUTH AND GUNS.

Further Reading: *New York Times* (March 25, 1998), p. A1; Violence Policy Center, "Arkansas School Shooting Focuses New Attention on Youth Gun Culture," March 26, 1998.

K

Kates, Don B., Jr. (1941–)

For over 20 years, Don B. Kates, Jr., has served as one of the more avid spokespersons for an individual right to keep and bear arms. Kates has developed arguments about the meaning of the Second Amendment, rejecting the collective view in favor of the individualistic interpretation of the right to keep and bear arms. He contends that the word "people" used in the Second Amendment has the same referent as it does in other amendments; it indicates individual persons. Aside from the constitutional arguments regarding firearms ownership as an individual right, Kates claims that gun control fails to produce the results its proponents profess. He asserts that such measures as banning handguns would have little effect on the level of violence in society. Instead, violence can be reduced only through changes in social and economic institutions and in the basic beliefs and values of the population.

Kates received a B.A. from Reed College in Portland, Oregon, and a law degree from Yale University. In the 1960s, he was a civil rights worker, assisting such civil rights lawyers as William Kunstler. Helping with the federal War on Poverty program, Kates focused on civil rights and police misconduct cases. He began carrying a firearm for self-protection during the more violent period of the civil rights movement. After teaching constitutional law and criminal procedure at St. Louis University Law School, Kates opened a private law practice in San Francisco.

In an article published in 1976, Kates explained why he, a civil libertarian, opposed gun control. He explained that a civil libertarian must not trust the military and the police, who have a monopoly on armament, with the authority to decide who may possess firearms. Kates adhered to the replacement hypothesis: those who want to commit violence will do so, whether with a gun, knife, or other device. A firearm simply serves as one instrument for criminal activity.

In the 1990s, Kates focused on the public health researchers who were employing an epidemiological approach to investigating firearms and violence. He accused such researchers—whom he called "health sages"—not only of conducting bad science, but of intellectual dishonesty, "systematically inventing, misinterpreting, selecting, or otherwise manipulating data to validate preordained political conclusions." Questioning the integrity of health care researchers, Kates charged them with "fraudulent omission of material fact" and "overt misrepresentation of facts." He accused these researchers of suppressing information about declines in accidental gun fatalities and accidental child gun deaths, and misrepresenting the relationship between gun ownership and the homicide rate. Kates objected especially to the assumption that ordinary law-abiding citizens are more likely to commit murder simply because they own firearms, citing evidence indicating that murders are most often committed by those who already have a criminal history. He concluded that little can be gained by denying the average citizen the right to own a firearm.

While accusing health professionals of bias due to their close relationship to gun control lobbying groups, Kates himself is closely related to pro-gun organizations. For instance, the National Rifle Association (NRA) has retained him to represent firearms owners in lawsuits. In a 1998 article entitled "Trigger Points," Bob Thompson noted that while Kates might be correct in his claim that public health research on firearms is biased, he may have made the effort to discover the truth about the issue more difficult with his lawyer's tendency to impeach the credibility of the opposition as forcefully as possible. *See also* DOCTORS FOR INTEGRITY IN POLICY RESEARCH; HEALTH CARE PROFESSIONALS; NATIONAL RIFLE ASSOCIATION; SECOND AMENDMENT.

Further Reading: Don B. Kates, "Handgun Prohibition and the Original Meaning of the Second Amendment," *Michigan Law Review* 82 (November 1983); Don B. Kates and Gary Kleck, *The Great Gun Debate: Essays on Firearms and Violence* (San Francisco: Pacific Research Institute for Public Policy, 1997); Don B. Kates, Henry E. Schaffer, John K. Lattimer, and George B. Murray, "Guns and Public Health: Epidemic of Violence or Pandemic of Propaganda," *Tennessee Law Review* (1995); Bob Thompson, "Trigger Points," *Washington Post Magazine* (March 29, 1998), 12-16, 23-24, 26-27.

Kellermann, Arthur (1955–)

Arthur Kellermann is a physician who has conducted research suggesting that the presence of firearms contributes independently to a higher level of violence. The claim often made in the media that "a gun in the home triples the risk of a homicide in the home" originated in Kellermann's research reports. Kellermann has been strongly criticized by gun rights organizations and by other researchers who have concluded that firearms can serve as effective instruments of self-defense. Kellermann is often portrayed as the pro-gun control movement's equivalent to Gary Kleck, the researcher who has concluded that firearms are used for self-defense

much more often than they cause injuries to the innocent. Kleck has criticized Kellermann for failing to recognize that violence may lead to increased ownership of firearms for self-defense, thus reversing the suggested cause-effect relationship

Kellermann received an undergraduate degree in biology from Rhodes College and a masters degree in public health from the University of Washington. He graduated from the Emory University School of Medicine in 1980. Kellermann became chief of emergency medicine at the University of Tennessee at Memphis, medical director of the emergency department at the Memphis County Hospital, and medical director to the Memphis Fire Department and Emergency Medical Services Bureau. In 1993, the Rollins School of Public Health at Emory University recruited Kellermann to establish and serve as director of the Center for Injury Control. He has conducted clinical research on various subjects dealing with emergency medicine and has published papers on emergency treatment of asthma, cardiopulmonary resuscitation, defibrillation methods, and emergency department drug screening.

Kellermann first became concerned about firearms violence in 1984 while a graduate student at the University of Washington. The shooting death of soul singer Marvin Gaye, who was killed by his own father, motivated Kellermann to examine the criminological and medical literature on firearms. When he discovered that little relevant research had been conducted, he decided to begin his own work on the question. Along with King County medical examiner Donald Reay, Kellermann studied gunshot deaths in the Seattle area. Kellermann and Reay determined that there occurred "43 suicides, criminal homicides, or accidental gunshot deaths involving a gun kept in the home for every case of homicide for self-protection." In 1986, these research results were published in the *New England Journal of Medicine*, thus giving wide circulation to Kellerman's contention that guns should be considered an independent variable in explaining violent behavior.

In 1988, Kellermann published a paper that summarized the results of his research, which was partially funded by the Centers for Disease Control (CDC), comparing crime rates in Seattle and the neighboring Canadian city of Vancouver. Kellermann reported that while the two cities' crime rates were similar, firearm-related assaults were seven times greater in Seattle. Other researchers were especially critical of this study, focusing their attacks on the methodology Kellermann employed.

Continuing the investigation of the effects of keeping firearms in the home, Kellermann and nine colleagues conducted a six-year study employing the case control method, which, according to Kellermann, was designed to eliminate other potential causes of violence in the home besides the presence of firearms. In 1993, the *New England Journal of Medicine* published the study in which Kellermann concluded that the presence of firearms in the home was "strongly and independently associated with an increased risk of homicide."

Kellermann has moved on to investigate the implementation and evaluation of various methods of violence prevention. The Center for Injury Control received a $500,000 grant to conduct a study titled "Youth, Firearms and Violence in Atlanta: A Problem-Solving Approach." As differing strategies are implemented, changes in handgun-related crime rates will be monitored. The expectation is that this study will permit the redirection of resources to those methods of violence reduction that prove successful. *See also* ACCIDENTS INVOLVING GUNS; FATALITIES; KLECK, GARY; VIOLENT CRIME RATE.

Further Reading: Arthur Kellermann and Donald Reay, "Protection or Peril? An Analysis of Firearm-Related Deaths in the Home," *New England Journal of Medicine* (June 12, 1986), 1557-60; Arthur Kellermann, et al., "Suicide in the Home in Relation to Gun Ownership," *New England Journal of Medicine* 327 (August 13, 1992), 467-72; John D. Thomas, "Accidents Don't Happen: Arthur Kellermann Addresses Gun Violence and Injuries as Preventable Public Health Problems," *Emory Magazine* (Summer 1995); Bob Thompson, "Trigger Points," *Washington Post Magazine* (March 29, 1998), 12-16, 23-24, 26-27.

Kelley v. R.G. Industries, Inc. (1983)

The Court of Appeals of Maryland, in *Kelley v. R.G. Industries, Inc.* (304 Md. 124, 1983), dealt with the question of whether a manufacturer or marketer of handguns could be found liable for injuries caused by one of its handguns during the commission of a crime. In consciously revising common law, the court decided that although standard liability claims did not apply in this case, a claim based on the predictable use of a so-called Saturday night special was appropriate under Maryland law.

An assailant shot and wounded Olen J. Kelley, a grocery store clerk, during an armed robbery. The handgun was a Rohm Revolver, assembled and sold by R.G. Industries, Inc., of Miami, Florida, a subsidiary of Rohm Gesellschaft, a German company. Kelly subsequently sued R.G. Industries, employing several theories of liability. R.G. Industries, in a motion to dismiss, argued that the handgun was not defective in that it performed as expected, and that the company could not be held responsible for the actions of the assailant.

The court rejected Kelley's first two claims of strict liability—that the manufacture and marketing of handguns is an "abnormally dangerous activity" and that handguns are "abnormally dangerous products." The court rejected the applicability of the doctrine of liability in this case because when a handgun injures an individual toward whom it is aimed, it performs just as intended and the product has no flaw. The court concluded that the misuse of handguns by others cannot justify, under Maryland law, imposing strict liability on the manufacturers of handguns for resulting injuries. A handgun cannot be ruled defective simply because it can be used in criminal activity. Hence, Kelley's argument confused the normal function of a product with a defect in design or manufacture.

Nonetheless, the court identified a possible avenue still open for determining liability. Saturday night specials, defined as poorly made, inexpensive, lightweight, easily concealed handguns that are inaccurate and unreliable, have no legitimate uses in law enforcement, sport, or for personal protection, but are primarily weapons employed by criminals. The court argued that this type of handgun has been appropriately and officially branded unique from all others in its lack of use except in criminal activity. The court referred to testimony before Congress that labeled the Saturday night special dangerous to intended victims and bystanders, subject to backfire, and extremely inaccurate except at close range. Disparaging comments toward the Saturday night special made by Maxwell Rich, executive vice president of the National Rifle Association (NRA), made during testimony before the U.S. Senate, were quoted in the decision. The court concluded that both the U.S. Congress and the Maryland General Assembly had established that Saturday night specials are a unique type of handgun distinct from all others.

Referring to the Gun Control Act of 1968, the court noted the ban on the importation of any firearm that fails to qualify for use in law enforcement, the military, or sport. Also noted during congressional hearings were references to Saturday night specials as "bellyguns" and "manstoppers," indicating what the court concluded was the true purpose of such handguns. Their major value is limited to criminal activity due to their concealability and low cost.

After establishing that the Saturday night special is a unique weapon distinct from all other handguns, the court asserted that the manufacturer or sellers of a Saturday night special should know that the product in which he or she is dealing has primarily a criminal utility. Such uses can be clearly foreseen by manufacturers and marketers. Therefore, the court concluded that holding manufacturers and sellers of Saturday night specials strictly liable to persons who suffer injuries from their criminal use is consistent with established public policy on the state and national levels. The court thereby established a limited area of strict liability for the misuse of handguns of a particular type. If a court establishes that the weapon used to cause injury can be clas-

sified as a Saturday night special, the manufacturer or anyone engaged in the sale of the weapon may be held liable. The wrongful act involved is marketing such guns to the public with the knowledge that they have "little or no legitimate use."

The court determined whether, in the present case, the Rohm Revolver could be categorized as a Saturday night special. Citing a handgun identification study, the weapon was placed in the category of the least expensive handguns of poorest quality, and therefore the general basis for liability was established in this specific case. *See also* GUN CONTROL ACT OF 1968; NATIONAL RIFLE ASSOCIATION; SATURDAY NIGHT SPECIAL.

Further Reading: *Kelley v. R.G. Industries, Inc.*, 304 Md. 124 (1983).

Kennesaw, Georgia

In 1982, Kennesaw, Georgia, a small town on the northern outskirts of Atlanta, gained nationwide publicity when its city council unanimously passed an ordinance that required residents to have a firearm in their homes. The ordinance read in part: "To provide for and protect the safety, security, and general welfare of the city and its inhabitants, every head of household residing in the city limits is required to maintain a firearm, together with ammunition." A member of the city council indicated that Morton Grove, a village in Illinois that had banned the possession of handguns by all residents, was a major reason for Kennesaw's mirror-image ordinance.

Darwin Purdy, mayor of Kennesaw, stated that the measure's purpose was to ensure the safety of the local population. He did not think that the ordinance would have the effect of increasing gunshot wounds among the 7,000 residents, but suggested that the rate of injury to criminals might well increase. He was expressing the belief that widespread ownership of firearms by citizens deters crime. Police Chief Robert Ruble claimed that the crime rate had risen 16 percent in Kennesaw from 1980 to 1981, thus spurring passage of the new legislation. However, when broken down into actual categories, that estimate did not appear nearly as significant for a small town with a population of 7,000. Armed robberies had increased from one in 1980 to four in 1981, and the number of homicides decreased from two in 1980 to none in 1981. These figures suggest that reaction to the Morton Grove ordinance played a major role in the decision to pass the Kennesaw measure.

The Kennesaw City Council established a minimal fine for violation of the ordinance ($50) and exempted certain groups within the population, including those with disabilities that would prevent them from using a firearm, those who oppose the use of firearms due to religious beliefs, and convicted felons. Police Chief Ruble suggested that the Morton Grove police department send to the Kennesaw police department all the guns that they had confiscated. Morton Grove officials declined the offer. The nationwide publicity led to some sympathetic response among gun rights supporters. The Kennesaw police chief received offers from groups in New York, California, Texas, and Oklahoma to send weapons to the small town. The chief of police indicated that he intended to accept all donations.

Before the ordinance could go into effect, the city council wanted to establish firearm safety classes. The council delayed the effective date twice to have a firing range prepared for those citizens who wished to undergo training in the use of a firearm. When the ordinance finally took effect June 1, 1982, the mayor indicated that most residents already were in compliance. On June 1, the American Civil Liberties Union (ACLU) challenged the new ordinance as unconstitutional, but made little headway in the courts.

Although no attempt was made to enforce the gun law, city officials estimated that 85 percent of residents were in compliance. Two years after passage, the police reported a decline in house burglaries. However, with a significant growth in the town's population, the burglary rate began to increase once more. New Chief of Police Dwaine L. Wilson reported that in 1987 the burglary rate was 4.3 per 1,000 residents whereas the year before

it had been 3.8 per 1,000. Given the small population, these figures do not amount to a large number of burglaries (39 in 1987). The police chief attributed the growing incidence of crime to the increased population and the fact that burglars were taking advantage of residents who worked during the day. Firearms cannot deter crime when home owners are not there to use them. This time the town responded to the increased crime rate by initiating a Neighborhood Watch program. The 1982 ordinance is still in effect, but not stringently enforced. *See also* AMERICAN CIVIL LIBERTIES UNION; MORTON GROVE, ILLINOIS.

Further Reading: *New York Times*, March 16, 1982, p. 14; March 17, 1988, p. 18; March 18, 1982, p. 26; March 23, 1982, p. 18; May 1, 1982, p. 10; June 2, 1982, p. 18; July 31, 1988, p. 38.

Klanwatch Project

An affiliate of the Southern Poverty Law Center, the Klanwatch Project was founded in 1980 to accumulate data about the activities of the Ku Klux Klan and convey that information to government officials and the general public. The organization employs the legal structure to sue those responsible for intimidating other citizens and to pass legislation that protects those groups that have been the target of Klan attacks. In the 1980s and 1990s, Klanwatch enlarged its campaign to include various militia groups it believed were influenced by racist elements. Although the organization recognizes the right of citizens to lobby against gun control legislation peacefully and to take part in various firearms sports, it observes that some gun rights advocates tend to use their opposition to gun control legislation as an excuse to form militia organizations that pose a threat to others.

In the 1980s, Klanwatch filed various lawsuits against the Ku Klux Klan and neo-Nazi groups. In 1984, the organization confronted Glenn Miller and his organization, the Carolina Knights of the Ku Klux Klan, which had been coercing minority groups in that area. After Klanwatch filed a lawsuit, Miller agreed to a settlement that required him to cease harassing blacks and to discontinue militia activities. However, two years later Miller began a militia organization called the White Patriot Party, an organization dedicated to establishing a "White Republic" in the American South. Klanwatch discovered that Miller had accumulated a large stash of stolen military weaponry and had engaged present military personnel to train the militia in the use of various military arms. The militia leader was arrested, tried, found guilty, and sentenced to prison. When set free on bond, Miller announced a personal declaration of war on the government and minorities. The Federal Bureau of Investigation (FBI) finally arrested Miller in Springfield, Missouri, in a van loaded with weapons. Because of this sort of incident, Klanwatch has supported the enforcement of federal gun control legislation to limit the potential for violence on the part of militia groups tinged with racist ideologies.

Three years after filing suit against Miller and his militia group, Klanwatch sued Klan groups that had attacked civil rights marchers in Georgia. The suits severely hampered the operation of such groups. Two years later, in Portland, Oregon, Klanwatch sued Tom Metzger, leader of the White Aryan Resistance (WAR), who had provided for the training of the skin-head group responsible for the violence. The multi-million-dollar judgment against Metzger shut down his operation. In 1994, observing increased activity among militia organizations, Klanwatch established the Militia Task Force to monitor the activities of white supremacists who were attempting to gain control of militia organizations. Klanwatch feared that combining arms with racial hatred was an explosive combination.

In March 1995, Klanwatch's Militia Task Force held a conference on militias, which was attended by 24 law enforcement officers at all levels of government. Those attending the conference heard reports regarding the activities and intentions of militia groups, their opposition to gun control legislation, and their accumulation of illegal weapons. Gun rights supporters argue that no inference should be drawn regarding any violent intentions and activities of militia groups,

even though they insist on stockpiling firearms. However, Klanwatch is far less sanguine about the close connection between the strong opposition of militia groups to gun control legislation and their insistence on bearing arms as a protection against what they consider a tyrannical government. Klanwatch has looked approvingly on the enforcement of gun control legislation to check the development of such groups. *See also* KU KLUX KLAN; MICHIGAN MILITIA; MILITIA OF MONTANA; MILITIA WATCHDOG.

Further Reading: Morris Dees, *Gathering Storm: America's Militia Threat* (New York: Harper Collins, 1996).

Kleck, Gary (1950–)

In the early 1990s, Gary Kleck, professor of criminology and criminal justice at Florida State University, became a controversial figure in the gun control debate. Kleck's studies of gun control set the standard for social science research on the question and he assumed near-legendary status among gun rights advocates for suggesting that firearm ownership could contribute to a reduction in violent crime. His research publications are the origin of the frequent claims that firearms are used defensively as many as 2.5 million times each year. Reputedly once a gun control advocate, Kleck has become skeptical about the potential success of gun regulations. Although he makes clear that he is affiliated with no gun rights organizations and that he is concerned solely with objective scientific investigation, various pro-gun groups see him as a major proponent for their cause.

Kleck received a Ph.D. in sociology from the University of Illinois at Urbana in 1979. Since then he has published two books and several articles and book chapters on various sociological topics, including questions related to firearms, self-defense against crime, and gun control. He has been interviewed numerous times on television and radio and is a contact person for such publications as *Newsweek, Time, U.S. News and World Report,* the *New York Times,* and the *Washington Post.* Kleck's research has been concerned with determining the costs versus the benefits of firearms ownership and gun control, the number of lives lost to the criminal use of firearms versus the number of lives saved by the defensive use of firearms, and the number of robberies or assaults involving a firearm versus the number of such events deterred by potential victims who own firearms. In 1993, Kleck's book, *Point Blank,*

The research of Gary Kleck, professor of criminology and criminal justice at Florida State University, has suggested that firearms ownership can reduce violent crime. *Courtesy of Gary Kleck.*

won the Michael Hindelang Award of the American Society of Criminology for the best book in criminology.

Several of Kleck's conclusions have been subject to criticism. Some question his claim that as many as 2.5 million defensive gun uses occur each year. In *The Politics of Gun Control* (1998), Robert J. Spitzer noted that Kleck began in 1991 by estimating between 606,000 and 960,000 defensive uses, but rounded that figure up to one million. Spitzer observed that by 1994 Kleck's estimate had increased to 2.4 million. Spitzer claimed that Kleck failed to distinguish between actual and imagined instances of self-defense uses of firearms. He concluded that "the numerous problems with Kleck's data are ironic in the

light of his harsh criticism of the methodologies of those with whom he disagrees." Kleck, in a revised version of *Point Blank,* titled *Targeting Guns,* reported additional findings derived from a National Self-Defense Survey to provide evidence of *at least* 2.5 million defensive gun uses.

Kleck's investigations have led to the conclusion that not only can firearm ownership have significant positive results, its negative impact is not nearly as severe as previously assumed. Contrary to the assertions of many groups advocating more stringent gun control, Kleck states that fatal gun accidents seldom involve pre-adolescent children. He suggests that limitations on a specific group of firearms, such a handguns, would lead to the substitution of other, perhaps more lethal, types of weapons. In the case of suicide, Kleck concludes that limitations on the accessibility to firearms would lead to the substitution of other methods.

Responding to criticisms of his work on gun control that claim to find flaws in his data and methodology, Kleck states that scholars "are never entitled to ignore or discount strong and relevant evidence merely because it is flawed, for the simple reason that all evidence is flawed." He recommends that his critics employ more constructive strategies rather than engage in "scholarly misconduct" and apply the same level of skepticism to their own investigations of firearms.

Further Reading: Gary Kleck, *Targeting Guns: Firearms and Their Control* (Hawthrone, NY: Aldine de Gruyter, 1997); Gary Kleck, *Point Blank: Guns and Violence in America* (Hawthorne, NY: Aldine de Gruyter, 1991); Robert J. Spitzer, *The Politics of Gun Control,* 2nd ed. (New York: Chatham House, 1998).

Knox, Neal (1935–)

For over two decades, more hardline gun rights coalitions in the National Rifle Association (NRA) and other organizations have looked to Neal Knox for leadership. He has headed some of the more aggressive campaigns against gun control. A former newspaperman, Knox first came to prominence in the NRA in 1977 when he led a revolt by members who were dissatisfied with the organization's apparent willingness to compromise on gun control issues and concerned about lags in the membership roles. That year, at the annual meeting in Cincinnati, Ohio, the organization selected Harlon Carter, also an uncompromising opponent of gun control, as the new executive vice president. Carter appointed Knox to head the NRA's lobbying organization, the Institute for Legislative Action (ILA).

Knox wanted to weaken the Gun Control Act of 1968. He strongly supported passage of the McClure-Volker firearms decontrol bill (also known as the Firearms Owners Protection Act), which Congress enacted in 1986. This law altered major provisions in the 1968 legislation. In addition, Knox focused the NRA's attention on the Bureau of Alcohol, Tobacco, and Firearms (BATF), the federal agency responsible for enforcing national firearms legislation. When Republican Ronald Reagan became president in 1981, Knox led an NRA campaign to weaken the BATF. At congressional hearings, a proposal arose that would place gun regulation authority in another governmental agency. However, Knox expressed reservations about such a move and finally opposed it. One possible reason for Knox's opposition to this proposal was concern that another government agency might prove far more efficient in executing gun control legislation. Although the agency was not destroyed, Congress limited its funding and authority.

Knox's uncompromising position on gun control led to the alienation of some police organizations from the NRA. In the early 1980s, when moves first began to limit armor-piercing, so-called "cop-killer," bullets, Knox was quoted as saying that there is no such thing as a good bullet or a bad bullet. Police organizations did not appreciate what they considered an anti-police position on the issue. In 1981, when the communist leadership imposed martial law in Poland, Knox placed advertisements in newspapers titled "An Open Letter to all Polish Americans" in which he stated that Poland had exactly the firearms laws that the NRA had prevented from being enacted in the United States and

that the Second Amendment guarantee of the right to keep and bear arms, if observed, would prevent similar events from occurring in the United States.

In 1982, Knox was ousted from his position as director of the Institute for Legislative Action. In response, he established the Firearms Coalition, which operated from his consulting firm, Neal Knox Associates. In July 1984, he became a registered lobbyist representing the Coalition. In 1991, Knox campaigned to reestablish his position in the NRA. He informed members that the NRA was losing members and that J. Warren Cassidy, the current executive vice president, was responsible. He accused Cassidy of bad management practices and claimed that the organization faced bankruptcy under current leadership. At the 1991 annual meeting, Knox and 22 supporters won 23 of the 26 seats up for election on the board. The election results indicated that the NRA once again was moving toward a more hardline policy. Knox continued to write his column, "Knox's Notebook," for the NRA's *American Rifleman* and *Shotgun News*. In recent years, his column has dealt with such topics as President Bill Clinton's call for trigger locks, the defense of Saturday night specials or "junk guns," gun shows, the activities of the BATF, and various legislative proposals.

At the 1997 NRA annual meeting in Seattle, Knox lost his position on the board of directors, indicating that political struggles among factions in the NRA continue. Knox maintains a faithful following among pro-gun activists and remains a vocal advocate in the gun rights movement. Knox has been a vocal critic of NRA president Charlton Heston and the current organization leadership. *See also* AMERICAN RIFLEMAN; BUREAU OF ALCOHOL, TOBACCO, AND FIREARMS; CLINTON, WILLIAM JEFFERSON (BILL); FIREARMS COALITION; FIREARMS OWNERS PROTECTION ACT; GUN CONTROL ACT OF 1968; HESTON, CHARLTON; INSTITUTE FOR LEGISLATIVE ACTION; NATIONAL RIFLE ASSOCIATION; REAGAN, RONALD; SATURDAY NIGHT SPECIAL; SECOND AMENDMENT; *SHOTGUN NEWS*; TRIGGER LOCKS.

Further Reading: Firearms Coalition Web site <www.nealknox.com>; Josh Sugarmann, *National Rifle Association: Money, Power and Fear* (Washington, DC: National Press, 1992).

Kopel, David B. (1960–)

David B. Kopel, research director since 1992 for the Colorado-based Independence Institute, has written extensively on the issue of gun control. He has criticized various proposals to restrict firearm ownership, including waiting periods and bans on semi-automatic assault weapons. He emphasizes that the Second Amendment guarantees the right to possess firearms for defense against the lawless as well as the government, and that the amendment's reference to a militia assures the right of individuals to own military-type weapons.

In 1982, Kopel received a B.A. in history from Brown University and graduated magna cum laude from the University of Michigan Law School in 1985. He was assistant district attorney for the borough of Manhattan and assistant attorney general for Colorado where he represented state agencies in the enforcement of environmental laws. In addition to his position at the Independence Institute, Kopel is an associate policy analyst at the Cato Institute, a technical consultant for the International Wound Ballistics Association, and an adjunct professor at New York University Law School. Kopel has conducted research in many policy areas, including hazardous waste law, abortion, media violence, and criminal sentencing.

In 1992, Kopel published *The Samurai, the Mountie, and the Cowboy: Should America Adopt the Gun Controls of Other Democracies?* The book is an exploration of gun control policies in Japan, Great Britain, Canada, Australia, New Zealand, Jamaica, and Switzerland. Kopel looked at the broader historical, political, and cultural contexts of firearms policies in these varied countries, investigating the possibility of introducing into the United States the programs these countries have followed. Two later chapters deal with American culture and the prospects for the success of gun control in the United

States. He declared that the proliferation of firearms in the United States is not directly related to a high crime rate. Countering a fundamental assumption of pro-gun control forces that firearms are an independent cause

David B. Kopel, research director of the Independence Institute, has written extensively on gun control and has criticized various proposals to restrict firearms ownership, including waiting periods. *Courtesy of the Independence Institute.*

of greater levels of violence, Kopel argued instead that "America's crime has much more to do with the absence of internal social controls than with the absence of statutory gun controls."

In response to the Stockton, California, school shooting committed by a lone gunman using an assault weapon, Kopel cautioned against outlawing such weapons. He claimed that the core of the Second Amendment is the militia, not hunting. The constitutional guarantee of a popular militia ensures the existence of a force "capable of overthrowing a domestic tyrant, or of resisting an invasion by a foreign one." In response to gun control groups that contend the idea of a militia is obsolete, Kopel argued that citizen forces were still important to defense against invasion or during times of internal disruption.

Kopel predicted that any additional controls, including waiting periods and background checks, would have little effect on criminals' acquisition of firearms. He compared the situation to the restrictions on ownership of automatic weapons that have been in place since enactment of the National Firearms Act of 1934, claiming that "the system is a total failure" because such weapons are "readily obtainable, even by teenage gang members." Kopel concluded that the only control that could have prevented the Stockton killings was keeping the shooter in prison when authorities had the opportunity.

In 1997, Kopel coauthored with Paul H. Blackman *No More Wacos: What's Wrong with Federal Law Enforcement, and How to Fix It*. Kopel viewed the federal law enforcement agencies as increasingly militaristic, violent, and lawless. In addition to the Waco standoff, Kopel discussed the Randy Weaver shooting and other cases of the use of federal law enforcement agents. Kopel made several proposals for altering federal law enforcement agencies, including reforming forfeiture laws and revising arrest procedures, which would contribute to the maintenance of an individualistic interpretation of the right to keep and bear arms. *See also* ASSAULT WEAPONS BAN; AUSTRALIA; CANADA; INDEPENDENCE INSTITUTE; GUN CULTURE; MEDIA VIOLENCE; NATIONAL FIREARMS ACT OF 1934; NATIONAL INSTANT CHECK SYSTEM; RUBY RIDGE; SECOND AMENDMENT; STOCKTON, CALIFORNIA, SHOOTING; UNITED KINGDOM; WACO, TEXAS, RAID.

Further Reading: David B. Kopel, *The Samurai, the Mountie, and the Cowboy: Should America Adopt the Gun Controls of Other Democracies?* (Buffalo, NY: Prometheus, 1992); David B. Kopel, ed., *Guns: Who Should Have Them?* (Buffalo, NY: Prometheus, 1995); David B. Kopel and Paul H. Blackman, *No More Wacos: What's Wrong with Federal Law Enforcement, and How to Fix It* (Buffalo, NY: Prometheus, 1997).

Ku Klux Klan

Gun rights supporters refer to the American experience with the Ku Klux Klan to illus-

trate the fundamental advantages of gun ownership to maintaining rights of self-protection. They cite the Klan's objectives during the post-Civil War Reconstruction era to disarm blacks in the former slave states of the South. They also cite other incidents, running from the early post-war years through the civil rights movement of the 1960s, where blacks were successful in warding off Klan violence by possessing firearms and demonstrating a determination to use them if need be. The lesson for contemporary society supposedly is that gun control advocates can, just like the Klan, oppress those who have surrendered their right to keep and bear arms.

The original Klan was established by former Confederate groups who opposed the imposition of Reconstruction on the defeated southern states. The organization was founded in Pulaski, Tennessee, in May 1866, and the following year Nathan Bedford Forrest, a noted Confederate cavalry officer, assumed the position of Grand Wizard. In 1869, apparently concerned about the violent tactics of local Klan organizations, Forrest ordered that the Klan disband and stepped down as the organization's Grand Wizard. However, the Klan continued, determined to use violence and intimidation to keep blacks from voting or taking part in other political activities. Klan members adopted a wardrobe that included a flowing white robe, a white mask, and skulls on their saddle horns.

The original Klan subsided after the end of Reconstruction, but resumed in 1915 when William J. Simmons established a second Klan organization. The revived Klan endorsed a wider agenda, including anti-Catholic and anti-Jewish bias and a nativist platform reminiscent of the "Know Nothing" party in the 1850s. In the 1920s, the Klan reached a reported nationwide membership of 4 million. However, by 1930 the total number of Klansmen had declined to around 30,000. State laws forbidding the wearing of masks and the hard economic times brought on by the Great Depression contributed to the organization's demise. The Klan has had at least two resurrections since then, including Samuel Green's attempt to revive the organization in Georgia after World War II and Robert Shelton's efforts in Mississippi during the civil rights movement of the 1960s.

Although gun rights supporters suggest that citizens can resist oppression best if they possess the tools to protect themselves, some historians indicate that blacks after the Civil War faced significant handicaps in the effective use of firearms. The weapons they owned were usually shotguns, which did not match up against the Winchester rifles and the handguns that Klan members carried. Black military experience generally paled in comparison to Klansmen who had participated in the Civil War. Even when blacks had gained military experience, they were usually outnumbered by hostile whites who generally were well trained in the use of arms. Even when blacks successfully deterred Klan assaults, there was often a price to pay. Many blacks left their homes in anticipation of subsequent retaliation.

Although many blacks armed themselves for self-defense and organized themselves into militia groups, hostile whites often responded with great indignation and increasing violence. At times, opponents of Reconstruction took extreme measures to ensure white dominance in southern states. In certain parts of the South, it became apparent that any blacks who confronted the Klan with firepower would suffer dire consequences. In most instances, blacks found themselves in an unenviable dilemma: radical Republican officials usually hesitated to take measures to resist the Klan, and efforts at organized self-defense could result in intensified violence.

In Arkansas and Texas, where the legal order supported the black community, greater success was achieved in resisting the Klan. Arkansas Governor Powell Clayton employed the state militia, composed of blacks and whites loyal to the Republicans, to arrest suspected Klan members. A few were executed and many fled the state. In Texas, Governor Edmund J. Davis organized a state police force in which 40 percent of the membership was black. From 1870 to 1872, blacks were provided with effective protection as the state police suppressed the Klan, arresting over 6,000 suspected members. The success that Clayton and Davis experienced against the Klan indicated that a willingness to employ organized force sanctioned by government could be an effective tool against what otherwise appeared to be an unbeatable organization. However, the use of such force could backfire, as it did in North Carolina, where Governor William W. Holden's administration fell after his use of the state militia produced sympathy for the Klan.

Although contemporary gun rights advocates argue strongly in favor of upholding the right of self-protection, the example of the Ku Klux Klan suggests that individual resistance may produce complex consequences that limit the possibility of success, or even increase the probability of escalating the level of violence. *See also* AFRICAN AMERICANS AND GUNS; BLACK CODES; KLANWATCH PROJECT.

Further Reading: Robert J. Cottrol and Raymond T. Diamond, "The Second Amendment: Toward an Afro-Americanist Reconsideration," in David B. Kopel, ed., *Guns: Who Should Have Them?* (Amherst, NY: Prometheus, 1995); Barry A. Crouch, *The Freedmen's Bureau and Black Texans* (Austin: University of Texas Press, 1992); Eric Foner, *Reconstruction: America's Unfinished Revolution: 1863-1877* (New York: Harper and Row, 1988); Ku Klux Klan Web site <www.kukluxklan.org>.

L

LaPierre, Wayne (1950–)

In 1991, the National Rifle Association (NRA) board of directors elevated long-time pro-gun activist Wayne LaPierre to the position of executive vice president. LaPierre, director since 1986 of the NRA's lobbying arm, the Institute for Legislative Action (ILA), had gained a reputation for resolute support of gun rights and firm opposition to gun control measures. Although LaPierre appeared to lack some of the aggressive qualities of past presidents, his strong credentials for uncompromising stands on gun control led the nominating committee to submit his name alone to the board of directors. LaPierre promised a continuing fight against new proposals for firearms legislation.

LaPierre began his career with the NRA in 1978 at the age of 28 as a lobbyist in the state and local affairs division of the ILA. By 1986, he was serving as the director of federal affairs. When the NRA board removed G. Ray Arnett as executive vice president, LaPierre rose to the position of executive director of the ILA. Guiding the NRA's fortunes in the political arena, he pushed to have public officials favorable to the organization's agenda elected to office. For instance, in 1988, he informed NRA members that if Democratic presidential candidate Michael Dukakis won the election, the liberal president would use his influence over the Justice and Treasury Departments to ban guns in the United States. In March 1989, when President George Bush's director of the Office of Drug Policy, William Bennett, declared that the Bureau of Alcohol, Tobacco, and Firearms (BATF) would prohibit the importation of five types of assault weapons, LaPierre quickly met with White House chief of staff John Sununu regarding the proposed action. Blaming the press for the fear of assault weapons, the NRA held that such a ban would prevent law-abiding citizens from using the weapons for legitimate sporting purposes.

In 1988, the Maryland state legislature approved a measure that would limit the ability of citizens to sue gun manufacturers for injuries, but at the same time would prohibit the sale of Saturday night specials in the state. A state panel would have the authority to determine which handguns fit the criteria for a Saturday night special. Pro-gun residents of the state began a petition drive to have the legislation repealed by referendum. LaPierre came to the forefront in the struggle, predicting that Maryland citizens would overrule the state legislature. However, after devoting over $6 million to the fight, the NRA lost the battle when voters opted to retain the ban.

As executive vice president, LaPierre has maintained the NRA's tenacious stand against any measures intended to limit the possession or carrying of firearms. The title of his column in the *American Rifleman*, "Standing Guard," symbolizes his interpretation of

Wayne LaPierre (right), executive vice president of the National Rifle Association, speaks to reporters in June 1997 about a Supreme Court ruling that invalidated a portion of the Brady Handgun Violence Prevention Act. *REUTERS/ Ken Cedeno/Archive Photos.*

the executive vice president's role. He has warned the membership about the perceived intention of Democratic President Bill Clinton to limit the rights of firearms owners. LaPierre has called for unity in the NRA to oppose such measures at the national level through grassroots organizing and lobbying. He urges gun owners to join in protecting the Second Amendment against attacks that, he claims, could lead to more restrictive gun legislation, as occurred in Australia and the United Kingdom. LaPierre labels various proposed gun control measures as efforts to "disarm the innocent," leaving citizens exposed to criminal attack. To oppose such measures, LaPierre has called for the election of a pro-gun president, keeping a pro-gun Congress, and educating a pro-gun public. In 1997, he enlisted the assistance of actor Charlton Heston, NRA first vice president, to assist in a public relations campaign to publicize the NRA's positions on gun rights and gun con-

trol. Heston was subsequently elected president of the organization. *See also* AMERICAN RIFLEMAN; AUSTRALIA; BUREAU OF ALCOHOL, TOBACCO, AND FIREARMS; BUSH, GEORGE; CLINTON, WILLIAM JEFFERSON (BILL); HESTON, CHARLTON; NATIONAL RIFLE ASSOCIATION; SATURDAY NIGHT SPECIAL; SECOND AMENDMENT; UNITED KINGDOM.

Further Reading: Wayne LaPierre, *Guns, Crime, and Freedom* (Washington, DC: Regnery, 1994); Wayne LaPierre, "Standing Guard" (column), *American Rifleman*; Josh Sugarmann, *National Rifle Association: Money, Firepower and Fear* (Washington, DC: National Press, 1992).

Lautenberg, Frank R. (1924–)

U.S. Senator Frank Lautenberg, a liberal Democrat from New Jersey, has been a major supporter of gun control legislation. He is most well known for the Lautenberg Amendment, which he attached to the fiscal 1997 Omnibus Appropriations bill. This amendment prohibited anyone convicted of domestic violence against a spouse or child from owning a firearm. A member of the President's Commission on Aviation Security, Lautenberg successfully attached the proposal to the fiscal 1997 transportation appropriations bill that funded President Bill Clinton's request for airport security. In 1997, Lautenberg proposed additional firearms legislation. Along with Senator Joseph Biden, Democrat of Maryland, he called for regulations to increase security at gun shops, stating that "incredible as it may seem, there are no federal minimum standards for security of premises and merchandise at gun shops." The bill provided for the secretary of the Treasury to formulate regulations establishing minimum gun safety and security requirements for federally licensed firearms dealers. He stated that from 1994 to 1997 over 30,000 firearms were stolen from gun dealers.

The son of an immigrant silk mill worker, Lautenberg served in the U.S. Army during World War II and received a B.S. degree from Columbia University in 1949. He amassed a personal fortune in private business and became a major supporter for Democratic candidates, but never ran for public office before competing successfully for the U.S. Senate in 1982. Beginning in the 105th Congress in 1997, Lautenberg became the ranking Democrat on the Senate Budget Committee. Lautenberg was willing to work with committee chairman, Pete Domenici, and other Republican leaders in developing an agreement with the Clinton administration that promised to balance the federal budget by 2002. His ability to work with the Republican majority contributed to the success of his gun control amendment.

Lautenberg has gained the enmity of tobacco interests and pro-gun groups alike. In 1989, the senator, formerly a heavy smoker, backed a smoking ban on domestic airline flights. In 1993, he sponsored an amendment banning smoking in federal buildings. Lautenberg's reform efforts have extended into the environmental arena, where he fought against reductions in funding for environmental protection and advocated continued

Senator Frank Lautenberg (D-NJ) was the sponsor of the Lautenberg Amendment, which prohibits anyone convicted of committing an act of domestic violence against a spouse or child from purchasing or owning a firearm. *Courtesy of Senator Lautenberg's office.*

appropriations for cleanup efforts. From 1994 to 1996, Lautenberg was a member of a bipartisan task force to establish new guidelines for gifts from lobbyists. He objected to the political access that lobbyists were receiving from congresspeople that ordinary citizens do not have.

Lautenberg had his appropriations bill amendment passed despite strong resistance from the National Rifle Association (NRA), arguing that the provision would save the lives of many abused wives and children. While the NRA and other gun rights groups portray Lautenberg as a misguided individual who does not understand the true meaning of the Second Amendment and the defensive value of firearms, the senator regards gun organizations as major stumbling blocks to social reform. Gun control groups have a strong supporter in Lautenberg, but in February 1999 he announced that he would not run for a fourth Senate term in 2000. *See also* CLINTON, WILLIAM JEFFERSON (BILL); LAUTENBERG AMENDMENT; NATIONAL RIFLE ASSOCIATION; SECOND AMENDMENT.

Further Reading: "Antis Push Gun Shop Security Legislation," *Gun News Digest* (Winter 1997-1998),

9; Philip D. Duncan and Christine C. Lawrence, *Politics in America: The 105th Congress* (Washington, DC: CQ Press, 1997).

Lautenberg Amendment

In 1996, a gun control measure called the Lautenberg Amendment after Democratic Senator Frank Lautenberg of New Jersey, was attached to a continuing resolution approving federal spending. The measure is also called the Domestic Violence Offender Gun Ban. The legislation prohibits anyone convicted of committing an act of domestic violence against a spouse or child from purchasing or owning a firearm. Despite opposition from the National Rifle Association (NRA), other gun rights organizations, and Republicans in the House of Representatives, gun control advocates successfully included the amendment, which received little public notice.

Gun control supporters argued that the measure was necessary to close a loophole in existing legislation. Although laws prohibited convicted felons from purchasing firearms, no statute dealt with misdemeanor convictions. Because domestic violence and child abuse are often prosecuted as misdemeanors, those convicted of such acts remained free to purchase and possess firearms. The gun control measure prevents anyone who has been convicted of a misdemeanor in a domestic violence episode from owning, carrying, or transporting a gun. Supporters of the measure hoped that it would lessen the probability of family conflicts escalating into firearm-related violence.

The Senate passed the legislation in July 1996, but the Republican leadership prevented its approval in the House of Representatives. In September, the Senate again passed the measure by a vote of 97-2. However, still opposed to the original proposal, House Speaker Newt Gingrich of Georgia and other House Republicans formulated an alternative version of the bill that would exempt any individual convicted for a domestic violence misdemeanor by a judge rather than a jury. Because a large proportion of misdemeanor cases are tried before a judge rather

than a jury, many found guilty of domestic violence would have avoided the restriction on gun ownership. When Democratic President Bill Clinton and Senator Lautenberg refused to compromise on the measure, Speaker Gingrich and the House Republican leadership finally agreed to accept the original bill. Republicans did not want to be held publicly responsible for delaying the budget agreement between Democrats and Republicans, which was the major focus of the bill.

Soon after President Clinton signed the bill, the National Association of Police Organization and other police unions protested the gun control measure, claiming that it was unenforceable in the general public and would deny many police officers their jobs. Several police officers in major American cities discovered that they were disqualified from carrying a firearm because they had at sometime in the past been convicted of a misdemeanor involving a domestic violence charge. By December, some had already surrendered their guns and been told that they were reassigned to desk duty and could lose their jobs. In Minneapolis, Minnesota, four officers were reassigned to desk duty or put on paid leave. Trying a different strategy, the sheriff's department in Denver, Colorado, requested that deputies who had been convicted of misdemeanor convictions surrender their firearms before leaving work. The federal government began an honor system, asking all employees who carry weapons to state in writing that they had never been convicted of a misdemeanor involving domestic violence. Questions also arose regarding the application of the new legislation to military personnel.

While supporters of the measure argued that police officers should be able to meet a high standard of conduct on the job and off, opponents charged that the legislation amounted to an ex post facto law that punished individuals for crimes committed before the law was passed. They also argued that the law did not allow for the possibility that people who committed a misdemeanor years ago have altered their behavior since the offense. Several congresspeople called for an amendment that would make the law apply only to new cases, while gun rights groups, such as Gun Owners of America (GOA) advocated its complete repeal. The Clinton administration announced its opposition to any changes in the legislation and it remains in effect. *See also* CLINTON, WILLIAM JEFFERSON (BILL); GUN OWNERS OF AMERICA; LAUTENBERG, FRANK R.; NATIONAL ASSOCIATION OF POLICE ORGANIZATIONS; NATIONAL RIFLE ASSOCIATION.

Further Reading: *New York Times*, (October 1, 1996), p. 24; Larry Reibstein and John Engen, "One Strike and You're Out," *Newsweek* 128 (December 23, 1996), 53.

Law Enforcement Alliance of America (LEAA)

In 1989, the organization Law Enforcement for the Preservation of the Second Amendment was formed; in 1990, the group became the Law Enforcement Alliance of America (LEAA). The LEAA describes itself as a legislative advocacy organization comprised of law enforcement and corrections officers, private law enforcement personnel, crime victims, and "concerned citizens." The organization maintains its headquarters in Falls Church, Virginia. The founders of the LEAA received financial support from the National Rifle Association (NRA) to establish the organization. The LEAA has taken a strong position in opposition to additional gun control legislation, campaigning against the Brady Handgun Violence Prevention Act and bans on assault weapons. The Alliance has backed a national legislative proposal to allow police officers to carry weapons outside their jurisdictions, and various state proposals to liberalize carrying concealed weapons (CCW) laws.

The LEAA maintains that most police officers do not support gun control, which the organization defines as "restricting the rights of, and disarming, peaceable citizens." The organization maintains that, unlike other police organizations, it represents officers' views on gun control, contending that the "real cops" oppose "any and all efforts to erode Second Amendment rights." The only form of gun control the organization supports is keeping firearms away from violent felons, including habitual criminals, drug users, drug dealers, and those who arm themselves with illegal or altered firearms. The LEAA advocates severe penalties for those who use a firearm in the commission of crimes.

The LEAA claims that present federal firearms legislation provides sufficient legal measures to deter individuals from using firearms while committing crimes. James J. Fotis, executive director of the LEAA, notes that legislation bars convicted felons, illegal aliens, those dishonorably discharged from the armed forces, and those judged insane from purchasing, owning, selling, or using any firearm. Fotis observes that using a firearm during the commission of a crime can result in an additional five-year sentence and a $250,000 fine. He believes that such stiff penalties certainly will "catch the attention of even the most dense-skulled underworld neanderthal."

Unlike the LEAA, other law enforcement organizations, such as the Police Executive Research Forum, the International Association of Chiefs of Police, and the National Sheriffs Association, have supported gun control proposals, particularly the Brady law. The LEAA explains this support by noting that these organizations have received millions of dollars from the Justice Department in return for their support for gun control measures. The LEAA asserts that the rank and file members of other police organizations do not support the official pro-gun control positions of the leadership. *See also* ASSAULT WEAPONS BAN; BRADY HANDGUN VIOLENCE PREVENTION ACT; CONCEALED CARRY LAWS; INTERNATIONAL ASSOCIATION OF CHIEFS OF POLICE; NATIONAL RIFLE ASSOCIATION; POLICE EXECUTIVE RESEARCH FORUM; SECOND AMENDMENT.

Further Reading: James J. Fotis, "Criminals, Guns and the Law; Why Cops Do Not Support Gun Control," Law Enforcement Alliance of America Web site <www.leaa.org>; Josh Sugarmann, *National Rifle Association: Money, Firepower and Fear* (Washington, DC: National Press, 1992).

Law Enforcement Officers Protection Act

The Law Enforcement Officers Protection Act of 1986, which banned the sale of armor-piercing ammunition (so-called "cop-killer" bullets), had political significance beyond the immediate provisions of the legislation. Police organizations such as the International Association of Chiefs of Police found themselves on the opposite side of the issue from the National Rifle Association (NRA), which for four years opposed efforts to have Congress ban bullets that could pierce body armor that police often wear for self-protection. NRA opposition to the legislation allowed Handgun Control, Inc., the leading gun control organization, to forge alliances with police organizations that ultimately proved valuable in the effort to pass the Brady Handgun Violence Prevention Act in 1993.

Armor piercing bullets, also referred to as KTWs after their inventors, three individuals named Kopsch, Turcus, and Ward, are composed of hard metals such as tungsten alloys, steel, brass, bronze, iron, beryllium, copper, or depleted uranium. When first developed, the ammunition was considered to be of value to police officers for stopping automobiles used in a crime because the bullets could pierce engine blocks. Police departments ultimately discovered that the ammunition was impractical because it represented a significant risk of harm to innocent bystanders. When police officers discovered that the bullets could be used against them, they called for banning the sale of such ammunition to the general public.

The struggle for legislation to prohibit the manufacture and sale of armor piercing bullets began in 1982. An initial test of political strength came at the local level when the Brookhaven, Long Island, Town Board considered an ordinance to outlaw KTW bullets for handguns. The NRA opposed this local action and sent telegrams to members encouraging them to attend the meeting called to consider adoption of a ban. James Baker, a lobbyist for the NRA, presented the basic position of the organization: No amount of legislation can alter human behavior by attempting to control physical objects.

Although police officers expressed concern regarding their safety, the NRA made the controversial claim that no police officer wearing a bullet-proof vest had been wounded or killed by an armor-piercing bullet. The organization argued that the move to ban a type of ammunition represented just another tactic by gun control advocates to limit the right to keep and bear arms. Two top NRA officials, Neal Knox and J. Warren Cassidy, insisted that bullets by themselves are neither good nor bad and that the crucial factor is how they are used. Legislation banning ammunition would only limit law-abiding citizens and could not control criminal behavior.

A bill to ban KTW bullets was introduced into the U.S. Senate by Daniel Patrick Moynihan, Democrat of New York, and in the House by Mario Biaggi, Democrat of New York, a long-time veteran of the New York City Police Department. The initial bills defined armor piercing handgun ammunition in terms of their ability to penetrate at least 18 layers of Kevlar, the material used to manufacture bulletproof vests. The NRA objected that this criterion was far too broad and would ban many types of rifle as well as handgun ammunition.

In 1986, the NRA, concerned about gaining support for passage of the Gun Owners Protection Act and faced with the intense push by law enforcement organizations for legislation regulating ammunition, communicated its willingness to compromise. The compromise definition shifted the criterion from degree of penetration to the hard metal content of ammunition. The NRA removed its objections to the bill and it was passed by Congress and signed by Republican President Ronald Reagan in August 1986. The legislation outlawed the manufacture, import, or sale of KTW bullets, but exemptions were allowed for the manufacture of bullets for long guns used in hunting that are designed to meet federal and state environmental standards. Such ammunition must be marked and packaged with a label identifying it as armor-piercing. Anyone violating the law was made subject to a five-year mandatory sentence. *See also* BRADY HANDGUN VIOLENCE PREVENTION ACT; FIREARMS OWNERS PROTECTION ACT; HANDGUN CONTROL, INC.; INTERNATIONAL ASSOCIATION OF CHIEFS OF POLICE; KNOX, NEAL; NATIONAL RIFLE ASSOCIATION; REAGAN, RONALD.

Further Reading: Earl R. Kruschke, *Gun Control* (Santa Barbara, CA: ABC-CLIO, 1995); Robert J. Spitzer, *The Politics of Gun Control* (Chatham, NJ: Chatham House, 1995); Josh Sugarmann, *National Rifle Association: Money, Firepower and Fear* (Washington, DC: National Press, 1992).

Lawyer's Second Amendment Society (LSAS)

The Lawyer's Second Amendment Society (LSAS), a small organization of just over 200 members, has filed *amicus curiae* briefs in court cases involving firearms legislation. The organization holds that the Second Amendment affirms a "God-given and individual right" to keep and bear arms. Therefore, any law restricting that right lacks any authority. Noting that most judges deny this understanding of the right to bear arms, the organization strives to alter prevailing judicial interpretations of the Second Amendment. Part of the organization's strategy involves opposing judicial nominations of candidates who do not support an individualistic interpretation of the Second Amendment. For instance, the LSAS opposed Senate ratification of President Bill Clinton's federal court nomination of Margaret Morrow, who, as president of the California State Bar in 1993-94, strongly supported a gun control resolution. However, in 1998, the Senate ultimately confirmed Morrow's nomination.

The Society was established in 1994 and incorporated in 1996. It publishes a bimonthly newsletter, *Liberty Pole*, which has a circulation of 3,000. Steven A. Silver, LSAS vice president, edits the newsletter. Officers of the organization write Second Amendment pieces for newspapers and magazines. The LSAS holds "ATF Night" (a reference to the Bureau of Alcohol, Tobacco, and Firearms) every other month in a Culver City, California, café. At these meetings firearms advocates gather for "an informal evening of adult beverages, cigars and gun talk."

The Society professes four basic objectives: 1) to persuade other attorneys that the Second Amendment guarantees an individual right to keep and bear arms; 2) to fund and also engage in litigation to proclaim an individualistic interpretation of the Second Amendment; 3) to offer guidance for attorneys across the country regarding Second Amendment questions; and 4) to serve as a center for research and information on the Second Amendment. Recognizing that "reasonable limitations" may be placed on any of the rights identified in the Bill of Rights, the LSAS concedes that the right to keep and bear arms could be subject to restrictions.

In 1997, the LSAS, along with other gun rights organizations, strongly opposed a ballot initiative (I-676) in Washington state that would have required a license to purchase a handgun. Noting that gun control advocate Sarah Brady considered this proposal an initial step toward a similar law at the national level, the organization urged supporters to contribute to the forces opposing the legislation and contact public officials and others who advocate gun control. Washington voters ultimately defeated the measure.

Daniel J. Schultz, writing in *Liberty Pole*, defended the right of citizens to form militias, but cautioned prospective militia members about the negative media publicity that must be endured. He recommended that people arm and train themselves individually and suggested that individuals communicate with others interested in militia participation and join several gun rights organizations, including the National Rifle Association (NRA) and the Law Enforcement Alliance of America (LEAA). Schultz stated that such organizations deserve financial support for their struggle against the "gun grabbers." Militia participants were advised to protect themselves against possible informants by asking any participants straightforwardly if they work for, or represent, the government. *See also* BRADY, SARAH; BUREAU OF ALCOHOL, TOBACCO, AND FIREARMS; CLINTON, WILLIAM JEFFERSON (BILL); LAW ENFORCEMENT ALLIANCE

OF AMERICA; NATIONAL RIFLE ASSOCIATION; SECOND AMENDMENT.

Further Reading: Lawyer's Second Amendment Society Web site <www.mcs.net/~lpylepru/lsas>.

Legal Action Project (LAP)

Legal Action Project (LAP), an affiliate of the Center to Prevent Handgun Violence, was established in 1989 to advocate gun control policies in the courts and to facilitate litigation against gun manufacturers and dealers. LAP defends gun control laws at the national, state, and local levels against challenges initiated by such organizations as the National Rifle Association (NRA). The organization provides legal assistance to victims of gun violence seeking court-awarded damages. In addition to participating in litigation, lawyers associated with LAP have challenged the interpretation of the Second Amendment advocated by gun rights organizations. They have published articles and appeared in the media attacking the position that the Second Amendment guarantees an individual right to keep and bear arms.

One of the Project's major goals is the maintenance of previous legislative victories. LAP provides *pro bono* services to government attorneys who are defending gun control statutes. Among its services, the organization provides attorneys with data supporting gun control statutes, legal briefs that were filed in other cases, the outcomes of recent court rulings, suggestions for expert witnesses, and assistance with legal strategy. The Project files *amicus curiae* briefs to support government defense of firearms legislation. LAP participated in the defense of the temporary five-day waiting period, established in the Brady Handgun Violence Prevention Act in 1994, against NRA-backed lawsuits. The Project has assisted the California attorney general in court defenses of that state's ban on semi-automatic weapons and defended various state and local provisions against the charge that they violate state constitutional provisions regarding the right to keep and bear arms.

LAP calls for innovations in the design of firearms to reduce the potential danger such weapons present, especially to young people. Guns should include appropriate technology to prevent unauthorized use. Of special concern to the Project is the difficulty in determining whether a firearm has been completely unloaded. In addition to calling for design changes, the Project faults firearms manufacturers for marketing such guns as assault weapons and Saturday night specials that the organization considers only suitable for criminal use. Other products, such as so-called cop-killer bullets and mail-order parts that may be assembled into untraceable guns, are considered to have no legitimate use.

The Project attempts to hold gun dealers legally responsible for sales to individuals who are ineligible to purchase firearms. Open to criticism are dealers who provide inadequate security systems to prevent theft and dealers who take part in bulk purchases that are used to supply guns for criminal activity. LAP has addressed what it considers the serious problem of illegal sales at gun shows. The organization recommends limiting handgun sales to one per month to an individual to prevent "straw man" sales, prohibiting the sale of firearms at gun shows, and requiring improved security procedures at retail firearms outlets. LAP filed an *amicus curiae* brief in a Florida court case (*Kitchen v. K-Mart*, 1997) in which the state supreme court held that retail gun dealers are legally required to refuse selling a firearm to an intoxicated buyer and may be held liable for any harm resulting from a sale to such a person. In several legal actions, the Project has attempted to hold negligent owners responsible for the misuse of their firearms by others.

The Project has focused its attention on firearm advertising, contending that the firearms industry presents the false impression that a handgun will keep the purchaser safe from criminal attack. The Project makes three recommendations regarding firearms advertising. First, no claims about home and personal security should be made. Second, advertisements should not appeal to "the criminal element or others prone to violent behavior." Finally, no ads should appear in publications aimed at youth. *See also* ASSAULT WEAPONS BAN; BRADY HANDGUN VIOLENCE PREVENTION ACT; CENTER TO PREVENT HANDGUN VIOLENCE; FIREARMS LITIGATION CLEARINGHOUSE; GUN SHOWS; LEGAL COMMUNITY AGAINST VIOLENCE; NATIONAL RIFLE ASSOCIATION; PRODUCT LIABILITY LAWSUITS; SATURDAY NIGHT SPECIAL; SECOND AMENDMENT; YOUTH AND GUNS.

Further Reading: Legal Action Project Web site <www.handguncontrol.org/legalaction>.

Legal Community Against Violence (LCAV)

The Legal Community Against Violence (LCAV), based in San Francisco, California, was established in 1993 in reaction to the murder in that city of eight people and the wounding of six others. The organization is committed to reducing gun-related violence through legislative initiatives, participation in litigation, and support for educational programs. The LCAV invites those in the legal profession to assist in drafting model legislation, conducting legal research, and offering *pro bono* legal assistance to municipal and county governments that have enacted gun control ordinances. The organization maintains a library of local government ordinances and legal briefs regarding legal challenges to firearms legislation.

The LCAV offers government officials the legal means to enact firearms policies that the organization believes will save lives. The organization has provided legal assistance to local governments that face challenges from pro-gun groups. At the national level, the LCAV supported passage of the Brady Handgun Violence Prevention Act and the assault weapons ban. In California, lobbying efforts have contributed to passage of state laws to deny firearm access to minors, to grant judges the authority to order the confiscation of weapons from individuals subject to restraining orders, and to hold gun owners responsible if minors injure themselves or others with a firearm that was negligently made available to them. The organization opposes legislative initiatives from pro-gun organizations, such as attempts to repeal the national assault weapons ban and proposed legislation in California to permit most adults to carry concealed weapons.

As part of its Local Ordinance Project, the LCAV distributes the publication, "Addressing Gun Violence Through Local Ordinances, A Legal Resource Manual for California Cities and Counties." The manual argues that gun control measures are needed to curb what is considered an epidemic of gun violence. It examines possible legal challenges to local firearm regulations, based on the Second Amendment, the due process clause, and the equal protection clause of the U.S. Constitution. Preemption principles and related legal decisions are discussed. The manual contains descriptions of various local ordinances, including those that ban firearms dealerships in residential areas; require dealer licenses and employee background checks; establish taxation policy; prohibit sales of Saturday night specials; mandate trigger locks, warning labels, and safe storage; prohibit firing a weapon within the jurisdiction; and regulate gun shows.

The organization refers to a long series of legal precedents that associate the right to keep and bear arms with membership in an organized state militia, and quotes noted early Americans, such as James Madison and Patrick Henry, to support the position that the intent of the Bill of Rights was to allow states to maintain a military force independent of the national government. Going beyond legal arguments, the LCAV reports opinion poll results indicating that a large majority of Americans support "common sense gun control laws" such as statutes placing stricter controls on handguns. *See also* ASSAULT WEAPONS BAN; BRADY HANDGUN VIOLENCE PREVENTION ACT; CONCEALED CARRY LAWS; GUN SHOWS; SATURDAY NIGHT SPECIAL; SECOND AMENDMENT; STATE GUN STATUTES; TRIGGER LOCKS.

Further Reading: Legal Community Against Violence Web site <www.lcav.org>.

Lewis v. United States (1980)

The U.S. Supreme Court in *Lewis v. United States* (445 U.S. 55, 1980) upheld a lower court conviction under section 1202 (a) (1) of Title VI of the Omnibus Crime Control and Safe Streets Act of 1968. This provision states that any person convicted by a federal or state court of a felony shall be prohibited from possessing a firearm. The appellant had been convicted of the disabling charge prior to the Supreme Court decision in *Gideon v. Wainwright* (1963), which held that a state court felony conviction where the defendant did not have counsel and did not refuse counsel is unconstitutional under the Sixth and Fourteenth Amendments to the U.S. Constitution.

In 1961, George Calvin Lewis, Jr., arrested for breaking and entering, was found guilty of a felony in a Florida court upon pleading guilty to the charge. He was not represented by counsel. Lewis served a term in prison. Subsequently, the Supreme Court ruled, in *Gideon v. Wainwright*, that states must provide counsel to defendants who cannot afford legal defense in criminal cases. Lewis never appealed his conviction and it was never overturned. In January 1977, Lewis was arrested in Virginia for knowingly receiving and possessing a firearm in violation of provisions in the Omnibus Crime Control Act. Lewis argued that because he had not been represented by counsel in the 1961 case, that conviction had violated his constitutional rights and therefore should not act against him in the present case.

The court rejected the argument, ruling that the constitutionality of the previous conviction was irrelevant in the present case. Lewis appealed the decision to the U.S. Court of Appeals for the Fourth Circuit, which affirmed the conviction for illegal gun possession. The Supreme Court, hearing the case on appeal from the Circuit Court, investigated the intentions of Congress when writing this provision. The Court found no evidence that Congress intended to allow a defendant to challenge the validity of the prior conviction as a defense of the firearm possession charge. Congress employed "sweeping" language,

including no restrictions on the term "convicted." Therefore, the felony conviction clearly results in a prohibition of firearm ownership until the conviction is canceled, or the felon either receives a pardon from the president or a state governor, or obtains permission from the secretary of the Treasury to possess a firearm.

In addition to a possible pardon or permission from the secretary of the Treasury, Lewis could challenge his previous conviction in the Florida state court system, seeking an official reversal of the original conviction. In any event, a defendant must clear his or her record prior to obtaining a firearm, thus complying with the intent of the law to "keep firearms away from the persons Congress classified as potentially irresponsible and dangerous." The Court concluded that Congress's intentions constituted a "rational basis" for legal distinctions and hence were in agreement with the Due Process Clause of the Fifth Amendment. In addition, the relationship between the right to keep and bear arms and the efficiency of a well regulated militia stated in the Second Amendment affords Congress the power to regulate firearms. The Court affirmed the ability of Congress constitutionally to prohibit certain activities on the part of a convicted felon and concluded that Congress was acting reasonably when it decided that a convicted felon fell in the category of those prohibited from dealing in or possessing firearms, even if the conviction occurred devoid of counsel. *See also* FOURTEENTH AMENDMENT; SECOND AMENDMENT.

Further Reading: *Lewis v. United States*, 445 U.S. 55 (1980).

Libertarian Party

The Libertarian Party, which believes that individuals possess the right to complete sovereignty over their own lives, liberty, and property—as long as they respect the equal rights of others—takes an uncompromising stand against the regulation of firearms. The party deems illegitimate any government interference in the private lives of citizens. Libertarians oppose victimless crime laws and any other government regulation of personal affairs and support private education, protection of property rights, and an unregulated free market economy. In its commitment to a classical liberal ideology, the party objects to such government activities as foreign aid, welfare, environmental regulations, and consumer protection laws. Because of their uncompromising position on limiting government involvement in the lives of private citizens, Libertarians oppose any government attempts to regulate the possession or carrying of firearms.

In their 1996 party platform, Libertarians expressed opposition to all laws at the local, state, and national levels "restricting, regulating, or requiring the ownership, manufacture, transfer, or sale of firearms or ammunition." Libertatians believe all laws requiring gun or ammunition registration should be repealed. The party rejected the argument that weapons or ammunition should be banned or regulated because they are unsafe, for this determination should reside with individuals, not the government. The party supported repeal of the National Firearms Act of 1934 and the federal Gun Control Act of 1968 and called for the abolition of the Bureau of Alcohol, Tobacco, and Firearms (BATF), the federal agency responsible for enforcing firearms legislation. Laws banning the concealment of weapons also came under attack, as did prohibitions on inexpensive handguns, or Saturday night specials, and semi-automatic assault weapons and magazines. Libertarians also oppose limitations on the use of other self-protection devices such as tear gas and mace, and believe all existing limitations should be eliminated.

The party argues against any gun control measures on theoretical as well as practical grounds. Libertarians contend that gun ownership as such harms no one else and thus is a matter of personal choice. Such ownership cannot justifiably lead to any criminal penalties. Practically, party members argue that gun control, like Prohibition and the present drug laws, is unenforceable. The true victims of gun control laws are honest citizens who have lost the right to defend themselves. The party holds that only if a large proportion of citizens are armed can the nation deter violent crime.

Libertarians support severe penalties for anyone who commits a crime using a gun. Any negligent gun user should be held fully responsible for any harm done to others. However, to the extent that citizens are well-armed and trained in the use of firearms, the party believes that the nation is better protected from crime and the threat of foreign invasion. The Libertarian Party does not indicate whether government should take the responsibility for assuring that firearms owners receive the appropriate training. However, given the party's individualist ideology, it is not likely to support granting this role to government. *See also* ASSAULT WEAPONS BAN; BUREAU OF ALCOHOL, TOBACCO, AND FIREARMS; GUN CONTROL ACT OF 1968; NATIONAL FIREARMS ACT OF 1934; SATURDAY NIGHT SPECIAL.

Further Reading: Libertarian Party, National Platform (Washington, DC: Libertarian National Committee, Inc., 1996); Libertarian Party, "Why Libertarians Support Equal Rights for America's Gun Owners," pamphlet (Washington, DC: Libertarian National Committee, Inc., n.d.); Libertarian Party Web site <www.lp.org>.

Littleton, Colorado, School Shooting

The Littleton, Colorado, school shooting, which occurred in April 1999, followed a series of similar incidents in 1997 and 1998. The shooting galvanized a national debate over what measures might be taken to curb incidents in which armed youth have killed and wounded fellow students and teachers. Soon after the incident President Bill Clinton unveiled several gun control proposals, initiating an extensive debate over the effectiveness of additional legislation in preventing gun-related violence.

On April 20, two students armed with semi-automatic weapons, sawed-off shotguns, and homemade bombs, attacked fellow students at Columbine High School in Littleton, a suburb of Denver, Colorado. The two male youths killed 12 students and 1 teacher and wounded several others before

Two weeks after the April 20, 1999, school shooting in nearby Littleton, Colorado, demonstrators outside the Adams Mark Hotel in Denver protest the NRA annual conference being held there. *Corbis/AFP.*

killing themselves as SWAT teams attempted to reach them. The national media gave the shootings extensive coverage and precipitated attempts to place blame and discover possible causes, including the ready availability of firearms. The National Rifle Association (NRA), which had scheduled its annual convention in Denver, announced that it would curtail, but not cancel, the meeting. When the NRA met on May 1, 8,000 people gathered to protest the meeting. Two measures to liberalize gun restrictions were removed from the Colorado state legislature's agenda.

President Clinton, who had been planning a series of new gun control proposals prior to the Colorado shooting, decided to make public his gun control agenda one week after the incident. Clinton called for banning gun sales and ownership to anyone under 21 years of age. Background checks would be required for the sale of firearms at gun shows and child safety locks would be mandated for each new firearm sold. Adults who allow children access to firearms would be subject to a prison term of 3 to 10 years and a fine of $10,000. Negligent parents would be held legally re-

sponsible if their children committed crimes with guns. Anyone committing violent crimes as juveniles would be subject to a lifetime ban on firearm ownership. In addition, Clinton called for the reintroduction of a waiting period for handgun purchases. The waiting period would be three days with a possible two-day extension if law enforcement officers needed the extra time to complete a check. Another measure would provide for treating explosives sales, including dynamite and blasting caps, the same as gun sales under the Brady Handgun Violence Prevention Act. Senator Charles Schumer, Democrat from New York, proposed allowing only licensed firearms dealers to have Web sites for trading in firearms.

While gun control advocates were proposing additional legislation, gun rights supporters were questioning the need for additional measures restricting firearms sales and ownership. Critics of additional gun control noted that no additional laws would have prevented the Littleton shooting, indicating that other causal factors, such as parental supervision and school security, must be addressed. Advocates of additional restrictions on guns argued that although such measures could not eliminate such incidents, the probability of violence could be minimized.

Stronger gun control provisions passed the U.S. Senate as part of a juvenile justice bill, including such requirements as background checks for purchasing firearms at gun shows, safety devices to be sold with handguns, raising the minimum age for purchasing a handgun from 18 to 21, and a ban on imported high capacity ammunition clips. However, the U.S. House of Representatives focused attention on other possible causes of violence, such as violence in the mass media, lack of parental supervision of youth, a too lenient juvenile justice system, and lack of respect for moral authority. A compromise gun control bill, proposed by John Dingell, Democrat from Michigan, failed to gain passage. A coalition of conservative Republicans and Democrats, including Dingell, opposed the measure. President Bill Clinton attributed the defeat of strong gun control legislation in the House to the lobbying efforts of the NRA. *See also* ASSAULT WEAPONS BAN; BRADY HANDGUN VIOLENCE PREVENTION ACT; CLINTON, WILLIAM JEFFERSON (BILL); JONESBORO, ARKANSAS, SCHOOL SHOOTING; NATIONAL INSTANT CHECK SYSTEM; NATIONAL RIFLE ASSOCIATION; SCHOOLS AND GUNS; SCHUMER, CHARLES; STOCKTON, CALIFORNIA, SHOOTING; TRIGGER LOCKS; YOUTH AND GUNS.

Further Reading: Matt Bai, "Anatomy of a Massacre," *Newsweek* (May 3, 1999), 22–31; Matt Bai, "Caught in the Cross-Fire: How Gun Control Turned Into a Casualty of the Capital Wars," *Newsweek* (June 28, 1999), 31–32; Michael Bane, "A Gun Owner Looks Into His Heart: The Tragedy in Littleton, Colorado," *Handguns* 13 (August 1999), 22–23; Neal Knox, "NRA At Denver," *Shotgun News* 53 (June 1, 1999), 7.

Long Gun

Gary Kleck defines a long gun as "a larger firearm with a long barrel and a buttstock, designed to be fired with the buttstock held against the shoulder." Long guns, which include rifles and shotguns, are generally associated with hunting and other sports activities. In contrast, handguns, which include revolvers and semi-automatic pistols, more often bring to mind use in criminal activities. The distinction between handguns and long guns–real and perceived–have resulted in gun control advocates focusing primarily on the control or banning of handguns, while allowing the continued ownership and use of long guns.

A rifle is a long gun that has a rifled barrel—the inside of the barrel has spiraled grooves. Usually firing one round with each pull of the trigger, rifles may place bullets in firing position in one of two different methods: cartridges may be placed into position by the mechanical action of a manually operated bolt, lever, or pump, or a semi-automatic mechanism places a new round in the chamber as the gun is fired. Shotguns are constructed with one or two barrels and fire a shell containing many round pellets, or possibly a rifled slug. A shotgun may require reloading after each firing of the barrels, or may have a semiautomatic mechanism that usually holds two-to-five shells, but can contain as many as 20. Older models that require manual reloading may also have hammers that must be cocked for each firing.

Gun control advocates argue that long guns are of less concern for potentially illegal use because they are not nearly as easy to conceal as handguns. Sawed-off versions of long guns are an exception, and have been banned by federal firearms legislation. Also subject to control are assault rifles, which have been defined as rifles with military characteristics that are capable of semi-automatic fire. Critics of current gun control efforts note that in many cases rifles not covered by present legislation actually have far more destructive effect than handguns or assault rifles.

Critics of the gun control agenda assert that a policy of classifying firearms for purposes of regulation cannot succeed in bringing about reduced rates of firearm use in criminal acts because to ban one type of weapon will lead to substituting others. They claim that far more deadly weapons, such as long guns, will be used more frequently than handguns for illicit purposes should handguns be banned. In addition, critics claim that any weapon that can be used by a criminal to commit a crime can also be valuable to the potential victim for self-defense. Not long guns, but the smaller handgun can be concealed on the person for self-defense when in public, or kept in an available place in the home should the need arise. Gun control advocates respond that the very availability of handguns makes them far more dangerous than long guns. For instance, they claim that children are major potential victims of accidents involving handguns. In addition, gun control advocates reject the notion of allowing large numbers of citizens to carry concealed weapons in public places.

Critics of gun control note that because long guns are more powerful than handguns, they have a far greater potential of harming a bystander when a confrontation occurs between a criminal and an armed victim. They claim that bullets shot from long guns can penetrate walls of homes and can possibly hit people passing by outside or living next door. Rather than focusing on the type of weapon to be banned, allow the "law abiding" citizen to own the weapon of choice, whether a long gun or handgun, and forbid sales to those with criminal records. The chances for the success of such a policy would depend on the possibility that, counter to the critics' arguments, handguns by themselves represent a significantly greater chance of being used in violent confrontations than do long guns. *See also* ASSAULT WEAPONS BAN; KLECK, GARY; SAWED-OFF SHOTGUN; YOUTH AND GUNS.

Further Reading: Gary Kleck, *Targeting Guns: Firearms and Their Control* (Hawthorne, NY: Aldine de Gruyter, 1997).

Lott, John R., Jr. (1958–)

John R. Lott, Jr., has gained widespread attention for publishing research results indicating that "shall issue" concealed carry laws contribute to reduced crime rates. Increased gun ownership leads to less, not more crime. Lott is the John M. Olin Visiting Law and Economics Fellow at the University of Chi-

cago, where he teaches criminal deterrence and law and economics. Lott's book, *More Guns, Less Crime*, published in 1998, elicited a large response from both sides of the gun control debate. The book contains a complex analysis of a huge data set derived from Federal Bureau of Investigation (FBI) yearly crime reports. Many of the findings had already been published in a paper by Lott and David B. Mustard titled "Crime, Deterrence, and Right-to-Carry Concealed Weapons."

Lott received his B.A., M.A., and Ph.D. in economics from the University of California at Los Angeles. Before arriving at the University of Chicago in 1994, Lott held positions at several educational institutions, including Cornell University Law School, the University of Pennsylvania, Rice University, and Texas A&M University. From 1988 to 1989, he was chief economist for the U.S. Sentencing Commission in Washington, D.C.

Lott's study involved crime data for the nation's 3,054 counties for the 14-year period extending from 1977 to 1994. He concluded from his analysis that various gun control measures, such as waiting periods, gun buyback programs, and background checks, have little effect on crime reduction. His study discovered that one gun policy yielded significant results: "right to carry" laws that allow citizens to have concealed weapons. Lott notes that the 31 states that have adopted shall-issue laws, which allow adults who do not have a criminal record or a history of mental illness to carry concealed handguns, have contributed to declining crime rates.

According to Lott, states with concealed carry laws on average reduced the murder rate by 8.5 percent, rapes by 5 percent, aggravated assaults by 7 percent, and robbery by 3 percent. He estimated that if those states without concealed carry laws had permitted concealed handguns in 1992, the number of murders would have been reduced by 1,570, rapes by 4,177, aggravated assaults by 60,000, and robberies by 12,000. Lott claimed that crime rates fall each year a concealed-carry law is in effect: murder by 3 percent, rape by 2 percent, and robbery by 2 percent. Countering those who fear the occurrence of multi-victim shootings, such as those committed at public schools in 1997, 1998, and 1999, Lott asserted that states passing concealed carry laws experienced an 84 percent decline in such events.

Lott concluded that two factors explain the lower rates of violent crime in states with concealed carry laws. First, such laws act as a deterrent to crime. Although a small proportion of the population carries concealed weapons, those contemplating a crime cannot tell who is armed and who is not. Second, those carrying firearms are able to defend themselves if an attack occurs. Lott asserted that a handgun provides women a much greater defensive capability than it does men, measured by the reduction in the murder rate.

The Violence Policy Center (VPC), focusing on Lott's political leanings, has criticized his findings. The Center portrayed Lott as a political extremist who has argued that a certain amount of crime can be beneficial to a society, that government regulation of indoor smoking is unjustified, and that global warming and ozone depletion are myths. The VPC claims possible conflict of interest because Lott has a fellowship from the John M. Olin Foundation, which has links to the Olin Corporation, owner of Winchester Ammunition. According to the VPC, "the Lott study is indelibly stained with the taint of the gun industry." Lott supporters respond that there are no administrative links between the Olin Foundation and the Olin Corporation. Lott critics regret such personal attacks in part because they give his research greater credibility than is deserved.

The Johns Hopkins Center for Gun Policy Research and the Pacific Center for Violence Prevention have focused on what they consider weaknesses in Lott's methodology. For instance, Lott is criticized for reliance on inappropriate statistical models, faulty categorization of concealed carry laws, and misstating implementation dates for concealed carry laws. Stephen Teret, writing for the Johns Hopkins Center, notes that the concealed carry laws apparently had the

greatest effect on rape, aggravated assault, and murder. However, theoretically, "shall issue" laws should have less effect on such crimes, which are most often committed by someone known to the victim. Teret also notes that the Lott study fails to take into account the possible effects of other gun laws.

Jens Ludwig of the Georgetown Public Policy Institute has concluded that Lott's statistical analysis does not support his conclusion that allowing law-abiding citizens to carry concealed handguns will save lives. Although Lott includes a chapter in which he replies to his critics, Ludwig claims that he fails to confront the criticisms of D.A. Black and D.S. Hagin, who focus on Lott's methodology. Employing Lott's data, Black and Hagin do not arrive at the same conclusion that concealed carry laws reduce crime. *See also* CONCEALED CARRY LAWS; GUN BUYBACK PROGRAMS; JOHNS HOPKINS CENTER FOR GUN POLICY RESEARCH; LUDWIG, JENS OTTO; PACIFIC CENTER FOR VIOLENCE PREVENTION; SCHOOLS AND GUNS; STATE GUN STATUTES; VIOLENCE POLICY CENTER.

Further Reading: John R. Lott, Jr., *More Guns, Less Crime: Understanding Crime and Gun Control Laws* (Chicago: University of Chicago Press, 1998); John R. Lott, Jr., and David B. Mustard, "Crime, Deterrence, and Right-to-Carry Concealed Handguns" (University of Chicago, 1996); Jens Ludwig, "Review of *More Guns, Less Crime: Understanding Crime and Gun Control Laws* by John R. Lott, Jr.," *Washington Monthly* (June 1998), 50-51; Stephen Teret, "Critical Commentary on a Paper by Lott and Mustard" (Report of the Johns Hopkins Center for Gun Policy and Research, August 1996); Daniel W. Webster, "The Claims that Right-to-Carry Laws Reduce Violent Crime Are Unsubstantiated" (Report of the Pacific Center for Violence Prevention, March 1997).

Ludwig, Jens Otto (1968–)

In his brief academic career, Jens Otto Ludwig has had a prolific research and publication record, including collaborative projects dealing with firearms. As a graduate student, Ludwig worked with firearms researcher Philip Cook at Duke University. He has challenged claims that firearms can be valuable for self-defense and has participated in debates on the issue. In 1998, he appeared as an expert witness before the Committee on Public Safety of the California Assembly, providing testimony on proposed carrying concealed handgun legislation.

Ludwig received a B.A. in economics from Rutgers College in 1990 and an M.A. and a Ph.D. in economics from Duke University in 1992 and 1994, respectively. His primary areas of specialization are econometrics and labor economics. An assistant professor of public policy at Georgetown University, Ludwig served in 1998 as a visiting scholar at the Northwestern University/University of Chicago Poverty Center. In addition to his research on firearms, Ludwig has studied education issues, including such subjects as school choice, determinants of academic achievement, and the effects of private schooling on the probability of juvenile criminal involvement. Ludwig has conducted research on the effects of family structure on various forms of youth delinquent behavior.

Ludwig participated in a study titled *Guns in America: National Survey on Private Ownership and Use of Firearms,* which was supported by the U.S. Justice Department's National Institute of Justice (NIJ). The results of the study, which involved a 1994 telephone survey of over 2,500 adults, were released in May 1997. Ludwig observed that fewer people are keeping firearms for hunting and recreational use while the ownership of firearms for self-protection is increasing. The survey results estimated that 42 percent of men and just 9 percent of women own firearms. At the study's release, Attorney General Janet Reno, commenting on the finding that over half of firearms kept in the home are unlocked, advocated legislation to require child-proof safety locks on newly sold firearms.

In 1997, Ludwig submitted an affidavit in support of the Canadian Firearms Act, which includes stringent controls on handguns. He has criticized John Lott's research results, which indicate that state laws permitting carrying concealed weapons deter crime.

In January 1998, Ludwig appeared with Lott in a forum held at Washburn University that was sponsored by the Koch Crime Commission. Ludwig focused his comments on what he perceived to be flaws in Lott's methodology and analysis of the data. He claimed that Lott failed to take account of other variables affecting the violent crime rate, such as gang activity, poverty levels, and the crack cocaine epidemic. Ludwig concluded that there is no compelling evidence that laws permitting carrying concealed weapons have deterred crime. In response to Lott's contention that concealed carry laws could deter multiple shootings, Ludwig commented that although such events were important from a public health position, they were too infrequent to draw a statistical conclusion.

Ludwig has suggested that a more valid measure of the effects of liberalized concealed carry laws would involve an examination of trends in the gap between adult and juvenile homicide victimization. He argues that because states with concealed carry laws require permit holders to be at least 18 years old, and in many cases 21, the deterrent effect should differentially benefit adults. Therefore, the gap between adult and juvenile victimization rates should be expected to narrow in states with liberalized laws. Ludwig states that his analysis of homicide data at the state level for the years 1977 to 1994 indicate no such effect. *See also* CONCEALED CARRY LAWS; COOK, PHILIP J.; LOTT, JOHN R.; RENO, JANET; TRIGGER LOCKS; YOUTH AND GUNS.

Further Reading: Philip J. Cook and Jens Ludwig, *Guns in America: Results of a Comprehensive Survey on Private Firearms Ownership and Use* (Washington, DC: National Institute of Justice, NCJ 165476, 1997); Jens Ludwig, "Do Carry-Concealed Weapons Laws Deter Crime?" *Spectrum: The Journal of State Government* 70 (Spring 1997), 29, 31; Daniel W. Webster, John S. Vernick, Jens Ludwig, and Kathleen Lester, "Flawed Gun Policy Research May Endanger Public Safety," *American Journal of Public Health* 87 (June 1997), 918-21.

M

Mailing of Firearms Act (MFA)

Prior to the major push for gun control legislation in the 1930s that ultimately resulted in passage of the National Firearms Act of 1934 and the Federal Firearms Act in 1938, the Mailing of Firearms Act of 1924 (MFA), also known as the Miller Act, was one of the few successes for gun control advocates. The law, which is still in effect today, prohibits sending through the United States Post Office pistols and other firearms that could be concealed on the person.

Consideration of the MFA followed soon after the introduction of another gun control bill supported by Senator John K. Shields, Democrat of Tennessee. The Shields bill would have prohibited the interstate shipment of all handguns except service revolvers, the so-called "big pistols" that Shields considered appropriate for home protection. The bill received legislative consideration in 1921, but extensive opposition developed. Because firearms manufacturing companies were highly concentrated geographically, the bill would have had a significant effect on the industry. Representatives of gun interests argued that the bill's restrictions might jeopardize national defense. Senator Frank Brandegee, Republican from Connecticut, a major gun manufacturing state, strongly opposed the bill and kept it from ever leaving the Judiciary Committee. When Shields lost his reelection bid in 1924, the bill died forever.

Republican Representative John F. Miller experienced much greater success in gaining passage of a gun control bill. Miller's constituents in Seattle, Washington, concerned with the mail-order sales of handguns, pressed him to introduce legislation to prohibit mail shipments of handguns. Unlike the Shields bill, Miller's proposal received wide support. An organized letter writing campaign informed Republican President Calvin Coolidge that the availability of pistols through the mail was tempting young people into criminal activity. A resolution from the United National Association of Post Office Clerks supported the legislation. The opposition of gun advocates could not overcome the strong support for the bill. No representatives from small arms manufacturers appeared at the hearings. One witness, a spokesman for the American Reclamation Society of Detroit, presented an argument that would be heard many times in the coming decades: The small number of firearms in Great Britain was responsible for that nation's low crime rate and therefore more stringent gun control legislation was also needed in the United States.

In the debate on the House floor, congressmen from the gun manufacturing states of Massachusetts and Connecticut offered no opposition to the bill. What opposition developed came from congressmen from southern and western states, who objected to the bill because they believed it violated the Second Amendment right to keep and bear arms. At a time when states rights predominated, they argued that the legislation would result in the proliferation of federal officials intent on violating state sovereignty. Congressman Thomas Blanton, Democrat of Texas, offered an anti-gun control argument that continues to be used: Despite the legislation, criminals would acquire guns, while law abiding citizens would have their constitutional rights violated.

Once the bill was approved by both houses, President Coolidge signed it into law in February 1927. His support of the legislation notwithstanding, Coolidge remained skeptical regarding the prospects for success of gun control legislation, especially in view of the miserable experience with federal enforcement of Prohibition. As the *Saturday Evening Post* observed, "If the Federal government cannot prevent the landing and distribution of shiploads of rum, how can it stop the criminal from getting the most concealed and vital tool of his trade?" The MFA effectively stopped mail shipments of handguns, but the measure had limited scope. In the meantime, firearms manufacturers were successful in opposing other legislation, and were also able to gain protection from foreign competition when Congress passed the Fordney-McCumber Tariff of 1922 and the Hawley-Smoot Tariff of 1930. The legislative battles of the 1920s established the pattern for future political struggles over gun control proposals. *See also* FEDERAL FIREARMS ACT; NATIONAL FIREARMS ACT OF 1934; SECOND AMENDMENT; UNITED KINGDOM.

Further Reading: Lee Kennett and James La Verne Anderson, The Gun in America: The Origins of a National Dilemma (Westport, CT: Greenwood, 1975); *New York Times* (February 10, 1924), 46.

Maryland One-Gun-Per-Month Law

Although the U.S. Congress has not enacted a one-gun-per-month statute that would limit an individual to purchasing just one firearm in a 30-day period, Maryland enacted such a law in October 1996. The statute provided the opportunity for interests on both sides of the gun control debate to evaluate the effectiveness of the measure. The number of purchases involving two or more handguns at a time declined from 7,569 in the 12 months before the law went into effect to 1,618 during the subsequent 12 months (the law allowed the continuation of multiple sales to gun collectors). Total handgun sales declined in Maryland from 41,726 in 1994 to 21,500 in 1997.

The purpose of a one-gun-per-month statute is to restrict "straw purchases," the practice of buying a large number of guns legally and then selling them on the street to be used for criminal purposes. Democratic Governor Parris N. Glendening, who signed the bill into law, claimed that the provision has been effective in keeping illegal handguns off Maryland streets. Preliminary data support Glendening's claim. From 1995 to 1997, the number of guns sold in multiple sales that were involved in crimes in the District of Columbia declined from 23 to 0, and in Baltimore from 26 to 0. However, studies indicate that Maryland remains the primary source of firearms for the District.

Critics claim that due to the new statute, criminals have substituted other weapons for handguns. The increase in police seizures of long guns relative to handguns lend support to this claim. While the seizure of handguns in Baltimore increased 23 percent from 1995 to 1997, the seizure of long guns increased 63 percent. Data from other locations in Maryland followed the same trend: The rate of increase in long gun seizures outpaced that of handguns, suggesting that those engaged in criminal activities were substituting long guns for handguns.

Lieutenant Governor Kathleen Kennedy Townsend, a Democrat, asserted that in 1997 the new law was responsible for a 9 percent decline in homicides, rapes, robberies, and aggravated assaults in Maryland. However, because the crime rate declined nationwide during the same period, many doubted that the new law could take sole credit for the reduction in Maryland.

One possible unintended consequence of the law might have been an increase in gun shop burglaries. State police reported that in the 18 months prior to passage of the legislation, two gun dealers reported burglaries, while in the 18 months following passage, 13 burglaries were reported. Criminals unable to bypass limitations on acquiring firearms by resorting to straw purchases may have resorted to theft.

While overall sales of handguns declined following the bill's passage, opponents of the measure argued that a general business downturn resulted in reduced sales. In addition, they argued that multiple sales of handguns never were common and that gun stores had not served as major sources of weapons for criminals. While the new law may deter a minor source of illegal handguns, opponents argue it inconveniences legitimate buyers. *See also* LONG GUN; VIOLENT CRIME RATE.

Further Reading: Philip P. Pan, "Maryland Handgun Sales Down 25 Percent: Drop Comes Year One-a-Month Buying Limit Was Imposed," *Washington Post* (May 27, 1998), A1.

Maryland v. United States (1965)

The U.S. Supreme Court decision in *Maryland v. United States* (381 U.S. 41, 1965) affects the question of gun control only indirectly, but has more direct significance for the status of state militias. In its decision, the Court commented that the National Guard constitutes the militia reserved to the states in Article I, section 8, clauses 15 and 16 of the U.S. Constitution. Although gun rights advocates argue that so-called "unorganized" militias established by private citizens fall under the claimed Second Amendment guarantee to keep and bear arms, the Court's interpretation of the modern militia leaves little room for informal organizations whose members claim to constitute the militia sanctioned by the Constitution.

The case arose from a collision between a commercial airliner and a Maryland Air National Guard jet trainer. In a suit brought against the United States under the Federal Tort Claims Act by the estates of the pilot and co-pilot of the commercial plane and the airline company, both parties accepted the trainer pilot's negligence. The main question

to be decided was whether the National Guard pilot was acting in his military capacity or as a civilian at the time of the accident. The district court ruled that the pilot had acted as a civilian under the supervision of the federal government and therefore the federal government was liable for his actions. Because two separate district court rulings and subsequent appeals came to different conclusions, the Supreme Court agreed to hear the case.

The Supreme Court ruled that whether the pilot was acting in his military or civilian capacity, he remained an employee of Maryland, not of the United States. The National Guard constitutes the modern equivalent of the militia provided for under Article I, section 8, clause 16 of the Constitution, which reserves to the states "the appointment of the officers, and the authority of training the militia according to the discipline prescribed by Congress." In 1916, to provide state militia organizations with the equipment and training they had previously lacked, Congress passed the National Defense Act. Under the act, the federal government allocated military equipment to militias, with the condition that states "make adequate provision, to the satisfaction of the Secretary of War, for the protection and care of such property."

Even though military members of the National Guard are paid by the federal government and must abide by federal regulations for training and promotion, state authorities appoint them and maintain direct control over personnel. The Court decided that "civilian caretakers" occupy the same status. Even though they have responsibility for maintaining federal property to keep the state militia in readiness, they are immediately responsible to the respective states in performing their duties. The Court declared that Congress intended the caretakers to be employed by the states and that, appointed by each state's adjutant general, they are responsible to state authorities for the performance of their duties.

The Court ruled that the Tort Claims Act did not apply in this case because both military and civilian personnel of the National

Guard are considered employees of the states, not the national government. Thus the decision blocked any legal action by the claimants against the national government. More generally, the case firmly cemented the view that the National Guard constitutes the state militia organizations envisioned by the constitutional framers. Many gun rights advocates maintain that privately organized militia groups, like private citizens, have the right to conduct training operations and to possess firearms. However, gun control advocates claim that court decisions such as the Maryland case contradict the further claim that private militia organizations have some special protection under Article I, section 8 and the Second Amendment to the Constitution. That status has been reserved for organizations established by the respective states and supported by the federal government. This position, argue gun control advocates, contributes to claims for the constitutionality of various restrictions on firearms possession. *See also* SECOND AMENDMENT.

Further Reading: *Maryland v. United States*, 381 U.S. 41 (1965).

Massachusetts Gun Violence Prevention Law

Gun control advocates have labeled the Massachusetts Gun Violence Prevention Law, enacted in July 1998, a model for other states and for Congress. The law's many provisions include increased penalties for illegal use of firearms, child accident prevention measures, and revised gun licensing regulations. Its introduction into the state legislature initiated an intense lobbying battle between pro- and anti-gun control forces. The final measure, signed by Massachusetts Governor Paul Cellucci, a Republican, is considered the most stringent gun control legislation in the United States. While Massachusetts Attorney General Scott Harshbarger, a Democrat, has called the law "a victory for common sense and for the protection of our children and our neighborhoods," gun rights organizations, extremely unhappy with the legislative outcome, quickly challenged the new law in the courts.

Among its provisions, the Massachusetts law establishes the responsibility of firearms owners for the safe storage of their guns. Criminal penalties are provided for negligent storage. The law increases penalties for such gun-related crimes as committing a felony with a firearm, illegal gun trafficking, illegal sale of a firearm to a minor, and illegal possession by a felon. Penalties were established for the possession of a firearm while intoxicated. The law prohibits possession or sale of sawed-off shotguns and any firearms that cannot be detected by metal detectors and X-ray machines. Through the codification of consumer protection regulations by the state attorney general, the sale of Saturday night specials, or "junk" guns, is prohibited.

The law created a new licensing system for all firearms, making Firearms Identification (FID) Cards renewable every four years, instead of for life as provided under previous regulations. Licenses to Carry (LTCs) are renewable every five years. While FID Cards are issued to any eligible person, LTCs are issued at the discretion of local police chiefs. The legislation provides for a club license that allows the possession of large capacity weapons for shooting ranges that can stock these weapons for use by members or visitors while on the premises. The statute includes additional bases for rejecting an application for an FID Card or LTC. These include conviction for a violent misdemeanor or the existence of an outstanding warrant against the applicant. Persons convicted of violent crimes or drug or firearms trafficking violations are subject to a life-long prohibition on obtaining an FID Card.

The law established a firearms Record-keeping Trust Fund that receives half of the licensing fees to finance the conduct of background checks and to maintain the Massachusetts firearms record keeping system. Firearms dealers are required to verify the validity of FID Cards, LTCs, and purchase permits before they may sell a gun. To ensure better record keeping, beginning September 1, 1999, gun dealers must operate from a location distinct from their residential address.

Broad policy changes such as the 1998 Massachusetts gun law can create unintended consequences. A provision within the law banning the open carrying of a rifle or shotgun unless while hunting or transporting the weapon in a case inadvertently prohibited veterans from carrying weapons during parades. When veterans' groups protested, the bill's original sponsors declared that their intention was never to prohibit veterans from carrying firearms during parades. The state legislature passed an amendment eliminating the unintended prohibition. *See also* Saturday Night Special; Sawed-Off Shotgun.

Further Reading: Join Together Online Web site <www.jointogether.org>.

McClure, James Albertas (1924–)

James McClure, a former Republican Senator from Idaho, pushed hard during the early 1980s for the adoption of firearms legislation that would amend what he considered the deficiencies of the Gun Control Act of 1968. He, along with Representative Harold L. Volkmer, Democrat from Missouri, sponsored the Firearms Owners Protection Act of 1986, a statute that significantly altered the original provisions of the 1968 act. Gun control advocates claimed that the 1986 act severely restricted the ability of the national government to limit the violent use of firearms. With the lobbying assistance of the National Rifle Association (NRA), the Gun Owners of America (GOA), and the Citizens Committee for the Right to Keep and Bear Arms (CCRKBA), McClure's firearms bill passed the U.S. Senate in 1985.

After serving in the U.S. Navy during World War II, McClure attended the Idaho College of Law, receiving a law degree in 1950. He became the prosecuting attorney of Payette County, a position he held until 1956. He was city attorney for Payette from 1953 to 1966 and served in the Idaho State Senate from 1961 to 1966. McClure campaigned successfully for the U.S. House of Representatives in 1966 and served three terms. In 1972, he was elected to the U.S. Senate, and was reelected in 1978 and 1984.

In 1986, McClure, a conservative, received a perfect score from the American Conservative Union for his senatorial voting record. The 1980 election, which brought Republican President Ronald Reagan into office, also gave Republicans control of the U.S. Senate. With a legislative body likely to be more sympathetic to gun rights interests, McClure began his efforts to enact a new firearms law.

While admitting that Congress intended the Gun Control Act of 1968 to restrict violent crime by regulating the sale, transportation, and possession of firearms, McClure claimed that the law had failed to achieve its objectives. He argued that those most affected by the law were not violent criminals, but innocent citizens who did an inadequate job of completing mandated paperwork. Law enforcement agencies, he contended, too often harassed law-abiding gun owners but did little to target dangerous criminals. The proposed legislation was intended to "provide for the legal protection" of citizens against the encroachment of law enforcement agents. He believed that the new legislation would bring firearms statutes in line with the original intent of Congress, "directing enforcement effort away from insignificant paperwork errors and toward willful violations of Federal firearms law."

McClure believed that his proposed bill struck a balance between the necessity of effective law enforcement and preserving the constitutional rights of law-abiding citizens. He emphasized the merits of specific provisions within the bill, including liberalization of interstate sales of firearms when they are legal in both the state of sale and the state of purchase; the necessity of demonstrating criminal intent in the prosecution of federal firearms law violations; clarification of sales procedures for private collectors; establishment of mandatory penalties for using a firearm during a federal crime; limitation of the legal seizure of firearms; provision for the return of seized firearms; and government payment of attorney's fees in frivolous suits. McClure assured skeptics that the legislation would not allow mail-order sales of firearms, permit unlicensed pawn shop gun sales, or restrict "legitimate" inspection of dealer records.

When McClure retired from the Senate in January 1991, the movement was already well under way to strengthen firearms legislation, which he had been instrumental in limiting through the Firearms Owners Protection Act. His efforts to amend the Gun Control Act of 1968 had the unintended consequences of alienating police organizations from the gun rights movement and energizing renewed efforts by gun control advocates to pass various firearms proposals, including what would become the Brady Handgun Violence Prevention Act. *See also* BRADY HANDGUN VIOLENCE PREVENTION ACT; CITIZENS COMMITTEE FOR THE RIGHT TO KEEP AND BEAR ARMS; COLLECTORS; FIREARMS OWNERS PROTECTION ACT; GUN CONTROL ACT OF 1968; GUN OWNERS OF AMERICA; NATIONAL RIFLE ASSOCIATION; REAGAN, RONALD; VOLKMER, HAROLD LEE.

Further Reading: James A. McClure, "Should Congress Adopt Proposed Relaxation of Handgun Controls?" *Congressional Digest* 65 (May 1986), 146, 148; Robert J. Spitzer, *The Politics of Gun Control* (Chatham, NJ: Chatham House, 1995).

McCollum, William (Bill) (1944–)

Republican William McCollum, U.S. representative from the eighth congressional district of Florida, serves as chairman of the Judiciary Subcommittee on Crime. In that capacity, McCollum has taken a strong interest in measures to reduce the national crime rate. Many consider him a major legislative authority on crime issues. However, the congressman has opposed gun control legislation and supported measures to weaken existing gun laws. In 1993, McCollum voted against final passage of the Brady Handgun Violence Prevention Act, and in 1994 he opposed passage of the ban on assault weapons. Both measures ultimately became law. In 1996, McCollum voted in favor of repealing the 1994 ban on semi-automatic assault weapons, a measure that passed the House of Representatives but failed in the Senate.

McCollum received a B.A. in 1965 and a J.D. in 1968 from the University of Florida.

After serving in the Navy from 1969 to 1972, he joined an Orlando law firm, becoming a partner in 1975. McCollum served as Seminole County Republican Executive Committee chairman from 1976 to 1980, when he was elected to the House of Representatives. Among his assignments, he co-chaired joint congressional hearings inquiring into the federal government raid on the Branch Davidian compound in Waco, Texas.

In June 1997, following a Supreme Court decision invalidating part of the Brady law that required local law enforcement authorities to conduct criminal background checks on handgun purchasers, the congressman commented that the decision would have little effect because the national instant check system was scheduled for implementation in November 1998. McCollum promised that his subcommittee would closely monitor the Federal Bureau of Investigation's (FBI) operation of the instant check system. He noted that the background check system does not prevent criminals from acquiring firearms because weapons are available from illegal sources. The congressman concluded that

Representative Bill McCollum (R-FL) supports measures to reduce the violent crime rate, but opposes gun control legislation and voted against the Brady Handgun Violence Prevention Act. *Courtesy of Rep. McCollum's office.*

additional measures, especially sentence enhancement laws, are needed to deter criminals from using firearms in violent crimes and drug trafficking.

Although he has opposed specific gun control measures, gun rights advocates might feel uneasy about some of the positions that McCollum has taken on crime policy issues. He supports anti-terrorism measures that would grant increased law enforcement powers to federal agents and advocates allowing prosecutors to conduct warrantless searches as long as police officers act "in good faith." Many, including gun rights groups, regard such legislation as being potentially in conflict with Fourth Amendment guarantees against unreasonable searches and seizures.

Although the violent crime rate has declined in the mid-1990s, McCollum believes there has not been nearly enough progress in bringing crime under control. He notes that while the number of violent crimes per 100,000 population was 160 in 1960, in 1995 that rate stood at 685. Noting the high crime rates among youths and young adults, McCollum has recommended legislation that would assist states in improving their juvenile justice systems. In return for federal assistance, states would be asked to institute such policies as allowing prosecutors to charge as adults anyone who is at least 15 years old and who commits murder, rape, or assault with a firearm. While not rejecting prevention measures, McCollum places special emphasis on deterrence as a way of combating youth as well as adult crime. *See also* ASSAULT WEAPONS BAN; BRADY HANDGUN VIOLENCE PREVENTION ACT; NATIONAL INSTANT CHECK SYSTEM; VIOLENT CRIME RATE; WACO, TEXAS, RAID.

Further Reading: Philip D. Duncan and Christine C. Lawrence, *Politics in America: The 105th Congress* (Washington, DC: CQ Press, 1997); Congressman Bill McCollum Web site <www.house.gov/mccollum>.

Media Violence

People on both sides of the gun control debate decry the prevalence of media violence, but draw different conclusions regarding its relationship to firearms. Movies, television, and popular music lyrics have come under criticism for their portrayal of violent acts. Gun control supporters tend to identify media violence with the danger of guns, while gun rights advocates, believing that guns don't kill people, people kill people, blame gun violence not on guns themselves, but on various other possible causes, among which could be the effects of violence in the mass media. Charlton Heston, when first vice president of the National Rifle Association (NRA), announced that he pressured Time-Warner to fire Ice-T because of the rapper's obscene lyrics. For gun control advocates, the media, venerate violence *and* guns; for gun rights advocates, the media glorify the *misuse* of guns.

Media critics such as Michael Medved have criticized the increased use of violence in films and television. For example, he reports that in the movies *Die Hard 2* and *Rambo III*, respectively, 264 and 106 people were killed. Current movies not only have far more acts of violence compared to past films, but the violence has become increasingly graphic. Movie makers appear to be forced to invent ever more explicitly violent acts to shock audiences who are becoming habituated to violent portrayals. Prime-time television programs depict an average of 3.6 crimes per episode, 25 percent of which are murders. Medved has expressed concern that movies increasingly portray violence as comedy. After killing someone, the hero often makes a humorous remark, thereby minimizing the significance of the violent act. Violence becomes entertainment to be enjoyed.

Defenders of the media argue that simply counting the number of violent acts committed in movies or television shows has no particular relevance to making inferences about effects on viewers. Some in the media argue that viewing violent acts can have a cathartic effect, thus actually reducing the probability that the viewer will commit an act of violence. However, several studies dealing especially with the behavior of children suggest that viewing violence encourages aggressive behavior. While media defenders argue that violent acts can be symbolic, representing a deeper lesson beyond the physical act itself, critics respond that an appeal to symbolism cannot erase the portrayal of violence against a human being. In another defense of the portrayal of violent acts, television dramas are described as morality plays in which the "bad guys" receive their just punishment. Critics reject this defense, arguing that younger children cannot always relate an act of violence to the ultimate retribution sometime later in the story.

Media defenders argue that violence in the mass media simply mirrors the actions and values of contemporary society. Therefore, they contend, critics are blaming the messenger, and ignoring the true source of the problem. Critics respond that films exaggerate the nature of physical violence. Fistfights and gunfights are made to last far longer than is usually the case in reality. In addition, the media exaggerate the frequency with which violent acts occur. Medved reports that a television character has an 8.6 percent chance of becoming a victim of violence, while the average American has a yearly chance of 0.5 percent. The media do not just mirror reality, but vastly over-represent one aspect of it.

To the extent that the media affect perceptions, people believe they are in greater danger of being victims of violent crime than is in fact the case. The fear of violent crime may affect behavior by, for instance, encouraging citizens to isolate themselves in anticipation of becoming a victim, and to believe that methods of self-defense, such as owning a firearm, are effective responses. However, while gun control advocates argue that perceptions have been distorted by the media, the gun rights supporters contend that the danger of crime is real.

Those people concerned with violence in the media have proposed possible palliatives to the problem of violence in the media. In the late 1980s, Democratic Senator Paul Simon of Illinois encouraged the entertainment industry to develop voluntary guidelines regarding the portrayal of violence, but had little success. Other than adding a computer chip to television sets that allows parents to block certain programs and establishing rating systems for movies and television programs, little has been done, and perhaps can be done, to deal with the problem of violence in the media. In the meantime, the First Amendment will enter the debate, and so will the Second Amendment, at least to the extent that critics associate media violence with the availability of firearms. *See also* NATIONAL RIFLE ASSOCIATION; SECOND AMENDMENT; VIOLENT CRIME RATE; YOUTH AND GUNS.

Further Reading: Carl M. Cannon, "Honey, I Warped the Kids," *Mother Jones* (July/August 1993), 17-21; Michael Medved, *Hollywood vs. America* (New York: Harper Collins, 1993).

Mennonite Central Committee (MCC)

The Mennonite Central Committee (MCC) has taken a strong stand in favor of various gun control proposals. The MCC advocates proposals intended to reduce the availability of guns and to regulate their use. The organization, calling itself a "peace church," encourages "people of faith" to surrender any firearms that are kept for self-defense, claiming that such actions will serve as an example to others of a "commitment to non-violence in a society that has become engulfed by violence." The Committee focuses its concern on handguns, noting that they constitute one-third of all firearms in the United States and are used in 80 percent of all firearm homicides.

The Mennonite Central Committee was founded in 1920 as a relief and development organization within the American Mennonite and Brethren in Christ churches. The MCC sends volunteers to work in approximately 50 countries. These volunteers are involved in various areas of development, including agriculture, health care and maintenance, education, and social services. In the United States and Canada, the organization conducts programs dealing with mental illness, disabilities, job creation, and services to criminal offenders. The organization's basic nonviolent stand has been a major factor in its support for gun control policy.

The MCC has employed poignant symbolism to convey its anti-gun message. In

September 1997, the Committee dedicated a 16-foot-high sculpture at a plaza located across from the District of Columbia police headquarters. Esther Augsburger and her son Michael, members of the Mennonites, created the sculpture, titled "Guns into Plowshares," using 3,000 guns collected in a gun buyback program by the District of Columbia Metropolitan Police Department.

Mennonites have served in various locations around the world where violence prevails. Carol Rose, a Mennonite worker who has worked in Central America, Thailand, and the Philippines, commented in 1995 after a year's tour of duty in Lancaster, Pennsylvania, that she witnessed more violence during her first year in that American city than during any other tour of duty outside the United States. She attributed the violence to the "easy accessibility to guns."

The MCC backs continuation of the prohibition on assault weapons passed in 1994 and opposes efforts in Congress to repeal the ban, claiming that such firearms "are part of the culture of death." Claiming that these guns are "a favorite among criminals," the Committee supports an extension of the ban on "junk guns," or Saturday night specials, to include those weapons manufactured in the United States. Additional proposals supported by the Committee include registering firearms, licensing, requiring that gun owners have liability insurance, establishing competency tests for potential gun owners, increasing penalties for misuse of firearms, creating regularized gun transfer procedures, and establishing gun owners' civil liability for the misuse of weapons. In addition to legislative proposals, the MCC educates people about the dangers of firearms, discouraging the keeping of handguns in the home and offering assistance to victims of gun violence. The organization distributes a study guide that provides information about firearms violence, gun control laws, the Mennonite position on gun violence, and suggestions for ameliorating the problem of firearm-related violence. *See also* ASSAULT WEAPONS BAN; CANADA; GUN BUYBACK PROGRAMS; GUN CULTURE; SATURDAY NIGHT SPECIAL.

Further Reading: "Gun Violence Packet" (Washington, DC: Mennonite Central Committee, 1997); Mennonite Central Committee Web site <www.mcc.org>.

Metaksa, Tanya K. (1936–)

Tanya Metaksa, who served as executive director of the National Rifle Association's (NRA) Institute for Legislative Action (ILA) from 1994 to 1998, has been an avid spokesperson and effective lobbyist for gun rights advocates. She adheres to the position that guns themselves are innocent of any wrongdoing; people commit crimes of violence, not the weapons they misuse. As a high official in an organization composed mostly of men, Metaksa represents the new image the NRA is attempting to convey to the American public.

Metaksa has taken strong stands on contemporary issues regarding firearms and gun control. Noting that over 200,000 machine guns are legally in private hands today, she accepts legitimate private ownership and use of such weapons. She denounces attempts to outlaw assault weapons, a term she claims has come to mean any firearm that gun control advocates want to ban. Metksa defines an assault weapon more stringently as "a fully automatic firearm used in time of war by the ordinary soldier" and labels as "stupid" the attempt to define assault weapons on the basis of what she considers cosmetic features.

With regard to so-called cop-killer bullets, Metaksa claims that most ammunition can penetrate protective vests. Besides, she has commented, most police officers who have been killed have been shot in the head. Focusing on the individualistic interpretation of the Second Amendment, Metksa admonishes the American Civil Liberties Union (ACLU) for failing to come to the defense of the right to keep and bear arms. She takes a cautious position on requiring the placement of taggants in gunpowder, which are intended to facilitate the tracing of terrorist bombers. She calls for further testing before being willing to accept their inclusion in explosives. However, Metaksa suggests their use be limited to commercial explosives. Those who make ammunition from gun powder should be exempt.

Metaksa, whose father escaped from Russia after the communist revolution, acquired a strong suspicion of governments, which is reflected in her opposition to any official effort to control private ownership of firearms. She views the organization for which she has labored the "only bulwark of defense" against advocates of gun control. Metaksa graduated from Smith College in 1958, becoming a medical photographer in a New York hospital. She and her husband George settled in Connecticut where Metaksa became a housewife and raised a family. In the late 1960s, she became active in the gun rights cause. She worked for three years as legislative director for Alfonse D'Amato, former Republican Senator from New York.

In 1977, Metaksa became director of state and local affairs in the NRA's Institute for Legislative Action. In 1979, she became deputy executive director of the Institute, but left that position in 1980, apparently over a disagreement with NRA executive vice president Harlon Carter. In 1991, Metaksa returned to a leadership position in the NRA as a member of the board of directors. In 1993, her company, Bullet Communications, was granted a $90,000 contract to create ILA's electronic bulletin board. Although Metaksa received criticism from within the NRA for this no-bid contract, she weathered the storm, and in 1994 rose to head the ILA. In 1998, NRA executive vice president Wayne LaPierre moved Metaksa out of the ILA, appointing James Jay Baker as the executive director. Metaksa continued to serve the NRA as a senior adviser to LaPierre. *See also* AMERICAN CIVIL LIBERTIES UNION; ASSAULT WEAPONS BAN; INSTITUTE FOR LEGISLATIVE ACTION; LAPIERRE, WAYNE; NATIONAL RIFLE ASSOCIATION; RUSSIA; TAGGANTS.

Further Reading: Barbara Grizzuti Harrison, "Cease Fire," *Mother Jones* (March/April 1997), 33-36; Tanya K. Metaksa, "Sliding Down the Slippery Slope," *American Rifleman* 145 (June 1997), 30-31.

Mexico

Mexico has had an uneasy relationship with the United States with regard to the regulation of firearms. Mexico has stringent gun regulations and does not have an armaments industry. Guns larger than .38-caliber are restricted to military use only. Officials generally associate the carrying of firearms with possible criminal activity. However, the country has a serious problem with violent crime, particularly organized crime syndicates linked to the drug trade, and political unrest at times has resulted in guerilla uprisings. The Mexican Foreign Relations Ministry reported that from 1995 to 1997 over 1,000 illegal weapons were confiscated each month, 40 percent of which were associated with drug cartels. The Mexican government contends that the large number of firearms available for illegal use originated in the United States. For example, the gun used to assassinate presidential candidate Luis Donaldo Colosio in 1994 was discovered to have originated with a Texas gun dealer.

To control the illegal gun trade, the Mexican government has clamped down on the transfer of firearms across the U.S.-Mexican border, enforcing restrictions on the importation of firearms and ammunition. Those convicted of firearms smuggling face prison terms up to 30 years. The U.S. embassy in Mexico reported that in 1998 over 120 U.S. citizens were arrested in Mexico on weapons charges, over half of whom were being held in Mexico at the end of the year. Some U.S. citizens used to carrying firearms who took guns inadvertently into Mexico have been arrested and detained. The U.S. government conducted an information campaign, including placing signs along highways leading to the Mexican border, warning U.S. citizens that they should not take guns into Mexico. U.S. citizens are warned that Mexican cities may have ordinances banning possession of other weapons, such as knives.

Just as the U.S. government has complained about the transfer of drugs from Mexico to the United States, Mexico has objected to the flow of illegal weapons from the United States into Mexico. Mexican officials

Zapatista rebel leader Subcomandante Marcos, a leader of the rebellion in the Mexican state of Chiapas, hands over his weapons as he prepares for talks with the Mexican government in June 1996. Mexico has strict gun regulations, but serious problems with violent crime and internal political unrest. *REUTERS/Andrew Winning/Archive Photos.*

claim that thousands of firearms make their way past U.S. Customs Service officials. U.S. officials have responded to the Mexican concerns by training dogs to sniff for ammunition, employing X-ray machines to detect firearms in trucks crossing the border, and intensifying the effort to trace guns confiscated in Mexico.

Because some U.S. citizens have apparently been detained in Mexico for innocently transporting a firearm into the country, the Mexican Congress considered new legislation in 1998 that would grant to border officers greater discretion in situations involving visitors to Mexico who unintentionally bring firearms with them. However, the new law also established harsher penalties for attempting to smuggle arms into Mexico, making more weapons offenses subject to long prison terms.

Some in the United States are concerned about the Mexican government's stringent gun control policies, given reports about the repression of political opposition. Amnesty International, the organization that monitors government violence against citizens, has protested reported violence against Mexican citizens. For instance, in November 1997, 45 people in the state of Chiapas were killed by gunmen believed to be members of a paramilitary group. Amnesty International has also protested the disappearance of political dissidents and reported incidents of torture. Pro-gun rights groups are especially suspicious of restrictions on gun ownership in such circumstances, arguing that the right to keep and bear arms is a major defense against an oppressive government.

Further Reading: Amnesty International Web site <www.amnesty.org.uk>; Jim Galasyn, "Mexican Congress Takes Aim at Illegal Guns from U.S.," *Los Angeles Times* (September 7, 1998), A3, A24; Clifford Krauss, "Harried Over Drugs, Mexico Presses Own Peeve: U.S. Guns" (March 18, 1997), located at LatinoLink Web site <www.latinolink.com/news>.

Michigan Militia (MM)

The Michigan Militia (MM) is an organization of people who believe in the right to organize armed military groups to protect themselves against perceived government oppression. The MM is an example of a more extreme element in the anti-gun control movement. The organization's pro-gun position is fueled by the belief that gun control legislation coincides with a much larger plan to enslave the American people.

Norman Olson, a Baptist minister and gun store owner, and Ray Southwell, a real estate agent, established the Michigan Militia in 1994. Southwell approached Olson after losing a struggle over educational policy with a local school board. He was concerned that the introduction of a curriculum advocated by the federal government would result in the debasement of the entire education system. To resist federal government intervention into education and other areas, Olson and Southwell formed a militia to defend what they believed to be their constitutional rights.

Olson and Southwell believed that too many state laws had been supplanted by federal restrictions. They saw the Environmental Protection Agency (EPA) as a clear example of such unwarranted intervention. A central issue for them was the preservation of the right to keep and bear arms. The Second Amendment, they argued, is the most important ingredient in the Bill of Rights because the other freedoms could easily be lost without the right to protect them by threat of force against the machinations of "tyrants."

After its founding, the Michigan Militia quickly increased its membership to as many as 7,000. When Mark Koernke joined the organization, he was working as a janitor at the University of Michigan. Not satisfied with the MM, he established the Michigan Militia at Large, considered a more extreme version of the MM. In the evenings, he broadcast an hour-long shortwave radio program, "Intelligence Report," on which he referred to himself simply as "Mark from Michigan." Koernke identified the New World Order as the enemy against which Americans must defend themselves and claimed that the federal government was involved in an elaborate conspiracy to disarm the American public. Supposedly involved in this conspiracy was a national police force composed of National Guardsmen, Los Angeles street gangs,

Nepalese Gurkhas, and Russian troops prepared to take armed control of the United States, all in the name of the United Nations. He foresaw the Federal Emergency Management Agency (FEMA) creating a provisional government in preparation for the New World Order. Koernke produced a videotape, *America in Peril,* which was distributed to militia groups around the country.

Immediately following the Oklahoma City bombing in April 1995, Koernke faxed a brief message to then-U.S. Representative Steve Stockman, Republican of Texas, stating: "Seven to 10 floors only. Military people on the scene." Later he professed no foreknowledge of the bombing, but claimed that in contacting Stockman, he was hoping to get the media to the scene. A few days after the bombing, Koernke claimed that federal agents had given Timothy McVeigh orange clothing so that potential snipers would have a better target.

The MM gained further publicity when leaders of the organization indicated that Terry Nichols, since convicted of complicity in the Oklahoma bombing, had attended meetings, bringing Timothy McVeigh with him to at least one gathering. When federal agents searched the farm of Nichols's brother, they discovered several papers associated with the MM. Olson and Southwell claimed immediately after the Oklahoma bombing that they believed the Japanese were responsible for the attack. These statements led the commanders of the MM to force the two leaders to resign. Claiming that the MM had been captured by moderates, Olson and Southwell formed the Northern Michigan Regional Militia. *See also* JAPAN; MILITIA OF MONTANA; OKLAHOMA CITY BOMBING; RUSSIA; SECOND AMENDMENT.

Further Reading: Morris Dees and James Corcoran, *Gathering Storm: America's Militia Threat* (New York: HarperCollins, 1996); Thomas Halpern, David Rosenberg, and Irwin Suall, "Militia Movement: Prescription for Disaster," in Frank McGuckin, ed., *Terrorism in the United States* (New York: H.W. Wilson, 1997), 51-63; Jonathan Karl, *The Right to Bear Arms: The Rise of America's New Militias* (New York: HarperCollins, 1995); Michigan Militia Web site <www.michiganmilitia.org>.

On June 15, 1995, Norman Olson (right) of the Northern Michigan Militia shakes hands with Senate Judiciary Committee Chairman Arlen Specter (R-PA) before the start of hearings on militias in the United States. *REUTERS/Gary A. Cameron/Archive Photos.*

Militia Act of 1792

According to the Militia Act of 1792, more formally titled "An Act more effectually to provide for the National Defense by establishing an Uniform militia throughout the United States," all free white male citizens, from 18 to 45 years old, were subject to militia duty. Every militiaman was required to furnish a musket or firelock, bayonet and belt, spare flints, knapsack, and a pouch containing not less than 24 cartridges. By establishing these requirements, the Militia Act in effect placed a tax on men 18 to 45 years of age. For 111 years, the act provided the basic structure for the militia system, although it was largely unused for much of that time.

In 1790, President George Washington's Secretary of War, Henry Knox, proposed a plan for an organized militia that called for national government control over military units established in the states. The states disliked the plan because it provided for more national government intervention in state affairs than they were willing to tolerate. In 1792, Congress passed a considerably weakened version of the Knox proposal. While Knox had recommended the organization of the militia into three age classes (18-20, 21-45, and 46-60), with military training appropriate for each class, the final bill called for all eligible men between 18 and 45 to be enrolled in an undifferentiated militia.

Congressional discussions of the Militia Act reveal no evidence that any legislator doubted citizens should have the right to own firearms. Legislators demonstrated a desire that the population should be armed, but at minimal cost to the average citizen. The act reflected the contemporary social conditions and demonstrated racial prejudice, for it prohibited slaves, freed blacks, and Indians from serving in the militia. While the Knox plan included prescriptions for militia organization, the Militia Act only made recommendations. The act intended that the United States would have a uniform militia, with units from the various states being essentially interchangeable. However, the law qualified this provision by stating "if the same be convenient," which it was not for many states.

As the only uniformity requirement, the act called for each state to have an adjutant general and an inspector for each brigade. The adjutant generals were given the responsibility of maintaining uniformity among the various state militias; each adjutant general was to report the condition of his state's militia each year to the governor and the president of the United States. Beyond this requirement, the act contained no sanctions against state governments or individual officials for failure to comply with its provisions. The potential force to be organized under the act numbered over a half million men. The states had neither the capacity nor the inclination, given the lack of penalties, to carry out the provisions of the Militia Act.

During the War of 1812, the state militias provided the vast majority of the American forces. The last time the national government made significant use of the militia system was during the Seminole War from 1836 to 1842. In the war against Mexico in 1846–1848, only 12 percent of American forces originated with state militias, and the remainder were national troops. In 1820, Secretary of War John C. Calhoun had recommended an army appropriation that emphasized a professional, national military force, thus focusing on a centralized military system in contrast to dependence on state militias. During the Civil War in the 1860s, less than 50,000 Union troops were derived from state militias. Rather than establishing a militia system according to the recommendations of the 1792 law, states depended on the organization of voluntary companies, a far cry from the universal militia service originally envisioned.

In 1808, Congress established a permanent annual appropriation of $200,000 to purchase muskets that would be distributed to the states in proportion to militia enrollments. A congressional decision in 1855 indicated the failure of the militia system. States that had failed to enroll a militia and therefore were receiving little of the grant money insisted on altering the basis for distribution. Rather than militia enrollments, Congress established a new standard that employed the number of senators and representatives from each state to determine each state's allotment.

Ultimately, the Dick Act of 1903 brought an end to the militia system of universal service established in the 1792 act and officially replaced it with a voluntary system of militia service called the National Guard. *See also* DICK ACT.

Further Reading: John K. Malton, *History of the Militia and the National Guard* (New York: Macmillan, 1983); William H. Riker, *Soldiers of the States: The Role of the National Guard in American Democracy* (Washington, DC: Public Affairs Press, 1957).

Militia of Montana (MOM)

Organized in February 1994 by John Trochmann along with his brother and a nephew, the Militia of Montana (MOM) has avidly opposed any gun control measures, considering them to be a violation of the Second Amendment right to keep and bear arms and to organize militia groups for self-protection. MOM established its base of operations in Noxon, Montana, just 50 miles from Ruby Ridge, Idaho, where in 1992 family members of white supremacist Randy Weaver were killed by FBI agents in an armed standoff. Trochmann was present at the police line during the siege of Ruby Ridge. Following the standoff, he joined with others to assist Weaver by forming United Citizens for Justice. Although the organization soon disbanded due to internal strife, it became the base for the Militia of Montana and other paramilitary groups.

MOM established a mail-order business, offering members and interested people books, videotapes, and handbooks that provided advice on forming a militia organization and obtaining military training. Among the items listed in its catalog is a training manual, which contains instructions for the conduct of guerrilla warfare and provides biblical justifications for subversive activity. Among the topics included in the manual are tactics for raiding military armories to obtain weapons and ammunition, the organization of sabotage attacks, and the conduct of domestic terrorism campaigns.

Trochmann associated gun control with his vision of an evil New World Order. To him, the Brady Handgun Violence Prevention Act represented an initial stage in the plans of those wishing to establish a world government to control American citizens. Ruby Ridge and the standoff at the Branch Davidian compound in Waco, Texas, provided evidence for Trochmann and MOM of a huge conspiracy to take firearms away from citizens. To prevent further incidents and to resist future "gun grabs," Trochmann advocated a coalition of unorganized militias throughout the United States. Simply having guns in the home would not preserve freedom. Citizens must train in military tactics and possess the appropriate equipment to resist with arms any government use of force.

MOM claimed that firearms provided a means to defend a way of life being threatened by government taxation, permissive abortions, and regulation of home schooling. Affirmative action programs came under attack, as well as such trade treaties as the General Agreement on Tariffs and Trade (GATT) and the North American Free Trade Agreement (NAFTA), which were perceived as threats to the livelihood of white American males. The organization saw evidence of a huge government conspiracy to disarm patriotic Americans, institute burdensome taxation, and destroy constitutional rights, all in the name of world government. Trochmann claimed that unorganized militias provided the only way to defend against this conspiracy. Just like the Minutemen of 1775, members of MOM believed they must be prepared to fight in a revolution. To this end, the organization encouraged members to arm themselves with semi-automatic weapons and to learn guerrilla warfare tactics.

MOM holds that the people have a right to arm themselves against their own government. Thus, unorganized militias become the primary line of defense if the government becomes oppressive, as MOM and other militia groups believe it has. With the assumption that government has become the major threat to individual freedom, gun control measures become especially objectionable because they amount to the oppressor disarming citizens and leaving them defenseless.

Critics of this view note the incongruity of arguing that a constitution, intended to establish a stable government, would at the same time make provision for the instrument of its own demise. Governments can and do at times violate citizen rights, but one of them is not the right to prepare for revolution. *See also* AMERICAN REVOLUTION; BRADY HANDGUN VIOLENCE PREVENTION ACT; MICHIGAN MILITIA, MILITIA ACT OF 1792; MILITIA WATCHDOG; MINUTEMEN, REVOLUTIONARY; RUBY RIDGE; SECOND AMENDMENT; WACO, TEXAS, RAID.

Further Reading: Morris Dees and James Corcoran, *Gathering Storm: America's Militia Threat* (New York: Harper Collins, 1996); Jonathan Karl, *The Right to Bear Arms: The Rise of America's New Militias* (New York: HarperCollins, 1995); Militia of Montana Web site <www.nidlink.com/~bobhard/mom.html>.

Militia Watchdog

The Militia Watchdog is a Web site devoted to monitoring the militia movement. The Militia Watchdog maintains information on the historical development and legal standing of militia groups and provides information on associations such as the patriot movement, common law courts, and tax resisters that are collaborating to create "an illegal 'shadow' government, heavily armed, answerable to no authority, and motivated by bizarre conspiracy theories." Although the Web site states that it does not take a position on the issues of gun control and the right to keep and bear arms, it does comment that paramilitary groups have "cloaked themselves in the Constitution," which includes an appeal to the Second Amendment to justify not only a right to keep and bear arms, but to organize militia groups to oppose the government itself.

Mark Pitcavage founded the Militia Watchdog as a way of informing the public about the operations of militia groups. The site does not claim to be objective, stating that it believes militia groups present a danger about which citizens must be warned. It wishes to expose what it considers misinterpretations of the history and law of the militia. Along with Sheldon Sheps, a Canadian

who has investigated U.S. right-wing/populist movements, Pitcavage developed a list of "Frequently Asked Questions" about the militias that they made available on the Web site. They claim that the militias lack legitimacy and legality, having little in common with the original constitutional and statutory establishment of military groups. Headquartered in Columbus, Ohio, the Militia Watchdog maintains a list of other Web sites and materials, including news items and profiles of individuals in the movement. It welcomes requests for information from individuals, the press, and law enforcement officials, and maintains a mailing list for professionals, including academics, lawyers, and public officials.

According to the Militia Watchdog, the militia movement reemerged in the 1990s, energized by those who perceived that the federal government was about to confiscate firearms. Following the confiscation, the United States would supposedly be overrun by a United Nations-operated "New World Order." The Militia Watchdog identifies common law courts, sovereign citizens (those who recognize only citizenship in a particular state), tax protesters, Christian patriots, and white supremacists as the "vanguard of antigovernment extremism." Among the events leading to the creation of militias are the 1992 Ruby Ridge standoff, the 1993 Waco raid on the Branch Davidian compound, and the passage of the Brady Handgun Violence Prevention Act and the assault weapons ban.

Despite an official disclaimer regarding any position on the gun control issue, Pitcavage provides a critical appraisal of the National Rifle Association (NRA) and other gun rights organizations. He focuses attention on the prevalence of firearms among militia groups and the presence of militia organizations at gun shows. Pitcavage notes that while the Brady waiting period was in effect, many people purchased firearms at gun shows because no waiting period was required to purchase from a private owner. He observes that the NRA has distanced itself from the militia movement, "despite the increasingly erratic actions of leader Wayne LaPierre." *See also* BRADY HANDGUN VIO-

LENCE PREVENTION ACT; GUN SHOWS; LAPIERRE, WAYNE; MICHIGAN MILITIA; MILITIA ACT OF 1792; MILITIA OF MONTANA; NATIONAL RIFLE ASSOCIATION; RUBY RIDGE; SECOND AMENDMENT; UNITED NATIONS; WACO, TEXAS, RAID.

Further Reading: Militia Watchdog Web site <http://www.militia-watchdog.org>; Mark Pitcavage, "Welcome to a New World (Disorder): A Visit to a Gun Show," *The Militia Watchdog*, <www.militia-watchdog.org/gunshow.htm>.

Miller v. Texas (1894)

The U.S. Supreme Court decision in *Miller v. Texas* (153 U.S. 535, 1894) provides an early example of the Court's unwillingness to interpret the Second Amendment of the U.S. Constitution as limiting the ability of state governments to restrict an individual citizen's right to keep and bear arms. The Court expressly stated that the Second Amendment applies only to the federal government and therefore does not have force regarding the proceedings of state courts. The decision occurred prior to the "selective incorporation" process in more recent Court decisions that has made much of the Bill of Rights applicable to the states. However, the Court's ruling in this case regarding the Second Amendment has so far not been altered.

A Dallas County, Texas, grand jury indicted Franklin P. Miller for a murder that occurred in June 1892. He was convicted in July of that year and sentenced to death. His appeal of the conviction to the Court of Criminal Appeals of Texas resulted in an affirmation of the guilty verdict, whereupon Miller filed a writ of error to the U.S. Supreme Court, claiming that the law under which he was originally arrested violated the U.S. Constitution. He contended that the Texas statute prohibiting the carrying of dangerous weapons infringed his rights as a citizen of the United States and violated the Second Amendment to the U.S. Constitution, noting that the original court had charged the jury that by carrying a pistol on a public street, he was violating the law. Further, he claimed that the arrest without warrant of a person carrying a weapon in violation of the statute violated the Fourth Amendment to the U.S.

Constitution, which proscribes unreasonable searches and seizures. Finally, Miller argued that the Texas statute violated the Fifth and Fourteenth Amendments, which provide, respectively, that no person shall be deprived of life, liberty, or property without due process of law, and that no state shall pass any law that abridges the privileges or immunities of citizens of the United States.

The Court's decision did not rely primarily on the substantive claims of the writ of error. The Court noted that no objection involving a federal question was raised either during the trial and before the judgment, or during the original appellate court hearing, but only arose before the appellate court on a motion for a rehearing, which was overruled. Therefore, the writ of error was dismissed because no objection raising a federal question had been introduced during the original trial. However, the Court did speak to the claims made by the defendant in the motion for a rehearing.

With regard to the claim that the Texas statute forbidding the carrying of weapons and allowing for the arrest without warrant of anyone violating this law was in conflict with the Second and Fourth Amendments to the U.S. Constitution, the Supreme Court stated that it could not discover where the defendant was denied any rights provided for in those amendments. Even if the defendant had been denied such protection, the Court ruled that the amendments apply only to the federal government and have no application to state courts. With regard to the Fourteenth Amendment, the Court indicated that the defendant's claim that his rights as a United States citizen had been abridged could not be considered because it was not presented in the trial court, and further stated that there had been no denial of due process of law with regard to the ordinary procedures of the court, nor did the Texas statute prohibiting the carrying of dangerous weapons abridge the privileges of citizens of the United States. *See also* FOURTH AMENDMENT; FOURTEENTH AMENDMENT; SECOND AMENDMENT.

Further Reading: *Miller v. Texas*, 153 U.S. 535 (1894).

Minutemen, Modern

The Minutemen, a para-military group that operated during the 1960s and early1970s, was a precursor to the right-wing militia groups of the 1990s. Founded in 1960 by Robert Bolivar DePugh, a chemist from Norborne, Missouri, the organization advocated citizen preparedness for a possible communist takeover of the United States. Members of the Minutemen were encouraged to become adept at guerrilla war tactics and to stockpile firearms and ammunition for use in a future conflict to defend the nation against invasion. The emphasis on the acquisition and stockpiling of guns resulted in the arrest and indictment of the organization's leadership for violations of federal firearms laws.

Due to DePugh's fanatical concern for super-secrecy to protect the membership should a communist takeover occur, the group was said to have been organized into squads of up to 25 individuals who supposedly had no knowledge of each other's identities. No membership roles were to be kept and only the state commanders were to know the identity of squad leaders. It is difficult to imagine how any organization could operate effectively under such conditions, and the Minutemen organization itself apparently did not. DePugh's most notable success was his ability to gain headlines, not for what the organization did, but for the violent actions he claimed the organization would take to save the nation.

The total Minutemen membership likely was never very large. DePugh at different times provided membership figures of anywhere from 600 to 25,000. In 1968, J. Edgar Hoover, head of the Federal Bureau of Investigation (FBI), claimed that the organization could not depend on more than 50 individuals as active participants. Others estimated an active membership of no more than 200 with possibly another 400 who donated money to the organization and subscribed to its publications.

Early in its existence, the organization's leaders ran afoul of federal firearms legislation. DePugh, taking his cue from communist strategy, claimed that one of the Minutemen's fundamental objectives was to incite the government into taking repressive measures against citizens to alienate the population from their government. This tactic included a belligerent rhetoric, with references to assassination and terrorism, as well as activities at the edge of the law. Richard Lauchli, for a time one of DePugh's associates, was arrested several times for various violations of firearms laws. In 1960, he was fined $500 for stealing 23 bazookas, and in 1964, he was indicted for allegedly transporting illegal firearms as part of a deal to sell guns to anti-Castro Cubans.

In 1966, DePugh was indicted for possession of bombs, but in March 1967 a judge dismissed the charge. In the meantime, the Minutemen leader was charged with firearms possession while under indictment. DePugh and two associates were convicted of violating the National Firearms Act of 1934 for receiving, transferring, and possessing automatic weapons and silencers. Depugh and another associate, Wally Peyson, were charged with, among other things, illegal possession of a machine gun and failing to pay a $200 tax under the National Firearms Act. In February 1968, DePugh was accused of bank robbery while free on appeal of his sentence of four years, but the charge was ultimately dropped.

At this time, DePugh and Peyson disappeared, prompting a 17-month FBI manhunt. When the two men were captured in Truth or Consequences, New Mexico, in July 1969, they had in their possession a number of homemade bombs, grenades, rifles, and handguns. In February 1970, DePugh was sentenced to four years for his disappearance while under bond. Shortly thereafter, he was convicted of federal firearms violations and in October was sentenced to 10 years in federal prison. He remained imprisoned from 1970 to 1973.

While DePugh languished behind bars, a leadership struggle among his would-be successors tore the Minutemen organization apart. The FBI continued its efforts to infiltrate the organization with informants and to destroy it from within. DePugh was released in May 1973, but his efforts to revive the Minutemen failed. For a time, he tried to coordinate the activities of several right-wing groups, but with little success due to internecine squabbles among the leadership. His final efforts at organization included the formation of the Committee of Ten Million in 1976, which involved holding "Patriots Leadership Conferences" in Kansas City, Missouri. After the organization ceased to exist in 1981, DePugh began a tabloid, *The American Patriot*, but the publication lasted only a short time. This publication marked the end of DePugh's career in radical politics. Far from considering his activism a failure, he claimed to have paved the way for the victory of conservative Republican Ronald Reagan in the 1980 presidential election.

In 1991, DePugh, who was then running a modeling school and agency, was arrested for sexual exploitation of a minor. Officials searched his wife's home back in Norborne and discovered several weapons undoubtedly stored there during the active days of the Minutemen. DePugh was indicted on four counts of firearms violations and was convicted on three of them. *See also* NATIONAL FIREARMS ACT OF 1934; REAGAN, RONALD.

Further Reading: John George and Laird Wilcox, *Nazis, Communists, Klansmen, and Others on the Fringe* (Buffalo, NY: Prometheus, 1992); Harry J. Jones, *A Private Army* (Toronto: Macmillan, 1969).

Minutemen, Revolutionary

The revolutionary minutemen captured the imagination of generations of Americans who admired the legendary exploits of these revolutionary patriots. Beginning with the 1960s, many extremist groups who have advocated military preparedness of private citizens and engaged in the caching of firearms have patterned their organizations to some extent after romantic perceptions of the revolutionary minutemen. The minutemen were militia units organized in the early days of the American Revolution in Massachusetts and a few other colonies. In 1774, in Worcester County, Massachusetts, military regiments were reorganized to eliminate officers and members loyal to Great Britain. New members were selected according to their political preferences and became known for their loyalty to the revolutionary cause.

In October 1774, the Massachusetts revolutionary convention designated a portion of the militia that was to be prepared to take up arms at "a minute's notice" when and where needed. These militiamen became known as minutemen, and the revolutionary convention adopted the name. To be prepared for immediate call, each militia member was expected to have a powder horn and bullet pouch, a bullet mold, and extra flints.

The minutemen are most closely associated with the battles of Lexington and Concord, fought on April 19, 1775. During the night, Paul Revere brought the alarm to Lexington that British regulars were on their way to capture a store of weapons. A company of minutemen responded to the urgent message. When no further news came, some of the minutemen returned home and others waited at a local tavern. At dawn the minutemen, under the command of Captain Jonas Parker, gathered again on Lexington Common. When the British troops arrived, the minutemen appeared on the verge of retreat when a musket shot brought a volley from the British. Eight minutemen were killed and ten more lay wounded. The British soldiers then reorganized for a march to Concord.

In Concord, several hundred minutemen had gathered with muskets. Hearing of the events in Lexington, two companies of minutemen began a march to aid their fellow patriots. However, when the group encountered a British column on the road, they decided it was the better part of valor to reverse direction and retreat back to Concord. They in effect led the way for the British along the road to Concord. The minutemen did not engage the British regulars. Instead, as the enemy made its way back to Boston, snipers, hidden in the thick brush beside the road, picked off many of the marchers. At Menotomy (now called Arlington), a group of 1,800 militiamen fired into the British column, killing a number of the enemy. By the end of the day, 273 British troops out of a total of 1,800 had been killed, wounded, or were missing. Of the minutemen, 49 were killed and 46 were wounded or missing.

Despite the fame that this group of militia attained, they existed for only a short time. The same month as the battles of Lexington and Concord, the Continental Congress decided not to rely on militia and minutemen but instead to recruit men for the regular army. Minuteman units continued for no more than six months, and the last units to be formed existed for only a few days. In the overall conduct of the war, the minutemen played a small role. Minuteman units had brief occasions of activity in other states. For instance, the defensive actions of minutemen maintained the American lines against British attack on Long Island. Minutemen were also active in Virginia.

The route of the minuteman march back to Concord leads to Minuteman National Park, which commemorates the storied exploits of this famous group of men. The vision of the minuteman standing watch pervades patriotic memorials. Although the minutemen, the most well-known portion of the militia, played a minimal role in the American Revolution, in the popular mind they were central to the fight for independence. It is not surprising that contemporary groups have attempted to pattern themselves after the image of a personally armed force ready at any moment to defend the community against outside invasion and what they perceive is a tyrannical government.

Further Reading: William J. Casey, *Where and How the War Was Fought: An Armchair Tour of the American Revolution* (New York: William Morrow, 1976); Christopher Ward, *The War of the Revolution* (New York: Macmillan, 1952).

Morton Grove, Illinois

In 1981, the Village of Morton Grove, Illinois, gained the attention of the nation when authorities approved an ordinance regulating firearms. Rather than attempting to regulate or ban one or a few guns, the Morton Grove ordinance (No. 81–11) instituted a general ban on firearms. The ordinance contained an especially controversial provision banning handgun ownership within the boundaries of the village. Although the ordinance led to intense debates regarding the appropriate area of activity of a municipality, it was upheld in court, and led the National Rifle Association (NRA) and other pro-gun groups to seek local preemption laws from state legislatures to reserve the making of gun control policy for the states.

Following passage of the ordinance, those council members supporting the measure presented their justification for adopting an ordinance regulating firearms and other weapons. They explained that the regulation of the possession of firearms could be justified by the village's responsibility to promote the welfare of its citizens. While not specifying a specific increase in crime within the corporate limits of the village, they argued that the widespread accessibility of firearms had increased the *possibility* of deaths and injuries related to the presence of such weapons. Narrowing the focus to handguns, the council members observed that these weapons were generally related to assault, armed robbery, and accidental injuries and death.

The ordinance was troubling to pro-gun interests for its sweeping provisions. It read in part:

> No person shall possess, in the Village of Morton Grove the following:
>
> (1) Any bludgeon, black-jack, slug shot, sand bag, metal knuckles or any knife, commonly referred to as a switchblade knife . . .
>
> (2) Any weapon from which 8 or more shots or bullets may be discharged by a single function of the firing device, any shotgun having one or more barrels less than 18 inches in length, sometimes called a sawed off shotgun or any weapon made from a shotgun . . . or any bomb, bombshell, grenade, bottle or other container containing an explosive substance . . .
>
> (3) Any handgun, unless the same has been rendered permanently inoperative.

Specific prohibitions did not apply to peace officers, wardens, and superintendents of prisons, and members of the active or reserve armed forces of the United States, the Illinois National Guard, employees of a railroad or public utility who perform police functions, security guards, agents of the Illinois Legislative Investigating Commission authorized to carry weapons, licensed gun collectors, licensed gun clubs, or those possessing antique firearms.

Due in part to the wide sweep of the ordinance, the council found it necessary to define what constituted a firearm: "any device, by whatever name known, which is designed to expel a projectile or projectiles by the action of an explosion, expansion of gas or escape of gas." A handgun was defined as any firearm that can be fired with one hand, or has a barrel less than 10 inches long, or is small enough to be concealed on the person. The ordinance also included a list of objects that were excluded from the category "firearm," such as any pneumatic, spring, or B-B gun; any device the sole purpose of which is to signal; antique firearms; and model rockets.

Although those debating the effectiveness of gun control measures have attempted to use the Morton Grove case as an example, the village did not have a serious problem with crime prior to passage of the ordinance, and did not make a concerted effort to enforce the ordinance once it went into effect. Of significance was a legal action precipitated by the law. In *Quilici v. Village of Morton Grove* (1981), a U.S. Appeals Court upheld the ordinance. Pro-gun forces feared that Morton Grove might become a model for other local jurisdictions that would enact a wide variety of limitations on gun ownership within a single state. Due to the efforts of pro-gun groups, 31 states have enacted preemption laws denying localities the power to enact gun control ordinances. *See also* KENNESAW, GEORGIA; NATIONAL RIFLE ASSOCIATION; *QUILICI V. VILLAGE OF MORTON GROVE* (1981); SAWED-OFF SHOTGUN.

Further Reading: Gregg Lee Carter, *The Gun Control Movement* (New York: Twayne, 1997); Alan M. Gottlieb, *The Rights of Gun Owners* (Bellevue, WA: Merril, 1991); Earl R. Kruschke, *Gun Control* (Santa Barbara, CA: ABC-CLIO, 1995).

Mothers Against Violence in America (MAVIA)

Founded in January 1994, Mothers Against Violence in America (MAVIA) encourages community activities to protect young people from violence. The organization has cooperated with medical, legal, and law enforcement organizations to educate youth and adults about what it considers the potentially devastating consequences of firearms and has supported firearms legislation as part of its campaign to create a safer environment for youth. With headquarters in Seattle, Washington, MAVIA initially concentrated efforts in its home state, but has begun to establish organizations in California, New York, and several other states. Chapters of Students Against Violence Everywhere, one of MAVIA's programs, have been established in elementary, middle, and high schools to provide students with the abilities and motivation to resolve conflict nonviolently. Over 32 chapters have been organized in Washington and California schools.

Pamela Eakes, an advertising and public relations professional, founded MAVIA. She had served as deputy chief of staff to Tipper Gore, Vice President Al Gore's wife, during the 1992 presidential election campaign. Pam Bartlett, who has years of experience as a speaker and performance coach, chairs the board of directors. Eakes and Bartlett, along with other staff members, have the public relations skills necessary to publicize the goals and recommendations of their organization. MAVIA claims a membership of 4,000.

MAVIA maintains a speakers bureau that includes presentations on several topics related to violence prevention. Presentations are made to schools, law enforcement organizations, community service groups, and conferences. Believing that gun violence has become a national epidemic, with more people between 15 and 24 years old killed by firearms than die from all natural causes combined, the speakers bureau places special emphasis on the prevention of gun violence. One presentation, titled "Gun Violence Prevention," attempts to explain why so many gun-related injuries and deaths occur each year and offers alternatives to guns for settling conflicts. MAVIA has sponsored a "Day of National Concern About Young People and Gun Violence" in Washington state in which thousands of students have pledged "never to use a gun to settle a dispute."

In Washington state, the organization supported legislation that raised the legal age for possessing firearms from 14 to 18, and advocated a measure that expanded the sentencing ranges for those convicted of manslaughter. MAVIA has focused on the dangers of weapons in homes, advising people to deliberate very seriously before purchasing a firearm, especially if there are children in the home. Recognizing that the debate over the benefits and costs of firearms continues to rage, MAVIA urges that guns at least be securely stored to keep children away from them. Noting that many gun owners keep firearms unlocked in a bedroom or closet, the organization urges owners to store firearms in a lockbox, gun safe, or with a trigger lock attached, and to keep keys to storage boxes or trigger locks hidden in a separate place. Children must be told never to play with guns and they should be educated about the potential for firearms to cause severe injury. The organization has produced a public service announcement to encourage gun owners to store their firearms responsibly.

MAVIA advocates various strategies for reducing the level of violence in the United States. People should refuse to purchase products that companies advertise on violent television programs. Conflict resolution skills should be taught in the schools as well as at home. Parents are urged to become familiar with their children's friends and their parents to determine if their children may be exposed to firearms. Neighbors should be urged to practice safe gun storage techniques. *See also* TRIGGER LOCKS.

Further Reading: Mothers Against Violence in America Web site <www.mavia.org>.

Muscarello v. United States (1998)

In *Muscarello v. United States* (Docket No. 96-1654, U.S. Supreme Court, 1998), the U.S. Supreme Court dealt with appeals of convictions based on a section of federal firearms statutes that imposes a five-year mandatory prison term for any person who "uses or carries a firearm . . . during and in relation to" a "drug trafficking crime" [18 U.S.C. 924 (c) (1)]. The decision hinged on the meaning of the word "carry." The Court held that the phrase "carries a firearm" can refer to the possession and conveyance of firearms in a vehicle, even if the firearm is kept in a locked glove compartment or trunk.

The Court combined two cases in its final decision. In the first, Frank J. Muscarello was charged with unlawfully selling marijuana. When police officers searched his truck, they found not only the marijuana, but a handgun locked in the glove compartment. In the second case, Donald Cleveland and Enrique Gray-Santana placed several firearms in the trunk of their car before proceeding to a scheduled drug purchase, intending instead to steal the drugs. When police arrested Cleveland and Gray-Santana, they found both the drugs and the guns. The Courts of Appeals determined that the defendants had carried the guns "during and in relation to a drug trafficking offense."

The Supreme Court heard the case on appeal to determine whether guns kept in a locked glove compartment or an automobile trunk constituted "carrying" a firearm under federal statute 924 (c) (1). The defendants argued that carrying meant "bearing" a firearm, or keeping it on the person; the statute did not apply to situations in which a person kept a firearm in a locked glove compartment or car trunk. However, the Court favored the "ordinary English meaning," which included the possibility of carrying in a "wagon, car, truck, or other vehicle that one accompanies."

The Court's decision depended upon what it considered Congress's intentions in using the word "carry." Examining the law's purpose and legislative history, the Court found no support for restricting the word to instances in which a weapon is kept on the person. Given that the law's purpose involved decreasing the probability of violence associated with the illegal drug trade, firearms kept in cars are not less dangerous than guns kept on the person.

The defendants argued that to move beyond an application of "carrying" to keeping on the person made the term equivalent to "transporting." The Court rejected this contention, specifying the basic distinctions in meaning between the two terms. The defendants also referred to the Court's previous narrow interpretation of the phrase "uses . . . a firearm," a related term appearing in the law. The Court responded that the limitation of "use" to "active employment" does not affect the meaning of "carry" which does not necessarily signify a similar active utilization. The Court ruled it could not interpret "carry" in a similarly narrow sense as "uses" without "undercutting the statute's basic objective."

The defendants argued that such a broad reading would expand the instances in which the law applies. However, the Court noted that the statute contains limiting conditions for the application of the carrying provision:

A defendant carries a gun "during and in relation to" a drug crime. Circumstances in which a gun is "immediately accessible" and circumstances in which a firearm is carried in a trunk or locked glove compartment are, according to the Court, "logically difficult to distinguish." Finally, with regard to an argument for invoking the rule of lenity due to the ambiguity of statutory wording, the Court responded that ambiguity to some extent characterizes all statutes. Congress's meaning is not "grievously ambiguous" and therefore the Court did not depend on simply guessing legislators' intent. *See also* BAILEY *v.* UNITED STATES (1996); FIREARM SENTENCE ENHANCEMENT LAWS.

Further Reading: *Muscarello v. United States*, Docket No. 96-1654 (U.S. Supreme Court, 1998); Nancy Norell, "High Court Uses Fiction, Newspapers to Define 'Carry' Under Federal Law," *Gun News Digest* (Fall 1998), 24-25, 46.

N

National Association of Federally Licensed Firearms Dealers (NAFLFD)

Established in 1973, the National Association of Federally Licensed Firearms Dealers (NAFLFD) represents those individuals who have obtained a license from the federal government to sell firearms. The organization provides its approximately 12,000 members with information about legislative action important to firearms dealers and disseminates material supporting the gun rights position. The NAFLFD distributes to members production and sales information regarding the firearms industry, descriptions of new products, and advice about conducting a retail business. In addition, the organization gathers data on the import, export, and domestic production of firearms. The Association publishes the *American Firearms Industry*, a monthly magazine that reports on firearms and outdoor sports, cutlery, and archery. The magazine reports on the current political scene with regard to firearms policy.

Although officially opposed to further gun control legislation, the organization assists its members in complying with existing rules and regulations in federal firearms law that are administered largely by the Bureau of Alcohol, Tobacco, and Firearms (BATF). The organization sells its members a Firearms Record Book to assist them in keeping accurate records of serial numbers, and the makes and models of firearms in case any are stolen, thus protecting the dealer from possible liability.

The Association supports claims that firearms possession by law-abiding citizens results in less, not more, crime. The NAFLFD asserts that gun ownership can give women an advantage against an attacker who likely is much stronger than his victim. The organization has cited approvingly the work of University of Chicago Law School Professor John R. Lott, Jr., whose research indicates that concealed carry laws deter crime. Lott has concluded that rarely do gun owners with concealed handgun permits commit violent crimes. Further, the claim is made that the number of accidental deaths attributed to firearms is minimal and that lenient state concealed carry laws add little to accidental firearms deaths, while deterring many more acts of violence.

The NAFLFD contests many of the claims of pro-gun control groups. The organization notes that since 1970 fatal gun accidents among children have declined 65 percent even though the number of firearms available to Americans has greatly increased. Citing gun researcher Gary Kleck, the organization disputes the estimate that 135,000 school children carry guns to school every day. The Association claims that the actual figure is closer to 16,000-17,000. The group also challenges the claim that the leading cause of death among all older teenagers in the United States is guns, claiming instead that this is true only of African-American males.

The Association affirms the view that the reduction of street crime in the United States is in the hands of the average, armed citizen. Supporters of gun control, skeptical of such claims, note the financial link between more citizens owning guns and the NAFLFD: Federally licensed firearms dealers would be the source of weapons in a new wave of purchases by private citizens. The Association counters by noting that the "crime-bureaucratic complex" in the United States, composed of lawyers, the courts, insurance companies, and public officials, profit from the existing level of crime.

Arguing in favor of the armed citizen, the Association asserts that the individual cannot expect protection from the approximately 150,000 police officers assigned to protect a population of over 250 million. The claim is made that background checks lead to gun registration and licensing, which in turn can result in confiscation of firearms. Employing the argument that gun ownership is a constitutional right, the Association claims that licensing and registration cannot be imposed on a constitutional right. Supporting the sale of assault rifles, which many people consider useless for any legitimate hunting purpose, the organization has argued that large curved magazines, one of the characteristics of such rifles, can be crucial to a citizen's defense when facing criminals on alcohol and drugs or a large group of people involved in civil disorder.

NAFLFD members believe that the problem of crime in the United States results from a circumstance that allows criminals to get what they want with minimal risk to personal safety or minimal chance of legal punishment. Association members sell a product that they claim is part of the answer to violent crime. Criminals must be deterred from committing criminal acts, and the Association envisions private citizens armed with guns as a key link in crime reduction, along with stiffer sentencing and the more frequent use of the death penalty. *See also* Assault Weapons Ban; Bu-

reau of Alcohol, Tobacco, and Firearms; Concealed Carry Laws; Kleck, Gary; Lott, John R, Jr.

Further Reading: American Firearms Industry magazine; National Association of Federally Licensed Firearms Dealers Web site <www.amfire.com>.

National Association of Police Organizations (NAPO)

In 1985, the National Association of Police Organizations (NAPO) joined with several other groups representing police officers in an unsuccessful attempt to prevent passage of the McClure-Volkmer Act, also known as the Firearms Owners Protection Act. NAPO opposed provisions of the legislation that weakened the Gun Control Act of 1968, believing the law placed law enforcement personnel in greater danger. Since 1985, organization members have continued to pass resolutions on gun control issues. A major motivation on this and any public policy issue has been the safety and rights of organization members.

Composed of 4,000 police organizations, 220,000 law enforcement officers, and 3,000 retired officers, plus an estimated 100,000 other individuals, NAPO represents the interests of law enforcement through legislative lobbying, legal advocacy, and educational and research programs. In 1991, the organization established the Police Research and Education Project (PREP) to "promote the well-being of police officers and their families and to educate the public about the role of law enforcement officers in a democratic society." In cooperation with the National Institute of Justice, PREP has investigated the effects of stress on law enforcement officers and their families. NAPO's National Law Enforcement Officers' Rights Center defends officers' legal and constitutional rights. The Center has assisted police officers and their families by, for instance, filing *amicus curiae* briefs in court cases involving officers.

Among its many issue positions, NAPO has supported legislation that would allow qualified active and former law enforcement officers to carry concealed weapons in any jurisdiction in the United States. This measure would limit concealed carrying to current and former law enforcement officers and would not apply to the general population. NAPO supports legislation that would establish the death penalty for killing a law enforcement officer or a federal correctional official. In addition, NAPO backs appropriations to hire additional law enforcement officers nationwide to reach the 1994 legislatively mandated objective of 100,000 additional officers.

NAPO supported the 1994 Violent Crime Control and Law Enforcement Act, which widened the ban on armor piercing ammunition. Although gun rights groups have expressed doubts about the existence of specifically armor-piercing ammunition, popularly called "cop-killer" bullets, NAPO contends that such ammunition can be distinguished by its ability to penetrate a bulletproof vest. The organization supports legislation banning mail-order sales of bullet-proof vests. Calling it "every law enforcement officer's worst nightmare," NAPO is concerned about violent criminals who wear body armor while committing crimes, thus putting police in greater danger of being injured or killed by a criminal's return fire.

NAPO supports legislation that would modify the prohibition on possession or ownership of firearms by anyone, including police officers, convicted of domestic violence misdemeanor charges. The proposal would establish an "official use" exception for law enforcement officers while on duty. A "capable and qualified" officer found guilty of domestic violence would be prohibited from keeping firearms in the home, but could carry a gun while at work. *See also* FIREARMS OWNERS PROTECTION ACT; GUN CONTROL ACT OF 1968; MCCLURE, JAMES ALBERTAS; VOLKMER, HAROLD LEE.

Further Reading: National Association of Police Organizations Web site <www.napo.org>.

National Association of School Psychologists (NASP)

The National Association of School Psychologists (NASP) supports gun control measures as a means of protecting the physical and psychological well-being of children, and promotes policies in schools and communities that deal effectively with the possible physical and psychological harm that firearms may cause children. The organization assists policy makers, community leaders, educators, and school psychologists in creating a safe school environment for children. NASP collaborates with other organizations, such as the American Psychological Association, in furthering its position on firearms and other issues.

Membership in NASP is open to anyone who works, or is qualified, as a school psychologist, a consultant or a supervisor of psychological services, or is engaged primarily in training school psychologists. NASP has over 20,000 members. Members elect delegates to the Delegate Assembly, which makes policy that is implemented by the Executive Council. The Council is composed of officers, program managers, regional directors, and delegate representatives. The organization publishes a newsletter, the *Communique*, eight times a year, as well as the quarterly *School Psychology Review* and books, monographs, and papers on various subjects, including youth violence and its relation to firearms.

In April 1998, Scott Poland, director of psychological services for a Houston, Texas, school district, represented NASP in testimony before the U.S. House of Representatives Committee on Education and the Workforce. Poland served as a leader for teams of psychologists that were sent to Paducah, Kentucky, and Jonesboro, Arkansas, following school shootings in these cities. Poland claimed that firearms "represent the single greatest threat to education and school children," citing estimates that as many as 270,000 firearms "go to school in America." He told the committee that the availability of firearms to children must be reduced, stating that, "There is a gun in every third home and almost every child can obtain a gun in a few hours." Gun access was cited as one of the predictive factors of youth violence. He questioned the wisdom of gun ownership, asserting that a gun in the home is more likely to kill a family member by accident, homicide, or suicide than to be used in defense against an intruder. Poland stated that he supports legislation that penalizes firearms owners whose weapons are used by children to injure or kill themselves or others.

In an article that appeared in the November 1998 NASP newsletter, Jeremy Shapiro reported on research dealing with attitudes of youth toward guns and violence. Shapiro stated that the number of handguns available in society is directly related to the level of violence, citing Arthur Kellermann's claim that the presence of a firearm in a conflict increases the probability that serious injury and death will occur. Shapiro summarized the results of the Attitudes Toward Guns and Violence Questionnaire (AGVQ) administered to students in four school systems, concluding that exposure to guns, including witnessing a shooting and having a gun in the home, increased scores on such factors as associating guns and violence with feelings of safety and power and expressing comfortable acceptance of violence. Shapiro noted that the greater attraction of guns and violence in adolescents made them less responsive to "preventive interventions" than younger children. *See also* JONESBORO, ARKANSAS, SCHOOL SHOOTING; KELLERMANN, ARTHUR; LITTLETON, COLORADO, SCHOOL SHOOTING; SCHOOLS AND GUNS; STOCKTON, CALIFORNIA, SHOOTING; YOUTH AND GUNS.

Further Reading: National Association of School Psychologists Web site <http://www/naspweb.org>.

National Center for Injury Prevention and Control (NCIPC)

The Centers for Disease Control and Prevention (CDC) established the National Center for Injury Prevention and Control (NCIPC) in June 1992 to conduct and support research on various causes of injury and possible injury prevention measures. In 1995, the agency came under attack from gun rights organizations such as the National Rifle Association (NRA), which claimed that the firearms research funded by the NCIPC was biased against gun ownership. Critics argued that the NCIPC duplicated the work of other federal agencies and therefore ought to be disbanded. The agency survived such attacks, although with a smaller budget, and continues to conduct research on many causes of injury, including firearms.

Firearms injuries research represents a small portion of the NCIPC's activities. The agency engages in studies of such injury-related factors as falls, fires and burns, drowning, poisoning, automobile accidents, and playground accidents. The NCIPC believes that accidents are not random occurrences and therefore are preventable. Along with health professionals, the agency advocates the same scientific procedures, including the epidemiological approach, employed in research on the causes and prevention of disease. Epidemiology involves investigations of the incidence, geographic and demographic spread, and control of disease. The treatment of firearms injuries from an epidemiological perspective has raised charges that public health researchers judge guns as a causal factor in injuries and therefore as something to be eliminated.

In response to charges of anti-gun bias, the NCIPC claims it is an organization that stands above the debate between gun rights groups and those who wish to institute a ban on firearms. In 1996, Mark Rosenberg, the agency's director, argued that the research the Center supports can offer such beneficial outcomes as improved gun design and better methods of firearm storage. The Center's defenders maintain that the public health perspective should offer the middle ground that will involve more people in discussions about the place of firearms in American society. However, the NRA and other pro-gun groups claim that the Center and health care professionals conducting research on firearms have ignored the findings of firearms researchers who take alternative perspectives. The NRA goes so far as to claim that NCIPC-funded researchers have provided misleading or false results to support their pre-drawn conclusions. Center representatives respond that pro-gun groups have reacted so negatively to research results because objective data have not supported the pro-gun position.

In a 1997 publication dealing with fatal firearm injuries from 1962 to 1994, the NCIPC observed that in 1994 firearm injuries represented the ninth leading cause of death, and the second leading cause of death among those between ages 10 and 24. From 1962 to 1994, the number of deaths due to firearms rose from 16,720 to 38,505, a 130-percent increase. The agency estimated that gun assaults on family members and other close acquaintances are 12 times more likely to lead to death than assaults with other weapons. The Center noted that people living in households containing firearms have a five times greater risk of suicide than non-gun owning households.

In 1992, CDC joined with the Consumer Product Safety Commission to establish the National Electronic Injury Surveillance System (NEISS) to assist in collecting data about firearms-related injuries. The system gathers information about gun injuries from 91 hospitals around the country. Firearms injury surveillance systems are being developed in seven states that also monitor safe storage policies and carrying concealed weapons laws. *See also* CONCEALED CARRY LAWS; DOCTORS FOR INTEGRITY IN POLICY RESEARCH; HEALTH CARE PROFESSIONALS; NATIONAL RIFLE ASSOCIATION.

Further Reading: "Fatal Firearm Injuries in the United States, 1962-1994," *Violence Surveillance Summary Series*, No. 3 (Atlanta: Centers for Disease Control and Prevention, National Center for Injury Prevention and Control, 1997); Helen K. Metaksa, "NRA Responds to Washington Post Editorial on CDC," *NRA Public Affairs* (June 12, 1996); National Center for Injury Prevention and Control Web site <www.cdc.gov/ncipc>; David Satcher, "In NRA Attack on Firearms Studies, Scientific Truth Is the Most Important Casualty," *Washington Post* (November 6, 1995).

National Center for Policy Analysis (NCPA)

In 1983, John Goodman established the National Center for Policy Analysis (NCPA) at the University of Dallas as a nonpartisan public policy research institute. The NCPA has opened an office in Washington, D.C., where its scholars often testify before congressional committees and brief congressional aides on policy issues. The Center has conducted studies in many policy areas, including health care, taxes, Social Security, welfare, criminal justice, education, and environmental regulation. The NCPA, which advocates free market solutions to policy questions, has published commentaries critical of gun control measures and in support of the right of citizens to own and carry firearms for self-protection.

Goodman serves as president of the Center. His areas of expertise include tax, welfare, and Social Security policy and health care reform. He has appeared on the major television network news programs and has co-hosted *Firing Line* with William F. Buckley, Jr. Pete du Pont is the policy chairman for the NCPA. He has made presentations on various subjects, including tax reform, economic growth, education, and health care. The NCPA includes centers for health policy studies, tax policy, the environment, and criminal justice. The Center's budget grew from $1 million in 1990 to $5 million in 1998.

In its support of the right of individual citizens to possess and carry firearms for self-protection, the NCPA notes that while government has a general duty to enforce laws, it does not have a specific legal obligation to protect individuals. Therefore, to the extent that government denies law-abiding citizens the right to own firearms for self-protection, it denies them the means to protect themselves. The Center notes that each year armed civilians kill almost 3,000 criminals, which is over three times the number killed by police. Civilians wound another 9,000 to 17,000 criminals each year. The organization argues that civilians armed with concealed weapons are a major deterrent to crime.

The NCPA has criticized the call for legislation to require that gun safety locks be provided with each new handgun. Because manufacturers of locks recommend that guns be kept unloaded, the Center contends that locked and unloaded firearms are made less useful for self-defense. While intended to make guns child-safe, gun locks "make homes easier targets for criminals" and can actually increase the number of deaths resulting from crime. Citing surveys in which criminals reported being more fearful of armed homeowners than of the police, the Center places great importance on the ability of private citizens to defend themselves.

The NCPA opposes bans on assault weapons, claiming that these weapons are not functionally different from other semi-automatic firearms, including guns used for hunting and target shooting. The Center notes that since 1934 a special license has been required for a civilian to possess automatic firearms; but "no civilian has ever used a legally owned machine gun in a violent crime." According to the Center, neither automatic nor semiautomatic weapons are used often in the commission of crimes. The NCPA argues that while assault weapons bans have little effect on criminals, they create significant problems for law-abiding citizens who are prevented from owning such weapons for self-defense.

The NCPA has criticized the Brady Handgun Violence Prevention Act, claiming that it has had little effect on the availability of firearms to criminals while it wasted law enforcement resources by requiring background checks. The organization observes that in the act's first 15 months of operation, only three people were successfully prosecuted using the law. Supporters of the Brady Act respond that convicted felons, aware of the background check, simply do not try to purchase firearms legally. *See also* ASSAULT WEAPONS BAN; BRADY HANDGUN VIOLENCE PREVENTION ACT; CONCEALED CARRY LAWS; HEALTH CARE PROFESSIONALS; TRIGGER LOCKS; YOUTH AND GUNS.

Further Reading: National Center for Policy Analysis Web site <www.ncpa.org>.

National Concealed Carry Incorporated (NCCI)

On its Web site, National Concealed Carry Incorporated (NCCI) is described as "a group of conservative second amendment activists who support the right to carry a concealed weapon in all fifty states." However, the NCCI states elsewhere in its material that there is no membership. The organization strives to have all 50 states recognize a valid concealed carry permit for all citizens licensed

to carry a weapon. The NCCI believes that there should be a national reciprocity standard under which each state recognizes the concealed carry permits of every other state. The organization contends that in the states that have adopted concealed carry laws, crime has diminished significantly.

The NCCI considers gun control organizations such as Handgun Control, Inc. and Cease Fire, Inc. "the world's worst nightmare come true," contending that such groups base their proposals on a gun control law from Nazi Germany. Like other gun rights organizations, the NCCI claims a close similarity between the German legislation and the Gun Control Act of 1968. The organization asks, if firearms are banned, "will ovens once again become the tool of choice?" Gun control advocates dismiss such charges, arguing that tyranny arises when a government fails to protect its citizens from societal violence. They refer to the inability or unwillingness of the Weimar Republic to control the tactics of intimidation used by the Nazis. The NCCI states that elected officials who do not comply with its concealed carry objectives should be removed "by any means deemed necessary."

The NCCI states that the word "incorporated" in its title "does not signify the establishment of a legal business for tax exempt purposes," which apparently means that the organization is not incorporated in any legal sense. The NCCI claims that "incorporated in this case only signifies the unity of every concerned citizen or political activist who believes in the right to keep and bear arms" and is used "for recognition purposes only." *See also* CONCEALED CARRY LAWS; GUN CONTROL ACT OF 1968; HANDGUN CONTROL, INC.; CEASE FIRE, INC.

Further Reading: National Concealed Carry Incorporated Web site <www.moa.sonnet.com/nvrpc>.

National Crime Prevention Council (NCPC)

The National Crime Prevention Council (NCPC) is a national organization that develops strategies to deter criminal activities, including those involving firearms. The organization was established in 1982 to manage a national advertising campaign featuring McGruff, the "take a bite out of crime" dog, and to coordinate programs for the Crime Prevention Coalition. The NCPC urges Americans to become aware of steps they can take to reduce the chances of being victims of crime and encourages non-violent ways of resolving conflicts. Among its recommendations, the Council discourages the use of firearms for self-protection.

The NCPC focuses much of its energies on ways of preventing youth violence. In March 1998, at the Eleventh National Youth Crime Prevention Conference, NCPC executive director John A. Calhoun referred to recent school shootings and declared that firearms should be considered hazardous consumer products that ought to be subject to strict safety regulation, like children's toys. He noted that gun ownership requires few if any of the standards established for driving automobiles, including education, competency tests, licensing, and insurance. Calhoun urged his young audience to contact political leaders and policy makers about the personal, economic, and social costs of firearm accessibility, asking "How many more Jonesboros will it take before we stop the killing?"

Although the Council provides recommendations for maintaining a home safe from crime, having a handgun in the home is not considered a viable option for defense. The Council advises people to "think long and hard" about keeping a firearm, claiming that a gun in the home is far less likely to stop a crime than it is to harm or kill a family member. Other ways of protecting the home are recommended, including improving locks, having a dog, introducing an alarm system, and joining a Neighborhood Watch program.

If there is a firearm in the home, the NCPC recommends that all family members receive instruction in firearm safety. Children should be taught that if they discover a gun they should follow the instructions of the National Rifle Association's (NRA) Eddie Eagle: "Stop, Don't Touch, Get Away, and Tell a Trusted Adult." However, unlike gun rights advocates, who regard firearms as an effective means of home defense, simple educa-

tion is not considered a sufficient safety measure by itself. Firearms should be safely stored in gun cases or pistol boxes and should be kept unloaded and with a trigger lock. Such measures would decrease the probability that a firearm would accidentally harm a family member, especially a child.

The NCPC has developed a series of public service announcements intended to make the general public aware of the dangers of gun violence. In one 30-second announcement, the group Peter, Paul, and Mary sing a rendition of Pete Seeger's "Where Have All The Flowers Gone" (retitled "Where Have All The Children Gone") as a handgun fires and the screen reports the toll of killed and wounded at three high school shootings: Thurston High School in Springfield, Oregon; Westside High School in Jonesboro, Arkansas; and Pearl High School in Pearl, Mississippi. The announcement ends with scenes of crying children. In another spot showing graphic scenes of gun violence, the announcer claims that gunfire kills 10 children each day and concludes, "Not one more lost life, not one more grieving family. Not one more." Such announcements are intended to "spur people to take action to reduce the effects of gun violence on children." *See also* EDDIE EAGLE; JONESBORO, ARKANSAS, SCHOOL SHOOTING; LITTLETON, COLORADO, SCHOOL SHOOTING; NATIONAL RIFLE ASSOCIATION; SCHOOLS AND GUNS; STOCKTON, CALIFORNIA, SHOOTING; TRIGGER LOCKS; YOUTH AND GUNS.

Further Reading: National Crime Prevention Council Web site <www.ncpc.org>.

National Education Association (NEA)

Although the National Education Association (NEA) holds that the problem of violence in public schools is not nearly as serious as the mass media suggest and that most schools maintain a safe environment for students, the organization still recognizes school violence and the presence of firearms as real problems that need to be addressed. In 1998, NEA president Bob Chase was quoted as stating, "America's culture of violence has breached the boundaries of the schoolhouse." In 1997, the NEA made the maintenance of school safety one of its major priorities. While primarily advocating school-community alliances to minimize the occurrence of violence, the NEA has also supported legislation at the state and national levels aimed at limiting youth access to firearms.

Founded in 1857, the NEA is the largest organization representing public school teachers. With a membership of nearly 2.4 million educators at all levels, from preschools to universities, affiliate organizations in all states, and 13,000 local groups, the Association has significant influence on education policy. The NEA's policy positions are set at an annual meeting of the Representative Assembly, which is composed of more than 9,000 delegates from the state and local organizations. Between meetings of the Representative Assembly, the elected Board of Directors and the Executive Committee serve as the decision-making bodies for the Association.

The NEA has declared its concern over the easy accessibility youth have to firearms. Citing data indicating that in 1989 and 1990, 75 people were killed in schools and another 200 were wounded, the organization has called for responsible gun ownership, including safe storage. The organization has presented data from the U.S. Centers for Disease Control and Prevention (CDC), claiming that 20 percent of high school students surveyed reported carrying a weapon at least once in the last month.

The NEA has called for a "zero tolerance" approach to firearms in schools: Any student found with a firearm should be expelled immediately and those who sell firearms and other weapons to students should be subject to severe penalties. The Association supports the strict regulation of the manufacture, importation, distribution, sale, and resale of handguns and ammunition. The organization has passed a resolution calling for a ban on the private possession of automatic firearms and semi-automatic assault weapons. The NEA supports the reintroduction of a waiting period before the sale of firearms to allow for a more thorough background check.

The resolution also supports educational programs for gun owners that emphasize responsible handling and safe storage of guns.

The NEA's program for violence reduction in public schools extends beyond the elimination of firearms in and around school campuses. Students must feel that they need not arm themselves for self-protection. Various educational strategies are recommended that promote nonviolent resolution of conflicts. Although discipline in the schools plays a crucial role in minimizing violence, the NEA believes the family and the larger community are important sources of violent behavior among students. Therefore, any effective procedure for violence control must include parental and community participation. In 1998, Reginald Weaver, NEA vice president, announced the organization's support for a Children's Gun Violence Prevention Act. According to Weaver, the Gun-Free Schools Act of 1994 has resulted in several thousand student expulsions for carrying firearms on school campuses. *See also* ASSAULT WEAPONS BAN; GUN-FREE SCHOOLS ACT; JONESBORO, ARKANSAS, SCHOOL SHOOTING; LITTLETON, COLORADO, SCHOOL SHOOTING; SCHOOLS AND GUNS; STOCKTON, CALIFORNIA, SHOOTING; YOUTH AND GUNS.

Further Reading: National Education Association Web site <www.nea.org>.

National Firearms Act

The National Firearms Act of 1934 was the first gun law to have national application. In 1934, congressional hearings were called to consider firearms regulation because the violence related to the gangsterism and organized crime of the Prohibition era, and to the criminal activities of such notorious outlaws as John Dillinger led many to believe that national regulation of firearms was necessary. Democratic President Franklin Delano Roosevelt played a role in the push toward legislation. While governor of New York, Roosevelt had lobbied for handgun licensing laws and the banning of machine guns, and continued that agenda when he became president in 1933. His administration took steps to improve the welfare of the nation, and gun control could be seen as one aspect of that objective. More immediately, an attempt had been made on Roosevelt's life in Miami in 1933. The assassination attempt resulted in a call for legislation to limit firearms.

Roosevelt's attorney general, Homer Cummings, was strongly committed to gun control measures, stating at one point, "Show me a man who does not want his gun registered and I will show you a man who should not have a gun." He believed that the sale of machine guns in particular should be regulated and that owners should register with the government, but ultimately held that all firearms should be registered. In 1934, a bill was introduced in Congress that provided for regulation of the sale of machine guns and a requirement to register all handguns.

The National Rifle Association (NRA), whose leadership at this time was not completely opposed to firearms legislation, was nonetheless unwilling to accept handgun registration, regarding it as an unwarranted invasion of the rights of law-abiding citizens. Ironically, the Roosevelt administration's emphasis on gangsterism as the major threat probably contributed to the success of the NRA and other groups in narrowing the bill to gangster-type weapons. The NRA activated those in the sporting community through editorials and press releases to write their congresspeople to oppose national registration. With a deluge of antiregistration mail, the term "all weaponry" in the bill was deleted and replaced with "machine guns and sawed-off shotguns." The NRA supported passage of the amended bill.

The act called for the taxation of the manufacture, sale, and transfer of weapons and associated materials most often connected to gangster activities, including machine guns, sawed-off shotguns, sawed-off rifles, and silencers. Purchasers of weapons covered by the act had to undergo background investigations by the Federal Bureau of Investigation (FBI) and were required to provide a photograph and submit to fingerprinting to determine past criminal activity. The legislation then required that the weapon be registered. Table 10 lists the number of firearms registered under the National Firearms Act as of December 31, 1996. The law imposed a transfer tax of $200 on the seller of the weapon. If someone's application to purchase a weapon were approved, that person was then required to gain the approval of local law enforcement officials to have the weapon in that local jurisdiction.

Although Roosevelt's Justice Department continued to advocate handgun registration, the National Firearms Act represented the last time the president himself took an active role in encouraging such legislation. The legislation was a factor in the NRA's establishment of a legislative division to deal with any further gun related legislation. *See also* NATIONAL RIFLE ASSOCIATION; SAWED-OFF SHOTGUN; TOMMY GUN.

Further Reading: Lee Kennet and James La Verne Anderson, *The Gun in America: The Origins of a National Dilemma* (Westport, CT: Greenwood, 1975); Earl Kruschke, *Gun Control* (Santa Barbara, CA: ABC-CLIO, 1995); Robert J. Spitzer, *The Politics of Gun Control*, 2nd ed. (Chatham, NJ: Chatham, 1995).

National Firearms Association (NFA)

The National Firearms Association (NFA) claims that the Second Amendment guarantees the right of citizens to own automatic, or military, firearms (classified under the National Firearms Act of 1934 as Class III firearms), and semi-automatic versions of such weapons. Despite the general public's unsympathetic perception of automatic firearms, organization members consider themselves to be an elite among gun owners. The organization, headquartered in Fairfax, Virginia, claims that for citizens to defend their country, they must be adequately trained, equipped, and prepared to use current military weaponry. In advocating the right of private citizens to own automatic weapons, the NFA takes a position that many other progun organizations are unwilling to support actively. The organization subscribes to what it calls the "NATO Pact Doctrine of Gun Ownership:" "Any attack on any firearms owner shall be viewed as an attack on us all, and shall be defended by all gun owners."

TABLE 10

NATIONAL FIREARMS ACT INVENTORY, BY STATE OF CURRENT OWNER, THROUGH DECEMBER 31, 1996

State	MG	SI	SR	SS	DD	AW	UNC	Total
Alabama	9571	1194	357	1129	7292	934	15	20,492
Alaska	1051	390	43	179	1218	268	18	3167
Arizona	8221	3528	608	715	20,343	704	33	34,152
Arkansas	2492	884	137	402	2469	428	28	6840
California	12,625	1375	980	3945	53,841	3439	90	76,295
Colorado	3104	991	244	784	7891	758	35	13,807
Connecticut	14,118	1840	355	383	2730	530	34	19,990
Delaware	113	17	31	121	239	31	–	552
District of Columbia	1847	58	28	144	2240	61	–	4378
Florida	13,439	6278	406	1417	33,567	2109	66	57,282
Georgia	16,841	7430	344	4562	6701	1315	63	37,256
Hawaii	224	13	39	30	416	35	4	761
Idaho	1591	420	133	192	2677	454	22	5489
Illinois	8461	324	380	1149	14,334	935	57	25,640
Indiana	9815	2495	217	2570	11,223	871	75	27,266
Iowa	1050	73	162	472	3606	850	26	6239
Kansas	1209	68	174	489	4885	642	21	7488
Kentucky	4316	840	226	590	3900	570	38	10,480
Louisiana	3268	702	181	527	10,021	483	20	15,202
Maine	1896	425	148	205	862	625	20	4181
Maryland	6651	1753	239	553	15,972	677	33	25,878
Massachusetts	4055	202	271	402	2468	773	56	8227
Michigan	5824	688	337	666	5305	1040	59	13,919
Minnesota	2816	480	236	721	7252	1360	67	12,932
Mississippi	2302	81	106	364	1374	299	10	4536
Missouri	3677	357	307	1219	6175	1128	64	12,927
Montana	1232	56	119	158	868	328	11	2772
Nebraska	1303	188	155	386	1247	631	25	3935
Nevada	3853	864	109	257	3397	345	14	8839
New Hampshire	3536	390	88	108	797	260	12	5191
New Jersey	3270	547	133	686	14,340	407	28	19,411
New Mexico	2209	445	155	265	6802	188	17	10,081
New York	4432	175	415	1310	9452	1047	51	16,882
North Carolina	5605	1433	238	720	9260	600	42	17,898
North Dakota	863	988	61	120	418	154	7	2611
Ohio	11,263	2241	580	1313	22,394	1452	133	39,376
Oklahoma	6887	1375	331	836	2930	920	40	13,319
Oregon	4168	1987	572	737	4573	1217	59	13,367
Pennsylvania	11,986	2326	648	1068	8254	1352	209	25,843
Rhode Island	357	10	32	53	736	40	6	234
South Carolina	2369	273	193	817	3897	550	20	8119
South Dakota	690	69	60	129	561	323	12	1844
Tennessee	5251	1988	227	941	9040	1182	35	18,664
Texas	17,732	15,291	1224	3406	23,004	3134	210	64,001
Utah	6071	357	73	252	3265	190	11	10,219
Vermont	839	41	41	49	2661	203	6	3840
Virginia	11,782	1972	373	1505	19,364	1549	55	36,600

TABLE 10 *(CONT.)*							
Washington	1806	357	460	493	9230	1270	27	13,643
West Virginia	1370	205	163	184	544	323	3	2790
Wisconsin	3513	880	191	669	8198	636	22	14,109
Wyoming	1091	104	78	186	25,853	279	13	27,604
Puerto Rico	642	4	6	2	34	1	–	689
Virgin Islands	29	–	–	–	–	–	–	–
Total	254,726	67,470	13,414	40,580	420,120	39,954	2022	838,286

MG=Machine Gun; SI=Silencer; SR=Short Barreled Rifle; SS=Short Barreled Shotgun; DD=Destructive Device; AW=Any Other Weapon; UNC=Unclassified.

Source: Bureau of Alcohol, Tobacco and Firearms; reprinted in Dan Shea, "BATF Charted Territory," *Small Arms Review* 1 (October 1997), p. 50. Reprinted with permission from Dan Shea.

The NFA and other small gun rights groups consider themselves the "conscience" of the National Rifle Association (NRA).

In September 1986, a group of individuals claiming the right under the Second Amendment to own automatic weapons met in Houson, Texas, to form the NFA. Although the McClure-Volkmer Gun Owners Protection Act of 1986 has been considered a major victory for gun rights advocates, the NFA founders considered it a major setback for gun rights because a provision in the 1986 legislation prohibited the future manufacture of automatic firearms for sale to private citizens. Holding to an absolute interpretation of the Second Amendment, the NFA brands this prohibition unconstitutional. More recent bans on semi-automatic assault weapons are considered a natural outcome of the initial prohibition on automatic weapons.

The NFA, which is led by a president and a five-member board of directors elected for two-year overlapping terms, offers an opportunity for those having an interest in automatic weapons to unite in a common organization. The organization has regional offices, each with its own chairman, and keeps abreast of regulatory questions and impending legislation related to automatic weapons at the national, state, and local levels. The organization supports candidates for office at the state and national levels who are willing to support an uncompromising position on the Second Amendment, and opposes legislation it believes violates the right to keep and bear arms.

The NFA, which established the rules and regulations for submachine gun competitions, organizes shooting contests for owners of automatic and semi-automatic firearms. The 1998 meet, which drew participants from across the nation, was held in Pleasant Grove, Alabama. The NFA supports the National Range Officer Academy, which is held in conjunction with shooting contests. Those already experienced in submachine gun competition are invited to prepare for conducting and judging automatic weapons events. The Academy provides training in firearm safety, scoring at shooting contests, rules for competitive shooting with automatic firearms, and target and course design. *See also* ASSAULT WEAPONS BAN; FIREARMS OWNERS PROTECTION ACT; MCCLURE, JAMES ALBERTAS; NATIONAL FIREARMS ACT OF 1934; NATIONAL RIFLE ASSOCIATION; SECOND AMENDMENT; VOLKMER, HAROLD LEE.

Further Reading: National Firearms Association Web site <www.quancon.com/~nfa>; Josh Sugarmann, *National Rifle Association: Money, Firepower and Fear* (Washington, DC: National Press Books, 1992).

National Firearms Association (NFA) of Canada

The National Firearms Association (NFA) of Canada was formed in the late 1980s to defend the right to keep and bear arms in Canada and to "battle for effective and fair firearms legislation." The NFA opposed those political interests that called for more stringent gun control. Holding that gun control and human rights abuses go hand in hand, the Association hopes to protect the rights of Canadian firearms owners. Based in Edmonton, Alberta, the organization claims to represent the interests of 7 million firearms owners in Canada. The Association encourages businesses to become members, a list of which the organization provides on its Web site. The NFA provides detailed information to members about Canadian firearms legislation and the activities of the Canadian Firearms Centre (CFC).

The organization offers advice on various legal matters and offers information to executors of estates with firearms regarding the applicability of the law. The Association makes recommendations to firearms owners about what to do if police arrive with a search warrant. The NFA has provided members with an "8-pack" of transcripts from favorable court decisions involving charges of unsafely storing firearms, claiming that this information most likely provides sufficient precedent to win acquittal. The organization comments that "simply showing the NFA 8-pack to the Crown prosecutor is enough to have him drop the charges before trial."

The NFA has four stated objectives: "to promote, support, and protect all safe recreational firearms activities; to promote, support, and protect all educational firearms activities; to promote natural justice for all firearms activities; to serve and inform responsible owners and users of recreational firearms." The organization provides expert witnesses for firearms-related court cases and lobbies for changes in firearms regulations. It encourages grassroots political activity in all Canadian political parties. Emphasizing that it is nonpartisan, the NFA urges individual members to become involved in the party of their choice. Participation in the selection of nominees for public office is considered especially important.

To attract and retain members, the NFA offers $2 million in liability insurance coverage at a low yearly charge and provides advice over the phone on various matters related to firearms, including shooting range construction, and provides transcripts of court cases dealing with firearms, including NFA

legal test cases. The NFA's Patches Program encourages Canadian gun owners to practice gun safety and to undergo training in the use of firearms. *Pointblank* is the official newsletter of the organization, which also produces "Alerts" and "Bulletins" that are available by mail and on the NFA Web site. The bulletins present firearms regulations with commentary and analysis. The NFA supports the *Canadian Hunting and Shooting, Bowhunting,* and *Angler* magazines.

Like the National Rifle Association (NRA), the NFA has expressed concern about United Nations (UN) conferences to discuss possible international controls on the small arms trade. The organization has urged its members to support a petition drive to inform the UN and member countries supporting "world disarmament" about the views of firearms owners. *See also* CANADA; CANADIAN FIREARMS CENTRE; NATIONAL RIFLE ASSOCIATION; UNITED NATIONS.

Further Reading: National Firearms Association of Canada Web site <www.nfa.ca>.

National Instant Check System (NICS)

The Brady Handgun Violence Prevention Act mandated that a National Instant Check System (NICS) be put into effect by November 1998. The statute initially established a five-day waiting period for purchasing a handgun to allow authorities to check a prospective purchaser's background. The instant check was intended to replace the waiting period after a national computer system containing federal and state records had been established. Nine categories of individuals are disqualified from purchasing a handgun under federal law: those convicted or under indictment on felony charges, fugitives, those determined to be mentally ill, those dishonorably discharged from the military, those who have renounced U.S. citizenship, illegal aliens, illegal drug users, those convicted of domestic violence misdemeanors, and those under domestic violence restraining orders. While some firearms organizations, such as the

National Rifle Association (NRA) supported NICS, other organizations, such as Gun Owners of America (GOA), opposed any check system at all. Gun control supporters doubted the effectiveness of the proposed computer system in conducting background checks on prospective handgun purchasers.

Thirty-one states are covered in the new instant check system, which involves federally licensed firearms dealers making a toll-free call directly to NICS. The remaining 19 states are responsible for conducting their own background checks. Larger retail outlets may use a computerized system that further increases the speed of the check. Each dealer has an identification number and password to access the system. Prior to initiation of the system, the Federal Bureau of Investigation (FBI) estimated that the average check would take approximately two minutes. In cases where delay occurs, the FBI has up to three days to approve or deny the sale. With 450 personnel taking calls, the system is geared to process 9,000 background inquiries per hour. The system operates seven days a week from 9:00 a.m. to 2:00 a.m. EST.

As the deadline for NICS to become operational approached, many people expressed concern about the completeness of records. Although Sarah Brady, president of Handgun Control, Inc., praised the new instant check system, she raised concerns about the absence of crucial information, such as the records of mental patients, to run a comprehensive background check. In 1992, just 18 percent of complete and accurate state criminal records were available on computer. The percent of state criminal records that were computer accessible increased to 33 percent by 1995, when states started to receive federal funds to improve their records systems. The Justice Department hoped that NICS would be at 50 percent efficiency by the time the system became active. When the system first went into effect, some state and local records involving involuntary mental hospital admissions, domestic violence misdemeanors, and recent arrests not yet computerized were unavailable for the checks.

Before NICS began, Democratic President Bill Clinton expressed his hope that the five-day waiting period would remain in effect to discourage purchases made in the heat of anger. While many pro-gun advocates, such as Wayne LaPierre of the NRA, lobbied strongly for replacement of the five-day waiting system with the instant check, some gun rights activists expressed as much opposition to NICS as they did to the original five-day waiting period. They argued that background checks have failed to reduce crime and violence and claimed that records may be inaccurate, containing initial arrest data but lacking ultimate disposition of many cases, including those in which the suspect was cleared of committing any crime. The FBI stated that it would retain information from checks for 18 months to assist with auditing, to check the system's security, and to track its success. For some people, any record keeping at all amounts to a national system of gun registration. Concerns have been raised about whether those running the checks would maintain the privacy of records. *See also* BRADY, SARAH; BRADY HANDGUN VIOLENCE PREVENTION ACT; BACKGROUND CHECKS; CLINTON, WILLIAM JEFFERSON (BILL); GUN OWNERS OF AMERICA; HANDGUN CONTROL, INC.; LAPIERRE, WAYNE; NATIONAL RIFLE ASSOCIATION.

Further Reading: American Shooting Sports Council, "Update on NICS" (April 28, 1998); Gun Owners of America, "Brady Gun Control Shows Its Ugly Face" (December 1998), <www.gunowners.org>.

National Muzzle Loading Rifle Association (NMLRA)

Founded in 1933, the National Muzzle Loading Rifle Association (NMLRA) is composed of individuals who are muzzle loading shooters and hunters. Members have a deep interest in preserving and celebrating the heritage of American firearms. While gun control advocates express concern about the American gun culture that extends back historically to the late eighteenth and early nineteenth centuries, members of the NMLRA consider firearms a crucial part of American history. The organization prides itself on being the defender of members' rights to own, shoot, and hunt with muzzle loading firearms. Because the muzzle loading rifle requires the use of black powder or black powder substitutes, members look with suspicion on calls for taggants in black powder, which they fear may alter the performance of this key ingredient in muzzle loader shooting.

The organization holds two major types of shooting events. In the first event, the rendezvous, members emphasize historical accuracy, priding themselves on preserving the black powder tradition. They attempt to "recreate the historical and aesthetic qualities of muzzleloader shooting," dressing in clothing and using equipment common to the eighteenth and early nineteenth centuries and using targets from that era. The second type of event, the local or national shoot, focuses on shooting skills rather than historical accuracy. The NMLRA conducts the National Shoots each year near the organization's headquarters in Friendship, Indiana. From the beginning of the organization in 1933 to the 1990s, the number of competitors has increased from 100 to nearly 2,000. Over 500 other matches are held around the nation. The organization's publication, *Muzzle Blasts*, contains entertaining articles that describe the frontier heritage, report on shooting events, and provide news items of interest to members.

The National Muzzle Loading Rifle Association defends the rights of shooters and hunters who use muzzle loading firearms, such as the nineteenth-century muzzleloader pictured here. *Corbis/Bettmann.*

The fascination with muzzle loader shooting is closely tied to "the pungent aroma of blackpowder smoke, the necessity of making one shot do the job, and the link to history." Many enjoy the challenge of slow ignition times. Others are attracted to the organization because most states grant early or special hunting seasons for primitive firearms. The organization emphasizes that the sport is a highly individualized activity. Rifle owners can mix their own powder, cast their own lead balls or bullets, and determine their own accessories. In shooting matches, participants employ a wide variety of rifles, but must be within the guidelines established in the NMLRA's "Range Rules and Regulations."

With approximately 25,000 members, the NMLRA does not have the political influence of the National Rifle Association (NRA) and other gun rights organizations. However, to the extent that the gun control debate includes a struggle over cultural perspectives, the members of this organization, who through their activities honor the history of firearms, oppose attempts to portray firearms as inherently dangerous instruments that should be subject to further government controls. *See also* GUN CULTURE; NATIONAL RIFLE ASSOCIATION; TAGGANTS.

Further Reading: *Muzzle Blasts Magazine*; National Muzzle Loading Rifle Association Web site <www.nmlra.org>.

National Organization of Black Law Enforcement Executives (NOBLE)

Established in 1976 by African-American law enforcement executives attending a conference on crime in urban low income areas, the National Organization of Black Law Enforcement Executives (NOBLE) strives to increase the voice of black law enforcement officers regarding the problems of crime in metropolitan areas. The organization, which represents over 3,000 members, works to have its public policy views made known to public officials and to the general public. NOBLE expresses a special concern for African-American youths, noting that the rate of murder among young black males is 11 times greater than that among young white males. The organization supports policies, including various gun control measures, that it believes will contribute to reducing the level of violence among minority youth. Because handguns are considered a major threat, the organization discourages their use by private citizens and opposes any attempts to weaken federal gun control legislation.

NOBLE lobbies for greater minority participation in the various levels of law enforcement. It has strongly supported the continuation of affirmative action programs, arguing that only through such policies have greater numbers of minorities entered law enforcement and other professions. It has advocated special recruitment projects at predominantly black colleges to attract more minorities into police work. The organization endeavors to develop greater community cooperation with law enforcement agencies, provides a means of greater communication among minority law enforcement executives, and contributes to the conduct of criminal justice research. The organization expresses special concern for the use of excessive or unnecessary deadly force by law enforcement officers and has developed formal guidelines for law enforcement agencies regarding its use.

Noting that the only use for certain types of ammunition is to kill or wound those wearing body armor, NOBLE supports the banning of armor-piercing bullets. The organization recommends that the National Institute of Justice (NIJ) be given the responsibility of testing bullet proof vests to determine which ammunition can pierce body armor. The organization has called for the U.S. attorney general to determine which types of ammunition shall be banned. Noting that between 1985 and 1995, 61 law enforcement officers were killed or injured by individuals wielding assault weapons, NOBLE supports continuation of the assault weapons ban enacted in 1994. The organization has resolved to work toward the elimination of such weapons, which have contributed to "the genocide of our youth."

NOBLE takes a strong stand against the trend in state legislatures to enact measures permitting the carrying of concealed weapons. It has concluded that carrying concealed weapons imperils the safety of citizens and law enforcement officers. Such laws present an especially serious danger because the weapons training required is inadequate for the responsibility involved in carrying a concealed weapon. NOBLE notes that 14 "shall issue" states require no safety training at all. Contrary to the claims of gun rights supporters, NOBLE cites a 1995 study indicating that three states where concealed carry laws were weakened experienced an overall 26 percent increase in gun-related homicides. The organization urges its members, community leaders, and public officials to oppose further attempts to liberalize concealed carry laws. *See also* AFRICAN AMERICANS AND GUNS; ASSAULT WEAPONS BAN; CONCEALED CARRY LAWS: YOUTH AND GUNS.

Further Reading: National Organization of Black Law Enforcement Executives Web site <www.noblenatl.org>.

National Rifle Association (NRA)

While many look to the National Rifle Association (NRA) as the foremost champion of the right to keep and bear arms, others consider the NRA a powerful and uncompromising opponent to reasoned policies to control the violence stemming from the use of firearms, and still others see the organization as far too moderate in its opposition to gun control. Although the NRA is the largest gun rights advocacy group, with a membership of approximately 2.5 million, other groups, like the Second Amendment Foundation and Gun Owners of America (GOA), with considerably smaller memberships, act as the "conscience" of the NRA, keeping its leadership from straying too far from the orthodox anti-gun control stance.

William Conant Church and George Wood Wingate, Union veterans of the Civil War, are recognized as the founders of the NRA. An advocate of military marksmanship, Church called for the establishment of an association, similar to the National Rifle Association of Great Britain, that would encourage systematic training in rifle shooting. In

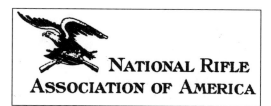

The logo of the National Rifle Association, one of the country's leading pro-gun rights groups. *UPI/Corbis-Bettmann.*

1871, New York State granted a charter to the newly formed National Rifle Association to encourage rifle practice and target shooting among the militia of New York and other states. The state provided the funds to purchase land on Long Island, called Creedmoor, to construct a site for rifle practice. The early days proved difficult for the fledgling organization, and in 1892 the NRA returned the land to New York and ceased activities. However, eight years later the organization came to life once more, due to increased interest in competitive shooting. In 1909, the NRA increased its board membership to include three appointments by the secretary of war and two from the secretary of the Navy, and directors of the state National Guard units were also added to the board. For many years, the organization benefited from the discount sale of surplus military rifles and ammunition to gun clubs, which proved to be an incentive for people to join the organization.

The NRA's first encounter with gun control occurred in 1911 when it opposed a gun control bill in New York State, which nevertheless became the Sullivan Law. In 1934, the NRA once more took an active role in gun control legislation when Congress considered a measure that ultimately became the National Firearms Act. That same year the organization established a Legislative Division. The NRA lobbied successfully against the inclusion of handgun regulation in the bill. Other measures, such as a proposal to keep on file for identification purposes ammunition fired from all new handguns and machine guns, were defeated. In 1938, when the gun control legislation that would become the Federal Firearms Act was proposed, the NRA successfully opposed more innovative proposals, such as bringing handguns under the provisions of the National Firearms Act. However, the organization failed to have the original provisions of the1934 legislation altered.

Political assassinations in the 1960s prompted renewed concern for controlling firearms. The NRA took a cautious approach to congressional proposals, but when Democratic President Lyndon Johnson called for a more stringent ban on mail-order shipments of firearms, gun owner licensing, and registration of firearms, NRA president Harold Glassen claimed that such measures would bring an end to shooting sports and ultimately result in disarming Americans. However, NRA officials were willing to entertain a ban on Saturday night special handguns.

The willingness of NRA officials to take a relatively moderate approach to certain gun control measures ended following the 1977 annual meeting in Cincinnati, Ohio. The old leadership, accused of abandoning the Second Amendment, was removed and a more militant contingent succeeded in electing Harlon Carter to the office of executive vice president. Carter committed the organization to an absolutist interpretation of the Second Amendment and appointed Neal Knox, equally as uncompromising on the gun control issue, to head the Institute for Legislative Action (ILA), which was responsible for encouraging the political activity of members and lobbying the national and state legislatures. Carter increased funding for this relatively new office within the NRA. In the 1980s, the NRA focused on two major political objectives: passing the McClure-Volkmer bill, which would weaken many of the provisions of the Gun Control Act of 1968, and limiting the authority of the Bureau of Alcohol, Tobacco, and Firearms (BATF), the federal agency responsible for enforcing federal firearms legislation.

In the 1980s, the NRA began an intense effort to increase membership. By 1984, the organization claimed a membership of nearly three million. Despite political successes, internal conflicts continued. When Carter retired in 1984, the board of directors chose

Ray G. Arnett as the new executive vice president. Arnett, a former member of Republican President Ronald Reagan's administration, soon faced a recall effort and in May 1986 the executive committee decided to suspend him without pay. ILA director J. Warren Cassidy replaced Arnett as executive vice president. During Cassidy's leadership, NRA membership declined and the organization faced increasing opposition to the preferred sale of surplus military weapons. Cassidy's willingness to reconsider waiting periods for the purchase of handguns and his unwillingness to endorse those advocating the right to own machine guns eroded his support base. In February 1991, Cassidy announced his resignation. The board of directors selected ILA director Wayne LaPierre to succeed Cassidy as the new executive vice president.

The NRA's initial opposition to such measures as the banning of armor-piercing bullets, plastic handguns, and assault rifles threatened organization support among police organizations. Declining support for the NRA gave impetus for passage of the Brady Handgun Violence Prevention Act of 1994. To regain momentum on the gun control issue, the NRA has taken steps to mend fences with law enforcement officials and has reached out to a group of potential new members and supporters, establishing the Women's Issues and Information Office in 1990 and in 1993 launching the "Refuse to Be a Victim" program, including a self-defense seminar for women.

The NRA continues to campaign against gun control proposals at the state and national levels. The organization opposed such proposals as required trigger locks on new handguns and a ban on multiple handgun sales. It has consistently opposed a waiting period for a handgun purchase. In 1997, the NRA enlisted the services of actor Charlton Heston as a spokesman and lobbyist for the organization. In 1998, Heston was chosen the organization's new president. Despite reports that the NRA has experienced a serious loss of influence in national and state politics, the organization still maintains much of its influence by supporting candidates politically and financially through its political action committee, the Political Victory Fund. *See also* ASSAULT WEAPONS BAN; BRADY HANDGUN VIOLENCE PREVENTION ACT; BUREAU OF ALCOHOL, TOBACCO, AND FIREARMS; BUSH, GEORGE; CLINTON, WILLIAM JEFFERSON (BILL); EDDIE EAGLE; FEDERAL FIREARMS ACT; FIREARMS OWNERS PROTECTION ACT; GUN OWNERS OF AMERICA; HESTON, CHARLTON; INSTITUTE FOR LEGISLATIVE ACTION; KNOX, NEAL; LAPIERRE, WAYNE; MCCLURE, JAMES ALBERTAS; NATIONAL FIREARMS ACT; REAGAN, RONALD; SATURDAY NIGHT SPECIAL; SECOND AMENDMENT; SECOND AMENDMENT FOUNDATION; STATE GUN STATUTES; SULLIVAN LAW; TRIGGER LOCKS; UNITED KINGDOM; VOLKMER, HAROLD LEE; WOMEN AND GUNS; YOUTH AND GUNS.

Further Reading: Jack Anderson, *Inside the NRA: Armed and Dangerous* (Beverly Hills, CA: Dove, 1996); Osha Gray Davidson, *Under Fire: The NRA and the Battle for Gun Control*, expanded ed. (Iowa City: University of Iowa, 1998); Wayne R. LaPierre, *Guns, Crime, and Freedom* (Washington, DC: Regnery, 1994); National Rifle Association Web site <www.nra.org>; Josh Sugarmann, *National Rifle Association: Money, Firepower, and Fear* (Washington, DC: National Press, 1992).

National SAFE KIDS Campaign

The National SAFE KIDS Campaign, headquartered in Washington, D.C., claims to be "the first and only national organization dedicated solely to the prevention of unintentional childhood injury," which the organization states is the major cause of death among children aged 14 and under. The organization encourages safe handling of guns by adults and supports additional legislation to protect children from accidental firearm injuries. Former U.S. Surgeon General C. Everett Koop chairs the Campaign and Vice President Al Gore and his wife Tipper serve as honorary chairs. In addition to the national office, there are over 250 state and local SAFE KIDS coalitions. Besides firearms safety, the coalitions develop strategies for injury prevention in such areas as bicycle safety, home fire detection, and burn prevention.

The Campaign labels firearms a "prevalent health hazard," claiming that in 1990 several states had more firearm-related deaths than fatalities caused by motor vehicle accidents. Access to loaded firearms increases the probability of unintentional death and injury to children. The organization believes that many adults underestimate children's ability to gain access to firearms and overestimate children's ability to distinguish real guns from toys and to handle guns safely and with good judgment. The Campaign reports that every year approximately 1,500 children aged 14 and under receive emergency room treatment for injuries from gun-related accidents. In 1996, over 14,000 children aged 14 and under received emergency room treatment for injuries caused by such non-powder weapons as BB and pellet guns.

For those who have firearms in the home, the Campaign recommends several safety rules. Keep the gun unloaded and always keep the safety on, even when unloaded. Store firearms in a locked cabinet or drawer and keep ammunition in a separate locked container. Treat all firearms as though they were loaded. Take a gun safety course, teach gun safety in the home, and tell children never to touch a gun. If someone has a history of depression or has discussed suicide, do not keep a firearm in the home.

The organization cites evidence that a gun in the home seldom is used for protection and is much more likely to be used to harm a family member or friend, a claim that is disputed by several firearms researchers and gun rights advocates. The Campaign claims that 30 percent of unintentional firearms fatalities could be prevented if handguns were equipped with gun locks and load indicators and notes with approval that 15 states have Child Access Prevention (CAP) laws, which hold adults legally responsible for failure to store firearms safely or to use locking devices on guns. The organization claims that the year after Florida passed a CAP law, unintentional firearm fatalities for children aged 14 and under was reduced 50 percent.

The Campaign notes that firearms are unregulated consumer products. No government agency regulates the safety of handguns and most gun laws focus on the gun users, not the firearms manufacturers. The organization cites public opinion surveys showing strong support for regulating the safety design of firearms and for making handguns child-resistant. The organization believes that in addition to saving lives, such measures would be financially prudent, given its estimate that the annual cost of unintentional injuries and deaths of children aged 14 and under that are attributed to firearms exceeds $3.7 billion. *See also* ACCIDENTS INVOLVING GUNS; FATALITIES; SCHOOLS AND GUNS; SUICIDE; TRIGGER LOCKS; YOUTH AND GUNS.

Further Reading: National SAFE KIDS Campaign Web site <www.safekids.org>.

National School Safety Center (NSSC)

In 1984, a directive from Republican President Ronald Reagan created the National School Safety Center (NSSC). Supported by congressional appropriations, the Center assists public school systems to implement programs geared to eradicate crime, violence, and drug use from schools, and to devise strategies to keep firearms away from school grounds. The NSSC, in cooperation with the Centers for Disease Control (CDC), monitors the number of school-associated deaths each year. The NSSC offers help in developing programs to deal with student discipline and attendance policy, provides legal and legislative assistance, distributes publications and films, conducts training programs, and provides technical assistance for those in education, law enforcement, and government. Center staff have given testimony before congressional and state legislative committees regarding school safety policy. In April 1998, Ronald D. Stephens, executive director of the NSSC, testified before the U.S. House Subcommittee on Early Childhood, Youth and Families, warning congresspeople about the wide availability of firearms to youth.

The NSSC has identified several causal factors in the occurrence of violence at schools and has developed an assessment tool composed of 20 items that help to identify those students likely to become violent. An action plan is provided that includes 40 steps that parents, school administrators, and the community can take to make schools safer for teachers and students. In this material, firearms appear as one factor contributing to a higher probability of violence. Two of the 20 items on the assessment tool concern firearms and other weapons. The NSSF, in cooperation with the CDC, has monitored school-associated violent deaths. Of the 105 deaths occurring from 1992 to 1994, a majority were firearms related. In 79 of these deaths in which a primary offender could be identified, 72 offenders were found to have previously brought a weapon to school. The Center cites data indicating that in 1995 ten percent of high school students questioned in a survey reported having carried a weapon to school in the last 30 days.

Although the Center has not taken explicit positions on gun control issues, it reports that "the easy accessibility of weapons to young people in this country is staggering." The NSSC comments that, due to the availability of firearms, the level of violence has increased over the years. The Center recommends a "zero tolerance" policy, in which any weapons violation results in expulsion from school. Any charge of weapons possession should lead to immediate investigation and "prompt and reasonable action."

The Center distributes reports on firearms violence prepared by other organizations. For instance, the Center makes available the results of a survey of 2,508 students in 96 public and private schools, grades 6 through 12, sponsored by the Harvard School of Public Health. Fifteen percent of respondents reported having carried a handgun in the month before the survey. Nine percent stated they had shot a firearm at someone, 39 percent reported they knew someone personally who had been killed or injured by a gun, and 59 percent claimed they had access to a handgun. *See also* JONESBORO, ARKANSAS, SCHOOL SHOOTING; LITTLETON, COLORADO, SCHOOL SHOOTING; REAGAN, RONALD; SCHOOLS AND GUNS; STOCKTON, CALIFORNIA, SHOOTING; TRIGGER LOCKS; YOUTH AND GUNS.

Further Reading: National School Safety Center Web site <www.nssc1.org>.

National Shooting Sports Foundation (NSSF)

The National Shooting Sports Foundation (NSSF) was established in 1961 to represent the hunting and shooting sports industry. According to the Foundation, its mission is "to bring a positive message about the shooting sports to the news media, to a new generation of shooters and to decision makers on all levels," and to promote active participation in the various shooting sports, especially among those who have not previously participated. More than 1,400 companies are members of the Foundation, including manufacturers, distributors, wholesalers, and retailers of shooting sports equipment, in addition to other associations related to shooting sports, publishing enterprises, and individuals.

The Foundation recognizes that the shooting sports industry has been supported primarily by the 18 to 20 million Americans who engage in hunting. This group represents two-thirds of the shooting sports market. Although in the past the industry could depend on hunters passing the tradition from one generation to the next, demographic changes such as greater urbanization may result in a significant decrease in the number of hunters. Therefore, the Foundation recognizes the need for more aggressive promotion through the mass media and safety education campaigns to attract new participants. The organization strives to have shooting covered just like any other sport. An ESPN cable series supported by the NSSF reports on target shooting. In another promotional effort, the NSSF produced a segment for MTV titled "Introduction to Sporting Clays." Such programs are meant to influence general public opinion about shooting sports and to attract new participants by presenting shooting as an enjoyable activity comparable to biking and skating.

The NSSF emphasizes that shooting is a safe sport, noting that "bowlers receive over seventeen times as many injuries as hunters," but without indicating the relative severity of injuries. The organization focuses on gun safety and frequently presents basic rules of safe handling, recognizing that a beneficial side effect of education programs can be the development of interest in the sport. The Foundation provides advice to members about attracting new shooters. For instance, a video featuring retired General Norman Schwarzkopf includes "the right mix of command presence and gentle persuasion to communicate a key message: Club members and leaders must treat new shooters in a welcoming and encouraging manner."

Youth, the source of future participants in the shooting sports, are a primary focus for gun safety programs. Young people are encouraged to attend hunter education courses before hunting for the first time. Three youth magazines, *Boy's Life, Scouting,* and *New Horizons* (a publication of Future Farmers of America) contain an annual shooting sports section. The organization promotes shooting programs with various youth organizations, including 4-H Clubs, and supports the Team Youth Development Program and the Hunter Education Association, whose estimated 50,000 volunteer instructors train several hundred thousand new hunters each year. The Foundation offers advice to parents taking a young person hunting for the first time. Parents should make sure that clothing is appropriate to the weather, provide an extra change of clothes, and make activities interesting, all geared to ensure that the youth will want to continue participating in the sport.

The NSSF has expanded the traditional father-son relationship to include daughters in shooting sports. In its efforts to change traditional attitudes about women's involvement in shooting sports and to encourage women to participate, the Foundation created the Women's Shooting Sports Foundation (WSSF), which sponsors women's-only and couples shotgun and handgun shooting events. *See also* AMERICAN SHOOTING SPORTS COUNCIL; WOMEN AND GUNS; YOUTH AND GUNS.

Further Reading: National Shooting Sports Foundation Web site <www.nssf.com>.

National Tracing Center (NTC)

The Bureau of Alcohol, Tobacco, and Firearms (BATF) maintains a National Tracing Center (NTC), which tracks the history of firearms recovered during or following the commission of crimes, from the sources (either manufacturers or importers) through the wholesale and retail enterprises to the persons who ultimately purchased the weapons. The Center can have a potentially significant effect on controlling the illegal firearms trade, both nationally and internationally, depending on its ability to provide useful information to law enforcement officials. However, gun control advocates argue that the strong opposition by gun rights groups to a firearms registration system severely hampers the ability of the NTC to conduct effective traces.

Law enforcement agencies at the local, state, national, and international levels can request information from the NTC database, which includes information about individuals who have engaged in unlicensed firearms dealing. The Center accumulates information about multiple firearms sales, stolen guns, and firearms with serial numbers that have been eliminated. Multiple sales may indicate "straw purchases," which involve persons acquiring firearms and then transferring them to others to conceal the actual receivers of the weapons. A federal statute enacted in 1975 requires federally licensed firearms dealers to report multiple sales to the BATF.

The Center identifies firearms trafficking "corridors," routes that illegal traffickers recurrently use to transport firearms. Such routes include interstate highways, bus lines, railways, airlines, and such carriers as United Parcel Service and the U.S. mail. A firearms trafficking "gateway" is a location, such as a border crossing point, seaport, airport, or train station, through which illegal traffickers frequently pass during the transport of firearms to final destinations. A market area is any locality where firearms are sold illegally or transferred to criminals and others prohibited from possessing firearms, including juveniles. In addition to conducting firearms traces and identifying illegal sources and transportation routes, the Center has responsibility for maintaining the records of federally licensed firearms dealers who have ceased doing business.

The BATF has established a computerized illegal firearms trafficking information system, called Project LEAD, which is responsible for providing assistance to law enforcement in the conduct of investigations through analysis of the crime data collected by the National Tracing Center. The Project is intended to reduce violent crime committed with firearms by determining multiple sales that may indicate illegal firearms trafficking and by assisting in the prosecution of those who illegally supply firearms to violent criminals. One indicator the Project uses to determine illegal firearms trafficking is the "time-to-crime" rate, which is the number of days between retail acquisition of a firearm and its recovery during or following the commission of a crime.

The Project reports that the newer the weapon the more easily it can be traced back to the original buyer and seller. Several short time-to-crime traces to the same dealer may indicate illegal trafficking. The Project can assist other countries in identifying persons residing in the United States who are illegally trafficking in firearms in other countries. A major objective is to eliminate criminals' sources of firearms. The NTC issues several trace analysis reports, including those that provide information about the total number of crime gun trace requests, types of crime guns, information by community, analyses of successful traces, summarization of incomplete traces, and categorization by age of those discovered to possess firearms illegally.

The NTC is affiliated with the BATF's Juvenile Firearms Violence Initiative, which traces firearms found on school grounds or taken from juveniles who used them to commit violent crimes. The Initiative is intended to reduce the number of young people who use firearms in the commission of violent acts, to identify and cut off the sources of firearms for juveniles and other violent users of firearms, and to arrest and prosecute adults who supply firearms to juveniles. *See also* BUREAU OF ALCOHOL, TOBACCO, AND FIREARMS; YOUTH AND GUNS.

Further Reading: Bureau of Alcohol, Tobacco, and Firearms Web site <www.atf.treas.gov/about/prog/trace.htm>.

Native Americans

In their attempt to confirm the liberty-destroying nature of gun control efforts, gun rights advocates argue that any time a government attempts to take firearms from a group, such as Native Americans (American Indians), the intent is ultimately to subjugate the group and to establish a tyranny. They note that the conquest of the North American continent and the extermination of Indian tribes was accomplished through the active complicity of federal government troops. The genocidal programs of such twentieth-century dictatorships as the Soviet Union and Nazi Germany are compared with the federal government's treatment of Native Americans.

However, to be *disarmed*, American Indians first had to be *armed*. Over a long period of time, European settlers provided firearms to Native Americans. Indians, recognizing the advantages of the new technology, avidly accepted the new weapons and abandoned their bows and arrows. Dutch traders reaped huge profits from trading guns for beaver pelts. Ironically, acceptance of firearms made the Indians dependent on the colonists for lead, powder, and the maintenance of weapons. In the seventeenth century, the British government officially opposed providing Indians with firearms, but the practice became so profitable for traders that by 1650 there was no way to stop the further spread of weapons among native tribes. Such trading somewhat lessened the disparity of weaponry between whites and Indians. Traders surrendered European military superiority and ultimately the lives of colonists for the opportunity to make large profits.

Despite early attempts to discourage gun trading, the French and British, when at war, enlisted the assistance of Indian tribes as allies, providing them with firearms. In Virginia,

Indians allied with the English colony were granted the right to firearms and gunpowder. Indian tribes desired firearms to give them the advantage in their own conflicts with other tribes. An early form of the arms race developed, with the tribe first able to gain modern weapons establishing supremacy over rival tribes. Indians less successful in acquiring the new technology became subordinated not only to the Europeans, but to Indian tribes that possessed firearms. European countries provided several hundred thousand firearms to Indians over a 200-year period. To gain new weapons, Indians efficiently used guns they had already acquired to kill game to trade more furs for additional weapons. In the process, wildlife on the North American continent was significantly reduced.

By the time the 13 colonies became a nation, Native Americans had several hundred years of experience with firearms. Although the Militia Act of 1792 excluded blacks, whether free or slave, and Indians from serving in the militia, the U.S. government followed the tradition established by European nations of providing firearms to the Indians, who could legally acquire rifles under the Indian Intercourse Act of 1834. A government-established factory and trading post system offered Indians firearms in exchange for furs and other goods. The government enticed Native Americans to move westward with the promise of additional firearms and gunsmiths to repair the weapons.

Although American Indians possessed weapons inferior to whites during the first half of the nineteenth century, after the Civil War, many Indians acquired rifles superior to those used by U.S. army soldiers. General George Armstrong Custer, who in 1876 was killed with his whole command by the Sioux and other tribes at the Little Bighorn River in the Dakota Territory (now Montana), once complained sarcastically that Indian warriors were well armed "through the foresight and strong love of fair play which prevails in the Indian Department" which did not effectively limit Indian acquisition of firearms.

History weaves a complex relationship between the firearm and the subjugation of the American Indian. European colonists possessed a major technological advantage over Native Americans when they first arrived bearing firearms. Later, western settlers clamored for federal government protection against Indian attacks. Over hundreds of years Native Americans suffered devastating losses. However, their plight did not arise from a consistent policy of denying firearms to them. The tragic struggle of Native Americans to resist the increasing waves of European immigration was doomed to failure. That struggle appears to offer no clear generalizations for pro- or anti-gun control groups regarding current laws or proposals. *See also* AMERICAN REVOLUTION; MILITIA ACT OF 1792; UNITED KINGDOM

Further Reading: Lee B. Kennett and James La Verne Anderson, *The Gun in America: The Origins of a National Dilemma* (Westport, CT: Greenwood, 1975); David B. Kopel, "Assault Weapons," in David B. Kopel, ed., *Guns: Who Should Have Them?* (Amherst, NY: Prometheus, 1995), 159-232; Carl P. Russell, *Guns on the Early Frontier* (New York: Bonanza Books, 1957).

Ninth Amendment

Some legal scholars have appealed to the Ninth Amendment to claim that the U.S. Constitution guarantees a right to keep and bear arms for self-defense. The amendment states that, "The enumeration in the Constitution, of certain rights, shall not be construed to deny or disparage others retained by the people." Particular rights, if not explicitly mentioned in the Constitution, are not thereby excluded from protection, but remain viable against encroachment by government. Among those rights considered so protected through the Ninth Amendment is self-protection and the ownership and carrying of firearms for that purpose. In his article "Beyond the Second Amendment: An Individual Right to Arms Viewed Through the Ninth Amendment" (1992), Nicholas Johnson argued that if the amendment is seen as a support for such things as "a right to engage in sodomy," "a right to wear long hair," and "protection against imprisonment in maximum security," it can be persuasively argued to protect a right to bear arms for self-defense. Even if the Second Amendment is interpreted to protect only a collective right of the states to maintain a militia, strong supporters of the right to keep and bear arms, such as Johnson, argue that the Ninth Amendment prevents the government from denying individuals the ability to defend themselves from others.

Johnson claimed that if we recognize that firearms in the United States have been traditionally regarded and still are widely accepted as especially useful tools for self-defense, then "we might view possession of arms for individual defense to be as basic as the right to choose a heavy coat against the cold." Johnson suggested that the common law tradition inherited from Great Britain recognizes a right to bear arms for self-defense, which is implicitly guaranteed by the Ninth Amendment. Similarly, Alan M. Gottlieb, chairman of the Citizens Committee for the Right to Keep and Bear Arms, argued in *The Rights of Gun Owners* (1991) that although the U.S. Constitution does not specifically guarantee the right to armed defense, this traditional common-law right is not nullified, but is protected by the Ninth Amendment.

Appealing to a natural rights view, Johnson suggested that not only do individuals have a right to arms, but that right cannot be restricted by the larger community, even by means of a constitutional amendment. He concluded that the individual's interest in self-preservation cannot be legitimately surrendered to society's interest in order. Pragmatically, the individual cannot always depend on the resources of the collective for personal security. In addition, the government itself may pose a threat to individual security, thereby requiring that people have the ability to resist such misuse of power through the use of force. Human rights principles within international law may be appealed to in establishing Ninth Amendment guarantees. The United Nations Charter recognizes the right of individual and collective self-defense and the Universal Declaration of Human Rights supports the right of individuals to life, liberty, and security.

In arguing for a right to personal protection and the related right to bear arms, Johnson noted that "guns equalize power relationships." The physical strength of an attacker can be resisted if the intended victim has a firearm. If the potential attacker is armed, the person who is the focus of the attack is better off armed, according to the principle that "increasing the cost of violence decreases its likelihood." For government to deny the tools of self-defense to its citizens is to leave them potential victims of the strong and the ruthless. Even though the danger exists that firearms will be misused in an armed society, Johnson concluded that individuals cannot be required to surrender their right to self-protection to benefit collective interests.

Although the argument from natural rights to certain guarantees within the Ninth Amendment may be tenuous, Johnson argued that the de facto resistence of citizens to surrendering the right of self-protection may be a significant affirmation of such a right. He argued against an elitist position, contending that government officials must be equally willing to surrender the right if they expect citizens to do so. Gun control advocates would claim that the argument for the right to bear arms based on Ninth Amendment, even if valid, does not establish an absolute protection. Although "disarming" citizens may not be constitutionally legitimate, such provisions as requiring registration and licensing, preventing felons from possessing firearms, and banning ownership of certain weapons, such as machine guns, could be considered reasonable precautions taken to ensure an ordered society. *See also* FOURTH AMENDMENT; FOURTEENTH AMENDMENT; GOTTLIEB, ALAN MERRIL; SECOND AMENDMENT; UNITED KINGDOM; UNITED NATIONS.

Further Reading: Alan M. Gottlieb, *The Rights of Gun Owners* (Bellevue, Washington: Merrill, 1991); Nicholas J. Johnson, "Beyond the Second Amendment: An Individual Right to Arms Viewed Through the Ninth Amendment," *Rutgers Law Journal* 24 (Fall 1992), 1-81.

Nunn v. Georgia (1846)

In *Nunn v. Georgia* (1 Ga. 243, 1846), the Supreme Court of Georgia overruled a lower court decision convicting Hawkins H. Nunn of carrying a pistol, contrary to an 1837 statute. The Supreme Court declared that both the U.S. and state constitutions guaranteed the right to keep and bear arms, anticipating some of the more recent arguments of gun rights supporters, including the appeal to common law and the natural rights tradition.

The state law in question prohibited "any merchant or vender of wares or merchandize in this State, or any other person or persons whatever, to sell, or to offer to sell, or to keep or to have about their persons, or elsewhere, any of the herein-after-described weapons, to wit: Bowie or any other kinds of knives, manufactured and sold for the purpose of wearing or carrying the same as arms of offence or defence; pistols, dirks, sword-canes, spears, & etc., shall also be contemplated in this act, save such pistols as are known and used as horseman's pistols."

Nunn was charged with carrying a pistol in his hand "which was not a horseman's pistol, but a breast pistol." Found guilty in the lower court, Nunn appealed the conviction, arguing that the 1837 statute under which he was convicted violated both the U.S. and Georgia constitutions, and that the indictment did not show that he had carried the pistol secretly. The Georgia Supreme Court, in rendering its decision, provided a broad interpretation of the right to bear arms, concluding that the state legislature had no authority to deny citizens the right to bear a weapon.

The court traced the historical roots of the right to bear arms, stating that "this is one of the fundamental principles, upon which rests the great fabric of civil liberty, reared by the fathers of the Revolution and of the country." The court held that the right antedated the U.S. Constitution, which "only reiterated a truth announced a century before, in the act of 1689." The court further ruled that the Second Amendment applied to both the federal and state governments, arguing that by denying the federal government power to forbid the right to bear arms, the people could not have intended to grant that authority to state governments. Referring to the maintenance of a well-regulated militia, the court noted that the state legislature cannot jeopardize the security of the people by disarming them.

The court called the right to bear arms a natural right and "unlimited," stating that "any law, State or Federal, is repugnant to the Constitution, and void, which contravenes this *right*, originally belonging to our forefathers, trampled under foot by Charles I and his two wicked sons and successors, re-established by the revolution of 1688, conveyed to this land of liberty by the colonists, and finally incorporated conspicuously in our own *Magna Charta*!" However, the court pulled away from an absolutist interpretation of the right by declaring that the law in question was valid to the extent that it "seeks to suppress the practice of carrying certain weapons *secretly*." Only insofar as the law forbade bearing arms openly was it contrary to the Constitution and void. *See also* SECOND AMENDMENT; UNITED KINGDOM.

Further Reading: *Nunn v. Georgia*, 1 Ga. 243 (1846).

O

Oklahoma City Bombing

The April 1995 Oklahoma City bombing in which the Alfred P. Murrah Federal Building was destroyed and 168 men, women, and children lost their lives is commonly associated with three events that had occurred in the two years preceding the bombing: the standoff at Ruby Ridge, Idaho in 1992 in which two members of Randy Weaver's family were killed by federal agents; the tragic ending to the confrontation at the Branch Davidian compound just outside Waco, Texas, in 1993; and the passage in 1994 of the Brady Handgun Violence Prevention Act. Each of these events involved federal firearms legislation. Federal officials wanted to arrest Randy Weaver for the illegal possession and sale of two sawed-off shotguns; Branch Davidian leader David Koresh was accused of possessing illegal automatic weapons; and the Brady Act imposed a waiting period and background check on anyone wishing to purchase a handgun. Timothy McVeigh, a gun enthusiast and prime suspect in the bombing, had expressed his extreme dislike for the federal government.

On April 19, 1995, two years to the day after federal agents stormed the Branch Davidian compound, a truck containing a 4,800-pound home-made bomb exploded in front of the Oklahoma City federal building. The building contained several federal offices, including the Bureau of Alcohol, Tobacco, and Firearms (BATF), an agency that many perceive as a major enemy of the right to bear arms. Ninety minutes after the blast, Timothy McVeigh, a 27-year-old former Army sergeant, was stopped by a state trooper for speeding along Interstate 35. McVeigh's automobile had no license plates, and he was carrying an unregistered 9-mm Glock semi-automatic pistol that was loaded with Black Talon bullets. The trooper arrested McVeigh and transported him to the Perry, Oklahoma, county jail, where he stayed for two days until the Federal Bureau of Investigation (FBI) traced him through his social security number. Using the computer system at the National Crime Information Center, the FBI discovered that their prime suspect was being held in Perry. They contacted the sheriff's office, requesting that McVeigh, who was about an hour away from release, be held for transfer to federal authorities.

In the first days following the bombing, some militia groups claimed that the devastation had been committed by the federal government to lay blame on militia groups, to manipulate Congress into giving law enforcement greater power, and to justify the repression of militia members and gun owners generally. However, the quick arrest of McVeigh and claimed co-conspirator Terry Nichols put to rest, for all but the most extreme militia members, claims of federal government involvement. In August 1995, McVeigh and Nichols were indicted by a federal grand jury.

On April 29, 1995, recovery workers search the inside of the bombed out shell of the U.S. federal building in Oklahoma City, Oklahoma. *REUTERS/Jim Bourg/Archive Photos.*

On June 2, 1997, a federal court jury found McVeigh guilty of the Oklahoma City bombing. He was convicted of first-degree murder in the deaths of eight federal law-enforcement officers who were working in the building. The defense had argued that McVeigh was innocent and that the true perpetrators, sponsored by a foreign government, had still not been found. However, the amount of evidence the prosecution was able to bring forward left any alternative explanation for the crime unconvincing. Before the bombing, McVeigh had told his sister to expect "something big." He had often expressed his hatred for the federal government and the BATF. McVeigh's favorite reading, a right-wing novel titled *The Turner Diaries*, contained a description of a similar bombing event against a government building. Although McVeigh's views gave some hint as to his motives, the conviction rested on the

impressive amount of evidence that the prosecution had amassed against the defendant. At the sentencing stage, McVeigh received the death penalty. Terry Nichols was subsequently convicted and sentenced to a life term for his part in the bombing plot.

While most people on both sides of the gun control issue behave within the legal confines of the system, a complete treatment of the gun control debate must recognize that some people view gun control advocates not only as mistaken in their interpretation of the Second Amendment, but anxious to wrest freedom away from average Americans who can depend only on themselves for self-protection. Indeed, the federal government is viewed as the great oppressor that, among other tyrannous acts, intends to disarm all Americans. This view, while highly implausible, apparently motivated McVeigh to take the use of force into his own hands. *See also*

BLACK TALON BULLET; BRADY HANDGUN VIOLENCE PREVENTION ACT; BUREAU OF ALCOHOL, TOBACCO, AND FIREARMS; RUBY RIDGE; SECOND AMENDMENT; TURNER DIARIES; WACO, TEXAS, RAID.

Further Reading: Morris Dees, *Gathering Storm: America's Militia Threat* (New York: HarperCollins, 1996); Jonathan Karl, *The Right to Bear Arms: The Rise of America's Militia Movement* (New York: HarperCollins, 1995); *New York Times*, June 3, 1997, 1, 18, 19.

P

Pacific Center for Violence Prevention (PCVP)

Located within the Trauma Foundation of San Francisco General Hospital, the Pacific Center for Violence Prevention (PCVP) strives to reduce youth violence. The Trauma Foundation, headed by Andrew McGuire, has engaged in a number campaigns to improve the safety of citizens, including advocacy of fire-safe cigarettes, mandatory seat belt laws, motorcycle helmet statutes, an increase in the liquor tax, regulation of alcohol advertising to prohibit demeaning images of women, and health care for battered women.

The Trauma Foundation began in 1973 as the Burn Council, an organization devoted to preventing burn injuries to children. The Council advocated such measures as requiring flame resistant children's sleepwear. In 1979, the organization was expanded to deal with all injuries. Firearms were identified as one of the unsafe products for younger people that should be given attention. The Pacific Center, which has focused on gun control as one means of preventing violence especially among youth, is the policy headquarters of the Violence Prevention Initiative, a collaboration of community groups engaged cooperatively in local violence prevention. The Center offers various services to communities, including media and policy advocacy training and information resources.

The Pacific Center has established three major objectives. First, it supports a policy shift away from institutional confinement for youth who commit violent acts toward community-based crime prevention programs that regard youth as a resource to be developed. Second, the Center works to reduce the access youth have to alcohol and other drugs by increasing the excise tax on beer, limiting youth-oriented advertising of alcoholic products, and allowing local communities to regulate alcohol sales. Finally, the organization hopes to initiate policies to limit firearm possession among youth.

The Policy Center considers youth access to firearms, as well as firearms possession generally, a major contributor to high levels of violence in California and across the nation. The organization notes that in California, firearms have become the leading cause of death for those aged 1 to 19. In California, 80 percent of homicides involving youth are committed with firearms. Also of concern is the large number of nonfatal gun injuries. From June 1992 to May 1993, approximately 99,000 such injuries were reported nationally.

The Center has supported several proposals to keep firearms away from youth. It promotes a total ban on the sale and possession of Saturday night specials, or junk guns, which are still produced in the United States even though the Gun Control Act of 1968 prohibited foreign imports. Although this proposal has experienced serious opposition in California, where several manufacturers are located, the Center strongly advocates such a ban, reporting that junk guns made in California are often used in crimes. The Center promotes home rule legislation that allows local communities to establish firearms limitations independent of state government. Gun rights organizations have strongly opposed such provisions, advocating instead state laws that preempt localities from approving gun control ordinances. The organization supports uniform penalties for carrying concealed weapons. In 1989, during the debate over an assault weapons ban, the Pacific Center, along with a coalition of health care workers and community leaders, campaigned for the bill's passage.

In working toward its goals, the Center collaborates with other organizations, including the Berkeley Media Studies Group, which assists with media advocacy training and news monitoring; the California Child Youth and Family Coalition, an organization concerned with the basic causes of violence; and the Urban Strategies Council, a group that examines the social factors affecting the level of violence in a community. *See also* ASSAULT WEAPONS BAN; CONCEALED CARRY LAWS; GUN CONTROL ACT OF 1968; HEALTH CARE PROFESSIONALS; SCHOOLS AND GUNS; SATURDAY NIGHT SPECIAL; YOUTH AND GUNS.

Further Reading: Pacific Center for Violence Prevention Web site <www.pcvp.org/firearms>.

Paladin Press

Paladin Press, headquartered in Boulder, Colorado, offers a list of books and video tapes on such controversial topics as weaponry and combat shooting, sniping, espionage, explosives, achieving revenge, and establishing a new identity. Paladin publishes a catalog, containing over 800 titles, which is also available on the Internet. Among the listed categories most relevant to firearms and gun control are "exotic weapons," "firearms," "sniping," and "explosives and demolitions."

In 1970, Peder Lund and Robert K. Brown joined forces to establish Paladin Press, which had previously been known as Panther Publications. Lund and Brown decided on the new name, fearing that the company might otherwise be confused with the Black Panther Party, a radical African-American group. During its first four years, Paladin limited its offerings primarily to government military manuals. When Brown left the company in 1974 to found *Soldier of Fortune* magazine, Lund expanded the publication list beyond military subjects to include how-to manuals dealing with such topics as identity change, bounty hunting, explosives, sniping, and martial arts.

Paladin offers several publications on firearms, some of which describe how to make guns at home. For instance, a description of *A Do-It-Yourself Submachine Gun* by Gerard Metral, states that, "You'll never have to worry about which submachine guns turn up on the banned-import list again. Now you can build your own simply by following the complete step-by-step plans and machinist's drawings." However, the description concludes by stating: "*Warning*. All BATF rules apply to the construction of this firearm. This book is presented for *academic study only*." Advertisements for a series of books by Bill Holmes dealing with the home manufacture of firearms contain the same disclaimer. A similar disclaimer follows a depiction of *Full-Auto Conversion of the SKS Rifle* by "Powder Burns," which is described as containing "complete plans for putting together a fully automatic weapon 'powerful enough to make would-be tyrants tremble in their jackboots.'" In response to those who express reservations about publishing such how-to books, Lund has been quoted as saying, "I've never seen a man killed by a book."

Some of the advertised publications express an explicit anti-gun control position. Alan M. Rice's *Lethal Laws* asserts a relationship between a government's tendency to control the ownership of guns and its intentions to engage in genocide. In *Gun Control: Gateway to Tyranny*, Jay Simkin and Aaron Zelman argue that U.S. gun control legislation was inspired by gun laws in Nazi Germany. The authors compare the Gun Control

Act of 1968 and Nazi laws to demonstrate "the fascist roots of American anti-gunners' progressive firearm confiscation policies."

The Paladin catalog describes Ragnar Benson's *Modern Weapons Caching* as a manual for hiding weapons from the authorities: "Firearms owners must literally take their weapons underground–bury them–or be prepared to have them confiscated." *Boston on Guns and Courage* by "Boston T. Party" is said to deal with such topics as which firearms to purchase, why the gun owner may not wish to apply for a concealed carry permit, and what guns are likely to be outlawed. The catalog also describes John Ross's novel, *Unintended Consequences*, which deals with the events surrounding a man's refusal to submit to "the increasingly heavy-handed tactics of the BATF." *See also* BLACK PANTHER PARTY; BUREAU OF ALCOHOL, TOBACCO, AND FIREARMS; CONCEALED CARRY LAWS; GUN CONTROL ACT OF 1968; *SOLDIER OF FORTUNE*.

Further Reading: Paladin Press Catalog (Boulder, Colorado, 1998); Paladin Press Web site <www.paladin-press.com>.

Paul, Ron (1935–)

Ron Paul, a conservative Republican congressman from Texas and an avid supporter of the individualist interpretation of the Second Amendment guarantee of the right to keep and bear arms, has advocated the virtual elimination of restrictions on gun ownership for law-abiding citizens. Paul has championed several conservative causes, including abolition through constitutional amendment of personal income, estate, and gift taxes and a prohibition on federal government business activities that compete with private citizens. Paul has proposed a constitutional amendment authorizing state governments to prohibit destruction of the U.S. flag and empowering Congress to prohibit destruction of federally owned flags. In 1997, the congressman sponsored a bill that would have withdrawn the United States from the United Nations. Paul was sharply criticized that year for commenting in a televised interview that he feared being "bombed by the federal government at another Waco."

An obstetrician and gynecologist, Paul received degrees from Gettysburg College and Duke University School of Medicine. After serving as a flight surgeon in the U.S. Air Force, he moved to Texas in 1968. Paul was first elected to the U.S. House of Representatives in 1976. He believes that the federal government should cease to play a role in education, leaving this function to state and local governments. A supporter of term limits, Paul did not run for reelection in 1984, choosing instead to return to his medical practice. In 1988, he ran for president as the Libertarian Party candidate. In 1996, Paul returned to the House of Representatives after wresting the party nomination from the Republican incumbent who had the support of the state and national Republican establishment.

In 1997, Paul sponsored a bill called the Second Amendment Restoration Act, which would repeal federal prohibitions on semiautomatic firearms and large capacity ammunition clips. The act would amend the federal criminal code and the Violent Crime Control and Law Enforcement Act of 1994, repealing prohibitions on "the manufacture, possession, transfer, and use of semiautomatic assault weapons and large capacity ammunition feeding devices." The act would acknowledge that the Second Amendment guarantees an individual right to keep and bear arms, including semi-automatic firearms, and declare that Article I, section 8 of the U.S. Constitution, which enumerates the powers of Congress, does not grant Congress authority to enact gun control legislation.

Continuing his efforts to dismantle federal gun control legislation, in October 1997 Paul introduced a proposal, called the Second Amendment Protection Act, which would repeal the Brady Handgun Violence Prevention Act, amend provisions of the Internal Revenue Code regarding the taxation of machine guns, and eliminate the provisions of the Gun Control Act of 1968 that distinguish among firearms on the basis of sporting purposes.

Wishing to establish a national right to carry a concealed weapon, Paul introduced a bill to provide for reciprocity among states in recognizing such a right. The legislation would establish that an individual who is not prohibited by federal law from possessing, transporting, shipping, or receiving a firearm, who has a valid state license to carry a concealed weapon, and "who is otherwise entitled to carry a concealed firearm in and pursuant to the law of the state of . . . residence" may carry a concealed firearm "in accordance with the terms of the license or with the laws of the state of the person's residence." Paul established the legal basis of the act in Article IV section 1 of the U.S. Constitution, which requires that each state give "full faith and credit" to the public acts, records, and judicial proceedings of every other state. *See also* ASSAULT WEAPONS BAN; BRADY HANDGUN VIOLENCE PREVENTION ACT; CONCEALED CARRY LAWS; GUN CONTROL ACT OF 1968; LIBERTARIAN PARTY; SECOND AMENDMENT; UNITED NATIONS; WACO, TEXAS, RAID.

Further Reading: Philip D. Duncan and Christine C. Lawrence, *Politics in America 1998: The 105th Congress* (Washington, DC: Congressional Quarterly, 1997); Congressman Ron Paul's Web site <www.house.gov/paul>.

Paul Revere Network (PRN)

The Paul Revere Network (PRN) was founded as an Internet Web page in August 1995 by Leroy Pyle, a former National Rifle Association (NRA) director and veteran of the San Jose, California, police force. The PRN is described as "a coast-to-coast network of committed grass-roots gun rights activists who rely upon computer bulletin board systems for their primary mode of communication." The organization considers the Second Amendment guarantee of the right to keep and bear arms to be the cornerstone of the Bill of Rights. Pyle is the director of the Network, which is headquartered in Chicago, Illinois. Regional coordinators are located in Kansas City, Missouri; San Jose, California; Los Angeles, California; Greenville, North Carolina; and Lansdowne, Pennsylvania. In addition to the regional coordinators, the PRN contains approximately 200 nodes, each of which contains large

amounts of data on firearms, the Second Amendment, opinion pieces, legislative updates, newsletter articles, and information about local and regional activities. The PRN issues an occasional newsletter.

Pyle, a firearms expert and police gun safety training officer, testified before the California legislature's Public Safety Committee against banning assault weapons in the state. An assault weapons ban gained extensive support in California following the schoolyard shooting in Stockton. By speaking out against the ban, Pyle contradicted the position of San Jose police chief Joseph McNamara, a proponent of gun control. The PRN claims that gun control legislation has been ineffective in reducing crime and that greater gun ownership in the population contributes to lowering the incidence of crime. The Network holds that assault rifles are indistinguishable from sporting and hunting firearms, except for cosmetic features, and therefore bans are unwarranted limitations on the Second Amendment right to keep and bear arms.

The PRN supports the "NEW NRA," in other words, a gun rights group unwilling to compromise on the issue of gun control. The Network expresses its attitude toward gun control organizations by declaring "No Negotiation with Terrorists!" Pyle believes that the Network gives Second Amendment activists an advantage over the gun control opposition. He expects that ultimately the Web site will facilitate supporters in the coordination of massive letter and telegram campaigns to contact public officials about firearms issues.

The organization is concerned about the various gun control proposals being initiated at all levels of government, which it claims will place serious limitations on the rights of gun owners. The Network applauds gun owners who have demanded a "stronger NRA" and contacted their legislators. Local efforts are seen as the best way gun owners can "halt the erosion of their gun freedoms." The Network hopes to unite the various local and regional efforts and to enlist politically inactive gun owners through a computer bulletin board system. *See also* ASSAULT WEAPONS BAN; NATIONAL RIFLE ASSOCIATION; SECOND AMENDMENT; STOCKTON, CALIFORNIA, SHOOTING.

Further Reading: Paul Revere Network Web site <www.paulrevere.org>.

PAX

PAX works to create wide public support for social and political solutions to the problem of firearms violence. The organization intends to create attention through the mass media for the gun violence issue and activate a grassroots movement demanding changes in policy. PAX was established in 1997 by Talmage Cooley and Daniel Gross, who serve as co-executive directors of the organization. PAX numbers among its trustees and advisers James and Sarah Brady of Handgun Control, Inc., Mayor Rudolph Giuliani of New York City, Richard Aborn, former president of Handgun Control, Inc., and Democratic Senators Frank Lautenberg and Charles Schumer. The organization's list of sponsors includes MTV Network, Calvin Klein, HBO, Time Warner Cable, and Broadway Video.

A Wall Street trader from 1983 until 1993, Cooley left the world of finance to become a writer, director, and photographer. In 1995, he established The Gun Violence Project to develop media strategies to assist in the development of an anti-gun violence movement. In 1997, Cooley merged The Gun Violence Project with PAX. That year, Gross's brother Matthew, a rock singer, was wounded in the Empire State Building shooting. Following the incident Gross became involved in anti-gun violence efforts, making appearances on television and radio and writing about the need to curb gun violence. He resigned a position in an advertising firm to co-found PAX.

PAX notes a General Accounting Office (GAO) report indicating that in 60 percent of gun-related fatal accidents the firearm was located "near the home." Advocating that states pass laws to mandate that firearms owners keep guns locked and safely stored to prevent children from having access to

weapons, PAX notes that 15 states presently have such laws. Focusing on school violence, the organization refers to a Department of Education report that 6,000 students were expelled in the 1996-97 school year for taking guns to school. PAX cites survey data indicating that over 80 percent of the U.S. population support legislation to make new handguns "childproof."

PAX recommends that parents familiarize themselves with the dangers of firearms, speak with their children about the dangers, and strive to keep them away from guns. Gun owners are advised to keep firearms locked and inaccessible to everyone but themselves. Those concerned about gun violence are encouraged to discover the position on gun control of their representatives in state legislatures and Congress; PAX suggests that individuals organize petition and letter-writing campaigns to lobby for proposals and take part in education programs to limit firearm violence. PAX supports the effort to have school children sign a pledge not to take a firearm to school and not to use a gun to settle disputes. In 1998, the organization conducted an awareness campaign that included public service announcements and a media event at a New Jersey elementary school that involved local and national public officials. *See also* BRADY, JAMES; BRADY, SARAH; EMPIRE STATE BUILDING SHOOTING; HANDGUN CONTROL, INC.; LAUTENBERG, FRANK R.; SCHOOLS AND GUNS; SCHUMER, CHARLES; TRIGGER LOCKS.

Further Reading: PAX Web site <www.paxusa.org>.

Perpich v. Department of Defense (1990)

Although the decision in *Perpich v. Department of Defense* (496 U.S. 334, 1990) does not relate directly to the right to keep and bear arms, gun rights advocates consider that the U.S. Supreme Court's ruling in the case supports an individualist interpretation of the Second Amendment, and conclude that the Court's affirmation of congressional power over state militias argues against the pro-gun control position that the Second Amendment guarantees only a communal right of the states to establish militia organizations independent of the national government.

In presenting its decision, the Court examined the history of the militia system in the United States. In 1916, Congress enacted a statute requiring all members of National Guard organizations in the states to take a dual oath, obligating themselves to obey the president of the United States as well as the governor of the state. The legislation authorized the president to draft members of the Guard into federal service. Democratic President Woodrow Wilson used that power during World War I to call up troops. In 1933, Congress amended the 1916 act, creating two overlapping organizations: the several state National Guards and the National Guard of the United States. Since 1933, anyone enlisting in a state's National Guard simultaneously enlists in the National Guard of the United States.

While originally the president was empowered to order National Guard units to active duty only in periods of national emergency, in 1952 Congress authorized the president to order units to "active duty or active duty for training" without the emergency requirement. However, the law specified that such orders required gubernatorial consent. In 1985, the governor of California refused to agree to a training mission in Honduras for 450 California National Guard personnel. The following year, Congress responded by enacting the Montgomery Amendment, which stated that, "the consent of a Governor . . . may not be withheld (in whole or in part) with regard to active duty outside the United States, its territories, and its possessions, because of any objection to the location, purpose, type, or schedule of active duty."

The governor of Minnesota objected to the Montgomery Amendment, arguing that it violated the two militia clauses of the Constitution. The governor contended that, according to the traditional understanding, the militia may be employed only "to execute the Laws of the Union, suppress Insurrections and repel Invasions." The Court observed that

members of the state National Guards "must keep three hats in their closets—a civilian hat, a state militia hat, and an army hat—only one of which is worn at any particular time." Situations may arise when state affiliation ceases and complete federal affiliation begins. Congress, which initially granted governors veto power over the use of state National Guard units in their respective states, has the authority to limit that power. Therefore, the Court concluded that the Montgomery Amendment does not violate the Constitution's militia clauses.

The governor contended that such an interpretation of the militia clauses would end in "nullifying an important state power that is expressly reserved in the Constitution." The Court responded that the Constitution simply recognizes federal supremacy in military affairs: "The Federal Government provides virtually all of the funding, the material, and the leadership for the State Guard units." The president's requiring a portion of a state guard to participate in a training exercise affects only slightly the overall guard unit in a state. In addition, the Court noted that Congress has passed legislation allowing a state to "provide and maintain at its own expense a defense force that is exempt from being drafted into the Armed Forces of the United States." Contrary to the claims of gun rights advocates in this case, gun control forces may use the Court's understanding that the states have maintained their unique position in sustaining the National Guard to argue for the communal interpretation of the Second Amendment. *See also* MILITIA ACT OF 1792; SECOND AMENDMENT.

Further Reading: *Perpich v. Department of Defense,* 496 U.S. 334 (1990).

Physicians for Social Responsibility (PSR)

Physicians for Social Responsibility (PSR), a network of physicians and public health professionals with national headquarters in Washington, D.C., develops strategies to decrease the dangers of nuclear weapons, environmental pollution, and gun violence. The organization calls itself "the active conscience of American medicine." Adhering to an epidemiological model of gun violence, the PSR engages in developing a national violence prevention coalition to reduce the number of firearms and the level of domestic violence. The organization is active in recruiting interested people locally to provide information about violence and to persuade local, state, and national representatives to support violence-prevention legislation. The Chicago chapter of the PSR has developed a slide show and speakers' bureau that includes color slides showing the medical consequences of handgun violence, a speakers' guide, and training for speakers.

The PSR rejects the individualistic interpretation of the Second Amendment, emphasizing that the federal court system has never struck down legislation regulating the private ownership of firearms on Second Amendment grounds. The PSR has taken stands on several public policy issues regarding firearms, supporting additional legislation and other actions the organization believes will decrease gun violence. For instance, legislation should be approved that limits handgun purchases to one per month to stop volume sales to underground dealers. In addition, just as consumer product safety regulations were instituted, such as child-resistant packaging for prescription drugs and air bags in automobiles, standards should be established for firearms safety and design. The organization has supported federal legislation to prevent foreign visitors from buying or carrying firearms while in the United States. Another favored piece of legislation would grant to the Bureau of Alcohol, Tobacco, and Firearms (BATF) the authority to regulate the manufacture, distribution, and sale of firearms and ammunition, and subject guns to safety restrictions.

The PSR supports enactment of child access prevention (CAP), or safe storage, laws. Already approved in 15 states by 1997, such laws are credited with preventing unauthorized use of firearms by minors. The organization advocates personalized gun technology that would prevent persons other than the gun owner from firing the weapon. If manufacturers do not introduce this technology voluntarily, state and national legislatures should approve legislation requiring the addition of such devices. The organization opposes the enactment of state concealed carry laws. Of greatest concern are "shall issue" laws that mandate the issuance of licenses virtually on demand to anyone not specifically prohibited from owning a firearm.

The PSR supports banning specific types of weapons. The organization advocates broadening the ban on the importation of junk guns, or Saturday night specials, that was instituted in the Gun Control Act of 1968. Not only foreign handguns, but domestically produced models should be subject to the ban. Claiming that "assault weapons are vectors of America's gun violence epidemic as surely as bacteria and viruses are vectors of infectious disease," the PSR opposes efforts backed by the National Rifle Association (NRA) to repeal the 1994 assault weapons ban. Estimating the costs of firearms deaths and injuries at $20 billion per year, the organization backs legislation to increase federal taxes on firearms. The additional revenue would be used to support victims of gun violence.

The PSR encourages physicians and other health care workers to inform families of the dangers of firearms to bring about greater numbers of gun-free homes. Concerned about the intensified marketing of firearms to women and arguing that guns do not offer the protection that gun manufacturers claim, the organization recommends that people not rely on firearms for self-protection. *See also* ASSAULT WEAPONS BAN; BUREAU OF ALCOHOL, TOBACCO, AND FIREARMS; GUN CONTROL ACT OF 1968; HEALTH CARE PROFESSIONALS; NATIONAL RIFLE ASSOCIATION; SATURDAY NIGHT SPECIAL; SECOND AMENDMENT; WOMEN AND GUNS.

Further Reading: Physicians for Social Responsibility Web site <www.psr.org>.

Police Executive Research Forum (PERF)

The Police Executive Research Forum (PERF), a group that represents those in leadership positions in municipal, county, and state law enforcement agencies, has taken stands in favor of several gun control proposals. Believing that the Gun Control Act of 1968 provided uniform national policy necessitated by the widely varying statutes among the states, PERF joined other law enforcement organizations to oppose provisions of the 1986 McClure-Volkmer Firearms Owners Protection Act that weakened the 1968 legislation. Since then PERF has supported firearms policies the organization believes will increase the safety of police officers.

The Forum began in 1975 when a small group of police executives from major cities met to discuss their concerns about policing. Two years later, it was incorporated as an organization dedicated to professionalizing policing at all levels of government. Based in Washington, D.C., the organization engages in and encourages research and public discussion to increase knowledge about law enforcement. Also emphasized are the encouragement of high ethical standards, integrity, responsibility, and accountability to the public. PERF receives support from government grants and contracts and from private organizations. The Forum supports the Senior Management Institute for Police (SMIP), a developmental program for current and future police executives.

Noting that keeping a loaded and unsecured handgun around children is "a tragedy waiting to happen," PERF supports the use of locks on handguns. The organization has backed such security devices since 1984, when it published guidelines for handgun safety that included a recommendation to owners to use trigger locks. The organization applauded the agreement between President Bill Clinton and representatives of several firearms companies to provide child safety mechanisms with newly manufactured handguns. Noting that from 1985 to 1994 the lives of over 2,000 police officers were saved by bulletproof vests, the Forum has supported legislation in Congress that would establish a grant program to assist local law enforcement agencies to purchase bulletproof vests for police officers. PERF has expressed support for the Brady Handgun Violence Prevention Act's criminal background check system for those wishing to purchase a handgun.

In a survey of 375 PERF members conducted in 1996, 92 percent of the respondents opposed legislation permitting the carrying of concealed weapons (CCW) laws, especially "shall issue" statutes that deny police officials discretion in granting permits. Members expressed doubt that concealed carry laws will reduce gun-related crime and feared that such laws threaten the safety of police officers. In addition to concern about "shall issue" CCW laws in general, PERF has objected to a legislative proposal that would exempt present and retired police officers from state laws that prohibit carrying concealed weapons. In 1997, John S. Farrell, legislative committee chairman for PERF and chief of police for Prince George's County, Maryland, presented reservations about such a law before the House Judiciary Committee's Subcommittee on Crime.

Farrell stated that although on some subjects a national policy is needed, the issue of CCW laws is best left to the individual states, especially provisions related to police officers carrying weapons. He expressed concern about former police officers being granted the right to carry a concealed weapon, raising questions about responsibility for regular training and possible legal liability. Who would be held responsible for an off-duty police officer who misuses a weapon in another state? Even if the final ruling determines that no liability exists, a police agency may be faced with significant legal expenses defending itself against claims of responsibility for a police officer who misuses his or her firearm off-duty. Although many police officials express support for such a law, noting that police officers may be the target of retaliation while off-duty or even after retirement, PERF urged serious consideration of the potential dangers to police officers the legislation would pose. For instance, an officer faced with using a firearm may not have the other standard equipment carried by a uniformed officer. In addition, a police officer who uses a firearm while dressed in plain clothes may face an identification problem when approached by on-duty police. *See also* BRADY HANDGUN VIOLENCE PREVENTION ACT; CLINTON, WILLIAM JEFFERSON (BILL); CONCEALED CARRY LAWS; FIREARMS OWNERS PROTECTION ACT; GUN CONTROL ACT OF 1968; MCCLURE, JAMES ALBERTAS; TRIGGER LOCKS; VOLKMER, HAROLD LEE.

Further Reading: Police Executive Research Forum Web site <www.policeforum.org>.

Potomac Institute

The Potomac Institute, located in Bethesda, Maryland, takes a contemporary liberal perspective on the issue of gun control in opposition to what it considers a joint conservative and libertarian position advocated by gun rights organizations. The Institute has supplanted the discontinued publication *Firearms Policy Journal*, which was distributed by Phoenix Publications of Hyattsville, Maryland. The Institute's motto is "It's not about guns . . . it's about citizenship," which emphasizes the role of citizens in a government-controlled militia rather than the individual right to possess firearms. The Institute advocates the registration of firearms, following what it considers the policy established by the Militia Act of 1792, which called for each citizen to be "enrolled" in the militia. The right to bear arms included a necessary obligation to serve the community.

The Institute claims that by registering all firearms the illegal trafficking in firearms could be significantly reduced primarily through the enforcement of local firearms regulations. Registration creates accountability in firearms ownership by connecting individuals to the uses to which their guns may be put. While the Institute regards as illegitimate the claims of gun rights advocates who assert a civil right to remain armed independent of the law, it also considers the agendas of gun control organizations ineffective in challenging the constitutional claims of pro-gun groups.

Among its activities, the Institute serves as a news service to report on gun violence and firearms policy, investigates and reveals the financial backing that gun rights groups provide for scholars, examines the background, objectives, and effectiveness of firearms legislation, analyzes the impact of current gun control strategies such as the public health approach, and encourages public debate of the gun control issue. The Institute holds that public health groups and gun control supporters must respond to the claim made by gun rights advocates that there is a right "to be armed outside the law."

The Institute rejects defenses of an individualistic right to keep and bear arms guaranteed in the Second Amendment, referring to them as "pseudoscholarship" conducted by researchers who receive support from conservative foundations. According to the Institute, articles appearing in law journals have contributed "enormous respectability to gun lobby claims and posturing." The gun rights-supported doctrine of an armed populace is considered incompatible with a society ruled by law. In a broad ideological swipe at the pro-gun movement, the Institute claims that opposition to gun control can be seen as part of a right wing reaction to New Deal reforms initiated by Democratic President Franklin Roosevelt's administration. Referring to the "libertarian fantasy" of individual sovereignty, the Institute contends that the gun rights agenda ultimately leads to support for anarchy.

While the Institute recognizes self-defense as a legitimate use of force, it contends that the National Rifle Association (NRA) exploits that claim to further the unacceptable position that individual sovereignty supports the right to possesses arms unhindered by government and as a potential means to oppose the government. The Institute sees no contradiction between the right to use firearms for self-defense and accountability to authority. Without legal controls, the individual possession of firearms could result in a domestic arms race that would fulfill the "anarchic libertarian fantasy" and facilitate gun interests' encouragement of gun ownership for self-defense purposes. The Institute holds that citizens may limit government coercion most effectively through the use of free institutions, not through a right outside the law to carry arms: "There can be no constitutional right to outflank this government with 'armed citizen guerrillas.'" *See also* HEALTH CARE PROFESSIONALS; LIBERTARIAN PARTY; MILITIA ACT OF 1792; NATIONAL RIFLE ASSOCIATION; SECOND AMENDMENT.

Further Reading: Potomac Institute Web site <www.us.net/potomac/index.html>.

Pratt, Larry (1943–)

Larry Pratt, executive director of Gun Owners of America (GOA), has for years represented the more fervent segment of the gun rights movement. He strongly opposes such measures as the Lautenberg Amendment (Domestic Violence Offender Gun Ban), which denies firearms ownership to anyone convicted of domestic violence, and the National Instant Check System (NICS) for those intending to purchase a firearm. He considers such measures intermediate steps toward the total banning of firearms. Pratt served as a Virginia state legislator and briefly as a Pat Buchanan campaign co-manager during Buchanan's run for the Republican presidential nomination in 1996.

Pratt vehemently opposes any government regulation of firearms, arguing that the greatest murderers of the twentieth century were governments. Victims of government are most often unarmed citizens. Pratt declares that proposals to have the Consumer Product Safety Commission regulate firearms are unconstitutional, and violate what he considers the clear meaning of the Second Amendment. Pratt believes that firearms in the possession of private citizens provide a major deterrent to and defense against crime.

Contrary to gun control advocates who point to such incidents as the Empire State Building shooting in their push for more stringent legislation, Pratt claims that such tragedies can occur only because citizens are largely unarmed and thus present easy targets for predators. He observes that although the shooter in the Empire State Building incident purchased a firearm in Florida, he did not use it there. Pratt claims that a more lenient concealed carry law in that state deterred the man. He has suggested that Rodney King, the African American in California who was beaten by police, would have been at a greater advantage had he been armed to defend himself.

Pratt entered the political limelight in 1996 when he resigned as one of Pat Buchanan's campaign co-chairpersons following news reports that he had spoken at meetings organized by white supremacists. One such meeting was held in Estes Park, Colorado, following the 1992 shoot-out between Randy Weaver and federal agents. Pete Peters, leader of Christian Identity, organized the meeting. It was also revealed that Pratt had appeared several times on Peters's radio talk show. Despite Buchanan's initial defense of Pratt against charges of associating with anti-

Larry Pratt is executive director of Gun Owners of America and a strong supporter of the right to keep and bear arms. *Courtesy of Gun Owners of America.*

Semitic groups, the GOA director left the campaign.

In his book, *Armed People Victorious*, published in 1990, Pratt defended the establishment of militias. He described efforts that were taken in Guatemala to develop armed civilian patrols and recommended that the United States reintroduce an armed citizenry for more effective defense. Basing his advocacy of the right to bear arms not only on the Second Amendment but also on biblical interpretation, Pratt contended that scripture goes beyond establishing a right to keep and bear arms and mandates the carrying of weapons. In defending militias, Pratt argued that "virtually all militias are lawful," that no laws regulating militias are needed, and that Congress should not investigate militia groups.

Pratt also argues that the provision of the Brady Handgun Violence Prevention Act calling for an instant check system for those wishing to purchase a handgun amounts to a "massive scheme to register law-abiding gun owners." He has criticized the National Rifle Association (NRA) for failing to express concern about a system he believes involves registration "by its very design." Pratt argues that the system, meant to eliminate the five-day waiting period, violates existing law and the Second Amendment. Pratt takes an all-or-nothing stand on the Lautenberg Amendment. He contends that simply modifying the original provision to, for instance, eliminate its retroactive nature, would make it more difficult to achieve a complete repeal in the future. Arguably, Pratt's more intense positions on firearms issues have inhibited more moderate gun rights advocates from compromising on gun control issues. *See also* BRADY HANDGUN VIOLENCE PREVENTION ACT; EMPIRE STATE BUILDING SHOOTING; GUN OWNERS OF AMERICA; LAUTENBERG AMENDMENT; NATIONAL INSTANT CHECK SYSTEM; NATIONAL RIFLE ASSOCIATION; RUBY RIDGE; SECOND AMENDMENT.

Further Reading: Gun Owners of America, "Brady Part II Launches Gun Registration Scheme," Press Release, June 1998; Gun Owners of America Web site <www.gunowners.org>; Larry Pratt, letter to Representative Bob Barr (May 23, 1997); Larry Pratt, "What Does the Bible Say About Gun Control?" (Springfield, VA: Gun Owners of America, n.d.); "Who Is Larry Pratt?" *New Republic* (March 11, 1996), 9.

Presbyterian Church (U.S.A.) (PCUSA)

Since the late 1960s, the Presbyterian Church (U.S.A.) (PCUSA), and its predecessor organizations have taken a resolute stand in favor of more stringent gun control regulations at the national and state levels. The General Assembly of the PCUSA called for "control [of] the sale and possession of firearms of all kinds." In 1976, the General Assembly reaffirmed this statement, but modified the resolution to exclude "shotguns and rifles used legitimately by sportsmen." At the 1988 meeting of the General Assembly, the Church again affirmed its position on gun control.

The PCUSA was formed in 1983 through a union of the Presbyterian Church in the U.S. (PCUS), known as the "southern branch," and the United Presbyterian Church in the U.S.A. (UPCUSA), called the "northern branch." The Presbyterian church is generally considered a part of mainstream Christian churches and representative of their views. The Presbyterian Church in the United States has been noted for developing various factions and coalitions. In the 1920s, J. Gresham Machen, a conservative Presbyterian theologian, left Princeton Theological Seminary to found a more conservative wing of the Presbyterian Church. Contemporary theological descendants of Machen and the Westminster Theological Seminary that he founded are far less sympathetic to such social issues as gun control.

In 1990, the PCUSA General Assembly approved a more extensive statement on gun control, supporting "gun control at federal, state, and local levels as the most effective response to the present crisis of gun violence." The General Assembly called for the federal government to enact legislation to regulate the importation, manufacture, sale, and possession of firearms and ammunition by the general public, and suggested that legislation could include the registration and licensing of gun purchasers and owners; background checks to determine possible disqualifying circumstances, such as a criminal conviction; and waiting periods for those intending to purchase firearms. The Assembly recommended "regulation of subsequent sale." The Church called for laws to be enacted at the state and local levels if federal legislation were delayed, a strategy that gun control advocates have pursued. Finally, the Assembly requested that government agencies at all levels provide "significant assistance" to victims of gun violence and their families.

Further Reading: Presbyterian Church (U.S.A.) Web site http://www.pcusa.org; Presbyterian Church (U.S.A.), Public Policy Statements of the Presbyterian Church (U.S.A.): "Gun Control" (Louisville, KY: PCUSA, 1996).

Presser v. Illinois (1886)

In *Presser v. Illinois* (116 U.S. 256, 1886), the U.S. Supreme Court heard an appeal from Herman Presser who was charged and convicted in 1879 of violating sections five and six of the Military Code of Illinois. The Code made it illegal for any group of individuals other than the organized volunteer militia of Illinois and U.S. troops to combine as a military organization or to parade with arms in any municipality of the state without first receiving a license from the governor.

Presser belonged to an organization called the *Lehr und Wehr Verein* (Education and Defense Society), which had been incorporated under the General Incorporation Laws of Illinois for the purpose of "improving the mental and bodily condition of its members, so as to qualify them for the duties of citizens of a republic." Among other activities, the members were to receive training in military exercises. In December 1879, Presser led a group of 400 members in a parade through the streets of Chicago. The members were armed with rifles and Presser, on horseback, carried a cavalry sword. The company of men had not received a license from the governor to parade as part of the state militia, was not a segment of either the organized state militia or the U.S. military, and had no official status under the national militia law.

After being found guilty of violating the Illinois Military Code, Presser appealed to the Supreme Court of Illinois, which affirmed the original decision. Presser then appealed the conviction to the U.S. Supreme Court on a writ of error. The plaintiff argued for the invalidity of the statute under which he was indicted and convicted, claiming that the Illinois legislature had wielded a power reserved to the national government under Article I, sections 8 and 10, and the Second Amendment of the U.S. Constitution. Presser also maintained that sections five and six of Article XI of the Military Code violated the protection against bills of attainder and ex post facto laws within Article I, section 9 of the U.S. Constitution (a claim the Court quickly dismissed), and the prohibition against states making laws abridging the privileges of U.S. citizens found in the Fourteenth Amendment to the U.S. Constitution

The Court ruled that the sections of the Military Code of Illinois that forbade groups of individuals from associating as military organizations or to parade with arms in municipalities unless the organization has received authorization did not violate the right of the people to keep and bear arms. Although the Court indicated that states cannot prohibit people from keeping and bearing arms, thus hindering a national resource for maintaining public security, it concluded that the sections at issue did not lead to that result.

The right to associate voluntarily as a military organization and to parade with arms independent of congressional or state legislative sanction fails as a claimed attribute of national citizenship. Because establishing a military organization and parading with arms are actions fundamentally under the control of government, no right to do so can be claimed without legal authorization. If this authority were denied to government, the Court reasoned, then the state would lack the ability to disperse groups intent on sedition and could not put down armed mobs about to riot.

Responding to Presser's claim that the articles at issue in the Code conflict with acts of Congress dealing with the organization of the militia, the Court stated that the purpose of these sections was to prohibit voluntary military groups with no legal authorization from organizing or parading with arms, and from obstructing the organization of the militia authorized by Congress. Therefore, these sections do not conflict with laws of Congress dealing with the militia. To the charge that the incorporation of the *Lehr und Wehr Verein* under the laws of Illinois constituted a license from the governor to parade, the Court stated that this was not a federal question and therefore was not an appropriate subject for a federal court ruling. *See also* Fourteenth Amendment; Militia Act of 1792; Second Amendment.

Further Reading: Earl R. Kruschke, *The Right to Keep and Bear Arms: A Continuing American Dilemma* (Springfield, IL: Charles C. Thomas, 1985); *Presser v. Illinois*, 116 U.S. 256 (1886).

Printz v. United States (1997)

In *Printz v. United States* (Docket No. 95-1478, U.S. Supreme Court, 1997), the U.S. Supreme Court held unconstitutional a provision of the Brady Handgun Violence Prevention Act that required chief law enforcement officers in local jurisdictions to conduct background checks on prospective handgun purchasers. Jay Printz, sheriff of Ravalli County, Montana, challenged the authority of the federal government to require him to assume a function of the national government, arguing that the federal mandate diverted critical resources from local law enforcement responsibilities. While invalidating mandated background checks, the Court left intact the law's five-day waiting period provision and the requirement that gun dealers submit to local authorities information about gun purchasers, with the proviso that any background check conducted by local officials must be voluntary.

The background check requirement fell victim to the Court's increased concern for maintaining state sovereignty. In the 5-to-4 decision, Justice Antonin Scalia, speaking for the majority, stated that, "Congress cannot compel the states to enact or enforce a federal regulatory program." The majority found no evidence in constitutional history for the claim that the national government may issue commands to state and local executive officials without the consent of the respective states.

The Court's decision was consistent with the 1995 ruling in *United States v. Lopez* in which the Court determined that Congress had exceeded its authority to regulate interstate commerce by banning guns within 1,000 feet of public schools. In the *Printz* ruling, the majority relied on the doctrine of dual sovereignty, holding that both the federal and state governments retain an inviolable realm of action independent of the other. What might otherwise by considered a legitimate power derived from the Necessary and Proper Clause of Article I, Section 8 of the Constitution is invalid because the Brady law violates the constitutional system of state sovereignty.

In his dissent from the majority decision, Justice John Paul Stevens emphasized national concern over the role of handguns in violent crime. Congress should have the right to deal with a national emergency, enlisting the help of local officials. He compared the background check to a federal requirement that local police officers report to the federal government the names of missing children. Stevens further argued that the majority, intending to protect state sovereignty, ironically had invited the federal government to create a large new bureaucracy to administer the policy.

Gun control opponents hailed the decision as a victory for their side. They focused particularly on the separate opinion of Justice Clarence Thomas, who, although in the majority, went further than his colleagues in suggesting that the Second Amendment protection of the right to keep and bear arms limits the national government's authority to control guns. Supporters of the Brady law, who claimed the decision was only a minor setback, gave their attention to Justice Sandra Day O'Connor's opinion, also in the majority, that the Court's ruling did not spell the end of the objectives of the law, for local police may still voluntarily conduct background checks and Congress may legitimately provide financial help to local law enforcement agencies that continue the checks.

The decision was expected to have minimal impact on the operation of the Brady law, especially since the federal government was in the process of developing a national computerized system for conducting background checks that became operational in November 1998. The Court declined to rule on the appropriateness of the waiting period and the requirement that gun dealers provide information to government officials. *See also* BRANDY HANDGUN VIOLENCE PROTECTION ACT; NATIONAL INSTANT CHECK SYSTEM; SECOND AMENDMENT; STATE GUN STATUTES; *UNITED STATES V. LOPEZ* (1995).

Further Reading: *Printz, Sheriff/Coroner, Ravalli County, Montana v. United States,* Docket No. 95-1478 (U.S. Supreme Court, 1997).

Product Liability Lawsuits

Gun control advocates argue that product liability lawsuits can provide opportunities to control the ill effects of firearms that legislative efforts have failed to bring about because of opposition from gun rights forces. They claim that the civil justice system can help reduce violence associated with firearms in two ways. First, firearms producers may be sued for defects in the design and manufacture of firearms and ammunition that lead to injuries to gun owners. Second, manufacturers and sellers of firearms may be held financially responsible for injuries or deaths because they sold firearms to individuals they should have known were highly likely to use the weapons illegally. Table 11 provides a breakdown of causes of injury deaths in the United States, indicating that firearms are the second most frequent cause of such deaths.

Recent lawsuits indicate that the judicial systems at the state and national levels are more willing to entertain the possibility of product liability in the case of firearms. For instance, in 1979, the Supreme Court of Alaska affirmed a punitive damage award to a plaintiff who was injured by the Old Model Ruger single-action revolver. While loading the revolver, it slipped from his hand and fired, shooting him in the leg. Claims were made that there had been over 600 accidental discharges of the revolver, which was manufactured from 1953 to 1972. The Supreme Court of Alaska ruled that although the manufacturer was aware of the defective design and that injuries and deaths had resulted, production of the revolver continued.

A 1994 lawsuit in Texas involved the Remington Model 700 rifle. The plaintiff charged that the Remington Company knew that the rifle could fire without the trigger being pulled, but did not take steps to improve the design. The jury awarded the plaintiff $15 million in punitive damages. The manufacturers of Saturday night specials also have been the target of civil suits. Although gun rights advocates claim that such firearms can be excellent defensive weapons, others argue that they often fail to meet minimum safety and design standards. Of five California companies that manufacture such weapons, at least two have faced product liability lawsuits.

Lawsuits have been filed to recover damages from firearms manufacturers and sales outlets for injuries caused by so-called "high-risk" gun owners. A California gun store was sued for failing to conduct a sufficiently accurate identification of an assault weapon purchaser. The owner used the gun to shoot and kill a man, whose widow filed suit against the gun outlet. She recovered $400,000 in an out-of-court settlement. Such cases, gun control advocates argue, encourage firearms dealers to take greater care that they sell weapons only to purchasers qualified under the law.

Wayne LaPierre, executive vice president of the National Rifle Association (NRA), has expressed his support for the firearms industry's attempts to bring about tort reform to limit punitive damage awards in civil suits. He has argued that frequent lawsuits tend to restrict manufacturers and lead to higher prices for the consumer. In early 1996, Congress passed legislation that would bring about tort reform, but President Bill Clinton vetoed the bill, giving as one of his reasons the unacceptable effect of the legislation on the victims of firearms violence. Gun control supporters assert that the legislation would have severely limited the ability of victims to gain compensation and would have reduced the motivation of firearms manufacturers to improve the safety of their products. *See also* CLINTON, WILLIAM JEFFERSON (BILL); CONSUMER PRODUCT SAFETY; LAPIERRE, WAYNE; NATIONAL RIFLE ASSOCIATION: REMINGTON, ELIPHALET, II; RUGER, WILLIAM BATTERMAN (BILL); SATURDAY NIGHT SPECIAL.

Further Reading: Kristen Rand, *Lawyers, Guns, and Money: The Impact of Tort Restrictions on Firearms Safety and Gun Control* (Washington, DC: Violence Policy Center, 1996); Josh Sugarmann and Kristen Rand, *Cease Fire: A Comprehensive Strategy to Reduce Firearms Violence* (Washington, DC: Violence Policy Center, 1997).

TABLE 11	
LEADING CAUSES OF INJURY DEATH BY MANNER OF DEATH: UNITED STATES, 1995	
Motor Vehicles	29%
Firearms	24%
Poisonings	11%
Falls	8%
Suffocation	7%
Drowning, fire and burns, and cutting and piercing injuries	9%
Other	12%

Source: Health, United States 1996–97 and *Injury Chartbook* (Washington, DC: Department of Health and Human Services, 1997), p. 24.

Project Exile

Project Exile, a joint federal and state government effort begun in Richmond, Virginia, charges felons found in possession of firearms with violation of federal firearms restrictions. Although recent years have seen a general nationwide drop in violent crime, Republican Governor James Gilmore attributed a significant drop in the Virginia murder rate to the initiation of Project Exile. The U.S. Attorney's Office in Richmond estimated that the number of gun deaths in Richmond declined 41 percent from the start of the Project in February 1997 until October 31, 1998.

Beginning in November 1998, Governor Gilmore, a member of the National Rifle Association (NRA), appeared in NRA print advertising praising Project Exile and stating that Virginia had "put politics aside" for a truly effective policy toward crime. The NRA considers Project Exile one way of reducing crime without restricting what it considers the rights of law-abiding gun owners and recommends that it be used nationwide. The project adheres to the advice of many gun rights advocates, who have asserted that existing legislation should be strictly enforced against criminals.

The joint federal-state program had been extended to Hampton Roads in December 1997 and to Norfolk early in 1998. The governor noted that through the federally supported program, 350 felons were arrested for illegal possession of firearms and 418 weapons had been confiscated. In October 1998, Governor Gilmore announced that the program would be expanded throughout the state as a way of punishing repeat offenders, recommending that the state Assembly pass the needed legislation. The state Assembly approved the legislation in March 1999 and Governor Gilmore signed it into law in April. Among its provisions, the law called for any person convicted of 1) possessing a firearm on school grounds, intending to use it or showing it in a threatening manner, 2) possessing a firearm after having been convicted of a violent felony, or 3) possessing a firearm while intending to sell drugs, shall be ineligible for probation and shall receive a minimum mandatory sentence of five years.

The governor pledged that Virginia law enforcement officials will prosecute repeat offenders "in a prompt and efficient manner." Other states were looking to Virginia for continued indication that Project Exile has a genuine impact on violent crime. However, some researchers have already concluded that enhanced sentencing laws have little effect on the rate of illegal firearm use. *See also* NATIONAL RIFLE ASSOCIATION.

Further Reading: James Gilmore, "Project Exile for the Commonwealth," Office of the Governor Press Office, October 6, 1998, <www.state.va.us/governor/speech/exilesp.htm>; Holly A. Heyser, "Gov. Gilmore's Latest Role: Starring in an NRA Ad," *Pilot Online News*, November 13, 1998, <http://

/ss003.infi.net/pilot/pilotonline/news/
nw1113nra.html>.

Project Lifeline

Project Lifeline is an appendage of the Center to Prevent Handgun Violence (CPHV) and is sponsored by the Handgun Epidemic Lowering Plan (HELP) and Physicians for Social Responsibility (PSR), organizations of health care professionals striving to prevent firearm violence. Project Lifeline declares that it is not involved in government lobbying and does not promote a ban on handguns. The organization emphasizes three basic messages to discourage the ownership of firearms: 1) guns are the most lethal means of violent injury; 2) handguns are responsible for the highest number of gun-related deaths and injuries; and 3) handgun injuries and deaths are preventable. The organization encourages health care professionals to educate the public regarding the dangers of handguns and possible preventive strategies to reduce deaths and injuries related to firearms. Advising parents to think carefully before allowing a firearm into the home, the organization claims that a child can more easily empty a handgun than a bottle of aspirin. The organization distributes a quarterly newsletter that keeps members informed about strategies for firearm injury prevention and about the experiences of various participants in the program.

Project Lifeline has over 47 national health-related organizations serving as partners, including the American Academy of Child and Adolescent Psychiatry, the American Academy of Pediatrics, the American Association of Public Health Physicians, and the American Public Health Association. In addition, the Project has 2,000 individual members, primarily health professionals. Although the Project assesses no membership fees, organizations that become partners agree to distribute materials and individual members promise to offer public education regarding firearms in their local communities. The organization makes available to partners one-minute radio spots that convey a message warning about the dangers of firearms and offers sample letters to the editor that members may then send to local newspapers.

The Project, which discourages keeping firearms in the home, has publicized the claim that guns kept in the home are 43 times more likely to kill a member of the family or a friend than to kill an intruder, an assertion that gun rights advocates have vigorously challenged. The organization disseminates data indicating that in 1995 fourteen children aged 19 and younger were killed by firearms each day. In 1994, the leading cause of death among black males aged 15 to 34 was firearms-related homicide. In 1995, the overall death toll from firearms in the United States was nearly 36,000. This figure includes deaths from all causes, including homicide, accident, and suicide. The organization notes that in 1996, 10,744 people were murdered with firearms. That figure represented roughly two-thirds of all homicides. Eighty percent of firearms-related murders were attributed to handguns. The Project further claimed that only 176 of the gun-related killings were justifiable homicides. The organization takes special note of the rate of handgun-related murders in various countries, observing that in 1996 there were 2 handgun-related murders in New Zealand, 15 in Japan, 30 in Great Britain, and 9,390 in the United States. Noting that there are nearly 200 million privately owned firearms in the United States, the Project contends that the large difference in the rates between the United States and other nations is strongly related to the availability of guns. *See also* CENTER TO PREVENT HANDGUN VIOLENCE; PHYSICIANS FOR SOCIAL RESPONSIBILITY.

Further Reading: Project Lifeline Web site <www.handguncontrol.org/protecting/D3/d3pr/ife.htm>.

Q

Quilici v. Village of Morton Grove (1981)

In an appeal from the U.S. District Court for the Northern District of Illinois, Eastern Division, the U.S. Court of Appeals for the Seventh Circuit in *Quilici v. Village of Morton Grove* (532 F. Supp. 1169 N.D. Ill., 1981) affirmed the decision of the district court that the Village of Morton Grove's Ordinance No. 81-11, which prohibits the possession of handguns within the borders of the village, is constitutional. In the ordinance, Morton Grove officials declared that the availability of firearms increased the probability of gun-related deaths and injuries and that handguns are strongly related to the commission of such crimes as homicide, assault, and armed robbery, and are responsible for accidental injuries and deaths.

Victor Quilici began his challenge of the ordinance in state court, but at the instigation of Morton Grove, the case was shifted to the federal court system and combined with two additional challenges to the ordinance. The plaintiffs claimed that the ordinance violated article I, section 22 of the state constitution of Illinois, which states that, "Subject only to the police power, the right of the individual citizen to keep and bear arms shall not be infringed." In addition, the claim was made that the ordinance violated the Second, Ninth, and Fourteenth Amendments to the U.S. Constitution.

Morton Grove held that section 22 of the state constitution guaranteed the keeping of some, but not all, firearms. The court of appeals agreed with the district court that the police power in Illinois justifies limiting the right to keep and bear arms. The court argued, first, that the state constitution grants the right to keep and bear arms, but not specifically handguns, and second, that although the constitutional framers intended handguns to be among those firearms conditionally protected, they also intended that local governments could employ their police power to restrict or prohibit the possession of handguns.

In response to the appellants' argument that allowing municipalities to exercise the police power to enact dissimilar gun control laws would lead to an absurd situation involving a crazy quilt of various ordinances across the state, the court declared that the state constitution allows home rule charters for local governments, permitting them to govern their own affairs as they deem appropriate in a wide number of areas, including regulation for protection of the public health, safety, morals, and welfare, and to tax and assume debt. Whether wise policy or not, municipalities may set their own standards regarding gun control because the state constitution only prohibits a ban on all firearms. As long as the Morton Grove ordinance does not prohibit all firearms, it does not violate the provisions of the state constitution. In addition, the court noted that there exists empirical evidence that such legislation may lower the number of accidents and deaths attributed to handguns. The court of appeals concurred with the district court's ruling that the ordinance is intended to preserve the health and safety of Morton Grove residents, is a valid exercise of the municipal police power, and does not violate any rights guaranteed by the state constitution.

As for the Second Amendment, the court of appeals noted that this provision of the national Constitution, according to *Presser v. Illinois* (1886), is applicable to the national Congress and not state legislatures. The appellants argued that, given the large number of provisions of the Bill of Rights that have been determined to apply to the states via the Fourteenth Amendment, the Second Amendment has been implicitly made applicable to the states along with other rights. The court rejected this argument, noting that the U.S. Supreme Court has explicitly rejected the assumption that the entire Bill of Rights now applies to the states. The court associated the right to bear arms with the preservation of state militias. Arguing that individually owned handguns are not military weapons, they concluded that the national Constitution does not protect a right to keep and bear handguns.

The appellants argued that the Morton Grove ordinance violates the Ninth Amendment to the U.S. Constitution, which involves the protection of "certain rights" other than those enumerated in the constitution. The appellants had in mind an unwritten, fundamental right to own or possess firearms. The court rejected this idea, indicating that the Supreme Court has never identified any specific right protected by this amendment. The court concluded that the Morton Grove ordinance banning handguns is a proper exercise of the police power that violates neither article I, section 22 of the Illinois state constitution nor the Second, Ninth, or Fourteenth Amendments to the U.S. Constitution.

One justice filed a dissenting opinion, raising the potential difficulty of a hodgepodge of local ordinances applicable not only to local residents but also to those traveling through the local area. Such ordinances were an undue limitation on the right to travel and interfered with commerce. The judge focused on a basic constitutional right to protect home and family, believing that the ordinance violates the fundamental right to "privacy in the home," limited, according to the judge, only by private, noncommercial activities, as long as the general welfare is not endangered. He concluded that the prohibition on handgun possession is not necessary to protecting the public welfare. *See also* FOURTH AMENDMENT; MORTON GROVE, ILLINOIS; NINTH AMENDMENT; *PRESSER V. ILLINOIS* (1886); SECOND AMENDMENT.

Further Reading: Earl R. Kruschke, *The Right to Keep and Bear Arms* (Springfield, IL: Charles C. Thomas, 1985); *Quilici v. Village of Morton Grove,* 532 F. Supp. 1169 N.D. Ill. (1981).

R

Reagan, Ronald (1911–)

Ronald Reagan, who served as U.S. president from 1981 to 1989, gained a reputation as an uncritical supporter of gun rights. In 1980, Reagan, a Republican, became the first presidential candidate to receive the official endorsement of the National Rifle Association (NRA). Although Reagan had narrowly escaped a 1981 assassination attempt in which his press secretary James Brady was critically wounded, in 1983 he became the first president to attend the NRA annual convention, where he pledged to support the goals of the organization. Reagan declared that the U.S. Constitution does not ordain the right to keep and bear arms, but states that the pre-existing right to keep and bear arms shall not be infringed. The president, a life member of the NRA, promised that, "We will never disarm any American who seeks to protect his or her family from fear or harm."

The Republican platform on which Reagan campaigned in 1980 stated that the party supported the right of citizens to keep and bear arms, announced opposition to federal registration of firearms, and supported longer sentences for using firearms in the commission of a crime. The platform went on to advocate the repeal of provisions of the Gun Control Act of 1968 that "do not significantly impact on crime but serve rather to restrain the law-abiding citizen in his legitimate use of firearms." The 1984 platform on which Reagan ran for re-election stated that citizens should not be criticized for "exercising their constitutional rights." The 1980 platform foreshadowed the Firearms Owners Protection that was passed by Congress and signed by Reagan in 1986. However, the Reagan administration played a minimal role in passage of the legislation.

In his first year as president, Reagan moved against the Bureau of Alcohol, Tobacco, and Firearms (BATF), the agency responsible for administering federal firearms legislation and one of the NRA's major targets. The president stated his intention to abolish the agency, shifting responsibilities to the Internal Revenue Service (IRS) and the Customs Service. Agents involved in explosives and arson regulation and enforcement would be transferred to the Secret Service. Although the NRA ultimately withdrew its support for the proposal to eliminate the BATF, the agency underwent budget cuts during the Reagan presidency.

Despite his staunch support for gun rights organizations, Reagan signed two gun control measures. In 1986, Reagan signed a bill banning so-called armor piercing bullets (bullets composed of certain hard metals such as tungsten alloys, steel, or bronze). The NRA had raised no objections to this measure. In November 1988, he signed a bill that prohibited the production, importation, and sale of weapons composed primarily of plastic that could not be sensed by metal detectors. However, in May 1986, Reagan signed into law a more significant measure, the Firearms Owners Protection (McClure-Volkmer) Act, which significantly weakened the Gun Control Act of 1968 by, for instance, limiting the BATF's record keeping authority and allowing resumption of mail-order ammunition sales.

After leaving office Reagan altered his stand on gun control legislation. In March 1991, on the tenth anniversary of the assassination attempt, he announced his support for the Brady Handgun Violence Prevention Act and urged Congress to pass the measure. He spoke to President George Bush at the White House, urging him to shift his position on the bill. In an article published in the *New York Times*, Reagan speculated that the attempt on his life might never have occurred if the Brady bill had been law in 1981. However, some on both sides of the gun control debate were quick to observe that the would-be assassin would not have been prevented from purchasing the weapon and that the waiting period would not have made any difference because the gun was purchased five months before the attempted assassination. In addition to supporting the Brady bill, Reagan argued in favor of a ban on assault weapons. Although not the crucial factor in passage of further gun control legislation, Reagan's support added to the momentum of the pro-gun control forces. *See also* BRADY, JAMES; BRADY HANDGUN VIOLENCE PREVENTION ACT; BUREAU OF ALCOHOL, TOBACCO; AND FIREARMS; BUSH, GEORGE; FIREARMS OWNERS PROTECTION ACT; GUN CONTROL ACT OF 1968; MCCLURE, JAMES ALBERTAS; NATIONAL RIFLE ASSOCIATION; VOLKMER, HAROLD LEE.

Further Reading: Gregg Lee Carter, *The Gun Control Movement* (New York: Twayne, 1997); Steven A. Holmes, "Gun Control Bill Backed by Reagan in Appeal to Bush," *New York Times* (March 29, 1991); Ronald Reagan, "Why I'm for the Brady Bill," *New York Times* (March 29, 1991); Robert J. Spitzer, *The Politics of Gun Control*, 2nd ed. (New York: Chatham House, 1998); Josh Sugarmann, *National Rifle Association: Money, Firepower and Fear* (Washington, DC: National Press, 1992).

Remington, Eliphalet, II (1793–1861)

A gunsmith and firearms manufacturer, Eliphalet Remington II added significantly to the mystique of firearms in the United States. The Remington company provided military weapons to the United States during major conflicts and still produces rifles today. Throughout its existence, the company has attempted to diversify, engaging in production of typewriters and sewing machines as well as firearms.

Remington's father, who built a forge after he moved to Staley Creek, New York, trained his son in blacksmithing. In August 1816, Remington manufactured his first rifle at his father's blacksmith shop. He traveled to Utica, New York, to have the barrel rifled, and when he returned, Remington added the other essential parts of the weapon, including hand-made screws and pins. Remington soon gained a reputation for gunmaking in New York. After four years, he had sold 200 gun barrels and complete rifles.

In 1828, Remington purchased 100 acres on the Mohawk River for an arms factory. When the building was completed in 1832, the new factory doubled the output of Remington's enterprise. With increased capacity, Remington began traveling to advertise his product. When his son Philo was old enough, Remington brought him into the business.

The war with Mexico in 1846 proved fortuitous for the Remington gun making operation. When the John Griffiths Company of Cincinnati, Ohio, failed to meet a government contract to produce 5,000 muskets, Remington bought the contract. In 1847, the Remington company added to its business, filling a contract with the U.S. Navy.

In 1849, the company experimented with the handgun market, but no model it produced represented a serious challenge to Colt or Smith and Wesson. With the onset of the Civil War in 1861, Remington expanded the production plant in anticipation of what would amount to $30 million in government contracts. By the end of the war, the com-

Eliphalet Remington II was one of the foremost American gunmakers of the nineteenth century. *Corbis-Bettmann.*

pany was producing nearly 1,000 rifles per day. Remington, approaching 70 years of age, drove himself too hard in the early days of wartime production. He died in August 1861 and his son Philo succeeded him as company president.

Following the war, the company continued to diversify, producing agricultural implements. With surplus military rifles on the American market, the company sought foreign business, particularly with the French government, and had significant success selling the Rolling Block rifle. This rifle also became a preferred weapon among frontiersmen. In the 1870s, Remington produced other goods, including fire engines and steam trolley cars, none of which returned significant profits. The company introduced the typewriter in 1873, but when sales were disappointing, Philo sold this portion of the business to support the armory. Ironically, the typewriter enterprise subsequently proved profitable, while the Remington Company sank inexorably into bankruptcy.

In March 1888, Marcellus Hartley, founder of the Union Metallic Cartridge Company, participated in a buyout of Remington. Hartley became president of the newly renamed Remington Arms Company.

Following Hartley's death in 1902, his grandson, Marcellus (Marcy) Hartley Dodge assumed control of the company. The company employed exhibitions to market its firearms and sponsored Annie Oakley's trick-shooting performances and other shooting events designed to attract and entertain prospective customers.

As World War I began in 1914, Remington geared up for war production. Both Great Britain and France signed contracts with the company. An agreement with Czar Nicholas II was nullified by the Russian Revolution of 1917, but the U.S. government ultimately agreed to purchase most of the rifles produced for the Russian sale. Remington produced nearly 70 percent of the rifles used by American forces in World War I. Following the war and the resulting fall in demand for new firearms, Remington diversified once more, introducing such products as knives and cash registers, but the company also responded to the increasing demand for hunting rifles and ammunition.

In 1933, Charles Davis assumed the office of company president. Despite the Depression, the new president succeeded in keeping the company in the black while at the same time increasing employee wages, establishing a standard 40-hour work week, and introducing such innovations as a bonus plan and improved employee insurance. World War II brought another vast expansion in demand for rifles. In 1943, the number of workers was 20 times the number employed in 1939. Even though Remington planned for decreasing production over a year before the war's end, peace brought an oversupply of ammunition, an important component of production. The company quickly introduced new sporting-gun models, which continue to the present to be the primary focus of its firearms production. *See also* COLT, SAMUEL; RUGER, WILLIAM BATTERMAN (BILL); SMITH AND WESSON; WINCHESTER, OLIVER FISHER.

Further Reading: K.D. Kirkland, *America's Premier Gunmakers* (New York: Mallard, 1990); Wayne Van Zwoll, *America's Great Gunmakers* (Hackensack, NJ: Stoeger, 1992).

Reno, Janet (1938–)

Conservatives, gun rights organizations, and militia groups have targeted President Bill Clinton's attorney general, Janet Reno, for her active support of gun control legislation. Stating in 1993 that youth violence was "the greatest single crime problem faced in America," Reno has focused attention primarily on preventing firearm violence among youth, supporting various programs of the U.S. Department of Justice (USDOJ) that are intended to keep guns away from young people. She received severe criticism from pro-gun organizations for her approval of the Federal Bureau of Investigation (FBI) raid on the Branch Davidian headquarters in Waco, Texas, in 1993.

Reno received a B.S. in chemistry from Cornell University in 1960 and a law degree from Harvard Law School in 1963. She served as staff director of the judiciary committee of the Florida House of Representatives, contributing to a state constitutional revision that paved the way for a reorganized state court system. She was counsel for the Florida senate's criminal justice committee for the revision of the state criminal code. Reno was ultimately appointed state attorney for Dade County and was elected for successive terms in 1978, 1981, 1985, 1989, and 1991. President Clinton appointed her U.S. attorney general in 1993. As attorney general, Reno has a reputation for fierce independence from partisan considerations.

In 1994, Reno announced several Department of Justice youth grant programs, including efforts to upset the illegal firearms trade, to reduce youth demand for guns, and to make travel to school safer. The attorney general announced that such action was necessary to prevent gun use from becoming a normal part of the lives of youths. The crime bill approved that year included a federal ban on youth handgun possession, punishments for those selling guns to minors, and crime prevention programs aimed at youth.

When the Republicans won control of both houses of Congress in 1994, Reno and the president not only found it more difficult to push for new gun control initiatives, but had to fight attempts to repeal existing legislation. In 1996, the House of Representatives approved a repeal of the 1994 assault weapons ban. When the Senate considered the same measure, the attorney general stated publicly that such a repeal would be completely unjustified, claiming that the number of assault weapons associated with criminal activity had fallen 18 percent during the ban's first year of operation. Although the repeal ultimately failed, the president and the attorney general were even opposed by several Democrats in Congress.

Janet Reno, attorney general in the Clinton administration, has angered conservative and gun rights groups with her strong support for gun control legislation. *Courtesy of the U.S. Department of Justice.*

Responding to a series of school shootings, Reno announced in June 1998 a renewed commitment to reducing youth violence through a number of initiatives, including limiting access to firearms. Regretting Congress's failure to pass legislation mandating safety locks for new handguns, Reno pledged to continue efforts to pass this legislation, which she termed a "common sense, reasonable solution to make sure that guns are not accessible to children."

Reno announced a new advertising campaign developed through cooperation between the Office of Juvenile Justice and Delinquency Prevention in the Bureau of Justice Assistance and the National Crime Prevention Council. One purpose of the campaign is to inform parents of the risks that children face when an unlocked gun is kept in the home. The attorney general noted that school officials are encouraged to deal seriously with threats of violence and gang activity. *See also* ASSAULT WEAPONS BAN; BUREAU OF ALCOHOL, TOBACCO, AND FIREARMS; CLINTON, WILLIAM JEFFERSON (BILL); JONESBORO, ARKANSAS, SCHOOL SHOOTING; LITTLETON, COLORADO, SCHOOL SHOOTING; SCHOOLS AND GUNS; TRIGGER LOCKS; WACO, TEXAS, RAID.

Further Reading: Michael Isikoff, "NRA Fires Lobbyist Over Reno Rumor," *Washington Post* (March 1993), A1; Janet Reno, *News Conference, United States Department of Justice*, July 23, 1998; U.S. Department of Justice Web site <www.usdoj.gov>.

Roberti-Roos Assault Weapons Act

In 1989, the California legislature passed the Roberti-Roos Assault Weapons Act, which became the first measure in the United States to prohibit the sale, possession, and manufacture of semi-automatic, military style firearms. The assault weapons ban had heightened political significance because it was enacted despite major opposition from pro-gun organizations, particularly the National Rifle Association (NRA). During legislative consideration of the measure, the NRA enlisted the services of an ad agency that placed several newspaper and television advertisements criticizing the bill. The organization referred to the ban as "unworkable, inefficient, and money-wasting." Gun control supporters were encouraged by the bill's passage, looking forward to campaigns for legislation in other states and at the national level. Some of those active in the California battle were requested to support ban efforts in other parts of the country.

The Assault Weapons Act demonstrates the tendency of public officials to push for new gun control legislation immediately following a multiple murder incident involving the use of firearms. The campaign for an assault weapons ban began in fall 1988, gathering major support particularly in the Oakland and San Francisco areas. Various public officials, including police chiefs and prosecutors, held public hearings, conducted legal research, and assisted in preparing draft legislation. However, supporters of the ban admitted that the tragic murder of five schoolchildren in Stockton, California, by a man wielding a Chinese-made AK-47 semi-automatic rifle electrified the movement to work for passage. Supporters ultimately won the necessary votes in the California legislature for final passage.

The proposed ban, sponsored by Democrat David A. Roberti in the California Senate and Democrat Mike Roos in the Assembly, received support from leading public officials. Governor George Deukmejian, a conservative Republican who generally opposed additional gun control legislation, backed the assault weapons ban. Two other influential officials, Daryl F. Gates, Los Angeles police chief, and Sheriff Glen Craig of Sacramento County, came out in favor of the bill. Although similar bills in 1985 and 1986 had failed to gain legislative approval, the broad support of public officials and the groundswell of approval in the general public convinced enough legislators to support this measure.

The Assault Weapons Act banned over 20 specific assault weapons, including the AK-47, one of the more widely used weapons worldwide. The act allowed private citizens already legally in possession of assault weapons to keep them. However, owners were required to register the weapons. Because a ban in one state would have limited effect due to the possibility of weapons being brought into the state illegally, the legislation appeared to argue forcefully for the nationwide ban that was finally enacted in 1994. State actions like the Roberti-Roos Act have forced the NRA and other pro-gun groups to pay greater attention to state legislative actions nation-wide. *See also* AK-47; ASSAULT WEAPONS BAN; NATIONAL RIFLE ASSOCIATION; STOCKTON, CALIFORNIA, SHOOTING.

Further Reading: *New York Times*, March 14, 1989, A2, D28; March 19, 1, 5.

Ruby Ridge

The unfortunate outcome of the standoff at Ruby Ridge, Idaho, in 1992 heightened suspicion of legal authority and led to the formation of militia groups that insisted upon the right to defend themselves with firearms, not only against criminals, but in opposition to government. The events at Ruby Ridge incurred the special ire of gun organizations, for the case began with an illegal weapons charge against Randy Weaver. Before Weaver finally surrendered in August 1992, three people lay dead from gunfire: a U.S. marshall and Weaver's wife and son.

Randy and Vicki Weaver became involved in the Christian Identity movement soon after their 1971 marriage in Cedar Rapids, Iowa. They adhered to a doctrine of white supremacy that claimed the United States had come under the control of ZOG, Zionist Occupied Government, an organization controlled by Jews who were carrying out a master plan to establish the New World Order. In 1983, Weaver moved his family from Iowa to Ruby Ridge, located in an isolated section of Idaho close to the Canadian border. He accumulated several weapons, including two semi-automatics, a rifle, a shotgun, a revolver, and a 9-mm pistol. Although Weaver never joined a militia group, he and his wife periodically visited the Aryan Nations compound located 60 miles from their home. Weaver sold two sawed-off shotguns to an individual who was actually a government informant. After Weaver refused to accept a deal in which the federal government would drop the gun charges in return for his agreement to become an informant for the Federal Bureau of Investigation (FBI) against the white supremacist movement, he was indicted on the gun charge. When Weaver failed to appear

Randy Weaver (left) confers with his attorney, Gerry Spence, at the 1995 Senate committee hearings on the FBI raid at Ruby Ridge, Idaho. *REUTERS/Mike Theiler/ Archive Photos.*

for trial in February 1991, the Ruby Ridge standoff began.

For 17 months, U.S. marshals kept watch on the Weaver home. On August 21, 1992, marshals decided to conduct a surveillance of the area around the house. When Weaver's dog began to bark at the approaching lawmen, Weaver, his 14-year-old son Sam, and friend Kevin Harris went to investigate. When one of the marshals shot the dog, an exchange of gunfire began, leaving Sam Weaver and a deputy marshal dead. The following day a sharpshooter for the Federal Bureau of Investigation, operating under revised regulations to shoot at any armed man outside the house, fired at Harris, but hit and killed Vicki Weaver as she stood in the doorway holding her infant son. Both Harris and Weaver were wounded. Harris, needing medical assistance, surrendered on August 30, and Weaver came out the next day, thus ending the siege.

In 1994, Weaver was brought to trial for the murder of the deputy marshal and found innocent. A jury also acquitted him of the illegal gun selling charges. His lawyer argued that Weaver had been entrapped by government officials who wanted to enlist Weaver as an informant. The defense argued that the government targeted Weaver for his unpopular beliefs and association with the Aryan Nations, a neo-Nazi organization. Weaver was convicted only of failing to appear at his February 1992 trial. Weaver ultimately received a $3.1 million out-of-court settlement from the federal government for the deaths of his wife and son.

In September 1995, Senator Arlen Specter, a Pennsylvania Republican, held hearings on the Ruby Ridge incident at which 62 witnesses testified. The committee's report criticized the FBI for a number of deficiencies, including the revised sharpshooter rules, poor intelligence gathering rules, and questionable internal investigations following the event. The FBI, which had assisted many Americans in their fight against hate groups, had suffered a blow to its reputation. The Bureau of Alcohol, Tobacco, and Firearms (BATF) was singled out by pro-gun organizations as particularly at fault. In a fund-raising letter, the National Rifle Association (NRA) compared the BATF agents to Nazi storm troopers. Former Republican President George Bush, upset by the NRA's intemperate language, resigned from the organization.

Although the general public had little sympathy for the racist beliefs of the Weavers and groups such as Aryan Nations, the failure of the FBI and the BATF to bring the situation to a peaceful conclusion harmed the reputation of two key agencies of the federal government. The inclusion of the gun rights issue heightened the post-event criticisms of government officials. This event, along with the Waco raid in 1993, motivated those who took part in the 1995 Oklahoma City bombing. *See also* BUREAU OF ALCOHOL, TOBACCO, AND FIREARMS; BUSH, GEORGE; NATIONAL RIFLE ASSOCIATION; OKLAHOMA CITY BOMBING; SAWED-OFF SHOTGUN; WACO, TEXAS, RAID.

Further Reading: Morris Dees, *Gathering Storm: America's Militia Threat* (New York: HarperCollins, 1996); Jonathan Karl, *The Right to Bear Arms: The Rise of America's New Militias* (New York: HarperCollins, 1995).

Ruger, William Batterman (Bill) (1916–)

Since the 1940s, Bill Ruger has offered a wide variety of firearms to a receptive public. Ruger resembles the famed armsmakers of the nineteenth century, for his entrepreneurial abilities contributed to the construction of a firearms business on a par with those of his predecessors. Like Samuel Colt, he constructed firearms for mass distribution. Today anyone moderately familiar with guns has owned, or at least handled, a Ruger firearm.

When Ruger contracted scarlet fever at the age of 12, his father, Adolph, promised him that he would receive a Remington on his next birthday. Believing his father most likely meant a knife, Ruger was delighted when he received a Remington Model 12 pump gun. Thus began Ruger's great fascination with firearms. In his teens, he studied every gun he could acquire, and pored over issues of the *American Rifleman*. At 17, Ruger designed plans for a light machine gun. With resources obtained from a trust fund established by an aunt, he had an initial model made.

During the two years he attended the University of North Carolina, Ruger con-

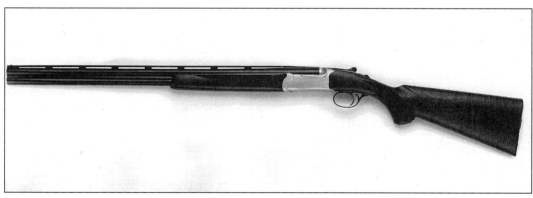

This shotgun is one of the weapons manufactured and sold by Sturm, Ruger & Company, the firm founded by William Batterman Ruger and Alexander Sturm in 1949. *Courtesy of Sturm, Ruger & Company.*

verted a lever-action rifle into a semi-automatic. A 1942 issue of the *American Rifleman* carried a report on his successful efforts. Impatient to continue his work with firearms, Ruger left college to seek a position with a gun company. He offered his machine gun design to Army Ordnance, but officials decided not to acquire it from Ruger. In 1939, he found a job at the Springfield Armory, but quickly became bored with the work, leaving the company in 1940. After returning to North Carolina, Ruger continued to work on a light machine-gun design for the military and took a position with Auto Ordnance Corporation, which was involved in producing the Thompson submachine gun. In 1946, unhappy about working for others, he began the Ruger Corporation in Southport, Connecticut.

The new business did not involve the production of firearms, but of tools such as screwdrivers and hand drills. The company did not do well and closed two years after its establishment. Alexander M. Sturm, a Yale Art School graduate, was impressed with Ruger's design for a high-quality but inexpensive .22 semi-automatic pistol and decided to join the gun designer in a new business enterprise, investing $50,000 in the project. The new enterprise was named Sturm, Ruger and Company. The first model, resembling the German Luger, went into production in 1949. The gun, costing $37.50, was advertised in the *American Rifleman* and became an immediate success. Sturm put his artistic talents to work designing the trademark, a round red medallion with a hawk spreading its wings. When Sturm died in 1951 at the age of 29, Ruger changed the color of the medallion to black as a memorial. It has remained so ever since.

Ruger continued to produce new models that generally were well received. In 1951, the Mark Series I appeared, an upgrade of the original Ruger. In 1953, Ruger revealed the Single Six, a Colt-like sixgun. In 1955, Ruger introduced another successful sidearm, the single-action Blackhawk, which could be used for target shooting. Subsequent Blackhawks were released in 1956 (44 Mag-

num), 1959 (Super Blackhawk), 1965 (41 Magnum), and 1967 (30 Carbine). These weapons and others, including the Bearcat, a revolver with a four-inch barrel, became some of the most popular firearms in the United States. Ruger also produced long guns, including the Model 77, a bolt-action big game rifle similar to the Mauser.

Over the years Sturm Ruger has expanded its operations. The company opened the Pine Tree Casting Division in Newport, New Hampshire, a facility larger than the home office in Southport, Connecticut. Ruger also runs a plant in Prescott, Arizona. In the early 1990s, company assets were estimated at about $100 million. By the late 1980s, Ruger, who suffers from rheumatoid arthritis, had allowed his two sons to assume management of the company's operations, although he continued to take part in the design of new firearms. *See also* AMERICAN RIFLEMAN; COLT, SAMUEL; REMINGTON, ELIPHALET, II; TOMMY GUN; WINCHESTER, OLIVER FISHER.

Further Reading: Sam Fadala, *Great Shooters of the World* (South Hackensack, NJ: Stoeger, 1990); Wayne Van Zwoll, *America's Great Gunmakers* (South Hackensack, NJ: Stoeger, 1992); R. L. Wilson, *Ruger and His Guns: A History of the Man, the Company and Their Firearms* (New York: Simon and Schuster, 1996).

Russia

Like the former Union of Soviet Socialist Republics (USSR), Russia maintains a strict policy regarding the availability of firearms and other weapons to private citizens. Gun rights advocates point out that despite stringent gun control in the former Soviet Union, the crime rate was high compared to nations such as Japan which also has strict limitations on firearm ownership, suggesting that factors other than legal rules limiting firearm possession are involved in determining the level of crime and violence. Similar questions are raised about the effectiveness of present Russian firearms restrictions.

Generally, Russian law prohibits the ownership of handguns and fully automatic weapons. Exceptions are made for military officers who may be awarded a firearm for meritorious service. Private citizens may own shotguns and rifles if they acquire a license. Among the conditions that can disqualify a private citizen from owning a firearm are hospitalization for alcohol or drug abuse, felony conviction, two misdemeanor convictions, an illness or physical disability that prevents appropriate gun handling, and absence of a permanent address. The high cost of firearms discourages many from acquiring them. All firearms must be kept in a locked location and ammunition must be stored separately. Guns can be transported only if they have been disassembled. Roman V. Isaev, a commentator on Russian firearms laws, notes that this regulation renders firearms useless for self-defense outside the home. However, a shotgun may be kept at home for protection.

Included among prohibited weapons are armor-piercing, burning, or exploding ammunition. Weapons containing nerve agents, poisons, and other toxic gases are banned. Non-firearm weapons such as throwing knives and boomerangs, and any instrument that can be used as a club are prohibited, but private ownership of low-energy air guns is permitted. Although restrictions are placed on more powerful air guns, they are not strictly enforced. Sprays such as CS gas can be purchased without a license. Firearms cannot be equipped with silencers or night vision devices and cannot be mailed. Carrying firearms and other weapons at political rallies and demonstrations is prohibited. To possess a firearm, a private citizen must be at least 18 years old. Smooth-bore firearms for hunting require a license. Rifled firearms may be acquired by professional hunters and those who have owned smooth-bore firearms for at least five years and have abided by the firearms regulations. Firearms must be registered within two weeks of purchase. Registration involves a test firing of the weapon at a soft target to obtain a bullet sample that is kept on file in case of future criminal use. Licenses must be renewed every five years. *See also* JAPAN.

Further Reading: Roman V. Isaev, "Brief Summary: Russian Laws for Civilians" (n.d.), <http://gunlab.com.ru/summary.html>; Roman V. Isaev, "Excerpts from Russian Law on Weapons" (n.d.), <http://gunlab.com.ru/excerpts.html>.

S

Safe Range Association (SafeRange)

The Safe Range Association (SafeRange), based in Austin, Texas, advocates passage of additional legislation to improve the safety of shooting ranges and to reduce the noise from such establishments. Claiming that it is not an anti-gun organization, SafeRange notes that many of its members are gun enthusiasts and hunters. The membership wishes to protect homes from stray bullets coming from gun ranges and from the impulse noise originating from these sites. The organization insists that, contrary to the claim of range owners that neighbors are encroaching on them, neighbors should have the right to use their land as they please without being impinged upon by the ranges. The organization reports on injuries that resulted because gun ranges did not institute sufficient safety features. Expressing its desire to work cooperatively with the National Rifle Association (NRA) and the Texas State Rifle Association (TSRA), SafeRange advocates that ranges follow the safety guidelines contained in the NRA Range Manual.

Focusing its attention on Texas, SafeRange argues that existing laws in that state are insufficient to assure the safety of neighbors of gun ranges. The organization advocates five minimum safety standards: 1) no bullets should ever leave firing ranges; 2) no noise in excess of 55 decibels should emanate from ranges; 3) no significant environmental damage, such as lead contamination, should occur at ranges; 4) ranges should be adequately fenced to prevent inadvertent trespass, particularly by children; and 5) no range should be able to operate without a permit certifying that it meets minimum standards, including overhead baffles, side walls, backstop, and bullet catchers. Among other safety measures for ranges, the organization advocates limiting the hours of operation, prohibiting the consumption of alcohol on the premises, and requiring "realistic" insurance coverage.

SafeRange claims that the Texas law regulating ranges is "poorly drafted and impossible to enforce." As for voluntary compliance with safety regulations, the organization contends that most ranges fail to meet adequate standards, having failed to invest the funds for needed improvements. In addition, the NRA and the TSRA have been ineffective in encouraging safe shooting ranges. Responding to the suggestion that requiring ranges to have liability insurance will lead insurance companies to mandate safer conditions at ranges, SafeRange responds that present law already requires insurance, but this has not resulted in improved safety conditions. SafeRange rejects the argument that actual or threatened lawsuits will foster improved safety measures simply because such improvements have not occurred at most ranges. The organization concludes that "leaving the decision on what is a safe facility to the owner or operator and hoping they will do the right thing has not and will not work."

Noting that law enforcement officers are important customers of shooting ranges, SafeRange recommends that law enforcement agencies should carefully examine the location and safety policy of ranges and their relations with neighbors before agreeing to conduct business with them. Only those ranges that have been designed with safety in mind, adhere to appropriate safety standards, and demonstrate consideration for those living near them should be awarded public money. The organization believes that more stringent standards regarding the use of shooting ranges by law enforcement officers could have a significant effect on safety policy. SafeRange strongly criticizes the practice of providing law enforcement officers with free access to ranges, which the organization considers a potential conflict of interest. *See also* NATIONAL RIFLE ASSOCIATION; NATIONAL SHOOTING SPORTS FOUNDATION.

Further Reading: Safe Range Association Web site <www.saferange.org>.

Safety for Women and Responsible Motherhood (SWARM)

Safety for Women and Responsible Motherhood (SWARM), headquartered in Wheat Ridge, Colorado, describes itself as a nonpartisan organization "dedicated to winning for women and all peaceable citizens across the U.S. the legal right to defend themselves with a firearm–not just in the home, but where most crimes occur, on the street." Formed in 1994 by a group of women in Colorado, the organization claimed to have over 3,000 members across the nation by 1998. SWARM advertises itself as the "first women's pro-firearm lobby in America." SWARM, which has gained national media attention, considers itself a "powerful catalyst in returning the media to reality concerning guns." It has among its advisers David Kopel, a pro-gun rights author and member of the Independence Institute, a Colorado-based "think tank."

SWARM strives to change state firearms laws it considers unfair to women. While allowing target shooting and hunting, laws in some states make illegal the use of guns as a self-defense tool. The organization considers such restrictions especially unfair to women who are usually much lighter than potential attackers and hence are rendered defenseless without some means of defense. It considers the especially liberal Vermont concealed carry law a model to be copied by other states.

Among its goals, SWARM strives to obtain the right of "decent, peaceable citizens" to defend themselves, their families, and their communities with firearms. The organization encourages all states to adopt "shall-issue" carrying concealed weapons (CCW) laws that allow anyone who is not specifically prohibited from doing so (for instance, convicted felons) to possess and carry a firearm. SWARM supports concealed carry permits that are similar to a driver's license in that each state grants reciprocity to all others—a permit to carry in one state is recognized in all other states. SWARM promotes firearms safety and training courses to prepare women to use guns effectively for self-defense. Concerned about the causes of crime, the organization recommends reform of the welfare and criminal justice systems. To achieve its goals, SWARM is conducting a nationwide membership drive and is striving to develop state organizations dedicated to liberalizing CCW laws. *See also* CONCEALED CARRY LAWS; INDEPENDENCE INSTITUTE; KOPEL, DAVID B.; STATE GUN STATUTES; WOMEN AND GUNS.

Further Reading: Safety for Women and Responsible Motherhood Web site <http://web.wn.net/~usr/chris/web/swarm.html>.

Saturday Night Special

For many years, the banning of the Saturday night special has been one of the causes célèbres of the gun control movement. Although lacking in any precise definition, the term is generally used to refer to a small, inexpensive, low-quality, low-caliber handgun with little or no sporting value, but which is nonetheless effective at close range when used in a holdup or to settle an argument. Prior to the Gun Control Act of 1968 such weapons were imported into the United States in large numbers and were easily obtainable in stores or by mail order.

The term "Saturday night special" has disputed origins. John Ciardi, the noted master of the written word, observed in his *A Browser's Dictionary* (1980) that the term refers to weapons that quickly transport the victims of robberies and crimes of passion to hospital emergency rooms, especially during the Saturday night "rush hour." Those who are unenthusiastic about gun control laws claim that the term was used in a derogatory way to characterize violent behavior among African Americans. Therefore, efforts to ban Saturday night specials in the 1960s and 1970s are regarded as examples of racial discrimination, an explanation that tends to oversimplify the train of events leading to passage of the 1968 legislation establishing limits on the importation of these weapons.

In 1961, Senator Thomas J. Dodd, Democratic senator from Connecticut and chairman of the Subcommittee on Juvenile Delinquency of the Senate Judiciary Committee, opened communications with the American firearms industry, the National Rifle Association (NRA), and other interested parties regarding the perceived problems of cheap handguns. The economy of Dodd's home state included firearms manufacturers who were concerned about the competition that cheap imported handguns represented.

Although the Gun Control Act of 1968 banned importation of Saturday night specials, a loophole in the law allowed the continued importation of parts for such handguns that could then be assembled in the United States. The domestic production of cheap handguns increased 16-fold from 1968 to 1970. Therefore, rather than providing for a ban on the Saturday night special, the law established trade protection for the domestic handgun industry.

In the early 1970s, Democratic Senator Birch Bayh of Indiana, concerned with the continued importation of cheap handgun parts, introduced a bill that would prohibit the domestic production and sale of cheap handguns that lacked any reasonable sporting purpose. The May 1972 attempted assassination of presidential candidate George Wallace, governor of Georgia, gave the Bayh bill momentum.

This small .38-caliber pistol is part of an easily concealable class of handguns known as Saturday night specials. *UPI/Corbis-Bettmann.*

The national response was so intense that even the executive vice president of the NRA, Maxwell Rich, testified before a Senate committee that the NRA basically agreed that "crudely made and unsafe handguns" should be banned from the American market. The Senate passed the ban on Saturday night specials by a wide margin, but the bill never reached the floor for a vote in the House of Representatives. Rich's support of a cheap handgun ban was in part responsible for a subsequent movement in the NRA that resulted in his removal from leadership.

The failure of Congress to deal with cheap handguns moved the issue to the courts, where litigants claimed that gun manufacturers should be held responsible for the damage their products caused. In 1985, in *Kelley v. R.G. Industries, Inc.*, a case before the Maryland Court of Appeals, the court held a manufacturer of Saturday night specials responsible for the way in which they were used.

The Firearms Owners Protection Act of 1986, although essentially an anti-control measure, introduced a ban on the importation of barrels for cheap handguns. Critics argue that a ban on Saturday night specials simply encourages criminals to use better weapons. From the perspective of gun control advocates, such a ban represents only one aspect of a larger program to limit the damage they attribute to firearms. *See also* DODD, THOMAS J.; FIREARMS OWNERS PROTECTION ACT; GUN CONTROL ACT OF 1968; *KELLEY V. R.G. INDUSTRIES, INC.*; NATIONAL RIFLE ASSOCIATION.

Further Reading: John Ciardi, *A Browser's Dictionary* (New York: Harper and Row, 1980); Lee Kennett and James La Verne Anderson, *The Gun in America: The Origins of a National Dilemma* (Westport, CT: Greenwood, 1975); Earl R. Kruschke, *Gun Control* (Santa Barbara, CA: ABC-CLIO, 1995).

Sawed-Off Shotgun

In the 1920s and 1930s, the sawed-off shotgun, like the machine gun, came to be regarded as a weapon whose use was confined solely to criminal activity, and therefore should be strictly controlled. A sawed-off shotgun is literally a shotgun with a barrel that has been sawed off, making it a formidable weapon at close range. Although this weapon became popular with gangsters in the

1920s, its history goes much further back. In 1898, the Winchester Company marketed a shotgun with a 20-inch barrel, touting it as a firearm that police could use to control riots. During World War I, the American army issued the weapon, termed a "trench gun," for use in hand-to-hand combat. The Germans protested its use, arguing that it violated the laws of war. The sawed-off shotgun's ultimate notoriety as a disreputable firearm developed after the war when gang members began to use it in criminal activities.

The sawed-off shotgun is legally defined as a shotgun with a barrel less than 18 inches in length from the breech to the muzzle, or less than 26 inches in overall length. Like an ordinary shotgun, the sawed-off version fires a shell containing as many as 400 small pellets. Some versions of the shotgun can contain two to five rounds, and some types used by police agencies contain 20 or more shells. It is an intimidating weapon that can coin-

This array of handguns includes two small Saturday night specials (center and bottom, right) and a sawed-off shotgun (top, right), which, because it can be so easily concealed under a jacket or coat, is often considered to be a type of handgun. *UPI/Corbis-Bettmann.*

cide nicely with criminal intentions. At close distances, it can have savage effects and can be used quickly because it does not require deliberate aiming. It is easily concealed on the person, either in a holster, as used by the notorious bank robber Clyde Barrow, who developed a quick-draw technique; or kept beneath a coat, dangling by a cord hung from the neck. Intention appeared to be a major factor in labeling the sawed-off shotgun a criminal weapon. By shortening the barrel, the shotgun was made virtually useless for hunting or any other legitimate purpose. The weapon's continued use in criminal activity sealed its fate in the 1934 National Firearms Act and the 1938 Federal Firearms Act, each of which banned the sale and possession of the weapon. During congressional hearings held prior to passage of the 1934 act, General M.A. Reckord, executive vice president of the National Rifle Association (NRA), expressed reservations about the legislation, but stated that the NRA had no objections to Congress's placing severe limitations on the ownership and sale of sawed-off shotguns and other "gangster type" weapons.

In 1939, the Supreme Court, in a challenge to the National Firearms Act (*United States v. Miller*), ruled that the sawed-off shotgun was not protected by the Second Amendment because it had no credible military use. Although the Court recognized the right of states to maintain militias, potentially composed of all physically fit males supplying their own arms, it could see no relationship between this weapon and the preservation of a well-regulated militia. Some people have noted that U.S. military forces employed the sawed-off shotgun in combat in the Vietnam War, arguing that military use makes the weapon eligible for private ownership under the Supreme Court's interpretation of the Second Amendment in the *Miller* case. Some gun rights advocates have pointed to the potential defensive and deterrent use of the sawed-off shotgun by private citizens, thus raising questions about the long-standing claim that the only intended use of such a weapon is criminal. However, gun control advocates counter that the potential devas-

tating effects of the sawed-off shotgun preclude any claimed defensive benefits. *See also* FEDERAL FIREARMS ACT; NATIONAL FIREARMS ACT; NATIONAL RIFLE ASSOCIATION; SECOND AMENDMENT; *UNITED STATES V. MILLER* (1939).

Further Reading: Gregg Lee Carter, *The Gun Control Movement* (New York: Twayne, 1997); Lee Kennett and James La Verne Anderson, *The Gun in America: The Origins of a National Dilemma* (Westport, CT: Greenwood, 1975).

Schools and Guns

Many Americans have expressed concern for the danger students and teachers face when youths take guns to school. Two major reasons are given to explain why students take guns to school: self-protection, and as a way of impressing fellow students. Various claims have been made regarding the number of guns taken to school each day. One estimate puts the number as high as 275,000 (Cox, 1997, p. 19), but others dispute such a high occurrence of gun carrying by students.

Usually following a violent incident, specific school districts have taken additional measures to prevent students from taking guns into school buildings. For instance, in 1993, following the deaths of two students, the Los Angeles Unified School District instituted a "zero-tolerance" policy that includes random gun sweeps in middle and high schools. In 1990, New York City began using metal detectors at schools with the greatest incidence of violence. Such efforts, combined with suspensions for students having guns or other weapons with them at school, are designed to keep schools "gun free."

In 1989, the School Crime Supplement to the National Crime Victimization Survey estimated that in the previous six months 2 percent of students had taken a weapon to school. In *Targeting Guns: Firearms and Their Control* (1997), gun control researcher Gary Kleck offered an estimate, based on the 1993 National Household Education Survey, that in 1992-93 approximately 46,000 students took a gun to school at least once, a figure one-fifth that of other estimates. Based on data from the Milwaukee County public

Students stand before a makeshift memorial to the victims (5 killed, 10 wounded) of two youths who opened fire on fellow students at Westside School in Jonesboro, Arkansas, on March 24, 1998. *REUTERS/Jeff Mitchell/ Archive Photos.*

school system, Kleck estimated that there are 4,300 gun confiscations at schools nationwide each year. Other data suggest that the range of gun confiscations could range from 4,300 to 17,300 per year. These figures likely include guns taken from students both on and off school property. Kleck estimated that from 24 to 96 guns are seized each school day across the nation, and that each year less than 0.1 percent of students are discovered with guns at school. Table 12 reports the various characteristics of students who took a gun to school, know a student who did, or saw a student with a gun.

Kleck suggested that surveys reporting numbers of students taking guns to school may over report such weapons actually taken into the classroom. This distinction may be significant because metal detectors would not discover guns hidden on school grounds or nearby, even though they would still be readily accessible. Kleck concluded that while the incidence of gun violence is high among adolescents, little of it takes place in schools, and while violence may be high in some schools, guns are seldom involved. He concluded that each year approximately seven firearm homicides are committed specifically in school buildings.

Gun control supporters are concerned about what students learn about guns while in school. The Violence Policy Center has criticized the National Shooting Sports Foundation (NSSF) for creating educational materials that are distributed to public and private schools as a means of introducing students to firearms. The NSSF's board of directors has contained members from the firearms and ammunition industry (including Colt, Remington, and Smith and Wesson), hunting publications, and conservation groups. The Center cites NSSF communications that encourage the development of various school programs that may nurture future gun buyers. NSSF materials intended for use in grades 4 through 12 discuss hunting and wildlife management. The NSSF receives federal assistance in distributing the materials, financed through the Pittman-Robertson Federal Aid in Wildlife Restoration Act. In 1993, the organization acquired a grant of $229,000 for its "Wildlife Management Education in Schools" program. The Center estimates that since 1980 the NSSF program has been distributed to thousands of schools. The Center, which is opposed to any encouragement given to youth to use firearms, recommends that a part of the Pittman-Robertson funds be used toward the health care costs caused by gun violence. *See also* GUN-FREE SCHOOLS ACT; JONESBORO, ARKANSAS, SCHOOL SHOOTING; KLECK, GARY; LITTLETON, COLORADO, SCHOOL SHOOTING; NATIONAL SHOOTING SPORTS FOUNDATION; STOCKTON, CALIFORNIA, SHOOTING; VIOLENCE POLICY CENTER; YOUTH AND GUNS.

Further Reading: Vic Cox, *Guns, Violence, and Teens* (Springfield, NJ: Enslow, 1997); Susan Glick and Josh Sugarmann, *"Use the Schools:" How Federal Tax Dollars Are Spent to Market Guns to Kids* (Washington, DC: Violence Policy Center, 1994); Gary Kleck, *Targeting Guns: Firearms and Their Control* (New York: Aldine De Gruyter, 1997).

TABLE 12

STUDENTS REPORTING GUNS AT SCHOOL BY SELECTED CHARACTERISTICS, UNITED STATES, 1995

Student Characteristics	Number of students (1,000's)	Took gun to school	Know student who took gun to school	Saw student with a gun at school
Total	23,933	0.1%	12.7%	5.3%
Sex				
Male	12,331	0.1	12.4	6.1
Female	11,602	0.0a	13.0	4.5
Race, ethnicity				
White	16,351	0.1	12.3	4.4
Black	3,752	0.1	15.5	8.7
Hispanic	2,898	0.1	11.8	6.2
Other	932	(b)	11.1	4.8
Age				
12 years	3,735	(b)	6.2	2.0
13 years	3,781	0.1	10.0	4.0
14 years	3,732	0.1	12.9	4.9
15 years	3,688	0.2	15.1	6.4
16 years	3,674	(b)	15.1	6.2
17 years	3,172	(b)	16.4	8.3
18 years	1,820	0.2	14.6	6.2
19 years	331	(b)	16.0	7.0
Grade				
Sixth	2,315	(b)	5.7	2.0
Seventh	3,736	(b)	8.9	3.0
Eighth	3,795	0.1	11.9	4.8
Ninth	3,689	0.3	15.1	6.2
Tenth	3,662	0.1	14.6	5.9
Eleventh	3,460	(b)	15.4	7.3
Twelfth	2,990	(b)	16.2	6.9
Other	285	(b)	5.3	4.3
Household Income				
< $7,000	1,487	(b)	10.9	5.2
7,500-9,999	783	(b)	12.4	8.3
10,000-14,999	1,657	(b)	12.1	6.2
15,000-24,999	3,130	0.3	14.7	7.0
25,000-29,999	1,729	(b)	13.7	5.7
30,000-49,999	6,295	0.1	12.2	5.0
50,00 and over	6,562	0.0a	12.6	4.4
Not ascertained	2,289	(b)	12.8	4.5
Place of Residence				
Central city	6,309	(b)	15.0	6.8
Suburb	11,341	0.1	12.3	4.8
Nonmetropolitan area	6,283	0.0a	11.1	4.8
School type				
Public	21,719	0.1	13.6	5.7
Private	2,163	0.1	4.4	2.0

aThere are cases in the cell but the estimate is less than 0.05%.
bNo cases of this type occurred in the data.

Source: Kathryn A. Chandler et al., *Student's Reports of School Crime: 1989 and 1995*, NCES 98-241/NCJ-169607 (Washington, DC: U.S. Department of Education and Justice, 1998), p. 20; adapted by Kathleen Maguire and Ann L. Pastore, eds., *Bureau of Justice Statistics Sourcebook of Criminal Justice Statistics–1997* (Washington, DC: U.S. Department of Justice, 1998), p. 232.

Schubert v. DeBard (1980)

The Court of Appeals of Indiana for the Third District ruled in *Joseph L. Schubert, Jr. v. Robert L. Debard, Indiana State Police Department* (398 N.E. 2d 1339, 1980) that Joseph Schubert had been arbitrarily denied the right to carry a handgun under Indiana law. Schubert applied in June 1975 for a permit to carry a handgun for self-protection. A state statute provided that an individual seeking such a license must apply to the chief of police or equivalent police officer in the municipality of residence, or to the sheriff of the county of residence. The officer shall then conduct an investigation to determine the applicant's "character and reputation" and ascertain the accuracy of information provided on the application. The information together with a recommendation shall then be forwarded to the superintendent of the Indiana State Police Department. If the law enforcement officer recommends to the superintendent that the request for a license be rejected, he shall provide reasons in writing for the recommendation. The superintendent may conduct a further investigation should he deem it necessary.

In providing evidence of his need to protect himself, Schubert offered two pieces of mail he received in 1975: a picture of a pig labeled with his name, and a letter demanding money that contained a death threat. Although Schubert suspected that his brother had sent the letters, he indicated that he had not spoken to his brother about them, nor had he contacted the police. He also reported that his brother had fired a rifle at the vehicle in which he was riding after a confrontation at their mother's home. Schubert believed that these incidents justified his application to carry a weapon for self-protection.

When Schubert's application was denied, he filed a petition for administrative review. Following the review, the superintendent of the Indiana State Police ruled that Schubert failed to demonstrate a proper reason for being granted a license and the permit was denied. Schubert then appealed to a trial court, claiming that his right to bear arms under the Indiana state constitution had been denied. The relevant provision within the constitution states that, "The people shall have a right to bear arms, for the defense of themselves and the State." A trial court upheld the superintendent's decision.

The Court of Appeals based its ruling on the appeal from the trial court decision on a previous decision (*Matthews v. State*, 1958) in which the state supreme court determined that the superintendent did not have the discretion to deny a license to an applicant who has met the conditions of the statute. In the Schubert case, the court determined that the status of the application was determined on the basis of the statutory authority of the superintendent to make a subjective evaluation of the need for self-defense. This authority, the court claimed, infringed on the constitutional right to bear arms. The court determined that Schubert's stated reason for wishing to obtain a license "stood unrefuted," and was an appropriate reason within the statute. Therefore, the case was returned to the lower court for a new hearing.

A judge dissenting from the majority opinion claimed that Superintendent DeBard had determined, in his appropriate role as factfinder, that Schubert's self-defense claim was not substantiated. The dissenting opinion further stated that should the present ruling set a precedent, the superintendent would have no choice but to grant licenses to carry handguns "to any 'proper' person who simply alleged a need for self-defense." While the judge admitted that there can be many "proper" persons, there may be only a few citizens who need to carry a handgun outside the home or business. Because the right to bear arms is not an absolute, those not satisfying the established standards for licensing could be denied the right. He expressed the opinion that Schubert's apparent need, considered psychological rather than actual, was not a satisfactory reason under the law to grant a license. The ultimate result of the majority decision, according to the dissenting judge, was to de-regulate handguns in the state of Indiana. However, statutory reasons for denying a license to bear a firearm still remained in effect. *See also* CONCEALED CARRY LAWS; STATE GUN STATUTES.

Further Reading: *Schubert v. DeBard*, 398 N.E. 2d 1339 (1980).

Schumer, Charles E. (1950–)

U.S. Senator Charles Schumer, Democrat from New York, has for the last several years been a major opponent of the legislative objectives of the National Rifle Association (NRA). During Democratic President Bill Clinton's first two years in office, Schumer, as a member of the U.S. House of Representatives, devoted his energies to winning passage of anti-crime legislation. As chairman of the Crime Subcommittee of the House Judiciary Committee, he led the way in developing the anti-crime bill that passed both houses of Congress in August 1994. Although the bill contained provisions to appeal to conservatives as well as liberals, and the total budget authorization was reduced to win Republican support, a faction of the NRA ran an ad in *USA Today* referring to Schumer as "the criminal's best friend." Schumer stated that he wore the allegation as "a badge of honor."

Schumer received a B.A. degree in 1971 and a law degree in 1974 from Harvard University. He served as legislative aide to New York state assemblyman Stephen J. Solarz, a Democrat from Brooklyn, before himself winning Solarz's seat in the Assembly in 1974 following his mentor's move to the U.S. House of Representatives. In 1980, after two terms in the state legislature, Schumer won election to the U.S. House of Representatives. Generally considered a liberal, he received a 1996 rating of 90 from the liberal Americans for Democratic Action and 5 from the American Conservative Union.

Schumer backed the 1993 Brady Handgun Violence Prevention Act and the 1994 ban on certain types of assault weapons, a measure included in the 1994 Violent Crime Control and Law Enforcement Act. When Republicans took control of both houses of Congress following the 1994 election, Schumer became a major defender of past legislative accomplishments against Republican attempts to weaken or repeal legislation.

Following the April 1995 bombing of the Alfred P. Murrah Federal Building in Oklahoma City, Oklahoma, Schumer supported President Clinton's efforts to pass anti-terrorism legislation. He strongly opposed an amendment by Representative Bob Barr, Republican of Georgia, that restricted the federal government's authority to prevent people associated with terrorist groups from entering the country and limited the government's ability to convict individuals accused of selling or trading guns that are subsequently used in a felony. Schumer blamed the NRA for what he considered a serious weakening of the legislation.

In July 1995, Schumer criticized hearings initiated by the Republican majority to investigate the actions of the Bureau of Alcohol, Tobacco, and Firearms (BATF) during the 1993 raid on the Branch Davidian encampment near Waco, Texas. He blamed the National Rifle Association for what he considered strong bias against the government agency. He claimed that the bias resulted from the NRA's long opposition to the organization that is primarily responsible for enforcing firearms legislation.

Senator Charles Schumer (D-NY) is a proponent of gun control legislation and a noted foe of the National Rifle Association. *Courtesy of Senator Schumer's office.*

Claiming in 1996 that NRA contributions had played an important role in electing a Republican majority to Congress in 1994, Schumer charged that the House vote to repeal the assault weapons ban was a direct payment for the monetary support. He criticized Republican Speaker Newt Gingrich of Georgia for demonstrating special deference to the NRA. Schumer also charged the Republicans with engaging in partisan rivalry, claiming that they wanted to deny the Democratic president a legislative victory. In 1998, Schumer won election to the U.S. Senate, where he can be expected to continue to fight for firearms legislation and to oppose attempts to weaken existing laws. *See also* ASSAULT WEAPONS BAN; BARR, BOB; BRADY HANDGUN VIOLENCE PREVENTION ACT; BUREAU OF ALCOHOL, TOBACCO, AND FIREARMS; CLINTON, WILLIAM JEFFERSON (BILL); NATIONAL RIFLE ASSOCIATION; OKLAHOMA CITY BOMBING; WACO, TEXAS, RAID.

Further Reading: Philip D. Duncan and Christine C. Lawrence, *Politics in America: The 105th Congress* (Washington, DC: CQ Press, 1997); Charles Schumer Web site <www.senate.gov/~schumer/>.

Scott v. Sanford (1857)

Gun rights advocates have cited a brief statement by Chief Justice Roger B. Taney in his majority decision in the case *Scott v. Sanford* (60 U.S. [19 Howard] 393, 15 L.Ed. 691, 1857) that appears to give credence to the claim that the Second Amendment protects the individual right of citizens to keep and bear arms. Taney rejected the claim that African Americans, either enslaved or free, have the rights of American citizens. Among the rights the chief justice insisted slaves could not enjoy was the right to keep and bear arms.

In 1834, Dred Scott, a slave, traveled with his owner, John Emerson, an army surgeon, from their home state of Missouri to Illinois. By this time Illinois had abolished slavery. Two years later, Emerson took Scott with him to Fort Snelling in the Louisiana territory, an area where slavery had been banned by the Missouri Compromise of 1820. In 1838, Scott returned with Emerson to Missouri. Following Emerson's death, a suit was brought on Scott's behalf in the Missouri state court system against Emerson's widow, claiming that Scott became free at the time he resided in a free territory. Although a lower court ruled in Scott's favor, the Missouri Supreme Court reversed the ruling in 1852, stating that Missouri law kept Scott a slave. In the meantime, ownership of Scott shifted to C.C. Chaffee, a Massachusetts abolitionist. Chaffee transferred ownership to his wife's brother, John Sanford, a New York resident. Chaffee was friendly toward Scott's cause, and arranged for an attorney to file suit for Scott. On appeal from the state court, the U.S. Supreme Court heard the case in February 1856, and again the following December.

Seven justices, including Taney, joined in a majority decision that denied to Scott his claim of freedom. Packed within this emotionally charged decision, gun rights advocates claim to find evidence to support their position on the Second Amendment. Referring to "the inferior and subject condition of that race at the time the Constitution was adopted," Taney imagined the state of affairs should African Americans be received into citizenship. Being recognized as citizens in one state, they would have the right to enter any other state of their own volition, "singly or in companies," without the need for any special permission, "to stay there as long as they pleased, to go where they pleased at every hour of the day or night without molestation." African Americans would have "the full liberty of speech in public and in private . . . to hold public meetings upon political affairs, *and to keep and carry arms wherever they went*" (emphasis added).

If some African Americans had these rights guaranteed by the constitutional system to all citizens of the United States, while at the same time slavery continued for most African Americans, Taney assumed that "discontent and insubordination" would result, thus "endangering the peace and safety of the State." The "great men" of the slaveholding states could not have had this intention when taking part in framing the Constitution. Taney appears to have concluded that the Bill of Rights applied to the states as well as to the national government. No constitutional interpretation prior to ratification of the Fourteenth Amendment in 1868 would support such a position. Taney apparently assumed that the Second Amendment did grant an individual right to keep and bear arms. However, he may have exaggerated his claim by implying that the Bill of Rights limited the actions of states.

Gun control advocates in the twentieth century are unconvinced by the authority of Taney's statement, given its alarmist nature. Not all members of the Court's majority in 1857 agreed completely with Taney' decision. Modern gun control advocates find unconvincing any interpretation of the nature of the constitutionally protected right to keep and bear arms based on one justice's brief comment in a case that did not deal directly with the subject. Nonetheless, gun rights advocates today believe Taney's brief comments contribute to the credibility of their Second Amendment interpretation. *See also* AFRICAN AMERICANS AND GUNS; BLACK CODES; FOURTEENTH AMENDMENT; SECOND AMENDMENT.

Further Reading: Alan M. Gottlieb, "Gun Ownership: A Constitutional Right," *Northern Kentucky Law Review* 10 (1982): 113-40; *Scott v. Sanford*, 60 U.S. (19 Howard) 393, 15 L.Ed. 691 (1857).

Second Amendment

Gun rights advocates look to the Second Amendment to the U.S. Constitution as the fundamental support in their cause. This amendment states, in typically laconic fashion, "A well regulated Militia, being necessary to the security of a free State, the right of the people to keep and bear arms shall not be infringed." Although the issues arising over the interpretation of the Amendment have been many, two tend to predominate. First, does it protect a collective (in other words, state), or an individual right, and second, assuming that it does in fact protect the right of individuals to keep and bear arms, does it apply to the states as well as the national government?

The Second Amendment was one of 12 constitutional amendments proposed by the first Congress in 1789. James Madison, a major architect of the Constitution, believed that the original document adequately protected citizens' rights. However, he agreed to propose to the first Congress amendments limiting government power to gain support for ratification from those who had qualms about the new government's powers. True to his promise, Madison submitted to Congress the amendments that would become the Bill of Rights. Ten of the 12 proposals were ratified by the required three-fourths of the state legislatures. The Second Amendment was ratified on December 15, 1791.

Gun rights advocates insist that the amendment protects two separate rights: first, the right to keep arms, and second, the right to bear arms. If this is so, they argue, then the amendment cannot be referring simply to the right of states to stockpile weapons at armories. The people, taken individually, are the ones who have a need to keep arms in their homes for both self-protection as well as to maintain readiness against a threat to the public peace. Supporters indicate that when the word "people" is used elsewhere in the Bill of Rights, as in the First and Fourth Amendments, it refers to individuals. Therefore, consistency requires that the Second Amendment also be interpreted as protecting an individual right.

Opponents of the individualist interpretation note that Madison's original proposal indicates his intent to provide a collective guarantee that states could maintain militias: "The right of the people to keep and bear arms shall not be infringed; a well armed and well regulated militia being the best security of a free country; but no person religiously scrupulous of bearing arms shall be compelled to render military service in person." Modifications were made in the final wording. First, "country" became "state," and "the best security of" became "necessary to." The guarantee that "religiously scrupulous" persons could not be compelled to serve in the military was dropped, possibly to prevent government officials from declaring some group "scrupulous" to exclude them from service. The amendment, according to this interpretation, deals solely with military questions, modifying the militia clause in Article I, section 8 of the original Constitution. Supporters of the individualist interpretation counter that the reference to the militia merely means that the individual right to keep and bear arms is conducive to the maintenance of a well-regulated militia.

Opponents of the individualist interpretation reject the claim that two rights are being protected: the right to keep and the right to bear arms. They claim that the phrase "to bear arms" has specific military reference, and can be taken as a synonym for waging war. According to gun control supporters, the phrase cannot be separated, but might best be rendered as one connected process, to-keep-and-bear, which most appropriately refers to a militia maintaining an arsenal of weapons on a continuing basis. While gun rights supporters claim that "the people" refers to all citizens as actual or potential members of the militia, who are thereby guaranteed the right to keep and bear arms, opponents note that all citizens were never considered part of the militia. Only those who have received appropriate training and have been received into a "well-regulated" militia as established under provisions of the Constitution can be considered a member of this portion of the people.

Some gun rights advocates claim that the militia extends beyond government-established militias, and argue that an individual right to possess arms was intended to be a strong deterrent against a government that might attempt to violate the rights of citizens. In effect, they contend that the Constitution, through the Second Amendment, guarantees a right of armed rebellion against the government of the United States. Opponents respond that finding such a right in the Second Amendment contradicts the provision in the original Constitution, found in Article III, that defines and provides punishment for treason. No government would provide the formal right to overthrow legally established institutions. Should a government become tyrannical, a right to revolution does not de-

pend upon any legal provision within the governing document.

In *United States v. Cruikshank* (1876) and *Presser v. Illinois* (1886), the U.S. Supreme Court ruled that the Second Amendment did not apply to the states, but only to the national government. Gun rights advocates consider these nineteenth-century cases to be antiquated because many of the guarantees in the Bill of Rights, which originally limited the authority only of the national government, have since been interpreted to limit state governments as well. However, no previous case dealing with another provision of the Bill of Rights can automatically be argued to grant the claimed individual protection within the Second Amendment. The Supreme Court has followed a "selective incorporation" policy whereby specific rights have been determined on a case-by-case basis to apply to states through the Fourteenth Amendment.

In *United States v. Miller* (1939), a case involving the National Firearms Act of 1934, the Court upheld a conviction for illegal possession of a sawed-off shotgun, ruling that such a firearm does not fit the category of weapons commonly used in the militia. Gun rights advocates have concluded that, conversely, an individual has the right to possess any weapon that is actually employed by the militia. Opponents argue that such an interpretation would lead to a *reductio ad absurdum*: the right of private citizens to possess a wide variety of weapons, including not only handguns and shotguns, but machine guns, grenade launchers, and anti-tank weapons, would be guaranteed as long as they were legitimate weapons of the militia.

Supporters of the individualist interpretation of the Second Amendment often refer to antecedent documents, such as the English Bill of Rights of 1689, which stated that Protestant subjects "may have arms for their defense and as allowed by law." They also appeal to common law within the American colonies which strongly suggests an individualist interpretation. Opponents argue that although such alternative sources as natural law, common law, and tradition may support a private right to own and employ firearms, the Second Amendment clearly has a military reference and hence cannot be used to defend such a private right. Gun rights advocates respond that a common law protection of the right to keep and bear arms is guaranteed through the Ninth Amendment. *See also* FOURTEENTH AMENDMENT; FOURTH AMENDMENT; NATIONAL FIREARMS ACT OF 1934; NINTH AMENDMENT; *PRESSER V. ILLINOIS* (1886); *UNITED STATES V. CRUIKSHANK* (1876); *UNITED STATES V. MILLER* (1939).

Further Reading: Alan M. Gottlieb, "Gun Ownership: A Constitutional Right," *Northern Kentucky Law Review* 10 (1982), 113-40; Stephen Halbrook, *A Right to Bear Arms: State and Federal Bills of Rights and Constitutional Guarantees* (Westport, CT: Greenwood Press, 1989); Joyce Lee Malcolm, *To Keep and Bear Arms: The Origins of an Anglo-American Right* (Boston: Harvard University Press, 1994); Gary Wills, "To Keep and Bear Arms," *The New York Review of Books* (September 21, 1995), 62-73.

Second Amendment Committee (SAC)

The Second Amendment Committee (SAC) is a little-known organization based in Hanford, California, which takes an uncompromising stand in support of gun rights. SAC focuses much of its attention on the Second Amendment, which it calls the "keystone amendment" within the Bill of Rights, claiming that the right to keep and bear arms, being "unalienable" is incapable of being repealed. Gun rights are seen as predating the Constitution and as embedded in the common law tradition. The Committee sees such a close relationship between the Second Amendment and other freedoms guaranteed in the Bill of Rights that it claims if firearms are eliminated, private ownership of land will disappear, the use of automobiles will be restricted, the right to vote will be eliminated, states will be eradicated, and people will no longer have religious freedom.

Bernadine Smith founded SAC in 1984 to provide information to those seeking to protect a right to keep and bear arms. For 30 years, Smith has conducted a campaign against what she considers a plan to disarm individual citizens. Considering the United

Nations a threat to individual rights, she has opposed U.S. membership in the international organization. Smith argues that the Second Amendment guarantees both a collective as well as an individual right to keep and bear arms, claiming that reference to "the people" means all the people when applied to citizen militias and each person individually when applied to the individual right to keep and bear arms.

According to the Committee, citizens must protect the right to possess firearms as an element of force they require to maintain control over a potentially despotic government, to protect themselves against the injustice and abuse of public officials, to defend liberty, and to secure the nation against foreign invasion. Privately owned firearms are needed for protection against criminals because the police cannot protect the people and the police may require assistance from private citizens to keep the peace.

SAC considers itself, not the National Rifle Association (NRA), the major defender of gun rights. The organization disagrees with the policy of the NRA and the Citizens Committee for the Right to Keep and Bear Arms (CCRKBA) that involves supporting state preemption laws intended to prevent local communities from enacting firearms legislation more restrictive than state laws. The Committee fears that uniform state regulations establish a dangerous precedent for a federal preemption law that could grant to the national government extensive authority over the regulation of firearms.

The Committee argues that those state and federal government officials who support gun control have violated their oaths of office by failing to uphold the Second Amendment, which is a part of the Constitution they have pledged to defend. Any actions to bring about "the complete disarmament of the United States and the people within" are labeled "acts which are against the law" and "acts of insurrection, rebellion, sedition, or tyranny against the laws of the United States." *See also* CITIZENS COMMITTEE FOR THE RIGHT TO KEEP AND BEAR ARMS; NATIONAL RIFLE ASSO-

CIATION; SECOND AMENDMENT; UNITED NATIONS.

Further Reading: Second Amendment Committee Web site <http://www.libertygunrights.com>.

Second Amendment Foundation (SAF)

The Second Amendment Foundation (SAF) focuses on the claimed constitutional right of individuals to keep and bear arms. Alan M. Gottlieb founded SAF in 1974 as a nonprofit corporation in the state of Washington. Since its founding, the organization has focused on ways to defend the right to keep and bear arms against advocates of firearms regulation. According to SAF literature, the organization is "dedicated to promoting a better understanding of the constitutional right of private citizens to keep and bear arms." SAF has headquarters in Bellevue, Washington (in a building named for James Madison, who introduced the proposal that ultimately became the Second Amendment), and has a publishing office in Buffalo, New York. The Foundation is administered by a seven-person board of trustees, of which Gottlieb is a member.

SAF supports several publications, including *Gun Week*, a publication devoted largely to news about efforts to protect the interests of gun owners and to counter the efforts of gun control advocates; *Women and Guns*, which focuses on women's right to bear arms; *Gun News Digest*, a quarterly publication advocating the right to bear arms; *SAF Reporter*, a quarterly newsletter; *Journal of Firearms and Public Policy*, an annual publication containing reprints of articles dealing with gun rights; and the *Gottlieb-Tartaro Report*, a monthly publication containing current information on gun issues from board members Gottlieb and Joseph P. Tartaro.

Since 1976, the Foundation has organized writers and scholars conferences to encourage research on the right to keep and bear arms. The organization has sponsored or co-sponsored training conferences, including the annual Gun Rights Policy Conference, legal conferences at universities, and leadership training conferences to prepare local activists. The Foundation employs various methods to make its message known to the general public. It distributes materials to high school and college students who are preparing class assignments on firearms issues and donates pro-gun works to public and school libraries. It also distributes position papers and commentaries on gun issues to media outlets. Representatives of the Foundation regularly appear on radio and television programs and contribute articles to newspapers and magazines. As one of the organization's major spokesmen, Gottlieb makes over 350 radio and television appearances each year.

The Foundation furthers the cause of gun rights by supporting cases in the courts and filing *amicus curiae* briefs advocating the right to keep and bear arms. Among its successful actions, the organization took part in a case overturning handgun bans in San Francisco, California, and New Haven, Connecticut. Other issues that have gained SAF's attention include carrying concealed weapons (CCW) license provisions that the organization considers unfair, and bans on firearms in several cities and states. For instance, the Foundation assisted in the successful court action to end restrictive CCW license policies in Los Angeles. The organization refers those involved in gun suits to attorneys who have had experience in dealing with firearms cases.

SAF produces advertisements that are placed in newspapers and magazines, and runs radio commercials daily across the country. The Foundation occasionally funds television commercials that advocate gun rights. In its many publications, radio and television advertisements, and appearances by members, SAF places great emphasis on suggesting to the grassroots gun advocate strategies that can be followed to advance the right to keep and bear arms. *See also* CONCEALED CARRY LAWS; GOTTLIEB, ALAN MERRIL; *GUN NEWS DIGEST*; GUN RIGHTS POLICY CONFERENCE; *GUN WEEK*; SECOND AMENDMENT; WOMEN AND GUNS; *WOMEN AND GUNS* MAGAZINE.

Further Reading: Second Amendment Foundation, "Creative Innovations in Public Education and Legal Action Since 1974" (Bellevue, WA, n.d.); Second Amendment Foundation Web site <www.saf.org>; Josh Sugarmann, *National Rifle Association: Money, Firepower and Fear* (Washington, DC: National Press, 1992).

Second Amendment Foundation v. City of Renton (1983)

In *Second Amendment Foundation v. City of Renton* (688 F.2d 596, 1983), the Court of Appeals of Washington upheld a city ordinance in Renton, Washington, which made it unlawful for a person within the city limits to carry a rifle, shotgun, or pistol in any place of business where liquor is sold by the drink. This ordinance applied to individuals whether or not they had a license or permit to carry a firearm, and regardless of whether the firearm was concealed.

Four residents of Renton, supported by the Second Amendment Foundation (SAF), sought an injunction against the new gun restrictions. They claimed that the ordinance violated the state constitutional provision that granted the right of citizens to bear arms both for individual defense and for the defense of the state. The only apparent limitation on the right to bear arms involved a prohibition on any individuals or groups to organize or maintain an armed organization. SAF also claimed that the ordinance violated the Second Amendment to the U.S. Constitution, which the organization interpreted as granting individuals the right to keep and bear arms.

After the Superior Court of King County, the original trial court, ruled in favor of the city of Renton, SAF appealed the decision to the Court of Appeals. This court ruled that Renton acted appropriately when it passed the ordinance forbidding the carrying of firearms into bars. The court declared that while the state constitution did protect the individual right to bear arms, that right is liable to reasonable regulation under the state's police power. The extent of regulation depends on a balance between the good consequences expected from the specific limitation placed on the right and the extent to which the regulation impedes the intention of the constitutional provision.

The court ruled that the ordinance reduced the danger of armed encounters among those who had been drinking while minimally reducing the right to keep and bear arms. The court concluded that "on balance, the public's right to a limited and reasonable exercise of police power must prevail against the individual's right to bear arms in public places where liquor is served." The court was careful to note that had the municipality of Renton established a blanket ban on the possession of handguns even though individuals held state permits, the ordinance would have violated the state constitution and laws. However, the actual ordinance was limited in that it applied to particular places as a means to protect the public welfare, an accepted function of local government.

The court compared Washington to other states with constitutional provisions regarding the right to bear arms, noting that in all states with such provisions, the right has never been considered absolute. In addition, in five states having constitutional provisions similar to Washington's, the right to bear arms has been considered open to limitations under the police power. *See also* CONCEALED CARRY LAWS; *QUILICI V. VILLAGE OF MORTON GROVE*; SECOND AMENDMENT; SECOND AMENDMENT FOUNDATION.

Further Reading: Mark A. Siegel, Nancy R. Jacobs, and Carol D. Foster, *Gun Control: Restricting Rights or Protecting People?* (Wylie, TX: Information Plus, 1991); *Second Amendment Foundation v. City of Renton*, 688 F.2d 596 (1983).

Self-Defense

While the Second Amendment provides the foundation for a claimed constitutional justification of the right to keep and bear arms, the asserted self-defense value of guns presents the fundamental practical support for the right. The desire for a means of self-defense stands out as a major explanation for the steady increase in the total number of firearms available in the United States. Critics of gun control argue that the presence of firearms among the general population contributes to the safety of law-abiding citizens, helps to thwart criminal acts, and provides an effective deterrent to crime. However, gun control supporters claim that the number of gun accidents, homicides, and suicides each year far outweigh the defensive uses of firearms.

Depending on the type of evidence provided, either anecdotal or statistical arguments are given for the effectiveness of firearms in self-defense. Anecdotal arguments cite individual cases where a victim was able to avoid actual or potential harm because he or she carried a handgun. Gun magazines such as the *American Rifleman, Guns and Ammo*, and *Handguns* include such stories in each issue. Potential defensive users of firearms imagine themselves calling 911 after realizing their home has been invaded by someone who intends them injury. During the 10 to 15 minutes before help arrives, the victims are at the mercy of the criminal. Many conclude that having a firearm ready can provide the defense people require during those crucial minutes.

Supporters of the defensive use of firearms are careful to caution that with gun ownership comes great responsibility. The home owner should know the law. A person is permitted to use a firearm in self-defense to prevent immediate and unavoidable danger of bodily harm or death to himself or an innocent victim. These situations do not include stopping a fleeing robber, responding to a verbal insult, or stopping vandalism. In addition, the gun owner should be trained in marksmanship and combat tactics to assure proper use of firearms should an emergency situation occur. In response to those who counsel alternative methods of defense, Massad F. Ayoob, in *Armed and Alive*, has responded that the "gun is manageable. The gun is power out of the box. The gun is remote control. The gun is quickly learned. No other self-defense system ever came near this combination for effectiveness, nor did one ever approach the biggest factor of all in favor of the armed citizen's gun: deterrent effect." The Second Amendment Foundation (SAF) distributes a window sticker that de-

clares, "The owner of this property is armed and prepared to protect life, liberty and property from criminal attack. There is nothing inside worth risking your life for!"

The second strategy for supporting the self-defense value of firearms involves citing data from crime study surveys that indicate the overall defensive use of guns and their success. Critics of gun control estimate that anywhere from 800,000 to 3.6 million defensive gun uses (DGUs) occur in the United States each year. They argue that firearms provide assistance even when not used, for they deter criminals from even attempting to commit a robbery or a crime of violence when they face the possibility of armed resistance. Surveys of felons suggest that many criminals fear home owners and store owners who keep guns at the ready. Critics of gun control argue that carrying guns in public places also provides protection from criminal activity. Estimates vary from 670,000 to over 1.5 million DGUs per year related to gun carrying in public places.

Opponents of the general use of firearms for self-defense note that some researchers have over-estimated the defensive use of firearms. They note that in such studies, the definition of defensive use is left to the respondent. It is suggested that many instances may have been against animals and others may be hear-say experiences received from other family members. In 1987, it is estimated that out of over 5.5 million violent crimes, there were only 28,000 instances (half of 1 percent of the total) where victims, whether gun-owning or not, had access to a firearm. Gun control advocates contrast this figure with the thousands who die from gunshot wounds and over 150,00 who are injured each year. An estimate based on Federal Bureau of Investigation (FBI) data for 1991 indicates that for every use of a gun in a justifiable homicide, 48 lives are lost to handgun violence.

While gun advocates argue that gun owners receive a sense of security from having a firearm, opponents claim that this feeling of well-being is illusory. A firearm is an extremely deadly weapon that represents a greater threat to the residents themselves than to any potential intruder. The arguments over the self-defense value of firearms will continue, with many advocating the wide distribution of guns in the population as a deterrent to crime, and others supporting a ban on handguns. The near-universal possession of firearms could lead to a radical decrease in violent crime, or a major increase in gun accidents, suicide, and murder, or perhaps a combination of the two. *See also* ACCIDENTS INVOLVING GUNS; *AMERICAN RIFLEMAN*; AYOOB, MASSAD; *GUNS AND AMMO*; SECOND AMENDMENT; SECOND AMENDMENT FOUNDATION; SUICIDE; VIOLENT CRIME RATE.

Further Reading: Massad F. Ayoob, *Armed and Alive* (First Amendment Foundation, n.d.); Gary Kleck, *Targeting Guns: Firearms and Their Control* (New York: Aldine de Gruyter, 1997); Josh Sugarmann and Kristen Rand, *Cease Fire: A Comprehensive Strategy to Reduce Firearms Violence* (Washington, DC: Violence Policy Center, 1997); James D. Wright and Peter H. Rossi, *Armed and Considered Dangerous: A Survey of Felons and Their Firearms* (Hawthorne, NY: Aldine de Gruyter, 1986).

Shotgun News

Shotgun News, established in 1946, lists over 10,000 firearms in each issue and advertises itself as "the world's largest gun sales publication." Based in Peoria, Illinois, *Shotgun News* is an outlet for buying, selling, and trading firearms. It serves a wide range of gun enthusiasts, including hunters, collectors, target shooters, and those interested in personal defense. Thirty-six issues are published each year. In addition to advertising rifles, shotguns, and handguns, the magazine includes ads for ammunition, antique firearms, books, gun smithing services, and various accessories such as optics and mounts. Articles on gun collecting also appear in the publication. Readers are encouraged to purchase firearms advertised in the magazine through these dealers. The magazine offers a supplemental guide to federally licensed firearms dealers.

Shotgun News regularly publishes a column by Neal Knox, the "Neal Knox Report," in which the avid gun rights advocate presents news about government action relevant to firearms and reports on the political infighting within the gun rights movement, particularly the National Rifle Association (NRA). For instance, in an October 1998 issue, Knox reported on Tanya Metaksa's replacement as head of the Institute for Legislative Action, commenting that many in the NRA were unhappy with Metaksa's "tendency to ignore dissenting views from the grass roots, and her efforts to pass state 'Instant Check' laws." Knox claimed that Metaksa's replacement, James J. Baker, is considered to be the "father of the Instant Check," which Knox considers "the heart of a national registration system on all firearms."

As the 1998 session of Congress drew to a close, Knox reported on such political maneuvering as the amendment to a Justice Department appropriation proposed by Senator Bob Smith, Republican from New Hampshire, that called for the immediate destruction of all records kept on those who have applied successfully for a handgun purchase. Smith's amendment would prevent any fee being charged those whose backgrounds are being checked through the new national instant check system. The amendment would enable gun owners to sue the government if records were kept. *See also* INSTITUTE FOR LEGISLATIVE ACTION; KNOX, NEAL; METAKSA, TANYA K.; NATIONAL INSTANT CHECK SYSTEM; NATIONAL RIFLE ASSOCIATION; SAWED-OFF SHOTGUN.

Further Reading: *Shotgun News* magazine (Peoria, Illinois); Web site <www.shotgunnews.com>.

Sklar v. Byrne (1984)

Sklar v. Byrne (727 F.2d 633, 1984), a case that dealt with a Chicago, Illinois, ordinance prohibiting handgun registration after April 10, 1982, reinforced the state decision in the *Quilici v. Village of Morton Grove* (1981) case. Jerome Sklar, a handgun owner with a valid Illinois Firearms Identification Card, lived in Skokie, Illinois, when the Chicago ordinance was passed. Soon after April 10, 1982, Sklar moved to Chicago, where he discovered that the new law prevented him from registering his handgun. Therefore, he could not take the weapon with him to his new residence.

Sklar challenged the new firearms ordinance in court, arguing that Chicago had denied him the equal protection of the laws under the U.S. Constitution. Handgun owners living in Chicago before April 10, 1982, could maintain registration of their weapons, a right he was prevented from exercising. The U.S. District Court for the Northern District of Illinois ruled that the *Quilici* decision required a conclusion that the Chicago ordinance did not violate Sklar's constitutional rights. In response to Sklar's claim that Chicago could have employed alternative and more effective means of protecting citizens from the damaging consequences of firearms, the court stated that it could not invalidate a law simply because judges concluded that other policies would result in better outcomes. Only if a law were judged "wholly arbitrary" could it face the possibility of invalidation. Because the city pursued a legitimate objective, limiting the right of registration to individuals who had registered their firearms by a certain date could be considered a non-arbitrary, and hence legitimate, exercise of government power.

The district court concluded that Sklar had not been denied equal protection under the U.S. Constitution. The City of Chicago was not required to ban completely the registration of handguns. A policy-making body has the right to deal with a recognized harm piecemeal. By passing an ordinance that limited handgun ownership to those already possessing a valid registration, "a notable first step toward limiting the havoc and mayhem caused by firearms could be made."

In his appeal to the U.S. Court of Appeals for the Seventh Circuit, Sklar argued that because he could not travel to Chicago without surrendering his weapon, the city ordinance also violated his right to travel freely. The Court of Appeals, upholding the lower court ruling, denied that the case involved any constitutional issue. Because the city council had concluded that the presence of firearms and ammunition were associated with crimes, deaths, and injuries in the city,

it acted legitimately under the police power to protect the health and welfare of citizens.

Sklar further argued that the ordinance, by allowing some but not others to keep handguns, was arbitrary and unfair. The Court of Appeals rejected this argument, claiming that the grandfather clause allowing Chicago registrants to keep their handguns was a reasonable exception within the law. Although the city could have banned all handguns, the council had decided to make reasonable exceptions.

Sklar suggested that making a distinction based on qualifications for possessing a handgun constitutes a far more reasonable criterion for excluding some and not others from handgun registration. In a response similar to that given by the court of original jurisdiction, the Court of Appeals noted that the city council, as a political institution responding to many interests, could not be held to a standard of perfect consistency. A political body must be allowed the leeway to resolve a problem in the way it sees fit, which may mean only partial resolution of the difficulty. Provided that the city council devoted reasonable consideration to the question, the court should not impose its own substantive evaluation of what might constitute the best policy in a situation. *See also* QUILICI V. VILLAGE OF MORTON GROVE.

Further Reading: Mark A. Siegel, Nancy R. Jacobs, and Carol D. Foster, eds., *Gun Control: Restricting Rights or Protecting People?* (Wylie, TX: Information Plus, 1991); *Sklar v. Byrne*, 727 F.2d 633 (1984).

Small Arms Review

The *Small Arms Review* (*SAR*), which began publication in October 1997, is devoted to firearms and gun accessories restricted by the National Firearms Act, such as machine guns, silencers, short-barreled shotguns, and other "exotic weapons," including flame throwers. The magazine was established to increase interest in automatic weapons at the same time that the national government was attempting to place greater limitations on such firearms. The editorial staff contends that the National Firearms Act of 1934, which governs automatic weapons, is bad law and violates the U.S. Constitution. *SAR* provides information about various automatic weapons and reports on gun shows and shooting events involving the use of automatic weapons.

Many of *SAR*'s columns contain information and commentary on firearms legislation, particularly the National Firearms Act, which place limitations on the ownership and trade in automatic weapons. Dan Shea, the magazine's general manager, writes a column titled "Raffica," which means "burst" or "full auto" in Italian, a term that appears on the side of the author's Beretta Modello 12 submachine gun. Shea responds to readers' questions, many of which deal with interpretations of federal firearms legislation.

In the column "Industry News," Robert Hausman reports on recent developments by firearms manufacturers and sales figures for various companies. Hausman includes news items regarding gun policy, including legislation and court rulings, that could adversely affect firearms industry interests. "The Legal Side," a regular column by James Bardwell and Basil St. Clair, deals with many current legal issues regarding the possession of firearms. Bardwell and St. Clair have reported on cases that involve detailed Bureau of Alcohol, Tobacco, and Firearms (BATF) rulings about automatic weapons. The authors also deal with state court and liability cases involving firearms.

The magazine occasionally reports on the activities of related associations in a column titled "Association News." *SAR* has praised the National Rifle Association (NRA) for its Eddie Eagle Gun Safety Program and reported on that organization's construction of a National Firearms Museum. The Law Enforcement Alliance of America and Gun Owners of America (GOA) have been granted space in the magazine to describe their activities. GOA is quoted as claiming that it is "the only national organization fighting to repeal the Brady instant 'registration' check, and is alone in pushing truly constitutional CCW [carrying concealed weapons] legislation that allows honest citizens to carry a firearm without a permit." *See also* BRADY HANDGUN VIOLENCE PREVENTION ACT; BUREAU OF ALCOHOL, TOBACCO, AND FIREARMS; CONCEALED CARRY LAWS; EDDIE EAGLE; GUN OWNERS OF AMERICA; LAW ENFORCEMENT ALLIANCE OF AMERICA; NATIONAL FIREARMS ACT OF 1934; NATIONAL INSTANT CHECK SYSTEM; NATIONAL RIFLE ASSOCIATION; SAWED-OFF SHOTGUN.

Further Reading: *Small Arms Review*, (Moose Lake Publishing, Harmony, Maine); Web site <www.smallarmsreview.com>.

Smart Guns

The call for smart, or personalized, guns, firearms engineered so that only the legitimate owner may fire it, demonstrates the lack of consensus on either side of the gun control issue. Smart guns, along with trigger locks, would appear to be a proposal that gun control groups would support, but some gun control advocates are suspicious, claiming that the introduction of smart guns, assuming the technology is available, would have little preventive capacity for gun deaths and injuries in the United States. Because most firearms deaths result from suicides and homicides, simply preventing someone other than the owner from using the weapon will not prevent such violent uses of handguns.

The Violence Policy Center (VPC), an organization that advocates a handgun ban, questions the availability of technology to make the smart gun feasible. The organization expresses concern because gun control advocates who are willing to entertain smart guns would need to depend on the firearms industry to develop the technology to make a system of personalization workable. The VPC expresses skepticism about the motives of the firearms industry, which, the organization claims, is primarily interested in profits and limiting potential liability rather than improving gun safety. Therefore, the VPC resists the surface attractiveness of such mechanisms. Women, who demonstrate great concern for safety, may find the smart gun an attractive product, thus providing a new market for gun manufacturers. Gun control advocates claim that placing attention on smart gun technology could take attention away from other serious safety issues, such as the tendency of some handguns to fire without pulling the trigger when they are dropped or bumped. Therefore, the concern should be for establishing general safety standards.

Similar to gun advocates' arguments that gun locks may provide a false sense of security, some gun control supporters claim that personalized guns would give the impression that a firearm so equipped is safer than it actually is. Gun control advocates also express concern that the advocacy of smart guns creates the false impression that firearms can be beneficial for legitimate owners. They argue that firearms have little defensive value for private citizens. In contrast to the simple ban-no-ban dichotomy, smart guns would require a government bureaucracy to determine the suitableness of a particular technology and to oversee its implementation.

Comparing smart gun technology to putting filters on cigarettes, gun control supporters who advocate banning handguns fear that manufacturers will be able claim their products are far safer than they actually are. They claim that smart technology makes sense only for weapons used by law enforcement officers who run the risk of being shot by their own firearms.

Gun rights supporters resist any proposal that imposes controls on the gun owner, especially when the requirement may in some way restrict the normal use of firearms. The reaction to smart guns, similar to gun locks, will be cautious, depending on whether their use is made mandatory for all, and the extent to which the technology is considered intrusive. While some gun control supporters view smart guns as a possible strategy to expand the market for guns and to ward off more stringent safety measures, some gun advocates see them as a potential first step toward greater gun control and possible confiscation. *See also* TRIGGER LOCKS; VIOLENCE POLICY CENTER; WOMEN AND GUNS.

Further Reading: Violence Policy Center, "The False Hope of the 'Smart' Gun" (n.d.).

Smith and Wesson

Today the names Smith and Wesson elicit the image of powerful handguns. When Clint Eastwood, as movie character Dirty Harry, tells a suspect that "we" will arrest him, the suspect asks who "we" are. Eastwood responds: "Smith, Wesson, and me." The Smith and Wesson .44 Magnum handgun has achieved legendary status in American culture as "the most powerful handgun in the world." New police officers, impressed with the weapons, begin carrying them, only to shift to a smaller, less "powerful" but more easily handled weapon.

Horace Smith (1808–1893) and Daniel Baird Wesson (1825–1906) began the Smith and Wesson company. Smith began apprenticeship at the Springfield Armory in 1824 where his father had been working for some time. In 1842, he moved to Worcester, Massachusetts, where he worked for a tool-making firm. In the same year, having already demonstrated a keen interest in firearms, Wesson was indentured to his brother Edwin who operated a gunshop in Grafton, Massachusetts. By 1848, Wesson had learned the trade and he and his brother moved the operation to Hartford, Connecticut, renaming it the Wesson Rifle Company. After his brother's death in 1849, Wesson was forced to sell the estate.

In 1852, Smith and Wesson joined their independently developed talents to improve both ammunition and firearms. The two partners joined with Courtlandt Palmer to produce the Volcanic pistol, and developed the rimfire cartridge, considered a major advance in ammunition. In 1855, a group of investors, among them Oliver Winchester, bought out the Smith and Wesson operation, giving it the name Volcanic Repeating Arms Company. Wesson stayed with the company, but Smith returned to Springfield. In 1856, Wesson left Volcanic to rejoin his old partner, forming the Smith and Wesson Revolver Factory. The firm experienced success, especially in the manufacture and sale of ammunition. The Smith and Wesson Model 1 revolver and subsequent revisions proved very popular, and the Civil War boosted orders. In 1862, as the sole company that could legally produce cartridge revolvers, Smith and Wesson amassed orders that would take three years to fulfill.

In 1871, Smith, considerably older than his partner, sold out to Wesson. At that time the company received an order from the Russian government. In 1873, pleased with the results, the Russian government ordered an additional 20,000 revolvers, called the Model 3 Russian Second Model. The Japanese government bought 5,000 of these handguns, and over 6,000 were sold commercially. That same year Smith and Wesson signed a contract with the U.S. government to deliver 3,000 Schofield revolvers. After the Schofield, the company produced the New Model 3, which stayed in production for many years.

In 1917, during World War I, Smith and Wesson obtained several contracts to deliver military revolvers. Joseph Wesson, the new company president, had become ill and management of the operation suffered. Therefore, the U.S. government assumed control of the company for the duration of the war. Following the war, the company perceived three potential impediments to its continued success: 1) the surplus of weapons that dampened sales for newly manufactured guns; 2) competition from imported weapons; and 3) a developing political movement lobbying for firearms controls.

The company survived the difficult depression years of the 1930s to provide weapons during World War II. In 1946, Carl Hellstrom became the fifth individual to hold the presidency of the firm. Hellstrom avoided diversification, insisting that the company focus on gun production. During his administration, the company began producing the .44 Magnum. Hellstrom retained the presidency throughout the profitable 1950s. He was still president of the company when he died of a heart attack in 1963. When Smith and Wesson was offered a stock buyout, the company accepted. The new management insisted on product diversification and established an academy to train police officers.

By the 1990s, Smith and Wesson, unlike many gun manufacturers, was operating its facilities at near capacity, offering 187 variations of its assorted models. The company saw itself serving the interests of four categories of customers: hunters, competitive shooters, law enforcement officers, and the private person concerned with personal security. *See also* COLT, SAMUEL; REMINGTON, ELIPHALET, II; WINCHESTER, OLIVER FISHER.

Further Reading: Wayne Van Zwoll, *America's Great Gunmakers* (South Hackensack, NJ: Stoeger, 1992).

Smith v. United States (1993)

In *Smith v. United States* (508 U.S. 223, 1993), the U.S. Supreme Court examined what activities may be regarded as the "use" of a firearm in the commission of a drug crime. A federal statute [U.S.C. 924 (c) (1)] calls for mandatory prison sentences for a defendant who "during and in relation to . . . [a] drug trafficking crime uses . . . a firearm." A defendant who has used a firearm must be sentenced to five years in prison, and if the firearm is a machinegun or has been equipped with a silencer, the sentence is 30 years. Citing the dictionary definition of "use," the Court ruled that trading a firearm for drugs can count as a clear example of use within the wording of the statute. Although the dissenting justices wished to make a more definite distinction between the firing of a weapon and a firearm's involvement as an object for barter, the majority, led by Justice Sandra Day O'Connor, regarded a firearm as continually an instrument of deadly force.

Angus Smith traveled with a companion from Tennessee to Florida to purchase illegal drugs. He made a deal with an undercover policeman to receive two ounces of cocaine in return for a MAC-10 firearm, which had been converted to automatic mode capable of firing 1,000 rounds per minute. He was arrested and a federal grand jury indicted him for two drug trafficking crimes. The indictment also charged Smith with knowingly using the firearm and its silencer "during and in relation to a drug trafficking crime." Because the firearm in question had been converted to automatic operation, Smith was subject to a 30-year prison term. A jury convicted Smith on all charges.

The Court of Appeals for the Eleventh Circuit, which heard Smith's appeal, rejected his argument that the penalty established in 924 (c) (1) applies only to the use of a firearm as a weapon. Because another Court of Appeals had ruled that trading a gun in a drug transaction does not constitute a use of a firearm within the intention of the statute, the Supreme Court agreed to hear the case to resolve the disagreement. The Court noted that the prosecution had to satisfy two conditions: 1) prove that the defendant "used or carried a firearm" and 2) demonstrate that the use or carrying occurred "during and in relation to" a "crime of violence or drug trafficking crime."

Smith contended that a conviction required not only a demonstration that he used the firearm, but in addition that he used the firearm *as a weapon*. The Court observed that the words "as a weapon" appear nowhere in the statute. Although Smith appealed to what the average person would take "using a firearm" to mean, the Court ruled that the prevailing understanding does not preclude other meanings. The primary delimiter to the meaning of use, according to the Court, is whether the use occurred "during and in relation to" an incident of illegal drug trafficking.

Commenting that the meaning of a word such as "use" within a statute cannot be determined in isolation, the Court observed that the section of the federal statute dealing with forfeiture of firearms lists offenses involving the use of a firearm not only as a weapon, but also as "an item of barter or commerce." The majority held that Congress, when adding drug trafficking crimes to the statute in 1986, "employed the term 'use' expansively, covering both use as a weapon . . . and use as an item of trade or barter, as an examination of 924 (d) demonstrates."

The Court remarked further that Congress "was no doubt aware that drugs and guns are a dangerous combination," increasing the danger to the general public. The Court noted that in 1989, 80 percent of murders in Washington, D.C., were drug-related. In the *Smith* case, the firearm played an integral part in the drug transaction, which could not have proceeded without it. Therefore, finding no reason to believe that Congress did not intend a broader meaning of use, the Court upheld the lower court conviction.

Further Reading: *Smith v. United States*, 508 U.S. 223 (1993).

Soldier of Fortune

Soldier of Fortune (*SOF*) magazine opposes gun control in its own unique way. The magazine takes a survivalist attitude toward the purpose of firearms and other weapons. The magazine promotes the view that the world is a dangerous place and that each individual must become aware of the need for personal defense. The publication contains articles about mercenary activities, unusual weapons, and military conditions around the world. Each issue states this disclaimer: "There may be products in the magazine of which sale, possession or interstate transportation may be restricted, prohibited or subject to special licensing requirements in your state or nation." The magazine has begun a television series titled *Soldier of Fortune, Inc.*, which provides a video version of the articles appearing in the printed pages.

Robert Brown, a National Rifle Association (NRA) board member, publishes the magazine. He writes a column each month titled "Command Guidance," which sets the tone for each issue. Taking a conservative political stand, Brown has referred to former Representative Ron Dellums, Democrat from California, as being "as far left as one can be without having a likeness of Lenin tattooed on a visible body part." Referring to the "sissies of the Clinton Administration" and the "draft dodger" president, Brown labeled President Bill Clinton's policy toward women and homosexuals in the U.S. military one of "sissification." Brown takes the same resolute stand toward any attempt to regulate firearms.

Like other pro-gun publications, *Soldier of Fortune* targets the Bureau of Alcohol, Tobacco, and Firearms (BATF) for severe criticism. *SOF* has labeled this government agency the "Gun Gestapo." It has warned parents who educate their children at home that the Gun-Free Schools Act, which prohibits the possession of a firearm in schools, could be applied to private homes where schooling occurs. Suspicious of the BATF, *SOF* has claimed that this government agency could potentially interpret the law broadly, calling for the confiscation of firearms belonging to home-schooling families.

The magazine contains several columns that deal with political and military themes. "Slick Willie Watch" focuses on Washington politics and the policy moves of the Clinton administration. Coming under particularly intense scrutiny is the administration's military policies. Another column, "World Sitrep," a regular feature compiled in part from the biweekly newsletter *For Your Eyes Only: An Open Intelligence Summary of Current Military Affairs*, flags those points on a world map where significant political and military events and civil unrest are occurring around the world. David H. Hackwork, a retired army colonel, writes *Sound Off*, a commentary on civil-military relations.

The magazine contains advertising for many unconventional items. Its pages include several ads for locksmithing tools and instruction videos on the subject. Other ads tout martial arts training videos, "killing techniques," and the "Navy SEAL Fighting System." Paladin Press has run a two-page ad displaying books on such topics as weapons building, dirty tricks, "how to live hidden and free," how to beat drug tests, and how to change identities. Although few firearm ads appear in the magazine, accessories such as gun grips and ammunition are featured, and articles review new weaponry. A section toward the end of the magazine, called the "Supply Depot," advertises a wide variety of items, including ammunition, military products catalogs, night vision scopes, and knives. A classified section advertises such items as electronic surveillance devices, photo identification cards, and private investigator training schools. *See also* BUREAU OF ALCOHOL, TOBACCO, AND FIREARMS; CLINTON, WILLIAM JEFFERSON (BILL); GUN-FREE SCHOOLS ACT; NATIONAL RIFLE ASSOCIATION; PALADIN PRESS.

Further Reading: *Soldier of Fortune* (Mount Morris, Illinois).

Sonzinsky v. United States (1937)

In *Sonzinsky v. United States* (300 U.S. 506, 1937), the U.S. Supreme Court ruled on the constitutionality of section two of the 1934 National Firearms Act which imposed a $200 annual license tax on firearms dealers. The law required firearms dealers to register with the Internal Revenue Service (IRS) in the district in which they conduct business and to pay the special excise tax. Importers or manufacturers were taxed $500 per year. The law defined a firearm as a shotgun or rifle with a barrel less than 18 inches long, or "any other weapon, except a pistol or revolver, from which a shot is discharged by an explosive, if capable of being concealed on the person, or a machine gun, and includes a muffler or silencer for any firearm." Section three of the act imposed a tax of $200 on the transfer of each firearm, but the Court did not consider the constitutionality of that provision in its decision.

Harold Sonzinsky was convicted in a federal district court in Illinois on two counts of violating the Federal Firearms Act. The defendant appealed the case to the Circuit Court of Appeals, which reversed one conviction, but affirmed the conviction for dealing in firearms without paying the special occupational tax. The U.S. Supreme Court decided to grant certiorari to consider the original conviction. Although Sonzinsky admitted that Congress may tax his firearms business, he protested that the assessment in question was not a genuine tax, but a penalty the national legislature instituted to discourage traffic in certain types of weapons the government considered objectionable. Successive taxes imposed on dealers, manufacturers, importers, and purchasers amounted to a large penalty compared to the worth of the weapons involved, thus prohibiting trade in firearms. Sonzinsky further argued that the authority to regulate such weapons was reserved to the states.

The Court's decision did not rest on any interpretation of the Second Amendment, but rather on the taxing power of the federal government. The Court ruled that the Federal Firearms Act did not contain regulatory provisions related to the tax in such a way that the tax was primarily a means of enforcing the regulations. Section two contained no regulation other than the requirement to register as a firearms dealer, which assisted in the collection of revenues. Although Sonzinsky contended that the tax operated as a regulatory tool beyond the authority of Congress, the Court concluded that every tax is to some extent regulatory, imposing an "economic impediment" on the activity taxed in comparison to enterprises not taxed. The Court refused to speculate about the motives of Congress in establishing the $200 special occupational tax: "We are not free to speculate as to the motives which moved Congress to impose it, or as to the extent to which it may operate to restrict the activities taxed." Because the tax was not accompanied by an "offensive regulation" and did in fact operate as a tax, the provision fell within the federal taxing power. *See also* FEDERAL FIREARMS ACT; NATIONAL FIREARMS ACT OF 1934.

Further Reading: *Sonzinsky v. United States,* 300 U.S. 506 (1937).

Sporting Arms and Ammunition Manufacturers' Institute (SAAMI)

In 1926, the federal government requested that firearms and ammunition manufacturers establish the Sporting Arms and Ammunition Manufacturer's Institute (SAAMI) to develop and disseminate industry standards for firearms and ammunition, coordinate technical data, and promote safe use of firearms. SAAMI publishes over 700 voluntary standards for firearms and ammunition quality and safety. The organization notes approvingly that in 1972 Congress exempted firearms and ammunition producers from the provisions of the Consumer Safety Protection Act. The organization observes that other products are exempted, including automobiles, boats, and aircraft, and opposes any change in the firearms and ammunition exemption, objecting to the call for the regulation of firearms as a consumer product.

The Technical Committee, a subgroup of SAAMI, conducts the major work of the Institute in establishing industry standards. Two Product Standards Task Forces, one for firearms and one for ammunition, develop product standards. The SAAMI Logistics and Regulatory Affairs Committee (SLARAC), engages in the development of standards for the safe transportation and distribution of products manufactured by member companies. The committee offers advice regarding the classification, labeling, and packaging of small arms ammunition and conducts tests to confirm the safety of storage and transportation practices for small arms ammunition. SLARAC has issued a video, *Sporting Ammunition and the Firefighter,* which assures firefighters that they have little to fear when stores of ammunition are involved in a fire. No mass explosion will occur and any bullets that may be fired are of low velocity.

SAAMI publicizes firearms safety as one of its major concerns. In 1997, the organization established the Center for Firearms Safety and Responsibility, which conducts educational programs aimed at reducing the number of firearms accidents. Although SAAMI neither recommends nor discourages possession of firearms for self-protection, the organization advises those who do keep weapons in the home to abide by safe storage and handling methods. Firearms should be equipped with a locking device that is easily disengaged or kept in a locked case that can be quickly opened by the owner.

SAAMI has cited various estimates of the number of defensive uses of firearms, which have been estimated as high as 3.6 million per year. The organization has disseminated the claim that as many as 400,000 lives are saved each year through the use of firearms. Citing the research of John Lott, the organization emphasizes the deterrent effect of firearms. As for the risks of firearm ownership, the organization contends that dangers can be minimized through training and educational programs and safe handling and storage practices. According to SAAMI, the greatest danger of firearms exists outside the home and are associated with criminals on the streets.

In response to those who advocate additional gun control and the prohibition of certain types of firearms, SAAMI emphasizes that guns are "an acceptable, responsible, and desirable ingredient of our nation's heritage." In addition, the organization emphasizes the economic effects of the firearms and ammunition industry. Americans spend over $30 billion each year on hunting and shooting sports and the industry employs more than 986,000 people. Although this number of employees represents less than 1 percent of the nation's workforce, it is greater than all the people employed in both Wyoming and West Virginia. Over 1,100 manufacturers, 100 distributors, and 14,000 retailers are engaged almost totally in activities related to hunting and recreational shooting. *See also* TRIGGER LOCKS.

Further Reading: Sporting Arms and Ammunition Manufacturers' Institute Web site <www.saami.org>.

Sporting Purposes Test

Pro-gun interests have expressed their concern about the sporting purposes test for the importation of firearms, which was originally included in the Gun Control Act of 1968. In the article "The 'Sporting Purposes' Time Bomb" (1999), gun rights advocate Richard L. Gaynes contended that through the use of the sporting purposes criterion in the Gun Control Act, the Bureau of Alcohol, Tobacco, and Firearms (BATF) "has effectively provided support to the Disarm America political agenda and greatly damaged the Second Amendment rights . . . in the name of fighting violent crime." Gun control advocates consider the test necessary to keep out of the country weapons they consider devoid of any legitimate purpose.

Section 925, sub-section (d)(3) of the Gun Control Act states that "(d) The [Treasury] Secretary shall authorize a firearm or ammunition to be imported or brought into the United States or any possession thereof if the firearm or ammunition . . . (3) is of a type that does not fall within the definition of a firearm as defined in section 5845(a) [a machine gun] of the Internal Revenue Code of 1954 and is generally recognized as particularly suitable for or readily adaptable to sporting purposes, excluding surplus military firearms." In 1984, the Gun Control Act was amended by adding section (e) which states: "Notwithstanding any other provision of this title, the Secretary shall authorize the importation of, by any licensed importer, the following: (1) All rifles and shotguns listed as curios or relics by the Secretary pursuant to section 921(a)(13), and (2) All handguns, listed as curios or relics by the Secretary pursuant to section 921(a)(13), provided that such handguns are generally recognized as particularly suitable for or readily adaptable to sporting purposes."

Gaynes observed that, following the the murder of children at a Stockton, California, school by a deranged gunman wielding a semi-automatic assault rifle, BATF officials formed a working group to establish a basis within the Gun Control Act of 1968 to prohibit the importation of certain types of firearms, to determine firearms evaluation standards on which to make such prohibitions, and "to prohibit the domestic manufacture and sale of certain firearms." The focus for establishing bans was the sporting purposes test. The BATF developed a list of physical characteristics of firearms (for instance, the capability of accepting detachable magazines, the presence of a flash suppressor, or the inclusion of a separate pistol grip) that would be used to determine absence of sporting purpose. Gaynes offered several criticisms of the sporting purposes test, faulting the BATF for failing to demonstrate prevalent use of particular weapons in crimes. He charged that the BATF working group adopted a narrow interpretation of firearms to which the sporting purposes test would apply.

The group Jews for the Preservation of Firearms Ownership (JPFO) particularly opposes the sporting purposes test, associating it with a weapons law passed in Nazi Germany in 1938. The German law also contained a sporting purposes exception, permitting those who had acquired licenses to carry firearms designed for hunting game.

The JPFO is uncomfortable with the grant of authority to the Treasury secretary to determine which firearms have a sporting purpose because the Nazi law had a similar provision, granting to administrative officials and the courts the power to determine which firearms had a sporting purpose.

For gun control supporters, the sporting purposes test has none of the ominous significance attributed to it by pro-gun groups. Instead, the test has provided a basis on which to limit the importation of weapons that are considered to have no legitimate use by sporting persons and therefore are thought to be likely candidates for criminal use. *See also* BUREAU OF ALCOHOL, TOBACCO, AND FIREARMS; GUN CONTROL ACT OF 1968; JEWS FOR THE PRESERVATION OF FIREARMS OWNERSHIP; SECOND AMENDMENT; STOCKTON, CALIFORNIA, SHOOTING.

Further Reading: Richard L. Gaynes, "The 'Sporting Purposes' Time Bomb," *Guns and Ammo* 43 (January 1999), 14-17, 94, 100; Jews for the Preservation of Firearms Ownership Web site <www.jpfo.org>.

Staples v. United States (1994)

In *Staples v. United States* (U.S. Supreme Court, Docket No. 92-1441), the U.S. Supreme Court determined whether defendants had to know their actions were criminal (demonstration of mens rea) to find them guilty of the prohibited act. In this case, the offense involved a violation of a provision of the National Firearms Act of 1934 [(section 5861 (d)], which bans the possession of certain unregistered firearms, including fully automatic weapons (machine guns). Gun rights advocates had a special stake in the outcome of the case because they feared that otherwise law-abiding citizens might be prosecuted for inadvertent violations of federal firearms laws.

Local police and Bureau of Alcohol, Tobacco, and Firearms (BATF) agents, having acquired a search warrant, inspected the home of the defendant, Harold E. Staples III, and discovered an AR-15 assault rifle. This rifle is a civilian, semi-automatic version of the M-16. The M-16 contains a selector switch that allows the operator to switch from semi-automatic to automatic fire. Although the AR-15 and the M-16 have interchangeable parts, the AR-15 has a metal stop on its receiver to prevent fully automatic fire. The metal stop on the defendant's AR-15 had been filed down and a selector switch and other M-16 parts had been installed. Suspecting that the weapon was capable of fully automatic fire, BATF agents arrested Staples for violating 5861 (d). BATF testing confirmed that the AR-15 could fire more than one shot with a single pull of the trigger.

At his district court trial, the defendant testified that he was unaware of the rifle's automatic fire capability, arguing that his ignorance of the firearm's characteristics should shield him from criminal liability for failing to register the weapon. However, the court denied his request to instruct the jury that the government must demonstrate that he knew of the fully automatic capability of the firearm. He was found guilty of failing to register an automatic weapon.

On appeal, the U.S. Supreme Court rejected the government claim that Congress had not explicitly established criminal intent as a criterion for determining an offense. Justice Clarence Thomas, delivering the opinion for the Court, noted that in public welfare offenses involving especially dangerous objects, such as narcotics or hand grenades, demonstration beyond a reasonable doubt that a defendant has specific knowledge of a statutory prohibition is unnecessary to establish guilt. Noting that "there is a long tradition of widespread lawful gun ownership by private individuals in this country," the Court declared that firearms in general do not fall into the category of dangerous products. The Court further stated that "even dangerous items can, in some cases, be so commonplace and generally available that we would not consider them to alert individuals to the likelihood of strict regulation." Even though firearms may potentially cause harm, they "can generally be owned in perfect innocence."

The Court noted that to accept the government position that owners of dangerous and regulated items have an obligation to "inquire at their peril into compliance with regulations" would lead to unacceptable results, such as making it a crime to operate an automobile with an inoperative emission control system. The Court argued that in the same way the government's position would impose criminal penalties on individuals whose ignorance of the capabilities of weapons in their possession "make their actions entirely innocent."

In accepting the applicability of mens rea, the Court noted the severe penalties associated with violation of 5861 (d), which include a prison sentence of up to 10 years. Where harsh penalties are imposed, it is usually assumed that defendants must know their actions are illegal. While not attempting to define those crimes that require a "mental element," the Court concluded that Congress did not intend to "make outlaws out of gun owners who were wholly ignorant of the offending characteristics of their weapons." *See also* BUREAU OF ALCOHOL, TOBACCO, AND FIREARMS; NATIONAL FIREARMS ACT.

Further Reading: *Staples v. United States* (U.S. Supreme Court, Docket No. 92-1441, 1994).

State Firearms Preemption Laws

Responding to the policy enactments of local governments such as Morton Grove, Illinois, which in 1981 passed an ordinance banning handgun possession, gun rights groups have lobbied state legislatures to enact firearms preemption laws. Preemption measures establish state control over the issue of gun regulation and forbid local governments from enacting more stringent ordinances. Gun rights supporters considered this issue at least as important as the establishment of the right to carry concealed weapons. According to pro-gun interests, preemption laws prevent a confusing variety of local ordinances throughout a state. Local gun control measures, they argue, place gun owners in a difficult position. While crossing local jurisdiction lines within their state, they may confront widely varying ordinances regarding the right to possess and bear arms. Pro-gun forces have been successful in having preemption measures enacted in 37 states. In four other states, judicial decisions have effected policies similar to preemption. With such laws in place, local governing units are prevented from engaging in policy making in the area, thus allowing pro-gun interests to concentrate their efforts in state legislatures and the national Congress. At the same time, pro-gun control groups are denied an arena to pursue their agenda.

The case *Quilici v. Village of Morton Grove* (1981) let stand the local ordinance in Morton Grove, Illinois, banning handguns. The decision supported the argument that local governments are more suited to determine the special circumstances and needs of local citizens. While admitting that on many issues local control is preferable, pro-gun interests counter that measures dealing with the regulation of firearms are more appropriately established at the state rather than the local level. Matters most often subject to local control, pro-gun groups argue, concern real property policies and policies that have minor or no effects on those traveling through a local jurisdiction. On the other hand, local gun regulation measures have potentially serious consequences for gun owners traveling with their weapon.

Associating the preemption issue with concealed carry permits, gun rights advocates hold that local ordinances limiting the right to carry weapons nullify state-established concealed carry laws. Pro-gun interests argue that such ordinances violate the constitutionally protected right to bear arms and the individual right of self-defense. Adding to the difficulty of complying with widely varying ordinances and their legal complexities, supporters of preemption laws argue that a citizen cannot be expected to know all the various ordinances in local jurisdictions across the state. They argue that often a traveler may not know when he or she has crossed from one jurisdiction to another. *See also* KENNESAW, GEORGIA; MORTON GROVE, ILLINOIS; QUILICI V. VILLAGE OF MORTON GROVE.

Further Reading: Second Amendment Foundation, "State Firearms Preemption Laws" (Bellevue, WA, n.d.).

State v. Boyce (1983)

The Oregon case, *State v. Boyce* (658 P.2d 577, 1983), continued the trend of state courts deciding that the right to keep and bear arms, although protected in the state constitution, is subject to reasonable limitations. The city of Portland, Oregon, had passed an ordinance that prohibited anyone from carrying a loaded weapon in a public place or from driving with such a weapon in an automobile. The ordinance specified that ammunition must be absent from the weapon's chamber, cylinder, clip, or magazine. Michael Boyce, who was found guilty of violating the ordinance, appealed the conviction to the state court of appeals, arguing that the law violated the provision in the Oregon constitution that guaranteed the right to bear arms for self-defense and the defense of the state.

Boyce referred to a 1980 case (*State v. Kessler*) in which the Oregon State Supreme Court invalidated a state law that prohibited such weapons as switchblades and blackjacks. However, the appeals court refused to accept a direct correspondence between the two cases. While the law nullified by the Oregon Supreme Court forbade the very possession of certain weapons, the law at issue in *Boyce* had a more limited objective—to regulate possession in a circumscribed manner. The court ruled that such a limitation, if reasonable, could stand the test of constitutional validity.

The court commented that a government at times may pass legislation that affects a right guaranteed by the state or national constitution to protect the public safety, especially if the unlimited enjoyment of the right endangers the public welfare. Government is limited in that such restrictions must not unreasonably circumscribe the right. The court did not deny the right of individuals to protect themselves, a situation that may arise in public places. Individuals who find it necessary to protect themselves in such situations will be restricted in their right to self-defense to the extent that they must load the weapons. However, the court indicated that such an inconvenience is reasonable as a means of safeguarding the general public against pos-

sible acts of violence. *See also* STATE V. KESSLER (1980).

Further Reading: Mark A. Siegel, Nancy R. Jacobs, and Carol D. Foster, *Gun Control: Restricting Rights or Protecting People?* (Wylie, TX: Information Plus, 1991); *State v. Boyce*, 658 P.2d 577 (1983).

State v. Kerner (1921)

The 1921 case, *State v. Kerner* (181 N.C. 574, 107 S.E. 222, 1921), involves an appeal by the state of North Carolina to reverse a lower court ruling that the defendant was not guilty of violating a statute prohibiting the carrying of a pistol. The appeals court's decision focused upon an interpretation of Article I, section 24 of the North Carolina state constitution, which reads, "The right of the people to keep and bear arms shall not be infringed. . . . Nothing herein contained shall justify the practice of carrying concealed weapons or prevent the legislature from enacting penal statutes against said practice." The court ultimately ruled in Kerner's favor, ruling that the statute violated the provisions of the state constitution.

Kerner had been walking along the street when another individual accosted him. Kerner set down the packages he was carrying, went to his place of business to secure a pistol, and returned to the scene of the altercation with the weapon in open sight. He was arrested and indicted for violating Chapter 317, Public Laws 1919, which prohibited citizens of Forsyth County from carrying concealed weapons and required a permit to carry a weapon openly. Violation of the statute resulted in a misdemeanor violation. The court of original jurisdiction, concluding that the statute violated the constitutional guarantee of the right to bear arms, directed a verdict of not guilty. The state appealed the verdict.

The appeals court made the distinction between the "sacred right" to bear arms, and the "practice of carrying concealed weapons," which could be controlled to prevent assassinations and other "advantages taken by the lawless." The right to bear arms included the right to possess and carry a rifle, musket, shotgun, or pistol. The possession of any weapon in common use at the time the constitution was adopted could not be denied to citizens. However, the court rejected a constitutional right to carry and use more contemporary weapons, such as bombs dropped from a "flying machine," those used in submarines, or lethal gases.

The court concluded that the colonists successfully repulsed the British at Lexington in 1775 because the people had been "accustomed to bear arms." In like manner, the regular use of arms allowed pioneers to repulse Indian attacks and to defend the country against the French at New Orleans. The court revealed a contemporary interpretation of oppression, not in terms of government action, but the activities of powerful private groups. Corporations employing detectives or private police could intimidate and oppress the people, leaving them "completely at the mercy of these great plutocratic organizations," if they were denied the right to bear arms. Although a country often resorts to disarming the people when the use of force prevails, the court reasoned that the people should have the opportunity to "meet illegal force with legal force" to defend themselves.

The court recognized circumstances in which the right to bear arms could be limited, thus affirming the distinction between regulation and banning. Prohibitions on bearing firearms by those under the influence of alcohol were justified, as was the possession of deadly weapons in particular locations, such as church, polling places, or public assemblies, or to "inspire terror." Such limitations the court considered "mere regulations" unoffensive to the constitutional guarantee. In addition, the legislature could reasonably regulate the length of firearms to prevent their being concealed on the person.

Nonetheless, the basic right of the people to use firearms to protect themselves had to be guaranteed. The court objected especially to the statute at issue because it required citizens to apply to the municipal or superior court to receive permission to carry a firearm off their premises and mandated that a permit be purchased for each weapon. With such restrictions, the peaceful citizen would be at the mercy of the lawless should violent

disorder occur. Because Kerner had acted to protect himself and his property, the appeals court ruled that the court of original jurisdiction acted properly when it determined that he was not guilty because the statute was offensive to the state constitution. *See also* CONCEALED CARRY LAWS.

Further Reading: Earl R. Kruschke, *The Right to Keep and Bear Arms* (Springfield, IL: Charles C. Thomas, 1885); *State v. Kerner*, 181 N.C. 574, 107 S.E. 222 (1921).

State v. Kessler (1980)

The Court of Appeals of the state of Oregon, in *State v. Kessler* (Or. 614 P.2d 94, 1980), examined the right to bear arms for personal defense and protection of property. The case involved possession of a billy club, not a firearm, but the court's decision that having a club in the home is protected by the Oregon state constitution is relevant to firearms as well.

Randy Kessler had been engaged in an intermittent argument with his apartment manager. At first only verbal, the confrontation intensified into moderate physical violence, such as the defendant kicking the elevator door of the building. When the police came to arrest Kessler, they discovered two billy clubs in his apartment. He was charged with disorderly conduct and "possession of a slugging weapon." The defendant moved to dismiss the charge, arguing that no actual crime had been committed. The court denied the motion and found Kessler guilty as charged on both counts.

The defendant appealed the conviction to the Court of Appeals, asserting first of all that his actions did not constitute disorderly conduct, and second, that the statute under which he was charged for possession of a billy club violated Article I, section 27 of the Oregon state constitution by denying him the right to have a weapon for personal defense in the home. That section states that, "The people shall have the right to bear arms for the defence [sic] of themselves, and the State, but the Military shall be kept in strict subordination to the civil power." The Oregon statute prohibited the possession of a "billy," but allowed police officers to carry a billy club, or "blackjack."

The court entered into an analysis of the origins of the state constitutional provision, which can be traced to other state constitutions drafted in the revolutionary war era and shortly thereafter. These state constitutions often included a bill of rights patterned after the English Bill of Rights of 1689. Like that document, the state constitutions guaranteed the right to bear arms and betrayed a general suspicion of standing armies, especially in time of peace. The court traced the right contained in the state constitution of Oregon directly to the Indiana constitution adopted in 1816, and determined that the phrase "for defence of themselves, and the State" probably derived from either the Kentucky constitution of 1799 or the Ohio constitution of 1802. This wording also appeared in the constitutions of Oregon and seven other states. The identical language notwithstanding, differing interpretations of its significance have developed. The phrase was placed in these constitutions either to indicate a preference for a militia over a standing army, to provide for a curb on government abuse of authority, or to guarantee the right of personal defense.

The court noted that historically, the right to bear arms for personal defense and protection of property gained special significance in the United States due to the uncertainties of rural life in early America. The term "arms," the court argued, came to refer in state constitutions to all those objects that settlers used for personal as well as military defense, including guns, hatchets, swords, and knifes. The court concluded that more advanced weapons used in modern warfare were intended exclusively for military use and therefore their personal possession could not be justified as protected under the constitutional right of the individual to bear arms for purposes of self-defense. Therefore, while the legislature could limit the right to carry a concealed club in public, it could not institute a blanket prohibition on keeping a club in the home. *See also* CONCEALED CARRY LAWS.

Further Reading: Earl R. Kruschke, *The Right to Keep and Bear Arms* (Springfield, IL: Charles C.

Thomas, 1985); *State v. Kessler*, Or. 614 P.2d 94 (1980).

State v. Rosenthal (1903)

In *State v. Rosenthal* (75 Vt. 295, 55 A. 610, 1903), the Appeals Court of Vermont heard the claim that the Rutland city ordinance that forbade the carrying within city limits of "any steel or brass knuckles, pistol, slung shot, stiletto, or weapon of similar character," or a concealed weapon, except with the permission of the mayor or chief of police, violated the state constitution that guaranteed the right to bear arms. The court ruled in favor of Andrew Rosenthal, stating that individuals have the right, under the state constitution, to bear arms for their defense.

Rosenthal was charged with carrying a loaded and concealed pistol within the city limits in violation of the city ordinance. The defendant argued that the statute under which he was charged, by forbidding the carrying of a pistol, was in violation of the state constitutional provision granting to the people of the state the right to bear arms for self-defense and defense of the state. The court determined that the council had not been delegated the clear right to enact the ordinance at issue, especially given the constitutional guarantee of the right of the people to bear arms.

The court placed prime importance on the intent involved in carrying a firearm. It pointed to a state statute prohibiting the carrying of a deadly weapon, whether in the open or concealed, with the *intention* of harming another person. A further provision banned the carrying of a deadly weapon while the person was "in attendance upon a school," and another section of state law penalized the intentional pointing of a firearm toward another individual, or the firing of a weapon toward another person, whether or not injury resulted. However, these limitations did not apply when firearms were used for self-defense or carried by an officer of the law in the conduct of his duty, or in the case of justifiable homicide. Therefore, an individual not associated with a school may bear a firearm, whether in the open or concealed, unless the *intent* of the bearer is to injure another person.

Relying on precedent, the court noted that a land owner could employ reasonable force in deterring a trespasser and therefore could rightfully defend himself against assault from the trespasser. If the land owner intended to employ a pistol solely for self-defense, then bearing the firearm should be judged lawful. In contrast, the city ordinance of Rutland forbade the carrying of a weapon for any purpose prior to acquiring permission in writing from the mayor or police chief. Therefore, the ordinance did not consider the essential importance of the firearm bearer's intentions when determining whether an offense had occurred. Conversely, if a person acquired permission to carry a weapon, then even though the intent of carrying a weapon was to injure another person, there would be no violation of the ordinance. The ordinance prohibited the carrying of a weapon when the constitution and the laws of the state regarded such carrying as legal, but at the same time allowed the bearing of weapons when the general laws of the state considered it a crime. Therefore, the court determined that the city ordinance conflicted with the constitution and laws of the state. *See also* CONCEALED CARRY LAWS.

Further Reading: Earl R. Kruschke, *The Right to Keep and Bear Arms* (Springfield, IL: Charles C. Thomas, 1985); *State v. Rosenthal*, 75 Vt. 295, 55 A. 610 (1903).

Stevens v. United States (1971)

In *Stevens v. United States*, 440 F.2d 144, 149 (1971), the United States Court of Appeals for the Sixth Circuit upheld a provision of the Gun Control Act of 1968 [18 U.S.C. App. Section 1202 (a) (1)] that prohibits convicted felons from receiving, possessing, or transporting a firearm. In presenting its decision, the Appeals Court expressly rejected an individualist interpretation of the Second Amendment. The relevant portion of the statute states that, "Any person who has been convicted by a court of the United States or of a State or any political subdivision thereof of a felony . . . and who receives, possesses, or transports in commerce or affecting commerce, after the date of enactment of this Act, any firearm shall be fined not more than $10,000 or imprisoned for not more than two years, or both."

Frank James Stevens appealed his conviction for violating this provision. In 1958, a Kentucky court found him guilty of armed assault with intent to rob, and in 1962 he was found guilty of voluntary manslaughter. Following passage of the Gun Control Act of 1968, Stevens was charged with possessing a 9-mm Astra semi-automatic pistol. Not denying any of the facts in the prosecution's case against him, Stevens argued that the conviction should be dismissed because the indictment did not assert, and the evidence did not demonstrate, that his possession of a firearm was "in commerce or affecting commerce." The appellant argued that the phrase "in commerce or affecting commerce" modified all three actions, "receives," "possesses," and "transports," while the government contended that the phrase applies only to "transports." The court's ruling that Stevens's position lacked credibility depended on the absence of a comma in the statute after the word "transports." Independent of congressional intent, the appellant's argument could prevail only with a comma in place, which would indicate that the commerce phrase modified all three activities.

Recognizing Congress's determination that convicted felons who possess firearms pose a threat to interstate commerce, the court concluded that Congress has the constitutional authority to prohibit such possession. Congress reasonably considered the rate of recidivism and crimes such as bank robbery that impede commerce as relevant considerations in establishing the prohibition of gun ownership by felons. Stevens, twice convicted of a felony before being discovered in possession of a firearm, belonged to the class of individuals that Congress intended to deny the right to possess firearms. Although an individual case may appear to affect commerce remotely, the court declared that Congress need not wait until commerce has been severely interrupted before taking protective action.

While Stevens claimed that Congress had no authority under the Constitution to deny him the privilege of possessing a firearm, the court argued that the Second Amendment right to keep and bear arms refers to a state right to maintain a militia, not to an individual right to bear arms. The court declared that no serious claim could be made that individuals have an explicit constitutional right to possess firearms and concluded that Congress has the authority, under the commerce clause of the Constitution, to limit firearms possession. *See also* GUN CONTROL ACT OF 1968; SECOND AMENDMENT.

Further Reading: *Stevens v. United States,* 440 F.2d 144, 149 (1971).

Stockton, California, Shooting

The Stockton, California, shooting at an elementary school, in which several children were killed and wounded, sparked a fresh surge toward gun control legislation that resulted in passage of measures to limit the purchase and possession of assault rifles. On January 17, 1989, Patrick Purdy entered the school yard carrying a Chinese-made AK-47. Purdy was a drifter who had lived in Stockton, California, during his youth and had attended the school. He began shooting at the mostly Cambodian, Vietnamese, Chinese, and Hispanic children, killing five girls and wounding 29 others. Police estimated the shooter fired over 106 rounds in a matter of a few minutes. Purdy then took his own life with a pistol.

The previous August, Purdy had purchased the AK-47 from a gun dealer in Sandy, Oregon, for $349.95. At that time, only three states—Hawaii, Illinois, and Pennsylvania—required a waiting period to purchase a rifle or a shotgun. Purdy gave a false name on a federal form necessary for the purchase, which required each gun purchaser to state that he or she is not a convicted criminal, under indictment, a drug addict, or mentally ill. At that time, the federal government required no background check or waiting period. No effective means existed to verify the information required on the form. The dealer

had to inform the Bureau of Alcohol, Tobacco, and Firearms (BATF) of the sale, and provide a description and serial number of the weapon and the type of identification presented at the time of purchase. Nonetheless, the purchaser's name was not provided to the BATF. An assault weapon containing a high-capacity ammunition magazine could be purchased as easily as a rifle or a shotgun.

Following the Stockton shooting, supporters of more stringent gun control legislation moved quickly to enact measures to ban assault weapons. Within two weeks of the Stockton tragedy, bills were introduced into the California legislature to ban the manufacture, sale, and possession of various rifles and pistols. Senator Howard Metzenbaum, Democrat from Ohio, introduced similar legislation in Congress. Twenty-seven additional states were considering a variety of measures to limit or ban assault weapons. Ironically, the general call for a ban led to significantly increased sales of AK-47s, apparently fueled by gun enthusiasts who wished to beat the deadline for the beginning of the prohibition.

Amid the overall momentum for new legislation, opponents of any ban argued that an attempt to prohibit particular weapons would not achieve its objective. They recommended instead that sentences for using firearms in a crime be increased and enforcement of bans on the ownership of guns by convicted criminals and the mentally unstable be tightened. Don B. Kates, a major opponent of gun control legislation, attempted to focus the debate on the more basic causes of violence in our society: socio-economic and cultural factors such as poverty and broken families. He claimed that guns themselves did not affect the crime rate, and to institute a general gun ban only succeeded in taking firearms away from "good citizens" who would not misuse the weapons and who needed the guns for their own protection.

Despite opposition from pro-gun groups, within a month of the school shooting the city councils of Stockton and Los Angeles had approved bans on the sale or possession of semi-automatic weapons equipped with a detachable magazine that could hold at least

20 rounds. The measures, which also banned sawed-off shotguns holding at least six shells, made any violation a misdemeanor punishable by six months in prison and a maximum fine of $1,000. The Los Angeles City Council approved an ordinance on February 7 by a unanimous vote and Mayor Tom Bradley signed the measure that same day.

Beginning February 10, 1989, Senator Metzenbaum held hearings on banning a number of assault weapons, at which a teacher at the Stockton school described the shooting in vivid detail. Although progress toward a ban did not proceed as quickly on the national level, public outrage at the shooting led steadily toward limitations on assault weapons. Even former Republican President Ronald Reagan, who had strongly opposed gun control, expressed his cautious support for a ban on assault weapons.

The Stockton shooting put gun rights groups at a definite disadvantage in the struggle over gun control. Arguments about the defensive advantages of firearms and the underlying causes of gun violence in the United States did not sway the public away from the perception that a horrible person had killed and injured many children, and the instrument he used with frightening efficiency was an assault weapon. *See also* AK-47; ASSAULT WEAPONS BAN; BUREAU OF ALCOHOL, TOBACCO, AND FIREARMS; KATES, DON B.; REAGAN, RONALD; ROBERTI-ROOS ASSAULT WEAPONS ACT.

Further Reading: Wilbur Edel, *Gun Control: Threat to Liberty or Defense Against Anarchy?* (Westport, CT: Praeger, 1995); *New York Times*, January 19, 1989, p. B6; January 28, p. 1; February 4, p. 27; March 3, p. 20.

Stop Handgun Violence, Inc. (SHV)

Stop Handgun Violence, Inc. (SHV), was established in 1995 by businessmen and women concerned about the high number of firearms-related deaths in the United States. The founders were especially alarmed that children were the victims of firearms violence. Troubled by several school shootings in 1997 and 1998, the SHV called for greater efforts to reduce the access youth have to firearms.

Headquartered in Newton, Massachusetts, the SHV participates in public awareness campaigns, educational programs, and community outreach to inform the public about the dangers of firearms. To finance media presentations, the organization has conducted fund-raising events, such as benefit concerts, educational house parties, and t-shirt sales.

The SHV focuses its public awareness campaigns on highly emotional individual cases of firearms-related deaths, especially among young people. As its first project, the organization constructed a large "tribute wall" facing the Massachusetts Turnpike. Motorists could read the message, "The cost of handguns keeps going up. Fifteen kids killed every day." The pictures of 15 children under age 19 appeared below the message. Noting that the number of young people killed by firearms has declined in recent years, the organization claims that through its efforts as well as the work of law enforcement officials and other organizations, 10 rather than 15 children are killed by firearms each day.

The SHV is expanding its billboard messages throughout Massachusetts and other states and is working in cooperation with Cease Fire, Inc., to produce public service announcements to warn against the dangers of handguns. Believing that the use of trigger locks is an important step in preventing firearms accidents, especially those involving children, organization members have worked to establish community-based trigger lock distribution programs. Such programs have been conducted in Massachusetts cities as well as in New Hampshire, Maine, and Miami, Florida. Another project involves the development of a school curriculum geared to prevent firearm accidents among young people. At the state level, the SHV lobbied the Massachusetts legislature to pass legislation banning assault weapons. Such a bill was ratified in 1998, but did not ban any weapons not already prohibited by federal law.

Through its affiliated organization, Not Bulletproof, the SHV worked with Massachusetts state legislators to pass a gun safety bill that became law in July 1998. The law is considered the most comprehensive gun control legislation in the country. The SHV hopes to expand its agenda to the national level, advocating firearms training, gun licensing, and registration. Another objective of the SHV involves expansion of the national assault weapons ban to include prohibitions on the possession and sale of copycat weapons and high capacity magazines. The organization is a strong advocate of regulation of firearms by the Consumer Product Safety Commission in the same manner in which Massachusetts has come to regulate guns as consumer products. The organization supports one-gun-a-month legislation that would limit an individual to purchasing just one handgun in a 30-day period, and advocates the application of personalization technology to firearms so that only the intended user may fire a gun. *See also* ACCIDENTS INVOLVING GUNS; ASSAULT WEAPONS BAN; CEASE FIRE, INC.; JONESBORO, ARKANSAS, SCHOOL SHOOTING; LITTLETON, COLORADO, SCHOOL SHOOTING; SCHOOLS AND GUNS; TRIGGER LOCK; YOUTH AND GUNS.

Further Reading: Stop Handgun Violence, Inc., Web site <www.stophandgunviolence.com>; "Major Accomplishments" (SHV, 1998); "National Solutions to Gun Violence" (SHV, 1998).

Student Pledge Against Gun Violence

The Student Pledge Against Gun Violence, coordinated by Mary Lewis Grow and headquartered in Northfield, Minnesota, involves a campaign to have students pledge not to use firearms in anger. The Student Pledge states, "I will never bring a gun to school; I will never use a gun to settle a dispute; and I will use my influence with my friends to keep them from using guns to settle disputes. My individual choices and actions, when multiplied by those of young people throughout the country, will make a difference. Together, by honoring this pledge, we can reverse the violence and grow up in safety." Each fall since 1996 the pledge movement has sponsored a Day of National Concern about Young People and Gun Violence, involving students around the country.

In 1996, Grow originated the idea of the Student Pledge and the Day of National Con-

cern during a meeting with Bill Bradley, Democratic senator from New Jersey. Bradley introduced a Senate resolution calling for a Day of National Concern and the national distribution of the Student Pledge. In 1997, Senators Patty Murray, Democrat from Washington, and Dirk Kempthorne, Republican from Idaho, in a demonstration of bipartisan support for the Day of National Concern, sponsored a similar resolution. Each year the resolution passed by unanimous consent. On November 6, 1997, President Bill Clinton issued a proclamation calling for the observance of that day as one of concern for young people.

Various groups, including the American Federation of Teachers, Handgun Control, Inc., Physicians for Social Responsibility, the Educational Fund to End Handgun Violence, and the American Medical Association have endorsed the Student Pledge. For the 1998 Day of National Concern, various organizations cooperated in publicizing the event. The United Way of America sent packets to 600 chapters, the National Education Association distributed materials to its local organizations, and the American Federation of Teachers reported on the Student Pledge in its newsletter. Several cities, including New York, Philadelphia, Boston, Chicago, and Washington, D.C., distributed Pledge materials to local schools.

Organizers of the Student Pledge campaign encourage parents, community groups, and religious organizations to take part in the National Day of Concern. Teachers are asked to initiate special activities, such as art projects and writing assignments. Social studies teachers are encouraged to invite an emergency room physician to speak to students at an all-school assembly about the special problems involved in treating gun-shot wounds. Another suggestion is to ask someone who has lost a relative to gun violence, or a survivor of a gunshot wound, to speak to students. The organizers recommend the use of children's books to convey the message that carrying firearms is dangerous. During the 1998 Day of National Concern, programs in various states emphasized the dangers of firearms to youth, often presenting personal accounts of firearms violence. In the context of several highly publicized school shootings, many prominent public officials agreed to take part in encouraging young people to sign the Student Pledge. *See also* CLINTON, WILLIAM JEFFERSON (BILL); EDUCATIONAL FUND TO END HANDGUN VIOLENCE; HANDGUN CONTROL, INC.; MOTHERS AGAINST VIOLENCE IN AMERICA; NATIONAL EDUCATION ASSOCIATION; PHYSICIANS FOR SOCIAL RESPONSIBILITY.

Further Reading: Student Pledge Against Gun Violence Web site <www.pledge.org>.

Suicide

Pro-gun control groups have pointed to the prevalence of suicide involving guns as a reason for further legislation limiting the availability of firearms. Data indicate that guns are more frequently involved in suicides than in homicides. Evidence is also marshaled to demonstrate that gun suicide attempts are successful more often than other common methods of self-destruction, such as hanging, carbon monoxide poisoning, and drowning. The argument over gun control and suicide revolves around the interpretation of often inadequate statistical research and the attempt to determine whether gun availability itself contributes to a higher suicide rate.

Researchers disagree about whether stricter legislation would result in fewer suicides (or fewer successful attempts) overall. If guns were not as readily available, would other methods simply be substituted? Gun control opponents argue that prospective suicides have a number of means available to them and therefore the unavailability of guns would not affect the total number of people who commit suicide. Therefore, while limiting gun availability might reduce the number of suicides in that category, the overall suicide rate would remain largely unchanged. As Gary Kleck has commented, "Few people would argue . . . that it is a worthwhile goal of public policy merely to shift suicides from one method to another, without producing any net reduction in the total number of suicides." Much depends on the actual avail-

ability of other methods, the preferences for a method by those making the attempt (some might be committed to one method and would not initiate the act if it were not available), and the seriousness of intent. Perhaps those using less lethal methods do so because their resolve is less certain than those using firearms. Therefore, if guns were less available, the resolve of those who would otherwise choose this method would lead them to use equally lethal means.

Suicide among young people is an especially troubling problem. While the suicide rate for all age groups increased slightly from 1950 to 1980, the rate for adolescents tripled. Suicide has become the third most common cause of death among children and the second most common cause among older teenagers. In *The Politics of Gun Control* (1995), Robert Spitzer cited a study of adolescent suicide in Chicago that reported large numbers of adolescent suicides among the children of law enforcement officers. While the availability of guns may have only a modest effect on the overall suicide rate, there is evidence that such availability may have a far greater impact on the adolescent suicide rate. *See also* KLECK, GARY; YOUTH AND GUNS.

Further Reading: Gregg Lee Carter, *The Gun Control Movement* (New York: Twayne, 1997); Gary Kleck, *Point Blank: Guns and Violence in America* (New York: Aldine de Gruyter, 1991); Robert J. Spitzer, *The Politics of Gun Control* (Chatham, NJ: Chatham House, 1995).

Sullivan Law

In 1911, the New York State legislature, responding to a popular outcry against street violence in New York City, passed the Sullivan Dangerous Weapons Law, the most stringent gun control legislation up to that time. For 50 years, the law stood as the model for such legislation. It required individuals to acquire a license to possess or carry a concealable weapon and made it a felony to carry a firearm small enough to be concealed on the person. Because the law contained a provision making it illegal for aliens to possess firearms "in any public place," opponents of gun control legislation have pointed to the Sullivan

This turn-of-the-century cartoon, entitled "The Free and Untrammeled Revolver," illustrates the misuse of handguns that led to the passage of the Sullivan gun control law in New York State in 1911. *Corbis-Bettmann.*

law as an example of the ulterior motives behind, and hence the illegitimacy of, such measures.

Although the 1911 law applied to the entire state of New York, state legislators had New York City in mind when passing the measure. In the 1870s, New York City politicians first began to consider proposals to regulate the carrying of concealed handguns. The response of many resemble more recent opposition to gun control: only law-abiding citizens would be affected, thus decreasing their ability to defend themselves against criminals. Although the Board of Aldermen approved an ordinance in 1877 that required a permit to carry a concealed weapon, it was not effectively enforced. The Board of Aldermen approved another concealed weapons ordinance in 1905 that raised the penalties for violations.

As in more recent years, many shocking newspaper accounts of firearms violence moved New York politicians toward further legislation. In 1910, a disgruntled former public employee shot and seriously wounded Mayor William J. Gaynor. Newspapers covered the mayor's long recovery and frequently printed articles dealing with gun violence. Notable city residents formed a citizens committee that called for stronger legislation. As gun violence gained increasing public visibility, politicians were drawn to the issue. Timothy D. "Big Tim" Sullivan, a Tammany politician recently elected to the state senate, promised to introduce a bill to regulate the purchase, possession, and carrying of concealed weapons. In January 1911, after David Graham Phillips, a popular novelist, was shot and killed on a New York City sidewalk, the concern for concealed weapons increased considerably. A report issued shortly thereafter indicating that gun homicides had risen nearly 50 percent in the previous year gave legislators further incentive to act.

When the state senate held hearings, the only people who spoke against the new legislation were hardware merchants from New York City and lobbyists representing small arms manufacturing firms. The overwhelming sentiment was in favor of passing a more restrictive measure. New York City's judges, police officials, and magistrates almost without exception supported passage. A mood of optimism regarding the possible beneficial results of new legislation pervaded the legislature and New York newspapers. Sullivan declared, "If this bill passes, it will do more to carry out the commandment thou shalt not kill and save more souls than all the talk of all the ministers and priests in the state for the next ten years." With virtually no organized opposition, the bill passed by overwhelming majorities in both houses of the state legislature.

Among its provisions, the legislation made carrying an unlicensed firearm a felony, mandated a permit to possess a concealable firearm, and required that pistols be sold only to those who presented a permit for possessing or carrying a weapon. Anyone selling a firearm was required to keep records of sales, identifying the purchaser by name, age, occupation, and residence, and reporting the caliber, make, model, and manufacturer's number of the firearm. The law made a misdemeanor of the sale, loan, lease, or gift to a person under 16 years old of any firearm, air gun, or spring gun. Any unlawful weapons seized were to be destroyed or made useless by the chief law enforcement officer of the jurisdiction. The law applied to other weapons, making it a misdemeanor to make or have made, or sell or give "a blackjack, bludgeon, sandbag, sandclub, billy, sl[i]ngshot, metal knuckles, etc. to any other person."

The optimism that the new legislation would certainly reduce the number of homicides appeared to be substantiated by initial reports. The Coroner's Report for 1912 indicated that the number of firearm suicides had declined by 40 percent compared with the previous year. However, the number of homicides actually increased from 1910 to 1912, suggesting the difficulty that has existed ever since in attempting to interpret data regarding the effects of gun control legislation.

After the initial euphoria had subsided, objections began to arise. The National Rifle Association (NRA) complained that the law made it difficult for an "honest man" and "good citizen" to acquire a pistol. Many questioned the Sullivan Law's constitutionality, but it survived court challenges. The law is still in effect, despite many attempts at repeal. It has been amended many times, but the fundamental purpose has remained constant. Many claim that the law has done little to reduce crime in New York City, while others argue that the crime rate would have been even higher without it. Some note that New York residents have found it easy to transport guns from other jurisdictions with more lenient gun regulations and therefore advocate more stringent national legislation. *See also* CONCEALED CARRY LAWS; NATIONAL RIFLE ASSOCIATION.

Further Reading: Lee Kennett and James LaVerne Anderson, *The Gun in America: The Origins of a National Dilemma* (Westport, CT: Greenwood, 1975); *New York Times* (May 17, 1911), 12, (August 29, 1911), 5, (August 30, 1911), 6; Josh Sugarmann, *The National Rifle Association: Money, Firepower and Fear* (Washington, DC: National Press, 1992).

Survivalism

Survivalism involves the belief that world or national social, economic, and political systems will collapse in the foreseeable future, leaving each individual, or groups of individuals, to fend for themselves, including providing for personal security and defense. Therefore, the right to keep and bear arms has been a major concern of survivalists, who believe that firearms represent an important ingredient for surviving the anticipated conflagration. Among the possible sources of the expected disruption are natural disasters, famine and disease, terrorist attacks, economic collapse and resulting civil unrest, global warfare, government disintegration or tyranny, and class, race, or religious conflict.

Although survivalist groups tend to differ in the emphasis they place on firearms and other weapons, guns remain an important ingredient in most survival scenarios. Because firearms are often considered crucial to surviving a variety of perceived dangers, survivalists react strongly against those who advocate gun control, considering them enemies of the Bill of Rights and threats to the security of the nation. The Rocky Mountain Survival Group (RMSG), which takes a more moderate position on the possession and use of firearms, holds that the right to keep and bear arms includes rifles, pistols, and shotguns that are commonly used by military forces, but accepts limitations on the right to possess cannons, mines, tanks, and other weapons capable of causing mass destruction.

Meg Raven, who is associated with the RMSG, encourages careful thought before deciding to carry a firearm and emphasizes safe usage and maintenance, but claims that most firearms owners fail the safety criterion. Professional snipers and expert hunters possess the virtues of self-control and patience that the average shooter does not have. Raven notes that those not prepared to shoot a human being may have the weapon taken away from them and advises that they would be safer not acquiring guns and concentrating instead on "nonviolent methods of escape and evasion." Nonetheless, despite these cautions, the basic survivalist logic calls for some means of defense, and firearms are the most available solution.

Raven identifies five distinct types of survivalist groups. The first are called "low impact, back-to-nature" organizations that intend to rely on the natural environment for survival. They emphasize such skills as botany, meteorology, holistic medicine, and plant cultivation. The second, "primitive skills" groups, focus on developing non-technological skills and are often associated with religious organizations such as the Quakers and the Amish. The third, "high-tech" groups, expect to depend on advanced technology to support them during a catastrophe. Para-military groups concentrate on collecting firearms and conducting military training. Raven does not consider them true survivalists, labeling them "borderline terrorists" that law enforcement organizations are justified in suppressing. Raven believes that "positive action/combined skills" groups have the best strategy, which involves integrating the views of the previous four.

Several enterprises concentrate on providing services to survivalists. Some provide storable food supplies and others, such as S.T.A.R.T. (Survival Training and Reaction Team) offer survival preparation courses. Consumertronics sells publications in all areas of survivalism, including materials on homemade explosives, firearms, booby traps, and self-defense. *See also* GRITZ, JAMES (BO); SELF-DEFENSE.

Further Reading: Consumertronics Web site <http://www.tsc-global.com>; Rocky Mountain Survival Group Web site <http://www.artrans.com/rmsg>; Survival Training and Reaction Team Web site <http://members.aol.com/nesurvival>.

Switzerland

While gun rights supporters argue that Switzerland's experience with firearms confirms their opposition to gun control in the United States, gun control advocates conclude that the Swiss case supports their call for more stringent gun control legislation. Gun supporters note the widespread availability of guns in Switzerland (over 2 million in a population of just over 7 million), where the crime rate is low. For instance, in 1995, Switzerland had just 113 firearms-related homicides. However, gun control proponents point to the extensive regulations the federal and canton governments impose on firearms ownership. Some suggest that the Swiss culture is primarily responsible for the low crime rate in a nation with extensive private gun ownership.

Swiss attitudes toward weapons were forged in a 200-year revolutionary battle for independence that ended in 1499 when Emperor Maximilian finally granted Switzerland complete autonomy. In the following centuries, the country defended its independence against invaders, relying upon a militia composed of all able-bodied male citizens who, until the late nineteenth century, provided their own weapons. Switzerland maintained neutrality in conflicts among various European powers, but many Swiss, having acquired military training, became mercenaries, serving in foreign armies. From the thirteenth to the twentieth centuries, citizenship was closely associated with weapons possession and service in the militia. The close association of citizen rights and military service meant that women were traditionally excluded from political participation long after they had won political rights in other Western democracies. Today, women have the same rights as men, including the right to purchase firearms.

All able-bodied males must complete military service. Men between the ages of 21 and 32 serve as frontline troops, devoting three weeks each year to training. Servicemen are expected to keep a rifle, ammunition, and other equipment in their homes. Men aged 33 to 42 serve in the equivalent of the U.S. National Guard and participate in brief periods of training. Men in their 40s serve as a reserve force, receiving infrequent training. After leaving military service, each citizen may keep his rifle. The army sells various other weapons, including machine guns, howitzers, and anti-aircraft guns, to private citizens. The 2 million firearms in private hands include 600,000 automatic weapons and 500,000 handguns.

Although gun control organizations emphasize the registration requirements imposed by the Swiss federal government and the various cantons, gun rights advocates indicate that such controls are minimal. Long gun purchases require no special procedures, but a purchase certificate from a cantonal authority is needed to purchase a military size handgun. A certificate is routinely issued to anyone who is not disqualified due to criminal activity or mental instability. Switzerland has no significant limitations on the purchase of any firearms, and no registration requirements for gun purchases or restrictions on carrying long guns. The government only registers fully automatic long guns.

The high concentration of firearms in Switzerland appears to present a minimal crime problem. The murder rate is approximately 15 percent of the rate in the United States. Those more sympathetic to the gun rights cause suggest that the low crime rate may be explained in part by the awareness potential violent criminals have that possible victims are trained in armed and unarmed defense and may possess a firearm. However, Switzerland has a high suicide rate, with firearms involved in nearly one-quarter of the total. The country has experienced several widely publicized mass murders that have led to a call for increased gun regulation. Such events were responsible in part for new gun control laws that were enacted in 1996 and that established a system of registration and uniform national standards requiring police authorization to purchase firearms. *See also* AUSTRALIA; ISRAEL; JAPAN.

Further Reading: Catherine Foster, "Nations Around World Try to Get a Grip on Guns," *Christian Science Monitor* (May 15, 1996), 1, 10-11; David B. Kopel, *The Samurai, the Mountie, and the Cowboy: Should America Adopt the Gun Controls of Other Democracies?* (Buffalo, NY: Prometheus, 1992).

T

Taggants

Bombing incidents, particularly at the World Trade Center in New York in 1993, the Alfred P. Murrah Federal Building in Oklahoma City in 1995, and the Centennial Olympic Park in Atlanta in 1996, have increased calls for federal legislation requiring the inclusion of chemical tags, or taggants, in materials that can be used to produce explosives. Such taggants also could be included in black and smokeless powder for the identification of gun users. National Rifle Association (NRA) officials have expressed their skepticism regarding the use of taggants, arguing on the basis of a 1980 study that such additions could destabilize gunpowder. The Antiterrorism and Effective Death Penalty Act of 1996 originally contained a provision to fund a six-month study of taggants to be conducted by the Treasury Department. However, the NRA and other organizations lobbied successfully to exclude gunpowder from the study.

In the early 1970s, Richard G. Livesay developed the first tags, which were tiny particles approximately a tenth of a millimeter in diameter consisting of layers of colored melamine plastic, a chemically inert substance likely to survive an explosion. Distinctive layering permits identification of the manufacturer, the production date, and the distributor of the explosive. Fluorescent materials included in the taggant assisted in detection. The magnetized taggants, when placed over a magnet, reveal their unique color coding. This type of taggant, called Microtaggant, is produced by Microtrace, a company that sells its product primarily to Switzerland, where since 1980 all explosives have been tagged. From 1984 to 1996, the Swiss used Microtaggants to solve over 500 bombing cases.

More recently, researchers have developed another type of taggant—nonradioactive heavy-isotope variations of molecules already present in the explosives. These isotopes of hydrogen, carbon, nitrogen, and oxygen vary only in atomic weight from materials already in the explosive. Potentially millions of distinct codes can be written as identifiers of specific explosive compounds. Identifying the tags requires relatively sophisticated laboratory analysis. Two companies, Microtrace of Minneapolis, Minnesota, and Isotag of Houston, Texas, provide isotope tags for many business firms for such products as shampoo, paint, gasoline, perfume, and glue to protect brand name products from counterfeiting and dilution. Taggant producers enthusiastically recommend the use of their products for those materials employed in the production of explosives, such as flammable liquids, black powder, smokeless powder, fireworks powders, ammonium nitrate fertilizer, and fuel oil.

Manufacturers demonstrate less enthusiasm for taggants. The Institute of Makers of Explosives contends that the inclusion of taggants is still too expensive. Tagging the approximately 2.5 million tons of dynamite and other high explosives produced in the United States each year would add an additional $12.5 to $37.5 million per year to the cost of production. It is estimated that to tag the 8.3 million tons of ammonium nitrate fertilizer produced each year would cost from $41.5 to $124.5 million. To prevent contamination of taggants from one batch to another, manufacturers contend that the production line would have to be cleaned thoroughly after each run, thus further increasing costs.

According to supporters of taggants, their extensive use in Switzerland demonstrates the safety of such materials. The more recent isotope taggants further obviate the concern about the older plastic version. Policy makers are left to decide whether the objective of apprehending those who have committed crimes using explosive materials and deterring such crimes is worth the financial costs involved. Record keeping by chemical manufacturers and retail store owners may prove burdensome. In the case of powder-containing bullets, retail outlets would have to determine the name of each purchaser and maintain the records. *See also* NATIONAL RIFLE ASSOCIATION; OKLAHOMA CITY BOMBING; SWITZERLAND.

Further Reading: Michael Kramer, "Without a Clue: Why Congress Balks at a Method for Tracing Bombs," *Time* 148 (August 12, 1996), 27; Robert F. Service, "NRC Panel Enters the Fight Over Tagging Explosives," *Science* 275 (January 24, 1997), 474-75; Corinna Wu, "Tagged Out: New Markers for Explosives May Lay Old Safety Questions to Rest," *Science News* 150 (September 14, 1996), 168-69.

Texas Tower Shooting

The Texas Tower shooting, which occurred at the University of Texas at Austin in August 1966, initiated public discussion regarding the dangers of firearms and provided a rationale for Democratic President Lyndon Johnson and the national Congress to push for gun control legislation, which was approved two years later. A lone gunman climbed to the observation deck of the university tower, called the Main Building, lugging a trunk containing several firearms, ammunition, food and water, and other provisions. For 80 minutes, Charles J. Whitman, a 25-year-old architectural student, sprayed bullets from all sides of the University of Texas landmark.

A Marine Corps veteran, Whitman had received two rifleman ratings, "marksman" and "sharpshooter." Whitman shot and killed his mother and stabbed his wife to death the night before the tower shooting. That morning he purchased a .12-gauge semi-automatic shotgun at a Sears store and cut off a portion of the stock and barrel. He also carried into the tower a 6-mm Remington rifle with a telescopic sight, a Remington .35-caliber reconditioned Army carbine, a .357 magnum pistol, a 9-mm Luger pistol, and a Bowie knife. Following the shooting, police found three rifles and two Derringers in his home.

His first victim at the tower was the elevator attendant. She was shot at her position at the visitors' register. Dragging the trunk to the observation platform, Whitman was in position to begin shooting just before noon. He succeeded in killing 12 people and wounding 33 others. The killing rampage ceased only when Romero Martinez, an off-duty policeman, made his way up the tower and shot Whitman six times with his service revolver and once with a shotgun. The final death toll, including Whitman and his wife and mother, was 15 people. An autopsy conducted soon after the event discovered that the gunman had a brain tumor, which might have contributed to the young man's rage.

President Johnson announced the day following the shooting that easy access to firearms must be given some of the blame for the incident. He urged Congress to take prompt action on a gun control bill that had been languishing in Congress, claiming that the bill would help restrict firearms sales to those who were not qualified to possess or use them. Senator Thomas Dodd, Democrat of Connecticut, the bill's major sponsor, also saw some remedy for this kind of act with passage of the pending legislation.

Gun control opponents maintained their resistance to new legislation, arguing that the tower shooting had no relevance at all to either a judgment on guns as such or on their use for marksmanship training. They further argued that additional legislation would not have prevented Whitman from committing his horrendous acts of violence. Not until 1968, with further public reaction against gun violence, particularly following the assassinations of Robert Kennedy and Martin Luther King, Jr., did the national legislature approve the first significant piece of gun control legislation in 30 years. *See also* DODD, THOMAS J.; GUN CONTROL ACT OF 1968; SAWED-OFF SHOTGUN.

Further Reading: Gary M. Lavergne, *A Sniper in the Tower: The Charles Whitman Murders* (Denton, TX: University of North Texas Press, 1997); *New York Times*, August 2, 1966, pp. 1, 15; August 3, 1966, p. 1.

Thompson, Linda (1952–)

In the two years following the federal government attack on the Branch Davidian compound in Waco, Texas, in 1993, Linda Thompson, founder of the American Justice Federation and advocate of extreme militia politics, energetically disseminated materials arguing the existence of a vast government conspiracy to destroy the militia movement and take control of the country. Thompson has been identified as the most significant person in making the Waco event a rallying cry for the militia and patriot movements. Thompson produced two video tapes, *Waco: The Big Lie* and *Waco: The Big Lie Continues*, in which she claimed that government tanks used flame throwers against the Branch Davidian compound during the attack of April 19, 1993. Thompson and her husband Al attributed the 1995 Oklahoma City bombing to a government plot to encourage a backlash against the militia movement. They expressed a similar skepticism about highly visible acts of gun violence that occurred just as Congress was considering new gun control legislation.

Before Thompson became involved in the militia movement, she worked as a civil rights attorney in her native Georgia. The events at Randy Weaver's cabin at Ruby Ridge, Idaho,

in 1992 altered her view of government. Six months later, soon after the siege at the Davidian compound had begun, Thompson traveled to Waco to offer her legal services to David Koresh, the leader of the Davidians. After a disagreement with another Koresh supporter, she left, but returned two weeks later to call for militant action to support the Davidians. Following the raid, Thompson began her campaign against a government she claimed was guilty of murderous activities.

On April 19, 1994, the first anniversary of the raid on the Branch Davidian compound, Thompson sent registered letters to each member of the U.S. House of Representatives and the Senate. Her "ultimatum" made a number of demands, including a complete government investigation of the Waco siege, repeal of the Fourteenth Amendment, and repeal of the Brady Handgun Violence Prevention Act, which imposed a waiting period and background check on those wanting to purchase a handgun. If Congress did not act by September 19, 1994, she declared that its members would be branded traitors, tried by a people's court, and executed. She identified herself as the acting adjutant general of the Unorganized Militia of the United States of America. At rallies across the country, Thompson advocated trials for leading government officials like Attorney General Janet Reno and then-Secretary of the Treasury Lloyd Bentsen, who had ultimate responsibility for the Bureau of Alcohol, Tobacco, and Firearms (BATF), the agency in charge of enforcing federal gun control legislation.

Thompson called for militias to travel to Washington, D.C., on September 19, armed, in uniform, and ready to take congresspeople into custody, try them for their crimes, and execute them. When militia organizations failed to respond to her call, Thompson canceled the event, saying that she never intended to carry out her threats. The self-proclaimed leader of the American militia movement had lost her credibility even among the most extreme militia organizations. In July 1994, she was arrested for attempting to use her car to block a bus loaded with supporters of Democratic President Bill Clinton's health care plan. Her car contained a .45-caliber pistol, a derringer, and an assault rifle, along with nearly 300 rounds of ammunition. She was arrested once again, in May 1995, for carrying a concealed firearm into the Marion County, Indiana, prosecutor's office.

Thompson took the gun rights argument that firearms are necessary for citizens to protect themselves from their own imminently oppressive government to its most extreme point. The ultimate oppressor, the United Nations, supposedly already had secret forces in the United States and was preparing for the final takeover. The telltale signs of such a force were the alleged black helicopters of an invading force that flew over her house to maintain surveillance on her activities. Within this paranoid scenario, gun control legislation fit neatly into a grander scheme to enslave the American people. Therefore, such legislation became not just a policy to be considered unwise and possibly unconstitutional, but part of a declaration of war by a government on its people. Not even the most radical groups were willing to accept Thompson's perception of reality, much less to act on that perception. *See also* BRADY HANDGUN VIO-LENCE PREVENTION ACT; BUREAU OF ALCOHOL, TOBACCO, AND FIREARMS; CLINTON, WILLIAM JEFFERSON (BILL); FOURTEENTH AMENDMENT; OKLAHOMA CITY BOMBING; RENO, JANET; RUBY RIDGE; UNITED NATIONS; WACO, TEXAS, RAID.

Further Reading: Morris Dees, *Gathering Storm: America's Militia Threat* (New York: Harper Collins, 1996); Alex Heard, "The Road to Oklahoma City," *The New Republic* 212 (May 15, 1995): 15-20; Jonathan Karl, *The Right to Bear Arms: The Rise of America's New Militias* (New York: HarperCollins, 1995); Jason Vest, "Leader of the Fringe," *The Progressive* 59 (June 1995): 28-29; Maryanne Vollers, "The White Woman from Hell," *Esquire* 124 (July 1995): 50-51.

Tommy Gun

The Tommy gun exemplified lawlessness and gangsterism that characterized much of the 1920s. Current gun control critics who oppose isolating particular types of weapons as "criminal," independent of who owns them, can find the source of the policy banning the Tommy gun in this era of American history. Colonel John M. Thompson developed the weapon during World War I for use by American troops. To distinguish it from larger and heavier automatic weapons used at the time, Thompson called the weapon a submachine gun. The Thompson submachine gun, or Tommy gun, fired .45 caliber bullets without interruption with one pull of the trigger.

Following the war, Thompson attempted to market his submachine gun as a police weapon, but police departments showed little interest. The national government also exhibited a lukewarm response. In 1926, the Treasury Department had only four Tommy guns. As demand for the weapon failed to increase, the price dropped from $225 to $50. Colt originally manufactured 15,000 guns, but by 1925 only 3,000 had been sold. Desperate to increase sales, salesmen looked for customers where they could. The Irish Republican Army placed a large order, but the federal government subsequently seized the shipment.

Chicago gangsters determined the Tommy gun's fate. Historians claim that the Joe Saltis and Frank McErlane gang, which controlled the Southwest Side of Chicago, first introduced the submachine gun for criminal purposes. However, others claim that the Tommy gun, also known in underworld slang as the "Chicago Piano," was first used in 1926 to murder two gunmen for the O'Donnell gang, Jim Doherty and Tom Duffy, and assistant state's attorney William H. McSwiggin. Others speculate that the notorious Chicago gangster Al Capone pulled the trigger. In 1927, the gun appeared in Philadelphia and in 1928 New York gangsters had acquired the weapon. The crime wave of the 1930s brought nationwide notoriety to the submachine gun, which had become the preferred weapon of such notorious outlaws as Pretty Boy Floyd and Ma Barker. The Tommy gun possessed advantages that attracted outlaws and gang members. It was an uncomplicated weapon, weighed just eight and one-half pounds, and could fire a withering hail of bullets, approaching 1,000 rounds per minute. The gun was conveniently available by mail order.

This Thompson machine gun, or Tommy gun, dates from about 1928. *Archive Photos.*

The Tommy gun became so closely associated with criminal activity that it was commonly regarded as a firearm that no respectable, law-abiding citizen would want to possess. During Democratic President Franklin Roosevelt's first administration, the criminal use of this weapon, along with such other weapons as the sawed-off shotgun, instigated the call for gun regulation. The 1934 National Firearms Act regulated the sale of machine guns, establishing taxation and regulation of the interstate sale or transfer of the weapons. The legislation focused almost exclusively on so-called "gangster weapons" such as the Tommy gun, leaving handguns and other weapons largely unregulated.

With government controls on the sale of firearms, gangsters sought alternative ways of acquiring the Thompson submachine gun. A black market developed, with the price of the weapon significantly higher than the original $225 price tag. Nonetheless, the new controls had some effect, and despite loopholes, the criminal use of submachine guns subsided.

Ever since restrictions were placed on the sale and ownership of the Tommy gun and other automatic weapons, gun advocates have protested that they possess a constitutional right to own such firearms. The controversy continues, with more uncompromising groups and elements within the National Rifle Association (NRA) calling for repeal of restrictions on the private ownership of machine guns. *See also* NATIONAL FIREARMS ACT OF 1934; NATIONAL RIFLE ASSOCIATION; SAWED-OFF SHOTGUN.

Further Reading: Bill R. Davidson, *To Keep and Bear Arms* (New Rochelle, NY: Arlington House, 1969); Lee Kennett and James La Verne Anderson, *The Gun in America: The Origins of a National Dilemma* (Westport, CT: Greenwood, 1975); Carl Sifakis, *Encyclopedia of American Crime* (New York: Facts on File, 1982).

Trigger Locks

In 1997, mandatory tricker locks on handguns became a prominent issue in the gun control debate. In his State of the Union Address in January, President Bill Clinton advocated legislation to require newly manufactured handguns to be sold with such devices, also called "child safety locks." Gun rights advocates demonstrated immediate skepticism, claiming that such devices were not the best way to ensure the safety of children. Instead, education and training efforts such as the National Rifle Association's (NRA) Eddie Eagle program could best prevent the gun accidents that prompted the proposal. Citing long-term data, opponents of such a measure claimed that education had already significantly reduced the number of accidents involving children each year.

The Clinton administration attempted to attach an amendment to a juvenile justice

In 1997, President Bill Clinton proposed that trigger locks, such as the one pictured here, be sold with every new handgun manufactured. *Supplied by Cristen Cervellini-Calfo of Franzen Security Products.*

reform measure mandating trigger locks and different proposals were considered in each house of Congress. In the Senate, an amendment softened the gun lock provision to require that gun dealers simply make gun locks available to customers who wished to purchase them. In October 1997, following meetings of representatives of the Sporting Arms and Ammunition Manufacturers' Institute (SAAMI), the American Shooting Sports Council (ASSC), and executive and legislative branch officials, some gun manufacturers agreed to provide gun locking devices. On October 9, representatives of some firearms manufacturing companies, including the executive director of the ASSC and officials from Beretta, Glock, H&R 1871, Heckler and Koch, O.F. Mossberg and Son, SIGArms, Smith and Wesson, and Taurus stood with President Clinton in the Rose Garden as he announced an agreement to include gun locks on newly manufactured weapons. Other companies not represented expressed their intention to support the agreement.

This announcement did not settle the issue of gun locks. Tanya Metaksa, executive director of the NRA's Institute for Legislative Action (ILA), insisted that the "one-size-fits-all" gun lock requirement did not work and that the most effective way of dealing with the gun accident problem was through "ef-

fective safety strategies." Charlton Heston, NRA first vice president, submitted a letter to the *New York Times* stating that he supported the agreement, but still thought that education was the most important factor in gun safety and that a loaded gun provided the best protection against criminal assault. Some pro-gun control forces also expressed reservations about the agreement. For instance, Sarah Brady, director of Handgun Control, Inc., although congratulating President Clinton for gaining a concession from gun manufacturers, indicated that much still needed to be done to improve firearm safety.

Representatives of Sturm, Ruger and Company cast doubt on the significance of the agreement. In open letters, Sturm, Ruger emphasized that the company believed proper instruction had led to the lowest level of gun accidents in the twentieth century. The company indicated that by taking part in the agreement, it was only continuing a policy that was begun 10 years before—to ship pistols in lock boxes with a padlock, a practice that was expanded to most of the handguns the company manufactured. The letters also expressed doubts about the safety of trigger locks, opting instead for the company's lockable boxes.

In the meantime, gun manufacturers and gun accessory companies began to advertise various types of trigger locks in gun magazines. Taurus began equipping its handguns with a locking device that appeared to avoid the safety criticisms leveled against other products, ensuring that the weapon would not fire as the owner disengaged the lock. The Taurus system involved a mechanism integral to the firearm that locked the hammer with a special key. Of importance to gun rights advocates, the owner could use the locking system as he or she wished, thus avoiding the perception of government mandate and preserving freedom of choice.

Other proposals at the national and state levels were made in an effort to provide for safer handguns, particularly in the presence of children. Some people have advocated devices that would only allow the owner to disengage the lock, so-called "user-sensitive" locking devices. However, gun advocates continue to claim that such mechanisms should never substitute for education and "common sense," arguing that if gun owners rely on them too much, trigger locks may actually lead to more accidents. *See also* AMERICAN SHOOTING SPORTS COUNCIL; BRADY, SARAH; CLINTON, WILLIAM JEFFERSON (BILL); EDDIE EAGLE; HANDGUN CONTROL, INC.; HESTON, CHARLTON; INSTITUTE FOR LEGISLATIVE ACTION; METAKSA, TANYA K.; NATIONAL RIFLE ASSOCIATION; SMART GUNS; SMITH AND WESSON; SPORTING ARMS AND AMMUNITION MANUFACTURERS' INSTITUTE.

Further Reading: James Jay Baker, "Gun Legislation," *Shooting Times* (January 1998), 10-13; News Briefs, "Reports Confuse Clinton, Industry Gun Lock Deal," *Gun News Digest* (Winter 1997-1998), 8-9; Staff Report, "Taurus Security System: Internal Mechanism Locks Revolver," *Gun World* (February 1998), 79-81.

The Turner Diaries

The Turner Diaries, a novel by William Pierce, a former college instructor in Oregon, was first published in 1978 under the pseudonym "Andrew MacDonald." The novel has been blamed for inspiring members of militia organizations to acts of terrorism. Supporters have called *The Turner Diaries* "the book most hated by the gun control crowd." Critics have labeled the book "a blueprint for Nazi terror," an "explicit terrorism manual," and "the bible of the racist right." The cover depicts a man and woman firing a pistol and automatic weapon. Originally available only through the National Alliance and other right-wing groups, the book was republished in 1996 by Barricade Books, a New York publishing house that printed 50,000 copies of the novel. The book has also been made available on audio cassette. Pierce has also published a sequel, *Hunter* (second edition, 1998), which portrays a drive-by shooter who murders interracial couples.

The book is a fictional account of violent acts committed in the 1990s by a racist and anti-Semitic underground military group called the "Organization." The Organization gains power in the United States and ultimately in the world, killing members of minority groups. Various terrorist acts are depicted, including a mortar attack on the Capitol building and the bombing of public utilities and communications networks.

Timothy McVeigh, the convicted bomber of the Murrah Federal Building in Oklahoma City in 1995, avidly promoted the book. He reportedly sent copies to friends, encouraging them to read the novel, and sold the book at guns shows. One friend testified that when he heard of the Oklahoma City bombing, he was reminded of a similar event in the novel and informed the Federal Bureau of Investigation (FBI) about his suspicions. In the novel, Organization members steal ammonium nitrate fertilizer from a farm-supply warehouse, mix it with heating oil, and load bags of the explosive material in a stolen truck. At 9:15 in the morning they explode the truck at the FBI building in Washington, D.C. McVeigh reportedly mailed portions of *The Turner Diaries* to his sister, who burned them after hearing about the Oklahoma City bombing. Police found a passage from the book in the car McVeigh drove on the day of the bombing. The passage stated in part that "[politicians and bureaucrats] learned today that not one of them is beyond our reach. They can huddle behind barbed wire and tanks in the city, or they can hide behind the concrete walls and alarm systems of their country estates, but we can still find them and kill them." Critics charge that other acts of violence by paramilitary organizations were inspired by the novel. Pierce has acknowledged that his book may have had some influence on those involved in the Oklahoma City bombing, but commented that the incident was not politically relevant because the perpetrators lacked sustained organization. *See also* OKLAHOMA CITY BOMBING.

Further Reading: Anti Defamation League Web site < http://www.adl.org/explosion_of_hate/intro_turner.html >; William Pierce ("Andrew Macdonald"), *Hunter*, 2nd ed. (Hillsborough, WV: National Vanguard Books, 1998); William Pierce ("Andrew Macdonald"), *The Turner Diaries* (New York: Barricade Books, 1996).

U

Undetectable Firearms Act

The Undetectable Firearms Act, also known as the Terrorist Firearms Detection Act, banned the manufacture, importation, possession, receipt, and transfer of plastic and ceramic guns that are undetectable by magnetometers and X-ray machines in airports and other public places. The act specified that a firearm must contain a minimum of 3.7 ounces of metal to make it detectable.

When Congress began consideration of a ban on plastic weapons, the National Rifle Association (NRA) expressed its opposition. In Senate hearings, an NRA representative labeled proposed legislation a "Trojan horse" intended to compromise the gun ownership rights of law-abiding citizens. The organization claimed that simply because terrorists might employ a product does not justify denying its use to the general public. Gun supporters claimed that the new weapons, which were not yet in production, had definite advantages over existing firearms. They would be lighter and more easily used, and would not rust. However, supporters of a ban defined the issue not as one of gun control, but of safety, for the guns were considered a major threat to the security of citizens if they could not be detected by standard equipment.

In February 1988, Vice President George Bush brought the issue into the national headlines. Participating in a debate among candidates for the Republican nomination for president sponsored by Gun Owners of New Hampshire, Bush showed the audience a small .22-caliber plastic pistol lent to him by the Treasury Department. While reiterating his support for the right of citizens to bear arms, he stated that Congress must deal with new firearms that are virtually undetectable by existing devices. The audience showed its approval and the other candidates quickly agreed with Bush, indicating widespread support for legislation banning plastic guns.

However, Senator James A. McClure, Republican of Idaho, one of the original authors of the Firearms Owners Protection Act, had introduced a weakened measure as an alternative to the one sponsored by Senators Strom Thurmond, Republican of South Carolina, and Howard Metzenbaum, Democrat of Ohio. McClure's proposal, supported by the NRA, would ban guns made entirely of plastic, but would allow the production of firearms with minimum amounts of metal. The NRA expressed its concern that the Thurmond-Metzenbaum legislation would lead to a ban on some existing weapons. Police organizations objected to the McClure proposal, claiming that the standard would allow the production of guns that could not be detected by existing devices.

Representatives of 12 police organizations met with Republican President Ronald Reagan's Attorney General, Edwin Meese, who had indicated his support for the alternative measure. Although the Justice Department initially indicated that advances in electronic equipment would improve the ability to detect weapons, thus obviating the need for stricter standards, the Reagan administration ultimately agreed to change its position and support the more restrictive provisions. In discussions among representatives of the Justice, Treasury, and Transportation Departments and a Law Enforcement Steering Committee representing law enforcement organizations, a compromise level of 3.7 ounces of metal was reached. When the NRA was assured that no existing gun would be banned under this standard, the organization dropped its opposition to the measure.

With all concerned groups supporting the same principle, the House of Representatives and the Senate passed slightly different versions of the bill in May 1988. The final legislation, approved by both houses in October and signed by President Reagan in November 1988, required all guns to set off metal detectors at a level equivalent to a firearm containing 3.7 ounces of stainless steel, or to be detectable by X-ray machines. *See also* BUSH, GEORGE; FIREARMS OWNERS PROTECTION ACT; MCCLURE, JAMES ALBERTAS; NATIONAL RIFLE ASSOCIATION; REAGAN, RONALD.

Further Reading: *New York Times* (February 3, 1988), 21A; (March 15, 1988), 20A; (April 27, 1988), 19A; (May 26, 1988), 25A; Josh Sugarmann, *National Rifle Association: Money, Firepower and Fear* (Washington, DC: National Press, 1992).

United Kingdom

Great Britain's experience with firearms has been used by both pro- and anti-gun control groups in the United States to argue for their respective positions. Gun rights advocates note that the Magna Carta, signed by King John in 1215, granted rights and freedoms to free men, including the possession of arms for defense and protection against government tyranny. However, over the centuries the British government did not follow a consistent policy on the right to keep and bear arms, at times taking steps to protect, and at other times to limit, that right.

In 1819, Parliament, fearful of civil unrest, passed the "Six Acts," which included a ban on drilling and training in the use of arms and an authorization to search and seize weapons in private homes. In 1903, Parliament, like other European legislatures, passed legislation (the Pistol Act) reacting to violent crime and the perceived threat of insurrection that arose from the social and economic pressures of industrialization. The Firearms Act was passed in 1920, and in 1937 economic and political unrest combined with international instability led to further firearms legislation in the United Kingdom and other European countries. After World War II, such laws were strengthened even further. In 1988, an additional statute placed even more restrictions on firearms ownership.

Most recently, the British Parliament has acted to ban all handguns and many Britons have advocated a complete prohibition on all firearms. Those on both sides of the gun control debate have disputed the success of gun control policy in the United Kingdom, where even prior to the call for a gun ban, strict regulations had been enacted. Gun control supporters argue that the relatively low homicide rate in Great Britain can be attributed to the country's stringent gun control legislation, while opponents attribute this phenomenon to cultural factors. Advocates of the defensive use of firearms suggest that the inability of the average Briton to deter crime through gun ownership can help to explain the high rate of robbery in Great Britain—criminals have little to fear from their victims.

By the early 1990s, British gun regulations required all firearms owners to have licenses for their weapons and to register them. Identification of the person seeking a permit must be established, including photographs and the verification of another individual who knows the applicant. To receive a permit, applicants must not have any criminal record, mental problems, or history of drug or alcohol abuse. The applicant must have sufficient reason to own a firearm, which cannot include defense of the home or personal protection. A weapon must be stored in a secure place, and the applicant must have a safe location to shoot the weapon. No semi-automatic weapons are permitted. Purchasers of long guns, including shotguns, must acquire a police certificate. Possessing a firearm with criminal intent could lead to a maximum punishment of life imprisonment, and simple illegal possession can bring a three-year sentence. Although the tradition in Great Britain was not to arm the police, in recent years that practice has been modified. Some police are now regularly armed and others can be quickly provided with weapons to meet extraordinary dangers. Still, the use of firearms by police is generally considered a last resort, limited to situations where such use can prevent the loss of life.

Warning against hasty conclusions from cross-national comparisons, Gary Kleck, in *Targeting Guns: Firearms and Their Control* (1997), criticized the association of lower rates of violence in Great Britain with more stringent gun legislation, a relationship that Kleck considered spurious. Kleck noted that in 1919, when British gun laws were far less strict, the homicide rate for England and Wales was 0.8 per 100,000, while the rate for the United States in the same year was 9.5, or 11.9 times as great as Great Britain. The homicide rate in the United States in the period 1983 to 1986 was 7.59 per 100,000, 11.3 times as great as the British rate of 0.67. Kleck concluded that after over six decades of stricter gun laws in Great Britain, the difference between British and American homicide rates actually declined slightly, implying that more stringent gun regulations had no effect on the homicide rate. However, hidden within that finding may be other factors such as a low rate of gun ownership in Great Britain that extends from 1919 to the present, and the enactment of many gun control laws in the United States at all levels of government.

Proposals for even more severe gun restrictions surfaced after the 1996 shooting of 16 schoolchildren and their teacher in the Scottish town of Dunblane. The call for additional gun control in the British public was far more extreme than has occurred in the United States in similar circumstances. In 1997, Parliament approved firearms legislation that outlawed handguns larger than .22 caliber. Handguns of .22 caliber or less must be stored at gun clubs. The legislation granted police greater discretion in licensing procedures and required all people who use a handgun to have a license. In addition, strict controls were placed on expanding ammunition and mail order sales of firearms. *See also* KLECK, GARY.

Further Reading: Wilbur Edel, *Gun Control: Threat to Liberty or Defense Against Anarchy?* (Westport, CT: Preager, 1995); Gary Kleck, *Targeting Guns: Firearms and Their Control* (New York: Aldine De Gruyter, 1997); David B. Kopel, *The Samurai, the Mountie, and the Cowboy: Should America Adopt the Gun Controls of Other Democracies?* (Buffalo, NY: Prometheus, 1992); Stryker McGuire, "The Dunblane Effect: Horror From the Massacre Prompts a Ban on Handguns," *Newsweek* 128 (October 28, 1996), 46; Pacific Center for Violence Prevention, "Handgun Ban Becomes Law," <http://www.pcvp.org/firearms> (1998); Gordon Witkin, "A Very Different Gun Culture: Britain Plans a Near Total Ban on Handguns," *U.S. News and World Report* 121 (October 28, 1996), 44.

United Nations (UN)

In recent years, United Nations (UN) agencies have investigated the possibility of international initiatives to control the world market in small arms. These investigations have raised concerns among gun rights organizations that multinational agreements might result in increased restrictions on gun ownership in the United States. In 1995, the Economic and Social Council, spurred by financial support from Japan, launched a global study of firearms ownership and use. The purpose of the study was to gain information about civilian possession of firearms, the use of firearms in crime, and the effectiveness of existing firearms regulations in approximately 50 countries. James Hayes of the Firearms Control Task Group of the Canadian Department of Justice became coordinator for the project.

UN agencies express concern that while trade in major weapons has declined, the spread of small arms has continued apace throughout the world. Those UN agencies that have been involved in discussions to pro-

The United Nations (its headquarters building in Manhattan is pictured here) has raised concerns among American gun rights groups with the recent efforts of some of its agencies to explore the possibility of international initiatives to control the world market in small arms. *UN Photo 165068/Lois Conner.*

pose controls on light weapons include the Disarmament Commission, the Panel of Governmental Experts on Small Arms, and the Economic and Social Council's Commission on Crime Prevention and Criminal Justice. Many participants support international agreements to control private arms trading, limit smuggling activities, and increase the security of police and military arms caches.

In May 1996, the UN Commission on Crime Prevention and Criminal Justice met in Vienna, Austria, to discuss summary information from a 25-country survey, which included data about gun-related accidents and suicides, transnational illicit trafficking in firearms, and regional legislation. A report from the secretariat included such possible action as making recommendations to governments about creating a database to facilitate sharing information worldwide about firearms and initiating cooperation among nations to control illegal firearms trafficking. Policy proposals included the destruction of small weapons remaining at the end of an armed conflict, the introduction of a techno-

logically sophisticated marking system to facilitate tracing of firearms, and establishing a global registry of firearms licenses.

Gun rights organizations have strongly criticized these initiatives, as well as what they consider inappropriate deliberative procedures within UN agencies. They fear that a proposed UN Declaration of Principles for the Regulation of Firearms could result in gun licensing and registration requirements imposed on the United States. Gun advocates refer to the UN treaty to ban landmines to illustrate the potential dangers of a firearms agreement for the United States, whose request for an exemption to keep landmines along the Korean demilitarized zone was rejected.

The National Rifle Association (NRA) obtained recognition as a nongovernmental organization to participate in various UN deliberations on the issue of gun control. In April 1998, Tanya Metaksa, then head of the NRA's Institute for Legislative Action (ILA), addressed a meeting of the UN Commission on Crime Prevention and Criminal Justice held in Vienna, Austria. Metaksa denounced various proposals to regulate firearms, contending that they went far beyond attempts to prevent illicit international arms trading and would seriously restrict the rights of law-abiding firearms owners. Responding to the exclusion of NRA representatives from certain UN agency meetings, Metaksa recommended a commitment to democratic processes within UN agencies and institutions. She urged an "open meeting" and "public records" policy for the UN, which would ensure greater access for pro-gun organizations like the NRA/ILA. *See also* CANADA; INSTITUTE FOR LEGISLATIVE ACTION; JAPAN; METAKSA, TANYA K.; NATIONAL RIFLE ASSOCIATION.

Further Reading: Ronald Bailey, "Global Gun Grabbers," *Weekly Standard* (February 23, 1998), 19-20; Robert M. Hausman, "Arms Ban Strategies Disclosed at UN Meeting," *Gun News Digest* (Spring 1998), 28-30; Helen Metaksa, "Metaksa Tells UN Commission on Crime to Open Closed Doors," *Gun Week* (June 20, 1998), 5; United Nations, "United Nations Global Study Begun on Civilian-Owned Firearms, Small Arms Trafficking, Firearms Regulations" (1995), <www.un.org>.

United States Conference of Mayors (USCM)

Since 1968, the United States Conference of Mayors (USCM) has advocated gun control policies. In 1994, the Conference adopted a resolution calling for several gun control measures, including a ban on the manufacture, sale, and possession of all semi-automatic weapons and component parts; a requirement to register all newly purchased and transferred firearms and the imposition of a registration fee; expansion of the Brady Handgun Violence Prevention Act background check to all firearms sales; a tightening of federal gun dealer licensing provisions; an increase in taxes on ammunition and firearms sales; a ban on armor-piercing and hollow-point ammunition; and the destruction of all firearms confiscated by law enforcement agencies.

The USCM was established in 1932 as a nonpartisan organization of mayors representing cities with populations of 30,000 or more. The Conference strives "to aid the development of effective national urban policy, strengthen federal-city relationships, ensure that federal policy meets urban needs, and provide mayors with leadership and management tools of value in their cities." An executive committee and an advisory board develop and guide policies and programs and the executive director, who is appointed by the executive committee, serves as the chief administrative officer. The Annual Conference is held each June.

In 1998, the USCM took active steps to initiate gun control provisions at the local, state, and national levels. In March, Chicago Mayor Richard M. Daley, president of the Conference, and Fort Wayne, Indiana, Mayor Paul Helmke, the vice president, met with Sarah and Jim Brady in a Capitol Hill press conference to announce proposed legislation to require all handguns sold to be equipped with safety locks. The Chicago City Council had just adopted an ordinance requiring that all handguns registered, sold, or transferred must be equipped with safety mechanisms, such as trigger locks, to prevent unauthorized use, especially by children, and load indica-

tors showing whether weapons contain ammunition.

The 1998 Annual Conference formed a mayoral task force that initiated discussions with gun manufacturers about measures that could be taken to make firearms safer and keep them out of the hands of criminals. Philadelphia Mayor Ed Rendell, chair of the task force, called for passage of a national Straw Purchaser Enforcement Act to prevent the purchase of large quantities of handguns by one person who then sells them to those prohibited from owning firearms. He asked the firearms industry to take precautions to prevent the stealing of guns from manufacturing plants and called for ammunition manufacturers to buy back armor-piercing bullets from retail outlets that still have them in stock.

In August 1998, Rendell, four other mayors, and representatives of the National Association of Counties met with Richard Feldman and others from the American Shooting Sports Council in St. Louis, Missouri, to discuss possible steps to reduce gun violence. The group discussed placing greater restrictions on selling firearms at gun shows and proposed legislation to limit individuals to purchasing one handgun a month. Rendell, who was scheduled to testify before a special Senate hearing on September 2 regarding restrictions on gun sales, invited the manufacturers to accompany him. However, Feldman later declined the request. Rendell testified at the hearing and several other members of the gun violence task force submitted letters supporting the proposed legislation.

The mayors of several cities initiated another strategy, filing lawsuits against firearms manufacturers and gun dealers to recover the medical and legal costs of violent crimes. In October 1998 New Orleans Mayor Marc H. Morial announced a lawsuit against 15 manufacturers, 3 trade associations, and several local pawnshops and gun dealers, and in November, Mayor Daley of Chicago announced a lawsuit against 12 gun shops in the suburbs surrounding Chicago, 22 gun manufacturers, and 4 gun distributors. Following the announcement, Daley wrote to

USCM executive director J. Thomas Cochran, encouraging other cities to consider filing similar suits. The Chicago lawsuit involved the claim that gun manufacturers had become a "public nuisance" by oversupplying gun shops outside the city's jurisdiction, intending that the handguns would be sold to city residents. In the article "Gun Shy" (1998), gun researcher John R. Lott, Jr., questioned such lawsuits, claiming that the economic benefits derived from the defensive use of firearms far outweigh the costs cities are attempting to recover. In early 1999, several other cities, including Boston, San Francisco, and Bridgeport, Connecticut, were taking steps to develop lawsuits against firearms manufacturers. Rendell proposed a simultaneous filing by up to 100 cities. To counter this strategy, gun interests began lobbying efforts to have state legislatures limit the authority of local jurisdictions to file such suits. *See also* AMERICAN SHOOTING SPORTS COUNCIL; BRADY, JAMES; BRADY, SARAH; BRADY HANDGUN VIOLENCE PREVENTION ACT; GUN SHOWS; LOTT, JOHN R.; TRIGGER LOCKS.

Further Reading: John R. Lott, Jr., "Gun Shy: Cities Turn from Regulation to Litigation in Their Campaign Against Guns," *National Review* 50 (December 21, 1998), 46-48; Roberto Suro, "Targeting Gun Makers with a Cigarette Strategy," *Washington Post National Weekly Edition* 16 (January 4, 1999), 30; United States Council of Mayors Web site <http://www.mayors.org>.

United States Practical Shooting Association (USPSA)

The United States Practical Shooting Association (USPSA), a promoter of practical shooting matches, conducts the Open and Limited National Championships each year. The organization is affiliated with the International Practical Shooting Confederation (IPSC) and sends the United States shooting team to the IPSC World Shoot every three years. The USPSA distributes *Front Sight*, a bi-monthly magazine containing articles and features on the various aspects of practical shooting, including improvement of competitive skills, reloading, practical shooting accessories, future matches, and views on practical shooting. Rifle and shotgun competitions are included in the organization's practical shooting program.

In addition to *Front Sight*, the organization distributes *In Touch*, a newsletter that frequently contains articles expressing the leadership's concern about various gun control efforts. In the February 1998 issue, Keith Milberger, Area 4 Director, discussed the lack of unity in the USPSA and other pro-gun organizations, in contrast to the singleness of purpose he perceived in pro-gun control groups. Milberger claimed that Handgun Control, Inc. (HCI) has been successful because it possesses a specific focus. He complained that pro-gun supporters seemed unable to agree on anything except that "the gun grabbers" are succeeding and no effective opposition is being mustered against them. Milberger suggested that to defend shooting sports, all members must "get along and work together or they just need to go."

The newsletter referred to potential problems resulting from allowing minor children to participate in shooting matches and the bad publicity generated by such "left wing, anti-gun" news anchors as Dan Rather and Tom Brokaw. The organization reported that it was developing policies to be adopted by the board of directors that were intended to "prevent any legal disaster that may befall us as well as any foreseeable personal disaster associated with a junior program." Proposed guidelines would include a statement holding a parent or guardian responsible for the safety of a minor and requiring parental presence when a minor is armed and shooting. Given that gun control organizations oppose the involvement of minor children in shooting events, the USPSA is sensitive to the possibility that any accident would not only lead to legal action, but also to greater limitations on the sport.

Like many other pro-gun organizations, the USPSA campaigned against the 1997 ballot initiative in the state of Washington that would have placed limitations on the ownership of handguns. The organization's newsletter stated that the proposal "originated in the White House." If the measure was successful in Washington, members were told they could expect similar measures in their own states. Members were advised to call legislators, write letters to local newspapers, and contact friends and acquaintances in Washington to offer assistance. The ballot measure ultimately failed.

Jeff Nelson, Area 2 Director, noted that the organization can find itself in a "Catch 22" situation when it discovers that a member legally should not be handling firearms, but have no way of excluding such a person without exposing the organization to a lawsuit. Nelson expressed frustration that the organization had no effective means of abiding by provisions of the Brady Handgun Violence Prevention Act. *See also* BRADY HANDGUN VIOLENCE PREVENTION ACT; HANDGUN CONTROL, INC.; INTERNATIONAL DEFENSIVE PISTOL ASSOCIATION.

Further Reading: United States Practical Shooting Association Web site <www.uspsa.org>.

United States v. Cruikshank (1876)

In *United States v. Cruikshank* (92 U.S. 542, 1876), the U.S. Supreme Court made its first major ruling on the Second Amendment right to keep and bear arms. The final decision limiting the right to bear arms was based on the Supreme Court's refusal to recognize that the Fourteenth Amendment protected the rights of American citizens from state action. The defendants were found guilty in federal district court of violating the sixth section of the Force Act of 1870 by conspiring to deprive two black men (Levi Nelson and Alexander Tillman) of their rights guaranteed by the First and Second Amendments to the U.S. Constitution to freedom of speech and assembly, and to bear arms. A circuit court of appeals overruled the district court, after which U.S. officials appealed the decision to the U.S. Supreme Court.

Among the various counts in the indictment, the defendants were charged with joining together with the intent to "injure, oppress, threaten, and intimidate" two citizens of African descent and "persons of color," with the objective of preventing their exercise of the right to peaceably assemble with others "for a peaceable and lawful purpose." Also included in the indictment was the charge that the defendants wished to prevent the exercise of "the right to keep and bear arms for a lawful purpose."

The Court stated that for the case to be placed under the statute, the rights that were violated must be ones granted by the Constitution or laws of the United States. If this were not the case, the criminal charges were not indictable by any act of Congress. The federal government was established for specific purposes, and could not grant or secure for citizens any right that the Constitution did not place under its jurisdiction. The Court understood national powers narrowly as only those powers expressly delegated to the national government.

Regarding the right of assembly, the Court ruled that it existed prior to the adoption of the U.S. Constitution and was not a right granted to the people by that document. The states had the obligation to protect this right, but the national government had no duty to require states to fulfill such an obligation. The First Amendment, which protects the right of assembly, only limits the power of the national government. For the people to enjoy its continued operation, they must appeal to the states.

The Court ruled similarly on the charge that the defendants hindered the right of the two African Americans to bear arms for a lawful purpose. Again, the Court stated that this right was not granted by the U.S. Constitution, nor was it dependent on the Constitution for its continued existence. Although the Second Amendment stated that the right to bear arms shall not be infringed, this meant, according to the Court, simply that Congress shall not place limitations on this right. Only the powers of the national government are restricted by this amendment. The people must look to the legal actions of the states, or what the Court termed the "internal police," to protect them against a violation of this right by fellow citizens.

With regard to the argument that the Fourteenth Amendment prohibits states from depriving any person of life, liberty, or property without due process of law, the Court ruled that this amendment contributed nothing to the rights that one citizen has against another, but offers an "additional guarantee" against the invasion by state governments of the rights that every member of society already has. Nothing was added to the rights any citizen possessed under the Constitution. The Court claimed that the duty of protecting citizens fell originally on the states, and that duty had not changed. The Fourteenth Amendment only guaranteed that states could not deny rights mentioned within it, and the power of the national government ended at that point. The Court ruled that the Civil Rights Act of 1866, intended to protect citizens of the United States against discrimination on the basis of race, color, or previous condition of servitude, did not apply in this case because the charges of violating the rights of citizens did not indicate that such violation was due to the race or color of the victims. *See also* FOURTEENTH AMENDMENT; SECOND AMENDMENT.

Further Reading: Earl R. Kruschke, *The Right to Keep and Bear Arms: A Continuing American Dilemma* (Springfield, IL: Charles C. Thomas, 1985); Mark A. Siegel, Nancy R. Jacobs, and Carol D. Foster, eds., *Gun Control: Restricting Rights or Protecting People?* (Wylie, TX: Information Plus, 1991).

United States v. Freed (1971)

The issues brought before the United States Supreme Court in *United States v. Freed* (401 U.S. 601, 1971) involved the frequent concerns expressed by gun rights advocates that gun control measures violate not only the Second Amendment but also infringe on the protection against self-incrimination guaranteed in the Fifth Amendment and in addition lead to punishment of a law-abiding individual who unknowingly breaks the law. In the *Freed* case, the defendants were charged with possessing and conspiring to possess hand grenades that had not been registered according to the provisions of federal firearms legislation.

The Supreme Court had previously held unconstitutional a portion of the National Firearms Act under the self-incrimination clause of the Fifth Amendment. The law levied a tax on certain classes of firearms that were used for unlawful purposes and provided for giving information about such weapons and their illegal owners to state and local government officials. In response to the Court's ruling, Congress amended the law to require only the lawful manufacturers and importers of firearms to register them. The amended law mandated that persons transferring weapons at issue identify themselves, describe the weapons, and provide the names and addresses of the persons to whom the weapons are transferred, along with their photograph and fingerprints. No information received by the federal government can be used against a registrant in a criminal proceeding dealing with a violation of the law that occurred before or concurrently with the application filing or registration. No information may be shared with other federal agencies or with state and local government officials.

Despite the amendments to the law, the defendants in the *Freed* case argued that the law compelled self-incrimination and that the law infringed on due process by omitting a specific knowledge of the law. In addition, the defendants maintained that the fingerprints and photograph requirement could lead to future incrimination. They argued that registering under federal law would have incriminated them under California law, which outlaws possession of hand grenades. The district court granted the defendants' motion to dismiss the case, arguing that the amended act, like the original legislation, violated the protection against self-incrimination.

Hearing the case on direct appeal, the U.S. Supreme Court reversed the lower court decision, concluding that the amended act presents no realistic possibility of violating the self-incrimination clause of the Fifth Amendment. The court observed that the transferor makes the potentially incriminating statements, not the person receiving the weapon. Although the law requires the receiver's fingerprints and photo, the process makes the recipient the lawful possessor of the weapon. Noting that the defendants asserted that the self-incrimination clause protects a person against past and present as well as future violations, the Court ruled that the clause cannot be stretched to supply "insulation for a career of crime about to be launched."

With regard to the defendants' scienter claim (that they lacked knowledge of the law they were accused of violating), the Court noted that the statute does not require demonstration of intent or knowledge that the hand grenades were unregistered, but simply makes it unlawful for a person "to receive or possess a [controlled] firearm which is not registered to him." The only knowledge necessary was that the thing possessed was a firearm. The Court did not consider the claimed lack of knowledge a disqualifying circumstance, noting that "one would hardly be surprised to learn that possession of hand grenades is not an innocent act." They are "highly dangerous offensive weapons," presenting a hazard to the public similar to that posed by narcotics. *See also* NATIONAL FIREARMS ACT OF 1934; SECOND AMENDMENT.

Further Reading: *United States v. Freed*, 401 U.S. 601 (1971).

United States v. Lopez (1995)

The U.S. Supreme Court, in *United States v. Lopez* (115 U.S. 1624, 1995), affirmed the reversal of conviction of Alphonso Lopez, Jr., by the Court of Appeals for the Fifth Circuit. Lopez had been found guilty in the U.S. District Court for the Western District of Texas of violating the Gun-Free School Zones Act of 1990. In this act, Congress had made it a federal crime for an individual knowingly to possess a firearm within a public, parochial, or private school, or within a zone extending 1,000 feet from the grounds of a school. In disallowing this gun control measure, the Court did not base its decision on the Second Amendment, but relied instead on an interpretation of Congress's commerce power.

On March 12, 1992, Lopez, a student, was discovered bearing a concealed .38 caliber handgun and ammunition at Edison High School in San Antonio, Texas. He was arrested for violating a state statute prohibiting

possession of a firearm on school grounds. When federal officials charged Lopez with violation of the Gun-Free School Zones Act, the state officials dismissed charges. Despite Lopez's objection at his trial that the national statute violated the U.S. Constitution, he was found guilty.

The majority decision of the Supreme Court involved a determination of the extent to which Congress may use the commerce power. The Court identified three areas that fall within Congress's constitutional power to regulate commerce: 1) activities involving channels of interstate commerce; 2) instrumentalities of, and persons or things in, interstate commerce; and 3) activities that have a "substantial relation" to interstate commerce. The Court rejected the first two categories as possible justifications of the commerce clause in this circumstance. Therefore, if the Gun-Free School Zones Act were to be held constitutional, it would need to be judged as regulating an activity that has a substantial effect on interstate commerce.

The Court determined that the statute deals with criminal activity and therefore has nothing to do with commerce or economic enterprise and has no essential relation to maintaining the regulation of an economic activity. Therefore, precedents established under the commerce power do not apply to the act. The elements of the statute demonstrate no relation between firearm possession and interstate commerce. The Court decided that the act represented a break with the previous constitutional standards for national firearms legislation.

The government argued that the considerable costs of violent crime spread beyond state boundaries, especially through the costs of insurance; that violent crime restricts people's disposition to travel to certain areas of the country; and that an educational process hindered by violence contributes to a less productive population. In rejecting these arguments, the Court reasoned that similar arguments could be employed to justify federal government involvement in a variety of areas, thus granting to it a wide police power traditionally determined to reside with the states.

In a dissenting opinion, Justice Stephen Breyer, joined by Justices John Paul Stevens, David Souter, and Ruth Bader Ginsberg, relied on three principles: the power to regulate commerce includes the ability to regulate local activities to the extent that they affect interstate commerce; ascertaining the effect of an activity requires considering not one action of an individual, but the effect of all related cases; and the granting of latitude to Congress in the determination of a connection between interstate commerce and an activity considered for regulation. Breyer argued that Congress could establish a reasonable link between education and the health of the national economy.

Although the Lopez decision did not alter precedents established by the Supreme Court regarding the Second Amendment, it did indicate that the Court had become less willing to allow Congress to intervene in new policy areas unless such intervention is solidly based on the constitutional powers delegated to the national legislature. *See also* Gun-Free Schools Act; Schools and Guns; Second Amendment.

Further Reading: Alpheus Thomas Mason and Donald Grier Stephenson, Jr., *American Constitutional Law*, 11th ed. (Upper Saddle River, NJ: Prentice Hall, 1996); *United States v. Lopez* (115 U.S. 1624, 1995).

United States v. Miller (1939)

Based on a challenge to the National Firearms Act of 1934, *United States v. Miller* (307 U.S. 174, 1939) involved an appeal by two individuals who had been convicted of transporting an unregistered sawed-off shotgun across state lines. The defendants based their challenge on the claim that the National Firearms Act violated the Second Amendment to the U.S. Constitution and that the act could not be justified under Congress's commerce power.

The defendants, Jack Miller and Frank Layton, were indicted in a federal district court in Arkansas for unlawfully transporting a double-barrel 12-gauge shotgun having a barrel less that 18 inches long. They allegedly transported the weapon from Claremore, Oklahoma, to Siloam, Arkansas, but had not registered the weapon as required under the National Firearms Act. The defendants, not disputing the facts of the case, claimed that the section of the law under which they were charged was not a revenue measure but rather sought to appropriate the police power retained by the states. The district court ruled that section 11 of the act violated the Second Amendment protection of the right to keep and bear arms.

The U.S. Supreme Court, receiving the case directly, first decided that the regulation of firearms could be encompassed under Congress's federal taxing power. The Court declared that the Second Amendment, according to its manifest purpose, assured the preservation of an effective militia in the states as provided for in Article 8 of the Constitution. Discovering no evidence demonstrating that a shotgun with "a barrel of less than eighteen inches in length" had at the time of the decision any connection to the maintenance of a well-regulated militia, the Court refused to conclude that the Second Amendment guaranteed the right to keep and bear such a weapon.

The Court related the Second Amendment to the power granted to Congress within the body of the original Constitution to make provision for activating the militia if needed to enforce national law, suppress insurrections, and repel invasions. Congress was to establish policy regarding the organization, provision of arms, and discipline of the militia, and for administering the portion of the militia that may be called into national service. The Court viewed the Second Amendment guarantee as a method of assuring that the effectiveness of militia forces would be continued. Citizens had a constitutionally protected right to bear arms only when such a right could be associated with militia service.

Later commentators on the case would contend that the Second Amendment guaranteed the possession of any weapon that has some connection to the national defense. However, subsequent federal court decisions did not support this view. Otherwise, individuals could legitimately claim the constitutional right to possess not only sawed-off shotguns (which were used in the Vietnam War), but a long list of other weapons from bazookas to nuclear weapons. *See also* NATIONAL FIREARMS ACT; SAWED-OFF SHOTGUN; SECOND AMENDMENT; *UNITED STATES V. WARIN* (1976).

Further Reading: *United States v. Miller*, 307 U.S. 174 (1939).

United States v. One Assortment of 89 Firearms (1984)

The U.S. Supreme Court, in *United States v. One Assortment of 89 Firearms* (465 U.S. 354, 1984), decided that federal authorities may proceed with the seizure of firearms even when the owner has been acquitted of criminal charges related to their possession, basing its decision on an interpretation of a section of the Gun Control Act of 1968 [18 U.S.C. 924 (d)], which provides for the seizure and forfeiture of firearms "involved in or used or intended to be used in, any violation of the provisions of this chapter." The decision overruled a precedent set in *Coffey v. United States* (1886).

In 1977, following a Bureau of Alcohol, Tobacco, and Firearms (BATF) raid on his home to seize a store of firearms, Patrick Mulcahey was charged with knowingly engaging in the firearms trade without a license, thus violating federal law (18 U.S.C. 922). At the trial, Mulcahey admitted to buying and selling firearms without a license, but argued that federal agents had entrapped him into the illegal activities. The jury returned a verdict of not guilty. Following the acquittal, the United States government began action to gain forfeiture of the seized firearms. Mulcahey attempted to stop the forfeiture, arguing that the criminal action had already settled the matter in his favor. The district court ruled that the firearms were subject to forfeiture.

The United States Court of Appeals for the Fourth District by a narrow margin reversed the lower court decision, arguing that the forfeiture proceeding was fundamentally criminal and punitive and therefore violated the constitutional guarantee against double jeopardy. The court ruled that the forfeiture action was based on the same information presented in the criminal case and therefore could not arrive at a ruling that contradicted the original decision. The court based its ruling on the Supreme Court's decision in *Coffey v. United States* (1886), which held that forfeiture action against distilling equipment could not proceed because the owner had been acquitted of charges related to the equipment.

The U.S. Supreme Court rejected the basis for the Court of Appeals decision, thus overruling the Coffey decision. Chief Justice Warren Burger, presenting the majority opinion, stated that "an acquittal on criminal charges does not prove that the defendant is innocent; it merely proves the existence of a reasonable doubt as to his guilt." The acquittal in the criminal case did not preclude a possible action in which the "preponderance of the evidence" could demonstrate that Mulcahey had conducted an unlicensed firearms business, and therefore that the relevant firearms should be forfeited according to section 924 (d).

The Court concluded that Congress, in establishing the forfeiture procedure, intended it as a "remedial civil action," not a criminal sanction. The purpose of section 924 (d) was to discourage unregulated trade in firearms and to prevent the trade of firearms "that have been used or intended for use outside regulated channels of commerce." By attempting to keep "potentially dangerous weapons" away from unlicensed dealers through the forfeiture provision, Congress had remedial, not punitive, goals in mind. Because the forfeiture process against the seized firearms did not constitute a criminal proceeding, the constitutional guarantee against double jeopardy does not apply.

Following the decision, gun rights groups, fearing a general confiscation of firearms, lobbied for changes in the Gun Control Act of 1968 that would provide greater assurance to gun owners acquitted in criminal proceedings that they would have appropriate procedures available to them to require the return of any seized firearms. The Firearms Owners Protection Act of 1986 provided such procedures to gun owners. Nonetheless, more recent federal forfeiture policies have again raised concerns among gun rights advocates about possible firearms seizures. *See also* BUREAU OF ALCOHOL, TOBACCO, AND FIREARMS; FIREARMS OWNERS PROTECTION ACT; GUN CONTROL ACT OF 1968; SECOND AMENDMENT.

Further Reading: *United States v. One Assortment of 89 Firearms*, 465 U.S. 354 (1984).

United States v. Powell (1975)

In *United States v. Powell* (423 U.S. 87, 1975), the U.S. Supreme Court examined the constitutionality of a federal statute (18 U.S.C. 1715) that prohibits the mailing of pistols, revolvers, and "other firearms capable of being concealed on the person," to determine whether the law applied to weapons such as sawed-off shotguns, which were considerably larger than handguns. The defendant, who was convicted of sending a sawed-off shotgun through the mail, claimed that the statute was so vague in its application as to be unconstitutional and that the law did not cover sawed-off shotguns. A Court of Appeals overturned the original conviction, arguing that the vagueness of the statute violated the Due Process Clause of the Fifth Amendment to the U.S. Constitution.

The U.S. Supreme Court, in deciding the Powell case, first dealt with the defendant's claim that the phrase "other firearms capable of being concealed on the person" does not apply to sawed-off shotguns but only to pistols and revolvers. Rejecting this contention, the Court argued that it would be justified in narrowing the scope of the statute only if there were evidence of congressional intent beyond the wording of the law. The Court observed that the stated purpose of the statute was "to avoid having the Post Office serve as an instrumentality for the violation of local laws which prohibited the purchase and possession of weapons," noting that local laws would more likely ban sawed-off shotguns than pistols and revolvers. The Court concluded that the defendant's narrow interpretation of the statute did not correspond to Congress's objective of making the acquisi-

tion of concealable weapons more difficult and therefore a jury could legitimately find that a 22-inch sawed-off shotgun was a "firearm capable of being concealed on the person."

Although recognizing that statutory vagueness can be a basis for overturning a conviction, the Court held that such a situation did not apply in this case. The Court commented that the relevant law "intelligibly forbids a definite course of conduct: the mailing of concealable firearms" and therefore gave "adequate warning" to the defendant that mailing a 22-inch sawed-off shotgun was a violation of the law. The language of the statute was sufficient to provide notice to potential violators what weapons were prohibited from mailing.

The Court of Appeals had argued that the "person" to which the statute refers may vary in physical characteristics to such an extent that what is a concealable weapon for one individual is not for another. Did the statute refer to the person mailing the firearm, the person receiving the weapon, or the average person? The Supreme Court responded that the commonsense meaning of person as an average individual "garbed in a manner to aid, rather than hinder, concealment of the weapons" most fairly represents the intentions of Congress. *See also* CONCEALED CARRY LAWS; SAWED-OFF SHOTGUN.

Further Reading: *United States v. Powell*, 423 U.S. 87 (1975).

United States v. Rene Martin Verdugo-Urquidez (1990)

Although the subject of *United States v. Rene Martin Verdugo-Urquidez* (494 U.S. 259, 1990) had nothing to do with gun control laws, the decision involved an interpretation of what "the people" means in various sections of the Constitution. According to gun advocates, the Supreme Court decision provides substantial support for an individualist interpretation of "the people" in the Second Amendment to the U.S. Constitution. The justices joining in the ruling noted that "the people" refers to "a class of persons who are part of a national community or who have otherwise developed sufficient connection with this country to be considered part of that community." The Court indicated that this definition applies not only to the Fourth Amendment, the focus for the decision, but also to the First, Second, Ninth, and Tenth Amendments.

The case had to do with the constitutionality of a search and seizure involving a non-U.S. citizen who resided outside the territory of the United States. The U.S. Drug Enforcement Agency (DEA) suspected that Rene Martin Verdugo-Urquidez, a citizen and resident of Mexico, was a leader of a drug-smuggling organization in Mexico. The DEA obtained a warrant for his arrest in August 1985, and in January 1986 Mexican police officials transported Verdugo-Urquidez to the U.S. Border Patrol station in Calexico, California, where he was arrested by U.S. marshals. Following the arrest, DEA officials decided to pursue a search of Verdugo-Urquidez's residences in Mexicali and San Felipe, Mexico, to acquire evidence of the defendant's illegal drug activities. In cooperation with Mexican officials, a search was conducted, revealing certain incriminating evidence.

The defendant claimed that the evidence had been obtained illegally because the DEA had not obtained a search warrant. The U.S. district court concluded that the Fourth Amendment protection against unwarranted searches and seizures applied in this case. The U.S. Court of Appeals for the Ninth Circuit affirmed the lower court decision, after which U.S. officials appealed the rulings to the U.S. Supreme Court.

The Supreme Court reversed the lower court rulings, arguing that the relevant portion of the Fourth Amendment, which states that, "The right of the people to be secure in their persons, houses, papers, and effects, against unreasonable searches and seizures, shall not be violated, and no Warrants shall issue, but upon probable cause, supported by oath or affirmation, and particularly describing the place to be searched, and the persons or things to be seized," protects specifically "the people of the United States." The Court

ruled that "the people" was a "term of art" used in certain portions of the Constitution to refer to a "person" or the "accused," as in the Fifth and Sixth Amendments involving criminal procedure. The term "people" refers to a class of persons that composes the national community. Those who have developed a sufficient connection with the nation may also be included in "the people." In the specific case, Verdugo-Urquidez, a citizen of Mexico who only entered the United States as a criminal defendant, did not satisfy the conditions to be considered a part of "the people" qualified to receive Fourth Amendment protections.

Gun rights supporters have focused on the Court's mention of the Second Amendment, along with other portions of the Bill of Rights, as protecting the right of the people as a class of persons closely associated with the American community. In the Second Amendment, "the right of the people to keep and bear Arms" is protected. Gun rights supporters have emphasized this brief mention of the Second Amendment because they see this as a promising foreshadowing of future Supreme Court rulings regarding the right to keep and bear arms. When the Court in the *Verdugo-Urquidez* case referred to a similar use of the term "people" in both the First Amendment, where rights definitely refer to those of individuals, and the Second Amendment, supporters had hope that the corporate notion of the people, as those involved in organized militias within states, would be defeated in favor of a more individualistic interpretation of the Second Amendment.

However, the *Verdugo-Urquidez* decision does not necessarily support the position of gun rights advocates. The Court's notion of the people as a class of persons who are part of the national community or have a close connection to the country could still be interpreted as a collective right exercised by the states in the formation of militia units. All that the Court ruled in the present case is that Verdugo-Urquidez lacked sufficient connection to the United States to be considered as part of "the people" as mentioned in the Fourth Amendment.

Even if the ruling indicates a willingness to view the Second Amendment right to keep and bear arms in the same way as the First Amendment guarantees of freedom of speech and press, only four Supreme Court justices adhered to such a notion (Chief Justice William Rehnquist and associate justices Byron White, Sandra Day O'Connor, and Antonin Scalia). Two other justices (Anthony Kennedy and John Paul Stevens) supported the ruling, but issued concurring opinions that declined to accept the idea of "the people" presented in the opinion written by Rehnquist. Three justices (William J. Brennan, Thurgood Marshall, and Harry Blackmun) dissented. Therefore, a minority of the Court adhered to the notion of "the people" and its application to the Second Amendment as well as to the First and Fourth Amendments. *See also* FOURTEENTH AMENDMENT; FOURTH AMENDMENT; NINTH AMENDMENT; SECOND AMENDMENT.

Further Reading: Alan M. Gottlieb, *The Rights of Gun Owners* (Bellevue, WA: Merril Press, 1991); *United States v. Rene Martin Verdugo-Urquidez*, 494 U.S. 259 (1990).

United States v. Tot (1942)

Frank Tot was tried in federal district court for unlawful possession of a firearm under a provision of the Federal Firearms Act of 1938 and found guilty. The act made it unlawful for anyone convicted of a violent crime "to receive any firearm or ammunition which has been shipped or transported in interstate or foreign commerce." In *United States v. Tot*, 131 F.2d 261 (1942), the U.S. Court of Appeals for the Third Circuit upheld Tot's conviction.

In September 1938, Tot was arrested at his Newark, New Jersey, home on a warrant charging that he had stolen cigarettes from an interstate shipment. Federal officers making the arrest found a .32 caliber Colt Automatic pistol at his residence. After his arrest, Tot requested that the pistol be returned to him and that the fact of its possession not be admitted at his trial, contending that officers had obtained it in violation of his Fourth Amendment guarantee against unreasonable searches and seizures. The court denied all of Tot's motions.

The Appeals Court ruled that the admission of the firearm into evidence was constitutional. First, the defendant had offered to produce the gun himself. Second, the U.S. Supreme Court had previously ruled that law enforcement officers may seize without a search warrant during a lawful arrest any weapons and other objects that could be used to assist the suspect in escaping from custody. Therefore, the court ruled that Tot could not legitimately claim any violation of Fourth Amendment rights against unwarranted search and seizure of the gun.

Tot also claimed the Federal Firearms Act violated the Second Amendment to the U.S. Constitution. In response to this contention, the court affirmed that this Amendment, unlike First Amendment guarantees, does not apply to the rights of individuals. Rather, the Amendment was adopted to protect states in their right to maintain militia organizations against interference from the national government. The Court indicated that Americans at the time wished to avoid the English experience under James II, when armed forces were lodged among a defenseless population. Many state constitutions adopted similar measures that, according to the court, supported this interpretation of the Second Amendment. In addition, the court referred to the common law tradition, which never treated the right to bear weapons as absolute, observing that regulation of the right to bear arms can be found in much earlier times, such as the Statute of Northampton in 1328.

The court dealt with the constitutionality of a provision that depends upon presumptive evidence, since it appears to violate the basic principle that a person is innocent until proven guilty. The notion of presumptive evidence seems to place the burden of proof on the defendant who is challenged to demonstrate his or her innocence in the face of assumed guilt. Citing precedent, the court ruled that the legislature may provide for the presumption of one fact from evidence of another, thus shifting the burden of proof without denying due process to the accused.

The Court observed that the gun in question had crossed state lines at least twice; it was originally shipped from Connecticut, the state of manufacture, to Illinois, and ultimately to New Jersey where it was found in Tot's possession.

The court then faced directly the question of the time at which Tot received the weapon. The statute went into effect on July 30, 1938. The trial judge had instructed the jury to presume that the gun was shipped in interstate commerce if the jury determined that Tot had obtained the weapon after the date the statute went into effect. At the trial, the only evidence presented for the defense was the testimony of Tot and his wife and sister. Jurors apparently did not believe their testimony. The defendant had the opportunity to present his evidence as to the time when he acquired the weapon. If, contrary to the actual outcome, he had been believed, this would have established that the defendant came into possession of the weapon prior to passage of the statute.

The Court noted that the legislation has a limited scope, dealing only with objects classified as firearms, and with a narrow group of people already convicted of violent crimes. In addition, the objective of the Federal Firearms Act, to protect society against violent individuals armed with dangerous weapons, can be considered fundamental to established government. The Court recognized that the national government can appropriately assist in the accomplishment of this objective. Therefore, the Court concluded that the means provided in the act to achieve the objective, while demanding, were not so arbitrary as to determine that Congress exceeded its authority. *See also* FEDERAL FIREARMS ACT; FOURTH AMENDMENT; SECOND AMENDMENT.

Further Reading: *United States v. Tot,* 131 F.2d 261 (1942).

United States v. Warin (1976)

The U.S. Court of Appeals for the Sixth Circuit, in *United States v. Warin* (530 F.2d 103, 1976), affirmed the U.S. District Court's judgment that Francis J. Warin had know-ingly possessed a firearm—a 9 mm prototype submachine gun—that he had not registered in the National Firearms Registration and Transfer Record as required under the National Firearms Act of 1934 as amended by the Gun Control Act of 1968. Warin, an engineer and designer of firearms, worked for a company that developed weapons for the government. He made the 9 mm submachine gun, which was of standard military design. Warin testified at the original trial that he had built the firearm to test and refine it for possible sale to the government as an improvement on military weapons then in use. He had not registered it as required by law.

A member of the Ohio "sedentary militia," Warin argued that the Second Amendment to the U.S. Constitution protected his right to possess a weapon that can be used by the armed forces of the United States. Basing his argument on *United States v. Miller* (1939), Warin argued that as a member of the sedentary militia, he could possess a weapon with military capability, and therefore the relevant provision of the National firearms Act was unconstitutional.

In disagreement with Warin's contention, the court ruled that when the U.S. Supreme Court in *Miller* determined that "a shotgun having a barrel of less than eighteen inches in length" had no reasonable connection to the maintenance of a well-regulated militia, the Court did not state that the Second Amendment is an absolute guarantee of the right to possess any weapon appropriate for military use. Citing the opinion in *Cases v. United States* (1942), the Court concluded that in *Miller* the Supreme Court made its ruling on the basis of the facts of that case, and was not establishing a broad ruling about the right to bear arms. The development of weaponry since World War II might be taken to indicate that only the most primitive of weapons could be regulated under the Warin decision. However, this would be an unacceptable conclusion in a time of nuclear weapons and other sophisticated instruments of destruction.

The court asserted that the Second Amendment clearly protects a collective, not an individual, right. It applies solely to the right of states to support a militia, not to an individual's right to bear arms. Therefore, an individual cannot legitimately claim to possess an unlimited constitutional guarantee to possess a firearm. In addition, Warin's membership, along with all adult citizens of Ohio, in the sedentary militia, did not confer on him the right under the Second Amendment to possess a submachine gun.

Citing *United States v. Tot* (1942), the court indicated that even when applicable, the Second Amendment did not confer an absolute right against congressional regulation of firearms. Going back as far as the fourteenth century, common law has not treated the bearing of weapons as an absolute right. Further, regulation of firearms can be justified by Congress's taxing power and the commerce power. Supreme Court rulings indicate that even First Amendment rights are not considered absolute, for such rights must be applied to achieve both liberty as well as an orderly life. Without an organized society where limitations may be placed on individual action, liberty would be lost to "unrestrained abuses."

The court rejected Warin's further argument that regulation of the manufacture of certain types of firearms was unconstitutional. The Appeals Court affirmed the district court's refusal to consider this argument because Warin was not charged with violating any law concerning the manufacture of firearms, but solely with the possession of an unregistered submachine gun. The court also agreed with the lower court regarding the argument that the statute under which Warin was charged violated the Ninth Amendment. The Court was not persuaded that possession of an unregistered submachine gun could be considered as a fundamental right guaranteed in this amendment. *See also* CASES V. UNITED STATES (1942); GUN CONTROL ACT OF 1968; NATIONAL FIREARMS ACT; NINTH AMENDMENT; SECOND AMENDMENT; *UNITED STATES V. MILLER* (1939); *UNITED STATES V. TOT* (1942).

Further Reading: *United States v. Warin*, 530 F.2d 103 (1976).

V

Violence Policy Center (VPC)

Established in 1988, the Violence Policy Center (VPC) is a Washington-based organization that conducts research on violence associated with firearms. In 1994, the Center joined with the Firearms Policy Project in supporting more stringent controls on the possession of handguns. Josh Sugarmann, executive director of the Center, has commented that few people have a true understanding of the gun control issue, arguing that the success of the National Rifle Association (NRA) and other pro-gun organizations stems in part from the lack of knowledge gun control organizations have about the issue. Therefore, the organization acts as an alternative source of information to pro-gun groups. The VPC has criticized the premier gun control organization, Handgun Control, Inc. (HCI), for accepting the NRA's major premise that not handguns, but handguns in the wrong hands, result in violence. The Center considers the NRA's well-known saying, "Guns don't kill, people do," as virtually identical to HCI's watchword, "Working to keep handguns out of the wrong hands."

According to the VPC, keeping handguns from the "wrong hands," in other words, from minors, criminals, alcoholics, drug users, and the mentally incompetent, does not address the major causes of gun violence. The organization holds that a major difficulty with guns derives from their use in suicides and homicides involving family members and acquaintances. The simple availability of firearms leads to violence. As Sugarmann has stated, "the 'right hands' have a nasty tendency to turn into the 'wrong hands.'" The Center has criticized the standard sorts of gun control measures advocated by the HCI, such as waiting periods. The VPC rejects the possible efficacy of other gun control measures, such as licensing, registration, safety training, or mandatory sentencing for those who use firearms in the commission of a crime. Legal handgun possession leads to major suffering without providing their owners with any significant self-defense advantage.

In effect, the VPC agrees with the NRA that waiting periods and background checks have extremely limited consequences for handgun violence, and that banning multiple handgun sales to the same person and mandatory trigger locks would have minimal influence on the reduction of violence associated with firearms. However, the agreement ends when the Center strongly advocates the banning of handguns, which the organization contends is the only way to deal with the problems of guns so widely available in the United States. According to the VPC, guns are a public health problem associated with a system of distribution that has allowed weapons to pervade society.

The organization distributes literature on such subjects as assault weapons; strategies to reduce firearms violence; various studies of women and guns, including an analysis of justifiable homicides committed by women and persuasive techniques employed by the firearms industry to appeal to potential female buyers; analyses of the firearms industry; firearms manufacturers in the United States; federally licensed firearms dealers; a study of caseless ammunition; and case studies of felons granted the right to own firearms despite the restrictions of federal firearms laws. *See also* GUN CULTURE; HANDGUN CONTROL, INC.; NATIONAL RIFLE ASSOCIATION; TRIGGER LOCKS; WOMEN AND GUNS.

Further Reading: Josh Sugarmann, *National Rifle Association: Money, Firepower and Fear* (Washington, DC: National Press, 1992); Violence Policy Center Web site <www.vpc.org>.

Violence Prevention Research Program (VPRP)

The Violence Prevention Research Program (VPRP), located at the University of California at Davis, focuses its research efforts on the causes, nature, and prevention of violence. Garen J. W. Wintemute, who practices emergency medicine at the UC Davis Medical Center in Sacramento, and is professor of epidemiology and preventive medicine at the UC Davis School of Medicine, serves as the Program's director. He has been a consultant for several organizations, including the National Institute of Justice, the World Health Organization (WHO), and the U.S. Centers for Disease Control and Prevention (CDC). Wintemute has engaged in a number of studies conducted by the Program that deal with the nature and prevention of violence and the development of strategies to prevent violent behavior. The Program has focused on the issue of gun violence from a health care perspective, which has drawn criticism from those less willing to concentrate on guns as an independent variable in the determination of the causes of violence.

Research conducted by the Program focuses on guns as in important ingredient in violent criminal behavior. According to a program report, illegal gun use adversely affects the lives of more than one million Americans each year, making the illegal use of firearms a "raging epidemic." VPRP-backed research focuses on acquiring greater information about firearms: the types that are more likely to be used in crime, the manufacturers, the users, the uses, where they are acquired (especially for illegal purposes), and where they are more prevalently used.

In 1997, the Program published a report on research conducted in Sacramento, California, which examined information about firearms that law enforcement officers confiscated during 1995. The researchers discovered that although those aged 12 to 24 represented 21 percent of Sacramento's residents, they constituted nearly half of those from whom weapons were taken. Several characteristics were found to be associated with criminal gun activity, including higher population density, higher unemployment rates, a greater proportion of younger residents, more single parents, lower housing values, fewer high school graduates, and more residents receiving public assistance. The Program suggests that these links demonstrate an association between criminal use of guns and poverty.

Because of the disproportionate involvement of youth in illegal gun activity, the Program recommended efforts to keep guns away from young people. Also recommended was an aggressive program of gun tracing to discover the source of firearms. Legal purchases that find their way into the illegal gun market (so-called straw purchases) and direct channels from manufacturers were identified as important sources to investigate. Because a large proportion of firearms are obtained through the illegal market, police officials must be able to penetrate this enterprise to prosecute those involved.

Because theft is an important source of weapons used in crimes, gun owners and dealers should become involved in anti-theft programs. Among the actions recommended to firearm owners are keeping serial numbers, locking guns away, and reporting any gun thefts. The Program advocates greater authority for police to destroy confiscated firearms, an action that may conflict with current federal law regarding a gun owner's right to repossess a confiscated weapon. Another recommended policy involves removing firearms from homes where domestic violence is likely to occur. As part of that recommendation, police officers should ask whether firearms are present where domestic violence has occurred or is likely to occur. Among proposed research studies, the Program intends to investigate relationships between gun confiscations in an area and the number of police calls recorded and the types of crimes committed. Another study would determine the characteristics of areas with the highest rates of gun thefts. *See also* HEALTH CARE PROFESSIONALS; TRIGGER LOCKS; WINTEMUTE, GAREN J.; YOUTH AND GUNS.

Further Reading: Don B. Kates, Henry E. Schaffer, John K. Lattimer, Geroge B. Murray, and Edwin H. Cassem, "Bad Medicine: Doctors and Guns," in David B. Kopel, ed., *Guns: Who Should Have Them?* (New York: Prometheus, 1995); E. Robinson-Haynes and Garen J. Wintemute, *Gun Confiscations: A Case Study of the City of Sacramento in 1995* (Sacramento, CA: Violence Prevention Research Program, 1997); Violence Prevention Research Program Web site <http://web.ucdmc.ucdavis.edu/vprp>.

Violent Crime Rate

In 1994, after several decades of seeming relentless increases, the violent crime rate began to fall, prompting questions about both the possible success of gun control legislation and the need for additional controls, as well as the success of concealed carry laws. From 1992 to 1996, the number of violent crimes declined 13 percent. The Federal Bureau of Investigation (FBI) released data in May 1998 indicating that violent crime had dropped an additional 5 percent during 1997. The number of murders decreased from 24,526 in 1993 to 19,645 in 1996, representing a 20-percent drop. The murder rate had declined from 9.5 to 7.4 per 100,000 residents.

Gordon Witkin, writing for *U.S. News and World Report* in May 1998, provided an analysis of possible explanations for the notable decline in violent crime. Some social scientists have suggested that an improved economy and low unemployment made crime a less appealing activity. However, although

economic conditions may be related to robbery offenses, the murder rate, the category that declined most dramatically, is far less likely to vary with economic conditions. While others suggested that organized youth activity and other crime prevention programs contributed to the drop, these sorts of initiatives have often been judged ineffective. Many analysts suggested that the increasing number of people held in prisons helped to explain the drop in crime. The rate of incarceration increased dramatically after 1974 and the number of people held in federal, state, and local jails rose from 744,000 in 1985 to over 1.7 million in 1997. When those convicted of crimes reside in jail, they obviously cannot commit additional crimes, at least in society.

Larger police forces and improved police procedures have also been credited with declining rates of violent crime. A notable example is New York City, where improved policing has been given as the reason for a dramatic decline in the number of murders from 1,946 in 1993 to 983 in 1996. Houston, which experienced a 58 percent drop in the murder rate, had added 1,400 new police officers since 1991. Although recognizing that the previously mentioned factors may have contributed to a portion of the decline in violent crime, Witkin ultimately focused on the crack cocaine trade that spread across the country beginning in 1985-86. Criminologists speculate that associated with the crack trade were large numbers of young people acting as street sellers. These youth, who carried drugs and money with them on the street, felt compelled to carry handguns to protect themselves from robberies. As the crack trade began to subside in the early 1990s, so did the murder rate.

Although guns often play an important role in the commission of violent crimes, Gary Kleck, in *Targeting Guns: Firearms and Their Control* (1997), cautioned against arriving at hasty conclusions. He highlighted three observations: 1) there are over 200 million guns in the United States, 2) the level of violence is high, and 3) a large proportion of homicides are committed with firearms. However, it is inappropriate to infer a causal relationship between a higher level of gun ownership in the United States and a corresponding higher violence rate. Kleck suggested that, in fact, high rates of violence could cause high levels of gun ownership. Nevertheless, firearms are used in a high proportion of homicide cases. Tables 13 and 14 provide data regarding felons' firearm preferences and the percentage of particular weapons used in committing murders.

In the case of the crack trade explanation, the ownership of guns by a specific group of people engaged in criminal activity is hypothesized to be the reason for a higher violent crime rate. Correspondingly, a decline in the crack trade, and hence in the number of people carrying guns, leads to a decline in the murder rate. Whether the murder rate would have been lower if gun control measures could have kept firearms out of the hands of those engaged in criminal activity is a matter for debate.

The decline in violent crime notwithstanding, the United States still has an exceptionally high rate of violent crime compared to many other developed nations. Therefore, gun control advocates continue to press for additional measures to check gun-related violence, while gun rights advocates proclaim that guns are a primary means for citizens to protect themselves from, and to deter, violent crime. Reports in 1998 indicated that at least a portion of the decline in violent crime was attributable to intentional under-reporting of crime in certain cities such as Philadelphia, New York, Atlanta, and Boca Raton, Florida. Law enforcement officials speculated that recent data indicating a decline in crime rates pressured police commanders to demonstrate even further declines, especially when such data are linked to promotions and pay raises. *See also* KLECK, GARY.

Further Reading: Gary Kleck, *Targeting Guns: Firearms and Their Control* (New York: Aldine De Gruyter, 1997); Gordon Witkin, "The Crime Bust," *U.S. News & World Report* 124 (May 25, 1998), 28-33, 36-37.

TABLE 13

WHAT FELONS LOOK FOR IN A HANDGUN

Trait	Very Important	Somewhat important	A little important	Unimportant	No. of cases	% 'single most important'
					(N)	(N=894)
Cheap	21	21	20	37	(14290)	6
Concealable	50	25	12	13	(1434)	13
Firepower	42	25	14	18	(1444)	22
Small caliber	11	20	22	47	(1382)	3
Large caliber	30	23	15	31	(1382)	4
Accurate	62	21	8	9	(1413)	9
Easy to shoot	54	24	10	12	(1427)	2
Scary-looking	21	18	16	44	(1421)	5
Well made	58	20	9	13	(1431)	17
Untraceable	60	12	9	19	(1434)	13
Easy to get	48	23	12	17	(1423)	4
Ammunition cheap	19	19	19	43	(1394)	—
Ammunition easy to get	45	26	11	18	(1436)	2

Source: Reprinted with permission from James D. Wright and Peter H. Rossi, *Armed and Considered Dangerous: A Survey of Felons and Their Firearms* (New York: Aldine de Gruyter, 1994), p. 163. Copyright © 1986 James D. Wright and Peter H. Rossi.

TABLE 14	
TYPES OF WEAPONS USED IN MURDERS, 1997 (PERCENT)	
Handguns	52.6%
Knives/cutting instruments	13.0
Firearms (type unknown)	13.2
Personal weapons (fists, feet, etc.)	6.3
Shotguns	4.2
Rifles	4.1
Other weapons	13.2

Source: *Crime in the United States, 1997* (Washington, DC: Federal Bureau of Investigation, 1998), derived from Table 20, p. 201 (Murder, State, Types of Weapons, 1997).

Volkmer, Harold Lee (1931–)

A strong advocate of the position that the Second Amendment establishes an individual right to keep and bear arms, Harold Volkmer, Democratic congressman from Missouri, worked for years to bring about passage of the Firearms Owners Protection Act of 1986, also known as the McClure-Volkmer Act. When Senator James A. McClure, Republican of Idaho, began backing the legislation in the Senate, Volkmer had already worked for several years to repeal major portions of the Gun Control Act of 1968. He first introduced a version of the Firearms Owners Protection Act in 1978, and played a key role in the bill's final passage in the House.

Volkmer received a law degree from the University of Missouri School of Law in Columbia in 1955. He served as assistant attorney general of Missouri in 1955 and, after a stint in the U.S. Army, established a private practice in Hannibal, Missouri, in 1958. He was prosecuting attorney for Marion County from 1960 to 1966 and served in the Missouri State House of Representatives from 1967 to 1976. Volkmer won election to the U.S. House of Representatives in 1976 and soon thereafter established himself as a major critic of the Gun Control Act of 1968.

Volkmer believed that the law was making criminals out of law-abiding citizens who inadvertently violated provisions of the act. Volkmer charged that the Bureau of Alcohol, Tobacco, and Firearms (BATF) was misapplying the law to the detriment of innocent gun owners. Rather than harassing law-abiding citizens, Volkmer wanted to require the BATF to focus its energies on those who violated the law through criminal activities. He included in the legislation provisions intended to protect citizens against the confiscation of property. The only weapons subject to seizure by law enforcement officials would be those actually involved in a crime. If charges were not filed within 120 days, the confiscated weapons were to be returned to the owners, and if the accused was acquitted, the law would require return of the seized firearms. If the government failed to return such weapons, the bill provided for the payment of attorney fees to a claimant in any lawsuit to obtain release of the firearms.

Although the Firearms Owners Protection Act passed the Senate in July 1985, by spring 1986 the bill was still in the House Judiciary Committee, where chairman Peter Rodino, Democrat of New Jersey, refused to take action. In April, Volkmer filed a discharge petition to release the bill from the Judiciary Committee. Infrequently attempted and even less frequently successful, a discharge petition requires the signatures of a majority of the House members (218) to bypass a committee and put a bill on the calendar for consideration by the whole House. When Volkmer's discharge petition received 200 signatures and appeared headed for a majority, the Judiciary Committee quickly released a compromise measure. Despite the conspicuous disapproval of a coalition of police organizations, the Volkmer bill, strongly supported by gun rights organizations, was substituted for the compromise bill.

Volkmer served in the House until January 1997, when he left after being defeated by his Republican opponent the previous November. Since 1986, he had witnessed some of the political fallout of his pro-gun bill. The McClure-Volkmer Act was a Pyrrhic victory for gun rights interests because it galvanized gun control supporters to work harder to pass more stringent gun control legislation. During Volkmer's tenure in the House, Congress passed the Brady Handgun Violence Prevention Act, the Un-Detectable

Firearms Act, and the assault weapons ban. *See also* BRADY HANDGUN VIOLENCE PREVENTION ACT; BUREAU OF ALCOHOL, TOBACCO, AND FIREARMS; FIREARMS OWNERS PROTECTION ACT; GUN CONTROL ACT OF 1968; MCCLURE, JAMES ALBERTAS; UNDETECTABLE FIREARMS ACT.

Further Reading: Earl R. Kruschke, *Gun Control* (Santa Barbara, CA: ABC-CLIO, 1995); Josh Sugarmann, *National Rifle Association: Money, Power and Fear* (Washington, DC: National Press, 1992).

W

Waco, Texas, Raid

The Waco, Texas, raid by federal law officials against David Koresh's Branch Davidian compound occurred less than one year after the tragedy at Ruby Ridge, Idaho, when two members of Randy Weaver's family and a federal marshal were killed during a standoff with federal agents. Each event began with a charge of violating federal firearms statutes. The Branch Davidians were accused of converting AR-15 semi-automatic rifles into machine guns, which are illegal under federal law. When the standoff ended on April 19, 1993, at least 80 people had lost their lives, including both members of the religious cult as well as law officers. The Waco raid galvanized militia movements, which believed that the federal government had declared war on the American people. Pro-gun groups took the opportunity to challenge the federal government's motives and tactics in enforcing gun control legislation.

The Branch Davidians, a religious sect that believed the apocalypse was near, also believed their leader, David Koresh, a 33-year-old erstwhile rock-and-roll band member, was the second Messiah. Approximately 130 Branch Davidians were living at the compound situated just seven miles northeast of Waco. Bureau of Alcohol, Tobacco, and Firearms (BATF) officials were concerned over the group's alleged stockpiling of illegal firearms and were considering how to serve an arrest warrant on Koresh and search the headquarters for illegal weapons with a minimum of disturbance.

On the morning of February 28, 1993, despite warnings that the Branch Davidians had received advance warning of a raid, 100 BATF agents jumped from cattle trailers and headed for the complex. Gunfire began as the agents attempted to enter the compound. When the shooting stopped, four BATF agents and six Branch Davidians, including Koresh's 2-year-old daughter, had been killed. The government then began a siege that lasted 51 days. More than 700 law enforcement officers from various jurisdictions, including the Federal Bureau of Investigation (FBI), the BATF, the Waco police, the National Guard, and the Texas Rangers took part in the extended standoff. Although the FBI successfully negotiated the release of 20 children, Koresh and his followers refused to surrender.

The FBI cut off electricity, used loudspeakers to play discordant music, and kept searchlights on the building during the night. None of these tactics appeared to create any dissension in the religious group or bring about any significant defections. Basing her decision on alleged child abuse among the Branch Davidians, Attorney General Janet Reno ordered an assault on the compound. Early on the morning of April 19, two tanks drove into the wall, and shot tear gas into the building. However, the occupants still refused

On April 19, 1993, the Branch Davidian compound near Waco, Texas, is engulfed in flames after being surrounded for 51 days by federal agents. *REUTERS/REED Schulman/Archive Photos.*

to leave. Around noon, smoke was seen coming from the windows, and soon the building was in flames. The government claimed that the Davidians had started the fires, but others insisted firing the tear gas had ignited the flames. Seventy-five people died in the fire, including 20 children.

The BATF took the brunt of criticism from many quarters, including pro-gun organizations like the National Rifle Association (NRA), which raised the fear that agents of the federal government were attempting to strip all Americans of their right to bear arms. The head of the BATF resigned under pressure from the Treasury Department and those responsible for the operation were demoted. Congress was highly critical of the government agencies involved in the raid. Militia groups concluded they had gained additional evidence that the federal government had declared war on them.

Because of the Waco raid, April 19 took on special significance for militia members and gun rights advocates. It was on that day in 1775 that the battles of Lexington and Concord occurred. British soldiers attempt-

ing to destroy a store of arms at Lexington engaged a group of Minutemen, American militiamen who were defending the towns. Contemporary militia members believed that just as the April 19, 1775, event had begun a revolutionary war, so would the April 19, 1993, raid against the Davidians begin a new revolution. In 1995, Timothy McVeigh, the convicted Oklahoma City bomber, chose this date for his act of terrorism to continue that revolutionary symbolism. *See also* AMERICAN REVOLUTION; BUREAU OF ALCOHOL, TOBACCO, AND FIREARMS; MINUTEMEN, REVOLUTIONARY; NATIONAL RIFLE ASSOCIATION; OKLAHOMA CITY BOMBING; RENO, JANET; RUBY RIDGE.

Further Reading: Morris Dees, *Gathering Storm: America's Militia Threat* (New York: HarperCollins, 1996); Jonathan Karl, *The Right to Bear Arms: The Rise of America's New Militias* (New York: HarperCollins, 1995).

Washington, D.C.

Advocates as well as opponents of gun control have pointed to Washington, D.C., the nation's capital, to bolster their respective positions regarding restrictions on firearms. In 1976, the District of Columbia came under the limitations imposed by the Firearm Control Regulations Act. The statute prohibits any new acquisition of handguns as well as semi-automatic firearms capable of using a detachable ammunition magazine with a capacity of more than 12 rounds. The only handguns that may be possessed are those that were registered before September 23, 1976 and re-registered by February 5, 1977. The District requires a permit to purchase a rifle or shotgun from a licensed dealer in the District. Criteria for such purchases include minimum age (21), physical fitness, knowledge of safe gun use, and no criminal record. Owners of registered firearms must keep them unloaded and disassembled or locked away unless being used for recreational purposes or when kept at a business. The penalty originally established for violating the firearms law was 10 days in jail and a $300 fine, but in 1981 the punishment was increased to a $1,000 fine and one year in jail.

Gun control supporters claim that the number of homicides committed in the District declined 25 percent from 1968 to 1987 (from 13.0 to 9.7) and estimate that 500 homicides were prevented in that time period. In the adjacent states of Maryland and Virginia, which did not have such stringent regulations, the monthly gun-related homicide rates experienced a more modest decline (from 5.8 in 1968 to 5.4 in 1987). However, the rate for the District remained considerably higher than for the two neighboring states despite the stricter firearms regulations. Those who question the effectiveness of gun control legislation note that the murder rate in the District remains the highest in the country. In addition, 85 percent of such cases in the District, compared to 68.3 percent of cases nationwide, were firearm-related.

In response to such criticisms, gun control supporters present two arguments. First, the murder rate for the District may be lower than it would have been without stringent gun control. Second, because surrounding states have far less stringent restrictions on the purchase and possession of firearms, individuals can easily acquire guns elsewhere and transport them into the District. The July 1998 shooting at the Capitol Building highlights the dilemmas of enforcing firearms restrictions locally. The assailant, who killed two security officers at the visitors' entrance, brought the weapon into the District with him.

The shooting did not lead to a call for more gun control legislation. Recent attempts to pass legislation concentrated on keeping firearms away from children and would have had no effect on the murder of the two security officers. Those on both sides of the gun control debate stated that little could have been done to prevent the shooting. Bob Walker, president of Handgun Control, Inc., admitted that more gun control legislation would not have kept the assailant from obtaining a handgun. Bill Powers, spokesman for the National Rifle Association (NRA), declared that existing laws did not keep firearms away from the shooter, who violated restrictions on bringing firearms into the District and taking guns onto the Capitol grounds. *See also* HANDGUN CONTROL, INC.; NATIONAL RIFLE ASSOCIATION; TRIGGER LOCKS; VIOLENT CRIME RATE.

Further Reading: Stephen P. Halbrook, "Second-Class Citizenship and the Second Amendment in the District of Columbia," *George Mason University Civil Rights Law Journal* (1995), 105-78; C. Loftin, et al., "Effects of Restrictive Licensing of Handguns on Homicide and Suicide in the District of Columbia," *New England Journal of Medicine* 325 (December 5, 1991), 1615-20; Kathleen Maguire and Ann L. Pastore, eds., *Bureau of Justice Statistics Sourcebook of Criminal Justice Statistics 1997* (Washington, DC: U.S. Government Printing Office, 1998).

Whitney, Eli (1765–1825)

The Militia Act of 1792 to establish a militia system in the United States, an act in 1798 to dispense weapons from the U.S. arsenals to the states, and an 1808 act to advance funds to states to finance militias provided the economic initiative to supplement Eli Whitney's inventive genius. By innovating the manufacturing process, Whitney was able to provide large numbers of muskets to the national and state governments in the early years of the nineteenth century. The federal government in the late eighteenth and early nineteenth centuries wanted to get guns into the hands of militia members and the regular military, and Whitney's work with standardized production increased the capacity to fulfill that policy goal.

Whitney's fame rests primarily on his invention of the cotton gin in 1792, a device that made the production of cotton profitable. Although the invention is credited with reshaping the whole economy of the South, the inventor gained little economically from his efforts. He shifted his attention to another enterprise—the manufacture of firearms. In January 1798, Whitney signed a contract with the national government to produce 10,000 muskets. He planned to manufacture the arms through a procedure that amounted to an early version of a system of interchangeable parts and mass production. Whitney put immense effort and time into developing the process, for at the time there existed neither the necessary machinery or the skilled labor.

Winchester, Oliver Fisher

He built a manufacturing plant, called Mill Rock, outside New Haven, Connecticut, using the funds invested by local residents to make the required tools and machines.

In October 1808, Whitney negotiated an agreement to produce 2,000 muskets for the New York State militia. At the same time, he pressed for a second contract with the federal government. In 1810, he obtained a contract to deliver 700 muskets, and the following year committed himself to producing 700 more. The approaching War of 1812 with Great Britain drew his interest because the nation would need additional weapons. In 1812 Whitney signed a contract with the secretary of war to deliver 15,000 muskets by the end of 1820.

Callender Irvine, commissary general of purchases for the federal government, discouraged Whitney's completion of the contract, hoping to end the gun maker's agreement with the federal government. Irvine wanted the U.S. War Department to adopt a musket in which he had a personal interest, and wished to maintain control over government procurement policies. Conflicts over payment and inspection standards delayed production. In 1814, Whitney appealed directly to Secretary of State James Monroe and in 1815 wrote to President James Madison. By appealing directly to officials at the highest levels of government, Whitney achieved a satisfactory resolution to the conflict over arms production.

In 1822, Whitney entered a third contract with the federal government, agreeing to deliver 15,000 additional muskets. During this time, Whitney introduced innovative tools, such as a milling machine, to improve production. Before Whitney's death late in 1824, his son, Eli, Jr., assumed management of the Mill Rock arms works, but lacked the ingenuity of his father. The factory became just one of many producers of arms. Not until the twentieth century did textbooks begin to recognize Whitney either as the inventor of the cotton gin or as an innovator in the production of firearms. *See also* COLT, SAMUEL; MILITIA ACT OF 1792; REMINGTON, ELIPHALET, II; RUGER, WILLIAM BATTERMAN (BILL); SMITH AND WESSON; WINCHESTER, OLIVER FISHER.

Further Reading: Green, Constance McLaughlin, *Eli Whitney and the Birth of American Technology* (Boston: Little, Brown, 1956).

Winchester, Oliver Fisher (1810–1880)

Many people regard early gun makers as heroic contributors to the establishment of the nation and none has gained a higher status than Oliver Fisher Winchester. To this day, the Winchester retains its reputation as the rifle that conquered the American West. By the end of western expansion, the Winchester company had become the foremost manufacturer of long guns. However, Winchester himself bore no resemblance to the rugged individual of the old West, for before entering the firearms business, he was a successful shirt salesman.

Samuel Winchester, Oliver's father, died the year after the birth in Boston, Massachusetts, of Oliver and his twin brother. From the age of 7, Winchester worked on local farms, which limited his schooling to winter months. At 14, he apprenticed to a carpenter who taught him construction skills. In 1834, Winchester entered the dry goods business, opening a men's store in Baltimore. In June 1855, Winchester, at the age of 45, joined a group of 40 businessmen to form and incorporate the Volcanic Repeating Arms Company, which bought out Smith, Wesson, and Palmer a month later. Although he held a minimal number of stock shares, Winchester was elected the company's director. The company was relocated from Norwich to New Haven, Connecticut. The poor performance of the Volcanic firearm forced Winchester and company president Nelson Gaston to secure loans through personal mortgages. After Gaston's death, Winchester became president. In February 1857, Volcanic was declared bankrupt, and the next month Winchester was able to purchase all company assets for $40,000. He began serving as the company's president and treasurer.

In 1858, Winchester asked B. Tyler Henry to modify the Volcanic rifle, for which he was

A factory worker examines rifle chambers at the Winchester Rifle factory, the firm begun by Oliver Winchester in the 1850s. *Archive Photos.*

well paid. Early in 1860, anticipating the Civil War, Winchester wrote to the U.S. government, requesting the military adoption of the Henry repeater. Like so many prophets of technology, Winchester predicted that major changes would result from the company's new rifle: "Probably it will modify the art of war; possibly it may revolutionize the whole science of war." However, Christopher Spencer received the major government contracts to supply the Union army with repeating rifles during the Civil War.

Following the war, pioneers moving west overwhelmingly chose the Winchester Model 1866, preferring its larger cartridge capacity and quickness. They found it an excellent weapon for defense against the dangers of the wilderness. When Nelson King solved a nagging problem with the ammunition magazine, Winchester dominated the market and Spencer's company could not survive. Customers chose the $50 Henry over the war-surplus Spencer, which sold for $7. The Model 1866 was so popular that it came to be known simply as "the Winchester." Throughout the 1870s, Winchester did well, making arms deals with foreign countries such as Turkey. With the Hotchkiss rifle (subsequently named the Model 1883), Winchester believed that the government contract that so far eluded the company could now be acquired. The Hotchkiss received superior ratings in tests conducted in 1878, but poor workmanship on the first shipment killed the deal. Winchester died in December 1880, and his son, whom he had expected to assume the presidency of the company, died of tuberculosis a few months later.

Concentrating on the civilian market, the Winchester Company around the turn of the century introduced "missionary" salesmen, entertainers who would not only make arms deals for the company, but would put on trick shot demonstrations to attract customers. Adolph (Ad) Topperwein, a circus performer since he was six years old, and his wife "Pinky" conducted tours on behalf of Winchester. At this time, Winchester produced other successful models, including the 94, which today is the rifle most often associated with Winchester.

During World War I, Winchester made large commitments to produce military arms. However, following the war, the drop in demand and inefficient production standards left the company $17 million in debt. Winchester had to borrow $3 million to pay taxes on wartime profits. Efforts in the 1920s to diversify and to open retail stores failed to raise the company out of debt. In January 1931, hit hard by the Great Depression, the company was forced into bankruptcy. After reorganization, the introduction of the Model 70, which became for the modern sportsman what the Winchester 66 had been for the post-Civil War settlers, improved the financial status of the company. World War II brought renewed government contracts.

In more recent times Winchester has gone through additional reorganizations, especially in 1984 when the company filed for bankruptcy under Chapter 11. In 1987, five investors bought the company. By the 1990s, managers had moved Winchester toward more aggressive sales strategies to maintain a share of the market. *See also* COLT, SAMUEL; REMINGTON, ELIPHALET, II; RUGER, WILLIAM BATTERMAN (BILL); SMITH AND WESSON; WINCHESTER, OLIVER FISHER.

Further Reading: Wayne Van Zwoll, *America's Great Gunmakers* (South Hackensack, NJ: Stoeger, 1992); K. D. Kirkland, *America's Premier Gunmakers* (New York: Mallard, 1990).

Wintemute, Garen J. (1951–)

Garen J. Wintemute, professor of medicine in the department of epidemiology and preventive medicine and director of the Violence Prevention Research Program at the University of California at Davis, has gained the critical attention of pro-gun groups and social science firearms researchers for his research on firearms and the gun manufacturing industry. Wintemute has published research findings dealing with accidental shootings committed by children, types of weapons used in suicides, hospital costs of firearm injuries, and firearms used in fatal shootings of law enforcement officers. Wintemute's 1994 study of southern California handgun manufacturers focused on what many gun control advocates consider the continuing problem of inexpensive handguns, or Saturday night specials, which Wintemute claims are disproportionately used in violent crime.

Wintemute received an undergraduate degree in biology from Yale University in 1973 and an M.D. from the University of California in 1977. In 1983, he was awarded a Master of Public Health degree from Johns Hopkins University. That year he became assistant professor of family practice at the University of California at Davis. In 1988, he was appointed director of the university's Family Practice Inpatient and Outpatient Services. An emergency room doctor, Wintemute became interested in firearm research when he realized that standard medical care was saving as many gunshot victims as possible and that any further improvements had to be made in the area of violence prevention.

Wintemute advocates the treatment of firearms as consumer products that should be subject to design, performance, safety, and reliability standards. Wintemute is especially concerned about U.S. manufacturers of inexpensive handguns. He calls the group of California companies (mostly belonging to the same family) that manufacture such weapons the "Ring of Fire." Wintemute is concerned about the availability of cheap handguns that are more powerful, more reliable, more accurate, and more easily used than previous models.

He is worried that, to increase sales, gun manufacturers have targeted new customers, particularly women. He contends that manufacturers lack a sense of responsibility for what happens to the firearms they produce. Wintemute believes that the Bureau of Alcohol, Tobacco, and Firearms (BATF) lacks the authority necessary to control firearms trafficking. Because the BATF is forbidden by law to keep a registry of firearms, the agency has a difficult task of tracing firearms used in crimes.

In a study of 88 unintentional shooting deaths of children in California from 1977 through 1983, Wintemute noted that 53 of the cases involved a child shooting another child. In 40 percent of these cases, the shooter was another family member. In 21 of the 88 shootings there was evidence that the child did not know the gun was loaded. In 1988, Wintemute participated in a California study of 5,360 authorized handgun purchasers between the ages of 21 and 25. He concluded that purchasers with a previous criminal history were more likely to acquire inexpensive handguns. Purchasers with no criminal history who acquired inexpensive handguns were nearly twice as likely to be charged with a crime of violence than purchasers of other types of handguns. Wintemute contends that these findings support other information indicating that cheap handguns are used disproportionately in the commission of crimes. *See also* BUREAU OF ALCOHOL, TOBACCO, AND FIREARMS; SATURDAY NIGHT SPECIAL; VIOLENCE PREVENTION RESEARCH PROGRAM.

Further Reading: Garen Wintemute, *Ring of Fire: The Handgun Makers of Southern California* (Sacramento, CA: Violence Prevention Research Program, 1994); Garen Wintemute, Carrie A. Parham, Mona A. Wright, James J. Beaumont, and Christiana M. Drake, "Weapons of Choice: Previous Criminal History, Later Criminal Activity, and Firearm Preference among Legally Authorized Young Adult Purchasers of Handguns," *Journal of Trauma Injury, Infection, and Critical Care* 44 (January 1998) 155–160; Garen Wintemute, S.P. Teret, J. Kraus, M.A. Wright, and G. Bradfield, "When Children Shoot Children: 88 Unintended Deaths in California," *Journal of the American Medical Association* 257 (1987), 3107-09.

Women Against Gun Control (WAGC)

Women Against Gun Control (WAGC), an organization headquartered in South Jordan, Utah, reflects the increasing interest women have shown in the acquisition of handguns for self-defense. The organization adheres to the position that "guns are the great equalizer. Guns give women a fighting chance," and claims that women attempting to fend off attacks from men can find a friend in firearms when police are not available to offer assistance. Therefore, any limitation on the right of law-abiding citizens to own firearms is viewed as preventing women from defending themselves in a dangerous environment. The WAGC warns against increasingly frequent attacks on the right to carry and use handguns and laments the tendency of women to support gun control. The organization criticizes such women as Sarah Brady, Dianne Feinstein, and Barbara Boxer for trying to turn women into helpless victims.

The organization believes that the Brady Handgun Violence Prevention Act, the Lautenberg Amendment, and various state and local laws have sharply limited the rights of gun owners. However, the WAGC applauds the laws various states have passed allowing for carrying concealed weapons.

In cooperation with other gun rights organizations, WAGC members take part in such political activities as petition gathering, letter writing to public officials, electoral politics, and testifying before state legislative and congressional committees. Following passage of the Lautenberg Amendment, which denied gun ownership to those found guilty of domestic violence, WAGC members took part in a press conference with pro-gun rights Representative Helen Chenoweth, Republican of Idaho. Although backers of the law touted it as an attempt to protect women against abuse, the organization called for its repeal, claiming that the law could be used to deny women the right to own firearms.

The WAGC monitors legislative proposals concerning gun control at all levels of government and reports findings to the membership in a quarterly newsletter, *BULLETin*.

Organization president, Janalee Tobias, provides information to women regarding self-defense and firearms. The organization hopes to promote common action by women worldwide to promote the right to keep and bear arms. Firearms instruction and safety training are additional activities in which members take part.

The WAGC has initiated a membership boycott against the Sara Lee Corporation. The corporation earned the gun organization's displeasure by awarding its Humanities award to Sarah Brady, one of the leading figures pushing for gun control. Sara Lee donated $50,000 to the Center to Prevent Handgun Violence, an organization affiliated with Sarah Brady's Handgun Control, Inc. The WAGC objected to the award because Sarah Brady has advocated banning "defensive weapons." The gun organization believes that any policy to ban handguns would be unconstitutional and would make law-abiding citizens easy prey for criminals. *See also* BOXER, BARBARA; BRADY, SARAH; BRADY HANDGUN VIOLENCE PREVENTION ACT; CHENOWETH, HELEN; FEINSTEIN, DIANNE; HANDGUN CONTROL, INC.; LAUTENBERG AMENDMENT; WOMEN AND GUNS.

Further Reading: Women Against Gun Control web site <www.wagc.org>.

Women and Guns

Traditionally, women and guns have been compared to oil and water: they simply do not mix. In 1934, when the National Rifle Association (NRA) successfully opposed the inclusion of handgun control measures in the National Firearms Act, the General Federation of Women's Clubs, representing 2 million members, reproached the NRA and approved a resolution calling for passage of the original bill. Sixty years later, results of a 1994 national survey conducted by the National Institute of Justice (NIJ) indicated that 42 percent of men, but only 9 percent of women owned guns. The contemporary feminist movement has been one of the most vocal supporters of gun control measures.

However, in the early 1990s, self-protection became a motivation to own a gun for women who were fearful of being victims of violent crime. Of the respondents in the NIJ survey, 41 percent of males, but 67 percent of females indicated that their primary purpose in possessing a gun was for protection against crime. At the same time, pro-gun organizations began a more serious effort to persuade growing numbers of women to become members and to convince them of the defensive value of gun ownership. In response to this increased interest by women in owning and learning to use firearms, women's magazines such as *Glamour*, *Ms.*, and *Vogue* printed articles questioning the value of gun ownership for women.

The NRA established the "Refuse to Be a Victim" program, which involves two initiatives. First, the NRA set up a toll-free number that women could call to receive a brochure informing them of self-defense techniques for women. The organization then established a three-hour self-defense seminar, costing participants $20. Anti-gun feminists responded skeptically to this program, charging that the NRA was primarily concerned with increasing membership in what previously had been a largely untapped segment of the population. In addition, gun control advocates claimed that the firearms industry, which had saturated the male market, had been searching for new customers and had found them in women. Sarah Brady, chair of Handgun Control, Inc., claimed that pro-gun advocates were cynically manipulating fear of crime among women to enlist new converts to their cause. "Refuse to Be a Victim" seminars were criticized for focusing on crimes committed by persons unknown to the victim, when the most common violent crime against women is rape and assault by a boyfriend or husband.

The NRA and other pro-gun advocates have presented gun ownership as an issue of choice, thus co-opting a major feminist theme often associated with the major feminist issue of reproductive rights. In response to the strong opposition to women owning firearms, pro-gun advocates contend that gun ownership should be, like other choices, one to be made by the individual woman. Pro-gun ad-

vocates, including some feminists, argue that gun ownership in the face of increasing violence represents a way that women can take control of their lives and can also act as a deterrent to the types of violent crimes that women now fear.

Women are becoming more active on both sides of the gun control debate. *Courtesy of Browning.*

In response to the arguments for choice, anti-gun feminists contend that the NRA offered no support for state legislative measures to authorize police to confiscate guns of men who assault women or who violate restraining orders. Given that so much violence against women occurs domestically, opponents also suggest that a woman who purchases a gun would more likely have it used against her by a male living with her than to use it to protect herself. In addition, the limited training women receive in the use of firearms may be insufficient to ensure their effective use. Those critical of gun ownership note that 16 percent of police officers who are murdered are shot with their own guns, despite the extensive training they receive in firearm use. However, the specter still remains of the woman, faced with a threatening boyfriend or husband or stranger, who, had she possessed the means of defense, might be alive today. Pro-gun advocates, considering themselves "pro-choice," criticize anti-gun feminists for attempting to deny individual women the right to take control of their own lives. The call not to be a victim has strong appeal for women concerned about their own safety.

Researchers Tom Smith and Robert Smith (1995) have challenged gun rights advocates' portrayal of women and guns. Employing General Social Survey data, they found no evidence that gun ownership among women is increasing. Smith and Smith estimate that less than 12 percent of women own a firearm, and less than eight percent own a handgun. They note that gun ownership is higher among married women residing outside large cities and is related to hunting rather than concerns for self-defense. *See also* BRADY, SARAH; HANDGUN CONTROL, INC.; NATIONAL FIREARMS ACT; NATIONAL RIFLE ASSOCIATION.

Further Reading: George Flynn and Alan Gottlieb, *Guns for Women: The Complete Handgun Buying Guide for Women* (Bellevue, WA: Merril, 1988); Ann Jones, "Living with Guns," *Ms.* (May/June 1994), 38-44; Ellen Neuborne, "Cashing In on Fear," *Ms.* (May/June 1994), 46-50; Paxton Quigley, *Armed and Female* (New York: St. Martin's, 1989); Tom W. Smith and Robert J. Smith, "Changes In Firearms Ownership Among Women, 1980–1994," *Journal of Criminal Law and Criminology* 86 (Fall 1995), 133–145. Mary Zeiss Stange, "Arms and the Woman: A Feminist Reappraisal," in David B. Kopel, ed., *Guns: Who Should Have Them?* (Amherst, NY: Prometheus, 1995).

Women and Guns Magazine

Established in 1989, *Women and Guns* magazine (*WG*) is published every other month by the Second Amendment Foundation. Julianne Versnel Gottlieb serves as the publisher. *WG* contains many of the same types of articles that appear in other gun publications, including reviews of new products, such as gun safes, gun locks, and handguns. The magazine profiles gun manufacturers' product lines, such as American Derringer's series of small handguns. American Derringer is even more attractive because the company's president is a woman. The magazine especially emphasizes self-protection themes. While gun advocates see it as providing women the opportunity to become acquainted with their right to bear arms, proponents of gun control claim the magazine is another example of the attempt to open a new market among women for gun manufacturers.

Peggy Tartaro, the executive editor, writes a column, "From the Editor," in which she touches on various political trends relevant to gun owners and the issue of gun control. The emphasis on self-defense is clear in a "News" column, which presents accounts of successful uses of firearms to thwart crime. The media are taken to task for focusing on incidents, such as the 1991 Kileen, Texas, shooting in which a gunman opened fire in a cafeteria, killing 22 people and injuring 23 others, and the 1989 Stockton, California, schoolyard shooting, while de-emphasizing the successful use of firearms to prevent other possible incidents. "Defensive Strategies," a column by Lyn Bates, a contributing editor, explores the sometimes complex circumstances of self-defense. In one issue, Bates introduced two scenarios, asking which of three options the reader would choose in each case. The reader was asked to consider not only whether the use of a firearm is justified, but if it is worth risking the consequences, which could involve criminal charges, expenditures for legal assistance, and law suits. The author mentioned three situations in which the gun owner should not hesitate to act: 1) when under deadly attack, 2) when being stalked by a killer, and 3) when family members are in serious danger. In all situations, Bates asserted, it is better to be armed than not.

Firearms are not the only weapons that *WG* encourages women to consider for self-protection. In an article by R.K. Campbell titled "Edged Weapon Options for Personal Protection," women are informed that even when in possession of a gun, they should consider carrying a knife as well. If a person cannot carry a gun, she has even greater use for a knife. Campbell notes that most types of knives are legal, inexpensive, easily purchased, and not dependent on one's physical strength. Women are advised to practice "slashing, striking, saber strikes and reverse slashes." Another *WG* article notes the advantages of a shotgun as a defensive weapon.

The column, "Legally Speaking" by Karen L. MacNutt, a contributing editor and consulting attorney for the Second Amendment Foundation, the National Rifle Association (NRA), and the Gun Owners' Action League, explores the legal implications of self-protection. In one issue, MacNutt discussed appropriate responses to verbal threats. She noted that "you may not use deadly force, nor should you display deadly force, if you are verbally threatened." Otherwise, the gun owner may risk a charge of assault with a deadly weapon. However, assault upon the gun owner would justify the use of deadly force as a self-defense measure. MacNutt also distinguished between making threats and informing someone of the legal consequences of their actions. *See also* GUN OWNERS' ACTION LEAGUE; NATIONAL RIFLE ASSOCIATION; SECOND AMENDMENT FOUNDATION; STOCKTON, CALIFORNIA, SHOOTING; WOMEN AND GUNS.

Further Reading: *Women and Guns* (Second Amendment Foundation, Buffalo, NY).

Women's Firearm Network (WFN)

The Women's Firearm Network, a Web site that provides firearms information to women, is maintained by Carole Walsh and Keeva Segal, computer graphics and design specialists. The site is dedicated to strengthening what is considered the individual right guaranteed in the Second Amendment to keep and bear arms and provides information on such topics as handguns, rifles, shotguns, hunting, and self-defense. Submissions from individuals and companies are welcome and the site features advertisements of new products such as handguns and firearm safety equipment. Various events, firearm training seminars, and personal protection courses are posted at the site.

The site features an article titled "Challenge" by Kathleen Gennaro, director of women's policy for Gun Owners of America. Gennaro challenges "the men of America who believe they really love their wives, their daughters, sons and their families" to consider their level of concern for the security of loved ones. According to Gennaro, "women do like feeling protected and cared for, I don't care what they NOW may say in opposition to it," referring to the greater tendency of women to prefer gun control. She advises family members to become knowledgeable about the Second Amendment and firearms laws. Men and their families are advised to determine the type of firearm best suited to their needs, to attend safety classes, and to learn how to clean the firearm and handle it properly. Gennaro claims that children, who learn how to play with a bat and ball at an early age and to read by the time they attend kindergarten, should also learn about firearms.

Gennaro states emphatically that she considers the Second Amendment to establish a right, not a privilege. She contends that although the nation has changed since revolutionary times and the rule of King George, the names of congressional leaders and the president could be substituted for that of the king and the situation would be the same. The Second Amendment is not a "man thing," but applies equally to women. Women are encouraged to become politically active, writing public officials, newspapers, and interest groups. The Network supports the boycott of products manufactured by Sara Lee Corporation as a way to "protect our freedom." Sara Lee named Sarah Brady, head of Handgun Control, Inc., a Forerunner Woman of the Year and gave her a $50,000 grant in recognition of her work with the nation's leading gun control organization. Women are asked to encourage their friends to support the boycott.

The WFN praises John R. Lott's book, *More Guns, Less Crime*, as the most thorough study of the effects of firearm ownership on the level of crime. The commentary emphasizes Lott's findings that waiting periods, gun buyback programs, and background checks have little effect on crime reduction, but that allowing the carrying of concealed handguns is "the most cost-effective method available for reducing violent crime." *See also* BRADY, SARAH; CONCEALED CARRY LAWS; GUN BUYBACK PROGRAMS; GUN OWNERS OF AMERICA; HANDGUN CONTROL, INC.; LOTT, JOHN R.; NATIONAL INSTANT CHECK SYSTEM; SECOND AMENDMENT; WOMEN AND GUNS.

Further Reading: Women's Firearm Network Web site <www.womenshooters.com>.

Y

Youth and Guns

Gun control advocates have focused much of their attention on gun violence among children and adolescents. They note that gunshot wounds are more likely to kill teenage males than all natural causes combined. From 1983 to 1995, the proportion of gun homicides in which juveniles used guns rose from 55 percent to 80 percent. These data are reflected in a 1993 Louis Harris poll, in which 35 percent of children from 6 to 12 years old said they feared for their lives because of gun violence. Although juvenile arrests for murder declined 14 percent during the period 1994–95, the levels of other types of violence remained high.

Some people have advocated the introduction of greater safety measures to curb youth injury and death due to firearms. For instance, in 1997 Democratic President Bill Clinton called for mandatory safety devices on guns to prevent accidents involving children. Although some argue for more stringent gun legislation, others contend that such legislation would have little effect on the overall level of gun possession and usage by youth. Gun researcher Gary Kleck has argued against mandating certain gun safety measures, claiming that they miss the true problem with gun violence. He notes that just 18 percent of accidental deaths from gun shots involved children 12 years of age or younger. He also notes that few young children have the strength to pull the trigger on the average handgun. Because children are seldom involved in gun accidents, Kleck argues that various safety devices cannot have a significant effect on the overall fatal gun accident (FGA) rate among young children.

Existing laws forbid juvenile purchases of handguns from retail stores or pawnshops; federal law restricts crossing state lines to purchase guns; theft of guns is illegal; transfer of stolen property is against the law; firing a gun inside the city limits is widely banned; and bearing a weapon on school property has been made illegal. Those who oppose further gun control legislation conjecture that better enforcement of the law could result in improved compliance. Although Joseph Sheley and James Wright, in their 1995 study of youth and firearms, conceded that more severe criminal penalties could have some positive effect in reducing gun violence, they concluded that the extent of the problem and the lack of resources have kept existing laws from having their intended effect. Controlling the supply of ammunition has also been suggested as a means of limiting gun violence. However, noting the experience with the illegal drug trade, some argue that a black market for ammunition would spring up quickly to meet the demand.

Sheley and Wright further argued that stiff new penalties would place the worst youth offenders in prison, but would ultimately prove futile because new offenders would soon replace those who have been taken off

A young boy receives instruction in the proper use of a handgun. *Courtesy of Browning.*

the streets. However, this objection fails to take into account the possible deterrent effect of harsher treatment of offenders. The recent decline in arrests for murder may have a number of causes, but one of them could be that a criminal justice system that has incarcerated larger numbers of offenders has deterred others from committing similar violent crimes.

Stuart Greenbaum (1997) emphasized the promising results of selected enforcement programs such as the Kansas City Gun Experiment, which targeted a limited area within the city to be patrolled intensively by police officers to disrupt the illegal gun trade. Greenbaum also emphasized programs that educate youth to the dangers of firearms, including the introduction of gun safety curricula in the public schools. To reduce juvenile gun possession, he noted that youth must be convinced they can cope with their environment without carrying weapons. However, Sheley and Wright noted that one of the major reasons youths carry weapons, at least in the inner city, is out of a need for self-protection, whether or not they are involved in the drug trade or in gang activities. They painted a grim picture of life for such youth, who have developed a "siege mentality." They fear for their safety and believe that carrying a gun is a reasonable step for them to take to preserve their lives. When living in disintegrating neighborhoods where police protection is virtually nonexistent and where schools are chaotic, carrying a gun can provide empowerment.

Sheley and Wright emphasized that gun possession as well as drug use and gang activity are all symptoms of a larger social breakdown. Assuming the legitimacy of this observation, others recognize that solving these larger problems will take a long and committed effort. In the meantime, we are thrown back on the struggle to find methods to control the instruments of violence. *See also* CLINTON, WILLIAM JEFFERSON (BILL); KLECK, GARY; SCHOOLS AND GUNS; TRIGGER LOCKS.

Further Reading: Stuart Greenbaum, "Kids and Guns: From Playgrounds to Battlegrounds," *Juvenile Justice* 3 (September 1997), 3-10; Gary Kleck, *Targeting Guns* (New York: Aldine de Gruyter, 1997);

David B. Kopel, "Children and Guns," in David B. Kopel, ed., *Guns: Who Should Have Them?* (Amherst, NY: Prometheus, 1995), 309-406; Joseph F. Sheley and James D. Wright, *In the Line of Fire: Youth, Guns, and Violence in Urban America* (New York: Aldine de Gruyter, 1995).

Youth Crime Gun Interdiction Initiative (YCGII)

The Bureau of Alcohol, Tobacco, and Firearms (BATF) began the Youth Crime Gun Interdiction Initiative (YCGII) in 1996 as a pilot program to identify and disrupt the illegal supply of firearms to youth. The YCGII was an expansion of the Juvenile Firearms Trace Initiative begun in 1993 and was intended to supplement the gun trafficking efforts of the BATF by focusing on youth and gun-related crime. Although the YCGII received limited funding from the U.S. Department of the Treasury ($1.175 million in fiscal 1996 and $2.49 million in fiscal 1997), the initiative addresses what many consider the serious problem of gun violence committed by those under 25 years of age. The Initiative traces recovered crime guns through the National Tracing Center and engages in analyses of crime gun data to identify trends involving the characteristics of recovered firearms.

The YCGII was begun in 17 cities, including Atlanta, Georgia; Cleveland, Ohio; Memphis, Tennessee; San Antonio, Texas; and Washington, D.C. Ten of the sites were cities that already received funding from the Office of Community Oriented Policing Services (COPS) for initiatives to control juvenile crime. The National Institute of Justice (NIJ) had research activities already underway in three other sites. The municipal governments of all 17 cities expressed their commitment to engage the problem of armed youth crime.

After the first year, 10 additional cities were added to the initiative. They included Chicago, Detroit, Miami, and Philadelphia. Cities selected included those with populations over 250,000 with a high rate of gun-related violent crimes committed by youths and juveniles, and cities with a population over 100,000 that the U.S. attorney general had included in the Special Cities Project because violent crime had increased each year from 1993 to 1996.

The police departments in the participating cities signed a "memorandum of understanding," agreeing to trace all recovered firearms. The YCGII is committed to coordinating federal and state court prosecutions of illegal firearms trafficking involving youth. The initiative uses the services of Project LEAD, the computerized illegal firearms trafficking information system maintained by the BATF. The YCGII provided each site with a laptop computer capable of operating the Project LEAD software. The use of this software facilitates ongoing analyses of firearms trace information.

The BATF believes that the initiative may prove a valuable tool for controlling violent crime, especially because the population of juveniles is projected to increase significantly in the coming years, producing what has been termed a "demographic crime bomb." Because firearms used in crimes committed by juveniles have a briefer "time to crime" (the time in days from initial purchase to criminal use), there is a greater probability that attempts to trace such weapons will end successfully.

During the first year of operation, more than 36,000 firearms were traced in the initial 17 sites. The YCGII trace analysis reports provided basic information about crime guns and their users. Data analyses indicate that 4 of every 10 guns that law enforcement officials recover are traced to individuals aged 24 and younger. Eight out of ten guns recovered from youths and juveniles are handguns. The initiative reports that guns diverted from federally licensed firearms dealers contribute to the availability of firearms on the black market. The YCGII concludes from its analyses that law enforcement agencies can increase their capacity to reduce the rate of armed crimes through sharing crime gun information with other communities through the program. *See also* Bureau of Alcohol, Tobacco, and Firearms; National Tracing Center; Youth and Guns.

Further Reading: Youth Crime Gun Interdiction Initiative Web site <www.atf.treas.gov/core/firearms/ycgii/overview/overview.htm>.

Z

Zimring, Franklin E. (1942–)

Franklin E. Zimring, William F. Simon Professor of Law and director of the Earl Warren Legal Institute at the University of California at Berkeley, has conducted research on the causes and control of firearms violence. He published the first study of death rates from gun versus knife attacks and in 1968-69 served as director of research for the Task Force on Firearms of the National Violence Commission. Zimring adheres to the concept of instrumentality, that "a conflict is more likely to be lethal if a lethal weapon is at hand." He holds that if the death rate due to violence is a major problem, then handguns are a major part of that problem.

Zimring received a B.A. from Wayne State University and a J.D. from the University of Chicago. He has co-authored books with Gordon Hawkins dealing with penal confinement, drug control policy, and capital punishment. In 1987, he published *The Citizen's Guide to Gun Control*. Zimring has served as a member of the MacArthur Foundation Research Program on Adolescent Development and Juvenile Justice, the Center for Gun Policy and Research of the Johns Hopkins University, the Violent and Serious Juvenile Offender Project of the National Council on Crime and Delinquency, the National Policy Committee of the American Society of Criminology, and the National Academy of Sciences Panel on Violence.

Franklin Zimring, William F. Simon Professor of law and director of the Earl Warren Legal Institute at the University of California, Berkeley, has conducted research on the causes and control of firearms violence. *Photo by Michal Crawford Zimring.*

Zimring notes that firearm injury reduction might be viewed in the same way as attempts to reduce auto crashes, or, alternatively, like efforts to eliminate smoking as a hazardous activity. Although efforts to improve traffic safety led to successful strategies to improve automobiles and highways, Zimring identifies a weakness in applying the traffic safety model to firearms. Because firearms are designed to be lethal, it is extremely difficult to devise a safe handgun. Zimring notes one crucial area of correspondence between firearms and automobiles. Just as there are accident-prone individuals (for instance, those who drink and drive), there are people predisposed to conflict. Zimring suggests that the public health policy model for cigarettes, employed in the case of firearms, would call for the elimination of firearms (specifically handguns) as a health hazard.

In 1997, Zimring co-authored with Hawkins *Crime Is Not the Problem*, a book that challenged traditional understandings of crime in Western nations. Zimring argued that the United States does not have a greater crime problem, or even a greater violence problem than other nations, but does have a greater lethal violence problem. Rates of non-violent crime in the United States are comparable to, and sometimes lower than, rates in other countries. However, the rate of le-thal violence is far greater in the United States than in other Western nations. For instance, Zimring discovered that assaults lead to 11 times more deaths in New York City than in London. Explaining the gap, Zimring notes that while 81 percent of assaults in London occurred without the use of a weapon, only 13 percent of reported cases in New York involved no weapon.

Zimring claims that most killings in the United States are unrelated to criminal activity and therefore "get tough on crime" campaigns fail to distinguish between lethal violence and other crimes. Not only is the rate of deadly violence disproportionately high in the United States, but 70 percent of all killings are committed with firearms. Given the high level of lethal violence compared to other countries, Zimring recommends that lawmakers respond specifically to this problem, which in a high proportion of cases involves firearms. *See also* UNITED KINGDOM.

Further Reading: Thomas B. Cole, "Franklin E. Zimring on Law and Firearms," *Journal of the American Medical Association* 275 (June 12, 1996), 1709; Franklin E. Zimring and Gordon Hawkins, *Crime Is Not the Problem: Lethal Violence in America* (New York: Oxford University Press, 1997).

APPENDIX 1
State Constitutional Gun Rights Provisions

Forty-three states have constitutional provisions dealing with the right to keep and bear arms. The constitutions of seven states—California, Delaware, Iowa, Maryland, Minnesota, New Jersey, and Wisconsin—contain no such provision. The following listing presents the relevant wording of state constitutions.

Alabama: That every citizen has a right to bear arms in defense of himself and the state (art. I, para. 26).

Alaska: A well-regulated militia being necessary to the security of a free state, the right of the people to keep and bear arms shall not be infringed (art. I, para. 19).

Arizona: The right of the individual citizen to bear arms in defense of himself or the State shall not be impaired, but nothing in this section shall be construed as authorizing individuals or corporations to organize, maintain, or employ an armed body of men (art. II, para. 26).

Arkansas: The citizens of this State shall have the right to keep and bear arms for their common defense (art. II, para. 5).

Colorado: The right of no person to keep and bear arms in defense of his home, person and property, or in aid of the civil power when thereto legally summoned, shall be called in question; but nothing herein contained shall be construed to justify the practice of carrying concealed weapons (art. II, para. 13).

Connecticut: Every citizen has a right to bear arms in defense of himself and the state (art. I, para. 15).

Florida: The right of the people to keep and bear arms in defense of themselves and of the lawful authority of the state shall not be infringed, except that the manner of bearing arms may be regulated by law (art. I, para. 8).

Georgia: The right of the people to keep and bear arms, shall not be infringed, but the General Assembly shall have power to prescribe the manner in which arms may be borne (art. I, para. I).

Hawaii: A well regulated militia being necessary to the security of a free state, the right of the people to keep and bear arms shall not be infringed (art. I, para. 15).

Idaho: The people have the right to keep and bear arms, which right shall not be abridged; but this provision shall not prevent the passage of laws to govern the carrying of weapons concealed on the person nor prevent passage of legislation providing minimum sentences for crimes committed while in possession of a firearm, nor prevent the passage of legislation providing penalties for the possession of firearms by a convicted felon, nor prevent the passage of any legislation punishing the use of a firearm. No law shall impose licensure, registration or special taxation on the ownership or possession of firearms or ammunition. Nor shall any law permit the confiscation of firearms, except those actually used in the commission of a felony (art. I, para. II).

Illinois: Subject only to the police power, the right of the individual citizen to keep and bear arms shall not be infringed (art. I, para. 22).

Indiana: The people shall have a right to bear arms, for defense of themselves and the State (art. I, para. 32).

Kansas: The people have the right to bear arms for their defense and security; but standing armies, in time of peace, are dangerous to liberty, and shall not be tolerated, and the military shall be in strict subordination to the civil power (Bill of Rights, para. 4).

Kentucky: All men are, by nature, free and equal, and have certain inherent and inalienable rights, among which may be reckoned: . . . The right to bear arms in defense of themselves and of the State, subject to the power of the General Assembly to enact laws to prevent persons from carrying concealed weapons (para. I).

Louisiana: The right of each citizen to keep and bear arms shall not be abridged, but this provision shall not prevent the passage of laws to prohibit the carrying of weapons concealed on the person (art. I, para. 4).

Maine: Every citizen has the right to keep and bear arms for the common defense; and this right shall never be questioned (art. I, para. 16).

Massachusetts: The people have a right to keep and bear arms for the common defence [sic]. And as, in times of peace, armies are dangerous to liberty, they ought not to be maintained without the consent of the legislature; and the military power shall always be held in an exact subordination to the civil authority, and be governed by it (pt. I, art. 17).

Michigan: Every person has a right to keep and bear arms for the defense of himself and the state (art. I, para. 6).

Mississippi: The right of every citizen to keep and bear arms in defense of his home, person, or property, or in aid of the civil power where thereto legally summoned, shall not be called in question, but the legislature may regulate or forbid carrying concealed weapons (art. 3, para. 9, sec. 12).

Missouri: That the right of every citizen to keep and bear arms in defense of his home, person and property, or when lawfully summoned in aid of the civil power, shall not be questioned; but this shall not justify the wearing of concealed weapons (art. I, para. 23).

Montana: The right of any person to keep or bear arms in defense of his own home, person, and property, or in aid of the civil power when thereto legally summoned, shall not be called in question, but nothing herein contained shall be held to permit the carrying of concealed weapons (art. II, para. 12).

Nebraska: All persons are by nature free and independent and have certain inherent and inalienable rights: among those are life, liberty, the pursuit of happiness, and the right to keep and bear arms, for security or defense of self, family, home, and others, and for lawful common events, hunting, recreational use, and all other lawful purposes, and such rights shall not be denied or infringed by the state or any subdivision thereof. To secure these rights, and the protection of property, governments are instituted among people, deriving their just powers from the consent of the governed (art. I, sec. I).

Nevada: Every citizen has the right to keep and bear arms for security and defense, for lawful hunting and recreational use and for other lawful purposes (art. I, sec. 11-1).

New Hampshire: All persons have the right to keep and bear arms in defense of themselves, their families, their property, and the state (part first, art. 2a).

New Mexico: No law shall abridge the right of the citizen to keep and bear arms for security and defense, for lawful hunting and recreational use and for other lawful purposes, but nothing herein shall be held to permit the carrying of concealed weapons (art. II, para. 6).

New York: A well-regulated militia being necessary to the security of a free state, the right of the people to keep and bear arms cannot be infringed (New York Civil Right Law, sec. 4).

North Carolina: A well regulated militia being necessary to the security of a free State, the right of the people to keep and bear arms shall not be infringed; and, as standing armies in time of peace are dangerous to liberty, they shall not be maintained, and the military shall be kept under strict subordination to, and governed by, the civil power. Nothing herein shall justify the practice of carrying concealed weapons, or prevent the General

Assembly from enacting penal statutes against that practice (art. I, para. 30).

North Dakota: All individuals are by nature equally free and independent and have certain inalienable rights, among which are those of enjoying and defending life and liberty; acquiring, possessing and protecting property and reputation; pursuing and obtaining safety and happiness; and to keep and bear arms for the defense of their person, family, property, and the state, and for lawful hunting, recreational, and other lawful purposes, which shall not be infringed (sec. 1, art. 1).

Ohio: The people have the right to bear arms for their defense and security; but standing armies, in time of peace, are dangerous to liberty, and shall not be kept up; and the military shall be in strict subordination to the civil power (art. I, para. 4).

Oklahoma: The right of a citizen to keep and bear arms in defense of his home, person, or property, or in aid of the civil power, when thereunto legally summoned, shall never be prohibited; but nothing herein contained shall prevent the Legislature from regulating the carrying of weapons (art. II, para. 26).

Oregon: The people shall have the right to bear arms for the defense of themselves, and the State, but the Military shall be kept in strict subordination to the civil power (art. I, para. 27).

Pennsylvania: The right of the citizens to bear arms in defence [sic] of themselves and the State shall not be questioned (art. I, para. 21).

Rhode Island: The right of the people to keep and bear arms shall not be infringed (art. I, para. 22).

South Carolina: A well regulated militia being necessary to the security of a free State, the right of the people to keep and bear arms shall not be infringed. As, in times of peace, armies are dangerous to liberty, they shall not be maintained without the consent of the General Assembly. The military power of the State shall always be held in subordination to the civil authority and be governed by it. No soldier shall in time of peace be quartered in any house without the consent of the owner nor in time of war but in the manner prescribed by law (art. I, para. 20).

South Dakota: The right of the citizens to bear arms in defense of themselves and the state shall not be denied (art. VI, para. 24).

Tennessee: That the citizens of this State have a right to keep and to bear arms for their common defense; but the Legislature shall have power, by law, to regulate the wearing of arms with a view to prevent crime (art. I, para. 26).

Texas: Every citizen shall have the right to keep and bear arms in the lawful defence [sic] of himself or the State; but the Legislature shall have power, by law, to regulate the wearing of arms, with a view to prevent crime (art. I, para. 23).

Utah: The people have the right to bear arms for their security and defense, but the Legislature may regulate the exercise of this right by law (art. I, para. 6).

Vermont: That the people have a right to bear arms for the defence [sic] of themselves and the State–and as standing armies in time of peace are dangerous to liberty, they ought not to be kept up; and that the military should be kept under strict subordination to and governed by the civil power (ch. I, art. XVI).

Virginia: That a well regulated militia, composed of the body of the people, trained to arms, is the proper, natural, and safe defense of a free state, therefore, the right of the people to keep and bear arms shall not be infringed; that standing armies, in time of peace, should be avoided as dangerous to liberty; and that in all cases the military should be under strict subordination to, and governed by, the civil power (art. I, para. 13).

Washington: The right of the individual citizen to bear arms in defense of himself, or the state, shall not be impaired, but nothing in this section shall be construed as authorizing individuals or corporations to organize, maintain, or employ an armed body of men (art. I, para. 24).

West Virginia: A person has the right to keep and bear arms for the defense of self, family , home, and state, and for lawful hunting and recreational use (art. II, sec. 22).

Wyoming: The right of citizens to bear arms in defense of themselves and of the state shall not be denied (art. I, para. 24).

APPENDIX 2
Statutory and Constitutional Provisions Relating to the Purchase, Ownership, and Use of Firearms

The data included in the table on the following pages were compiled by the National Rifle Association of America, Institute for Legislative Action and appear in the *Sourcebook of Criminal Justice Statistics Online*, Table 1.87, <www.albany.edu/sourcebook>. In addition to state laws, the purchase, sale, and, in certain circumstances, the possession and interstate transportation of firearms are regulated by the Federal Gun Control Act of 1968 as amended by the Firearms Owners' Protection Act and other federal laws. Also, cities and localities may have their own firearms ordinances in addition to federal and state laws. A "Y" in the table indicates the existence of a state law or constitutional provision. However, many qualifications may apply. The source notes that state firearms laws are subject to frequent change. State and local statutes and ordinances, as well as local law enforcement authorities, should be consulted for the full text and meaning of statutory provisions.

A long gun is a rifle or shotgun. The source defines "constitutional provision" by citing Article 1, Section 15 of the Connecticut State Constitution as an example of the basic feature contained in the constitutions of many states. It reads: "Every citizen has a right to bear arms in defense of himself and the State."

Appendix 2: State Firearms Provisions

STATUTORY AND CONSTITUTIONAL PROVISIONS RELATING TO THE PURCHASE, OWNERSHIP, AND USE OF FIREARMS, BY STATE, AUGUST 1, 1999

State	NICS instant background check[a]	Exemptions to NICS	State waiting period (in days) Hand-gun	State waiting period (in days) Long gun	License or permit to purchase Hand-gun	License or permit to purchase Long gun	Registration Hand-gun	Registration Long gun	Record of sale sent to police	License or identification card	Certain firearms prohibited	State firearms preemption law[b]	Constitutional provision	Concealed carry law	Carrying openly prohibited	Hunter protection law[c]	Range protection law[d]	Firearm industry lawsuit preemption[e]
Alabama	Y[f]		2						Y[g]			Y[h]	Y	Y[j]	Y[n]	Y[i]		
Alaska	Y[f]	(k)										Y	Y	Y[j]		Y	Y	Y
Arizona	Y	(k)										Y	Y	Y[j]		Y	Y	Y
Arkansas	Y	(m)										Y	Y	Y[p]	Y[n]	Y	Y	Y
California	Y[f]		10	10					Y[g]		Y[o]	Y		Y[p]	Y[q]	Y	Y	
Colorado	Y[f]												Y	Y[p]		Y	Y	
Connecticut	Y[f]	(m)	14[r,s]	14[r,s]	Y[t]				Y[g]		Y[o]	Y[u]	Y	Y[p]	Y	Y	Y	
Delaware	Y[f]	(m)										Y	Y	Y[p]	Y	Y	Y	
Florida	Y[f]	(m)	3[r,s]									Y	Y	Y[p]	Y	Y	Y	Y
Georgia	Y[f]	(k)										Y[u]	Y	Y[p]	Y	Y	Y	
Hawaii	Y[f]	(w)			Y[t]		Y[x]	Y[x]	Y[g]		Y[o]	Y	Y	Y[y]		Y	Y	
Idaho	Y[f]	(k)										Y	Y	Y[p]		Y	Y	
Illinois	Y[f]		3	1	Y[t]	Y[t]	(y)	(y)	Y[g]	Y	Y[o]	Y[ab]		Y[z]	Y	Y	Y	
Indiana	Y[aa]	(k)			Y[t]				Y[g]			Y	Y	Y[p]	Y[p]	Y	Y	
Iowa	Y[ac]	(k,w)			(ad)		(ad)		Y[g]			Y		Y[p]	(ad)	Y	Y	
Kansas	Y[f]		(ad)		(ad)		(ad)					Y	Y	Y[z]	(ad)	Y	Y	
Kentucky	Y[f]	(m)							Y[g]			Y	Y	Y[p]		Y	Y	Y
Louisiana	Y[f]	(m)										Y	Y	Y[p]		Y	Y	Y
Maine	Y[f]											Y	Y	Y[p]		Y	Y	
Maryland	Y[aa]	(m)	7	7[ae]	(t)				Y[g]		Y[o]	Y[u]		Y[p]	Y	Y	Y	
Massachusetts	Y[ac]	(m)	7		Y[t]	Y[t]			Y[g]	Y		Y[u]	Y	Y[p]	Y	Y	Y	
Michigan	Y[ac]	(w)			Y[t]		Y		Y[g]			Y	Y	Y[p]	Y[p]	Y	Y	
Minnesota	Y[f]	(m)	7[r]	(r)	Y[t]	Y[t]			Y[g]		Y[o]	Y		Y[p]	Y	Y	Y	
Mississippi	Y[f]	(k)										Y	Y	Y[z]		Y	Y	
Missouri	Y[f]	(m)	7		Y[t]				Y[g]			Y	Y	Y[z]		Y	Y	Y
Montana	Y[f]	(k)											Y	Y[z]		Y	Y	
Nebraska	Y[ac]	(w)			Y							Y	Y	Y[z]		Y	Y	
Nevada	Y[f]	(k)	(ad)		(ad)		(ad)		Y[g]			Y	Y	Y[p]		Y	Y	Y
New Hampshire	Y[aa]	(k)			Y[t]	Y[t]			Y[g]	Y	Y[o]	Y	Y	Y[p]	Y	Y	Y	
New Jersey	Y[f]	(k)			Y[t]	Y[t]			Y[g]	Y	Y[o]	Y[u]		Y[p]	Y	Y	Y	Y

Purchase and ownership · Carrying

Purchase and ownership

State	NICS instant background check[a]	Exemptions to NICS	State waiting period (in days) Hand-gun	State waiting period (in days) Long gun	License or permit to purchase Hand-gun	License or permit to purchase Long gun	Registration Hand-gun	Registration Long gun	Record of sale sent to police	License or identification card	Certain firearms prohibited	State firearms preemption law[b]
New Mexico	Y[f]								Y[g]			Y
New York	Y[ac]	(w)			Y[t]	(t)	Y	(af)	Y[g]		(o)	Y[o]
North Carolina	Y[ac]	(k,w)			Y[t]				Y[g]	Y		Y[v]
North Dakota	Y[f]	(m)										Y
Ohio	Y[f]	(ad)	(ad)		(t)		(ad)		(ad)	(u)	(o)	
Oklahoma	Y[aa]	(m)										
Oregon	Y[aa]	(m)							Y[g]			Y
Pennsylvania	Y[f]	(m)							Y[g]			Y
Rhode Island	Y[f]		7	7					Y[g]			Y
South Carolina	Y[f]	(k)	(s)		(t)				Y[g]			Y
South Dakota	Y[f]	(m)	2						Y[g]		Y[o]	
Tennessee	Y[f]								Y[g]			Y
Texas	Y[f]	(k)										Y
Utah	Y[f]	(k)										Y
Vermont	Y[f]											Y
Virginia	Y[f]	(m)	(s,ad)		(t)				(ad)		Y[o]	Y
Washington	Y[aa]	(m)	5[ai]						Y[g]			Y
West Virginia	Y[f]											Y
Wisconsin	Y[aa]		2						Y[g]			Y
Wyoming	Y[f]	(k)										Y
District of Columbia	Y[f]	(m)			Y[t]		Y[v]	Y	Y[h]	Y	Y[o]	

Carrying

State	Constitutional provision	Concealed carry law	Carrying openly prohibited	Hunter protection law[c]	Range protection law[d]	Firearm industry lawsuit preemption[e]
New Mexico	Y	Y[z]				
New York		Y[p,i]	Y	Y	Y	
North Carolina	Y	Y[i]		Y	Y	
North Dakota	Y	Y[x]		Y	Y	
Ohio	Y	Y[z]	Y[p]	Y	Y	
Oklahoma	Y	Y[i]	(ad)	Y	Y	
Oregon	Y	Y[i]	Y[p]	Y		Y
Pennsylvania	Y	Y[i,ag]	Y[i]	Y	Y	
Rhode Island	Y	Y[p]	Y	Y		
South Carolina	Y	Y[i]	Y	Y	Y	
South Dakota	Y	Y[i]		Y		
Tennessee	Y	Y[i]	Y[n]	Y	Y	Y
Texas	Y	Y[i]	Y	Y	Y	Y
Utah	Y	Y[i]	Y[p]	Y		Y
Vermont	Y	Y[u,ah]	Y[n]	Y	Y	
Virginia	Y	Y[i]	(ad)	Y	Y	
Washington	Y	Y[i]		Y		
West Virginia	Y	Y[i]		Y	Y	
Wisconsin	Y	Y[z]		Y	Y	
Wyoming	Y	Y[i]		Y	Y	
District of Columbia	(aj)	Y[p]	Y		Y	Y

a The National Instant Check System (NICS), conducting records checks on retail firearm purchasers, took effect November 1998, replacing the Brady Act requirement that retail handgun sales be delayed until law enforcement authorities completed a check, or 5 business days passed, whichever came first.

b A State firearms preemption law prohibits local statutes more restrictive than the State's law regulating firearms.

c Hunter protection laws prohibit interference with lawful hunting activities.

d Range protection laws protect firearm ranges from nuisance and noise control actions intended to prevent a range's operation.

e Prohibits local jurisdictions from suing entities of the firearm industry.

f Checks are conducted by the FBI for retail firearm sales.

g On some or all firearm sales.

h Applies to handgun ordinances only.

i "Shall issue" permit system, liberally administered discretion by local authorities over permit issuance, or no permit required.

j Carrying a handgun in a motor vehicle requires a license, with exceptions.

k Firearm carrying permit holders are exempt. In Indiana, holders of personal protection or hunting and target shooting permits are exempt. Those not exempt: in Mississippi, permits issued to security guards; in Texas, peace officer licenses issued after NICS start date.

l Checks are conducted by the State for retail firearm sales.

m Holders of firearm carrying permits issued before Nov. 30, 1998 are exempt.

n Arkansas prohibits carrying a firearm with a purpose to employ it against a person. Tennessee prohibits carrying "with the intent to go armed." Vermont prohibits carrying with "the intent or purpose of injuring another."

STATUTORY AND CONSTITUTIONAL PROVISIONS RELATING TO THE PURCHASE, OWNERSHIP, AND USE OF FIREARMS, BY STATE, AUGUST 1, 1999 (CONT.)

o California, Connecticut, New Jersey, New York, New York City, other local jurisdictions in New York, and some local jurisdictions in Ohio prohibit "assault weapons." Hawaii prohibits "assault pistols." Illinois prohibits Federal firearms licensees from manufacturing or selling a handgun certain parts of which are made of certain metals and melt or deform below 800 degrees Fahrenheit; Chicago, Evanston, Oak Park, Morton Grove, Winnetka, Wilmette, and Highland Park prohibit handguns; some cities prohibit other kinds of firearms. Maryland prohibits several small, low-caliber, inexpensive handguns and "assault pistols." Minnesota prohibits licensed firearm dealers from selling a handgun any part of which melts below 1,000 degrees Fahrenheit or has an ultimate tensile strength less than 55,000 p.s.i. Ohio: Some cities prohibit handguns of certain magazine capacities. South Carolina prohibits licensed firearms dealers from possessing or selling a handgun the frame of which is of a certain construction and melts below 800 degrees Fahrenheit. Virginia prohibits "Street Sweeper" shotguns. The District of Columbia prohibits new acquisition of handguns and any semi-automatic firearm capable of using a detachable ammunition magazine of more than 12 rounds capacity. (With respect to some of these laws and ordinances, individuals may retain prohibited firearms owned previously, with certain restrictions.)

p Restrictively administered discretion by local authorities over permit issuance, or permits are unavailable and carrying is prohibited in most circumstances.

q Loaded.

r The State waiting period does not apply to a person holding a valid permit or license to carry a firearm. In Connecticut, a hunting license also exempts the holder for long gun purchases. In Indiana, only persons with unlimited carry permits are exempt.

s Purchases from licensed dealers only.

t A permit to purchase or a carry permit is required.

u Preemption through judicial ruling. Local regulation may be instituted in Massachusetts if ratified by the legislature.

v Previously by judicial ruling, adopted by law.

w Holders of State permits or licenses to possess or purchase firearms, or firearm identification cards, are exempt.

x Every person arriving in Hawaii is required to register any firearm(s) brought into the State within 3 days of arrival of the person or firearm(s), whichever occurs later. Handguns purchased from licensed dealers must be registered within 5 days.

y Chicago only. No handgun not already registered may be lawfully possessed.

z No permit system exists and concealed carry is prohibited.

aa Checks for retail handgun sales are conducted by the State; those for long guns, by the FBI.

ab Except for ordinances in Gary, East Chicago, and those enacted before January 1994.

ac State permit or license for all handgun purchases required; no NICS check. Checks for retail long gun sales are conducted by the FBI.

ad Local ordinance in certain cities or counties.

ae Maryland subjects purchases of "assault weapons" to a 7-day waiting period.

af New York City only.

ag Prior to 1995, the law did not apply to Philadelphia.

ah No permit is required to carry for lawful purposes.

ai May be extended by police to 30 days in some circumstances. An individual not holding a driver's license must wait 90 days.

aj The District of Columbia is subject to the Federal Constitution's second amendment.

Source: Table provided by the National Rifle Association of America, Institute for Legislative Action.

APPENDIX 3
List of Organizations

Listed below are organizations involved in gun rights and gun control issues, including addresses, phone numbers, and Web sites.

Academics for the Second Amendment
Joseph E. Olson, President
P.O. Box 131254
St. Paul, MN 55113

American Academy of Pediatrics
P.O. Box 747
Elk Grove Village, IL 60009-0747
(847) 228-5005
www.aap.org

American Bar Association
750 N. Lake Shore Drive
Chicago, IL 60611
(312) 988-5000
www.abanet.org

American Civil Liberties Union
125 Broad Street, 18th Floor
New York, NY 10004-2400
www.aclu.org

American Firearms Council
1845 The Exchange, Suite 150
Atlanta, GA 30339
(770) 933-0200
www.assc.org/afchome.html

American Jewish Congress
15 East 84th Street
New York, NY 10028
(212) 249-3672
www.ajcongress.org

American Shooting Sports Council
101 D Street SE
Washington, DC 20003
(202) 544-1610
www.assc.org

Americans for Democratic Action
1625 K Street, Suite 210
Washington, DC 20006
(202) 785-5980
www.adaction.org

Arming Women Against Rape and
    Endangerment
P.O. Box 242
Bedford, MA 01730-0242
(781)893-0500
www.aware.org

British American Security Information Council
1900 L Street NW, Suite 401
Washington, DC 20036
(202) 785-1266
www.basicint.org

Bureau of Alcohol, Tobacco, and Firearms
Washington, DC
(202) 927-8500
www.atf.treas.gov

Canadian Firearms Centre
284 Wellington Street
Ottawa, ON K1A OH8
Canada
(800) 731-4000
www.canadianfirearms.com

Cease Fire, Inc.
P.O. Box 33424
Washington, DC 20033-0424
(202) 429-1741
www.ceasefire.org

Center for the Study and Prevention of Violence
Institute of Behavioral Science
University of Colorado at Boulder
Campus Box 442
Boulder, CO 80309-0442
www.colorado.edu/cspv

Center to Prevent Handgun Violence
1225 Eye Street NW, Suite 1100
Washington, DC 20005
(202) 289-7319
www.handguncontrol.org

Central Conference of American Rabbis
355 Lexington Avenue
New York, NY 10017
(212) 972-3636
http://ccarnet.org

Children's Defense Fund
25 E. Street NW
Washington, DC 20001
(202) 628-8787
www.childrensdefense.org

Citizens Committee for the Right to Keep and
  Bear Arms
12500 N.E. Tenth Place
Bellevue, WA 98005
(206) 454-4911
www.ccrkba.org

Coalition To Stop Gun Violence
10001 6th Street NW. Suite 603
Washington, DC 20036
(202) 530-0340
www.gunfree.org

Congress of Racial Equality
817 Broadway, 3rd Floor
New York, NY 10003
(212) 598-4000
www.core-online.org

Democrats for the Second Amendment
P.O. Box 12061
Seattle, WA 98102
www.d2a.org

Doctors for Integrity in Policy Research
5201 Norris Canyon Road #220
San Ramon, CA 94583-5405
(510) 277-0333
www.dipr.org

Doctors for Responsible Gun Ownership
Claremont Institute
250 West First Street, Suite 330
Claremont, CA 91711
(909) 621-6825
www.claremont.org

Drive-By-Agony
3798 Martin Luther King Boulevard,
P.O. Box 762
Lynwood, CA 90262
(310) 537-8018
www.drive-by-agony.org

Educational Fund to End Handgun Violence
110 Maryland Avenue NE, Box 72
Washington, DC 20002
(202) 544-7227
www.gunfree.org/edfund/ceasefir.htm

Firearms Coalition
7771 Sudley Road #44
Manassas, VA 20109
(900) 225-3006
www.nealknox.com

Firearms Litigation Clearinghouse
1000 18th Street NW, Suite 603
Washington, DC 20036-5743
(202) 530-5888
www.firearmslitigation.org

Firearms Owners Against Crime
P.O. Box 75
Presto, PA 15142
(412) 221-4595
http://hhi.com/foac

Firearms Research and Identification
  Association
21465 East Fort Bowie Drive
Walnut, CA 91789
(909) 598-8919

Fraternal Order of Police
1410 Donelson Pike A-17
Nashville, TN 37217
(615) 399-0900
www.grandlodgefop.org

Gun Control Resource Center
John K. Hunka, Attorney At Law
21 South 12th Street, Suite 402
Philadelphia, PA 19107
http://astro.ocis.temple.edu/~hunka/
handgun.html

Gun Owners' Action League
37 Pierce Street, P.O. Box 567
Northboro, MA 01532
(508) 393-5333
www.goal.org

Gun Owners of America
8001 Forbes Place, Suite 102
Springfield, VA 22151
(703) 321-8585
www.gunowners.org

Handgun Control, Inc.
1225 Eye Street NW, Suite 1100
Washington, DC 20005
(202) 218-4641
www.handguncontrol.org

Harborview Injury Prevention and Research
    Center
325 Ninth Avenue, Box 359960
Seattle, WA 98104
(206) 521-1520
http://weber.u.washington.edu/~hiprc

Heartland Institute
19 South LaSalle Street #903
Chicago, IL 60603
(312) 377-4000
www.heartland.org

HELP Network
Children's Memorial Hospital
2300 Children's Plaza #88
Chicago, IL 60614
(773) 880-3826
www.childmmc.edu/help/helphome.htm

Independence Institute
14142 Denver West Parkway, Suite 185
Golden, CO 80401
(303)279-6536
www.i2i.org

Institute for Legislative Action
11250 Waples Road
Fairfax, VA 22030
(800)392-8683
www.nraila.org

International Association of Chiefs of Police
515 North Washington Street
Alexandria, VA 22314
(703) 836-6767
www.theiacp.org

International Brotherhood of Police Officers
159 Burgin Parkway
Quincy, MA 02169
(617) 376-0220
www.ibpo.org

International Defensive Pistol Association
P.O. Box 639
Berryville, AR 72616-0639
(870) 545-3886
www.idpa.com

Izaak Walton League of America
707 Conservation Lane
Gaithersburg, MD 20878
(301) 548-0150
www.iwla.org

Jews for the Preservation of Firearms
    Ownership
2874 South Wentworth Avenue
Milwaukee, WI 53207
(414) 769-0760
www.jpfo.org

John Birch Society
P.O. Box 8040
Appleton, WI 54913
(920) 749-3780
www.jbs.org

Johns Hopkins Center for Gun Policy and
    Research
624 North Broadway
Baltimore, MD 21205
(410) 955-3995
http://infosys.jhsph.edu/centers/gunpolicy

Klanwatch Project
400 Washington Avenue
Montgomery, AL 36104
(334) 264-0286

Ku Klux Klan
P.O. Box 2222
Harrison, AR 72601
(870) 427-3414
www.kukluxklan.org

Law Enforcement Alliance of America
7700 Leesburg Pike, Suite 421
Falls Church, VA 22043
(800) 766-8578
www.largo.org/LEAAfotis.html

Lawyer's Second Amendment Society
18034 Ventura Boulevard #329
Encino, CA 91316
(310) 479-0915 ext. 239
www.mcs.net/~lpyleprn/lsas

Legal Action Project
1225 Eye Street NW, Suite 1100
Washington, DC 20005
(202) 289-7319
www.handguncontrol.org/legalaction

Legal Community Against Violence
268 Bush Street, Suite 5555
San Francisco, CA 94104
www.lcav.org

Libertarian Party
2600 Virginia Avenue NW, Suite 100
Washington, DC 20037
(202) 333-0008
www.lp.org

Mennonite Central Committee
110 Maryland Avenue NE
Washington, DC 20002
(202) 544-6564
www.mcc.org

Michigan Militia
8808 Dennison
Detroit, MI 48210
(517) 694-6603
www.michiganmilitia.org

Militia of Montana
P.O. Box 1486
Noxon, MT 59853
(406) 847-2735
www.nidlink.com/~bobhard/mom.html

Militia Watchdog
P.O. Box 12606
Columbus, OH 43212

(614) 488-9141
www.militia-watchdog.org

Mothers Against Violence in America
105 14th Avenue, Suite 2A
Seattle, WA 98122
(206) 323-2303
www.mavia..org

National Association of Federally Licensed
  Firearms Dealers
2455 East Sunrise Boulevard, Suite 916
Fort Lauderdale, FL 33304
(800) 453-1643
http://amfire.com

National Association of Police Organizations
750 First Street NE, Suite 920
Washington, DC 20002-4241
(202) 842-3560
www.napo.org

National Association of School
  Psychologists
4340 East-West Highway #402
Bethesda, MD 20814
(301) 657-0270
http://naspweb.org

National Center for Injury Prevention and
  Control
4770 Buford Highway NE
Atlanta, GA 30341-3724
(770) 488-1506
www.cdc.gov/ncipc

National Center for Policy Analysis
727 15th Street NW, Fifth Floor
Washington, DC 20005
(202) 628-6671
www.ncpa.org

National Concealed Carry Incorporated
www.moa.sonnet.com/nvrpc

National Crime Prevention Council
1700 K Street NW, Second Floor
Washington, DC 20005
(202) 466-6272
www.ncpc.org

National Education Association
1201 16th Street NW
Washington, DC 20036
(202) 833-4000
www.nea.org

National Firearms Association
4610 Demby Drive
Fairfax, VA 22032-1707
(703) 503-2073
www.quancon.com/~nfa

National Firearms Association of Canada
Box 1779, Edmonton AB
T5J 2P1 Canada
(403) 439-1394
www.nfa.ca

National Muzzle Loading Rifle Association
P.O. Box 67
Friendship, IN 47021
(812) 667-5131
www.nmlra.org

National Organization of Black Law
  Enforcement Executives
4609 Pinecrest Office Park Drive,
Suite F
Alexandria, VA 22312-1442
(703) 658-1529
www.noblenatl.org

National Rifle Association
11250 Waples Mill Road
Fairfax, VA 22030
(800) 392-8683
www.nra.org

National SAFE KIDS Campaign
1301 Pennsylvania Avenue, Suite 1000
Washington, DC 20004-1707
(202) 662-0600
www.safekids.org

National School Safety Center
4165 Thousand Oaks Boulevard,
Suite 290
Westlake Village, CA 91362
(805) 373-9977
www.nssc1.org

National Shooting Sports Foundation
11 Mile Hill Road
Newtown, CT 06470-2359
(203) 426-1320
www.nssf.com

National Tracing Center
Washington, DC 20226
(202) 927-8500
www.atf.treas.gov/about/prog/trace.htm

Pacific Center for Violence Prevention
San Francisco General Hospital
San Francisco, CA 94110
(415) 821-8209
www.pcvp.org

Paul Revere Network
e-mail: lpyle@Paul Revere.org
www.paulrevere.org

PAX
P.O. Box 2151
New York, NY 10021
(212) 254-5300
www.paxusa.org

Physicians for Social Responsibility
1101 14th Street NW, Suite 700
Washington, DC 20036
(202) 898-0150
www.psr.org

Police Executive Research Forum
1120 Connecticut Avenue NW,
Suite 930
Washington, DC 20036
(202) 466-7820
www.policeforum.org

Potomac Institute
P.O. Box 5907
Bethesda, MD 20824-1396
www.us.net/potomac/index.html

Presbyterian Church (U.S.A.)
100 Witherspoon Street
Louisville, KY 40202-1396
(502) 569-5803
www.pcusa.org

Project Lifeline
1225 Eye Street NW, Suite 1100
Washington, DC 20005
(202) 289-7319
www.handguncontrol.org/protecting/D3/
d3prlife.htm

Safe Range Association
13740 Research Boulevard, Suite B-4
Austin, TX 78750
(512) 335-8123
http://saferange.org

Appendix 3: List of Organizations

Safety for Women and Responsible Motherhood
3440 Youngfield #204
Wheat Ridge, CO 80033
(303) 969-0708
http://web.wn.net/~usr/chris/web/swarm.html

Second Amendment Committee
P.O. Box 1776
Hanford, CA 93232
(209) 584-5209
www.libertygunrights.com

Second Amendment Foundation
12500 North East Tenth Place
Bellevue, WA 98005
(206) 454-7012
www.saf.org

Sporting Arms and Ammunition Manufacturers'
  Institute
11 Mile Hill Road
Newtown, CT 06470
(203) 426-1320
www.saami.org

Stop Handgun Violence
One Bridge Street
Newton, MA 02458
(617) 243-8174
www.stophandgunviolence.com

Student Pledge Against Gun Violence
112 Nevada Street
Northfield, MN 55057
(507) 645-5378
www.pledge.org

United States Conference of Mayors
1620 Eye Street NW
Washington, DC 20006
(202) 293-7330
www.mayors.org

United States Practical Shooting Association
P.O. Box 811
Sedro Woolley, WA 98284
(306) 855-2245
www.uspsa.org

Violence Policy Center
1350 Connecticut Avenue NW,
Suite 825
Washington, DC 20036
(202) 822-8200
www.vpc.org

Violence Prevention Research Program
University of California, Davis
2315 Stockton Boulevard
Sacramento, CA 95817
(916) 734-3539
http://web.ucdmc.ucdavis.edu/vprp

Women Against Gun Control
P.O. Box 95357
South Jordan UT 84095
(801) 328-9660
http://wagc.com

Women's Firearm Network
Shooters, P.O. Box 990
One Court Street
Exeter, NH 03833
(603) 778-4720
www.womenshooters.com

CHRONOLOGY

1775   Colonial militia, called the minutemen, defend a store of arms in Lexington, Massachusetts, against an attempt by British troops under the command of General Thomas Gage to confiscate weapons. The minutemen take on a reputation far beyond their contribution to the fight for independence, becoming a crucial ingredient in many Americans' positive attitudes toward firearms.

1789   James Madison fulfills a promise to submit 12 constitutional amendments in the first session of the new House of Representatives; the amendments are to constitute a Bill of Rights to the recently adopted U.S. Constitution. Although initially holding that a Bill of Rights is unnecessary, Madison agrees to support the idea to attain ratification of the Constitution. One of Madison's proposed amendments originally reads: "The right of the people to keep and bear arms shall not be infringed; a well-regulated militia being the best security of a free country: but no person religiously scrupulous of bearing arms shall be compelled to render military service in person." The amendment is revised to exclude a religious exemption and is submitted to the states as: "A well regulated Militia, being necessary to the security of a free State, the right of the people to keep and bear Arms, shall not be infringed." This Second Amendment to the U.S. Constitution is ratified on December 15, 1791.

1792   Congress passes the Militia Act, which establishes an organized militia and an enrolled militia composed of all free white males, who were expected to provide their own muskets, firelocks, and ammunition. The act is never truly implemented by the states.

1846   In *Nunn v. State*, the Supreme Court of Georgia overrules a lower court decision convicting Hawkins Nunn of carrying a pistol in violation of an 1837 state statute. The court finds that both the U.S. and Georgia state constitutions guarantee the right to keep and bear arms and traces the historical roots of the right, calling it "one of the fundamental principles, upon which rests the great fabric of civil liberty, reared by the fathers of the Revolution and of the country."

1857   The U.S. Supreme Court, in *Scott v. Sanford*, rules that the Bill of Rights does not apply to blacks. Chief Justice Roger Taney argues that if blacks were given full citizen status with free white men, they would have the right of free speech and the right "to keep and carry arms wherever they went."

1871	Colonel William C. Church and George W. Wingate, former Union army officers, collaborate in establishing the National Rifle Association (NRA). The NRA hopes to encourage rifle practice so that Americans will be better prepared militarily for any future conflict. New York State provides funds to purchase land on Long Island to establish a rifle range for NRA members.
1876	The U.S. Supreme Court, in *United States v. Cruikshank*, rules for the first time on the basis of the Second Amendment, declaring that the amendment applies to the national government only, and not to private groups. Among other charges, the defendants were originally indicted for preventing two African Americans from exercising "the right to keep and bear arms for a lawful purpose." The Court decided that only the states have the authority to protect citizens against such violations of their rights by private persons.
1881	A gun-wielding attacker assassinates President James Garfield, the second president to be killed in office.
1886	In *Presser v. Illinois*, Herman Presser, the appellant, appealed his state conviction for violating the Military Code of Illinois to the U.S. Supreme Court. Presser led a contingent of 400 armed men in a Chicago parade, himself carrying a cavalry sword, without receiving a license from the governor to parade as part of the state militia. The Supreme Court rules that the section of the Illinois statute banning armed parades without authorization does not violate the right of the people to keep and bear arms.
1901	President William McKinley is assassinated by a gunman.
1903	Congress passes the Dick Act, which repeals the Militia Act of 1792. The Dick Act is an attempt to revive state militias based on voluntary recruitment and greater national government control over the organization and operation of the National Guard.
1911	Responding to the outcry against street violence in New York City, the New York State legislature enacts the Sullivan Law, the most stringent gun legislation of the time. The statute requires a license to possess or carry a concealable weapon. One provision of the law forbids aliens to possess firearms in public.
1924	Congress passes the Mailing of Firearms Act, which prohibits sending pistols and other firearms that can be concealed on the person through the United States Post Office.
1934	Congress enacts the National Firearms Act, which focuses on limiting access to weapons commonly thought to be used primarily by gangsters. Over-the-counter sale of machine guns is prohibited, and automatic weapons, short-barreled rifles, and sawed-off shotguns must be registered.
1938	Congress passes the Federal Firearms Act, which is intended to regulate the interstate sale of firearms. Those wishing to manufacture, sell, or import firearms and ammunition must receive a license from the federal government's Internal Revenue Service (IRS), which is responsible for collecting the license fees.
1939	In *United States v. Miller*, the U.S. Supreme Court rules on a challenge to the National Firearms Act of 1934 that by prohibiting the transportation of a sawed-off shotgun across state lines the law violates the Second Amendment. The Court rejects the appeal, ruling that the Second Amendment does not protect

the possession of a sawed-off shotgun, which has no relation to the preservation of a well-regulated militia.

1958   The Federal Aviation Act prohibits the carrying of firearms on commercial aircraft.

1963   President John F. Kennedy is assassinated by a gunman using a mail-order rifle.

1966   Following the shooting incident at the University of Texas at Austin, in which 12 people are killed and 33 others wounded by a lone gunman, President Lyndon Johnson urges legislators to take action on gun control legislation before Congress.

1968   In separate incidents, Dr. Martin Luther King, Jr., and Senator Robert F. Kennedy are assassinated by gunmen.

Congress passes the Gun Control Act. Among its provisions, the law strengthens the firearms licensing process to limit foreign and interstate transport of firearms, prohibits the interstate shipment of pistols and revolvers to private individuals, and forbids certain criminals, the mentally incompetent, and drug addicts from shipping or receiving weapons through interstate commerce, and firearms dealers are prohibited from knowingly selling weapons to these categories of people.

1972   The Internal Revenue Service's Alcohol, Tobacco, and Firearms Division receives bureau status in the Department of the Treasury, but does not receive status as an independent regulatory agency, leaving it more open to political attacks.

1980   In *Lewis v. United States*, the U.S. Supreme Court upholds a lower court conviction under a provision of the Omnibus Crime Control and Safe Streets Act of 1968, which prohibits any person convicted by a federal or state court of a felony from possessing a firearm. The Court rules that Congress acted reasonably when it determined that a convicted felon should be prohibited from dealing in or possessing firearms, even if the conviction occurred without the benefit of counsel.

1981   The Village of Morton Grove, Illinois, receives national attention when it passes an ordinance to regulate the possession of firearms "and other dangerous weapons." No person may possess a handgun, unless it has been made permanently inoperable.

In *Quilici v. Village of Morton Grove*, a U.S. Circuit Court affirms the constitutionality of the Morton Grove ordinance. The court rules that local governments with home rule charters have the right to govern their own affairs.

1982   Inspired by the firearm ban enacted in Morton Grove, Illinois, in 1981, the city council of Kennesaw, Georgia, a small town north of Atlanta, passes an ordinance to require residents to keep firearms in their homes.

1986   President Ronald Reagan signs the Firearms Owners Protection (McClure-Volkmer) Act, which limits various provisions of the Gun Control Act of 1968. The act permits the sale of ammunition through the mail, allows weapons dealers to resume the interstate sale of rifles and shotguns, and relieves ammunition dealers of record-keeping requirements. The Bureau of Alcohol, Tobacco, and Firearms (BATF) is prohibited from centralizing records and from establishing a firearms registration system. Focusing on the misuse of firearms, the law requires mandatory penalties for such misuse.

1988   Congress passes the Undetectable Firearms Act, which bans the manufacture, importation, receipt, and transfer of plastic and ceramic guns that X-ray machines and magnetometers cannot detect. The law requires firearms to contain a minimum of 3.7 ounces of metal to make them detectable.

1989   Following a shooting incident at a Stockton, California, elementary school, in which a man wielding a Chinese-made AK-47 killed several children, the California legislature passes the Roberti-Roos Assault Weapons Act, which is the first statute in the United States to ban the sale, possession, or manufacture of semi-automatic, military style firearms.

1992   A standoff between Randy Weaver and federal government officers occurs at Ruby Ridge, Idaho. After Weaver tries to sell two sawed-off shotguns to a government informant, the Federal Bureau of Investigation (FBI) tries to recruit Weaver as an informant. He refuses. The resulting standoff leads to the death of a U.S. Marshall and Weaver's wife and son. The event heightens the suspicions that more extreme groups have about federal government firearms policy.

1993   Federal agents conduct a raid on the Branch Davidian compound in Waco, Texas, because the members of the religious group are suspected of weapons violations. Four BATF agents and six Branch Davidians die in the initial assault. After a 51-day siege, the compound is assaulted with tanks and tear gas. Seventy-five people, including 20 children, die in a fire apparently set by group members. The incident lowers the prestige of the BATF and increases the hatred some extremist groups have for the federal government.

1994   Congress passes the Brady Handgun Violence Prevention Act, which establishes a temporary five-day waiting period before individuals may purchase a handgun to run a background check to discover if potential purchasers are disqualified from owning a handgun.

Congress passes the Assault Weapons Ban Act, which prohibits the sale, manufacture, importation, or possession of 19 types of assault weapons.

1995   In *United States v. Lopez*, the U.S. Supreme Court affirms an appeals court reversal of a conviction based on the Gun-Free School Zones Act of 1990. Basing its decision on an interpretation of Congress's commerce power, the Court disallows the measure that made it a federal crime to knowingly possess a firearm within a public, parochial, or private school, or in a zone within 1,000 feet of school grounds.

1996   Maryland enacts a one-gun-per-month statute, which limits an individual to purchasing no more than one gun in a 30-day period. The legislative success of the statute inspires gun control advocates to push for a similar law on the national level.

1997   In *Printz v. United States*, the U.S. Supreme Court declares unconstitutional a provision of the Brady Handgun Violence Prevention Act that requires chief law enforcement officers in local jurisdictions to perform background checks on prospective handgun purchasers. Speaking for the majority, Justice Antonin Scalia states that Congress violated the constitutional system of state sovereignty by compelling states to enforce a federal regulatory program.

1998   A National Instant Check System (NICS) goes into effect on November 30, in which gun dealers must consult a computerized background check system to determine whether a prospective handgun purchaser is disqualified from owning a firearm. The National Rifle Association (NRA) quickly files a suit against the operation of the system, claiming that records are being kept illegally.

The Supreme Court rules in *Caron v. United States* that a felon may have the right to own firearms restored under federal law only if a state confers the right to own all types of firearms.

Two boys, aged 11 and 13, are arrested in Jonesboro, Arkansas, for shooting and killing four fellow students and one teacher, and wounding 11 others at the Westside Middle School. The incident sparks renewed debates about gun control.

1999

A jury in New York finds in favor of a handgun victim against several firearms manufacturers. Given the potential significance of the ruling for manufacturers, the decision is expected to be appealed.

Two students, aged 17 and 18, enter their high school in Littleton, Colorado, with automatic weapons, sawed-off shotguns, and homemade bombs, killing 12 students, one teacher, and themselves. The incident and its aftermath receive nationwide coverage, opening a debate over the need for additional gun control measures.

President Bill Clinton proposes several gun control measures, including the re-imposition of a waiting period to purchase a firearm, a prohibition on gun ownership for those under 21 years of age, and the establishment of penalties, including imprisonment and fines, for adults who give children access to firearms.

Although the U.S. Senate approves stronger gun control legislation, a coalition of conservative Republicans and Democrats defeat a considerably weakened measure in the U.S. House of Representatives. While rejecting a proposal to require labeling entertainment products with violent content, the House approves a measure allowing the posting of the Ten Commandments in schools and government buildings.

To counter cities such as Boston and San Francisco, which have initiated lawsuits against gun manufacturers and dealers to recover the costs of gun violence, the National Rifle Association lobbies state legislatures to limit the authority of local governments to file such suits.

BIBLIOGRAPHY

Ahern, Jerry. *CCW: Carrying Concealed Weapons, How to Carry Concealed Weapons and Know When Others Are*. Chino Valley, AZ: Blacksmith Corp., 1996.

Apel, Lorelei. *Dealing with Weapons at School and at Home*. New York: Rosen Publishing Group, 1996.

Ayoob, Massad F. *In the Gravest Extreme: The Role of the Firearm in Personal Protection*. Concord, NH: Police Bookshelf, 1980.

_____. *Gunproof Your Children: Handgun Primer*. Concord, NH: Police Bookshelf, 1986.

Bartone, John C. *Guns, the National Rifle Association, and Consumers as Armed Citizens*. Washington, DC: ABBE, 1994.

_____. *Guns and Their Importance to Americans Facing Crimes of Threat, Harm, and Property Invasion*. Washington, DC: ABBE, 1996.

Beckelman, Laurie. *Gun Control: You Decide*. Parsippany, NJ: Crestwood House, 1999.

Berands, Neal. *Gun Control*. San Diego: Lucent Books, 1992.

Bijlefeld, Marjolijn. *Gun Control Debate: A Documentary History*. Westport, CT: Greenwood, 1997.

Bird, Chris. *The Concealed Handgun Manual: How to Choose, Carry, and Shoot a Gun in Self Defense*. San Antonio: Privateer Publications, 1998.

Brennan, Jill W. *Gun Control in the 1990s*. Kettering, OH: PPI, 1996.

Bruce, John M. and Clyde Wilcox. *The Changing Politics of Gun Control*. Lanham, MD: Rowman and Littlefield, 1998.

Bureau of Alcohol, Tobacco, and Firearms. *Federal Firearms Regulations Reference Guide*. Washington, DC: U.S. Government Printing Office, 1995.

_____. *State Laws and Published Ordinances–Firearms*, 21st ed. Washington, DC: U.S. Government Printing Office, 1998.

Carter, Gregg Lee. *The Gun Control Movement*. New York: Twayne, 1997.

Cottrol, Robert J., ed. *Gun Control and the Constitution: Sources and Explorations on the Second Amendment*. New York: Garland, 1994.

Cox, Vic. *Guns, Violence and Teens*. Enslow, 1997.

Cozic, Charles P. *The Militia Movement*. San Diego: Greenhaven, 1997.

Cozic, Charles P., and Carol Wekesser, eds. *Gun Control*. San Diego: Greenhaven, 1992.

Davidson, Osha Gray. *Under Fire: The NRA and the Battle for Gun Control*. Iowa City: University of Iowa Press, 1998.

Dekker, Virginia M. *Guns and Firearms: Index of New Information with Social, Medical, Psychological and Legal Implications*. Washington, DC: ABBE, 1995.

Devour, Cynthia D. *Kids and Guns*. Minneapolis: Abdo and Daughters, 1994.

Diaz, Tom. *Making a Killing: The Business of Guns in America*. New York: New Press, 1999.

Bibliography

Dizzard, Jan E., Robert Merrill Muth, and Stephen P. Andrews, Jr., eds. *Guns in America: A Reader*. New York: New York University Press, 1999.

Dolan, Edward F. and Margaret M. Scariano. *Guns in the United States*. Danbury, CT: Franklin Watts, 1994.

Edel, Wilbur. *Gun Control: Threat to Liberty or Defense Against Anarchy?* Westport, CT: Praeger, 1995.

Fadala, Sam. *Great Shooters of the World*. South Hackensack, NJ: Stoeger, 1990.

Flynn, George and Alan Gottlieb. *Guns for Women: The Complete Handgun Buying Guide for Women*. Bellevue, WA: Merril, 1988.

Freedman, Warren. *The Privilege to Keep and Bear Arms: The Second Amendment and Its Interpretation*. New York: Quorum, 1989.

Fuller, Sharon. *The Gun Control Debate: An Update*. Upland, PA: DIANE Publishing, 1995.

Gottfried, Ted. *Gun Control: Public Safety and the Right to Bear Arms*. Brookfield, CT: Millbrook, 1993.

Gottlieb, Alan M. *Gun Rights Fact Book*. Bellevue, WA: Merril, 1989.

_____. *The Rights of Gun Owners*. Bellevue, WA: Merrill, 1991.

_____. *Politically Correct Guns*. Bellevue, WA: Merril, 1996.

_____. *The Gun Grabbers: Who They Are, How They Operate, Where They Get Their Money*, Reissue ed. Bellevue, WA: Merril, 1998.

Gottlieb, Alan M. and David B. Kopel. *Things You Can Do to Defend Your Gun Rights*. Bellevue, WA: Merril, 1993.

_____. *More Things You Can Do to Defend Your Gun Rights*. Bellevue, WA: Merril, 1995.

Halbrook, Stephen P. *Firearms Law Deskbook: Federal and State Criminal Practice*. New York: Clark Boardman Callaghan, 1995.

Hamilton, Neil A. *Militias in America*. Santa Barbara, CA: ABC-CLIO, 1996.

Hemenway, David. *Guns and the Constitution: The Myth of Second Amendment Protection for Firearms in America*. Northampton, MA: Aletheia, 1995.

Hook, Donald D. *Gun Control: The Continuing Debate*. Bellevue, WA: Merril, 1992.

Kates, Don B. and Gary Kleck, eds. *The Great American Gun Debate: Essays on Firearms and Violence*. San Francisco: Pacific Research Institute for Public Policy, 1997.

Kennet, Lee and James La Verne Anderson. *The Gun in America: The Origins of a National Dilemma*. Westport, CT: Greenwood, 1975.

Kleck, Gary. *Point Blank: Guns and Violence in America*. New York: Aldine De Gruyter, 1991.

_____. *Targeting Guns: Firearms and Their Control*. New York: Aldine De Gruyter, 1997.

Kopel, David B. *The Samurai, the Mountie, and the Cowboy: Should America Adopt the Gun Controls of Other Democracies?* Buffalo, NY: Prometheus, 1992.

_____, ed. *Guns: Who Should Have Them?* Amherst, NY: Prometheus, 1995.

Korwin, Alan, with Michael P. Anthony. *Gun Laws of America*. Phoenix: Bloomfield, 1997.

Krushke, Earl R. *The Right to Keep and Bear Arms: A Continuing American Dilemma*. Springfield, IL: Charles C. Thomas, 1985.

_____. *Gun Control: A Reference Handbook*. Santa Barbara, CA: ABC-CLIO, 1995.

Landau, Elaine. *Armed America: The Status of Gun Control*. Parsippany, NJ: Julian Messner, 1991.

LaPierre, Wayne R. *Guns, Crime, and Freedom*. Washington, DC: Regnery, 1994.

Larosa, Benedict D. *Gun Control*. San Antonio: Candlestick, 1997.

Larson, Erik. *Lethal Passage: The Story of a Gun*. New York: Vintage, 1995.

Levine, Herbert M. *Gun Control*. Chatham, NJ: Raintree Steck-Vaughn, 1997.

Lott, John R., Jr. *More Guns Less Crime: Understanding Crime and Gun Control Laws*. Chicago: University of Chicago Press, 1998.

MacNutt, Karen. *Ladies Legal Companion*. Boston: MacNutt Art Trust, 1993.

Mahon, John K. *History of the Militia and the National Guard*. New York: Macmillan, 1983.

Malcolm, Joyce Lee. *To Keep and Bear Arms: The Origins of an Anglo-American Right*. Cambridge, MA: Harvard University Press, 1994.

May-Hayes, Gila. *Effective Defense: The Woman, The Plan, The Gun*. Onalaska, WA: FAS Books, 1994.

Miller, Maryann. *Working Together Against Gun Violence*, Revised ed. New York: Rosen, 1997.

Murray, James M. *Fifty Things You Can Do about Guns*. San Francisco: Robert D. Reed, 1994.

Neaderland, Louise Odes. *The Case for Gun Control*. Brooklyn, NY: Bone Hollow Arts, 1994.

Nisbet, Lee, ed. *The Gun Control Debate: You Decide*. Amherst, NY: Prometheus, 1991.

O'Sullivan, Carol. *Gun Control: Distinguishing Between Fact and Opinion*. San Diego: Greenhaven, 1990.

Pontonne, S., ed. *Gun Control Issues*. Commack, NY: Nova Science, 1996.

Pratt, Larry. *Safeguarding Liberty: The Constitution and Citizen Militias*. Franklin, TN: Legacy Communications, 1995.

Prothrow-Stith, Deborah. *Deadly Consequences: How Violence Is Destroying Our Teenage Population and a Plan to Begin Solving the Problem*. New York: HarperCollins, 1991.

Quigley, Paxton. *Armed and Female: Twelve Million American Women Own Guns, Shouldn't You?* New York: St. Martin's, 1993.

Ragnar, Benson. *Modern Weapons Caching: A Down to Earth Approach to Beating the Government Gun Grab*. Boulder, CO: Paladin, 1990.

Robin, Gerald D. *Violent Crime and Gun Control*. Cincinnati: Anderson, 1991.

Roleff, Tamara L., ed. *Gun Control*. San Diego: Greenhaven, 1997.

Sawyer, C.W. *Firearms in American History 1600-1800*. Watchung, NJ: Albert Saifer, 1987.

Schulman, J. Neil. *Stopping Power: Why 70 Million Americans Own Guns*. Santa Monica, CA: Synapse-Centurion, 1994.

_____. *Self Control Not Gun Control*. Santa Monica, CA: Synapse-Centurion, 1995.

Sheley, Joseph F. and James D. Wright. *In the Line of Fire: Youth, Guns, and Violence in Urban America*. New York: Aldine De Gruyter, 1995.

Siegel, Mark A., Nancy R. Jacobs, and Carol D. Foster, eds. *Gun Control: Restricting Rights or Protecting People?* Wylie, TX: Information Plus, 1991.

Simkin, Jay, and Aaron S. Zelman. *Gun Control–Gateway to Tyranny: The Nazi Law 18 March 1938*. Milwaukee: Jews for the Preservation of Firearms Ownership, 1992.

Simkin, Jay, Aaron S. Zelman, and Alan M. Rice. *Lethal Laws: 'Gun Control' Is the Key to Genocide*. Milwaukee: Jews for the Preservation of Firearms Ownership, 1994.

Sinclair, Beth, Jennifer Hamilton, Babette Gutmann, Julie Daft, and Dee Bolcik, *Report on State Implementation of the Gun-Free Schools Act–School Year 1996-97*. Washington, DC: U.S. Department of Education, 1998.

Spitzer, Robert J. *The Politics of Gun Control*, 2nd ed. New York: Chatham House, 1998.

Sugarmann, Josh and Kristen Rand. *Cease Fire: A Comprehensive Strategy to Reduce Firearms Violence*. Washington, DC: Violence Policy Center, 1997.

Tonso, William R., ed. *The Gun Culture and Its Enemies*. Bellevue, WA: Merril, 1990.

Truby, J. David. *Zips, Pipes, and Pens: Arsenal of Improvised Arms*. Boulder, CO: Paladin, 1993.

Turley, Windle and James E. Rooks. *Firearms Litigation: Law, Science, and Practice*. New York: John Wiley and Sons, 1994.

Van Zwoll, Wayne. *America's Great Gunmakers*. South Hackensack, NJ: Stoeger, 1992.

Vizzard, William J. *In the Cross Fire: A Political History of the Bureau of Alcohol, Tobacco and Firearms*. Boulder, CO: Lynne Rienner, 1997.

Waters, Robert A. *The Best Defense: True Stories of Intended Victims Who Defended Themselves With a Firearm*, Nashville, TN: Cumberland House, 1998.

Weir, William. *A Well Regulated Militia: The Battle Over Gun Control*. North Haven, CT: Archon, 1997.

Whitman, Neil. *Gun Control War*. Kettering, OH: PPI, 1995.

Wilson, R.L. *Ruger and His Guns: A History of the Man, the Company and Their Firearms*. New York: Simon and Schuster, 1996.

Bibliography

Wintemute, Garen. *Ring of Fire: The Handgun Makers of Southern California*. Sacramento, CA: Violence Prevention Research Program, 1994.

Wright, James D. and Peter H. Rossi. *Armed and Considered Dangerous: A Survey of Felons and Their Firearms*. New York: Aldine De Gruyter, 1994.

Zimring, Franklin E., and Gordon Hawkins. *The Citizen's Guide to Gun Control*. New York: Macmillan, 1987.

_____. *Crime Is Not the Problem: Lethal Violence in America*. New York: Oxford University Press, 1997.

INDEX

by Glenn H. Utter

DEPARTMENTS

This Book Recommended For:

☐ Indiana C____

FOR REFERENCE ONLY

AD	FF	MU
AV	GR	NC
BO	HI	SJ
CL	HO	CN L
DS	LS	

DEC 1 3 99

THIS BOOK IS RENEWABLE BY PHONE OR IN PERSON IF THERE IS NO RESERVE
WAITING OR FINE DUE.

LCP #0390